10th International Natural Language Generation Conference (INLG 2017)

Santiago de Compostela, Spain
4 – 7 September 2017

ISBN: 978-1-5108-5291-4

INLG 2017

**The 10th International
Natural Language Generation conference**

Proceedings of the Conference

September 4-7, 2017
Santiago de Compostela, Spain

Introduction

Welcome to the Proceedings of the 10th International Natural Language Generation Conference (INLG 2017)! INLG is the annual meeting of the ACL Special Interest Group on Natural Language Generation (SIGGEN). The INLG conference provides the premier forum for the discussion, dissemination, and archiving of research and results in the field of Natural Language Generation (NLG). This edition is singular, since for the first time it absorbs under the INLG umbrella the former European Workshop on Natural Language Generation (ENLG) that was celebrated for many years. Previous INLG conferences have been held in Australia, Germany, Greece, Ireland, Israel, the UK and the USA. Prior to 2000, these meetings were held as international workshops with a history stretching back to 1983. In 2017, INLG was organized in Santiago de Compostela, Spain, a UNESCO World Heritage City since 1985. The venues were the School of Engineering and the Research Center in Information Tecnology of the University of Santiago de Compostela.

The INLG 2017 program included presentations of substantial, original, and previously unpublished results on all topics related to NLG. This year, INLG has hosted the following workshops on: Linguistic Resources for Automatic Natural Language Generation (LiRA 2017), Recent Advances in RST and Related Formalisms (RST 2017), Explainable Computational Intelligence (XCI 2017) and Computational Creativity in Natural Language Generation (CC-NLG).

This year we received 56 submissions (27 long papers, 23 short papers and 6 demos). 37 submissions were accepted, more specifically, 15 as long papers (11 oral presentations, 4 posters), 16 as short papers (3 oral presentations, 13 posters), and the 6 submitted demos. In addition, INLG 2017 included two invited talks by Gemma Boleda (Universitat Pompeu Fabra) and Frank Schilder (Thomson Reuters Research & Development). Also an invited tutorial by Ehud Reiter and the 2nd Edition of the SIGGEN Hackathon, organized by Yaji Sripada, were held during the Conference.

As the organizing committee, we would like to thank our invited speakers for agreeing to join us and to the authors of all submitted papers. In addition, we thank the program committee members and anonymous reviewers for their outstanding work. We have also received sponsorships from Arria, Accenture and Phrasee, for which we are extremely grateful. We hope that you have had an enjoyable and inspiring stay in Santiago de Compostela!

Jose M. Alonso, Alberto Bugarín and Ehud Reiter
INLG 2017 Co-Chairs

General and Programme Chairs:

Jose M. Alonso

Alberto Bugarín

Ehud Reiter

Workshop Chairs:

Pablo Gervás

Elena Lloret

Tutorial and Invited Talks Chair:

Dimitra Gkatzia

Hackathon Chair:

Yaji Sripada

Publicity Chair:

Ichiro Kobayashi

Publication Chairs:

Alejandro Ramos-Soto

Cristina Barros

Marta Vicente

Local Organization Committee:

Cristina Barros

Senén Barro

Susana Bautista Blasco

Manuel Lama Penín

Gonzalo Méndez

Manuel Mucientes Molina

Martín Pereira Fariña

Alejandro Ramos-Soto

Marta Vicente

Program Committee:

Jose M. Alonso

Anja Belz

Alberto Bugarín

Rodrigo de Oliveira
Nina Dethlefs
Nikolaos Engonopoulos
Macarena Espinilla
Claire Gardent
Albert Gatt
Pablo Gervás
Dimitra Gkatzia
Helen Hastie
David M. Howcroft
Amy Isard
Janusz Kacprzyk
John Kelleher
Ioannis Konstas
Emiel Krahmer
Cyril Labbe
Guy Lapalme
Elena Lloret
Saad Mahamood
David McDonald
Simon Mille
Elena Montiel-Ponsoda
Laura Perez-Beltrachini
Paul Piwek
François Portet
Alejandro Ramos-Soto
Ehud Reiter
Daniel Sánchez
David Schlangen
Advaith Siddharthan
Somayajulu Sripada
Amanda Stent
Kristina Striegnitz
Mariët Theune
Kees van Deemter
Ielka van der Sluis
Keith Vander Linden
Andreas Vlachos
Leo Wanner
Michael White
Sander Wubben
Sina Zarrieß

Session Chairs:

Claire Gardent
Susana Bautista

Emiel Krahmer

Helmut Horacek

Amy Isard

Yaji Sripada

Ehud Reiter

Jose M. Alonso

Albert Gatt

Siimon Mille

Kees van Deemter

Alejandro Ramos-Soto

Alberto Bugarín

Invited Speakers:

Gemma Boleda (Universitat Pompeu Fabra)

Frank Schilder (Thomson Reuters Research & Development)

Table of Contents

Conference Program

Monday, September 4, 2017

8:30–9:00	**Registration**
9:00–11:00	**Workshop: Linguistic Resources for Automatic Natural Language Generation (LiRA 2017)**
9:00–11:00	**Workshop: Recent Advances in RST and Related Formalisms (RST 2017)**
9:00–11:00	**Workshop: Explainable Computational Intelligence (XCI 2017)**
11:00–11:30	**Coffee Break**
11:30–13:30	**Workshop: Linguistic Resources for Automatic Natural Language Generation (LiRA 2017)**
11:30–13:30	**Workshop: Recent Advances in RST and Related Formalisms (RST 2017)**
11:30–13:30	**Workshop: Explainable Computational Intelligence (XCI 2017)**
13:30–14:30	**Lunch**

11:00–11:30   Posters and Demos with Coffee (Part 1, Chair: Susana Bautista)

Content Selection for Real-time Sports News Construction from Commentary Texts
Jin-ge Yao, Jianmin Zhang, Xiaojun Wan and Jianguo Xiao

Improving the Naturalness and Expressivity of Language Generation for Spanish
Cristina Barros, Dimitra Gkatzia and Elena Lloret

What is the Role of Recurrent Neural Networks (RNNs) in an Image Caption Generator?
Marc Tanti, Albert Gatt and Kenneth Camilleri

Exploring the Behavior of Classic REG Algorithms in the Description of Characters in 3D Images
Gonzalo Méndez, Raquel Hervás, Susana Bautista, Adrian Rabadan and Teresa Rodriguez

Co-PoeTryMe: a Co-Creative Interface for the Composition of Poetry
Hugo Gonçalo Oliveira, Tiago Mendes and Ana Boavida

Refer-iTTS: A System for Referring in Spoken Installments to Objects in Real-World Images
Sina Zarrieß, M. Soledad López Gambino and David Schlangen

11:30–12:30   Invited Talk (Chair: Emiel Krahmer)

11:30–12:30   *Finding the "right" answers for customers*
Frank Schilder

12:30–13:30	**Oral Session 2 (Chair: Helmut Horacek)**

12:30–13:00   *Referring Expression Generation under Uncertainty: Algorithm and Evaluation Framework*
Tom Williams and Matthias Scheutz

13:00–13:30   *Natural Language Descriptions for Human Activities in Video Streams*
Nouf Alharbi and Yoshihiko Gotoh

13:30–15:00   **Lunch**

15:00–16:00   **Oral Session 3 (Chair: Amy Isard)**

15:00–15:30   *PASS: A Dutch data-to-text system for soccer, targeted towards specific audiences*
Chris van der Lee, Emiel Krahmer and Sander Wubben

15:30–16:00   *Evaluation of a Runyankore grammar engine for healthcare messages*
Joan Byamugisha, C. Maria Keet and Brian DeRenzi

16:00–16:30   **Hackathon Presentation with Coffee (Chair: Yaji Sripada)**

16:30–18:00   **Special session on getting NLG into widespread real-world usage (Chair: Ehud Reiter)**

Tuesday, September 5, 2017 (continued)

20:30–21:30   **Welcome Reception**

Wednesday, September 6, 2017

9:00–10:00   **Invited Talk (Chair: Jose M. Alonso)**

9:00–10:00   *Talking about the world with a distributed model*
Gemma Boleda

10:00–11:00   **Special Session on Generation Challenges (Chair: Albert Gatt)**

The Code2Text Challenge: Text Generation in Source Libraries
Kyle Richardson, Sina Zarrieß and Jonas Kuhn

Shared Task Proposal: Multilingual Surface Realization Using Universal Dependency Trees
Simon Mille, Bernd Bohnet, Leo Wanner and Anja Belz

The WebNLG Challenge: Generating Text from RDF Data
Claire Gardent, Anastasia Shimorina, Shashi Narayan and Laura Perez-Beltrachini

11:00–11:30   **Posters and Demos with Coffee (Part 2, Chair: Simon Mille)**

A Commercial Perspective on Reference
Ehud Reiter

Integrated sentence generation using charts
Alexander Koller and Nikos Engonopoulos

Adapting SimpleNLG to Spanish
Alejandro Ramos Soto, Julio Janeiro Gallardo and Alberto Bugarín Diz

G-TUNA: a corpus of referring expressions in German, including duration information
David Howcroft, Jorrig Vogels and Vera Demberg

Toward an NLG System for Bantu languages: first steps with Runyankore (demo)
Joan Byamugisha, C. Maria Keet and Brian DeRenzi

A working, non-trivial, topically indifferent NLG System for 17 languages
Robert Weißgraeber and Andreas Madsack

11:30–13:30 Oral Session 4 (Chair: Kees van Deemter)

11:30–12:00 *Generating titles for millions of browse pages on an e-Commerce site*
Prashant Mathur, Nicola Ueffing and Gregor Leusch

12:00–12:30 *Towards Automatic Generation of Product Reviews from Aspect-Sentiment Scores*
Hongyu Zang and Xiaojun Wan

12:30–13:00 *A model of suspense for narrative generation*
Richard Doust and Paul Piwek

13:00–13:30 *Data-Driven News Generation for Automated Journalism*
Leo Leppänen, Myriam Munezero, Mark Granroth-Wilding and Hannu Toivonen

13:30–15:00 Lunch

Wednesday, September 6, 2017 (continued)

16:00–17:00   Oral Session 5 (Chair: Alberto Bugarín)

16:00–16:20   *Referential Success of Set Referring Expressions with Fuzzy Properties*
Nicolas Marin, Gustavo Rivas-Gervilla and Daniel Sanchez

16:20–16:40   *Neural Response Generation for Customer Service based on Personality Traits*
Jonathan Herzig, Michal Shmueli-Scheuer, Tommy Sandbank and David Konopnicki

16:40–17:00   *Neural Paraphrase Generation using Transfer Learning*
Florin Brad and Traian Rebedea

18:00–19:30   INLG Group Photo and Guided Tour to the Old City

21:00–23:30   Gala Dinner and Awards Ceremony

Thursday, September 7, 2017

**9:00–11:00   Invited Tutorial on Evaluating Natural Language Generation Systems, by
Ehud Reiter (Part 1)**

11:00–11:30   Coffee Break

Linguistic realisation as machine translation:
Comparing different MT models for AMR-to-text generation

Thiago Castro Ferreira[1] and **Iacer Calixto**[2] and **Sander Wubben**[1] and **Emiel Krahmer**[1]

[1]Tilburg center for Cognition and Communication (TiCC), Tilburg University, The Netherlands

[2]ADAPT Centre, Dublin City University, School of Computing, Ireland

`{tcastrof,e.j.krahmer,s.wubben}@tilburguniversity.edu`

`{iacer.calixto}@adaptcentre.ie`

Abstract

In this paper, we study AMR-to-text generation, framing it as a translation task and comparing two different MT approaches (Phrase-based and Neural MT). We systematically study the effects of 3 AMR preprocessing steps (Delexicalisation, Compression, and Linearisation) applied before the MT phase. Our results show that preprocessing indeed helps, although the benefits differ for the two MT models. The implementation of the models are publicly available[1].

1 Introduction

Natural Language Generation (NLG) is the process of generating coherent natural language text from non-linguistic data (Reiter and Dale, 2000). While there is broad consensus among NLG scholars on the output of NLG systems (i.e., text), there is far less agreement on what the input should be; see Gatt and Krahmer (2017) for a recent review. Over the years, NLG systems have taken a wide range of inputs, including for example images (Xu et al., 2015), numeric data (Gkatzia et al., 2014) and semantic representations (Theune et al., 2001).

This study focuses on generating natural language based on Abstract Meaning Representations (AMRs) (Banarescu et al., 2013). AMRs encode the meaning of a sentence as a rooted, directed and acyclic graph, where nodes represent concepts, and labeled directed edges represent relations among these concepts. The formalism strongly relies on the PropBank notation. Figure 1 shows an example.

AMRs have increased in popularity in recent years, partly because they are relatively easy to produce, to read and to process automatically. In addition, they can be systematically translated into first-order logic, allowing for a well-specified model-theoretic interpretation (Bos, 2016). Most earlier studies on AMRs have focused on text understanding, i.e. processing texts in order to produce AMRs (Flanigan et al., 2014; Artzi et al., 2015). However, recently the reverse process, i.e. the generation of texts from AMRs, has started to receive scholarly attention (Flanigan et al., 2016; Song et al., 2016; Pourdamghani et al., 2016; Song et al., 2017; Konstas et al., 2017).

We assume that in practical applications, conceptualisation models or dialogue managers (models which decide *"what to say"*) output AMRs. In this paper we study different ways in which these AMRs can be converted into natural language (deciding *"how to say it"*). We approach this as a translation problem—automatically translating from AMRs into natural language—and the key contribution of this paper is that we systematically compare different preprocessing strategies for two different MT systems: Phrase-based MT (PBMT) and Neural MT (NMT).

We look at potential benefits of three preprocessing steps on AMRs before feeding them into an MT system: *delexicalisation*, *compression*, and *linearisation*. Delexicalisation decreases the sparsity of an AMR by removing constant values, compression removes nodes and edges which are less likely to be aligned to any word on the textual side and linearisation 'flattens' the AMR in a specific order. Com-

---

[1]`https://github.com/ThiagoCF05/LinearAMR`

Proceedings of The 10th International Natural Language Generation conference, pages 1–10,
Santiago de Compostela, Spain, September 4-7 2017. ©2017 Association for Computational Linguistics

```
(a3 / attend-02~e.13
    :ARG0 (p2 / person~e.6)
    :ARG1~e.14 (b / birthday~e.18
    :poss~e.17 (p3 / person :wiki "Mao_Zedong"
            :name (n / name :op1 "Mao"~e.15 :op2 "Zedong"~e.16)))
    :time (s / since~e.1
    :op1 (t / turn-02~e.3
            :ARG1 p3~e.2
            :ARG2 (t2 / temporal-quantity :quant 80~e.4
                :unit (y / year))))
    :mod (a2 / also~e.0)
    :quant (m / more-and-more~e.10,11,12))
```

Also~0   since~1   he~2   turned~3   80~4   ,~5   people~6   had~7   been~8   paying~9   more~10   and~11
more~12   attention~13   to~14   Mao~15   Zedong~16   's~17   birthday~18   .~19

Figure 1: Example of an AMR

bining all possibilities gives rise to $2^3 = 8$ AMR preprocessing strategies, which we evaluate for two different MT systems: PBMT and NMT.

Following earlier work in AMR-to-text generation and the MT literature, we evaluate the system outputs in terms of fluency, adequacy and post-editing effort, using BLEU (Papineni et al., 2002), METEOR (Lavie and Agarwal, 2007) and TER (Snover et al., 2006) scores, respectively. We show that preprocessing helps, although the extent of the benefits differs for the two MT systems.

2   Related Studies

To the best of our knowledge, Flanigan et al. (2016) was the first study that introduced a model for natural language generation from AMRs. The model consists of two steps. First, the AMR-graph is converted into a spanning tree, and then, in a second step, this tree is converted into a sentence using a tree transducer.

In Song et al. (2016), the generation of a sentence from an AMR is addressed as an asymmetric generalised traveling salesman problem (AGTSP). For sentences shorter than 30 words, the model does not beat the system described by Flanigan et al. (2016). However, Song et al. (2017) treat the AMR-to-text task using a Synchronous Node Replacement Grammar (SNRG) and outperform Flanigan et al. (2016).

Although AMRs do not contain articles and do not represent inflectional morphology for tense and number (Banarescu et al., 2013), the formalism is relatively close to the (English) language. Motivated by this similarity, Pourdamghani et al. (2016) proposed an AMR-to-text method that organises some of these concepts and edges in a flat representation, commonly known as *Linearisation*. Once the linearisation is complete, Pourdamghani et al. (2016) map the flat AMR into an English sentence using a Phrase-Based Machine Translation (PBMT) system. This method yields better results than Flanigan et al. (2016) on development and test set from the LDC2014T12 corpus.

Pourdamghani et al. (2016) train their system using a set of AMR-sentence pairs obtained by the aligner described in Pourdamghani et al. (2014). In order to decrease the sparsity of the AMR formalism caused by the ratio of broad vocabulary and relatively small amount of data, this aligner drops a considerable amount of the AMR structure, such as role edges :ARG0, :ARG1, :mod, etc. However, inspection of the gold-standard alignments provided in the LDC2016E25 corpus revealed that this rule-based compression can be harmful for the generation of sentences, since such role edges can actually be aligned to function words in English sentences. So having these roles available arguably could improve AMR-to-text translation. This indicates that a better comparison of the effects of different preprocessing steps is called for, which we do in this study.

In addition, Pourdamghani et al. (2016) use PBMT, which is devised for translation but also utilised in other NLP tasks, e.g. text simplification (Wubben et al., 2012; Štajner et al., 2015). However, these systems have the disadvantage of having many different feature functions, and finding optimal settings for all of them increases the complexity of the problem from an engineering point of view.

An alternative MT model has been proposed: Neural Machine Translation (NMT). NMT models frame translation as a sequence-to-sequence problem (Bahdanau et al., 2015), and have shown strong results when translating between many different language pairs (Bojar et al., 2015). Recently, Konstas et al. (2017) introduce sequence-to-sequence models for parsing (text-to-AMR) and generation (AMR-to-text). They use a semi-supervised training procedure, incorporating 20M English sentences which do not have a gold-standard AMR, thus overcoming the limited amount of data available. They report state-of-the-art results for the task, which suggests that NMT is a promising alternative for AMR-to-text.

3 Models

We describe our AMR-to-text generation models, which rely on 3 preprocessing steps (*delexicalisation*, *compression*, and/or *linearisation*) followed by a machine translation and realisation steps.

3.1 Delexicalisation

Inspection of the LDC2016E25 corpus reveals that on average 22% of the structure of an AMR are AMR constant values, such as names, quantities, and dates. This information increases the sparsity of the data, and makes it arguably more difficult to map an AMR into a textual format. To address this, Pourdamghani et al. (2016) look for special realisation component for names, dates and numbers in development and test sets and add them on the training set. On the other hand, similar to Konstas et al. (2017), we delexicalised these constants, replacing the original information for tags (e.g., __name1__, __quant1__). A list of tag-values is kept, aiming to identifying the position and to insert the original information in the sentence after the translation step is completed. Figure 2 shows a delexicalised AMR.

3.2 Compression

Given the alignment between an AMR and a sentence, the nodes and edges in the AMR can either be aligned to words in the sentence or not. So before the linearisation step, we would like to know which elements of an AMR should actually be part of the 'flattened' representation.

Following the aligner of Pourdamghani et al. (2014), Pourdamghani et al. (2016) clean an AMR by removing some nodes and edges independent of the context. Instead, we are using alignments that may relate a given node or edge to an English word according to the context. In Figure 1 for instance, the first edge :ARG1 is aligned to the preposition *to* from the sentence, whereas the second edge with a similar value is not aligned to any word in the sentence. Therefore, we need to train a classifier to de-cide which parts of an AMR should be in the flattened representation according to the context.

To solve the problem, we train a Conditional Random Field (CRF) which determines whether a node or an edge of an AMR should be included in the flattened representation. The classification process is sequential over a flattened representation of an AMR obtained by depth first search through the graph. Each element is represented by their name and parent name. We use *CRFSuite* (Okazaki, 2007) to implement our model.

3.3 Linearisation

After Compression, we flatten the AMR to serve as input to the translation step, similarly as proposed in Pourdamghani et al. (2016). We perform a depth-first search through the AMR, printing the elements according to their visiting order. In a second step, also following Pourdamghani et al. (2016), we implemented a version of the 2-Step Classifier from Lerner and Petrov (2013) to preorder the elements from an AMR according to the target side.

2-Step Classifier We implement the preordering method proposed by Lerner and Petrov (2013) in the following way. We define the order among a head node and its subtrees in two steps. In the first, we use a trained maximum entropy classifier to predict for each subtree whether it should occur before or after the head node. As features, we represent the head node by its frameset, whereas the subtree is represented by its head node frameset and parent edge.

Once we divide the subtrees into the ones which should occur before and after the head node, we use a maximum entropy classifier for the size of the subtree group to predict their order. For instance, for a group of 2 subtrees, a maximum entropy classifier specific for groups of 2 subtrees would be used to predict the permutation order of them (0-1 or 1-0). As features, the head node is also represented by its PropBank frameset, whereas the subtrees of the groups are represented by their parent edges, their head node framesets and by which side of the head node they are (before or after). We train classifiers for groups of sizes between 2 and 4 subtrees. For bigger groups, we used the depth first search order.

```
(a3 / attend~e.13
      :ARG0 (p2 / person~e.6)
      :ARG1~e.14 (b / birthday~e.17
            :poss~e.16 (p3 / person :wiki "Mao_Zedong"
                  :name (n / __name1__~e.15)))
      :time (s / since~e.1
      :op1 (t / turn~e.3
            :ARG1 p3~e.2
            :ARG2 (t2 / temporal-quantity :quant __quant1__~e.4
                  :unit (y / year))))
      :mod (a2 / also~e.0)
      :quant (m / more-and-more~e.10,11,12))
```

Delexicalized, Compressed and Linearized AMR:

also~e.0   since~e.1   person~e.2   turn~e.3   __quant1__~e.4   person~e.6   more-and-more~e.10,11,12
attend~e.13   :ARG1~e.14   __name1__~e.15   :poss~e.16   birthday~e.17

Text:

Also~0   since~1   he~2   turned~3   __quant1__~4   ,~5   people~6   had~7   been~8   paying~9   more~10
and~11   more~12   attention~13   to~14   __name1__~15   's~16   birthday~17   .~18

Figure 2: Example of a *Delexicalised, Compressed* and *Linearised* AMR

3.4 Translation models

To map a flat AMR representation into an English sentence, we use phrase-based (Koehn et al., 2003) and neural machine translation (Bahdanau et al., 2015) models.

3.4.1 Phrase-Based Machine Translation

These models use Bayes rule to formalise the problem of translating a text from a source language f to a target language e. In our case, we want to translate a flat amr into an English sentence e as Equation 1 shows.

$$P(e \mid amr) = argmax\, P(amr \mid e)P(e) \quad (1)$$

The *a priori* function $P(e)$ usually is represented by a language model trained on the target language. The *a posteriori* equation is calculated by the log-linear model described at Equation 2.

$$P(amr \mid e) = argmax \sum_{j=1}^{J} \lambda_j h_j(amr, e) \quad (2)$$

Each $h_j(amr, e)$ is an arbitrary feature function over AMR-sentence pairs. To calculate it, the flat amr is segmented into I phrases $a\bar{m}r_1^I$, such that each phrase $a\bar{m}r_i$ is translated into a target phrase $\bar{e}_i$ as described by Equation 3.

$$h_j(amr, e) = argmax\, h_j(a\bar{m}r_i^I, \bar{e}_i^I) \quad (3)$$

As feature functions, we used direct and inverse phrase translation probabilities and lexical weighting; word, unknown word and phrase penalties.

We also used models to reorder a flat amr according to the target sentence e at decoding time. They work on the word-level (Koehn et al., 2003), at the level of adjacent phrases (Koehn et al., 2005) and beyond adjacent phrases (hierarchical-level) (Galley and Manning, 2008). Phrase- and hierarchical level models are also known as lexicalized reordering models.

As Koehn et al. (2003), given s_i the start position of the source phrase $a\bar{m}r_i$ translated into the English phrase $\bar{e}_i$, and f_{i-1} the end position of the source phrase $a\bar{m}r_{i-1}$ translated into the English phrase $\bar{e}_{i-1}$, a distortion model $\alpha^{|s_i - f_{i-1} - 1|}$ is defined as a distance-based reordering model. α is chosen by tunning the model.

Lexicalised models are more complex than distance-based ones, but usually help the system to obtain better results (Koehn et al., 2005; Galley and Manning, 2008). Given a possible set of target phrases $e = (\bar{e}_1, \ldots, \bar{e}_n)$ based on a source amr, and a set of alignments $a = (a_1, \ldots, a_n)$ that maps a source phrase $a\bar{m}r_{a_i}$ into a target phrase $\bar{e}_i$, a lexicalised model aims to predict a set of orientations $o = (o_1, \ldots, o_n)$ as Equation 4 shows.

$$P(o \mid e, amr) = \prod_{i=1}^{n} P(o_i \mid \bar{e}_i, a\bar{m}r_{a_i}, a_{i-1}, a_i)$$

$$(4)$$

Each orientation o_i, attached to the hypothesised target phrase e_i, can be a monotone (M), swap (S) or discontinuous (D) operation according to Equation 5.

$$o_i = \begin{cases} M, & \text{if } a_i - a_{i-1} = 1 \\ S, & \text{if } a_i - a_{i-1} = -1 \\ D, & \text{if } |a_i - a_{i-1}| \neq 1 \end{cases} \qquad (5)$$

In the hierarchical model, we distinguished the discontinuous operation by the direction: discontinuous right ($a_i - a_{i-1} < 1$) and discontinuous left ($a_i - a_{i-1} > 1$). These models are important for our task, since the preordering method used in the Linearisation step can be insufficient to adequate it to the target sentence order.

3.4.2 Neural Machine Translation

Following the attention-based Neural Machine Translation (NMT) model introduced by Bahdanau et al. (2015), given a flat $amr = (amr_1, amr_2, \cdots, amr_N)$ and its English sentence translation $e = (e_1, e_2, \cdots, e_M)$, a single neural network is trained to translate amr into e by directly learning to model $p(e \mid amr)$. The network consists of one *encoder*, one *decoder*, and one *attention mechanism*.

The encoder is a bi-directional RNN with gated recurrent units (GRU) (Cho et al., 2014), where one forward RNN $\overrightarrow{\Phi}_{\text{enc}}$ reads the amr from left to right and generates a sequence of *forward annotation vectors* $(\overrightarrow{h}_1, \overrightarrow{h}_2, \cdots, \overrightarrow{h}_N)$ at each encoder time step $i \in [1, N]$, and a backward RNN $\overleftarrow{\Phi}_{\text{enc}}$ reads the amr from right to left and generates a sequence of *backward annotation vectors* $(\overleftarrow{h}_N, \overleftarrow{h}_{N-1}, \cdots, \overleftarrow{h}_1)$. The final annotation vector is the concatenation of forward and backward vectors $h_i = [\overrightarrow{h}_i; \overleftarrow{h}_i]$, and $C = (h_1, h_2, \cdots, h_N)$ is the set of source annotation vectors.

The decoder is a neural LM conditioned on the previously emitted words and the source sentence via an attention mechanism over C. A multilayer perceptron is used to initialise the decoder's hidden state s_0, where the input to this network is the concatenation of the last forward and backward vectors $[\overrightarrow{h}_N; \overleftarrow{h}_1]$.

At each time step t of the decoder, we compute a *time-dependent* context vector c_t based on the annotation vectors C, the decoder's previous hidden state s_{t-1} and the target English word $\tilde{e}_{t-1}$ emitted by the decoder in the previous time step. A single-layer feed-forward network computes an *expected align-ment* $a_{t,i}$ between each source annotation vector h_i and the target word to be emitted at the current time step t, as in (6):

$$a_{t,i} = v_a{}^T \tanh(U_a s_{t-1} + W_a h_i). \qquad (6)$$

In Equation (7), these expected alignments are normalised and converted into probabilities:

$$\alpha_{t,i} = \frac{\exp(a_{t,i})}{\sum_{j=1}^{N} \exp(a_{t,j})}, \qquad (7)$$

where $\alpha_{t,i}$ are called the model's *attention weights*, which are in turn used in computing the time-dependent context vector $c_t = \sum_{i=1}^{N} \alpha_{t,i} h_i$. Finally, the context vector c_t is used in computing the decoder's hidden state s_t for the current time step t, as shown in Equation (8):

$$s_t = \Phi_{\text{dec}}(s_{t-1}, W_e[\tilde{e}_{t-1}], c_t), \qquad (8)$$

where s_{t-1} is the decoder's previous hidden state, $W_e[\tilde{e}_{t-1}]$ is the embedding of the word emitted in the previous time step, and c_t is the updated time-dependent context vector. Given a hidden state s_t, the probabilities for the next target word are computed using one projection layer followed by a soft-max, as illustrated in eq. (9), where the matrices L_o, L_s, L_w and L_c are transformation matrices and c_t is the time-dependent context vector.

3.5 Realisation

Since we delexicalise names, dates, quantities and values from AMRs, we need to textually realise this information once we obtain the results from the translation step. As we kept all the original information and their relation with the tags, we just need to replace one for the other.

We implement some rules to adequate our generated texts to the ones we saw in the training set. Different from the AMRs, we represent months nominally, and not numerically - month *5* will be *May* for example. Values and quantities bigger than a thousand are also part realised nominally. The value *8500000000* would be realised as *8.5 billion* for instance. On the other hand, names are realised as they are.

$$p(e_t = k \mid e_{<t}, c_t) \propto \exp(L_o \tanh(L_s s_t + L_w E_e[\hat{e}_{t-1}] + L_c c_t)). \tag{9}$$

4 Evaluation

4.1 Data

We used the corpus LDC2016E25 provided by the SemEval 2017 Task 9 in our evaluation. This corpus consists of aligned AMR-sentence pairs, mostly newswire. We considered the train/dev/test sets splitting proposed in the original setting, totaling 36,521, 1,368 and 1,371 AMR-sentence pairs, respectively. Compression and Linearisation methods, as well as Phrase-based Machine Translation models were trained over the gold-standard alignments between AMRs and sentences on the training set of the corpus.

4.2 Evaluated Models

We test models with and without the Delexicalisation/Realisation (-Delex and +Delex) and Compression (-Compress and +Compress) steps. In models without the Compression step, we include all the elements from an AMR in the flattened representation. For the Linearisation step, we flatten the AMR structure based on a depth-first search (-Preorder) or preorder it with our 2-step classifier (+Preorder). Finally, we translate a flattened AMR into text using a Phrase-based (PBMT) and a Neural Machine Translation model (NMT). In total, we evaluated 16 models.

Phrase-based Machine Translation We used a standard PBMT system built using Moses toolkit (Koehn et al., 2007). At training time, we extract and score phrase sentences up to the size of 9 tokens. All the feature functions were trained using the gold-standard alignments from the training set and their weights were tuned on the development data using k-batch MIRA with $k = 60$ (Cherry and Foster, 2012) with BLEU as the evaluation metric. A distortion limit of 6 was used for the reordering models. Lexicalised reordering models were bidirectional. At decoding time, we use a stack size of 1000.

Our language model $P(e)$ is a 5-gram LM trained on the Gigaword Third Edition corpus using KenLM (Heafield et al., 2013). For the models with the Delexicalisation step, we trained the language model with a delexicalised version of Gigaword by parsing the corpus using the Stanford Named Entity Recognition tool (Finkel et al., 2005). All the entities labeled as LOCATION, PERSON, ORGANISATION or MISC were replaced by the tag __nameX__. Entities labeled as NUMBER or MONEY were replaced by the tag __quantX__. Finally, entities labeled as PERCENT or ORDINAL were replaced by __valueX__. In the tags, X is replaced by the ordinal position of the entity in the sentence.

Neural Machine Translation The encoder is a bidirectional RNN with GRU, each with a 1024D hidden unit. Source and target word embeddings are 620D each and are both trained jointly with the model. All non-recurrent matrices are initialised by sampling from a Gaussian ($\mu = 0, \sigma = 0.01$), recurrent matrices are random orthogonal and bias vectors are all initialised to zero. The decoder RNN also uses GRU and is a neural LM conditioned on its previous emissions and the source sentence by means of the source attention mechanism.

We apply dropout with a probability of 0.3 in both source and target word embeddings, in the encoder and decoder RNNs inputs and recurrent connections, and before the readout operation in the decoder RNN. We follow Gal and Ghahramani (2016) and apply dropout to the encoder and decoder RNNs using the same mask in all time steps.

Models are trained using stochastic gradient descent with Adadelta (Zeiler, 2012) and minibatches of size 40. We apply early stopping for model selection based on BLEU scores, so that if a model does not improve on the validation set for more than 20 epochs, training is halted.

4.3 Models for Comparison

We compare BLEU scores for some of the AMR-to-text systems described in the literature (Flanigan et al., 2016; Song et al., 2016; Pourdamghani et al., 2016; Song et al., 2017; Konstas et al., 2017). Since the models of Flanigan et al. (2016) and Pourdamghani et al. (2016) are publicly available, we also use them with the same training data as our models. For Flanigan et al. (2016), we specifically use the version available on GitHub[2].

For Pourdamghani et al. (2016), we use the version available at the first author's website[3]. The rules used for the preordering model and the feature functions from the PBMT system are trained using alignments over AMR–sentence pairs from the training set obtained with the aligner described by Pourdamghani et al. (2014). We do not use lexicalised reordering models as Pourdamghani et al. (2016). Moreover, we tune the weights of the feature functions with MERT (Och, 2003).

Both models make use of a 5-gram language model trained on Gigaword Third Edition corpus with KenLM.

4.4 Metrics

To evaluate fluency, adequacy and post-editing effort of the models, we use BLEU (Papineni et al., 2002), METEOR (Lavie and Agarwal, 2007) and TER (Snover et al., 2006), respectively.

5 Results

Table 1 depicts the scores of the different models by the size of the data they were trained on. For illustration, we depicted the BLEU scores of all the AMR-to-text systems described in the literature. The models of Flanigan et al. (2016) and Pourdamghani et al. (2016) were officially trained with 10,313 AMR-sentence pairs from the LDC2014T12 corpus, and with 36,521 AMR-sentence pairs from the LDC2016E25 in our study (as our models). The ones of Song et al. (2016) and Song et al. (2017) were trained with 16,833 pairs from the LDC2015E86 corpus. Konstas et al. (2017), which presents the highest quantitative result in the task so far, also used the LDC2015E86 corpus plus 20 million English sentences from the Gigaword corpus with a semi-supervised approach. We report the results when their model were trained only with AMR-sentence pairs from the corpus, and when improved with more 20 million sentences.

Among the PBMT models, the Delexicalisation step (+Delex) does not seem to play a role in obtaining better sentences from AMRs. All the models with the preordering method in Linearisation

---

	Data Size	BLEU	METEOR	TER
(Flanigan et al., 2016)	~10K	22.1	–	–
(Pourdamghani et al., 2016)	~10K	26.9	–	–
(Konstas et al., 2017)	~17K	22.0	–	–
(Song et al., 2016)	~17K	22.4	–	–
(Song et al., 2017)	~17K	25.6	–	–
(Flanigan et al., 2016)	~36K	19.6	–	–
(Pourdamghani et al., 2016)	~36K	24.3	–	–
(Konstas et al., 2017)	~20M	<u>33.8</u>	–	–
NMT				
+Delex-Compress-Preorder		18.9	<u>26.6</u>	<u>66.2</u>
+Delex+Compress-Preorder		14.6	23.6	77.0
+Delex-Compress+Preorder		<u>19.3</u>	26.3	69.3
+Delex+Compress+Preorder	~36K	15.2	23.8	77.8
-Delex-Compress-Preorder		18.2	24.8	67.7
-Delex+Compress-Preorder		15.2	22.4	72.8
-Delex-Compress+Preorder		19.0	25.5	66.6
-Delex+Compress+Preorder		15.9	22.6	71.4
PBMT				
+Delex-Compress-Preorder		20.6	32.8	64.5
+Delex+Compress-Preorder		22.2	33.0	63.3
+Delex-Compress+Preorder		24.6	34.3	60.4
+Delex+Compress+Preorder	~36K	23.9	33.7	60.5
-Delex-Compress-Preorder		21.0	32.7	65.5
-Delex+Compress-Preorder		25.6	34.1	60.9
-Delex-Compress+Preorder		26.5	<u>34.9</u>	59.9
-Delex+Compress+Preorder		<u>26.8</u>	34.7	<u>59.4</u>

Table 1: MT scores for the evaluated models by the size of the training data. Best baseline, PBMT and NMT results were underlined.

(+Preorder) introduce better results than Flanigan et al. (2016) and Song et al. (2016), whereas only the lexicalised models with the preordering method (PBMT+Delex[+|-]Compress+Preorder) outperform Song et al. (2017) and introduce competitive results with Pourdamghani et al. (2016).

In our NMT models, apparently the Compression step is harmful to the task, whereas Delexicalisation and preordering in Linearisation lead to better results. However, none of the NMT models outperform neither the PBMT models nor the baselines.

6 Discussion

In this paper, we studied models for AMR-to-text generation using machine translation. We systematically analysed the effects of 3 processing strategies on AMRs before feeding them either to a Phrase-based or a Neural MT system. The evaluation was performed on the LDC2016E25 corpus, provided by SemEval 2017 Task 9. All the models had the fluency, adequacy and post-editing effort of their produced sentences measured by BLEU, METEOR and TER, respectively. In general, we found that processing AMRs helps, although the effects differ for the different systems.

Phrase-based MT Delexicalisation (+Delex) does not seem to play a role in obtaining better sentences from AMRs using PBMT. Our best model (PBMT-Delex+Compress+Preorder) presents competitive results to Pourdamghani et al. (2016) with the advantage that no technique is necessary to overcome data sparsity.

Compressing an AMR graph with a classifier shows improvements over a comparable model without compression, but not as strong as preordering the elements in the Linearisation step. In fact, preordering seems to be the most important preprocessing step across all three MT preprocessing metrics. We note that the preordering success was expected, based on previous results (Pourdamghani et al., 2016).

Neural MT The first impression from our NMT experiments is that using Compression consistently deteriorates translations according to all metrics evaluated. Delexicalisation seems to improve results, corroborating the findings from Konstas et al. (2017). While Delexicalisation is harmful and Compression is beneficial for PBMT, we see the opposite in NMT models. Besides the differences between these two MT architectures, applying preordering in the Linearisation step improves results in both cases. This seems to contradict the finding in Konstas et al. (2017) regarding neural models. We conjecture that the additional training data used by Konstas et al. (2017) may have decreased the gap between using and not using preordering (see also below). More research is necessary to settle this point.

PBMT vs. NMT PBMT models generate much better sentences from AMRs than NMT models in terms of fluency, adequacy and post-editing effort. We believe that the lower performance of NMT models is due to the small size of the training set (36,521 AMR-sentence pairs). Neural models are known to perform well when trained on much larger data sets, e.g. in the order of millions of entries, as exemplified by Konstas et al. (2017). PBMT models trained on small data sets clearly outperform NMT ones, e.g. Konstas et al. (2017) reported 22.0 BLEU, whereas Pourdamghani et al. (2016)'s best model achieved 26.9 BLEU, and our best model performs comparably (26.8 BLEU).

Model comparison While the best PBMT models are comparable to the state-of-the-art AMR-to-text systems, the current best results are reported by Konstas et al. (2017), showing the potential of applying deep learning onto large amounts of training data with a 33.8 BLEU-score. However, this result crucially relies on the existence of a very large dataset. Interestingly, when applied in a situation with limited amounts of data, Konstas et al. (2017) report substantially lower performance scores. In such situations, our PBMT models, like Pourdamghani et al. (2016), look appear to be a good alternative option.

7 Conclusion

In this work, we systematically studied different MT models to *translate* AMRs into natural language. We observed that the Delexicalisation, Compression, and Linearisation steps have different impacts on AMR-to-text generation depending on the MT architecture used. We observed that delexicalising AMRs yields the best results in NMT models, in contrast to PBMT models. On the other hand, for both PBMT models and NMT models, preordering the AMR in Linearisation introduces better results.

Among our models, PBMT generally outperforms NMT. Finally, the literature suggests that the improvements obtained by having more data are larger than those obtained with improved preprocessing strategies. Nonetheless, combining the right preprocessing strategy with large volumes of training data should lead to further improvements.

Acknowledgments

This work has been supported by the National Council of Scientific and Technological Development from Brazil (CNPq). Iacer Calixto has received funding from Science Foundation Ireland in the ADAPT Centre for Digital Content Technology (www.adaptcentre.ie) at Dublin City University funded under the SFI Research Centres Programme (Grant 13/RC/2106) co-funded under the European Regional Development Fund and the European Union Horizon 2020 research and innovation programme under grant agreement 645452 (QT21).

References

Yoav Artzi, Kenton Lee, and Luke Zettlemoyer. 2015. Broad-coverage ccg semantic parsing with amr. In *Proceedings of the 2015 Conference on Empirical Methods in Natural Language Processing*, pages 1699–1710, Lisbon, Portugal, September. Association for Computational Linguistics.

Dzmitry Bahdanau, Kyunghyun Cho, and Yoshua Bengio. 2015. Neural Machine Translation by Jointly Learning to Align and Translate. In *International Conference on Learning Representations, ICLR 2015*, San Diego, California.

Laura Banarescu, Claire Bonial, Shu Cai, Madalina Georgescu, Kira Griffitt, Ulf Hermjakob, Kevin Knight, Philipp Koehn, Martha Palmer, and Nathan Schneider. 2013. Abstract meaning representation for sembanking. In *Proceedings of the 7th Linguistic Annotation Workshop and Interoperability with Discourse*, pages 178–186, Sofia, Bulgaria, August. Association for Computational Linguistics.

Ondřej Bojar, Rajen Chatterjee, Christian Federmann, Barry Haddow, Matthias Huck, Chris Hokamp, Philipp Koehn, Varvara Logacheva, Christof Monz, Matteo Negri, Matt Post, Carolina Scarton, Lucia Specia, and Marco Turchi. 2015. Findings of the 2015 Workshop on Statistical Machine Translation. In *Proceedings of the Tenth Workshop on Statistical Machine Translation*, pages 1–46, Lisbon, Portugal, September. Association for Computational Linguistics.

Johan Bos. 2016. Expressive power of abstract meaning representations. *Comput. Linguist.*, 42(3):527–535, September.

Colin Cherry and George Foster. 2012. Batch tuning strategies for statistical machine translation. In *Proceedings of the 2012 Conference of the North American Chapter of the Association for Computational Linguistics: Human Language Technologies*, NAACL HLT '12, pages 427–436, Stroudsburg, PA, USA. Association for Computational Linguistics.

Kyunghyun Cho, Bart van Merrienboer, Dzmitry Bahdanau, and Yoshua Bengio. 2014. On the Properties of Neural Machine Translation: Encoder–Decoder Approaches. In *Proceedings of SSST-8, Eighth Workshop on Syntax, Semantics and Structure in Statistical Translation*, pages 103–111, Doha, Qatar, October.

Jenny Rose Finkel, Trond Grenager, and Christopher Manning. 2005. Incorporating non-local information into information extraction systems by gibbs sampling. In *Proceedings of the 43rd Annual Meeting of the Association for Computational Linguistics (ACL'05)*, pages 363–370, Ann Arbor, Michigan, June. Association for Computational Linguistics.

Jeffrey Flanigan, Sam Thomson, Jaime Carbonell, Chris Dyer, and Noah A. Smith. 2014. A discriminative graph-based parser for the abstract meaning representation. In *Proceedings of the 52nd Annual Meeting of the Association for Computational Linguistics (Volume 1: Long Papers)*, pages 1426–1436, Baltimore, Maryland, June. Association for Computational Linguistics.

Jeffrey Flanigan, Chris Dyer, Noah A. Smith, and Jaime Carbonell. 2016. Generation from abstract meaning representation using tree transducers. In *Proceedings of the 2016 Conference of the North American Chapter of the Association for Computational Linguistics: Human Language Technologies*, pages 731–739, San Diego, California, June. Association for Computational Linguistics.

Yarin Gal and Zoubin Ghahramani. 2016. A Theoretically Grounded Application of Dropout in Recurrent Neural Networks. In *Advances in Neural Information Processing Systems, NIPS*, pages 1019–1027, Barcelona, Spain.

Michel Galley and Christopher D. Manning. 2008. A simple and effective hierarchical phrase reordering model. In *Proceedings of the 2008 Conference on Empirical Methods in Natural Language Processing*, pages 848–856, Honolulu, Hawaii, October. Association for Computational Linguistics.

A. Gatt and E. Krahmer. 2017. Survey of the State of the Art in Natural Language Generation: Core tasks, applications and evaluation. *ArXiv e-prints*, March.

Dimitra Gkatzia, Helen Hastie, and Oliver Lemon. 2014. Comparing multi-label classification with reinforcement learning for summarisation of time-series data. In *Proceedings of the 52nd Annual Meeting of the Association for Computational Linguistics (Volume 1: Long Papers)*, pages 1231–1240, Baltimore, Maryland, June. Association for Computational Linguistics.

Kenneth Heafield, Ivan Pouzyrevsky, Jonathan H. Clark, and Philipp Koehn. 2013. Scalable modified kneser-ney language model estimation. In *Proceedings of the 51st Annual Meeting of the Association for Computational Linguistics (Volume 2: Short Papers)*, pages 690–696, Sofia, Bulgaria, August. Association for Computational Linguistics.

Philipp Koehn, Franz Josef Och, and Daniel Marcu. 2003. Statistical phrase-based translation. In *Proceedings of the 2003 Conference of the North American Chapter of the Association for Computational Linguistics on Human Language Technology - Volume 1*, NAACL '03, pages 48–54, Stroudsburg, PA, USA. Association for Computational Linguistics.

Philipp Koehn, Amittai Axelrod, Alexandra Birch, Chris Callison-Burch, Miles Osborne, and David Talbot. 2005. Edinburgh System Description for the 2005

IWSLT Speech Translation Evaluation. In *International Workshop on Spoken Language Translation*.

Philipp Koehn, Hieu Hoang, Alexandra Birch, Chris Callison-Burch, Marcello Federico, Nicola Bertoldi, Brooke Cowan, Wade Shen, Christine Moran, Richard Zens, Chris Dyer, Ondřej Bojar, Alexandra Constantin, and Evan Herbst. 2007. Moses: Open source toolkit for statistical machine translation. In *Proceedings of the 45th Annual Meeting of the ACL on Interactive Poster and Demonstration Sessions*, ACL '07, pages 177–180, Stroudsburg, PA, USA. Association for Computational Linguistics.

I. Konstas, S. Iyer, M. Yatskar, Y. Choi, and L. Zettlemoyer. 2017. Neural AMR: Sequence-to-Sequence Models for Parsing and Generation. *ArXiv e-prints*, April.

Alon Lavie and Abhaya Agarwal. 2007. Meteor: An Automatic Metric for MT Evaluation with High Levels of Correlation with Human Judgments. In *Proceedings of the Second Workshop on Statistical Machine Translation*, StatMT '07, pages 228–231, Prague, Czech Republic.

Uri Lerner and Slav Petrov. 2013. Source-side classifier preordering for machine translation. In *Proceedings of the 2013 Conference on Empirical Methods in Natural Language Processing*, pages 513–523, Seattle, Washington, USA, October. Association for Computational Linguistics.

Franz Josef Och. 2003. Minimum error rate training in statistical machine translation. In *Proceedings of the 41st Annual Meeting of the Association for Computational Linguistics*, pages 160–167, Sapporo, Japan, July. Association for Computational Linguistics.

Naoaki Okazaki. 2007. Crfsuite: a fast implementation of conditional random fields (crfs).

Kishore Papineni, Salim Roukos, Todd Ward, and Wei-Jing Zhu. 2002. Bleu: a method for automatic evaluation of machine translation. In *Proceedings of 40th Annual Meeting of the Association for Computational Linguistics*, pages 311–318, Philadelphia, Pennsylvania, USA, July. Association for Computational Linguistics.

Nima Pourdamghani, Yang Gao, Ulf Hermjakob, and Kevin Knight. 2014. Aligning english strings with abstract meaning representation graphs. In *Proceedings of the 2014 Conference on Empirical Methods in Natural Language Processing (EMNLP)*, pages 425–429, Doha, Qatar, October. Association for Computational Linguistics.

Nima Pourdamghani, Kevin Knight, and Ulf Hermjakob. 2016. Generating english from abstract meaning representations. In *Proceedings of the 9th International Natural Language Generation conference*, pages 21–25, Edinburgh, UK, September 5-8. Association for Computational Linguistics.

Ehud Reiter and Robert Dale. 2000. *Building natural language generation systems*. Cambridge University Press, New York, NY, USA.

Matthew Snover, Bonnie Dorr, Richard Schwartz, Linnea Micciulla, and John Makhoul. 2006. A study of translation edit rate with targeted human annotation. In *Proceedings of Association for Machine Translation in the Americas, AMTA*, pages 223–231, Cambridge, MA, USA.

Linfeng Song, Yue Zhang, Xiaochang Peng, Zhiguo Wang, and Daniel Gildea. 2016. Amr-to-text generation as a traveling salesman problem. In *Proceedings of the 2016 Conference on Empirical Methods in Natural Language Processing*, pages 2084–2089, Austin, Texas, November. Association for Computational Linguistics.

L. Song, X. Peng, Y. Zhang, Z. Wang, and D. Gildea. 2017. AMR-to-text Generation with Synchronous Node Replacement Grammar. *ArXiv e-prints*, February.

M. Theune, E. Klabbers, J. R. De Pijper, E. Krahmer, and J. Odijk. 2001. From data to speech: A general approach. *Nat. Lang. Eng.*, 7(1):47–86, March.

Sanja Štajner, Iacer Calixto, and Horacio Saggion. 2015. Automatic text simplification for spanish: Comparative evaluation of various simplification strategies. In *Proceedings of the International Conference Recent Advances in Natural Language Processing*, pages 618–626, Hissar, Bulgaria, September.

Sander Wubben, Antal van den Bosch, and Emiel Krahmer. 2012. Sentence simplification by monolingual machine translation. In *Proceedings of the 50th Annual Meeting of the Association for Computational Linguistics: Long Papers - Volume 1*, ACL '12, pages 1015–1024, Stroudsburg, PA, USA. Association for Computational Linguistics.

Kelvin Xu, Jimmy Ba, Ryan Kiros, Kyunghyun Cho, Aaron Courville, Ruslan Salakhudinov, Rich Zemel, and Yoshua Bengio. 2015. Show, attend and tell: Neural image caption generation with visual attention. In David Blei and Francis Bach, editors, *Proceedings of the 32nd International Conference on Machine Learning (ICML-15)*, pages 2048–2057. JMLR Workshop and Conference Proceedings.

Matthew D. Zeiler. 2012. ADADELTA: An Adaptive Learning Rate Method. *CoRR*, abs/1212.5701.

A Survey on Intelligent Poetry Generation: Languages, Features, Techniques, Reutilisation and Evaluation

Hugo Gonçalo Oliveira
CISUC, Department of Informatics Engineering
University of Coimbra, Portugal
`hroliv@dei.uc.pt`

Abstract

Poetry generation is becoming popular among researchers of Natural Language Generation, Computational Creativity and, broadly, Artificial Intelligence. To produce text that may be regarded as poetry, computational systems are typically knowledge-intensive and deal with several levels of language. Interest on the topic resulted in the development of several poetry generators described in the literature, with different features covered or handled differently, by a broad range of alternative approaches, as well as different perspectives on evaluation, another challenging aspect due the underlying subjectivity. This paper surveys intelligent poetry generators around a set of relevant axis – target language, form and content features, applied techniques, reutilisation of material, and evaluation – and aims to organise work developed on this topic so far.

1 Introduction

Interest in the development of automatic methods for generating poetry dates back to the 1960s, even before computers were accessible to everyone. A commonly cited example is the creation of a large number of new poems by interchanging the lines in a set of poems, always respecting the relative position of each line within a stanza (Queneau, 1961). Early approaches to (so-called) experimental poetry applied a set of combinatory processes to existing poems, in order to generate new ones. This challenge was embraced by different groups, such as the Portuguese movement of Experimental Poetry (PO.EX, see e.g. the collection by Torres and Baldwin (2014)), or

the French Atelier of Literature Assisted by Maths and Computers (ALAMO, see Oulipo (1981)). A notable work of the latter includes the *rimbaudelaires*, where the structure of a poem by Rimbaud is filled with vocabulary from Baudelaire's poems. At the time, interested people were mostly poets or researchers from the domain of humanities.

It was not until the turn of the millennium that this area started to get attention from the Computer Science community, mainly researchers in the domain of Artificial Intelligence (AI) and, specifically, Computational Creativity (Colton and Wiggins, 2012). Since the works of Gervás (2000) and Manurung (2003), the development of "intelligent" poetry generation systems has seen a significant increase. These systems are not limited to rewriting text in a poetic form. They are often knowledge-intensive natural language generation systems that deal with several levels of language (e.g. phonetics, lexical choice, syntax and semantics) to produce aesthetically-pleasing text with a creative value.

What makes this task more interesting is that some levels of language do not have to be strictly addressed. Writing poetic text does not have to be an extremely precise task (Gervás, 2000), as several rules, typically present in the production of natural language, need to be broken (Manurung, 2003). On the other hand, poetry involves a high occurrence of interdependent linguistic phenomena where features such as metre, rhyme, and the presence of figurative language play an important role. For instance, it might be ok to transmit a less clear message, in a trade-off for a pleasant sound given by a highly regular metre. In fact, the latter is easier to achieve by a

11

Proceedings of The 10th International Natural Language Generation conference, pages 11–20,
Santiago de Compostela, Spain, September 4-7 2017. ©2017 Association for Computational Linguistics

computer, while transmitting a clear message can be highly challenging, especially when constrained by the previous features.

Given the challenge involved and the range of possibilities, it is not surprising to see many poetry generators developed as serious research efforts where distinct approaches to tackle this common goal are explored, reported in scientific papers, with enough detail, and even compared to prior work. Besides the involved challenge, poetry generators can be useful for applications in different areas, such as education or electronic entertainment.

While not exactly an introduction to the topic, this paper surveys poetry generation systems according to relevant axis where different trends have emerged for the goal of generating poetry automatically – though not necessarily enough to cover every single detail in this topic. Instead of a full description of specific systems, it is organised around the identified axis and focuses on distinct ways they were handled by different systems. For those interested on the topic, this can be seen as a quicker reference for selecting suitable approaches, possibly tackling their limitations, or opt instead for alternative approaches, novel for poetry generation.

This paper is structured as follows: Section 2 enumerates the languages for which intelligent poetry generators have been developed. Section 3 overviews the most common poetic features considered by these systems. Section 4 focuses on the different approaches and resources that poetry generators resort to for selecting their content. Section 5 describes some of the AI techniques applied by these systems towards their goal. Section 6 is about the different degrees to which human-produced text is exploited or reused by different systems, for inspiration. Section 7 overviews distinct evaluation approaches applied to poetry generators. Given the subjectivity involved in poetry generation, not all surveyed systems have been evaluated, and most have only to a certain extent. Section 8 concludes this paper with some final remarks.

2 Languages

Poetry is an artistic expression of language. Humans have produced poetry in many languages and, due to their specificities, different languages happen to follow different poetic traditions, often focused on different forms. While the majority of poetry generation systems targets English and produces text in this language, there are systems of this kind in other languages, enumerated in this section.

Well-known early attempts to poetry generation included French (Queneau, 1961; Oulipo, 1981), but Spanish was one of the first languages where this topic was explored in the context of AI, and related issues were discussed (Gervás, 2000; Gervás, 2001). For Portuguese, another romance language, song lyrics have been automatically generated for a given melody (Gonçalo Oliveira et al., 2007), and poetry has been produced according to user-given structures that would set the number of lines, stanzas, syllables per stanza, or the rhyme pattern (Gonçalo Oliveira, 2012). In an effort to use the same architecture for generating poetry in different languages, the previous system was extended to cover also Spanish and English (Gonçalo Oliveira et al., 2017). Another poetry generator originally developed for English was also adapted to produce poetry in Spanish (Ghazvininejad et al., 2016).

Traditional eight-line Basque poems, aiming to be sung, have also been produced automatically (Agirrezabal et al., 2013). Although, as Portuguese and Spanish, Basque is spoken in the Iberian Peninsula, it has different origins and is significantly different from romance languages. Toivanen et al. (2012)'s system produced poetry in Finnish, another European language.

Asian languages have also been targeted, some of which with specific tonal and rhythm requirements in poetry generation. This includes the generation of song lyrics in Tamil (Ramakrishnan A et al., 2009; Ramakrishnan A and Devi, 2010), a phonetic language; ancient Chinese classic poetry (Yan et al., 2013; Zhang and Lapata, 2014; Yan, 2016), with strict tonal and rhythm requirements; follow-up lines in Bengali (Das and Gambäck, 2014), matching the rhythm of a user-given line; and poetry inspired by news articles, in Indonesian (Rashel and Manurung, 2014).

3 Form features

Despite all the levels of language involved in poetry, form is a key feature for, at the first glance, recognising the resulting text as poetic. Most common form-related features are, without a doubt, a regular metre and rhymes. When alone, both of them are quite straightforward to handle by computer programs, especially when compared with content features.

Metre is generally modelled with the number of syllables each line has, sometimes also considering the stress patterns (e.g. Manurung (2003), Gervás (2001), Tobing and Manurung (2015)), which indicate the position of the stressed syllables. Rhyme results from the repetition of certain sounds (e.g. in *great* and *mate*). End-rhymes, the most typical, occur when two lines end in the same sound. But some systems consider other kinds of rhyme, such as assonance or alliteration, which respectively involve the repetition of the same vowel or of a consonant sound throughout the poem.

For less phonetic languages, such as Portuguese (Gonçalo Oliveira et al., 2007) or Spanish (Gervás, 2001), it is often enough to design a set of orthography-based rules to handle metre and rhyme. For English, poetry generators (e.g. Manurung (2003), Colton et al. (2012), Tobing and Manurung (2015)) typically resort to a pronunciation dictionary for this purpose (e.g. CMU's[1]). Yet, automatic methods for the automatic scansion of poetry have also been developed (Agirrezabal et al., 2016).

Metre and rhymes are often organised according to a well-known poetry form and some systems are designed to produce only poems of specific forms. *Haikus* traditionally have 3 lines, respectively with 5, 7 and 5 syllables (Manurung, 2003; Netzer et al., 2009), but there are modern haikus with a different number (Wong and Chun, 2008). *Limericks* have five lines, with lines 1, 2 and 5 generally longer, and rhyme of the kind AABBA (Levy, 2001; Manurung, 2003). The *sonnet* is a classic form of poem with 14 lines, typically with 10-syllables each. Depending on the tradition, it might have different groupings, stress patterns and rhyming schemes, such as ABAB CDCD EFEF GG (Ghazvininejad et al., 2016). Spanish traditional forms (Gervás, 2000; Gervás, 2001) include the *romance*, lines of 8 syllables, where all even-numbered rhyme together; the *cuarteto*, a stanza with four 11-syllable lines, where

the two outer lines rhyme together; and *tercetos encadenados*, stanzas of three 11-syllable lines with the pattern ABA BCB CDC... *Bertsolaritza* is a Basque traditional verse with metre and rhyme constraints, typically sung (Agirrezabal et al., 2013). The generation of classic Chinese poetry has focused mostly on *quartrains*, four lines of 5 or 7 characters with a rigid tonal pattern where two kinds of tones are interleaved, and a rhyme scheme where the majority of the lines in the same poem end with the same vowel, but not the same character (Yan et al., 2013; Zhang and Lapata, 2014; Yan, 2016).

The poetry form can be decided from the initial data (Gervás, 2000), while other systems generate poetry in more or less any form, depending on a user-provided template, which might be strictly structural (Gonçalo Oliveira, 2012) or a poem, possibly with some words stripped (Toivanen et al., 2014). There are also systems focused on generating song lyrics, which have less traditional forms, but where metre is key for matching the rhythm, while other features should still be present. These include melodies where stressed and weak beats are identified (Gonçalo Oliveira et al., 2007; Ramakrishnan A et al., 2009; Gonçalo Oliveira, 2015), pop songs (Barbieri et al., 2012), or rap (Malmi et al., 2016; Potash et al., 2015) where, besides rhyme, assonance is modelled as the repetition of vowel phonemes (e.g. in *raps* and *tax*).

4 Content features

Even though form ends up shaping content, it is not enough for a poem to simply follow a recognisable form of poetry. According to Manurung (2003), besides *poeticness*, poetic text should hold two other fundamental properties: it must obey linguistic conventions, prescribed by a given grammar and lexicon (*grammaticality*); and it must convey a conceptual message, meaningful under some interpretation (*meaningfulness*). To some extent, following syntactic rules is often a consequence of most of the surveyed approaches, as they rely on text fragments, lexical-syntactic patterns or language models acquired from human-produced text (see following sections). On the other hand, meaningfulness is less trivial to handle automatically. Given the involved challenge, it is not always explicitly consid-

---

[1] `http://svn.code.sf.net/p/cmusphinx/code/trunk/cmudict/`

ered and is often only softly satisfied, for instance, by using words that belong to the same semantic domain. This section describes how different poetry generators select their content in order to transmit a meaningful message or, at least, to be, as much as possible, semantically coherent.

Intelligent poetry generation systems often exploit a model of semantics, either a semantic knowledge base, or a statistical model of distributional semantics. The former is usually a more theoretical view on linguistic knowledge, where words are connected according to labelled relations, with different meanings. Poetry generators have used knowledge bases with verbs and their restrictions and ontological categories (Ramakrishnan A and Devi, 2010); semantic networks extracted from dictionaries, that go beyond synonymy and hypernymy, and cover other relations such as causation, property and others (Gonçalo Oliveira, 2012); WordNet, a lexical knowledge base (Colton et al., 2012; Agirrezabal et al., 2013; Tobing and Manurung, 2015); and ConceptNet, a common sense knowledge base (Das and Gambäck, 2014). Those have been used not only to restrict the generated words to a common semantic domain, but also for increasing the paraphrasing power, towards higher variation and better covering of different metres.

Distributional models of semantics target how language is actually used, in a collection of documents, and consider that words that occur in similar contexts have similar meanings. These include vector space models, either based on words (Wong and Chun, 2008; McGregor et al., 2016), also including word embeddings learned from collections of poems (Yan, 2016) or from Wikipedia (Ghazvininejad et al., 2016), or based on sentences (Malmi et al., 2016), both used to compute the semantic relatedness with the cosine similarity; or word associations (Netzer et al., 2009; Toivanen et al., 2012) which, according to some authors, capture relations in poetic text better than WordNet-like lexical knowledge bases.

In some systems, text is generated according to a grammar for handling syntax, possibly also considering semantic features (Manurung, 2003). In Gonçalo Oliveira (2012)'s system, the grammar is tightly related to the semantics, as each rule transmits a known semantic relation and can be instantiated with any pair of words sharing relations of that kind (e.g. *vehicle-car* or *fruit-mango*, for hypernymy).

Yet, in order to enable some kind of interpretation, the poem must actually be about something or, at least, be different for different stimuli, reflected in its content. Stimuli can be given in different forms, with different degrees of precision, namely: a list of semantic predicates (e.g. *love(John, Mary)*) (Manurung, 2003); one (Netzer et al., 2009; Toivanen et al., 2013; Ghazvininejad et al., 2016) or more (Wong and Chun, 2008; Gonçalo Oliveira, 2012; Zhang and Lapata, 2014; Yan, 2016) keywords that will, somehow, set a semantic domain and constraint the generation space; a line of text (Das and Gambäck, 2014) or a sequence of lines (Malmi et al., 2016) to be followed; a textual document, which can either be a single sentence with a message (Gervás, 2001), or a longer text from a blog (Misztal and Indurkhya, 2014) or newspaper (Díaz-Agudo et al., 2002; Colton et al., 2012; Rashel and Manurung, 2014; Toivanen et al., 2014; Tobing and Manurung, 2015; Gonçalo Oliveira and Alves, 2016).

In order to extract meaningful information to be used in the poem, different systems process the input document differently. For instance, Toivanen et al. (2014) acquire novel associations from the document (e.g. *bieber* and *alcohol*, in opposition to *pop* and *star*), identified by contrast with well-known associations. Tobing and Manurung (2015) extract dependency relations from the document and use them to constrain the generated poem. They argue that, though not a genuine semantic representation, dependency relations are a useful abstraction of the text and end up conveying its semantics. In fact, some dependency relations include semantic relations (e.g. *agent-of*, *subject-of*, *object-of*). A final example (Gonçalo Oliveira and Alves, 2016) extracts concept maps from the input document, and uses them as a semantic network.

Towards an improved interpretation, Colton et al. (2012)'s system produces natural language commentaries for each generated poem, providing some generation context. A similar feature is presented by Gonçalo Oliveira and Alves (2016) or Gonçalo Oliveira et al. (2017). In this case, semantic relation instances explaining the connection between the input keywords and the words used can be provided either in raw format or, if a grammar exists for this purpose, in natural language.

Additional semantic features captured by poetry generators include sentiment (Gervás, 2000; Colton et al., 2012; Gonçalo Oliveira et al., 2017), which typically involves exploiting a polarity lexicon; or emotion (Misztal and Indurkhya, 2014), in this case achieved with the help of WordNet Affect.

Figurative language is often implicitly present as a consequence of reusing material from human-produced poetry, but its presence can also be explicitly handled, for instance, by exploiting similes mined from Google n-grams (Colton et al., 2012). Veale (2013) points out the importance of content-features and presents a system more relaxed on form but heavily influenced by figurative language. More precisely, similes (e.g. *politicians are crooks*) are exploited for generating metaphors (e.g. *he is a crook*) and conceptual blends (e.g. *sweet silence*).

Poetry generation systems handle a broad range of features both at the formal and at the content level. Dealing with so many constraints may actually turn out to be computationally impractical (see e.g. Tobing and Manurung (2015)). Yet, this also depends on the techniques adopted for handling all the constrains, surveyed in the following section.

5 Artificial Intelligence Techniques

Early poetry generators (e.g. Queneau (1961) or Oulipo (1981)) relied heavily on combinatory processes applied to a set of human-created poems. On the other hand, intelligent poetry generation systems consider semantics when selecting content and take advantage of computational techniques that add value to the generation process, with a more efficient exploration of the space of possible generations, also enabling to handle a larger number of features, often towards a predefined intention, and sometimes resulting in poems with higher novelty. This section enumerates some of those techniques, borrowed from the domain of AI.

The technique of Case-Based Reasoning exploits past solutions for solving new similar problems, in a four-step approach (*retrieve, reuse, revise, retain*). In the scope of poetry generation (Gervás, 2001; Díaz-Agudo et al., 2002), it has been instantiated as follows: *retrieve* vocabulary and line examples that suit fragments of a poem draft; *reuse* the part-of-speech (POS) structure of the example lines for producing new lines and combine them with the words in the vocabulary; present the resulting draft to the user, for *revision*; perform a linguistic analysis of the revised poems and *retain* it for further generations.

Chart Parsing is a known technique that employs dynamic programming for parsing text according to a context-free grammar. Chart Generation, used by some poetry generation systems (Manurung, 1999; Manurung, 2003; Tobing and Manurung, 2015; Gonçalo Oliveira, 2012), is the inverse of chart parsing. Given a grammar, a lexicon, and a meaning (e.g. as a set of predicates), chart generation produces all syntactically well-formed texts that convey the meaning. Charts store complete generated constituents (inactive edges) as well as incomplete (active edges), with dotted rules marking constituent portions yet to be generated.

Poetry composition can be seen as an incremental task, where initial drafts go through several iterations, each ideally better than the previous, until the final poem. The application of evolutionary algorithms to this task (Levy, 2001; Manurung, 2003) is thus natural. The basic idea is to generate an initial population of poems by a simple method, and then evolve it through several generations, towards more suitable poems, assessed by a fitness function that considers a set of relevant features for poetry. Changes in the population are obtained by the application of crossover and mutation operators. Crossover creates new poems from two other poems in the population. This can be achieved by adopting the syntax of the former but the words or the rhyme of the latter (Levy, 2001), or by swapping parts of the former with parts of the latter (Manurung, 2003). Mutation may involve the replacement of some words in all the poem, only in a certain line, or changing the rhyme (Levy, 2001). It may also consist of adding, deleting or changing contents of the poem, possibly considering the target semantics (Manurung, 2003).

Given the number of constraints involved in poetry generation, it is also natural to have this problem formulated as a Constraint Satisfaction approach (Toivanen et al., 2013; Rashel and Manurung, 2014). For this purpose, a constraint satisfaction solver explores the search space and produces solutions that match the input properties (how poems can be like), represented as predicates that indicate the poem structure and the vocabulary words to be used. Different constraints and their types can be set for different generations. Hard constraints are mandatory (e.g. number of lines, syllables per line), while soft constraints are optional (e.g. rhymes).

Language models have been used to generate poetic text, constrained by both a target style and a predefined form. These include Markov models (Barbieri et al., 2012) and models based on Deep Neural Networks (DNNs), including Recurrent Neural Networks (RNNs). Given a sequence of words, a RNN was used to predict the next word in rap lyrics (Potash et al., 2015). Or given the line history, RNNs can be used for generating new lines incrementally, considering their respective phonetics, structure and semantics (Zhang and Lapata, 2014; Yan, 2016). There may be one neural network (NN) for selecting the structure of lines and another for guiding the generation of single words within a line. Towards better poeticness, Yan (2016) goes further and adds poem refinement iterations to the previous process. The RNN language model may also be guided by a Finite-State Acceptor that controls rhyme and metre (Ghazvininejad et al., 2016). Malmi et al. (2016) use a DNN and the RankSVM algorithm to predict the next full line, from a knowledge base of human-produced lyrics, considering rhyme, structure and semantic similarity.

Support Vector Machines (SVMs), trained in a poetry corpus, were also used to predict follow-up lines with certain syllabic and rhyming properties (Das and Gambäck, 2014). And classic NNs were also used to measure the fitness of poems generated by an evolutionary approach (Levy, 2001). In the latter case, the NN was trained on human judgments of creativity in a selection of *limericks*, half by humans and another half randomly generated.

Misztal and Indurkhya (2014) adopted a Multi-Agent approach where a set of artificial experts, focused on a particular aspect of poetry generation, interact by sharing results on a blackboard. Experts can contribute with words matching a given topic or emotion (*word-generating*), arrange words in the common pool into phrases (*poem-making*), or select the best solutions according to given constraints and heuristics (*selection experts*), among others.

Poetry generation has also been tackled as a Generative Summarization framework that incorporates poetic features as constraints to be optimised (Yan et al., 2013). Candidate poems are retrieved for a set of keywords, they are segmented into constituent terms and clustered given their semantics. Lines that conform the structural constraints, each using terms from the same cluster and with some correlation, are then selected. Suitable term replacements are finally made iteratively, in order to improve structure, rhyme, tonality and semantic coherence.

6 Reutilisation of Materials

To avoid the generation of poems completely from scratch, most poetry generators take shortcuts and rely on human-created text, usually poems, for inspiration. Different systems exploit the inspiration set differently, generally for the acquisition of useful knowledge or guidelines that will simplify how certain features (e.g. form, syntax or even figurative language) are handled, and also to help modelling the produced poems towards recognisable poetry. This is also reflected on how the inspiration contents are reused in the produced poems.

Some systems acquire full lines or fragments from human-created poems (Queneau, 1961), rap lyrics (Malmi et al., 2016), blog posts (Wong and Chun, 2008), or tweets (Charnley et al., 2014), and recombine them in new poems, considering features such as metre, rhymes, presence of certain words or semantic similarity. On the one hand, these solutions minimize the issues of dealing with syntax and do not require an underlying generation grammar or template. On the other hand, from the point of view of novelty, they are poor, as lines from known texts can be spotted in the middle of the produced poems. If precautions are not taken, this can even lead to licensing issues.

Other systems operate on templates to be filled with new words. Templates can be handcrafted and cover variations of similes and key phrases from newspapers (Colton et al., 2012), or they can be extracted automatically from text. The latter kind may be based on full poems or on single lines, where some words are replaced by others with similar grammatical features, possibly further constrained on metre, rhyme, POS or semantics. For instance, full poems can have content words stripped (Toivanen et al., 2012; Toivanen et al., 2013; Toivanen et al., 2014; Rashel and Manurung, 2014). Systems that reuse full fragments may also include an additional step where certain words are replaced, in order to better satisfy the target features (Yan et al., 2013).

Line templates can be extracted fragments where a semantic relation must be held between stripped words (e.g. *dark $<x>$ on a dangerous $<y>$*, where *partOf(x, y)*) (Gonçalo Oliveira, 2012; Gonçalo Oliveira and Alves, 2016; Gonçalo Oliveira et al., 2017), or sequences of POS-tags (e.g. *NN-NN-JJ-VB*) (Gervás, 2000; Gonçalo Oliveira et al., 2007; Agirrezabal et al., 2013). To some extent, POS-tag templates can be seen as flat grammars.

A different way of exploiting the inspiration set involves acquiring a lexicon with the most common words used in this set, and using it for guiding the generation process (Wong and Chun, 2008).

7 Evaluation

Poetry generation is becoming a mature research field, which is confirmed by several works that go beyond the production and exhibition of a few interesting poems that, to some extent, match the target goals. Despite the subjective aspect that makes poem evaluation far from trivial, it is more and more common to explore different ways for assessing both the obtained results and the generation process.

Claiming that the intended audience of poetry consists of people, the evaluation of computer generated poetry has often resorted to human judges, who assess produced poems according to a set of predefined dimensions. For instance, although, to some extent, the properties of *poeticness*, *grammaticality* and *meaningfulness* can be validated by the methods applied (Manurung, 2003; Misztal and Indurkhya, 2014), they can also be assessed by the observation of the obtained results. Having this in mind, some researchers (Yan et al., 2013; Das and Gambäck, 2014; Zhang and Lapata, 2014; Yan, 2016) evaluated the output of their system based on the opinion of human judges on a set of produced poems, who answered questionnaires designed to capture the aforementioned properties. Still relying on human opinions, other authors took conclusions on the quality of their results with questions

that rated slightly different dimensions, though with some overlap. Those include the typicality as a poem, understandability, quality of language, mental images, emotions, and liking (Toivanen et al., 2012); or structure, diction, grammar, unity, message and expressiveness (Rashel and Manurung, 2014).

Some of the previous systems ended up conducting a Turing test-like evaluation, where the scores of the systems produced by their poems were compared to those for human-created poems (Netzer et al., 2009; Toivanen et al., 2012; Agirrezabal et al., 2013; Rashel and Manurung, 2014). Despite also relying on human evaluation, other researchers compared poems produced only by their systems but using different parameters or strategies (Gervás, 2000; Gonçalo Oliveira et al., 2007; Barbieri et al., 2012; Yan et al., 2013; McGregor et al., 2016); or poems produced by other systems with a very similar purpose (Zhang and Lapata, 2014; Yan, 2016).

Established methods to evaluate human creativity, from the psychology domain, have also been proposed to assess computational creativity, including automatically generated poetry. van der Velde et al. (2015) present a map of words related to creativity (e.g. unconventional, spontaneitiy, imagination, planning, craftmanship, art), obtained from an association study. These words were clustered and may be used to define relevant dimensions for evaluating creativity, for instance, in a poem, and in its creation process. Another study employing methods from psychology (Lamb et al., 2016) resorted to human experts for rating the creativity of poems, some written by humans and others generated automatically, by different creative systems. Judges were not informed of this and, despite some consensus on the best and worst poems, they disagreed on the remaining, which made the authors unsure on the suitability of their approach for computer-generated poetry.

There has been a huge discussion on the suitability of the Turing test for evaluating computational creativity approaches (Pease and Colton, 2011). The main criticism is that it is focused on the resulting products and not on the involved creative process, which encourages the application of simpler processes, some of which might be merely concerned with tricking the human judge into thinking their outputs were produced by a human.

The FACE descriptive model (Colton et al., 2011)

has been proposed to evaluate the creative process and was used in the evaluation of poetry generation systems (Colton et al., 2012; Misztal and Indurkhya, 2014). To be assessed positively by this model, a creative system must create a concept (C), with several examples (E), include an aesthetic measure (A) for evaluating the concept and its examples, and provide framing information (F) that will explain the context or motivation of the outputs. Yet, other experiments (McGregor et al., 2016) suggest that framing, which can be provided as a natural language commentary, does not make a big difference in human assessment of the creativity, meaningfulness or general quality of computer-generated poems.

In many systems, the evaluation of certain features is part of the process, as it happens for Misztal and Indurkhya (2014)'s automatic experts, or with the large number of systems that assess the metre, rhymes and other properties of produced texts during generation time. Few approaches have tried to evaluate poetry generation systems or their results automatically, and these often tackled less subjective dimensions of poems. Those include the application of metrics typically used in the scope of automatic summarization and machine translation, such as ROUGE, to access the performance of a poetry generator based on Generative Summarization (Yan et al., 2013); or BLEU, to assess the ability to generate valid sequences of lines (Zhang and Lapata, 2014; Yan, 2016). ROUGE was also used to assess variation in poems generated by the same system with the same parameters (Gonçalo Oliveira et al., 2017). Moreover, the perplexity of the learned language model has been compared to human-produced poetry with a similar style (Zhang and Lapata, 2014; Yan, 2016); the average cosine similarity of the lines in automatically-created *haikus* has been compared to the same value for awarded *haikus* by humans, to conclude that semantic coherence is similar (Wong and Chun, 2008); and Pointwise Mutual Information, computed on Wikipedia, has been used to measure the association between seeds and words effectively used (Gonçalo Oliveira, 2015; Gonçalo Oliveira et al., 2017).

Other systems focused on measuring the novelty of their results, especially those that reuse more material or try to model an artist's style. The main goal is to generate poems that share some similarities with the inspiration set, but are different from any existing poem. Potash et al. (2015) compute the cosine similarity between the automatically generated lines and the original lines by the target artist (the lower cosine, the higher the novelty). To compute similarity, the number of rhyming syllables is divided by the total number of syllables (rhyme density) and the result is compared to the same number for the lyrics of the target artist. Rhyme density is also computed by Malmi et al. (2016) and, to some extent, by Gonçalo Oliveira et al. (2017). In the latter case, it is given by the number of lines with an end-rhyme divided by the total number of lines.

8 Final discussion

Many computational systems that tackle the complexity of poetry generation from an AI perspective have been developed and thoroughly described in scientific literature. We can thus say that this topic, with interest for the communities of Computational Creativity and Natural Language Generation, is today an established research field.

Intelligent poetry generators were surveyed in this paper, around a set of relevant axis where alternative approaches have been explored. Poetry has been automatically generated in different languages and forms, considering different sets of features, and through significantly different approaches. Poetry generators have been developed with different goals and intents, each with their stronger and weaker points (though this is out of the scope of the current paper), which adds to the subjectivity involved in the evaluation of poetry, even for humans. This explains the broad range of approaches explored for poetry generation, though not one can be said to be better than the others. Nevertheless, many researchers are making progress towards the evaluation of the generation process and its impact on the obtained results.

We do hope that this paper can be used as a future reference for people working or considering to work on poetry generation. Many of the approaches described have room for further exploration, not to mention that several alternative features, constraints or AI techniques are still left to be explored in this scope. Some of which might result in surprisingly interesting results, with potential applications in education or entertainment.

References

Manex Agirrezabal, Bertol Arrieta, Aitzol Astigarraga, and Mans Hulden. 2013. POS-tag based poetry generation with wordnet. In *Proceedings of the 14th European Workshop on Natural Language Generation*, pages 162–166, Sofia, Bulgaria, August. ACL Press.

Manex Agirrezabal, Iñaki Alegria, and Mans Hulden. 2016. Machine learning for metrical analysis of english poetry. In *Proceedings of 26th International Conference on Computational Linguistics: Technical Papers*, pages 772–781, Osaka, Japan, December. COLING 2016 Organizing Committee.

Gabriele Barbieri, François Pachet, Pierre Roy, and Mirko Degli Esposti. 2012. Markov constraints for generating lyrics with style. In *Proceedings of 20th European Conference on Artificial Intelligence (ECAI)*, volume 242 of *Frontiers in Artificial Intelligence and Applications*, pages 115–120. IOS Press.

John Charnley, Simon Colton, and Maria Teresa Llano. 2014. The FloWr framework: Automated flowchart construction, optimisation and alteration for creative systems. In *Proceedings of 5th International Conference on Computational Creativity, ICCC 2014*, Ljubljana, Slovenia, June.

Simon Colton and Geraint A. Wiggins. 2012. Computational creativity: The final frontier? In *Proceedings of 20th European Conference on Artificial Intelligence (ECAI 2012)*, volume 242 of *Frontiers in Artificial Intelligence and Applications*, pages 21–26, Montpellier, France. IOS Press.

Simon Colton, John Charnley, and Alison Pease. 2011. Computational creativity theory: The face and idea descriptive models. In *Proceedings of the 2nd International Conference on Computational Creativity*, page 90–95, México City, México, April.

Simon Colton, Jacob Goodwin, and Tony Veale. 2012. Full FACE poetry generation. In *Proceedings of 3rd International Conference on Computational Creativity, ICCC 2012*, pages 95–102, Dublin, Ireland.

Amitava Das and Björn Gambäck. 2014. Poetic machine: Computational creativity for automatic poetry generation in Bengali. In *Proceedings of 5th International Conference on Computational Creativity*, ICCC 2014, Ljubljana, Slovenia, June.

Belén Díaz-Agudo, Pablo Gervás, and Pedro A. González-Calero. 2002. Poetry generation in colibri. In *Proceedings of 6th European Conference on Advances in Case-Based Reasoning (ECCBR 2002)*, pages 73–102, London, UK. Springer.

Pablo Gervás. 2000. WASP: Evaluation of different strategies for the automatic generation of spanish verse. In *Proceedings of AISB'00 Symposium on Creative & Cultural Aspects and Applications of AI & Cognitive Science*, pages 93–100, Birmingham, UK.

Pablo Gervás. 2001. An expert system for the composition of formal Spanish poetry. *Journal of Knowledge-Based Systems*, 14(3–4):181–188.

Marjan Ghazvininejad, Xing Shi, Yejin Choi, and Kevin Knight. 2016. Generating topical poetry. In *Proceedings of the 2016 Conference on Empirical Methods in Natural Language Processing*, pages 1183–1191, Austin, Texas, November. ACL Press.

Hugo Gonçalo Oliveira, F. Amílcar Cardoso, and Francisco Câmara Pereira. 2007. Tra-la-Lyrics: an approach to generate text based on rhythm. In *Procs. of 4th International Joint Workshop on Computational Creativity*, pages 47–55, London, UK. IJWCC 2007.

Hugo Gonçalo Oliveira. 2012. PoeTryMe: a versatile platform for poetry generation. In *Proceedings of the ECAI 2012 Workshop on Computational Creativity, Concept Invention, and General Intelligence*, C3GI 2012, Montpellier, France, August.

Hugo Gonçalo Oliveira and Ana Oliveira Alves. 2016. Poetry from concept maps – yet another adaptation of PoeTryMe's flexible architecture. In *Proceedings of 7th International Conference on Computational Creativity*, ICCC 2016, Paris, France.

Hugo Gonçalo Oliveira, Raquel Hervás, Alberto Díaz, and Pablo Gervás. 2017. Multilanguage extension and evaluation of a poetry generator. *Natural Language Engineering*, page in press. (online since June 2017).

Hugo Gonçalo Oliveira. 2015. Tra-la-lyrics 2.0: Automatic generation of song lyrics on a semantic domain. *Journal of Artificial General Intelligence*, 6(1):87–110, December. Special Issue: Computational Creativity, Concept Invention, and General Intelligence.

Carolyn Lamb, Daniel Brown, and Charles Clarke. 2016. How digital poetry experts evaluate digital poetry. In *Proceedings of 7th International Conference on Computational Creativity*, ICCC 2016, Paris, France.

R. P. Levy. 2001. A computational model of poetic creativity with neural network as measure of adaptive fitness. In *Proceedings of the ICCBR'01 Workshop on Creative Systems*.

Eric Malmi, Pyry Takala, Hannu Toivonen, Tapani Raiko, and Aristides Gionis. 2016. Dopelearning: A computational approach to rap lyrics generation. In *Proceedings of 22nd SIGKDD International Conference on Knowledge Discovery and Data Mining*, pages 195–204, San Francisco, CA, USA, August. ACM Press.

Hisar Manurung. 1999. A chart generator for rhythm patterned text. In *Proceedings of 1st International Workshop on Literature in Cognition and Computer*.

H. M. Manurung. 2003. *An evolutionary algorithm approach to poetry generation*. Ph.D. thesis, University of Edimburgh, Edimburgh, UK.

Stephen McGregor, Matthew Purver, and Geraint Wiggins. 2016. Process based evaluation of computer generated poetry. In *Proceedings of the INLG 2016 Workshop on Computational Creativity in Natural Language Generation*, pages 51–60, Edinburgh, UK, September. ACL Press.

Joanna Misztal and Bipin Indurkhya. 2014. Poetry generation system with an emotional personality. In *5th International Conference on Computational Creativity, ICCC 2014*, Ljubljana, Slovenia, 06/2014.

Yael Netzer, David Gabay, Yoav Goldberg, and Michael Elhadad. 2009. Gaiku: generating haiku with word associations norms. In *Proceedings of the Workshop on Computational Approaches to Linguistic Creativity*, CALC'09, pages 32–39. ACL Press.

(Association) Oulipo. 1981. *Atlas de littérature potentielle*. Number vol. 1 in Collection Idées. Gallimard.

Alison Pease and Simon Colton. 2011. On impact and evaluation in computational creativity: A discussion of the turing test and an alternative proposal. In *Proceedings of the 3rd AISB symposium on AI and Philosophy, University of York, York, UK.*

Peter Potash, Alexey Romanov, and Anna Rumshisky. 2015. GhostWriter: Using an LSTM for automatic rap lyric generation. In *Proceedings of the 2015 Conference on Empirical Methods in Natural Language Processing*, EMNLP 2015, pages 1919–1924, Lisbon, Portugal. ACL Press.

R. Queneau. 1961. *100.000.000.000.000 de poèmes*. Gallimard Series. Schoenhof's Foreign Books, Incorporated.

Ananth Ramakrishnan A and Sobha Lalitha Devi. 2010. An alternate approach towards meaningful lyric generation in tamil. In *Proceedings of the NAACL HLT 2010 2nd Workshop on Computational Approaches to Linguistic Creativity*, CALC'10, pages 31–39. ACL Press.

Ananth Ramakrishnan A, Sankar Kuppan, and Sobha Lalitha Devi. 2009. Automatic generation of Tamil lyrics for melodies. In *Proceedings of Workshop on Computational Approaches to Linguistic Creativity*, CALC'09, pages 40–46. ACL Press.

Fam Rashel and Ruli Manurung. 2014. Pemuisi: A constraint satisfaction-based generator of topical Indonesian poetry. In *Proceedings of 5th International Conference on Computational Creativity*, ICCC 2014, Ljubljana, Slovenia, June.

Berty Chrismartin Lumban Tobing and Ruli Manurung. 2015. A chart generation system for topical metrical poetry. In *Proceedings of the 6th International Conference on Computational Creativity, Park City, Utah, USA*, ICCC 2015, Park City, Utah, USA, Jun.

Jukka M. Toivanen, Hannu Toivonen, Alessandro Valitutti, and Oskar Gross. 2012. Corpus-based generation of content and form in poetry. In *Proceedings of the 3rd International Conference on Computational Creativity*, ICCC 2012, pages 211–215, Dublin, Ireland, May.

Jukka M. Toivanen, Matti Järvisalo, and Hannu Toivonen. 2013. Harnessing constraint programming for poetry composition. In *Proceedings of the 4th International Conference on Computational Creativity*, ICCC 2013, pages 160–167. The University of Sydney.

Jukka M. Toivanen, Oskar Gross, and Hannu Toivonen. 2014. The officer is taller than you, who race yourself! using document specific word associations in poetry generation. In *5th International Conference on Computational Creativity, ICCC 2014*, Ljubljana, Slovenia, 06/2014.

Rui Torres and Sandy Baldwin, editors. 2014. *PO.EX: Essays from Portugal on Cyberliterature and Intermedia by Pedro Barbosa, Ana Hatherly, and E.M. de Melo e Castro*. West Virginia University Press / Center for Literary Computing.

Frank van der Velde, Roger A Wolf, Martin Schmettow, and Deniece S Nazareth. 2015. A semantic map for evaluating creativity. In *Proceedings of the 6th International Conference on Computational Creativity June*, page 94.

Tony Veale. 2013. Less rhyme, more reason: Knowledge-based poetry generation with feeling, insight and wit. In *Proceedings of the 4th International Conference on Computational Creativity*, pages 152–159, Sydney, Australia.

Martin Tsan Wong and Andy Hon Wai Chun. 2008. Automatic haiku generation using VSM. In *Proceeding of 7th WSEAS International Conference on Applied Computer & Applied Computational Science*, ACACOS '08, Hangzhou, China.

Rui Yan, Han Jiang, Mirella Lapata, Shou-De Lin, Xueqiang Lv, and Xiaoming Li. 2013. I, Poet: Automatic Chinese poetry composition through a generative summarization framework under constrained optimization. In *Proceedings of 23rd International Joint Conference on Artificial Intelligence*, IJCAI'13, pages 2197–2203. AAAI Press.

Rui Yan. 2016. i, Poet: Automatic poetry composition through recurrent neural networks with iterative polishing schema. In *Proceedings of 25th International Joint Conference on Artificial Intelligence*, IJCAI 2016, pages 2238–2244, New York, NY, USA, July. IJCAI/AAAI Press.

Xingxing Zhang and Mirella Lapata. 2014. Chinese poetry generation with recurrent neural networks. In *Proceedings of 2014 Conference on Empirical Methods in Natural Language Processing*, EMNLP 2014, pages 670–680, Doha, Qatar, October. ACL Press.

Cross-linguistic differences and similarities in image descriptions

Emiel van Miltenburg
Vrije Universiteit Amsterdam
emiel.van.miltenburg@vu.nl

Desmond Elliott
University of Edinburgh
d.elliott@ed.ac.uk

Piek Vossen
Vrije Universiteit Amsterdam
piek.vossen@vu.nl

Abstract

Automatic image description systems are commonly trained and evaluated on large image description datasets. Recently, researchers have started to collect such datasets for languages other than English. An unexplored question is how different these datasets are from English and, if there are any differences, what causes them to differ. This paper provides a cross-linguistic comparison of Dutch, English, and German image descriptions. We find that these descriptions are similar in many respects, but the familiarity of crowd workers with the subjects of the images has a noticeable influence on description specificity.

1 Introduction

Vision and language researchers have started to collect image description corpora for languages other than English, e.g. Chinese (Li et al., 2016), German (Elliott et al., 2016; Hitschler et al., 2016; Rajendran et al., 2016), Japanese (Miyazaki and Shimizu, 2016; Yoshikawa et al., 2017), French (Rajendran et al., 2016), and Turkish (Unal et al., 2016). The main aim of those efforts is to develop image description systems for non-English languages and to explore the related problems of cross-lingual image description (Elliott et al., 2015; Miyazaki and Shimizu, 2016) and machine translation in a visual context (Specia et al., 2016; Hitschler et al., 2016). We view these new corpora as sociological data that is in itself worth studying. Our research stems from the following question: *To what extent do speakers of different languages differ in their descriptions of the same images?* Considering this question, we developed a (non-exhaustive) list of factors that may influence the descriptions provided by crowd workers. Understanding the effect of these factors will enable us to improve the data collection process, and help us appreciate the challenges of natural language generation in a visual context:

1. **Task design effects**: There are many possible approaches to collecting descriptions of images. Previous research has re-used the Flickr8K (Hodosh et al., 2013) template and methodology. Baltaretu and Castro Ferreira (2016) showed that task design may influence the form of crowd-sourced descriptions.

2. **(Perceived) audience**: Speakers adapt the style of their messages to their audience (Bell, 1984). Knowing how the descriptions will be used may affect the style or quality of the corpora.

3. **Individual/Demographic factors**: Individual features, like the demographics or personal preferences of the workers, may explain part of the variation in the descriptions.

4. **Differences in (background) knowledge**: Workers can only provide as much information as they know. Besides educational factors, the background knowledge of a person can be influenced by where they currently live and where they have previously lived.

5. **Language differences**: Languages differ in how they package information, which may be reflected in the descriptions. This is close to, but separate from *linguistic relativity* (see e.g. (Deutscher, 2010; McWhorter, 2014)).

Proceedings of The 10th International Natural Language Generation conference, pages 21–30,
Santiago de Compostela, Spain, September 4-7 2017. ©2017 Association for Computational Linguistics

6. **Cultural differences**: Culture may influence the descriptions on a group level by affecting the social perspective of a population.

This paper focuses on the last three factors in a cross-linguistic corpus study of Dutch, German, and English image descriptions. Our work is a starting point for understanding the differences in descriptions between languages. The focus on the last three factors is a consequence of our corpus study: the first two factors require manipulating the experimental set-up, and the third factor requires data about the crowd workers that is not known (and should ideally also be controlled). As we will see in Sections 4 and 5, we *can* make claims about the last three factors based on the workers' language and geolocations.

We believe that studying differences between languages shows us which phenomena are robust across languages and thus important to consider when implementing and deploying models. Also, differences between languages can inform us about the feasibility of approaches to image description in different languages by translating existing English data (Li et al., 2016; Yoshikawa et al., 2017).

Our analysis combines quantitative and qualitative studies of a trilingual corpus of described images. We use the Flickr30K (Young et al., 2014) for English, Multi30K for German (Elliott et al., 2016), and a new corpus of Dutch descriptions (Section 3). We build on earlier work that studies the semantic and pragmatic properties of English descriptions (van Miltenburg, 2016; van Miltenburg et al., 2016). Those works study ethnicity marking, negation marking, and unwarranted inferences about the roles of people. The main finding of our analysis is that all of these properties are stable across Dutch, US English, and German (Section 4). We also show how differences in background knowledge can affect description specificity (Section 5). We make the Dutch corpus available online and we also release software to explore image description corpora with the descriptions in different languages side-by-side to encourage future work with different language families.[1]

2 Related work

We review work on the theory about the image description process, and work on automatic image de-

---

[1]See: https://github.com/cltl/DutchDescriptions

scription in other languages.

Describing an image. Erwin Panofsky's (Panofsky, 1939) hierarchy of meaning was originally intended as a guide for interpreting works of art. It has since been applied by Shatford (1986) and Jaimes and Chang (1999) in the context of indexing and searching for images in libraries. The hierarchy consists of three levels that build on each other.

1. **Pre-iconography**: giving a factual description of the contents of an image, and an expressional indication of the mood it conveys.
2. **Iconography**: giving a more *specific* description, informed by knowledge of the cultural context in which the image is situated.
3. **Iconology**: interpreting the image, establishing its cultural and intellectual significance.

This hierarchy is useful to think about for descriptions of images (Hodosh et al., 2013). As Panofsky (1939) notes, these levels require more knowledge as we move up the hierarchy. If we apply this hierarchy to the image description domain, we can say that image description corpora typically cover the first two levels. An important factor in the 'quality' of a description is the amount of *cultural* or *background* knowledge that informs the description. We will explore the influence of this factor in Section 5.

Descriptions in other languages. Work on image description in other languages generally focuses on system performance rather than cross-linguistic differences (Elliott et al., 2015; Li et al., 2016; Miyazaki and Shimizu, 2016). Thus far, any differences have only been anecdotally described.

Li et al. (2016) collected Chinese descriptions of images in the Flickr8K corpus (Hodosh et al., 2013). They highlight the differences between Chinese and English descriptions using a picture of a woman taking a photograph. The English annotators describe the woman as *Asian*, whereas Chinese annotators describe her as *middle-aged*. The authors note that "Asian faces are probably too common to be visually salient from a Chinese point of view."

Miyazaki and Shimizu (2016) collected Japanese descriptions for a subset of the MS COCO dataset, which mostly contains pictures taken in (or by people from) Europe and the United States (Lin et al., 2014). They note that in their pilot phase, the images appeared "exotic" to Japanese crowd workers, who would frequently use adjectives like *foreign* and *overseas*. The authors actively tried to combat this by modifying their guidelines to explicitly prevent crowd workers using these phrases, but the observation remains that perspective can strongly influence the nature of the descriptions.

In this paper we collect a new dataset of Dutch image descriptions, but our work differs from previous work in two ways: (i) we aim to provide a more systematic overview of the differences between descriptions in three languages, and therefore (ii) we do not empirically evaluate system performance in reproducing the descriptions.

3 Collecting Dutch descriptions

We used Crowdflower to annotate 2,014 images from the validation and test splits of the Flickr30K corpus (Young et al., 2014) with five Dutch descriptions.

Following other work, our goal is to create a parallel corpus of image descriptions, using the images as pivots. This requires us to stay as close to the original task setup as possible, thus fixing the effect of Task Design factor. We base our task on the template used by (Hodosh et al., 2013) to collect English descriptions, and by (Elliott et al., 2016) for German descriptions. In this design, images are annotated in batches of five images. The task for our participants is to describe each of those images "in one complete, but simple sentence." Before starting on the task, we ask participants to read the guidelines, and to study a picture with example descriptions ranging from *very good* to *very bad*. We include the instructions for our task in the supplementary materials.

Participants. Crowdflower does not offer the option to select Dutch participants based on their native language. Instead, we restricted our task to level 2 (experienced and reasonably accurate) workers in the Netherlands. We had to continuously monitor the task for ungrammatical descriptions in order to stop contributors from submitting low-quality responses.

Other settings. Following (Elliott et al., 2016), we set a reward for $0.25 per completed task (or $0.05 per image), and required participants to spend at least 90 seconds on each task, resulting in a theoretical maximum wage of $10 per hour. We initially limited the number of judgments to 250 descriptions per participant, but due to the small size of the crowd

we increased this limit to 500.

Results. A total of 72 participants provided 10,070 valid descriptions in 116 days, at a cost of $821.40. We were surprised by the number of participants who presumably used Google Translate to submit their responses. These are identifiable through their ungrammaticality, usually due to incorrectly inflected verbs. An example is given in (1), with a literal translation and original English description (verified using Google Translate).

(1) Response generated with Google Translate.

a. *Een paar kussen   (Description)
  'A couple of kisses'   (Translation)
  A couple kisses   (Original)

Altogether, we had to remove 60 participants due to either submitting ungrammatical responses (60%), Lorum Ipsum text (12%), random combinations of characters (9%), non-Dutch responses (6%), or otherwise low-quality responses (13%).

We conclude that crowdsourcing is a feasible way to collect Dutch data, but it may still be faster to collect image descriptions in the lab (in terms of time to collect the data, not counting the time spent as an experimenter overseeing the task). For large-scale datasets, such as Flickr30K or MS COCO, the Dutch crowdsourcing population seems to be too small to collect descriptions for *all* the images in a reasonable amount of time. This is a problem; with the current data-hungry technology, low-resource languages and languages with smaller pools of crowd workers are in danger of being left behind. For example, Sprugnoli et al. (2016) note that for Flemish, an example of a *small-pool language*, they "were not able to get a sufficient response from the crowd to complete the offered transcription tasks."

4 Characterizing English, German, and Dutch image descriptions

We now examine the descriptions between languages in more detail, focusing on the *validation* subset of the Multi30K dataset (1,014 images, with 5,070 descriptions per language).

4.1 General statistics

Table 1 shows the mean sentence length (in tokens and words) for the three languages. The English descriptions are the longest, followed by the Dutch and

	Tokens	σ	Words	σ
Dutch	11.14	4.5	10.32	4.3
English	13.60	5.6	12.48	5.3
German	9.76	4.2	8.81	3.9

Table 1: Mean sentence length across languages.

the German ones. However, German has the longest average word length (5.25 characters per word), followed by Dutch (4.62) and English (4.12). This difference seems due to German and Dutch compounding, which is confirmed by the number of word types: German has 31% more types than English (5709 versus 4355). Dutch has 19% more (5193).

Definiteness. The five most frequent bigrams that start a description (showing the typical subjects of the images) are given in Table 2. The majority starts with an indefinite article, which is in line with the *familiarity theory of definiteness*: the function of definite articles is to refer to familiar referents, whereas indefinite articles are used for unfamiliar referents (Christophersen, 1939; Heim, 1982). The distribution of (in)definite articles follows from the fact that the participants have never seen the images before, nor any context for the image in which the referents could be introduced. A corollary is that systems trained on this data are more likely to produce indefinite than definite articles, and need to be told when definites should be used.

4.2 Replicating previous findings for negation and ethnicity marking

Previous work has studied the use of negation and ethnicity marking in English image description datasets (van Miltenburg et al., 2016; van Miltenburg, 2016) We now attempt to replicate these findings in the Dutch and German data.

Negations. van Miltenburg et al. (2016) performed a corpus study to categorize all uses of (non-affixal) negations in the Flickr30K corpus. Negations are interesting in descriptions because they describe images by saying what is *not* there. Negations may be used because something in the picture is unexpected, goes against some social norm, or because non-visible factors are relevant to describe the picture. If annotators consistently use negations, this can be seen as evidence that the negated information is part of their shared background knowledge and is a strong

requirement for producing human-like descriptions. We readily found examples of negations in both the Dutch and the German data. Some examples are given in (2) and (3), respectively.

(2) Examples from the Dutch descriptions

  a. De kinderen dragen **geen** kleding.
     'The kids are **not** wearing any clothing.'
  b. Vrouw snijdt broodje **zonder** te kijken(!)
     'Woman slices a bun **without** looking(!)'

(3) Examples from the German descriptions

  a. Zwei Buben **ohne** T-Shirt setzen auf der Straße.
     'Two boys without T-shirt sitting on the street.'
  b. Eine Ansammlung von Menschen [. . .] schaut auf ein Ereignis, das **nicht** im Bild ist.
     'A crowd of people is watching an event not shown in the picture.'

In total, we found 11 Dutch and 20 German descriptions containing explicit negations in the corpus, while van Miltenburg et al. (2016) found 27 in English for the same images (excluding false positives). This confirms that workers in different languages mark negations at approximately the same rate, given a sample size of 5,070 sentences. We found almost no images that consistently attracted the use of negations in all three languages: we found only four examples of co-occurring negation between languages. One image is described by speakers of all three languages using a negation (a man with two prosthetic legs, described as having no legs), and there are three other images (all of shirtless individuals) where both English and German workers use negations.

Racial and ethnic marking. van Miltenburg (2016) found that the descriptions in the Flickr30K data have a skewed distribution of racial and ethnic markers: annotators used terms like *asian* or *black* much more often than *white* or *caucasian*. If we find the same disproportionate use of ethnicity markers in Dutch and German, then we can conclude that this is not a quirk in the English data, but a systematic linguistic bias (Beukeboom, 2014).

Indeed, we did find that non-white people were often marked with adjectives such as *black, dark-skinned, Asian, Chinese*. In Dutch and German, white people were only marked to indicate a contrast between them and someone of a different ethnicity in the same image. The English data contains five

Dutch	Gloss	Count	English	Count	German	Gloss	Count
Een man	A man	517	A man	760	Ein Mann	A man	584
Een vrouw	A woman	252	A woman	367	Eine Frau	A woman	296
De man	The man	105	A young	223	Zwei Männer	Two men	120
Een jongen	A boy	92	A group	211	Ein Junge	A boy	108
Twee mannen	Two men	92	Two men	127	Der Mann	The man	93

Table 2: Top-5 most frequent bigrams at the start of a sentence, with their English translation.

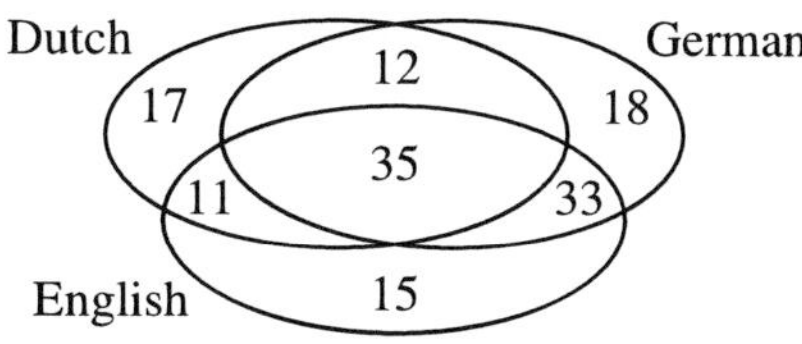

Figure 1: Venn diagram of ethnicity markers by Dutch, English, and German workers. Counts correspond to images.

exceptions to this rule, where white individuals were marked without any people of another ethnicity being present in the image. We do have to note, however, that there are other ways to *indirectly* mark someone as white, e.g. using adjectives like *blonde* or *brunette*.

Figure 1 shows a Venn-diagram of the use of race/ethnicity markers in Dutch, English, and German. We observe that English and German workers use these markers slightly more often than Dutch workers. However, we do *not* claim that this is evidence that people living in Germany and the U.S.A. are *more racist* than people living in the Netherlands. Rather than trying to interpret the meaning of this difference, we ask a different question: what drives people to mention racial or ethnic features?

There are several reasons why people may mark race/ethnicity in their descriptions. One common theme is that annotators mark images where the people are dressed in traditional outfits. Examples include traditional dancers from South-East Asia, and Scotsmen wearing kilts. These items of clothing are *meant to* signal being part of a group, and the annotators picked up on this.

The distribution of the labels may be explained in terms of markedness (Jakobson, 1972) and reporting bias (Misra et al., 2016). In this explanation, white is seen as the unmarked default, as it is the dominant ethnicity in all three countries.[2] The marker *white*

is only used to be consistent in the use of modifiers within same sentence. This reasoning also explains the observation by Miyazaki and Shimizu (2016) that Japanese crowd workers often used the labels *foreign* and *overseas* for the MS COCO images.

A final reason for crowd workers to mention ethnicity and skin color may be that the images are visually less interesting, but the description task still demands that the workers provide a description. Workers are thus pressured to find *something* worth mentioning about the image, because too general descriptions might get their work rejected. This is a general task effect that may have implications beyond racial/ethnic marking.

Speculation. van Miltenburg (2016) also found that that annotators often go beyond the content of the images in their descriptions, making *unwarranted inferences* about the pictures. If we find that Dutch and German crowd workers also make such inferences, we conclude that image descriptions in all three languages are *interpretations* of the images that may not necessarily be true.

We observed unwarranted inferences throughout the Dutch and German data, especially about women with infants, who were often seen as the mother. Figure 2 shows an image where both Dutch, English, and German workers suggested the woman is the *grandmother*. In the most extreme case, two KLM stewards in pantsuits were described by a German worker as well-dressed *Lesben* ('lesbians'). It would be undesirable for a model to associate all unseen images of air stewards with lesbians. We expect that having multiple descriptions alleviates this type of extreme example, but there is an open question about how to deal with more common types of speculation.

---

[2]The US population is 75% white, according to the 2010 census (Humes et al., 2011). The Dutch and German census bureaus do not monitor ethnicity, and instead report that 77% of the Dutch population is Dutch/Frisian (Centraal Bureau voor de Statistiek, 2016) and 80% of the German population is German (Statistisches Bundesamt, 2013).

Figure 2: Image 4634063005. The older woman in the picture was often seen as the grandmother.

5 Familiarity and cultural differences

As the speakers of Dutch, English, and German have different backgrounds, some images may be more familiar to one group than to the others. Familiarity enables speakers to be more specific (but doesn't necessarily cause them to *be* more specific). We will look at three kinds of examples (selected after inspecting the full validation set), where differences in familiarity lead to differences in the description of named entities, objects, and sports. These examples are illustrative of a larger issue, namely that descriptions in one language may not be adequate for speakers of another language (even if they were perfectly translated). We discuss this issue in §6.2.

5.1 Named entities

The Dutch, English, and German descriptions differ in their use of place and entity names. We study two cases: one image that is more likely to be familiar to European workers (German and Dutch), and one that is more likely to be familiar to US workers (English).

The Tuileries Garden. Figure 3 shows a scene from the Tuileries Garden in Paris, a popular tourist attraction. It may be more likely for a European crowd worker to have visited this location than for an American crowd worker. Three Dutch people indeed included references to the actual location in their description. One mentioned the Arc de Triomphe in the background, one said that this picture is from a square in Paris, and the most specific description (correctly) identified the location:

(4) Een man zit aan de vijver van het Tuilleries park in Parijs.

'A man is sitting by the pond of the Tuileries park in Paris.'

Neither the German nor the American workers identified the location or the monuments by name

Figure 3: Image 6408975653. This picture was taken at the Tuileries Garden in Paris, and shows the Luxor Obelisk and the Arc de Triomphe.

Figure 4: Image 4727348655. This picture shows a man wearing a Denver Broncos hat and jersey.

(though one American worker thought this picture was taken at the Washington Monument). Instead of mentioning the location, the English and German workers describe the scene in more general terms. Two examples are given in Example 5.

(5) a. A person in a white sweatshirt is sitting in a chair near a pond and monument.

   b. A man in a white hoodie relaxes in a chair by a fountain.

These examples reveal a common strategy to handle unfamiliarity: focus on something else you *do* know. This undermines the idea that crowd-sourced descriptions tell us what is relevant about the picture.

The Denver Broncos. Figure 4 shows a man wearing a Denver Broncos hat and jersey. The Denver Broncos are an American Football team, which is not so well-known in Europe. Two American crowd workers but neither the Dutch nor the German workers identified the Broncos jersey. Three out of five American workers also described the activity in the image as *tailgating*, a typical North-American phenomenon where people gather to enjoy an informal (often barbecue) meal on the parking lot outside a

Figure 5: Image 4897113571. This picture shows the back of a street organ in the Netherlands.

sports stadium. As this concept is not so prevalent in Dutch or German culture, there is no Dutch or German word, idiom, or collocation to describe tailgating. Such 'untranslatable' concepts are called *lexical gaps*. The presence of this gap means that the Dutch and German workers can only concretely describe the image without being able to relate the depicted event to any more abstract concept.

5.2 Objects

Familiarity also plays a role in labeling objects. Consider Figure 5, which shows (the backside of) a street organ in a shopping street in the Netherlands. All Dutch workers, as well as two German workers identified this object as a street organ, whereas the English workers are only able to provide very general descriptions (Example 6).

(6) a. A **yellow truck** is standing on a busy street in front of the Swarovski store.

b. A **strange looking wood trailer** is parked in a street in front of stores.

c. An **unusual looking vehicle** parked in front of some stores.

This example illustrates two strategies the crowd may use to provide descriptions for unfamiliar objects: (1) signal the unfamiliarity of the object using adjectives like *strange* and *unusual looking*. This is similar to the finding by Miyazaki and Shimizu (2016) that the Japanese crowd made frequent use of terms like *foreign* and *overseas* for the Western images from MS COCO. (2) use a more general cover term, like *vehicle*. Such terms may have a higher *visual dispersion* (Kiela et al., 2014), but they provide a safe back-off strategy.

5.3 Sports

We found that unfamiliarity with different kinds of sports leads to the misclassification of those sports. We focus on three sports: American Football, Rugby, and Soccer. Looking at images for these sports, we compared how the three different groups referred to them. We found that the German and Dutch groups patterned together, deviating from the American crowd workers.

As expected, the Dutch and German workers make the most mistakes categorizing American Football. For all seven pictures of American Football, there is at least one Dutch annotator who thinks it's a game of Rugby. For six of those, at least one German annotator made the same mistake. By contrast, workers from the US made more mistakes identifying rugby images. For all three pictures of Rugby, there is at least one American calling it Soccer or Football. For one of those images, a German annotator thought it was American Football. All Soccer images were universally recognized as Soccer.

6 Discussion

6.1 Description specificity

In Section 5 we observed that annotators differ in the specificity of their descriptions due to their familiarity with the depicted scenes or objects. One challenge for image description systems is to find the right level of specificity for their descriptions, despite this variation. If a system can identify the exact category of an object, it is probably more useful to produce e.g. *street organ* rather than *unusual looking vehicle*.

Besides familiarity, there are also other factors influencing label specificity. For example, cultures may have differences in their *basic level*; i.e. how specific speakers are generally expected to be (Rosch et al., 1976; Matsumoto, 1995). For this reason, *dog* is a more appropriate label than *affenpinscher* in most situations, even though the latter is more specific. Ideally, image description systems should recognize when to use a more general term, and when to go more into detail (Ordonez et al., 2015).

6.2 Limitations of translation approaches

One approach to image description in multiple languages is to use a translation system. For example, Li et al. (2016) compare two strategies: *early* versus *late* translation. Using early translation, image descriptions are translated to the target language before training an image description system on the translated descriptions. Using late translation, an image description system is trained on the original data, and the output is translated. Li et al. (2016) show that the former strategy achieves the best result, and argue that it is a promising approach because it requires no extra manual annotation.

Our observations in Section 5 show that there are limits to what a translation-based approach can achieve. While translation provides a strong baseline, it can only capture those phenomena that are familiar to the crowd providing the descriptions. The street organ example shows that there exists a 'knowledge gap' between Dutch and English. Dutch users would certainly not be satisfied with street organs being labeled as *unusual looking vehicles*. If the translation-based approach is to be successful, future research should find out how to bridge such gaps.

6.3 Limitations of this study

Our focus on Germanic languages from the Western world does not allow us to make general statements about how people describe images. A comparison with taxonomically and culturally different languages might help us uncover important factors that we have missed in this study. A surprising example comes from Baltaretu et al. (2016), who discuss how writing direction (left-to-right versus right-to-left) affects the way people process and recall visual scenes. This may have implications for the way that images are described by (or should be described for) speakers of languages differing in this regard.

Finally, there are limits to what a corpus study can show. The phenomena described here are presented with post-hoc explanations. Plausible as these explanations may be, they are still hypotheses. We think these hypotheses are useful guides in thinking about image description, but they still remain to be validated experimentally.

7 Conclusion

We studied a trilingually aligned corpus of described images to learn about how crowd workers of different languages described the same images. The main finding was that earlier observations about negation marking and ethnicity marking by English workers also hold for Dutch and German. Dutch and German workers also use negations in their image descriptions, showing that this is a robust phenomenon. Dutch and German workers also make unwarranted inferences about the images, this shows that crowd workers regularly include extra-visual information in their descriptions. In addition, Dutch and German workers also disproportionately mark non-white people in their descriptions, showing that image description corpora carry biases that we need to take into account when working with this data.

We also explored the role of familiarity in image description. We found images in our corpus that were easily described by workers of one language, but unidentifiable to the workers of another language. This has consequences for image description models trained on automatically translated training data: some images will not be properly described for the target audience. But the problem is more general. The success of image description systems trained on datasets of described images is limited by the knowledge of the annotators, regardless of the language. While the available data is useful for us to learn and discuss what human-like descriptions should look like, it can only take us so far. Full coverage systems that could tailor their descriptions to particular audiences are still out of reach.

We hope this work provides a starting point for conducting cross-linguistic comparisons of image descriptions. Future work includes replicating our analyses across more diverse families of languages, modifying the task design to contrast the results with our findings, and using our inspection tool to explore other linguistic phenomena. We are also interested in scaling up our analyses to larger corpora, which will require the development of automated comparison methods. We believe that these steps will bring us closer to an initial understanding of the diversity in image descriptions across different languages and social groups.

Acknowledgements

This research is funded through the NWO Spinoza prize, awarded to PV. DE is supported by an Amazon Research Award. We thank three anonymous reviewers for their questions and comments.

References

Adriana Baltaretu and Thiago Castro Ferreira. 2016. Task demands and individual variation in referring expressions. In *Proceedings of the 9th International Natural Language Generation conference*, pages 89–93, September 5-8.

Adriana Baltaretu, Emiel J Krahmer, Carel van Wijk, and Alfons Maes. 2016. Talking about relations: Factors influencing the production of relational descriptions. *Frontiers in psychology*, 7.

Allan Bell. 1984. Language style as audience design. *Language in Society*, 13(2):145—204.

Camiel J. Beukeboom. 2014. Mechanisms of linguistic bias: How words reflect and maintain stereotypic expectancies. In J. Laszlo, J. Forgas, and O. Vincze, editors, *Social cognition and communication*, volume 31, pages 313–330. Psychology Press.

Centraal Bureau voor de Statistiek. 2016. Bevolking; generatie, geslacht, leeftijd en herkomstgroepering, 1 januari. Part of the CBS database, last modified 15 September 2016, September.

Paul Christophersen. 1939. *The articles: A study of their theory and use in English*. Copenhagen: Munksgaard.

Guy Deutscher. 2010. *Through the language glass: How Words Colour Your World*. New York: Metropolitan Books.

Desmond Elliott, Stella Frank, and Eva Hasler. 2015. Multilingual image description with neural sequence models. *CoRR*.

Desmond Elliott, Stella Frank, Khalil Sima'an, and Lucia Specia. 2016. Multi30k: Multilingual english-german image descriptions. In *Proceedings of the 5th Workshop on Vision and Language*, pages 70–74.

Irene Heim. 1982. *The semantics of definite and indefinite noun phrases*. Ph.D. thesis, University of Massachusetts. New edition typeset in 2011 by Anders J. Schoubye and Ephraim Glick.

Julian Hitschler, Shigehiko Schamoni, and Stefan Riezler. 2016. Multimodal pivots for image caption translation. In *Proceedings of the 54th Annual Meeting of the Association for Computational Linguistics*.

Micah Hodosh, Peter Young, and Julia Hockenmaier. 2013. Framing image description as a ranking task: Data, models and evaluation metrics. *Journal of Artificial Intelligence Research*, 47:853–899.

Karen R. Humes, Nicholas A. Jones, and Roberto R. Ramirez. 2011. Overview of race and hispanic origin: 2010. Published by the United States Census Bureau, March.

Alejandro Jaimes and Shih-Fu Chang. 1999. Conceptual framework for indexing visual information at multiple levels. In *Electronic Imaging*, pages 2–15. International Society for Optics and Photonics.

Roman Jakobson. 1972. Verbal communication. *Scientific American*, 227:72–80.

Douwe Kiela, Felix Hill, Anna Korhonen, and Stephen Clark. 2014. Improving multi-modal representations using image dispersion: Why less is sometimes more. In *Proceedings of the 52nd Annual Meeting of the Association for Computational Linguistics*, pages 835–841.

Xirong Li, Weiyu Lan, Jianfeng Dong, and Hailong Liu. 2016. Adding chinese captions to images. In *Proceedings of the 2016 ACM on International Conference on Multimedia Retrieval*, pages 271–275.

Tsung-Yi Lin, Michael Maire, Serge Belongie, James Hays, Pietro Perona, Deva Ramanan, Piotr Dollár, and C Lawrence Zitnick. 2014. Microsoft coco: Common objects in context. In *European Conference on Computer Vision*, pages 740–755.

Yo Matsumoto. 1995. The conversational condition on horn scales. *Linguistics and philosophy*, 18(1):21–60.

John H McWhorter. 2014. *The language hoax: Why the world looks the same in any language*. Oxford University Press, USA.

Ishan Misra, C Lawrence Zitnick, Margaret Mitchell, and Ross Girshick. 2016. Seeing through the human reporting bias: Visual classifiers from noisy human-centric labels. In *Proceedings of the IEEE Conference on Computer Vision and Pattern Recognition*, pages 2930–2939.

Takashi Miyazaki and Nobuyuki Shimizu. 2016. Cross-lingual image caption generation. In *Proceedings of the 54th Annual Meeting of the Association for Computational Linguistics*, pages 1780–1790.

Vicente Ordonez, Wei Liu, Jia Deng, Yejin Choi, Alexander C. Berg, and Tamara L. Berg. 2015. Predicting entry-level categories. *International Journal of Computer Vision*, pages 1–15.

Erwin Panofsky. 1939. *Studies in Iconology*. Oxford University Press.

Janarthanan Rajendran, Mitesh M Khapra, Sarath Chandar, and Balaraman Ravindran. 2016. Bridge correlational neural networks for multilingual multimodal representation learning. In *Proceedings of the 2016 Conference of the North American Chapter of the Association for Computational Linguistics: Human Language Technologies*.

Eleanor Rosch, Carolyn B Mervis, Wayne D Gray, David M Johnson, and Penny Boyes-Braem. 1976. Basic objects in natural categories. *Cognitive psychology*, 8(3):382–439.

Sara Shatford. 1986. Analyzing the subject of a picture: a theoretical approach. *Cataloging & classification quarterly*, 6(3):39–62.

Lucia Specia, Stella Frank, Khalil Sima'an, and Desmond Elliott. 2016. A shared task on multimodal machine translation and crosslingual image description. In *Proceedings of the First Conference on Machine Translation*, pages 543–553.

Rachele Sprugnoli, Giovanni Moretti, Luisa Bentivogli, and Diego Giuliani. 2016. Creating a ground truth multilingual dataset of news and talk show transcriptions through crowdsourcing. *Language Resources and Evaluation*, pages 1–35.

Statistisches Bundesamt. 2013. Zensus 2011: 80,2 millionen einwohner lebten am 9. mai 2011 in deutschland. Press release, Nr. 188, May.

M. E. Unal, B. Citamak, S. Yagcioglu, A. Erdem, E. Erdem, N. Ikizler Cinbis, and R. Cakici. 2016. Tasviret: Görüntülerden otomatik türkçe açıklama oluşturma İçin bir denektaçı veri kümesi (tasviret: A benchmark dataset for automatic turkish description generation from images). In *IEEE Sinyal İşleme ve İletişim Uygulamaları Kurultayı (SIU 2016)*.

Emiel van Miltenburg, Roser Morante, and Desmond Elliott. 2016. Pragmatic factors in image description: the case of negations. In *Proceedings of the 5th Workshop on Vision and Language at ACL '16*.

Emiel van Miltenburg. 2016. Stereotyping and bias in the flickr30k dataset. In *Proceedings of Multimodal Corpora: Computer vision and language processing (MMC 2016)*, pages 1–4.

Yuya Yoshikawa, Yutaro Shigeto, and Akikazu Takeuchi. 2017. Stair captions: Constructing a large-scale japanese image caption dataset. *arXiv preprint arXiv:1705.00823*.

Peter Young, Alice Lai, Micah Hodosh, and Julia Hockenmaier. 2014. From image descriptions to visual denotations: New similarity metrics for semantic inference over event descriptions. *Transactions of the Association for Computational Linguistics*, 2:67–78.

Content Selection for Real-time Sports News Construction
from Commentary Texts

Jin-ge Yao   Jianmin Zhang   Xiaojun Wan   Jianguo Xiao

Institute of Computer Science and Technology, Peking University, Beijing 100871, China

The MOE Key Laboratory of Computational Linguistics, Peking University, China

`{yaojinge, zhangjianmin2015, wanxiaojun, xiaojianguo}@pku.edu.cn`

Abstract

We study the task of constructing sports news report automatically from live commentary and focus on content selection. Rather than receiving every piece of text of a sports match before news construction, as in previous related work, we novelly verify the feasibility of a more challenging setting to generate news report on the fly by treating live text input as a stream. We design scoring functions to address different requirements of the task and use stream substitution for sentence selection. Experiments suggest that our proposed framework can already produce comparable results compared with previous work that relies on a supervised learning-to-rank model.

1 Introduction

Live text commentary services are available on the web and are becoming increasingly popular for sports fans who do not have access to live video streams due to copyright reasons. Some people may also prefer live texts on portable devices. The emergence of live texts has produced huge amount of text commentary data. Currently there exists very few studies about utilizing this rich data source.

On the other hand, manually-written sports news for game reporting usually share the same information and vocabulary as live texts for the corresponding sports game. Sports news and commentary texts can be treated as two different sources of descriptions for the same sports events. It is tempting to investigate whether we can utilize the huge amount of live texts to automatically generate sports news for sports game reporting. Building an automatic sports news generation system will largely relax the burden of sports news editors, making them free from repetitive efforts for writing while producing sports news more efficiently and covering more sports games.

As a promising starting point, one recent study (Zhang et al., 2016) successfully demonstrated that it is technically feasible to generate sports news from given live text commentary scripts. They treat the task as a special kind of document summarization and adapt supervised learning-to-rank models to learn preference for which sentences should be extracted for construction.

However, sports news providers demand more on automatic generation, from a practical point of view. Taking this to the extreme, a sports news reporter typically starts writing early following the game proceeding, without even having seen an entire game played to the final minute. Manually written match reports usually get uploaded within a few minutes after the game, which is rather speedy. An automatic writer should likewise avoid long wait times until the game finished before the writing procedure. A more natural way to view the problem is to treat commentary texts as stream data, which come in to the system one by one as input. Unfortunately, previously used strategies cannot fulfill such requirements.

In this work we proposed a simple framework as a response to stream data requirements. By studying the properties of the task, we design scoring schemes to address different aspects of the problem. To extract the subset of commentary texts that maximize the score when the data come in stream, while considering a possible overall length budget constraint, we design an efficient stream substitution algorithm

31

Proceedings of The 10th International Natural Language Generation conference, pages 31–40,
Santiago de Compostela, Spain, September 4-7 2017. ©2017 Association for Computational Linguistics

that requires only single pass of data, based on a priority queue implementation. The overall framework forms a rather simple, efficient, practical approach that produces results comparable to the supervised learning-to-rank framework used by previous studies that involves rather heavy feature engineering, as shown on a real world dataset containing Chinese commentary texts.

2   Task Formulation

Following Zhang et al. (2016), we can also treat the task of constructing sports news from commentary texts as a special type of extractive summarization: extracting sentences from commentary scripts to form a news report for the described sports game. Formally, given the commentary texts for a sports match, containing a collection of candidate sentences $U = \{s_1, s_2, \ldots, s_n\}$, the goal is to extract a subset of sentences $S \in U$ to form a summary report for the match. For experimental comparison, we require the total length of selected extraction not to exceed a pre-specified length budget B measured by the total number of Chinese characters.

Compared with generic document summarization, the candidate sentence processed here has a richer structure. Other than commentary text, it also contains the time when the currently described action or event happens, along with a current scoreline. See Table 1 for an example segment of commentary texts that we used for experiments, consisting of texts crawled from easily available sports live texts.[1]

Time	Scoreline	Commentary Texts
21'	1-0	The flag is up for a foul from Costa.
22'	2-0	2-0! Goal for Everton!
22'	2-0	The substitute Naismith scored twice to establish the two-goal lead for his team.

Table 1: Example excerpt of commentary data format

More importantly, in this work we emphasize that our data are assumed to come in stream, provided in a real-time fashion. In other words, we receive commentary sentences one by one during the sports game playing, without seeing the description of future events. The goal here is to perform sentence extraction simultaneously, with the hope that once the game finishes, we immediately get the news report right in the first second to ensure that the automatic writer is faster than a human author.

As an additional comment, this setting directly blocks the possibility to apply standard document summarization methodologies as they often involve global optimization or sentence graph ranking, requiring global information that cannot be well captured by a partial stream of data.[2] The effective approaches based on learning-to-rank models used in (Zhang et al., 2016) cannot be adapted here either. Instead, structurally simpler frameworks should be used, such as element-wise regression or classification, direct function evaluation, etc. Since it is nontrivial to address the length budget as well as some other possible requirements when training a supervised learning model, we opt for an even more simpler way of designing characterizing functions to address different aspect of the task, followed by a properly designed stream algorithm for content selection.

3   Our Proposed Approach

The framework of the approach proposed in this paper has a rather simple nature. Once a piece of commentary data comes, the system immediately performs a scoring function evaluation for it, and store the top scoring pieces of text in memory, while conforming to the total length budget. See Figure 1 for an overview illustration of the framework we leverage in this study.

3.1   Sentence Scoring

The way to describe sports events in commentary is different from that in a written news report. There are multiple aspects that should be taken into consideration if we would like to use commentary sentences to construct sports news.

3.1.1   Importance of described actions

The most straightforward criterion for deciding whether to preserve a sentence for news construc-

---

[1] We will be using the data collected by previous work which contain Chinese texts only. For succinctness we only show corresponding English translations here in this paper.

[2] Exceptions mainly include methods that are based on singleton predictions by simply ignoring structural dependencies or relative preferences.

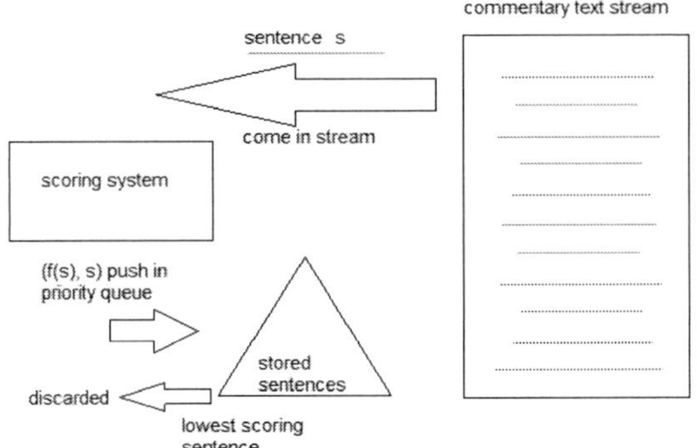

Figure 1: Overview of the framework

tion is to quantify the amount of importance for the described actions or events in the sports game. In sports events, actions are mostly described using verbs, nouns and compound nouns. Therefore, we count the main importance calculations on such types of words only for an efficient approximate processing. Specifically, we define *indicator words* to be all valid nouns and verbs that are not in the stop words list. Such words characterize the main indicative information described in the sentence, typically covering actions, events and locations (e.g. specific area of the pitch or arena). Note that here proper nouns such as team names or player names should be excluded, since almost every piece of commentary sentence contains such proper nouns, making these words not discriminative for our local decisions of sentence extraction.

For a given sentence s, we use $I(s)$ to denote the collection of the *indicator words*, i.e. all valid nouns and verbs contained in sentence s excluding proper nouns. The question is how to find those words that are more important and more indicative, and have a strong tendency to be selected to compose news reports.

We separately characterize two aspects: the *tendency* to be described in news reports, as well as individual *importance*. We rely on simple corpus statistics to address the estimation problem of each. Specifically, for *tendency* estimation we first align descriptions in live commentary texts to the corresponding human written news, utilizing the time stamps as well. We mark the frequency count of indicator words that can be aligned to manual news as $C_{aligned}(w)$, and use $C_{total}(w)$ to denote the total frequency of w appearing in the live texts. For *importance* estimation, we crawled another collection of sports news, without any need to be aligned to any commentary texts. We simply use the logarithm of frequency counts[3] of an indicator word appeared in manually written news, as an importance indicator.

In summary, the importance score for an indicator word w is defined as

$$imp(w) = \frac{C_{aligned}(w)}{C_{total}(w)} \log C_{news}(w), \quad (1)$$

In Table 2 we list a proportion of the top scoring indicator words (translated from original Chinese data) as calculated by the aforementioned method. We can observe that the words that are assigned to be indicator words are indeed intuitive as they capture the most important events, motions, or key locations in some cases, during a soccer game. In the implementation a few manual modifications of indicators have been made to promote more reasonable selection.

shoot (shè)	shot (shèmén)	substitution
find	score	penalty area
change	goal	red card
threat	one-on-one	top corner

Table 2: Example top scoring indicator words

3.1.2 Description style

Descriptive languages in sports commentary and news report are different in general. However, they also share some commonalities since they are describing the same events. For selecting sentences to form news reports, we may tend to preserve those that are close to the description of news already. With the minimum amount of post-editing they can almost be directly used for news construction.

To find sentences that are close to news descriptions style, we make use of the additionally crawled data used for calculating individual importance of indicator words, as described earlier. Specifically, we use log bigram frequency to conceptually simulate an effect of a n-gram language model. In this step we also exclude proper nouns as usual, to

---

[3] We do not use raw counts since they are in greater scale and the differences between words are huge and too sensitive to the specific corpus.

33

exclude pairs that are not generalizable to games played between different teams and different players. A bit more formally, we write $bigram(s)$ for a given sentence s to denote the description quality characterized by news bigrams:

$$bigram(s) = \sum_{b \in bigrams(s)} \log C_{news}(b) \quad (2)$$

In Table 3 we also show the top scoring bigrams to depict what kinds of local wording choices are typically used in sports news. The bigrams are formed with Chinese words, therefore they may not correspond to English bigrams formally. We fill some commonly appearing compositions in parentheses in order to show the use of bigrams with more clarity.

inside the penalty area	the shot was (saved)
was shown (the yellow card)	the shot from
hit the (bar/post)	minutes later
just wide	was over

Table 3: Example top scoring bigrams

Note that such scoring scheme may also partially characterize the preservation of important information from a slightly different angle, leading to possibly overlapping effects with the previous aspect as we described. Bigrams counts have been used to capture concept importance in previous work on summarization as well (Gillick et al., 2008; Gillick et al., 2009). In the implementation a few noisy bigrams have been manually filtered to promote more reasonable selection.

3.1.3 Closeness to key changes

For every type of sport there exist certain types of key events that should definitely be reported in the news, possibly in slightly more details. Take soccer for example, the most important change during a game is the scoreline change, triggered by goal scoring events. It is appropriate to assign related descriptions with higher sentence scores.

We characterize the closeness of a sentence at time t to the latest scoreline change point t' as:

$$sc(t, t') = \exp(-\frac{|t - t'|^2}{2\sigma^2}), \quad (3)$$

where σ is a width parameter for controlling the scale of difference. A larger σ assign less preference for those who are close to the scoreline change point, but not as close enough. For simplicity we directly set $\sigma = 1$ in this work.

3.1.4 Sentence scoring function in sum

Taking all three aspects we just described together, we form the scoring function for a given sentence s using a simple summation as follows:

$$f(s) = bigram(s) + \sum_{w \in I(s)} imp(w) + sc(s.time, t'), \quad (4)$$

where each term has been described in earlier subsections, addressing different aspects for the task respectively.

The overall target is then to select a subset S of sentences from the total commentary set U, under a length budget. The score of a subset S is simply $f(S) = \sum_{s \in S} f(s)$.

3.2 Stream Data Selection

Our ultimate goal is to select commentary texts that maximize the total score as defined in the previous section, aiming at keeping the most important, representative pieces of information. It is intuitive and easy to verify that when ignoring the third closeness term (3), the remaining bigram scores and indicator importance scores actually satisfy the *submodularity* property,[4] i.e. for $\forall S \subseteq T \subseteq U \setminus u$, we have:

$$f(S \cup \{u\}) - f(S) \geq f(T \cup \{u\}) - f(T). \quad (5)$$

As a result, our objective function consists of a submodular proportion along with a bounded term, as $sc() \leq 1$, which contributes a small, controllable proportion to the total score. Therefore we can treat our objective function as near-submodular.

There exist some studies exploring the strategies to approximately optimize a submodular function in stream data settings, also without seeing the entirety while only a small, constant proportion of memory usage is allowed. For example, the sieving approach proposed in (Badanidiyuru et al., 2014) provides an efficient streaming algorithm that has a constant factor of $1/2 - \epsilon$ of approximation guarantee to the optimal solution, while only requiring a

---

[4] They are in fact *modular*, i.e. both f and $-f$ are submodular.

data-independent size of memory and a single pass through the data stream.

Most off-the-shelf algorithms for submodular maximization in stream data settings are designed for cases where cardinality constraints are involved, i.e. restricting the total selected number by requiring $|S| \leq k$ where k is a predefined constant integer. This setting is different with what we care about in this work: a knapsack constraint $\sum_{s \in S} length(s) \leq B$ restricting the total length.

As a result, we develop a new stream algorithm called *heap substitution* that fits our target well and finds a good approximate solution. The algorithm can be treated as an adapted version of an earlier work (Krause and Gomes, 2010), which may not be optimal in a theoretical sense, but can achieve very good approximate solution. The nature of our algorithm is simple: keep a priority queue (implemented using a heap) for the currently selected sentences to be preserved. Once the budget constraint could be violated by introducing the current commentary sentence, we push it to the priority queue and pop out the sentence that is evaluated with the least amount of score in the queue. The algorithm is listed in pseudocode in Algorithm 1.

Algorithm 1 The heap substitution algorithm

Input:
    Sentences $\{s_i\}$ coming in stream; predefined budget B

Output:
    The sentence set S in the sports news;

1: **Initialize** $S = \emptyset$ stored in a minimal heap
2: **if** $f(s_i) > 0$ **then**
3:     **if** $|S \cup \{s_i\}| \leq B$ **then**
4:         $S = S \cup \{s_i\}$
5:     **else**
6:         Push s_i onto the heap S
7:         Pop the top (minimum score) element of S
8:     **end if**
9: **end if**
10: **return** S

As far as we know, currently there exist no study for stream submodular maximization under such knapsack constraints. As theoretical analysis is not the major focus of this work, we leave it as a future work to generalize the algorithm to more generic scenarios beyond sports news construction. Meanwhile, there exist additional stream algorithms with better theoretical or practical properties for cardinality constrained submodular maximization. The modified (multi-)sieve streaming algorithm described in (Badanidiyuru et al., 2014) can be served as an example. These algorithms may also be adapted, but perhaps technically more demanding for this study. We leave such further variants and comparisons to future work study.

4 Experiments

4.1 Data

There are not many datasets available for the particular stream data setting studied in this paper. However, generic datasets for sports news construction actually suffice for our purpose, as long as we treat the texts as stream data and simply ignore future observations during calculation and prediction, while consuming a tiny proportion of memory usage. To form direct comparison with previous work, we simply use the same dataset as constructed in (Zhang et al., 2016). The authors find Chinese commentary text rather easy to acquire and crawled 150 football matches on Sina Sports Live, each assigned with two manually written news reports for the purpose of training or evaluation.

Following previous work, we perform cross-validation during evaluation to utilize the dataset more sufficiently and to draw more reliable conclusions. Specifically, we randomly divide the dataset into three parts with equal sizes, each contains 50 pairs of live texts and gold-standard news. Each time we set one of them as the test set and use the remaining two parts for training, or specific types of corpus statistics as used in our method. We will mainly report the averaged results from all three folds.

4.2 Evaluation Metrics

Similar to the evaluation for traditional summarization tasks, we use the ROUGE metrics (Lin and Hovy, 2003) to automatically evaluate the quality of produced summaries given the gold-standard reference news. The ROUGE metrics measure summary quality by counting the precision, recall and F-score of overlapping units, such as n-grams and skip grams, between a candidate summary and the reference summaries.

Specifically, we report the F-scores of the following metrics in the experimental results: ROUGE-1 (unigram-based), ROUGE-2 (bigram-based) and ROUGE-SU4 (based on skip bigrams with a maximum skip distance of 4). Note that the ROUGE scores are computed for each document set, and then the scores are averaged. We use the ROUGE-1.5.5 toolkit to perform the evaluation.

Note that the results are slightly different with those reported in (Zhang et al., 2016). As we understand, in that work the ROUGE overlaps are calculated based on a rather weak word segmentation tool that breaks many named entities into separated characters or subwords, which boosts the ROUGE quantities slightly larger than expected and may incorrectly reflect the preference between each other. The ROUGE distance between system outputs and gold standard manually written news, which should be treated as an upper bound, is somewhat close. In this work the evaluation is based on another popular Chinese word segmentation toolkit called Jieba,[5] that performs word segmentation results with satisfactory level of accuracy, when provided external sports dictionary.

We also conduct manual evaluation in this study. Specifically, we use the pyramid method (Nenkova and Passonneau, 2004) and modified pyramid scores as described in (Passonneau et al., 2005) to manually evaluate the summaries generated by different methods. We randomly sample 20 games from the data set and manually annotate facts on the gold-standard news. The annotated facts are mostly describing specific events happened during the game. Each fact is treated as a Summarization Content Unit (SCU) (Nenkova and Passonneau, 2004). The number of occurrences for each SCU in the gold-standard news is regarded as the weight of this SCU.

Two types of scores for peers were computed from the peer annotations. Both scores are a ratio of the sum of the weights of the SCUs found in the generated summary (OBServed) to the sum for an ideal gold-standard news (MAXimum). If the number of SCUs of a given weight i that occur in a summary is O_i, the sum of the weights of all the SCUs in a summary is:

$$OBS = \sum_{i=1}^{n} i \times O_i$$

In the original pyramid scoring, the number of SCUs used in computing MAX is the same as the number used to compute OBS. The score is defined as the ratio OBS/MAX. In a more commonly used modified score, MAX_M is computed instead of MAX using the average number of SCUs found in all gold-standard news and the score is defined as the ratio OBS/MAX_M. This modified version avoids assigning high scores to summaries that have retrieved very few SCUs. We conform to the modified version during pyramid evaluation.

4.3 Baselines

The most straightforward baseline is directly performing singleton regression or classification. Specifically, the support vector machine (SVM) and support vector regression (SVR) model serve as strong supervised baselines. We utilize the LIBSVM implementation[6] (Chang and Lin, 2011) with the RBF kernel for classification/regression. We reimplemented the features described in (Zhang et al., 2016) which turn out to be effective for this task. As in stream data settings, features that depends on future observations are not used.

We also generate results from batch processing systems for reference. Specifically, we implemented graph-based document summarization approach including centroid-based summarization (Radev et al., 2000) and the well-known LexRank (Erkan and Radev, 2004). We also rebuilt the learning-to-rank system followed with a probabilistic greedy selection procedure, as used by (Zhang et al., 2016) based on random forests of LambdaMART rankers, and observed similar results as the authors reported. The produced results have been verified to be similar to those reported in their paper, if using the same word segmentation procedure.

4.4 Results

Table 4 lists the results for different output systems. The results of this work is significantly different ($p < 0.01$) with all baseline systems but LTR,

---

[5]https://github.com/fxsjy/jieba/

[6]http://www.csie.ntu.edu.tw/ cjlin/libsvm/

with the difference between LTR and the proposed method only at the significant level of 0.1. Bonferroni adjustment (Bonferroni, 1936; Bland and Altman, 1995) has been considered when calculating p-values for multiple comparisons.

From the table we can observe that our proposed method for stream settings clearly outperform graph-based baseline approaches as well as the singleton-prediction baselines of SVR and SVM, while producing comparable or better results compared with the state-of-the-art learning-to-rank system which involves heavy feature engineering.

Since SVR and SVM baselines are trained on labels derived from ROUGE values, they may not learn the discriminative behaviors between those features that lead to preservation or those that are not suitable to be preserved for news construction. Our proposed scoring function is able to address this issue by *direct word-level control*, therefore yielding better results. Note that conceptually the same issue exists in the learning-to-rank system as well and as a result one may observe that there exist a significant improve from the proposed method, in terms of the pyramid score.

Graph-based summarization approaches have been shown not suitable for the task of commentary based sports news construction. The results in this work also corroborate such observations.

Table 5 shows an example output[7] of extracted sentences by our method for the Everton vs Manchester City game played in the English Premier League at season 2015-2016. We can observe that our system is able to capture most of the possible key moments during the game, with a tiny proportion of less important descriptions. There also exist some more difficult problems which we do not focus in this study. For example, the second sentence clearly has a problem of zero anaphora, without clearly stating who is performing the long shot.

4.5 Ablation Analysis

To test the contribution of each component in the scoring scheme, we form combinations by removing each group of scoring respectively. Table 6 shows the results, with "-" denotes experiments without the corresponding group.

(Preview) Man City won only one out of the last six away games at Goodison Park.
(2') A long range effort is blocked.
(3') Corner for Man City. The ball is crossed to the middle and headed out by the defender.
...
(60') Sterling dribbles to the penalty area,
throughs the ball to Kolarov,
and Kolarov finds the net from a tight angle.
(63') Kone's shot in the box is blocked.
...
(89') A clever pass from Yaya Toure to the box,
Nasri moves forward, lobs the keeper to score.
(FT) The game finishes at 0-2.

Table 5: Example output for the Everton vs Man City game

System	R-1	R-2	R-SU4	Pyramid
All	0.33247	0.10223	0.13478	0.80759
-bigram	0.31262	0.09412	0.11628	0.77310
-import.	0.30759	0.08660	0.11744	0.65241
-closen.	0.31148	0.09064	0.11749	0.79034

Table 6: Score ablation results

We can observe that removing any of the three components degrades the overall performance. The results also suggest that the indicator word scores contribute the most. This is natural since the indicator part of score has some form of supervision from calculating statistics on aligned training data.

5 Related Work

5.1 Sports News Generation

To the best of our knowledge, generation of sports news by utilizing commentary texts is not a well-studied task in related fields. Very few related work can be backtracked other than the study of (Zhang et al., 2016) which treats the task as single document summarization and develop a supervised learning-to-rank framework to show the feasibility of this task. A few earlier studies attempted to generate sports report from structured data such as event tables (Lareau et al., 2011) and ontology-based knowledge base (Bouayad-Agha et al., 2011; Bouayad-Agha et al., 2012), based on predefined templates. There exist some related studies that focused on generating textual summaries for sports events from status up-

---

[7]We omit part of the extracted descriptions in the middle due to space limit.

System	ROUGE-1	ROUGE-2	ROUGE-SU4	Pyramid
Centroid	0.26201	0.05150	0.08146	0.32483
LexRank	0.24456	0.03533	0.06609	0.29034
SVR	0.30502	0.07371	0.10532	0.42828
SVM	0.30934	0.07482	0.10681	0.46276
LTR	0.32489	0.09464	0.12319	0.56621
This work	0.33247	0.10223	0.13478	0.80759
Gold-standard	0.40802	0.12924	0.16407	0.88219

Table 4: Evaluation results of different approaches

dates in Twitter (Nichols et al., 2012; Kubo et al., 2013; Tagawa and Shimada, 2016). There also exists earlier work from study groups that do not focus on text analysis or language processing, studying generation of sports highlight frames from sports videos, focusing on a very different type of data (Tjondronegoro et al., 2004).

5.2 Submodular Maximization

As we mentioned earlier, the designed scoring function is near submodular. Maximization of submodular functions is a well-studied topic in machine learning and algorithmic analysis, It has been applied to many tasks such as document summarization (Lin and Bilmes, 2010), sensor placement (Krause et al., 2006) network inference (Gomez Rodriguez et al., 2010) and many more applications, with the aim of balancing the coverage or quality measures of selected items while encouraging diversity in selection.

5.3 Stream Data Processing

Stream data settings are becoming popular due to the fact that it is natural in many tasks where enormous amount of data are coming one by one (Gaber et al., 2005). For maximizing submodular functions, there already exist a number of stream algorithms (Krause and Gomes, 2010; Badanidiyuru et al., 2014; Kumar et al., 2015). The heap substitution algorithm we designed in this work resembles the algorithm developed in (Krause and Gomes, 2010) that addresses cardinality constraints. In the task settings for this study the budget is limited in sentences lengths measured by total number of characters, which leads to a knapsack constraint rather than cardinality constraints that are easier to deal with.

5.4 Document Summarization

The approach of selecting sentences to construct news reports can be treated as a special kind of document summarization (Nenkova et al., 2011). Among the large number of papers in summarization literature, some of them are based on simple definitions of sentence scoring with different components addressing different requirements in specific task settings (Yih et al., 2007; Christensen et al., 2013; Macdonald and Siddharthan, 2016, for instance), which is similar to this paper. The main difference between document summarization and the task in this study is the way to characterize importance.

6 Conclusion

We study the task of constructing sports news in real time, treating live commentary texts as stream input. The nature of this setting blocks the use of preference learning or global optimization. As a result, we proposed a more straightforward procedure to perform online evaluation and prediction. We develop a simple heap substitution algorithm to decide which texts should be preserved, subject to a predefined length constraint. Experiments show that our proposed method works well on real world datasets and yields comparable results to the state-of-the-art learning-to-rank framework.

Acknowledgments

This work was supported by 863 Program of China (2015AA015403), NSFC (61331011), and Key Laboratory of Science, Technology and Standard in Press Industry (Key Laboratory of Intelligent Press Media Technology). We thank the anonymous reviewers for helpful comments. Xiaojun Wan is the corresponding author.

References

Ashwinkumar Badanidiyuru, Baharan Mirzasoleiman, Amin Karbasi, and Andreas Krause. 2014. Streaming submodular maximization: Massive data summarization on the fly. In *Proceedings of the 20th ACM SIGKDD international conference on Knowledge discovery and data mining*, pages 671–680. ACM.

J Martin Bland and Douglas G Altman. 1995. Multiple significance tests: the bonferroni method. *Bmj*, 310(6973):170.

Carlo E Bonferroni. 1936. *Teoria statistica delle classi e calcolo delle probabilita*. Libreria internazionale Seeber.

Nadjet Bouayad-Agha, Gerard Casamayor, and Leo Wanner. 2011. Content selection from an ontology-based knowledge base for the generation of football summaries. In *Proceedings of the 13th European Workshop on Natural Language Generation*, pages 72–81. Association for Computational Linguistics.

Nadjet Bouayad-Agha, Gerard Casamayor, Simon Mille, and Leo Wanner. 2012. Perspective-oriented generation of football match summaries: Old tasks, new challenges. *ACM Transactions on Speech and Language Processing (TSLP)*, 9(2):3.

Chih-Chung Chang and Chih-Jen Lin. 2011. Libsvm: a library for support vector machines. *ACM Transactions on Intelligent Systems and Technology (TIST)*, 2(3):27.

Janara Christensen, Mausam, Stephen Soderland, and Oren Etzioni. 2013. Towards coherent multi-document summarization. In *Proceedings of the 2013 Conference of the North American Chapter of the Association for Computational Linguistics: Human Language Technologies*, pages 1163–1173, Atlanta, Georgia, June. Association for Computational Linguistics.

Günes Erkan and Dragomir R Radev. 2004. Lexrank: Graph-based lexical centrality as salience in text summarization. *Journal of Artificial Intelligence Research*, pages 457–479.

Mohamed Medhat Gaber, Arkady Zaslavsky, and Shonali Krishnaswamy. 2005. Mining data streams: a review. *ACM Sigmod Record*, 34(2):18–26.

Dan Gillick, Benoit Favre, and Dilek Hakkani-Tur. 2008. The icsi summarization system at tac 2008. In *Proceedings of the Text Understanding Conference*.

Dan Gillick, Benoit Favre, Dilek Hakkani-Tur, Berndt Bohnet, Yang Liu, and Shasha Xie. 2009. The icsi/utd summarization system at tac 2009. In *Proceedings of the Second Text Analysis Conference, Gaithersburg, Maryland, USA. National Institute of Standards and Technology*.

Manuel Gomez Rodriguez, Jure Leskovec, and Andreas Krause. 2010. Inferring networks of diffusion and influence. In *Proceedings of the 16th ACM SIGKDD international conference on Knowledge discovery and data mining*, pages 1019–1028. ACM.

Andreas Krause and Ryan G Gomes. 2010. Budgeted nonparametric learning from data streams. In *Proceedings of the 27th International Conference on Machine Learning (ICML-10)*, pages 391–398.

Andreas Krause, Carlos Guestrin, Anupam Gupta, and Jon Kleinberg. 2006. Near-optimal sensor placements: Maximizing information while minimizing communication cost. In *Proceedings of the 5th international conference on Information processing in sensor networks*, pages 2–10. ACM.

Mitsumasa Kubo, Ryohei Sasano, Hiroya Takamura, and Manabu Okumura. 2013. Generating live sports updates from twitter by finding good reporters. In *Web Intelligence (WI) and Intelligent Agent Technologies (IAT), 2013 IEEE/WIC/ACM International Joint Conferences on*, volume 1, pages 527–534. IEEE.

Ravi Kumar, Benjamin Moseley, Sergei Vassilvitskii, and Andrea Vattani. 2015. Fast greedy algorithms in mapreduce and streaming. *ACM Transactions on Parallel Computing*, 2(3):14.

François Lareau, Mark Dras, and Robert Dale. 2011. Detecting interesting event sequences for sports reporting. In *Proceedings of the 13th European Workshop on Natural Language Generation*, pages 200–205, Nancy, France, September. Association for Computational Linguistics.

Hui Lin and Jeff Bilmes. 2010. Multi-document summarization via budgeted maximization of submodular functions. In *Human Language Technologies: The 2010 Annual Conference of the North American Chapter of the Association for Computational Linguistics*, pages 912–920. Association for Computational Linguistics.

Chin-Yew Lin and Eduard Hovy. 2003. Automatic evaluation of summaries using n-gram co-occurrence statistics. In *Proceedings of the 2003 Conference of the North American Chapter of the Association for Computational Linguistics on Human Language Technology-Volume 1*, pages 71–78. Association for Computational Linguistics.

Iain Macdonald and Advaith Siddharthan. 2016. Summarising news stories for children. In *Proceedings of the 9th International Natural Language Generation conference*, pages 1–10, Edinburgh, UK, September 5-8. Association for Computational Linguistics.

Ani Nenkova and Rebecca Passonneau. 2004. Evaluating content selection in summarization: The pyramid method.

Ani Nenkova, Kathleen McKeown, et al. 2011. Automatic summarization. *Foundations and Trends® in Information Retrieval*, 5(2–3):103–233.

Jeffrey Nichols, Jalal Mahmud, and Clemens Drews. 2012. Summarizing sporting events using twitter. In *Proceedings of the 2012 ACM international conference on Intelligent User Interfaces*, pages 189–198. ACM.

Rebecca J Passonneau, Ani Nenkova, Kathleen McKeown, and Sergey Sigelman. 2005. Applying the pyramid method in duc 2005. In *Proceedings of the Document Understanding Conference (DUC 05), Vancouver, BC, Canada*.

Dragomir R Radev, Hongyan Jing, and Malgorzata Budzikowska. 2000. Centroid-based summarization of multiple documents: sentence extraction, utility-based evaluation, and user studies. In *Proceedings of the 2000 NAACL-ANLP Workshop on Automatic summarization*, pages 21–30. Association for Computational Linguistics.

Yuuki Tagawa and Kazutaka Shimada. 2016. Generating abstractive summaries of sports games from japanese tweets. In *Advanced Applied Informatics (IIAI-AAI), 2016 5th IIAI International Congress on*, pages 82–87. IEEE.

Dian Tjondronegoro, Yi-Ping Phoebe Chen, and Binh Pham. 2004. Integrating highlights for more complete sports video summarization. *IEEE multimedia*, 11(4):22–37.

Wen-tau Yih, Joshua Goodman, Lucy Vanderwende, and Hisami Suzuki. 2007. Multi-document summarization by maximizing informative content-words. In *Proceedings of the 20th International Joint Conference on Artificial Intelligence*, pages 1776–1782, Hyderabad, India, January 6-12.

Jianmin Zhang, Jin-ge Yao, and Xiaojun Wan. 2016. Towards constructing sports news from live text commentary. In *Proceedings of the 54th Annual Meeting of the Association for Computational Linguistics (Volume 1: Long Papers)*, pages 1361–1371, Berlin, Germany, August. Association for Computational Linguistics.

Improving the Naturalness and Expressivity of Language Generation for Spanish

Cristina Barros
Department of Software
and Computing Systems
University of Alicante
Apdo. de Correos 99
E-03080, Alicante, Spain
cbarros@dlsi.ua.es

Dimitra Gkatzia
School of Computing
Edinburgh Napier University
Edinburgh, EH10 5DT, UK
d.gkatzia@napier.ac.uk

Elena Lloret
Department of Software
and Computing Systems
University of Alicante
Apdo. de Correos 99
E-03080, Alicante, Spain
elloret@dlsi.ua.es

Abstract

We present a flexible Natural Language Generation approach for Spanish, focused on the surface realisation stage, which integrates an inflection module in order to improve the naturalness and expressivity of the generated language. This inflection module inflects the verbs using an ensemble of trainable algorithms whereas the other types of words (e.g. nouns, determiners, etc) are inflected using hand-crafted rules. We show that our approach achieves 2% higher accuracy than two state-of-art inflection generation approaches. Furthermore, our proposed approach also predicts an extra feature: the inflection of the imperative mood, which was not taken into account by previous work. We also present a user evaluation, where we demonstrate that the proposed method significantly improves the perceived naturalness of the generated language.

1 Introduction

Improving the naturalness and expressivity of the generated language is key in the area of Natural Language Generation (NLG), which aims to automatically generate text from non textual inputs. Specifically, one way to address it is by enriching the language through its morphology. Existing NLG systems are usually applied to non-morphologically rich languages, such as English, where the *morphological realisation* (i.e. the production of well inflected sentences or words through the use of words' morpho-syntactic properties) of words during the generation can be done using hand-written rules or existing libraries such as SimpleNLG (Gatt and Reiter, 2009). However, the use of this type of rules

in morphologically rich languages, such as Spanish or German, can be expensive and lead to incorrect inflection of a word, thus generating ungrammatical or meaningless texts.

We propose a flexible and domain independent NLG approach for Spanish, focused on the surface realisation stage, which integrates an inflection module. This inflection module incorporates an ensemble of trainable algorithms to automatically inflect a sentence by learning the inflection of Spanish verbs in conjunction with some hand-crafted rules for inflecting others types of words.

Our contributions to the field are as follows: we propose a flexible NLG approach for Spanish, focused on the surface realisation stage, which includes a novel and efficient inflection module that tackles the challenge of inflection generation using an ensemble of algorithms together with some hand-crafted rules; we contribute a high-quality dataset which includes instances of Spanish verbs for all the grammatical moods (in contrast with the current inflection approaches which do not tackle the imperative mood); our inflection module achieves 2% higher accuracy than the state-of-the-art methods; and finally, the proposed method achieves significant improvement of the perceived naturalness of the generated language in terms of coherence, grammaticality and post-editing.

In the next section (Section 2), we refer to the related work on inflection generation in general and on inflection within NLG systems. In Section 3, we describe our overall surface realisation approach which consists of three modules, including the proposed inflection module for NLG. In Section 4, we

41

Proceedings of The 10th International Natural Language Generation conference, pages 41–50,
Santiago de Compostela, Spain, September 4-7 2017. ©2017 Association for Computational Linguistics

present the experimental setup for testing the inflection module both with automatic metrics against state-of-the-art approaches and with a user evaluation, and in Section 5, we discuss the results. Finally, in Section 6, directions for future work are discussed.

2 Related Work

An NLG system comprises a wide range of modules, commonly grouped into a pipeline of three broad stages: document planning, microplanning and surface realisation (Reiter and Dale, 2000). The latter is responsible for generating the output text in natural language, which includes the morphological realisation in order to make the generated language more natural and expressive.

Most of the existing NLG systems usually work with English where the morphological realisation does not represent a problem because of its simplicity. It can be addressed using existing libraries as in Khan et al. (2015) where the SimpleNLG software (Gatt and Reiter, 2009) is used to generate sentences from predicate argument structures. On the other hand, previous work has addressed the morphology employing information extracted from lexicons (Androutsopoulos et al., 2013) or has not included it (Ballesteros et al., 2015).

The grammatical richness of the Spanish language is a challenge for NLG. Existing methods to automatically learn/predict the inflection of the verbs for morphologically rich languages have used supervised or semi-supervised learning (Durrett and DeNero, 2013; Ahlberg et al., 2014; Nicolai et al., 2015; Faruqui et al., 2016) to learn morphological rules on word forms in order to inflect the desired words. Other approaches have relied on linguistic information, such as morphemes and phonology (Cotterell et al., 2016); morphosyntactic disambiguation rules (Suárez et al., 2005); and graphical models (Dreyer and Eisner, 2009).

Recently, the morphological inflection has been also addressed at SIGMORPHON 2016 Shared Task (Cotterell et al., 2016) where, given a lemma with its part-of-speech, a target inflected form had to be generated (Task 1). This task was addressed through several approaches, including align and transduce (Alegria and Etxeberria, 2016; Nicolai et al., 2016; Liu and Mao, 2016); recurrent neural networks (Kann and Schütze, 2016; Aharoni et al., 2016; Östling, 2016); and linguistic-inspired heuristics approaches (Taji et al., 2016; Sorokin, 2016). Overall, recurrent neural networks approaches performed better, being (Kann and Schütze, 2016) the best performing system in the shared task, obtaining around 98%. For the purpose of this task, a dataset in 10 languages, including Spanish[1], was provided. This dataset consisted of examples of word forms with its corresponding morphosyntactic descriptions.

Finally, the work described here differs from existing statistical surface realisation methods which use phrase-based or n-grams learning (e.g., (Konstas and Lapata, 2012; Angeli et al., 2010)) since they do not include morphological inflection. In this respect, our work is more similar to (Dušek and Jurčíček, 2013), where the inflected word forms are learnt through multi-class logistic regression by predicting edit scripts; and (Bohnet et al., 2010) where a statistical morphology generator (evaluated for English, Spanish, German and Chinese) was employed as a part of a support-vector-machines based surface realiser from semantic structures.

3 Surface Realisation Approach

This section describes the overall surface realisation approach for Spanish. The approach is divided in three modules as shown in Figure 1: (1) vocabulary selection, (2) generation of related sentences and (3) inflection generation.

The vocabulary selection module chooses the vocabulary that is used for text generation. This vocabulary is then used to generate a set of related sentences in lemma forms with the chosen content words (i.e. all of the words contained in the sentences are lemmas). This content is then used to generate related sentences in lemma form that also contain terms included in the previous sentence. Finally, the inflection module inflects all the content of the sentences generated into inflected sentences, that will be the final output of the approach.

---

[1]The dataset also includes the imperative mood, however it does not include examples for all the tenses for a concrete verb. For instance, which corresponding, for the verb "abacorar" there are only 2 examples which corresponding to the first person plural of the present of indicative. Therefore, we opted to create a wide-coverage dataset for this work.

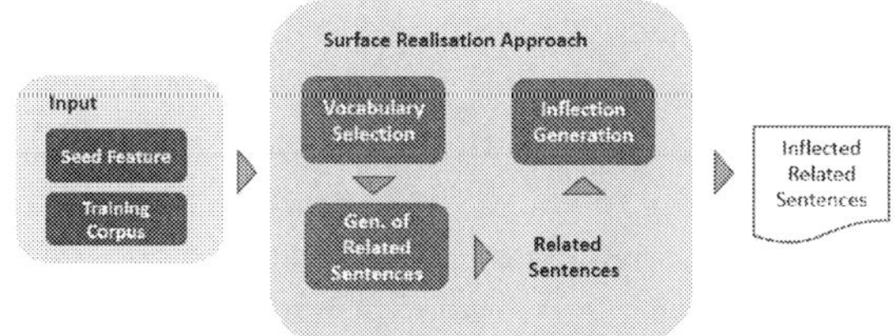

Figure 1: Diagram of the surface realisation approach divided in 3 modules: vocabulary selection, generation of related sentences and inflection generation.

3.1 Vocabulary Selection

As mentioned, the proposed approach mainly focuses on the surface realisation stage. Therefore, the content and the vocabulary needed to generate a sentence are determined by the input corpora and input *seed feature*. In general, a seed feature is an abstract object (which can be anything such as a topic, a sentiment, etc.) that is used to guide the generation process in relation to the most suitable vocabulary and content that the generated text will contain for a given domain (Barros and Lloret, 2015). The aim of the generated sentences is to meet the requirements expressed with this seed feature (e.g. to contain the maximum number of words for a specific phoneme, or to generate an opinionated sentence (Barros and Lloret, 2017)).

In this work, we selected phonemes (i.e. a small set of units different for each language, considered to be the basic distinctive units of speech by which morphemes, words, and sentences are represented) as the seed feature employed during the generation process. This approach will be useful in the context of assistive technologies for users with language impairments (e.g. dyslalia[2]) and the choice of the seed features is based on the end system. The generated sentences will contain the maximum number of words with the phoneme employed as the seed feature. These words are obtained from a part of the training corpus and stored into a bag of words that is used during the generation process. For example, for phoneme /d/, the bag of words could contain the words *delfín*-dolphin- or *dormir*-to sleep. The vocabulary contained in the bag of words is used to

guide the sentences to be generated as it will be explained in the next section.

3.2 Generation of Related Sentences

This module generates a set of related sentences whose words are in lemma form by choosing the words of a sentence using over-generation and ranking techniques (Barros and Lloret, 2016). Starting from a training corpus, an input seed feature and a bag of words with the vocabulary, a factored language model is learnt over it. Factored language models (FLM) are an extension of language models, proposed by Bilmes and Kirchhoff (2003), where a word is viewed as a vector of k factors such that $w_t \equiv \{f_t^1, f_t^2, \ldots, f_t^K\}$. These factors can be anything, including lemmas, stems, words or any other lexical, syntactic or semantic features. Our approach uses the lemmas and Part-of-Speech (POS) tags as factors, due to the variability that they can bring to the generated sentences. The words chosen for generation will be in a lemma form, therefore, they are able to be further inflected to improve the naturalness and expressivity of the generated language. Furthermore, for the purpose of this research, a simple grammar (based on the basic structure that divides a sentence into subject, verb and object), shown in Figure 2, is used to guarantee the appearance of some elements in the generated sentence.

$$S \rightarrow NP\ VP$$
$$NP \rightarrow D\ N$$
$$VP \rightarrow V\ NP$$

Figure 2: Basic clause structure grammar.

In order to generate a set of related sentences with related content, we first generate independently a sentence by employing over-generation techniques, where a set of candidate sentences is generated based on the probabilities given by the FLM and the seed feature selected. The generation process prioritises the selection of words from the bags of words in order to ensure that the generated sentences will contain the maximum number of words related with the input seed feature.

These candidate sentences are subsequently ranked in order to select one, based on the sentence probability. The probability of a sentence is computed by the chain rule where the probability can be

---

[2] A disorder in phoneme articulation which implies the inability to correctly pronounce certain phonemes or groups of phonemes.

calculated as the product of the probability of all the words:

$$P(w_1, w_2...w_n) = \prod_{i=1}^{n} P(w_i|w_1, w_2...w_{i-1}) \quad (1)$$

As suggested in Isard et al. (2006), the probability of a word is determined as the linear combination of FLMs, where a weight λ_i was assigned for each of them:

$$P(f_i|f_{i-2}^{i-1}) = \\ \lambda_1 P_1(f_i|f_{i-2}^{i-1})^{1/n} + \cdots + \lambda_n P_n(f_i|f_{i-2}^{i-1})^{1/n} \quad (2)$$

where f is the selected factors from the different FLMs and the total sum of the weights is 1.

After one sentence is generated, we perform pos-tagging, syntactic parsing and semantic parsing to identify different linguistic components of the sentence content (e.g. the subject, the object, name entities, etc.). To generate a sentence with related content, one of the identified linguistic components is chosen to influence the generation of the next sentence. This linguistic component is included in the sentence replacing the same type of linguistic component included in the next related sentence or it is used as a guide to select the content of the bag of words. For example, if the sentence generated by this module is *"mi padre tocar el suelo"*(my father to touch the ground), after performing the analysis of its content, this module would identify as linguistic components the subject (*"mi padre"*- my father) and the object (*"el suelo"* - the ground) of the sentence. The module would choose one of the two identified linguistic components, and would generate a sentence related to *"mi padre"*(my father) or a sentence related to *"el suelo"*(the ground).

Then, the remaining sentences are generated based on the probabilities estimated by the FLM, the input seed feature and the information extracted from the linguistic component.

3.3 Inflection Generation

After the set of related sentences are generated by the previous module, they are inflected by the last module integrated within the surface realisation approach (Barros et al., 2017). At this stage, we only address the inflection of Spanish verbs using supervised learning because of their complexity. The inflection of other simpler word types (e.g. determin-

ers, noun, adjectives, etc.) is done through a rule-based approach in order to ensure the gender and number concordance. In order to learn the inflection of Spanish verbs, we first created a dataset containing all the necessary information to inflect the verbs. The dataset was constructed by consulting the *Real Academia Española*[3] and the *Enciclopedia Libre Universal en Español*[4]. The dataset is composed of the following features: (1) *ending*, (2) *ending stem*, (3) *penSyl*, (4) *person*, (5) *number*, (6) *tense*, (7) *mood*, (8) *suff1*, (9) *suff2*, (10) *stemC1*, (11) *stemC2*, (12) *stemC3* (see also Table 1).

We considered that a word can be divided into three parts: (1) the *ending* (in Spanish the verbs are classified by their ending); (2) *ending stem* (i.e. the closest consonant to the ending); and (3) *penSyl* (i.e. the previous syllable of the ending formed by the whole syllable or its dominant vowel is extracted), as shown in Figure 3.

Suff1 and *suff2* are the inflection predicted for the suffix of the verb form; and *stemC1*, *stemC2* and *stemC3*, refer to the inflection predicted for the stem of the verb form.

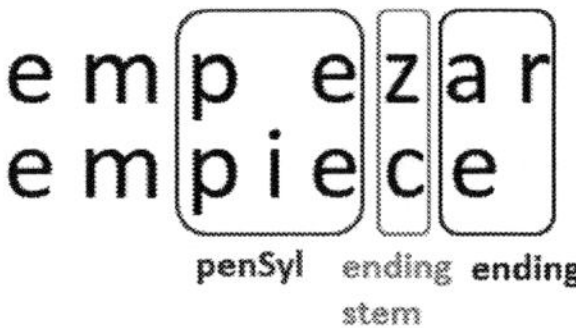

Figure 3: Division of the Spanish verb *to begin* and its inflection for the first singular person of the present tense and in the subjunctive mood.

We trained an ensemble of individual models for each of the features with a potential inflection value. We used the WEKA (Frank et al., 2016) implementation of the Random Forest algorithm to train the models for the *stemC3* and *stemC2* features, and the Random Tree algorithm to train the models for the *suff1*, *suff2* and *stemC1* features. We then predicted all the possible inflections given a verb in its base form, i.e., all the tenses for each mood in Spanish. For accomplishing this task, we first analysed the base form to extract the necessary features for the

---

[3]http://www.rae.es/diccionario-panhispanico-de-dudas/apendices/modelos-de-conjugacion-verbal

[4]http://enciclopedia.us.es/index.php/Categoría:Verbos

Feature	Description
(1) *ending*	ending of the verb that can be "-ar", "-er" and "-ir", used to classify the verbs in 1st, 2nd, and 3rd conjugation respectively.
(2) *ending stem*	the closest consonant or group of letters to the ending, being part of the same syllable of the ending
(3) *penSyl*	the previous syllable of the ending, consisting of the whole syllable or the dominant vowel
(4) *person*	grammatical distinction between references to participants in an event, which can be 1st (the speaker), 2nd (the addressee) and 3rd (others) person
(5) *number*	grammatical category that expresses count distinctions, which can be singular (one) or plural (more than one)
(6) *tense*	category that expresses time reference, in Spanish there are 17 different verb tenses
(7) *mood*	grammatical features of the verbs used for denoting modality (statement of facts, of desire, of commands, etc.), in Spanish there are three different moods
(8) *suff1*	one of the possible inflections for the ending
(9) *suff2*	one of the possible inflections for the ending
(10) *stemC1*	one of the possible inflections for the stem
(11) *stemC2*	one of the possible inflections for the stem
(12) *stemC3*	one of the possible inflections for the stem

Table 1: Detailed description of features. A specific verb tense in Spanish can have more than one valid inflection, being necessary to predict each variant of the tense.

inflection, and then we predicted its predicted inflection using the models. Finally, the predicted inflections were employed to replace the features previously identified in the base form, leading to the reconstruction of the base form into the desired inflection, as it can be seen in Figure 4.

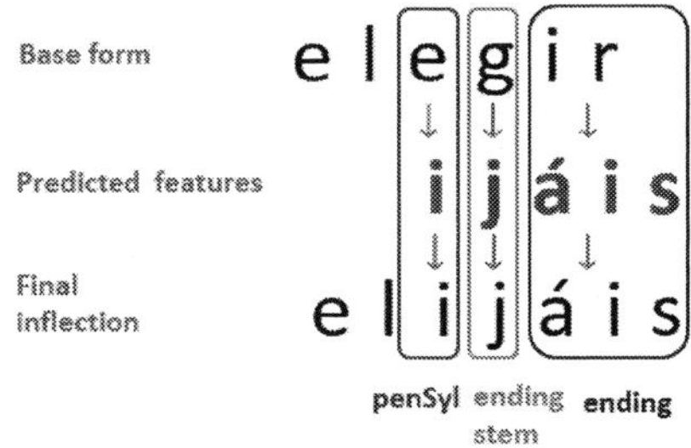

Figure 4: Reconstruction of the verb *elegir* (to choose) with the features predicted by the models.

4 Experiments

We performed two experiments: first, we tested the inflection module by comparing it against the state-of-the-art in order to ensure the accuracy for this task. Secondly, we generated and inflected the sentences using the whole surface realisation approach in order to test whether the quality of the generated sentences improved.

4.1 Experiments on Inflection Generation

For the first experiment, we compared our inflection module (RandFT) with two very competitive baselines by Durret13 (Durrett and DeNero, 2013) and Ahlberg14 (Ahlberg et al., 2014), by measuring the accuracy of their output for Spanish verb inflections under the same conditions. This experiment was done to validate the performing of the inflection module.

In order to compare our system with both baselines, we employed the test set of examples (200 different verbs) which was made available by Durrett and DeNero (2013), since this test-set included verbs with both irregular and regular forms. This test set does not include any of the entries used within our training dataset. For the experiments, we generated all the verb inflections for the 200 base forms.

Furthermore, the aforementioned baselines do not predict all the grammatical moods that exist in the Spanish language. Both baselines are only able to predict the indicative and subjunctive mood, but not the *imperative one*, which is complex especially for irregular forms. To tackle this, we used an additional test-set to evaluate this grammatical mood. We created the additional test-set by employing information from the Freeling's lexicon for the imperative forms of these 200 verbs (Padró and Stanilovsky, 2012).

4.2 Experiments on End-to-end NLG

For the second experiment, we integrated the inflection unit with the surface realisation approach described in Section 3 in order to test if the quality of the generated sentences improved. For this purpose, we generated a set of three related sentences for each Spanish phoneme (i.e. there are a total of 27 phonemes in Spanish). These sentences have related topics that will appear within the set so that the direct object of a sentence is used as the subject of the following sentence, obtaining a preliminary set of related sentences. We compared our realisation approach against a random baseline, where a random verb tense was assigned for each of the sentences forming the set. We set our proposed approach to a fixed tense, either present or indicative. These sentences were ranked according to the approach described in section 3.2 being the linear combination of FLM as follows: $P(w_i) = \lambda_1 P(f_i|f_{i-2}, f_{i-1}) + \lambda_2 P(f_i|p_{i-2}, p_{i-1}) + \lambda_3 P(p_i|f_{i-2}, f_{i-1})$, where f refers to a lemma, p refers to a POS tag, and λ_i are set $\lambda_1 = 0.25$, $\lambda_2 = 0.25$ and $\lambda_3 = 0.5$. These values were empirically determined by testing different values and comparing the results obtained.

For this experiment, we used a collection of Hans Christian Andersen tales, automatically gathered from *Ciudad Seva*[5], as a corpus. In order to train the FLM, used during the generation, we employed SRILM (Stolcke, 2002), a software that allows to build and apply statistical language models, which includes and implementation of FLM. In addition, we use Freeling language analyser (Padró and Stanilovsky, 2012) to tag the corpus with lexical information as well as to perform the analysis of the generated sentences.

5 Evaluation and Results

This section describes the results obtained with the experimentation carried out. First, the results obtained from the comparison of our inflection module in order to validate its performance are shown. Then, the results obtained from the integration of this module within the end-to-end NLG approach are described.

[5]http://ciudadseva.com/autor/hans-christian-andersen/cuentos/

5.1 Results for the Inflection Module

The results obtained are shown in Table 2, where we compared the inflection of the same verb tenses as Durret and Ahlberg using the test-set described in the previous section. Our inflection module, which includes an ensemble of classifiers (RandFT), trained with our generalised dataset for Spanish, obtained a higher overall accuracy (but not significantly) with respect to the state-of-the-art baselines systems.

Approach	Correctly predicted verb tables	Correctly predicted verb forms
RandFT	99%	99.98%
Durret13	97%	99.76%
Ahlberg14	96%	99.52%

Table 2: Accuracy of predicting inflection of verb tables and individual verb forms given only the base form, evaluated with an unseen test set of 200 verbs. For the imperative mood, our system achieves 100% accuracy, however the baselines do not predict the imperative form.

Base form–*Inflected form*
contar–*cuenta*; **errar**–*yerra*; **haber**–*he*; **hacer**–*haz*; **oler**–*huele*; **ir**–*ve*; **oír**–*oye*; **decir**–*di*

Table 3: Variability of inflection in the imperative mood for the 2nd person singular of the present.

In addition, our model can correctly perform the inflection of the imperative mood, which was not included in the baseline systems. This grammatical mood, which forms commands or requests, contains unique imperative forms among the irregular Spanish verbs, as shown in Table 3. For this experiment, our system achieves 100% accuracy when evaluated on the additional test-set.

5.2 Results for the Generated Text

We also performed a user evaluation with three evaluators in order to discern if the inclusion of the inflection module improved the naturalness and expressivity of the language.

Each evaluator was shown 27 sets of sentences with different kinds of inflections (i.e. without inflecting the sentences, with a fixed inflection and with a random inflection, as described in Section

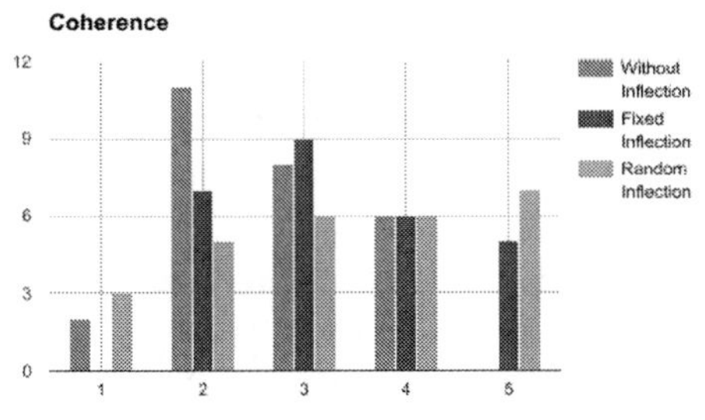

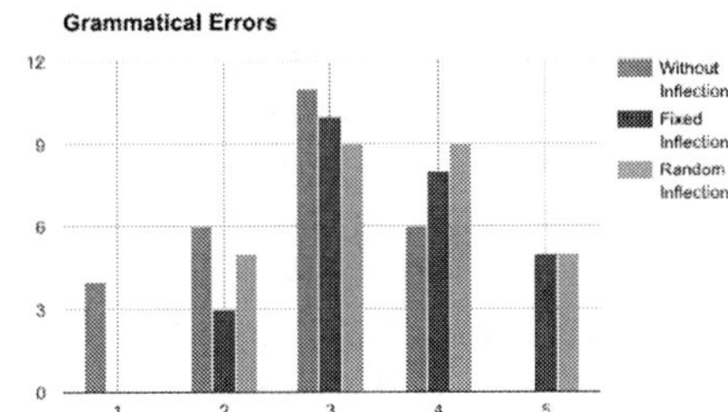

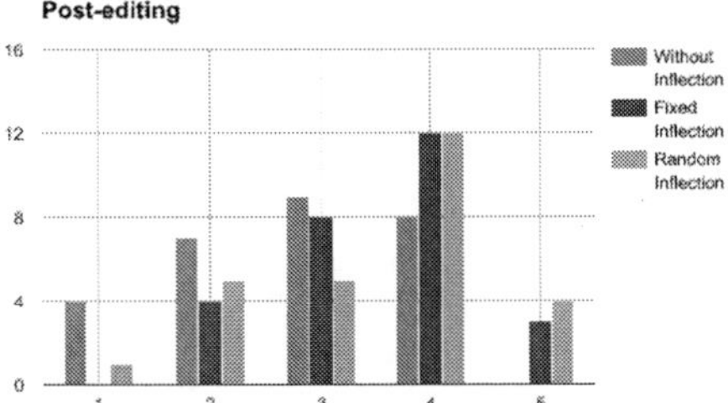

Figure 5: Number of sentences scored for each rating of the 5-pt Likert scale regarding the *coherence*, the *grammatical errors* and the *ease of correction*. The minimum values for the *coherence* indicate a lack of meaning of the sentences whereas the maximum values indicate a correct full meaning for a sentence. For the *grammatical errors* ratings, the minimum values represent a high number of errors in the sentences and the higher values indicate a lack of errors in the sentences. Finally, the minimum *ease of correction* values refers to a huge number of changes required to correct or improve the sentences while the maximum values indicates otherwise.

4.2) and had to overall rate each set using a 5-pt Likert scale, in terms of *coherence*, the *grammatical errors* an the *post-editing*. The *coherence*, which is very difficult to determine automatically being its analysis performed manually, refers to the meaning of the generated sentence, so that a sentence with no meaning would be rated with a 1 and a sentence with a full meaning would be rated with a 5. In contrast, the *grammatical errors* indicate the amount of errors in the sentence (i.e. fewer errors indicate a better sentence). The *post-editing* (ease of correction) refers to the amount of changes necessary to convert a sentence with many errors into one with no errors. In this sense, the lower values for the post-tagging indicates the need to make a lot of changes to the sentence whereas the higher values refers to not perform changes to the sentence. All the sentences contained in the sets were different since they were generated with each of the Spanish phonemes.

A summary of the results obtained can be seen in the Table 4. The results of inflecting a sentence in

Inflection Type	Coherence		Grammar errors		Post-editing	
	Mean	Mode	Mean	Mode	Mean	Mode
Without	2.65*	2	2.73*	3	2.75*	3
Fixed	**3.36***	3	**3.57***	3	**3.54***	4
Random	3.31*	5	3.51*	4	3.48*	4

Table 4: Results of the means and the modes of the 5-pt Likert scale with respect to the *coherence, grammatical errors* and *ease of correction*, of the inflected generated sentences. * denotes significance with $p < 0.01$.

contrast to not inflecting it are better, indicating that the quality of the generated sentences improved.

Figure 5 summarises the number of set of sentences (i.e. one set per phoneme) derived from the evaluation of the ratings mentioned before. As can be seen in the figure, the sentences without inflection are less coherent than the inflected sentences (both fixed and random inflection). In terms of grammaticality and ease of correction (post-tagging), the non-inflected sentences score lower than the inflected sentences. These ratings in concordance to the results given in Table 4 demonstrate the improvement of the quality obtained after applying inflection to the generated sentences. In contrast, the ratings obtained from the fixed inflection and random inflection are quite similar, standing out the ratings of this last one in *coherence*. This is due to the fact that the inflection of the verb is the only thing that can be random or fixed in the sentence; however a sentence can be meaningful with more than one verb tense. For instance, consider the following two sentences: "I am in the ground" and "I was on the ground". Both are meaningful, and grammatically correct.

Phoneme: /n/
Without Inflection
Cuánto cosa tener nuestro pensamiento.
(How much thing to have our thinking.)
Cuánto pensamiento tener nuestro corazón.
(How much thought to have our heart.)
Cuánto corazón tener nuestro pensamiento.
(How much heart to have our thinking.)

Fixed Inflection
Cuánta cosa tiene nuestro pensamiento.
(How much thing our thinking has.)
Cuánto pensamiento tiene nuestro corazón.
(How much thought our heart has.)
Cuánto corazón tiene nuestro pensamiento.
(How much heart our thinking has.)

Random Inflection
Cuánta cosa tiene nuestro pensamiento.
(How much thing our thinking has.)
Cuánto pensamiento tuviere nuestro corazón.
(How much thought our heart had.)
Cuánto corazón tenga nuestro pensamiento.
(How much heart our thinking had.)

Figure 6: Example of a generated set of sentences for the phoneme /n/ without inflection, with a fixed inflection (e.g. in present of indicative) and with random inflection (first sentence in present of indicative, second sentence in present of subjunctive and third sentence in past imperfect of subjunctive).

Some examples of the inflection of an automatically generated set of sentences by the described approach are shown in Figure 6.

5.3 Discussion

With the experimentation carried out, on the one hand, the inflection module obtained almost 100% of accuracy, being able to inflect almost all the verbs in Spanish. On the other hand, the introduction of an inflection module in a surface realisation approach improves the generated language. This inflection approach could be further used in phrase-based NLG systems (i.e. systems trained to generated text based on n-grams rather than linguistic rules), in order to enhance the naturalness, grammaticality and coherence of the generated text. However, at this stage, while the NLG without the inflection module is language independent, the inflection module is only able to learn the inflection for Spanish verbs.

6 Conclusion and Future Work

This paper presented a flexible and domain independent NLG approach for Spanish focused on the surface realisation stage. Within the NLG approach, a robust light-weight supervised inflection module to obtain the inflected form of any Spanish verb for any of its moods (indicative, subjunctive and imperative) was integrated. This inflection module obtained accuracy close to 100%, outperforming existing state-of-the-art approaches. In addition, the integration of this inflection module within a surface realisation approach improves the quality of the generated sentences, adding naturalness and expressivity to the generated language. In the future, we plan to learn the inflection for other types of words (not only verbs), seeking for a whole sentence inflection model. Moreover, we will test this inflection approach to other languages.

Acknowledgments

This research work has been partially funded by the Generalitat Valenciana through the projects "DIIM2.0: Desarrollo de técnicas Inteligentes e Interactivas de Minería y generación de información sobre la web 2.0" (PROMETEOII/2014/001); and partially funded by the Spanish Government through projects TIN2015-65100-R, TIN2015-65136-C2-2-R, as well as by the project "Análisis de Sentimientos Aplicado a la Prevención del Suicidio en las Redes Sociales (ASAP)" funded by Ayudas Fundación BBVA a equipos de investigación científica.

References

Roee Aharoni, Yoav Goldberg, and Yonatan Belinkov. 2016. Improving sequence to sequence learning for morphological inflection generation: The biu-mit systems for the sigmorphon 2016 shared task for morphological reinflection. In *Proceedings of the 14th Annual SIGMORPHON Workshop on Computational Research in Phonetics, Phonology, and Morphology*, pages 41–48. Association for Computational Linguistics.

Malin Ahlberg, Markus Forsberg, and Mans Hulden. 2014. Semi-supervised learning of morphological paradigms and lexicons. In *Proceedings of the 14th Conference of the European Chapter of the Association for Computational Linguistics*, pages 569–578.

Iñaki Alegria and Izaskun Etxeberria. 2016. Ehu at the sigmorphon 2016 shared task. a simple proposal: Grapheme-to-phoneme for inflection. In *Proceedings of the 14th Annual SIGMORPHON Workshop on Computational Research in Phonetics, Phonology, and Morphology*, pages 27–30. Association for Computational Linguistics.

Ion Androutsopoulos, Gerasimos Lampouras, and Dimitrios Galanis. 2013. Generating natural language descriptions from owl ontologies: the naturalowl system. *Journal of Artificial Intelligence Research*, 48:671–715.

Gabor Angeli, Percy Liang, and Dan Klein. 2010. A simple domain-independent probabilistic approach to generation. In *Conference on Empirical Methods in Natural Language Processing (EMNLP)*, pages 502–512, Cambridge, Massachusetts.

Miguel Ballesteros, Bernd Bohnet, Simon Mille, and Leo Wanner. 2015. Data-driven sentence generation with non-isomorphic trees. In *Proceedings of the 2015 Conference of the North American Chapter of the Association for Computational Linguistics: Human Language Technologies*, pages 387–397. Association for Computational Linguistics.

Cristina Barros and Elena Lloret. 2015. Input seed features for guiding the generation process: A statistical approach for Spanish. In *Proceedings of the 15th European Workshop on Natural Language Generation (ENLG)*, pages 9–17. Association for Computational Linguistics.

Cristina Barros and Elena Lloret. 2016. Generating sets of related sentences from input seed features. In *Proceedings of the 2nd International Workshop on Natural Language Generation and the Semantic Web (WebNLG 2016)*, pages 1–4. Association for Computational Linguistics (ACL).

Cristina Barros and Elena Lloret. 2017. A multilingual multi-domain data-to-text natural language generation approach. *Procesamiento del Lenguaje Natural*, 58(0):45–52.

Cristina Barros, Dimitra Gkatzia, and Elena Lloret. 2017. Inflection generation for spanish verbs using supervised learning. In *Proceedings of the 1st Workshop on Subword and Character LEvel Models in NLP (SCLeM)*. Association for Computational Linguistics.

Jeff A. Bilmes and Katrin Kirchhoff. 2003. Factored language models and generalized parallel backoff. In *Proceedings of the 2003 Conference of the North American Chapter of the Association for Computational Linguistics on Human Language Technology: Companion Volume of the Proceedings of HLT-NAACL 2003–short Papers - Volume 2*, pages 4–6.

Bernd Bohnet, Leo Wanner, Simon Mille, and Alicia Burga. 2010. Broad coverage multilingual deep sentence generation with a stochastic multi-level realizer. In *Proceedings of the 23rd International Conference on Computational Linguistics*, pages 98–106. Association for Computational Linguistics.

Ryan Cotterell, Christo Kirov, John Sylak-Glassman, David Yarowsky, Jason Eisner, and Mans Hulden. 2016. The sigmorphon 2016 shared task— morphological reinflection. In *Proceedings of the 2016 Meeting of SIGMORPHON*. Association for Computational Linguistics.

Markus Dreyer and Jason Eisner. 2009. Graphical models over multiple strings. In *Proceedings of the 2009 Conference on Empirical Methods in Natural Language Processing: Volume 1 - Volume 1*, pages 101–110. Association for Computational Linguistics.

Greg Durrett and John DeNero. 2013. Supervised learning of complete morphological paradigms. In *Proceedings of the North American Chapter of the Association for Computational Linguistics*, pages 1185–1195.

Ondřej Dušek and Filip Jurčíček. 2013. Robust multilingual statistical morphological generation models. In *51st Annual Meeting of the Association for Computational Linguistics: Proceedings of the Student Research Workshop*, pages 158–164. Association of Computational Linguistics.

Manaal Faruqui, Yulia Tsvetkov, Graham Neubig, and Chris Dyer. 2016. Morphological inflection generation using character sequence to sequence learning. In *NAACL HLT 2016, The 2016 Conference of the North American Chapter of the Association for Computational Linguistics: Human Language Technologies*, pages 634–643.

Eibe Frank, Mark A. Hall, and Ian H. Witten. 2016. *The WEKA Workbench. Online Appendix for "Data Mining: Practical Machine Learning Tools and Techniques"*. Morgan Kaufmann, 4 edition.

Albert Gatt and Ehud Reiter. 2009. Simplenlg: A realisation engine for practical applications. In *Proceedings of the 12th European Workshop on Natural Language Generation (ENLG)*.

Amy Isard, Carsten Brockmann, and Jon Oberlander. 2006. Individuality and alignment in generated dialogues. In *Proceedings of the Fourth International Natural Language Generation Conference*, pages 25–32. Association for Computational Linguistics.

Katharina Kann and Hinrich Schütze. 2016. Med: The lmu system for the sigmorphon 2016 shared task on morphological reinflection. In *Proceedings of the 14th SIGMORPHON Workshop on Computational Research in Phonetics, Phonology, and Morphology*, pages 62–70. Association for Computational Linguistics.

Atif Khan, Naomie Salim, and Yogan Jaya Kumar. 2015. A framework for multi-document abstractive summarization based on semantic role labelling. *Applied Soft Computing*, 30:737 – 747.

Ioannis Konstas and Mirella Lapata. 2012. Concept-to-text generation via discriminative reranking. In *Proceedings of the 50th Annual Meeting of the Association for Computational Linguistics*, pages 369–378.

Ling Liu and Lingshuang Jack Mao. 2016. Morphological reinflection with conditional random fields and unsupervised features. In *Proceedings of the 14th Annual SIGMORPHON Workshop on Computational Research in Phonetics, Phonology, and Morphology*, pages 36–40. Association for Computational Linguistics.

Garrett Nicolai, Colin Cherry, and Grzegorz Kondrak. 2015. Inflection generation as discriminative string transduction. In *NAACL HLT 2015, The 2015 Conference of the North American Chapter of the Association for Computational Linguistics: Human Language Technologies*, pages 922–931.

Garrett Nicolai, Bradley Hauer, Adam St. Arnaud, and Grzegorz Kondrak. 2016. Morphological reinflection via discriminative string transduction. In *Proceedings of the 14th Annual SIGMORPHON Workshop on Computational Research in Phonetics, Phonology, and Morphology*, pages 31–35. Association for Computational Linguistics.

Robert Östling. 2016. Morphological reinflection with convolutional neural networks. In *Proceedings of the 14th SIGMORPHON Workshop on Computational Research in Phonetics, Phonology, and Morphology*, pages 23–26. Association for Computational Linguistics.

Lluís Padró and Evgeny Stanilovsky. 2012. Freeling 3.0: Towards wider multilinguality. In *Proceedings of the Eight International Conference on Language Resources and Evaluation*.

Ehud Reiter and Robert Dale. 2000. *Building Natural Language Generation Systems*. Cambridge University Press.

Alexey Sorokin. 2016. Using longest common subsequence and character models to predict word forms. In *Proceedings of the 14th SIGMORPHON Workshop on Computational Research in Phonetics, Phonology, and Morphology*, pages 54–61. Association for Computational Linguistics.

Andreas Stolcke. 2002. Srilm - an extensible language modeling toolkit. In *Proceedings International Conference on Spoken Language Processing, vol 2.*, pages 901–904.

Octavio Santana Suárez, José Rafael Pérez Aguiar, Luis Javier Losada García, and Francisco Javier Carreras Riudavets. 2005. Spanish morphosyntactic disambiguator. In *Proceedings of the Association for Computers and the Humanities and the Association for Literary and Linguistic Computing*, pages 201–204.

Dima Taji, Ramy Eskander, Nizar Habash, and Owen Rambow. 2016. The columbia university - new york university abu dhabi sigmorphon 2016 morphological reinflection shared task submission. In *Proceedings of the 14th SIGMORPHON Workshop on Computational Research in Phonetics, Phonology, and Morphology*, pages 71–75. Association for Computational Linguistics.

What is the Role of Recurrent Neural Networks (RNNs) in an Image Caption Generator?

Marc Tanti   Albert Gatt
Institute of Linguistics
and Language Technology
University of Malta
marc.tanti.06@um.edu.mt
albert.gatt@um.edu.mt

Kenneth P. Camilleri
Deptartment of Systems
and Control Engineering
University of Malta
kenneth.camilleri@um.edu.mt

Abstract

In neural image captioning systems, a recurrent neural network (RNN) is typically viewed as the primary 'generation' component. This view suggests that the image features should be 'injected' into the RNN. This is in fact the dominant view in the literature. Alternatively, the RNN can instead be viewed as only encoding the previously generated words. This view suggests that the RNN should only be used to encode linguistic features and that only the final representation should be 'merged' with the image features at a later stage. This paper compares these two architectures. We find that, in general, late merging outperforms injection, suggesting that RNNs are better viewed as encoders, rather than generators.

1   Introduction

Image captioning (Bernardi et al., 2016) has emerged as an important testbed for solutions to the fundamental AI challenge of grounding symbolic or linguistic information in perceptual data (Harnad, 1990; Roy and Reiter, 2005). Most captioning systems focus on what Hodosh et al. (2013) refer to as *concrete conceptual* descriptions, that is, captions that describe what is strictly within the image, although recently, there has been growing interest in moving beyond this, with research on visual question-answering (Antol et al., 2015) and image-grounded narrative generation (Huang et al., 2016) among others.

Approaches to image captioning can be divided into three main classes (Bernardi et al., 2016):

1. Systems that rely on computer vision techniques to extract object detections and features from the source image, using these as input to an NLG stage (Kulkarni et al., 2011; Mitchell et al., 2012; Elliott and Keller, 2013). The latter is roughly akin to the microplanning and realisation modules in the well-known NLG pipeline architecture (Reiter and Dale, 2000).

2. Systems that frame the task as a retrieval problem, where a caption, or parts thereof, is identified by computing the proximity/relevance of strings in the training data to a given image. This is done by exploiting either a unimodal (Ordonez et al., 2011; Gupta et al., 2012; Mason and Charniak,) or multimodal (Hodosh et al., 2013; Socher et al., 2014) space. Many retrieval-based approaches rely on neural models to handle both image features and linguistic information (Ordonez et al., 2011; Socher et al., 2014).

3. Systems that also rely on neural models, but rather than performing partial or wholesale caption retrieval, generate novel captions using a recurrent neural network (RNN), usually a long short-term memory (LSTM). Typically, such models use image features extracted from a pre-trained convolutional neural network (CNN) such as the VGG CNN (Simonyan and Zisserman, 2014) to bias the RNN towards sampling terms from the vocabulary in such a way that a sequence of such terms produces a caption that is relevant to the image (Kiros et al., 2014b; Kiros et al., 2014a; Vinyals et

Proceedings of The 10th International Natural Language Generation conference, pages 51–60,
Santiago de Compostela, Spain, September 4-7 2017. ©2017 Association for Computational Linguistics

al., 2015; Mao et al., 2015a; Hendricks et al., 2016).

This paper focuses on the third class. The key property of these models is that the CNN image features are used to condition the predictions of the best caption to describe the image. However, this can be done in different ways and the role of the RNN depends in large measure on the mode in which CNN and RNN are combined.

It is quite typical for RNNs to be viewed as 'generators'. For example, Bernardi et al. (2016) suggest that 'the RNN is trained to generate the next word [of a caption]', a view also expressed by LeCun et al. (2015). A similar position has also been taken in work focusing on the use of RNNs as language models for generation (Sutskever et al., ; Graves, 2013). However, an alternative view is possible, whereby the role of the RNN can be thought of as primarily to encode sequences, but not directly to generate them.

(a) Conditioning by injecting the image means injecting the image into the same RNN that processes the words.

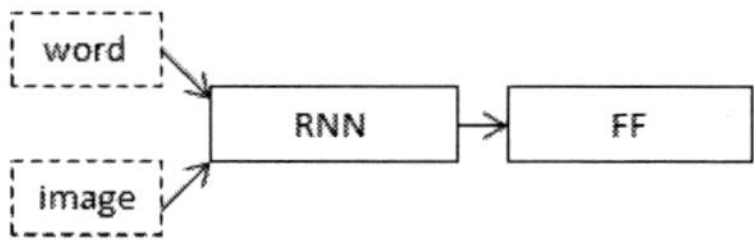

(b) Conditioning by merging the image means merging the image with the final state of the RNN in a "multimodal layer" after processing the words.

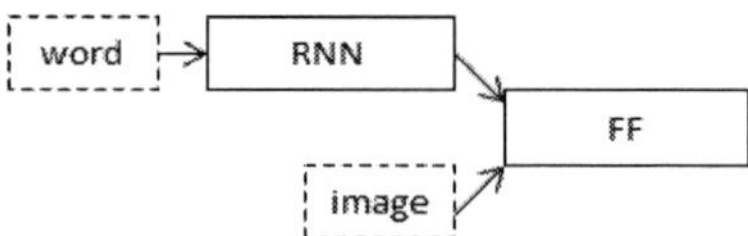

Figure 1: The inject and merge architectures for caption generation. The RNN's previous state going into the RNN is not shown. Legend: RNN - Recurrent Neural Network; FF - Feed Forward layer.

These two views can be associated with different architectures for neural caption generators, which we discuss below and illustrated in Figure 1. In one class of architectures, image features are directly incorporated into the RNN during the sequence encoding process (Figure 1a). In these models, it is natural to think of the RNN as the primary generation component of the image captioning system, making pre-

dictions conditioned by the image. A different architecture keeps the encoding of linguistic and perceptual features separate, merging them in a later multimodal layer, at which point predictions are made (Figure 1b). In this type of model, the RNN is functioning primarily as an encoder of sequences of word embeddings, with the visual features merged with the linguistic features in a later, multimodal layer. This multimodal layer is the one that drives the generation process since the RNN never sees the image and hence would not be able to direct the generation process.

While both architectural alternatives have been attested in the literature, their implications have not, to our knowledge, been systematically discussed and comparatively evaluated. In what follows, we first discuss the distinction between the two architectures (Section 2) and then present some experiments comparing the two (Sections 3 and 4). Our conclusion is that grounding language generation in image data is best conducted in an architecture that first encodes the two modalities separately, before merging them to predict captions.

2 Background: Neural Caption Generation Architectures

In a neural language model, an RNN encodes a prefix (for example, the caption generated so far) and either itself predicts the next item in the sequence with the help of a feed forward layer or else it passes the encoding to the next layer which will make the prediction itself. This new item is added to the prefix at the next iteration to predict another item, until an end-of-sequence symbol is reached. Typically, the prediction is carried out using a softmax function to sample the next item according to a probability distribution over the vocabulary items, based on their activation. This process is illustrated in Figure 2.

One way to condition the RNN to predict image captions is to inject both visual and linguistic features directly into the RNN, depicted in Figure 1a. We refer to this as 'conditioning-by-inject' (or *inject* for short). Different types of inject architectures have become the most widely attested among deep learning approaches to image captioning (Chen and Zitnick, 2015; Donahue et al., 2015; Hessel et al., 2015; Karpathy and Fei-Fei, 2015; Liu et al., 2016;

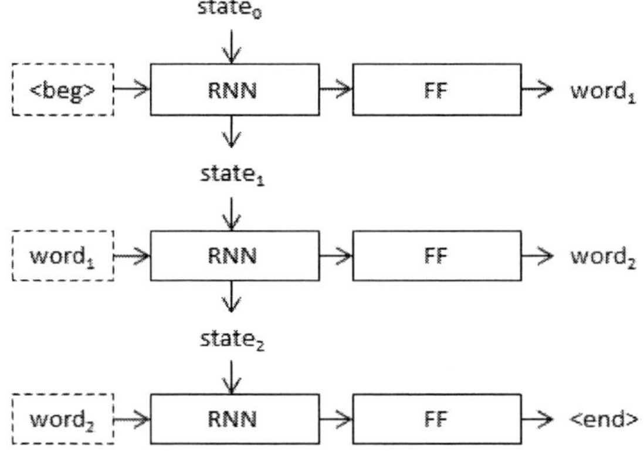

Figure 2: How RNNs work: each state of the RNN encodes a prefix, which incorporates the output word derived from the previous state. In practice the neural network does not output a single word but a probability distribution over all known words in the vocabulary. Legend: FF - feedforward layer; <beg> - the start-of-sentence token; <end> - the end-of-sentence token.

Yang et al., 2016; Zhou et al., 2016).[1] Given training pairs consisting of an image and a caption, the RNN component of such models is trained by exposure to prefixes of increasing length extracted from the caption, in tandem with the image.

An alternative architecture – which we refer to as 'conditioning-by-merge' (Figure 1b) – treats the RNN exclusively as a 'language model' to encode linguistic sequences of varying length. The linguistic vector resulting from this encoding is subsequently combined with the image features in a separate multimodal layer. This amounts to viewing the RNN as primarily an encoder of linguistic information. This type of architecture is also attested in the literature, albeit to a lesser extent than the inject architecture (Mao et al., 2014; Mao et al., 2015a; Mao et al., 2015b; Song and Yoo, 2016; Hendricks et al., 2016; You et al., 2016). A limited number of approaches have also been proposed in which both architectures are combined (Lu et al., 2016; Xu et al., 2015).

Notice that both architectures are compatible with the inclusion of attentional mechanisms (Xu et al., 2015). The effect of attention in the inject architec-

ture is to combine a different representation of the image with each word. In the case of merge, a different representation of the image can be combined with the final RNN state before each prediction. Attentional mechanisms are however beyond the scope of the present work.

The main differences between inject and merge architectures can be summed up as follows: In an inject model, the RNN is trained to predict sequences based on histories consisting of both linguistic and perceptual features. Hence, in this model, the RNN is primarily responsible for image-conditioned language generation. By contrast, in the merge architecture, RNNs in effect encode linguistic *representations*, which themselves constitute the input to a later prediction stage that comes after a multimodal layer. It is only at this late stage that image features are used to condition predictions.

As a result, a model involving conditioning by inject is trained to learn linguistic representations directly conditioned by image data; a merge architecture maintains a distinction between the two representations, but brings them together in a later layer.

Put somewhat differently, it could be argued that at a given time step, the merge architecture predicts what to generate next by combining the RNN-encoded prefix of the string generated so far (the 'past' of the generation process) with non-linguistic information (the guide of the generation process). The inject architecture on the other hand uses the full image features with every word of the prefix during training, in effect learning a 'visuo-linguistic' representation of each word. One effect of this is that image features can serve to further specify or disambiguate the 'meaning' of words, by disambiguating tokens of the same word which are correlated with different image features (such as 'crane' as in the bird versus the construction equipment). This implies that inject models learn a larger vocabulary during training.

The two architectures also differ in the number of parameters they need to handle. As noted above, since an inject architecture combines the image with each word during training, it is effectively handling a larger vocabulary than merge. Assume that the image vectors are concatenated with the word embedding vectors (inject) or the final RNN state (merge). Then, in the inject architecture, the number

---

[1]See Tanti et al. (2017) for an overview of different versions of the inject architecture and a systematic comparison among models. In this paper we focus on parallel-inject.

of weights in the RNN is a function of both the caption embedding and the images, whereas in merge, it is only the word embeddings that contribute to the size of this layer of the network. Let e be the size of the word embedding, v the size of the vocabulary, i the image vector size and s the state size of the RNN. In the inject case, the number of weights in the RNN is $w \propto (e+i) \times s$, whereas it is $w \propto e \times s$ in merge. The smaller number of weights handled by the RNN in merge is offset by a larger number of weights at the final softmax layer, which has to take as input the RNN state and the image, having size $\propto (s+i) \times v$.

A systematic comparison of these two architectures would shed light on the best way to conceive of the role of RNNs in neural language generation. Apart from the theoretical implications concerning the stage at which language should be grounded in visual information, such a comparison also has practical implications. In particular, if it turns out that merge outperforms inject, this would imply that the linguistic representations encoded in an RNN could be pre-trained and re-used for a variety of tasks and/or image captioning datasets, with domain-specific training only required for the final feedforward layer, where the tuning required to make perceptually grounded predictions is carried out. We return to this point in Section 6.1.

In the following sections, we describe some experiments to conduct such a comparison.

3   Experiments

To evaluate the performance of the inject and merge architectures, and thus the roles of the RNN, we trained and evaluated them on the Flickr8k (Hodosh et al., 2013) and Flickr30k (Young et al., 2014) datasets of image-caption pairs. For the purposes of these experiments, we used the version of the datasets distributed by Karpathy and Fei-Fei (2015)[2]. The dataset splits are identical to that used by Karpathy and Fei-Fei (2015): Flickr8k is split into 6,000 images for training, 1,000 for validation, and 1,000 for testing whilst Flickr30k is split into 29,000 images for training, 1,014 images for validation, and 1,000 images for testing. Each image

[2]http://cs.stanford.edu/people/karpathy/ deepimagesent/

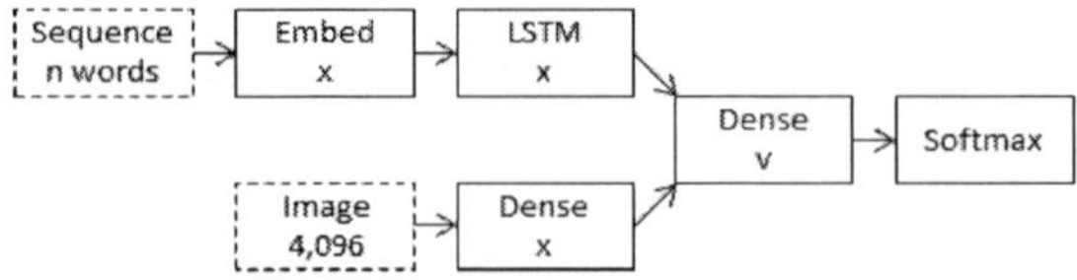

(a) The merge architecture.

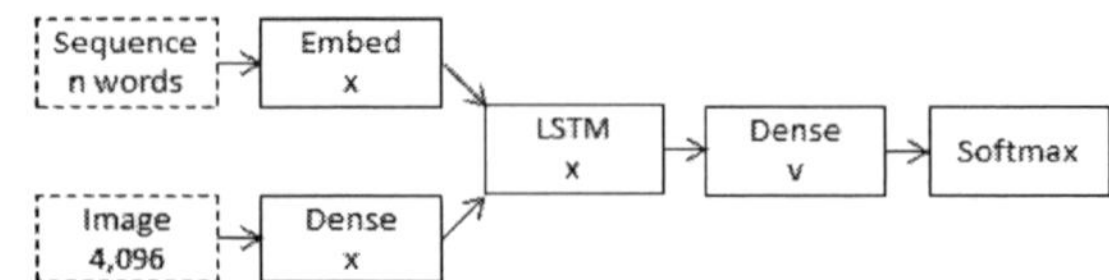

(b) The inject architecture.

Figure 3:   An illustration of the different architectures that are tested in this paper. The numbers or letters at the bottom of each box refer to the vector size output of a layer. 'x' is an arbitrary layer size that is varied in the experiments and 'v' is the vocabulary size which is also varied in the experiments. 'Dense' means fully connected layer with bias.

in both datasets has five different captions. 4,096-element image feature vectors that were extracted from the pre-trained VGG CNN (Simonyan and Zisserman, 2014) are also available in the distributed datasets. We normalised the image vectors to unit length during preprocessing.

Tokens with frequency lower than a threshold in the training set were replaced with the 'unknown' token. In our experiments we varied the threshold between 3 and 5 in order to measure the performance of each model as vocabulary size changes. For thresholds of 3, 4, and 5, this gives vocabulary sizes of 2,539, 2,918, and 3,478 for Flickr8k and 7,415, 8,275, 9,584 and for Flickr30k.

Since our purpose is to compare the performance of architectures, we used the 'barest' models possible, with the fewest number of hyperparameters. This means that complexities that are usually introduced in order to reach state-of-the-art performance, such as regularization, were avoided, since it is difficult to determine which combination of hyperparameters do not give an unfair advantage to one architecture over the other.

We constructed a basic neural language model consisting of a word embedding matrix, a basic LSTM (Hochreiter and Schmidhuber, 1997), and a softmax layer. The LSTM is defined as follows:

$$i_n = sig(x_n W_{xi} + s_{n-1} W_{si} + b_i) \qquad (1)$$
$$f_n = sig(x_n W_{xf} + s_{n-1} W_{sf} + b_f) \qquad (2)$$
$$o_n = sig(x_n W_{xo} + s_{n-1} W_{so} + b_o) \qquad (3)$$
$$g_n = \tanh(x_n W_{xc} + s_{n-1} W_{sc} + b_c) \qquad (4)$$
$$c_n = f_n \odot c_{n-1} + i_n \odot g_n \qquad (5)$$
$$s_n = o_n \odot \tanh(c_n) \qquad (6)$$

where x_n is the nth input, s_n is the hidden state after n inputs, s_0 is the all-zeros vector, c_n is the cell state after n inputs, c_0 is the all-zeros vector, i_n is the input gate after n inputs, f_n is the forget gate after n inputs, o_n is the output gate after n inputs, i_n is the input gate after n inputs, g_n is the modified input used to calculate c_n after n inputs, $W_{\alpha\beta}$ is the weight matrix between α and β, b_α is the bias vector for α, $\odot$ is the elementwise vector multiplication operator, and 'sig' refers to the sigmoid function. The hidden state and the cell state always have the same size.

In the experiments, this basic neural language model is used as a part of two different architectures: In the inject architecture, the image vector is concatenated with each of the word vectors in a caption. In the merge architecture, it is only concatenated with the final LSTM state. The layer sizes of the embedding, LSTM state, and projected image vector were also varied in the experiments in order to measure the effect of increasing the capacity of the networks. The layer sizes used are 128, 256, and 512. The details of the architectures used in the experiments are illustrated in Figure 3.

Training was performed using the Adam optimisation algorithm (Kingma and Ba, 2014) with default hyperparameters and a minibatch size of 50 captions. The cost function used was sum crossentropy. Training was carried out with an early stopping criterion which terminated training as soon as performance on the validation data started to deteriorate (validation performance is measured after each training epoch). Initialization of weights was done using Xavier initialization (Glorot and Bengio, 2010) and biases were set to zero.

Each architecture was trained three separate times; the results reported below are averages over these three separate runs.

To evaluate the trained models we generated captions for images in the test set using beam search with a beam width of 3 and a clipped maximum length of 20 words. The MSCOCO evaluation code[3] was used to measure the quality of the captions by using the standard evaluation metrics BLEU-(1,2,3,4) (Papineni et al., 2002), METEOR (Banerjee and Lavie, 2005), CIDEr (Vedantam et al., 2015), and ROUGE-L (Lin and Och, 2004). We also calculated the percentage of word types that were actually used in the generated captions out of the vocabulary of available word types. This measure indicates how well each architecture exploits the vocabulary it is trained on.

The code used for the experiments was implemented with TensorFlow and is available online[4].

4   Results

Table 1 reports means and standard deviations over the three runs of all the MSCOCO measures and the vocabulary usage. Since the point is to compare the effects of the architectures rather than to reach state-of-the-art performance, we do not include results from other published systems in our tables.

Across all experimental variables (dataset, vocabulary, and layer sizes), the performance of the merge architecture is generally superior to that of the inject architecture in all measures except for ROUGE-L and BLEU (ROUGE-L is designed for evaluating text summarization whilst BLEU is criticized for its lack of correlation with human-given scores). In what follows, we focus on the CIDEr measure for caption quality as it was specifically designed for captioning systems.

Although merge outperforms inject by a rather narrow margin, the low standard deviation over the three training runs suggests that this is a consistent performance advantage across train-and-test runs. In any case, there is clearly no disadvantage to the merge strategy with respect to injecting image features.

One peculiarity is that results on Flickr8k are better than those on Flickr30k. This could mean that Flickr8k captions contain less variation, hence are easier to perform well on. Preliminary results on the larger dataset MSCOCO (Lin et al., 2014) (currently in progress) show CIDEr results over 0.7

---

[3] https://github.com/tylin/coco-caption
[4] https://github.com/mtanti/rnn-role

Layer	Vocab.	% Vocabulary		CIDEr		METEOR		ROUGE-L	
		Merge	Inject	Merge	Inject	Merge	Inject	Merge	Inject
128	2539	**14.730 (0.40)**	10.555 (0.34)	**0.460 (0.01)**	0.431 (0.01)	**0.192 (0.00)**	0.183 (0.00)	**0.445 (0.00)**	0.430 (0.00)
128	2918	**13.719 (0.49)**	8.876 (0.24)	**0.456 (0.00)**	0.431 (0.00)	**0.191 (0.00)**	0.185 (0.00)	**0.437 (0.00)**	0.434 (0.00)
128	3478	**11.223 (0.35)**	8.175 (0.31)	**0.458 (0.01)**	0.433 (0.01)	**0.192 (0.00)**	0.187 (0.00)	**0.442 (0.00)**	0.432 (0.00)
256	2539	**15.439 (0.84)**	11.448 (0.71)	**0.462 (0.01)**	0.456 (0.01)	**0.192 (0.00)**	0.189 (0.00)	**0.439 (0.00)**	0.436 (0.00)
256	2918	**13.697 (0.19)**	10.430 (0.34)	**0.456 (0.01)**	0.451 (0.01)	**0.190 (0.00)**	0.189 (0.00)	0.438 (0.00)	**0.440 (0.00)**
256	3478	**11.252 (0.51)**	8.405 (0.39)	**0.470 (0.01)**	0.449 (0.02)	**0.191 (0.00)**	0.189 (0.00)	**0.439 (0.00)**	0.437 (0.00)
512	2539	**15.741 (0.40)**	12.761 (0.81)	0.452 (0.01)	**0.464 (0.00)**	0.191 (0.00)	**0.192 (0.00)**	0.437 (0.00)	**0.442 (0.00)**
512	2918	**13.114 (0.75)**	10.155 (0.42)	**0.469 (0.01)**	0.457 (0.00)	**0.193 (0.00)**	0.189 (0.00)	**0.440 (0.00)**	0.437 (0.00)
512	3478	**11.501 (0.49)**	8.587 (0.50)	**0.458 (0.01)**	0.439 (0.01)	**0.192 (0.00)**	0.188 (0.00)	**0.439 (0.00)**	0.434 (0.00)

(a) Flickr8k: % of vocabulary used, CIDEr, METEOR and ROUGE-L results.

Layer	Vocab.	BLEU-1		BLEU-2		BLEU-3		BLEU-4	
		Merge	Inject	Merge	Inject	Merge	Inject	Merge	Inject
128	2539	**0.600 (0.00)**	0.592 (0.01)	**0.410 (0.00)**	0.405 (0.01)	**0.272 (0.00)**	0.270 (0.01)	**0.179 (0.00)**	0.177 (0.00)
128	2918	**0.595 (0.01)**	0.590 (0.00)	0.405 (0.01)	**0.406 (0.00)**	0.267 (0.01)	**0.271 (0.00)**	0.175 (0.00)	**0.178 (0.00)**
128	3478	**0.608 (0.01)**	0.586 (0.01)	**0.416 (0.01)**	0.401 (0.01)	**0.276 (0.01)**	0.268 (0.01)	**0.182 (0.01)**	0.178 (0.01)
256	2539	**0.594 (0.00)**	0.591 (0.00)	0.407 (0.01)	**0.408 (0.00)**	0.269 (0.01)	**0.276 (0.00)**	0.176 (0.01)	**0.184 (0.00)**
256	2918	**0.596 (0.01)**	0.596 (0.01)	0.405 (0.01)	**0.413 (0.01)**	0.265 (0.00)	**0.278 (0.01)**	0.172 (0.00)	**0.184 (0.00)**
256	3478	**0.601 (0.00)**	0.596 (0.01)	**0.411 (0.00)**	0.409 (0.01)	0.272 (0.01)	**0.274 (0.01)**	0.179 (0.01)	**0.181 (0.01)**
512	2539	0.597 (0.01)	**0.603 (0.00)**	0.406 (0.01)	**0.419 (0.00)**	0.267 (0.01)	**0.283 (0.00)**	0.176 (0.01)	**0.188 (0.00)**
512	2918	**0.593 (0.01)**	0.589 (0.01)	0.404 (0.01)	**0.409 (0.00)**	0.268 (0.00)	**0.277 (0.00)**	0.177 (0.00)	**0.185 (0.00)**
512	3478	**0.597 (0.01)**	0.587 (0.00)	**0.407 (0.01)**	0.405 (0.00)	0.270 (0.01)	**0.272 (0.00)**	0.178 (0.00)	**0.180 (0.01)**

(b) Flickr8k: BLEU-n scores.

Layer	Vocab.	% Vocabulary		CIDEr		METEOR		ROUGE-L	
		Merge	Inject	Merge	Inject	Merge	Inject	Merge	Inject
128	7415	**6.253 (0.06)**	5.255 (0.02)	**0.362 (0.01)**	0.339 (0.01)	**0.174 (0.00)**	0.169 (0.00)	**0.417 (0.00)**	0.415 (0.00)
128	8275	**5.402 (0.20)**	4.939 (0.08)	**0.376 (0.00)**	0.351 (0.00)	**0.174 (0.00)**	0.171 (0.00)	**0.420 (0.00)**	0.417 (0.00)
128	9584	**4.793 (0.01)**	4.090 (0.18)	**0.378 (0.00)**	0.355 (0.00)	**0.175 (0.00)**	0.171 (0.00)	**0.420 (0.00)**	0.419 (0.00)
256	7415	**6.150 (0.18)**	5.597 (0.11)	**0.363 (0.00)**	0.361 (0.01)	**0.174 (0.00)**	0.173 (0.00)	0.414 (0.00)	**0.420 (0.00)**
256	8275	**5.559 (0.08)**	5.410 (0.10)	**0.364 (0.01)**	0.359 (0.00)	**0.174 (0.00)**	0.173 (0.00)	0.416 (0.00)	**0.417 (0.00)**
256	9584	**4.873 (0.07)**	4.309 (0.18)	**0.364 (0.01)**	0.359 (0.01)	**0.175 (0.00)**	0.173 (0.00)	0.416 (0.00)	**0.420 (0.00)**
512	7415	**6.330 (0.56)**	5.732 (0.32)	0.365 (0.01)	**0.367 (0.01)**	0.173 (0.00)	0.173 (0.00)	0.416 (0.00)	**0.422 (0.01)**
512	8275	**5.619 (0.09)**	5.221 (0.49)	**0.370 (0.00)**	0.369 (0.01)	**0.174 (0.00)**	0.174 (0.00)	0.419 (0.00)	**0.422 (0.00)**
512	9584	**4.887 (0.16)**	4.309 (0.25)	0.357 (0.01)	**0.360 (0.01)**	0.172 (0.00)	**0.172 (0.00)**	0.414 (0.00)	**0.417 (0.00)**

(c) Flickr30k: % of vocabulary used, CIDEr, METEOR and ROUGE-L results.

Layer	Vocab.	BLEU-1		BLEU-2		BLEU-3		BLEU-4	
		Merge	Inject	Merge	Inject	Merge	Inject	Merge	Inject
128	7415	**0.601 (0.01)**	0.595 (0.01)	**0.403 (0.01)**	0.400 (0.01)	**0.268 (0.01)**	0.265 (0.01)	**0.179 (0.01)**	0.175 (0.01)
128	8275	**0.605 (0.01)**	0.604 (0.00)	**0.411 (0.01)**	0.409 (0.00)	**0.276 (0.01)**	0.275 (0.00)	**0.185 (0.00)**	0.183 (0.00)
128	9584	**0.610 (0.01)**	0.605 (0.00)	**0.414 (0.01)**	0.411 (0.00)	**0.278 (0.00)**	0.275 (0.01)	**0.186 (0.00)**	0.184 (0.01)
256	7415	0.593 (0.01)	**0.606 (0.00)**	0.400 (0.01)	**0.412 (0.00)**	0.268 (0.01)	**0.277 (0.00)**	0.179 (0.01)	**0.186 (0.01)**
256	8275	0.594 (0.01)	**0.603 (0.01)**	0.402 (0.01)	**0.409 (0.00)**	0.269 (0.01)	**0.275 (0.00)**	0.180 (0.00)	**0.183 (0.00)**
256	9584	0.596 (0.01)	**0.614 (0.01)**	0.404 (0.00)	**0.419 (0.01)**	0.270 (0.00)	**0.283 (0.00)**	0.181 (0.00)	**0.189 (0.00)**
512	7415	0.598 (0.02)	**0.617 (0.01)**	0.404 (0.02)	**0.422 (0.01)**	0.270 (0.01)	**0.285 (0.00)**	0.181 (0.01)	**0.191 (0.00)**
512	8275	0.603 (0.00)	**0.609 (0.01)**	0.406 (0.00)	**0.419 (0.01)**	0.271 (0.00)	**0.284 (0.01)**	0.181 (0.00)	**0.191 (0.00)**
512	9584	0.596 (0.00)	**0.609 (0.01)**	0.399 (0.00)	**0.414 (0.01)**	0.265 (0.00)	**0.278 (0.01)**	0.177 (0.00)	**0.185 (0.00)**

(d) Flickr30k: BLEU-n scores.

Table 1: Results on the captions generated using the inject and merge architectures. Values are means over three separately retrained models, together with the standard deviation in parentheses. Legend: Layer - the layer size used ('x' in Figure 3); Vocab. - the vocabulary size used.

which means that either Flickr8k is too easy or Flickr30k is too hard when compared to the much larger MSCOCO.

The best-performing models are merge with state size of 256 on Flickr8k, and merge with state size 128 on Flickr30k, both with minimum token frequency threshold of 3. Inject models tend to improve with increasing state size, on both datasets, while the relationship between the performance of merge and the state size shows no discernible trend. Inject therefore does not seem to overfit as state size increases, even on the larger dataset. At the same time, inject only seems to be able to outperform the best scores achieved by merge if it has a much larger layer size. Therefore, in practical terms, inject models have to have larger capacity to be at par with merge. Put differently, merge has a higher performance to model size ratio and makes more efficient use of limited resources (this observation holds even when model size is defined in terms of number of parameters instead of layer sizes).

Given the same layer sizes and vocabulary, the number of parameters for merge is greater than for inject. The difference becomes greater as the vocabulary size is increased. For a vocabulary size of 2,539 and layer size of 512, merge has about 3% more parameters than inject whilst for a vocabulary size of 9,584 and layer size of 512, merge has about 20% more parameters. However, the foregoing remarks concerning over- and under-fitting also apply when the difference between the number of parameters is small. That is, the difference in performance is due at least in part to architectural differences, not just to differences in number of parameters.

Merge models use a greater proportion of the training vocabulary on test captions. However, the proportion of vocabulary used is generally quite small for both architectures: less than 16% for Flickr8k and less than 7% for Flickr30k. Overall, the trend is for smaller proportions of the overall training vocabulary to be used, as the vocabulary grows larger, suggesting that neural language models find it harder to use infrequent words (which are more numerous at larger vocabulary sizes, by definition). In practice, it means that reducing training vocabularies results in minimal performance loss.

Overall, the evidence suggests that delaying the merging of image features with linguistic encodings to a late stage in the architecture may be advantageous, at least as far as corpus-based evaluation measures are concerned. Furthermore, the results suggest that a merge architecture has a higher capacity than an inject architecture and can generate better quality captions with smaller layers.

5 Discussion

If the RNN had the primary role of generating captions, then it would need to have access to the image in order to know what to generate. This does not seem to be the case as including the image into the RNN is not generally beneficial to its performance as a caption generator.

When viewing RNNs as having the primary role of encoding rather than generating, it makes sense that the inject architecture generally suffers in performance when compared to the merge architecture. The most plausible explanation has to do with the handling of variation. Consider once more the task of the RNN in the image captioning task: During training, captions are broken down into prefixes of increasing length, with each prefix compressed to a fixed-size vector, as illustrated in Figure 2 above.

In the inject architecture, the encoding task is made more complex by the inclusion of image features. Indeed, in the version of inject used in our experiments – the most commonly used solution in the caption generation literature[5] – image features are concatenated with every word in the caption. The upshot is (a) a requirement to compress caption prefixes together with image data into a fixed-size vector and (b) a substantial growth in the vocabulary size the RNN has to handle, because each image+word is treated as a single 'word'. This problem is alleviated in merge, where the RNN encodes linguistic histories only, at the expense of more parameters in the softmax layer.

One practical consequence of these findings is that, while merge models can handle more variety with smaller layers, increasing the state size of the RNN in the merge architecture is potentially quite profitable, as the entire state will be used to remember a greater variety of previously generated words. By contrast, in the inject architecture, this increase in memory would be used to better accommodate information from two distinct, but combined, modalities.

---

[5]We are referring to architectures that inject image features in parallel with word embeddings in the RNN. In the literature, when this type of architecture is used, the image features might only be included with some of the words or are changed for different words (such as in attention models).

6 Conclusions

This paper has presented two views of the role of the RNN in an image caption generator. In the first, an RNN decides on which word is the most likely to be generated next, given what has been generated before. In multimodal generation, this view encourages architectures where the image is incorporated into the RNN along with the words that were generated in order to allow the RNN to make visually-informed predictions.

The second view is that the RNN's role is purely memory-based and is only there to encode the sequence of words that have been generated thus far. This representation informs caption prediction at a later layer of the network as a function of both the RNN encoding and perceptual features. This view encourages architectures where vision and langauge are brought together late, in a multimodal layer.

Caption generation turns out to perform worse, in general, when image features are injected into the RNN. Thus, the role of the RNN is better conceived in terms of the learning of linguistic representations, to be used to inform later layers in the neural network, where predictions are made based on what has been generated in the past together with the image that is guiding the generation. Had the RNN been the component primarily involved in generating the caption, it would need to be informed about the image in order to know what needs to be generated; however this line of reasoning seems to hurt performance when applied to an architecture. This suggests that it is not the case that the RNN is the main component of the caption generator that is involved in generation.

In short, given a neural network architecture that is expected to process input sequences from multiple modalities, arriving at a joint representation, it would be better to have a separate component to encode each input, bringing them together at a late stage, rather than to pass them all into the same RNN through separate input channels. With respect to the question of how language should be grounded in perceptual data, the tentative answer offered by these experiments is that the link between the symbolic and perceptual should be established late, once encoding has been performed. To this end, recurrent networks are best viewed as learning representations, not as generating sequences.

6.1 Future work

The experiments reported here were conducted on two separate datasets. One concern is that results on Flickr8k and Flickr30k are not entirely consistent, though the superiority of merge over inject is clear in both. We are currently extending our experiments to the larger MSCOCO dataset (Lin et al., 2014).

The insights discussed in this paper invite future research on how generally applicable the merge architecture is in different domains. We would like to investigate whether similar changes in architecture would work in sequence-to-sequence tasks such as machine translation, where instead of conditioning a language model on an image we are conditioning a target language model on sentences in a source language. A similar question arises in image processing. If a CNN were conditioned to be more sensitive to certain types of objects or saliency differences among regions of a complex image, should the conditioning vector be incorporated at the beginning, thereby conditioning the entire CNN, or would it be better to instead incorporate it in a final layer, where saliency differences would then be based on high-level visual features?

There are also more practical advantages to merge architectures, such as for transfer learning. Since merge keeps the image separate from the RNN, the RNN used for captioning can conceivably be transferred from a neural language model that has been trained on general text. This cannot be done with an inject architecture since the RNN would need to be trained to combine image and text in the input. In future work, we intend to see how the performance of a caption generator is affected when the weights of the RNN are initialized from those of a general neural language model, along lines explored in neural machine translation (Ramachandran et al., 2016).

Acknowledgments

This work was partially funded by the Endeavour Scholarship Scheme (Malta), part-financed by the European Social Fund (ESF).

References

Stanislaw Antol, Aishwarya Agrawal, Jiasen Lu, Margaret Mitchell, Dhruv Batra, C Lawrence Zitnick, and Devi Parikh. 2015. VQA: Visual Question Answering. In *Proc. ICCV'15*, pages 2425–2433, Santiago, Chile.

Satanjeev Banerjee and Alon Lavie. 2005. METEOR: An automatic metric for MT evaluation with improved correlation with human judgments. In *Proc. Workshop on Intrinsic and Extrinsic Evaluation Measures for Machine Translation and/or Summarization*, volume 29, pages 65–72.

Raffaella Bernardi, Ruket Cakici, Desmond Elliott, Aykut Erdem, Erkut Erdem, Nazli Ikizler-Cinbis, Frank Keller, Adrian Muscat, and Barbara Plank. 2016. Automatic Description Generation from Images: A Survey of Models, Datasets, and Evaluation Measures. *Journal of Artificial Intelligence Research*, 55:409–442.

Xinlei Chen and C. Lawrence Zitnick. 2015. Mind's eye: A recurrent visual representation for image caption generation. In *Proc. CVPR'15*.

Jeff Donahue, Lisa Anne Hendricks, Sergio Guadarrama, Marcus Rohrbach, Subhashini Venugopalan, Kate Saenko, and Trevor Darrell. 2015. Long-term Recurrent Convolutional Networks for Visual Recognition and Description. In *Proc. CVPR'15*.

Desmond Elliott and Frank Keller. 2013. Image Description using Visual Dependency Representations. In *Proc. EMNLP'13*, pages 1292–1302, Seattle, WA. Association for Computational Linguistics.

Xavier Glorot and Yoshua Bengio. 2010. Understanding the difficulty of training deep feedforward neural networks. In *Proc. 13th International Conference on Artificial Intelligence and Statistics*, pages 249–256.

Alex Graves. 2013. Generating Sequences with Recurrent Neural Networks. *CoRR*, abs/1308.0850:1–43.

Ankush Gupta, Yashaswi Verma, and C. V. Jawahar. 2012. Choosing Linguistics over Vision to Describe Images. In *Proc. AAAI'12*, pages 606–612.

Stevan Harnad. 1990. The symbol grounding problem. *Physica D*, 42:335–346.

Lisa Anne Hendricks, Subhashini Venugopalan, Marcus Rohrbach, Raymond Mooney, Kate Saenko, and Trevor Darrell. 2016. Deep Compositional Captioning: Describing Novel Object Categories without Paired Training Data. In *Proc. CVPR'16*.

Jack Hessel, Nicolas Savva, and Michael J. Wilber. 2015. Image Representations and New Domains in Neural Image Captioning. *CoRR*, abs/1508.02091.

Sepp Hochreiter and Jürgen Schmidhuber. 1997. Long short-term memory. *Neural computation*, 9(8):1735–1780.

Micah Hodosh, Peter Young, and Julia Hockenmaier. 2013. Framing Image Description as a Ranking Task: Data, Models and Evaluation Metrics. *Journal of Artificial Intelligence Research*, 47(1):853–899.

Ting-Hao Huang, Francis Ferraro, Nasrin Mostafazadeh, Ishan Misra, Aishwarya Agrawal, Jacob Devlin, Ross Girshick, Xiaodong He, Pushmeet Kohli, Dhruv Batra, C Lawrence Zitnick, Devi Parikh, Lucy Vanderwende, Michel Galley, and Margaret Mitchell. 2016. Visual Storytelling. In *Proc. NAACL-HLT'16*, pages 1233–1239.

Andrej Karpathy and Li Fei-Fei. 2015. Deep Visual-Semantic Alignments for Generating Image Descriptions. In *Proc. CVPR'15*.

Diederik P. Kingma and Jimmy Ba. 2014. Adam: A Method for Stochastic Optimization. *CoRR*, abs/1412.6980.

Ryan Kiros, Ruslan Salakhutdinov, and Richard S Zemel. 2014a. Multimodal neural language models. In *Proc. ICML'14*, page 595603.

Ryan Kiros, Ruslan Salakhutdinov, and Richard S Zemel. 2014b. Unifying visual-semantic embeddings with multimodal neural language models. *CoRR*, abs/1411.2539.

Girish Kulkarni, Visruth Premraj, Sagnik Dhar, Siming Li, Yejin Choi, Alexander C Berg, and Tamara L Berg. 2011. Baby Talk : Understanding and Generating Image Descriptions. In *Proc. CVPR'11*, pages 1601–1608, Colorado Springs.

Yann LeCun, Yoshua Bengio, and Geoffrey Hinton. 2015. Deep learning. *Nature*, 521(7553):436–444.

Chin-Yew Lin and Franz Josef Och. 2004. Automatic evaluation of machine translation quality using longest common subsequence and skip-bigram statistics. In *Proc. ACL'04*. Association for Computational Linguistics (ACL).

Tsung-Yi Lin, Michael Maire, Serge Belongie, James Hays, Pietro Perona, Deva Ramanan, Piotr Dollár, and C. Lawrence Zitnick. 2014. Microsoft COCO: Common objects in context. In *Proc. ECCV'14*, pages 740–755.

Siqi Liu, Zhenhai Zhu, Ning Ye, Sergio Guadarrama, and Kevin Murphy. 2016. Optimization of image description metrics using policy gradient methods. *CoRR*, abs/1612.00370.

Jiasen Lu, Caiming Xiong, Devi Parikh, and Richard Socher. 2016. Knowing when to look: Adaptive attention via A visual sentinel for image captioning. *CoRR*, abs/1612.01887.

Junhua Mao, Wei Xu, Yi Yang, Jiang Wang, and Alan L. Yuille. 2014. Explain images with multimodal recurrent neural networks. In *Proc. NIPS'14 Deep Learning Workshop*.

Junhua Mao, Wei Xu, Yi Yang, Jiang Wang, Zhiheng Huang, and Alan Yuille. 2015a. Deep Captioning with Multimodal Recurrent Neural Networks (m-RNN). In *Proc. ICLR'15*.

Junhua Mao, Wei Xu, Yi Yang, Jiang Wang, Zhiheng Huang, and Alan Yuille. 2015b. Learning like a Child: Fast Novel Visual Concept Learning from Sentence Descriptions of Images. In *Proc. ICCV'15*.

Rebecca Mason and Eugene Charniak. In *Proc. CONLL'14*, pages 11–20, Baltimore, MA.

Margaret Mitchell, Jesse Dodge, Amit Goyal, Kota Yamaguchi, Karl Stratos, Xufeng Han, Alyssa Mensch, Alex Berg, Xufeng Han, Tamara Berg, and Hal Daume III. 2012. Midge: Generating Image Descriptions From Computer Vision Detections. In *Proc. EACL'12*, pages 747–756, Avignon, France.

V Ordonez, G Kulkarni, and Tl Berg. 2011. Im2text: Describing images using 1 million captioned photographs. In *Proc. NIPS'11*, pages 1143–1151, Granada, Spain.

Kishore Papineni, Salim Roukos, Todd Ward, and Wei-Jing Zhu. 2002. BLEU: a method for automatic evaluation of machine translation. In *Proc. ACL'02*, pages 311–318.

Prajit Ramachandran, Peter J. Liu, and Quoc V. Le. 2016. Unsupervised pretraining for sequence to sequence learning. *CoRR*, abs/1611.02683.

E. Reiter and R. Dale. 2000. *Building Natural Language Generation Systems*. Cambridge University Press, Cambridge, UK.

Deb Roy and Ehud Reiter. 2005. Connecting language to the world. *Artificial Intelligence*, 167(1-2):1–12.

Karen Simonyan and Andrew Zisserman. 2014. Very Deep Convolutional Networks for Large-Scale Image Recognition. *CoRR*, abs/1409.1556.

Richard Socher, Andrej Karpathy, Quoc V Le, Christopher D Manning, and Andrew Y Ng. 2014. Grounded Compositional Semantics for Finding and Describing Images with Sentences. *Transactions of the Association for Computational Linguistics (TACL)*, 2(April):207–218.

Mingoo Song and Chang D. Yoo. 2016. Multimodal representation: Kneser-ney smoothing/skip-gram based neural language model. In *Proc. ICIP'16*.

Ilya Sutskever, James Martens, and Geoffrey Hinton. In *Proc. ICML'11*, pages 1017–1024, Bellevue, WA.

Marc Tanti, Albert Gatt, and Kenneth P. Camilleri. 2017. Where to put the image in an image caption generator. *CoRR*, abs/1703.09137.

Ramakrishna Vedantam, C. Lawrence Zitnick, and Devi Parikh. 2015. CIDEr: Consensus-based image description evaluation. In *Proc. CVPR'15*.

Oriol Vinyals, Alexander Toshev, Samy Bengio, and Dumitru Erhan. 2015. Show and tell: A neural image caption generator. In *Proc. CVPR'15*.

Kelvin Xu, Jimmy Ba, Ryan Kiros, Kyunghyun Cho, Aaron C. Courville, Ruslan Salakhutdinov, Richard S. Zemel, and Yoshua Bengio. 2015. Show, Attend and Tell: Neural Image Caption Generation with Visual Attention. In *Proc. ICML'15*.

Zhilin Yang, Ye Yuan, Yuexin Wu, Ruslan Salakhutdinov, and William W. Cohen. 2016. Encode, review, and decode: Reviewer module for caption generation. *CoRR*, abs/1605.07912.

Quanzeng You, Hailin Jin, Zhaowen Wang, Chen Fang, and Jiebo Luo. 2016. Image captioning with semantic attention. In *Proc. CVPR'16*.

Peter Young, Alice Lai, Micah Hodosh, and Julia Hockenmaier. 2014. From image descriptions to visual denotations: New similarity metrics for semantic inference over event descriptions. *Transactions of the Association for Computational Linguistics*, 2:67–78.

Luowei Zhou, Chenliang Xu, Parker Koch, and Jason J. Corso. 2016. Image caption generation with text-conditional semantic attention. *CoRR*, abs/1606.04621.

Exploring the Behavior of Classic REG Algorithms
in the Description of Characters in 3D Images [*]

Gonzalo Méndez and **Raquel Hervás** and **Susana Bautista** and **Adrián Rabadán** and **Teresa Rodríguez**
Facultad de Informática - Instituto de Tecnología del Conocimiento
Universidad Complutense de Madrid (Spain)
{gmendez,raquelhb,subautis}@fdi.ucm.es, {arabadan,teresaro}@ucm.es

Abstract

Describing people and characters can be very useful in different contexts, such as computational narrative or image description for the visually impaired. However, a review of the existing literature shows that the automatic generation of people descriptions has not received much attention. Our work focuses on the description of people in snapshots from a 3D environment. First, we have conducted a survey to identify the way in which people describe other people under different conditions. We have used the information extracted from this survey to design several Referring Expression Generation algorithms which produce similar results. We have evaluated these algorithms with users in order to identify which ones generate the best description for specific characters in different situations. The evaluation has shown that, in order to generate good descriptions, a combination of different algorithms has to be used depending on the features and situation of the person to be described.

1 Introduction

In every conversation, human beings refer to people, objects, places and situations, and we need to be able to describe them accurately so that the hearer knows who or what we are referring to. In order to be able to automatically create descriptions that can be useful in real life situations – such as generating descriptions for the visually impaired – where

the complexity of the information needed to generate them is noteworthy, we first need to tackle specific aspects of these problems that bring light to the more general problem we intend to solve.

In this work we focus on the description of people in snapshots from a 3D environment, considering that feature extraction can be perfectly performed. Whereas most approaches to image description work with real world images, we have opted for 3D images because they allow us to easily manipulate the entities and their features in order to test different hypothesis, and we can create more complex situations to test our algorithms. In addition, we only focus on the description of people. Except for the TUNA corpus (Gatt et al., 2007; Deemter et al., 2012), which contained a set of close-up photographs of people, and the algorithms that used it in the TUNA Challenges (Gatt and Belz, 2010), to the best of our knowledge there are no works only focusing on people when describing visual images taken in real environments. The insights obtained in our work can improve the generation of descriptions for images where people are detected, as the examples presented by other studies show how references to people do not work in the same way as references to other entities do.

As a first step towards the implementation of a REG algorithm for describing people in 3D environments, we have explored the performance of classic REG algorithms for the task. We chose two well-known algorithms that can be easily configured depending on the the type of entities to be described: the Greedy (Dale, 1992) and the Incremental Algorithms (Dale and Reiter, 1995).

[*] This research is supported by the IDiLyCo project (TIN2015-66655-R) funded by the Spanish Ministry of Economy, Industry and Competitiveness.

Proceedings of The 10th International Natural Language Generation conference, pages 61–69,
Santiago de Compostela, Spain, September 4-7 2017. ©2017 Association for Computational Linguistics

As these algorithms require a predefined list of attributes that define the referent's appearance, we carried out a small study in order to determine the attributes that people include when describing people in real-life images (section 3). Then, we implemented the algorithms (and some variations) taking into account the obtained results (section 4), and asked people to judge the quality of their output when generating descriptions of characters in a 3D environment (section 5).

For both evaluations, we have taken an approach similar to the one in (Koller et al., 2010), which consists of an internet-based evaluation that allows for lower costs (it becomes unnecessary to summon a group of subjects to try out the system in a specific place). Users could easily access each survey using a link we provided, and they could do this at any time and from any place.

2 Related Work

A referring expression is a description created with the intention of distinguishing a certain object or person (*referent*) from a number of other objects or people (*distractors*). It must identify the referent unambiguously, effectively ruling out all the distractors. Therefore, any sentence that meets these criteria can be called a referring expression. However, not all of them can be considered equally good. It is usually considered that an effective referring expression should only contain information that the user knows or can easily perceive, and preferably information that is perceptually salient. In addition, overspecification could be desirable when extra information can help the listener to find the target more easily (Paraboni and van Deemter, 2014).

2.1 Classical Referring Expression Generation Algorithms

The task of Referring Expression Generation (REG) has been explored for over forty years (Krahmer and van Deemter, 2012). Although there are many other approaches to solve this problem (graph-based algorithms, constraint-based algorithms or description logics), in this work we have chosen to focus on two classical algorithms and the incorporation of relations into them. These algorithms are appropriate for our work because they are oriented to general pur-

pose settings and therefore are easily configurable for different domains and situations.

The Greedy Algorithm (Dale, 1989; Dale, 1992) creates a reference by iteratively selecting the attribute with the highest discriminatory power which rules out most of the distractors. The algorithm continues working until there are no distractors left, or there are no attributes left (in which case the referring expression cannot successfully identify the referent). Since there is no backtracking, sometimes one of the attributes that has been included may become redundant as a result of the combination of other attributes used afterwards. For this reason the algorithm does not truly offer minimal referring expressions, but it does focus on the most salient properties of the referent.

The Incremental Algorithm (Reiter and Dale, 1992; Dale and Reiter, 1995) has been one of the most influential REG algorithms so far. It builds referring expressions incrementally, similarly to the Greedy Algorithm. The difference between the two is that the Incremental Algorithm has a list of attributes in a pre-established order, and in each iteration it picks the first one from the list that rules out at least one distractor. This method is more likely to lead to overspecification of the referring expression, since the algorithm does not allow backtracking. The order of the attributes is crucial, in this case the algorithm cannot select salient properties by itself, so this list should be chosen with care depending on the context or scene.

In addition to merely mentioning the properties of the referent, several algorithms have incorporated relations to other objects or people into their referring expressions, the first of which was the Relational Algorithm (Dale and Haddock, 1991). Since then, relations have been incorporated into other algorithms, but they are very often considered inferior to properties belonging to the referent itself, and are used only as a last resort when its attributes are not enough to distinguish it (Krahmer and Theune, 2002). However, there is also research that proves that people tend to use relations in their descriptions even when they are not necessary (Viethen and Dale, 2008). Works like the ones by Kelleher and Kruijff (2005) deal with the determination of the best landmarks to use in a referring expression depending on context.

2.2 Automatic Description of Visual Information

The automatic generation of image descriptions is a problem that has received a large amount of interest in recent years from both computer vision and natural language generation communities.

An extensive survey on this topic can be found in (Bernardi et al., 2016). The authors divide the existing approaches into two main groups based on the models used. *Direct generation models* follow a classical pipeline: they first extract image information in terms of entities, relations between them, etc., and then this information is used by a natural language generation algorithm to generate the final image description. *Retrieval models* attack the problem by searching for images that are similar to the one to be described and then building the final description based on the descriptions of the retrieved images. Because our work consists in the description of characters in an interactive setting, we are more interested in direct generation models where a previously available database of image and descriptions is not required.

Although direct generation models have the advantage of being able to produce novel descriptions without relying on a previously existing corpus of descriptions, they rely heavily on the quality of the conceptual information extracted from the original image. In order to tackle this issue, some authors have started to separate both problems and study the generation of image descriptions assuming that visual image recognizers have already achieved close to perfection identification of information in images (Elliott and Keller, 2013; Yatskar et al., 2014; Wang and Gaizauskas, 2015).

3 Identification of Features Used in Descriptions

We conducted a survey in order to identify what features are relevant for individuals when they have to describe other people. A total of 71 evaluators took part in this survey. They were presented with photographs taken in our university canteen which contained a high number of people (an example can be seen in Figure 1) and they had to complete two sets of tasks.

3.1 Part 1: Identifying People

In this part of the survey, the participants were provided with four pictures of the canteen, each of them accompanied by a description, and they were asked to *"Find the person described at the top of the screen"*.

In the first scene, the participants were asked to identify a boy with a black t-shirt. In this picture, four boys were dressed in black, but two of them were wearing coats instead of t-shirts. Any of the other two were considered as a correct answer. 32% of the people chose a boy wearing a black coat, who was the most visible person in the scene and the closest one to the observer. 49% chose either of the two boys wearing a black t-shirt (28% and 21%, respectively) and 7% did not know the answer. From these answers we concluded that people are more likely to notice someone who is closer to them, and that the color of a person's clothes is more important that the type of the clothes.

In the second scene, the participants were asked to identify a boy leaning against a wall. We intended to find out if it would be easier for the participants to identify a person when they are very close to an important area in the room. 94% chose the right individual. He is at the edge of the photo and he is not very visible, but he is the only one leaning on the wall. The conclusion in this scene is that, since the wall is an important part of the room, people's eyes are drawn to it quickly, making it easy for them to find the person they are looking for.

In the third scene, the participants were asked to identify a person sitting next to a window. This time, as well as choosing a person that is next to an important area of the room, we picked someone who was further away from the user, to see if this had any effect on the participants reactions. 96% of the participants chose the right boy. By mentioning a relevant element such as the window, people's attention seem to automatically go towards that area and ignore the rest of the picture, so it is easier for them to find the person who fits the description.

In the fourth scene, the participants were asked to identify a girl with black hair. We chose a person furthest away from the viewer, and we decided to pick one of the only two girls with dark hair in the whole photograph. 69% of the people chose the

Figure 1: Sample scene used in the first study

correct girl, even though, out of all the girls, she was the one that was the furthest away from the observer. 23% chose a girl with dark (not black) hair, closer to the observer than the right girl. Two people chose a blond girl at the front of the photo, and two more did not know the answer. From these answers we can see that people tend to focus on what they see first. For this reason, it may be a good idea to provide more details than necessary when describing a person that is further away.

3.2 Part 2: Describing People

In this part of the survey, participants were provided with several pictures and were asked to *"Describe the person number N"* (see Figure 1).

In the first scene, the participants had to describe a boy working with his laptop. 66% of the participants mentioned his posture in some way (e.g. leaning on the table, working with his laptop), and 36% mentioned his clothes. We can conclude that, in this case, since the referent was in a very particular pos-

ture (hands crossed beneath his chin and looking at his laptop), the users have a tendency to include this as the main part of their description. There is only one other person in the photograph with a laptop, and nobody else visible with their hands under their chin. For this reason his posture stands out as a very descriptive feature.

In the second scene, they had to describe a waitress of the canteen. Overall, 59% of the participants mentioned her clothes, and 41% mentioned her profession. We can infer that, when someone is recognizable by their type, this can be descriptive enough and we may not need to mention anything else.

In the third scene, the target boy was barely visible. 8% of the participants gave an exhaustive description of everything they could see, but a lot of people described him by his clothes (53%) even though there are other boys close in the picture who are wearing clothes of a similar description (white t-shirt with dark details). Even when there are several people in a scene wearing similar clothes, people often tend to include information about those clothes in their description.

In the fourth scene, 21% of the participants described the target person as the boy with the red shirt, and did not mention anything else, even though there is another boy that could also fit in that description. A few people also noticed his posture (24%) and the fact that he is within a group of people. This reinforces what we concluded in the first part of the survey: when people see someone who fits a description, they do not look any further to check if that description may apply to someone else.

In the fifth scene, the target boy is sitting with a group of friends and is wearing a red shirt, so his description might be very similar to one of his friends. This time, 31% of the people described his posture as well as his clothes, and said that he is talking to the boy next to him. 14% of the participants described only his clothes, but they mentioned that his top has long sleeves, in contrast to his friends t-shirt. Even when the color of their clothes alone is not enough to distinguish a person, if it stands out enough, users tend to mention only that.

In the sixth scene, the target boy's face is not visible, the color of his clothes does not stand out, and there seems to be nothing particularly eye-catching about him. In this case, 73% of the people described his posture (he is sitting facing away from the observer), and most mentioned that he is sitting next to a girl. Some even described the girl's clothes, because they stand out more than his. Here we can see that when a person does not stand out very much, people tend to notice something nearby that stands out more (in this case the girl he is sitting with, but it could also be a window, a door or an object like a laptop, as seen in previous scenes).

3.3 Results

This study provided us with two important insights. The first one was that distance (from the viewer and to landmarks) influences the identification of referents. We could observe in the survey that the test subjects sometimes focused on the people who were nearer to them in the scene, and if a distractor looked similar to the referent, even if not all the attributes in the description matched, they would settle for this distractor. It also seemed that referring expressions that include information about nearby objects or people were easier to understand.

The second insight obtained from the study was a list of preferred attributes when describing people in crowded environments. The type of the person (e.g. boy, girl, waitress) was mentioned very often, in an average of 73.11% of the description. The next most used attribute was the colour of the top garment, and the last attribute which stood out was posture (used on average in 57.31% of the descriptions). Interestingly, the test subjects only mentioned important areas of the room 13.91% of the time, and described nearby people a little more often, 17.21% of the time.

Finally, based on the results we have obtained, we have seen that, rather than giving the shortest and most efficient description possible, people often give more information than is needed. This makes it easier for us to find the right person quickly.

4 Implementation of Classic Algorithms

With the results obtained from the previous study we could implement algorithms that do not choose the included attributes arbitrarily, but based on the opinions of real test subjects. Some of the attributes mentioned by the evaluators were not used because they are either too subjective (attitude, personality, age, height, weight) or cannot be appreciated in an image (shoe type and colour). The resulting prioritized list of attributes for the Greedy and Incremental Algorithms is therefore the following (from most to least priority): (1) type; (2) top colour; (3) posture; (4) beard; (5) hair colour; (6) top type; (7) hair type/length; (8) bottom colour; (9) bottom type.

In light of the results of the previous survey, we decided to include information about whether the referent is close to or far away from the observer in order to distinguish the referent faster. Considering the size of the room used in the scenes, we divided the space into two halves. The distance in the environment was measured from the observer to each character, so the character who was furthest away dictated the maximum distance that would be considered, and this would be divided by two to create a halfway division. Every character who was between the observer and the division would be considered near, and the rest would be considered far. Since this is not strictly a physical attribute of the referent it was not included in the Greedy Algorithm. For example, distance could potentially discard a large amount of people in the Greedy Algorithm while not being clearly visible to the observer if they are all in a group but some of them are standing further back. Distance was mentioned only in the Incremental Algorithm and it was added at the end of the description.

In addition to the Greedy and Incremental Algorithms, we also included the Exhaustive Algorithm as a baseline, which offers a full description of the referent including all its features. This last type of referring expression can be overspecified or non-distinguishing, so it is not ideal for describing the referent. The sentence structure in the Exhaustive Algorithm, taking into account the previously prioritized list of attributes, is:

> *The Type with HairType HairColour hair [and a Beard], with the TopColour Top-Type and BottomColour BottomType.*

Finally, in order to take into account objects or people near the referent, we implemented two relational algorithms to be used in combination with the three previously mentioned. Therefore, the referent was described using one of the three previous algorithms and additional information about relevant people or objects was included in case there was any.

The Nearby Objects Algorithm checks if there are any significant areas or objects near the referent and mentions the closest one. The referent can be described using either of the three basic algorithms, which leaves us with three different versions of the Nearby Objects Algorithm.

The Nearby People Algorithm works in a similar way, but the distance required to consider a person next to the referent is a little longer than in the previous case, since people tend to keep slightly further away from other people than from objects (although this distance is known to be culture dependent).

Therefore, the final algorithms were the Exhaustive Algorithm (EA), the Incremental Algorithm (IA), the Greedy Algorithm (GA), Nearby Objects with Exhaustive Algorithm (NOEA), Nearby Objects with Incremental Algorithm (NOIA), Nearby Objects with Greedy Algorithm (NOGA), Nearby People with Exhaustive Algorithm (NPEA), Nearby People with Incremental Algorithm (NPIA) and Nearby People with Greedy Algorithm (NPGA). Out of these nine algorithms, NOEA and NPEA have been excluded from the evaluation, since the EA algorithm was included only as a baseline and some preliminary tests pointed out that the descriptions provided by NOEA and NPEA algorithms did not improve the ones provided by the other algorithms. On the contrary, overspecification decreased the quality of these descriptions.

5 Evaluation of Classic Algorithms

After implementing all the algorithms, we tested them in order to find out if there was one that worked better than the rest in all situations or which one worked best depending on the situation.

In this survey, we showed the participants snapshots of the university canteen taken in a 3D virtual environment built using the Unity 3D engine. The characters' clothes and postures were modified to imitate the ones in the pictures (see Figures 1 and 2). The use of a 3D environment aids in the personalization of the scene, facilitating experiments in which any number of people and objects can be represented. This way we were also able to appreciate the differences between the descriptions given for a photograph of a real scene, and a scene developed in a 3D virtual environment.

A total of fifty-two participants completed this survey: 54% were women and 46% were men; most of them (67%) were between eighteen and thirty years old, 17% were between thirty and forty years old, 4% were under eighteen, and 12% were over forty.

The structure of the survey and the order of the questions were carefully planned so they did not influence the users' opinions. We wanted them to offer their own descriptions first, before reading and judging the descriptions generated by the algorithms. We have also considered the effort and amount of time that they will have to spend on the survey, so they will not be tempted to leave it unfinished and we can get as many answers as possible.

Because both the way in which the test subjects describe someone in the 3D scene and their ability to recognize the target character given a referring expression were intended to be analyzed, this survey was divided in two parts.

Figure 2: Sample scene used in the second study

In the first part, each test subject was asked to describe a certain person from three different scenes. The goal was to examine whether their answers would be very different when faced with a 3D environment as opposed to photographs.

The results show that type, top color, top type and posture still were the most used attributes, and they were mentioned even more often than during the first survey. The difference between inclusion of the color of the top garment and its type increased slightly, confirming that the color is a more salient attribute. The inclusion of nearby people and nearby objects approximately doubled in both cases, possibly due to the simplified representation of the room and the characters. In the case of the nearby people, we could see that it is not always the closest person that gets mentioned, but the person that stands out the most among the closest ones.

The use of hair color decreased slightly, and hair type/length was rarely used, possibly because there were not many variations of hairstyles in the scene.

Even though two of the referents had a beard, the test subjects only mentioned it in 5.77% of the descriptions, much less than in the first survey and contrary to our hypothesis. This may be either due to the quality of the characters used or simply because the beard is not a very salient attribute.

Overall, the results showed a similar order in the preferred attributes, with relations to large areas and other people gaining more importance, and small details being used less.

For the second part of the survey, the test subjects were shown four scenes (see Figure 2), each of them with several referring expressions for one referent, created and linguistically realized by our algorithms. Then, they had to rate each of the descriptions on a five point Likert scale, the lowest value being "very bad" and the highest "very good". Not all the algorithms were rated in all the scenes, either because they did not provide any useful information (e.g. there were no nearby objects in scene 1, so NOGA and NOIA were discarded), or because they gener-

	EA	GA	IA	NOGA	NOIA	NPGA	NPIA
Scene 1	2.647	2.019	3.372	-	-	-	4.673
Scene 2	1.901	1.843	2.176	2.941	2.960	2.285	3.115
Scene 3	2.940	3.784	-	4.140	3.882	-	-
Scene 4	-	2.411	2.500	4.215	-	3.200	-

Table 1: Average scores obtained by the algorithms

ated results equivalent to those of other algorithms (e.g. NOIA and NOGA in scene 4). The following example shows the descriptions generated for Figure 2:

- Greedy (GA): *"The girl sitting down"*

- Incremental (IA): *"The girl in the white tank top who is sitting down. She is near."*

- Exhaustive (EA): *"The girl with medium length brown hair, with the white tank top and blue trousers."*

- Nearby Objects with Greedy (NOGA): *"The girl sitting down near the window."*

- Nearby Objects with Incremental (NOIA): *"The girl in the white tank top who is sitting down. She is near. She is near the window."*

- Nearby People with Greedy (NPGA): *"The girl sitting down next to the boy in the dark blue sweater."*

- Nearby People with Incremental (NPIA): *"The girl in the white tank top who is sitting down. She is near. She is next to the boy in the dark blue sweater."*

The obtained results are shown in Table 1, where the average score for the descriptions generated by the algorithms in each of the four scenes are shown. Relational algorithms have proved to have very high ratings. This suggests that, at least for the particular scenes and situations shown to the participants, relational algorithms which include nearby people or objects can be very useful if there are distractors or objects that stand out and can be related to the intended referent.

The results from the second survey also showed that users do not benefit from the inclusion of the beard or information about the referent's bottom garment or shoes, so we eliminated these from the attributes list. In scenarios in which people wear very unusual clothing this may not be a correct decision, but since we are working with characters with casual attire, the bottom half of their clothes are not different enough from each other to stand out. Additionally, many characters are sitting down or are partially covered and some parts of their clothes are often not visible to the observer.

6 Conclusions and Future Work

In the present work, we have described a user driven approach to automatically generate character descriptions in 3D environments. We have conducted two different surveys that have allowed us to identify, on the one hand, what attributes are more relevant for people when they describe another person, and on the other hand, what kind of description they understand better depending on the specific features and situation of the target subject of the description.

In our aim to build an algorithm that describes people in different, static, situations, the next step we must take is to design an strategy that, for a given scene, identifies the relevant features of the subject to be described and selects the most appropriate algorithm, among the studied ones, to generate a suitable description of this person.

In the long run, we intend to generate descriptions in closer to real life situations, where both the observer and the elements of the scene, either objects or people, can move and change, so that these changes have to be taken into account in order to modify the contents of the description in real time.

References

Raffaella Bernardi, Ruket Cakici, Desmond Elliott, Aykut Erdem, Erkut Erdem, Nazli Ikizler-Cinbis, Frank Keller, Adrian Muscat, and Barbara Plank. 2016. Automatic description generation from images: A survey of models, datasets, and evaluation measures. *Journal of Artificial Intelligence Research*, 55(1):409–442, January.

Robert Dale and Nicholas Haddock. 1991. Generating referring expressions involving relations. In *Proceedings of the 5th Conference of the European Chapter of the Association for Computational Linguistics*, pages 161–166, Germany.

Robert Dale and Ehud Reiter. 1995. Computational interpretations of the gricean maxims in the generation of referring expressions. *Cognitive Science*, 19(2):233–263.

Robert Dale. 1989. Cooking up referring expressions. In *Proceedings of the 27th Annual Meeting of the Association for Computational Linguistics*, pages 68–75, University of British Columbia, Vancouver, BC, Canada.

Robert Dale. 1992. *Generating Referring Expressions: Constructing Descriptions in a Domain of Objects and Processes*. MIT Press, Cambridge, Cambridge, MA, USA.

Kees van Deemter, Albert Gatt, Ielka van der Sluis, and Richard Power. 2012. Generation of referring expressions: Assessing the incremental algorithm. *Cognitive Science*, 36(5):799–836.

Desmond Elliott and Frank Keller. 2013. Image description using visual dependency representations. In *Proceedings of the 2013 Conference on Empirical Methods in Natural Language Processing (EMNLP-13)*, pages 1292–1302. Association for Computational Linguistics.

Albert Gatt and Anja Belz, 2010. *Introducing Shared Tasks to NLG: The TUNA Shared Task Evaluation Challenges*, pages 264–293. Springer Berlin Heidelberg, Berlin, Heidelberg.

Albert Gatt, Ielka van der Sluis, and Kees van Deemter. 2007. Evaluating algorithms for the generation of referring expressions using a balanced corpus. In *Proceedings of the Eleventh European Workshop on Natural Language Generation*, ENLG '07, pages 49–56, Stroudsburg, PA, USA. Association for Computational Linguistics.

John Kelleher and Geert-Jan Kruijff. 2005. A context-dependent algorithm for generating locative expressions in physically situated environments. In *Proceedings of the 10th European Workshop on Natural Language Generation*, pages 68–74, Aberdeen, UK.

Alexander Koller, Kristina Striegnitz, Donna Byron, Justine Cassell, Robert Dale, Johanna Moore, and Jon Oberlander. 2010. The first challenge on generating instructions in virtual environments. In E. Krahmer and M. Theune, editors, *Empirical Methods in Natural Language Generation*, volume 5790 of *LNCS*, pages 337–361. Springer.

Emiel Krahmer and Mariet Theune. 2002. Efficient context-sensitive generation of referring expressions. In Kees van Deemter and Rodger Kibble, editors, *Information Sharing: Reference and Presupposition in Language Generation and Interpretation*, pages 223–264. CSLI Publications, Stanford CA, USA.

Emiel Krahmer and Kees van Deemter. 2012. Computational generation of referring expressions: A survey. *Computational Linguistics*, 38(1):173–218.

Ivandr Paraboni and Kees van Deemter. 2014. Reference and the facilitation of search in spatial domains. *Language, Cognition and Neuroscience*, 29(8):1002–1017.

Ehud Reiter and Robert Dale. 1992. A fast algorithm for the generation of referring expressions. In *Proceedings of the 14th International Conference on Computational Linguistics*, pages 232–238, Nantes, France.

Jette Viethen and Robert Dale. 2008. The use of spatial relations in referring expression generation. In *Proceedings of the 5th International Conference on Natural Language Generation*, pages 59–67, Salt Fork, OH, USA.

J.K. Wang and R. Gaizauskas. 2015. Generating image descriptions with gold standard visual inputs: Motivation, evaluation and baselines. In *15th European Workshop on Natural Language Generation (ENLG)*, pages 117–126. Association for Computational Linguistics.

Mark Yatskar, Michel Galley, Lucy Vanderwende, and Luke Zettlemoyer. 2014. See no evil, say no evil: Description generation from densely labeled images. In *Proceedings of the Third Joint Conference on Lexical and Computational Semantics (*SEM 2014)*, pages 110–120. Association for Computational Linguistics.

Co-PoeTryMe: a Co-Creative Interface for the Composition of Poetry

Hugo Gonçalo Oliveira and **Tiago Mendes** and **Ana Boavida**
CISUC, Department of Informatics Engineering
University of Coimbra, Portugal
`hroliv@dei.uc.pt, tjmendes@student.dei.uc.pt, aboavida@dei.uc.pt`

Abstract

Co-PoeTryMe is a web application for poetry composition, guided by the user, though with the help of automatic features, such as the generation of full (editable) drafts, as well as the acquisition of additional well-formed lines, or semantically-related words, possibly constrained by the number of syllables, rhyme, or polarity. Towards the final poem, the latter can replace lines or words in the draft.

1 Context

PoeTryMe (Gonçalo Oliveira, 2012) is a platform for automated poetry generation from a set of initial parameters, such as the poetry form, the language (English, Portuguese or Spanish), a set of seed words or a surprise factor. A semantic network and a grammar are combined to produce semantically-coherent lines, using the seeds or words related to them, grouped according to the given poetry form, with the corresponding number of syllables, and often with rhymes.

This was originally an autonomous procedure, without user interaction but providing the initial parameters. Yet, after using PoeTryMe, creative writers and other interested people expressed their wish to make changes in the resulting poems or to interact with the system and take part in the creative process. Some even confessed to have generated several poems, keeping only some of the lines and, from their manual selection, created a new poem, more in line with their intents. Although the obtained results are generally ok, intention-related aspects can always be improved (Gonçalo Oliveira et al., 2017),

not to mention that assessing the quality of poetry is a subjective task and may diverge from user to user.

This was our main motivation for developing Co-PoeTryMe, a creativity-support application that enables the user to interact with some of the modules that constitute PoeTryMe. As it happens in the Poetry Machine (Kantosalo et al., 2014) and jG-noetry[1], specifically for poetry, or DeepBeat (Malmi et al., 2016) and LyriSys (Watanabe et al., 2017), for song lyrics, Co-PoeTryMe enables the collaboration between humans and a computational system towards the co-creation of poems. Co-PoeTryMe takes advantage of the architecture of PoeTryMe and its unique functionalities, and adopts a rational hands-on design, with few decorative elements, aiming to make the process of poetry composition visually more interesting.

2 Co-Creative Poetry Composition

Developing Co-PoeTryMe was eased by the modular architecture of PoeTryMe and its web API, that enables the production of full poems with a predefined structure; single lines, given a set of seed words; or words, semantically or structurally constrained. Co-PoeTryMe is a web-based application, developed in JavaScript, and thus portable, as it does not require the installation of additional software, only a browser and a working Internet connection.

Co-PoeTryMe is based on several visual modules, each covering a specific group of functionalities, and only visible when the actions they provide are available. Modules are placed around a central module that displays the current draft and en-

---

[1] `http://www.eddeaddad.net/jgnoetry/`

70

Proceedings of The 10th International Natural Language Generation conference, pages 70–71,
Santiago de Compostela, Spain, September 4-7 2017. ©2017 Association for Computational Linguistics

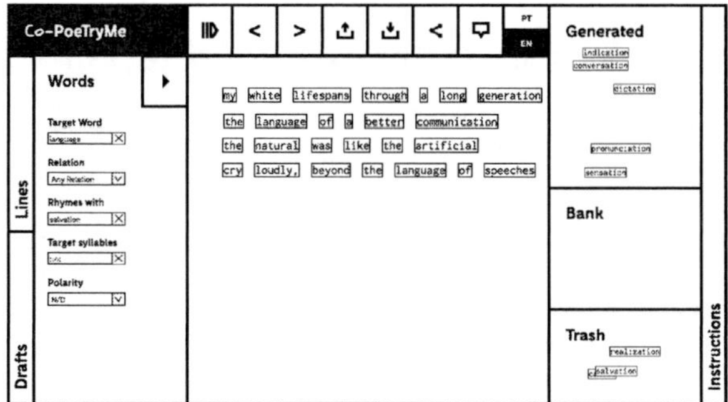

Figure 1: Poem edition and word generation.

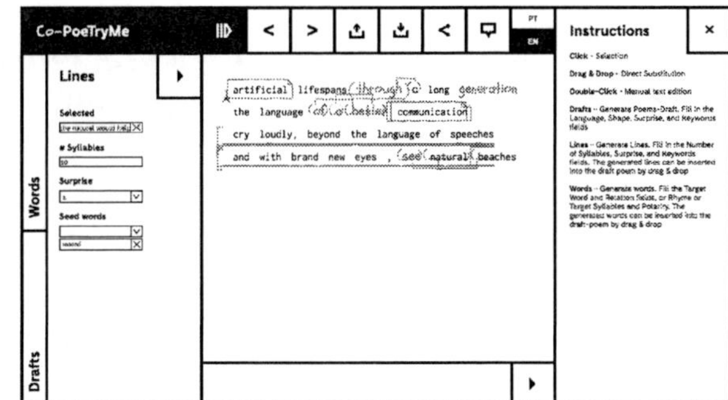

Figure 2: Line generation and visualizing the changes.

ables its edition (Figure 1). To start co-creating, the user can: (i) write a poem right away; (ii) import an existing poem draft from a text file; (iii) use the Drafts module, in the left-hand side, for generating a draft, given a target language (English, Portuguese or Spanish), a predefined or custom poetry form, a surprise factor (0-4), and a list of seed words for setting the semantic domain.

Once the central module has content, full lines or words can be selected to be edited, swapped, or to be used as input for the generation of new words or lines. Selecting a line reveals the Lines module (Figure 2, left), which enables the generation of alternative lines, using one of the given seeds and with a target number of syllables. Selecting a word reveals the Words module (Figure 1, left), which can be used for the acquisition of words combining a subset of the following constraints: semantically-related (synonym, hypernym or hyponym, co-hyponyn, antonym, or other), rhyming, or same number of syllables as the target word; or with a certain polarity (positive or negative). Retrieved words appear in the Generated module, on the right-hand side. They can be added or swapped with any word in the draft, or moved to the Bank, below, in order to be used later. Words that were once part of the draft appear in the Trash module. A similar set of modules exists for the lines.

The top module has utility buttons for selecting the application language (English or Portuguese), showing or hiding tooltips, importing or exporting a draft, sharing in social networks, undo, redo, as well as tool for visualizing the changes made from the initial draft to its current state (Figure 2).

Poem composition results from user interaction with the available modules and their underlying in-

teraction with PoeTryMe's API.

3 Conclusion

Co-PoeTryMe was developed to meet the wishes of PoeTryMe users, who can now play with the available functionalities, hopefully towards the creation of better poems. Co-PoeTryMe is freely available to be used by anyone, on the Web[2].

References

Hugo Gonçalo Oliveira, Tiago Mendes, and Ana Boavida. 2017. Towards finer-grained interaction with a Poetry Generator. In *Procs of ProSocrates 2017: Symposium on Problem-solving, Creativity and Spatial Reasoning in Cognitive Systems*, Delmenhorst, Germany.

Hugo Gonçalo Oliveira. 2012. PoeTryMe: a versatile platform for poetry generation. In *Procs of Workshop on Computational Creativity, Concept Invention, and General Intelligence*, C3GI 2012, Montpellier, France.

Anna Kantosalo, Jukka M. Toivanen, Ping Xiao, and Hannu Toivonen. 2014. From isolation to involvement: Adapting machine creativity software to support human-computer co-creation. In *Procs 5th Intl Conf on Computational Creativity*, ICCC 2014, Ljubljana, Slovenia.

Eric Malmi, Pyry Takala, Hannu Toivonen, Tapani Raiko, and Aristides Gionis. 2016. DopeLearning: A computational approach to rap lyrics generation. In *Procs 22nd SIGKDD Intl Conf on Knowledge Discovery and Data Mining*, pages 195–204, San Francisco, USA.

Kento Watanabe, Yuichiroh Matsubayashi, Kentaro Inui, Tomoyasu Nakano, Satoru Fukayama, and Masataka Goto. 2017. LyriSys: An interactive support system for writing lyrics based on topic transition. In *Procs 22nd Intl Conf on Intelligent User Interfaces*, IUI '17, pages 559–563, New York, NY, USA. ACM.

---

[2]`http://poetryme.dei.uc.pt/~copoetryme/`

Refer-iTTS: A System for Referring in Spoken Installments to Objects in Real-World Images

Sina Zarrieß and **David Schlangen**

Dialogue Systems Group // CITEC // Faculty of Linguistics and Literary Studies
Bielefeld University, Germany
`{sina.zarriess,david.schlangen}@uni-bielefeld.de`

Commonly, the output of a referring expression generation system is written text which is, typically, presented to a human user as a one-shot expression. Consequently, the majority of existing REG systems interact with users in a very rigid and strictly turn-based fashion: only after the system has fully completed and delivered the result of the REG process, the user is able to read it and react accordingly. A lot of human referential communication, however, happens in situated interaction and via spoken language. Theoretically, it is well known that this change in modality fundamentally changes human production of referring expressions: Given the real-time constraints of situated interaction, a speaker often has to start uttering before she has found the optimal expression, but at the same time, she can observe the listener's reaction while speaking and extend, adapt, or correct her referring expressions accordingly (Clark and Wilkes-Gibbs, 1986; Clark and Krych, 2004). Practically, spoken and interactive REG has been rarely studied empirically or implemented in realistic systems, but see (DeVault et al., 2005; Staudte et al., 2012; Striegnitz et al., 2012; Fang et al., 2014).

We present Refer-iTTS, a system that is meant to support research on real-time spoken REG and builds upon recent approaches to REG from real-world images (Kazemzadeh et al., 2014; Zarrieß and Schlangen, 2016). We use the recently proposed words-as-classifiers (WAC) model for generation from low-level visual inputs and integrate it with InproTk (Baumann and Schlangen, 2012b), an open-source framework for incremental dialogue processing (`http://wwwhomes.uni-bielefeld.`
`de/dschlangen/inpro/`). Importantly, InproTk features an incremental text-to-speech synthesis implementation (iTTS) (Baumann and Schlangen, 2012a) allowing for fine-grained, incremental manipulation of the audio signal (e.g. interruption, pausing, resumption, continuation).

We will show an interactive demonstration of the following set-up: the system presents an image with several objects in a visual scene on the screen and the user's task is to click on the object referred to. While generating and synthesizing the RE, the system continuously observes the non-verbal reactions of the user (i.e. her mouse movements) and adapts the generated utterances to these actions in an incremental fashion. At the same time, the system tries to be as cooperative as possible: if the user shows no reaction for a certain amount of time, the previous expression is expanded, i.e. the system splits its referring expression over several utterances, which is usually known as "reference in installments", cf. (Zarrieß and Schlangen, 2016).

Figure 1 illustrates the architecture of Refer-iTTS, which conceptually follows the framework of the Incremental Unit (IU) model (Schlangen and Skantze, 2009), and two example interactions. User actions and the system's generation and synthesis decisions happen concurrently, coordinated and monitored by an action manager (AM) module. Thus, besides decisions related to content planning and realization (e.g. attribute selection and ordering), a spoken installment-based REG system has to make a number of high-level decisions related to the delivery and timing of its own output. Using the Zarrieß and Schlangen (2016)'s generator, the system orders its

Proceedings of The 10th International Natural Language Generation conference, pages 72–73,
Santiago de Compostela, Spain, September 4-7 2017. ©2017 Association for Computational Linguistics

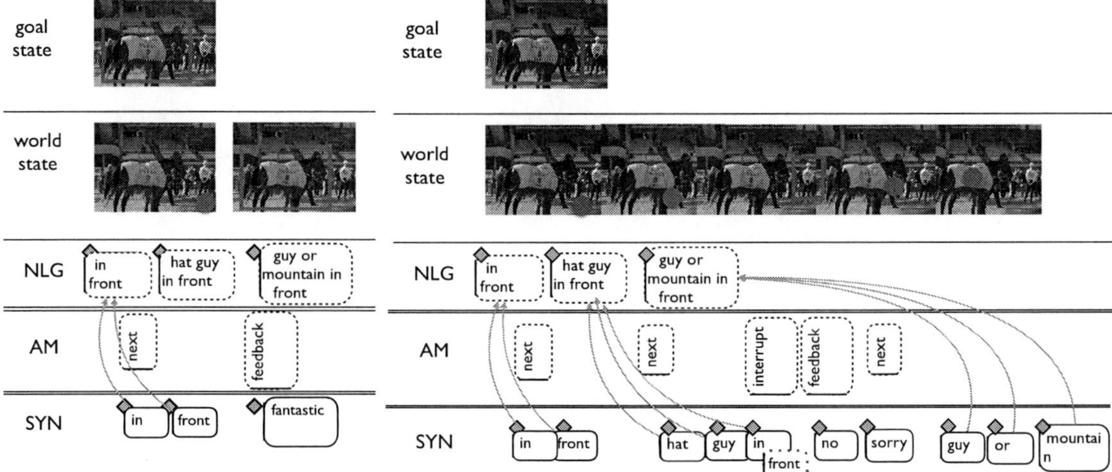

Figure 1: Two example interactions with Refer-iTTS, user actions (mouse movements and clicks are shown as red points and rectangles on the image), system decisions made by the NLG, AM (Action Manager) and SYN (synthesis) module are shown in rounded rectangles that correspond to incremental units (IUs) in InproTk, arrows between IUs indicate grounded-in links

installments according to its internal confidence, i.e. it first commits a phrase referring to the location, and then a phrase referring to the object's category. As shown in Figure 1, the Action Manager then decides when to initiate a new synthesis process for the next installment phrase (NEXT), when to interrupt the on-going formulation of an installment phrase, e.g. in case the user clicks on an objects while the synthesis is speaking (INTERRUPT) or when to provide FEED-BACK that reacts to a user click or action. This architecture allows for highly dynamic interaction with a user.

References

Timo Baumann and David Schlangen. 2012a. IN-PRO_iSS: A Component for Just-In-Time Incremental Speech Synthesis. In *Proceedings of the ACL 2012 System Demonstrations*.

Timo Baumann and David Schlangen. 2012b. The In-proTK 2012 release. In *Proceedings of the NAACL-HLT Workshop on Future directions and needs in the Spoken Dialog Community: Tools and Data (SDCTD 2012)*, pages 29–32, Montreal, Canada.

Herbert H. Clark and Meredyth A. Krych. 2004. Speaking while monitoring addressees for understanding. *Journal of Memory and Language*, 50(1):62–81.

Herbert H Clark and Deanna Wilkes-Gibbs. 1986. Referring as a collaborative process. *Cognition*, 22(1):1–39.

David DeVault, Natalia Kariaeva, Anubha Kothari, Iris Oved, and Matthew Stone. 2005. An information-state approach to collaborative reference. In *Proceedings of the ACL 2005 on Interactive poster and demonstration sessions*, pages 1–4.

Rui Fang, Malcolm Doering, and Joyce Y. Chai. 2014. Collaborative Models for Referring Expression Generation in Situated Dialogue. In *Proceedings of the 28th AAAI Conference on Artificial Intelligence*.

Sahar Kazemzadeh, Vicente Ordonez, Mark Matten, and Tamara L Berg. 2014. ReferItGame: Referring to Objects in Photographs of Natural Scenes. In *Proceedings of EMNLP 2014*, pages 787–798, Doha, Qatar.

David Schlangen and Gabriel Skantze. 2009. A general, abstract model of incremental dialogue processing. In *Proceedings of the 12th Conference of the European Chapter of the Association for Computational Linguistics (EACL 2009)*, pages 710–718, Athens, Greece.

Maria Staudte, Alexander Koller, Konstantina Garoufi, and Matthew W Crocker. 2012. Using listener gaze to augment speech generation in a virtual 3d environment. In *Proceedings of the 34th Annual Conference of the Cognitive Science Society*.

Kristina Striegnitz, Hendrik Buschmeier, and Stefan Kopp. 2012. Referring in installments: a corpus study of spoken object references in an interactive virtual environment. In *Proceedings of the 7th INLG Conference*, pages 12–16.

Sina Zarrieß and David Schlangen. 2016. Easy things first: Installments improve referring expression generation for objects in photographs. In *Proceedings of the 54th Annual Meeting of the Association for Computational Linguistics*.

Finding the "right" answers for customers

Frank Schilder
Thomson Reuters Research & Development

Abstract

This talk will present a few NLG systems developed within Thomson Reuters providing information to professionals such as lawyers, accountants or traders. Based on the experience developing these system, I will discuss the usefulness of automatic metrics, crowd-sourced evaluation, corpora studies and expert reviews. I will conclude with exploring the question of whether developers of NLG systems need to follow ethical guidelines and how those guidelines could be established.

Proceedings of The 10th International Natural Language Generation conference, page 74,
Santiago de Compostela, Spain, September 4-7 2017. ©2017 Association for Computational Linguistics

Referring Expression Generation under Uncertainty: Algorithm and Evaluation Framework

Tom Williams and Matthias Scheutz
Human-Robot Interaction Laboratory
Tufts University
williams@cs.tufts.edu, matthias.scheutz@tufts.edu

Abstract

For situated agents to effectively engage in natural-language interactions with humans, they must be able to *refer* to entities such as people, locations, and objects. While classic *referring expression generation* (REG) algorithms like the Incremental Algorithm (IA) assume perfect, complete, and accessible knowledge of all referents, this is not always possible. In this work, we show how a previously presented *consultant* framework (which facilitates *reference resolution* when knowledge is uncertain, heterogeneous and distributed) can be used to extend the IA to produce *DIST-PIA*, a domain-independent algorithm for REG under uncertain, heterogeneous, and distributed knowledge. We also present a novel framework that can be used to evaluate such REG algorithms without conflating the performance of the algorithm with the performance of classifiers it employs.

1 Introduction

For situated agents to effectively engage in natural-language interactions with humans, they must be able to *refer* to those entities of interest to their interlocutors, such as people, locations, and objects. This task, known as *referring expression generation (REG)* is typically split into two sub-tasks: *content determination* (deciding which properties to use to describe a target), and *linguistic realization*, (choosing which words to use to communicate those properties) (Krahmer and Van Deemter, 2012). In keeping with tradition, we refer to content determination algorithms as REG algorithms.

Traditionally, REG algorithms make use of a *domain* (comprised of target referent m and a set of distractors X), where each entity in that domain is represented by an *attribute set* of properties and relations that hold for that entity (Dale and Reiter, 1995). The most traditionally successful such algorithm has been Dale and Reiter's *Incremental Algorithm (IA)*, which additionally takes a *preference ordering P* in which attributes are to be considered.

A variety of factors prevent many *situated* agents from using algorithms from this tradition. Crucially, to check whether an entity has a certain attribute, *IA* simply checks whether that attribute is a member of that entity's attribute set, producing a clear and unambiguous answer. But for many agents, it is imperative to represent the *uncertainty* of knowledge. The knowledge bases (KBs) of these agents may thus be *unable* to definitively state whether or not a given attribute holds for a given entity.

While there have been previous approaches to generating referring expressions (REs) under uncertainty, those algorithms have been explicitly designed to refer to *objects* in visual scenes, and as such are tightly integrated with visual classifiers (Zarrieß and Schlangen, 2016; Roy, 2002; Meo et al., 2014). This is problematic for least two reasons: First, intelligent agents may need to generate REs for a much wider class of entities than those appearing in a visual scene (e.g., agents, locations, ideas, utterances), which may not be possible if an REG algorithm is tightly coupled with *visual* classifiers. Second, due to this tight coupling, the evaluation of these algorithms conflates the performance of the REG algorithms themselves with the perfor-

Proceedings of The 10th International Natural Language Generation conference, pages 75–84,
Santiago de Compostela, Spain, September 4-7 2017. ©2017 Association for Computational Linguistics

mance of the visual classifiers they employ. For these reasons, previous algorithms for generating REs under uncertainty have only been evaluated relative to different versions of themselves, and not to other algorithms or to humans. We believe it is important to be able to talk separately about the design, efficacy, and integration of REG algorithms and the design, efficacy, and integration of property classifiers used by those algorithms. In this paper we present an REG algorithm that is *not* tightly integrated with specific property classifiers, but is easily extensible to allow for arbitrary property classifiers to be utilized within a general framework.

In addition to these two primary concerns, we raise a third, specific to the realities of modern integrated agent architectures. In many integrated agent architectures, such as DIARC (Scheutz et al., 2013) and ROS (Quigley et al., 2009), information may be distributed across a number of architectural components, rather than being stored in a single centralized KB, meaning that no central attribute set can be expected to be ready and available for use by an REG algorithm. While there has been much research on merging disparate knowledge bases (Lin, 1996; Liberatore and Schaerf, 1998; Konieczny, 2000), this is not always feasible or even desirable in integrated architectures (Williams and Scheutz, 2016).

In this paper, we address three main research challenges. First and most crucially, we address the need for REG algorithms that take into account the generator's uncertainty regarding entities' attributes, and which are not tied to a particular domain (e.g., visible objects). Second, we address the lack of a rigorous evaluation framework for systematically evaluating such algorithms, in a way that allows REG algorithms in this class to be compared to both each other and to humans. Finally, we address the need for such algorithms to take into account the realities of the distributed knowledge representation schemes used by modern integrated agent architectures.

To address these challenges, we present *DIST-PIA*: an *IA*-inspired REG algorithm designed to operate within our previously presented *consultant framework* (Williams and Scheutz, 2016), which provides access to uncertain, heterogeneous, and distributed knowledge. Furthermore, we present a novel two-stage evaluation framework in which human participants first assess the uncertainty that various attributes hold within a domain and to generate novel REs, and then evaluate the effectiveness of REs created from both human- and machine-generated sets of properties within that domain.

2 Previous Work

"Referring" has been referred to as the "fruit fly" of language due to the amount of study it has attracted (Van Deemter, 2016). The bulk of such study has focused on the content determination stage of REG. As previously noted, classic REG algorithms (e.g., *Full Brevity*, the *Greedy Algorithm* (Dale, 1989), and the aforementioned *Incremental Algorithm* (Dale and Reiter, 1995)) operate under a number of simplifying assumptions (such as certain knowledge on the part of both speaker and listener) that are not tenable in realistic interaction scenarios.

In this section, we will not attempt to survey the full scope of REG algorithms developed in the past few decades (for an excellent primer, we recommend Van Deemter (2016)'s recent book on the subject), but will instead focus on REG algorithms that have relaxed the constraint of certain knowledge.

Horacek (2005) presents an algorithm that reasons about the certainty that *a listener* will be able to recognize that a target referent has certain attributes, choosing an utterance that minimizes recognition failure. This is an example of *audience design* in which the *listener's* knowledge and capabilities are taken into account. Horacek's algorithm does not, however, take into account the uncertainty of the *agent's* knowledge, which we argue must be taken into account before audience design is considered.

In the graph-based approach presented by Sadovnik et al. (2013), computer vision classifiers are used to assess both the uncertainty of the agent's knowledge as well as for audience design. If Sadovnik's algorithm cannot generate an RE that is sufficiently likely to disambiguate the target, it is re-run using the attributes of both the target and one of its neighbors. While this approach relaxes the assumption of completely certain knowledge, it imposes others, as it is specifically tailored to use vision-based techniques alone. Furthermore, by giving equal weight to the attributes of target and anchors, the algorithm generates REs that curiously under-describe the target relative to anchors (e.g.,

"The person on the right of a person who is not Asian and has eye glasses and is smiling and has bangs and whose mouth is not closed").

Finally, Fang et al. (2013) (see also (Fang et al., 2015)) present an approach which more systematically handles attributes by expanding a hypergraph of properties until the selected properties disambiguate the target referent. When choosing how to expand this hypergraph, Fang chooses the attribute of minimal cost, taking into account the uncertainty of the agent's knowledge as well as the preference of that attribute (in the sense used by the IA). While this approach moves in the right direction, it once again assumes the exclusive use of computer vision classifiers, that all entities are objects in a visual scene, and that information about all such entities is stored in a single, centralized data structure.

3   Consultant Framework

We previously presented a framework of "consultants" that allows information about entities to be assessed when knowledge is uncertain, heterogeneous, and distributed (Williams and Scheutz, 2016). Specifically, each consultant c facilitates access to one KB k, and must be capable of at least four functions:

1. providing a set c_{domain} of atomic entities from k,
2. advertising a list $c_{constraints}$ of constraints that can be assessed with respect to entities from c_{domain},
3. assessing constraints from $c_{constraints}$ with respect to entities from c_{domain}, and
4. adding, removing, or imposing constraints from $c_{constraints}$ on entities from c_{domain}.

While these capabilities were designed to facilitate reference resolution, they can also facilitate REG, which requires a set of distractors to rule out (Capability 1), a list of constraints that can be used to rule out those distractors (Capability 2), and a means of checking whether those constraints do in fact rule out distractors (Capability 3).

Recall, however, that the IA considers constraints according to a *preference ordering*. For example, it may be more preferable to use an entity's *type* to describe it than to use its *color*, more preferable to use color rather than size, and so on. To use the aforementioned consultant framework for REG, we thus require a more specific second capability:

2. advertising a list $c_{constraints}$ of constraints that can be assessed with respect to entities from c_{domain},

and that is ordered by descending preference.

With this modification, we now have a framework which provides access to uncertain knowledge from different domains and of heterogeneous representation which is distributed throughout a robot architecture, and which is configured to interface well with the IA. In the next section, we describe how we have similarly modified the IA in order to take advantage of this framework.

4   Algorithm and Walkthrough

In this section, we present *DIST-PIA*, the Distributed, Probabilistic Incremental Algorithm[1], a modified version of the *Incremental Algorithm (IA)* (Dale and Reiter, 1995). For each property p in the list of properties attributed to the target referent, *IA* checks whether p is *not* attributed to any distractors; if so, p is added to the list of properties to communicate, and the ruled-out distractors are removed from the set of distractors. This process terminates when all distractors are eliminated or there are no properties left to consider.

When information is uncertain and distributed across multiple KBs, however, the assumptions made by the *IA* are unlikely to hold. It is unlikely, for example, that the set of properties that hold for each entity will have been helpfully precomputed. As such, an REG algorithm operating under uncertain and distributed knowledge cannot rely on simple set-membership checks, but must instead explicitly check how probable it is that an entity has a particular property.

In this section, we present *DIST-PIA*, the Distributed, Probabilistic Incremental Algorithm which uses the aforementioned consultant framework to do just that. And we provide a walkthrough of this algorithm in an example scenario. Each step of this walkthrough is summarized in a row of Tab. 1 and denoted in the walkthrough in bold (e.g., **(1)**).

To illustrate the behavior of *DIST-PIA*, we will use an architectural configuration with three distributed consultants C for representing people (p), locations (l), and objects (o). If *DIST-PIA* (*DP* hereafter) is required, using this architecture, to refer to entity $m = p_5$, it will begin by creating an empty de-

---

[1]A preliminary description of this algorithm also appears in (Williams and Scheutz, 2017a).

Notation
C A set of *consultants* $\{c_0, \ldots, c_n\}$
c_m^{Λ} The set of formulae $\{\lambda_0, \ldots, \lambda_n\}$ advertised by the consultant $c \in C$ responsible for m.
M A robot's *world model* of entities $\{m_0 \ldots m_n\}$ found in the domains provided by C.
D The incrementally built up description, comprised of mappings from entities M to sets of pairs (λ, Γ) of formulae and bindings for those formulae.
D^M The set of entities $m \in M$ for which sub-descriptions have been created.
d^M The set of entities $m \in M$ involved in sub-description d.
P The set of candidate (λ, Γ) pairs under consideration for addition to a sub-description.
Q The queue of referents which must be described.
X The incrementally pruned set of distractors

Algorithm 1 $DIST\text{-}PIA(m, C)$

```
1:  D = new Map()  // The Description
2:  Q = new Queue(m)  // The Referent Queue
3:  while Q ≠ ∅ do
4:      // Consider the next referent
5:      mı = pop(Q)
6:      // Craft a description d for it
7:      d = DIST-PIA-HELPER(mı, C)
8:      D = D ∪ {m → d}
9:      // Find all entities used in d
10:     for all mıı ∈ dᴹ \ keys(D) do
11:         // And add undescribed entities to the queue
12:         push(Q, mıı)
13:     end for
14: end while
15: return D
```

Algorithm 2 $DIST\text{-}PIA\text{-}HELPER(m, C)$

```
1:  d = ∅  // The Sub-Description
2:  X = M \ m  // The Distractors
3:  // Initialize a set of properties to consider: those advertised
    by the consultant c responsible for m
4:  P = [∀λ ∈ cᴧₘ : (λ, ∅)]
5:  // While there are distractors to eliminate or properties to
    consider
6:  while X ≠ ∅ and P ≠ ∅ do
7:      (λ, Γ) = pop(P)
8:      // Find all unbound variables in the next property
9:      V = find_unbound(λ, Γ)
10:     if |V| > 1 then
11:         // If there's more than one, create copies of that prop-
            erty under all possible variable bindings that leaving
            unbound exactly one variable of the same type as the
            target referent
12:         for all Γı ∈ cross_bindings(λ, Γ, C) do
13:             // And push them onto the property list
14:             push(P, (λ, Γı))
15:         end for
16:         // Otherwise, if it is sufficiently probable that the
            property applies to the target referent...
17:     else if apply(cₘ, λ, Γ ∪ (v₀ → m)) > τ_dph then
18:         // And it's sufficiently probable that it does not apply
            to at least one distractor...
19:         X̄ = [x ∈ X | apply(cₓ, λ, Γ ∪ (v₀ → x)) > τ_dph]
20:         // Then bind its free variable to the target referent,
            and add it to the sub-description...
21:         if X̄ ≠ ∅ then
22:             // And remove any eliminated distractors
23:             d = d ∪ (λ, Γ ∪ (v₀ → m))
24:             X = X \ X̄
25:         end if
26:     end if
27: end while
28: return d
```

scription $D = \emptyset$ and a queue of referents to describe $Q = \{p_5\}$ (Tab. 1 Row **(1)**; Algorithm 1, Lines 1-2). Because there are still referents left to describe (Line 5), *DP* calls on its helper function *DIST-PIA-HELPER* (*DPH* hereafter) to craft a sub-description for p_5, which is popped off of Q (Line 7).

DPH begins by asking the consultant responsible for p_5 for a set of distractors X (e.g., $\{p_1, p_2, p_3, p_4\}$) and a set of properties P to consider (e.g., c_m^{Λ} = jim(X-p), jill(X-p), man(X-p), woman(X-p), lives-in(X-p,Y-l)), each of which *DPH* pairs with an empty set of bindings (Algorithm 2, Lines 1- 4). From this list, *DPH* pops the first unconsidered property (i.e., $jim(X - p)$) and its (empty) set of bindings. $jim(X - p)$ has exactly one unbound variable, so *DPH* will use **(2)** consultant p's *apply* method (as per Capability 3) to

ask how probable it is that $jim(X - p)$ applies to p_5. Suppose the returned probability is above threshold τ_{dph} (e.g., 60%). Because the chosen property does indeed apply to the target referent, *DPH* uses the same method to determine whether it also applies to any distractor x in X. Suppose this is only the case for p_2. The remaining distractors $\{p_1, p_3, p_4\}$ **(3)** will be removed from X and **(4)** $jim(p_5)$ will be added to sub-description d (Lines 17- 26).

DPH will then repeat this process with other properties. Suppose it is insufficiently probable that $jill(X - p)$ holds **(5)**: it will be ignored. Suppose it *is* sufficiently probable that $man(X - p)$ holds **(6)**, but that it is *also* sufficiently probable that it applies to the lone remaining distractor, p_2 **(7)**: it will

#	Act	Description	m	Sub-description	Distractors	Property	Property List
1	P	$\emptyset$	p_5	$\emptyset$	$\{p_1, p_2, p_3, p_4\}$	$\emptyset$	$\{jim(X\text{-}p), jill(X\text{-}p), man(X\text{-}p), wom(X\text{-}p), l\text{-}in(X\text{-}p, Y\text{-}l)\}$
2	A	$\emptyset$	p_5	$\emptyset$	$\{p_1, p_2, p_3, p_4\}$	$jim(X\text{-}p)$	$\{jill(X\text{-}p), man(X\text{-}p), wom(X\text{-}p), l\text{-}in(X\text{-}p, Y\text{-}l)\}$
3	E	$\emptyset$	p_5	$\emptyset$	$\{p_2\}$	$jim(X\text{-}p)$	$\{jill(X\text{-}p), man(X\text{-}p), wom(X\text{-}p), l\text{-}in(X\text{-}p, Y\text{-}l)\}$
4	d	$\emptyset$	p_5	$\{jim(p_5)\}$	$\{p_2\}$	$\emptyset$	$\{jill(X\text{-}p), man(X\text{-}p), wom(X\text{-}p), l\text{-}in(X\text{-}p, Y\text{-}l)\}$
5	A	$\emptyset$	p_5	$\{jim(p_5)\}$	$\{p_2\}$	$jill(X\text{-}p)$	$\{man(X\text{-}p), wom(X\text{-}p), l\text{-}in(X\text{-}p, Y\text{-}l)\}$
6	A	$\emptyset$	p_5	$\{jim(p_5)\}$	$\{p_2\}$	$man(X\text{-}p)$	$\{wom(X\text{-}p), l\text{-}in(X\text{-}p, Y\text{-}l)\}$
7	E	$\emptyset$	p_5	$\{jim(p_5)\}$	$\{p_2\}$	$man(X\text{-}p)$	$\{wom(X\text{-}p), l\text{-}in(X\text{-}p, Y\text{-}l)\}$
8	A	$\emptyset$	p_5	$\{jim(p_5)\}$	$\{p_2\}$	$wom(X\text{-}p)$	$\{l\text{-}in(X\text{-}p, Y\text{-}l)\}$
9	B	$\emptyset$	p_5	$\{jim(p_5)\}$	$\{p_2\}$	$l\text{-}in(X\text{-}p, Y\text{-}l)$	$\{l\text{-}in(X\text{-}p, l_1), l\text{-}in(X\text{-}p, l_2), l\text{-}in(X\text{-}p, l_3)\}$
10	A	$\emptyset$	p_5	$\{jim(p_5)\}$	$\{p_2\}$	$l\text{-}in(X\text{-}p, l_1)$	$\{l\text{-}in(X\text{-}p, l_2), l\text{-}in(X\text{-}p, l_3)\}$
11	E	$\emptyset$	p_5	$\{jim(p_5)\}$	$\emptyset$	$l\text{-}in(X\text{-}p, l_1)$	$\{l\text{-}in(X\text{-}p, l_2), l\text{-}in(X\text{-}p, l_3)\}$
12	d	$\emptyset$	p_5	$\{jim(p_5), l\text{-}in(p_5, l_1)\}$	$\emptyset$	$\emptyset$	$\{l\text{-}in(X\text{-}p, l_2), l\text{-}in(X\text{-}p, l_3)\}$
13	D	$\{jim(p_5), l\text{-}in(p_5, l_1)\}$	$\emptyset$	$\emptyset$	$\emptyset$	$\emptyset$	$\emptyset$
14	P	$\{jim(p_5), l\text{-}in(p_5, l_1)\}$	l_1	$\emptyset$	$\{l_2, l_3\}$	$\emptyset$	$\{som(X\text{-}l), cam(X\text{-}l), mass(X\text{-}l), in(X\text{-}l, Y\text{-}l)\}$
15	A	$\{jim(p_5), l\text{-}in(p_5, l_1)\}$	l_1	$\emptyset$	$\{l_2, l_3\}$	$som(X\text{-}l)$	$\{cam(X\text{-}l), mass(X\text{-}l), in(X\text{-}l, Y\text{-}l)\}$
16	E	$\{jim(p_5), l\text{-}in(p_5, l_1)\}$	l_1	$\emptyset$	$\emptyset$	$som(X\text{-}l)$	$\{cam(X\text{-}l), mass(X\text{-}l), in(X\text{-}l, Y\text{-}l)\}$
17	d	$\{jim(p_5), l\text{-}in(p_5, l_1)\}$	l_1	$\{som(l_1)\}$	$\emptyset$	$\emptyset$	$\{cam(X\text{-}l), mass(X\text{-}l), in(X\text{-}l, Y\text{-}l)\}$
18	D	$\{jim(p_5), l\text{-}in(p_5, l_1), som(l_1)\}$	$\emptyset$	$\emptyset$	$\emptyset$	$\emptyset$	$\emptyset$

Table 1: WALKTHROUGH SUMMARY.
Column Two summarizes action taken: **P**repare, **A**ssess, **E**liminate, **B**ind, **d**-append, or **D**-append.
Some predicates are abbreviated, and predicate/binding tuples are rewritten as bound predicates.

be ignored. Suppose it is insufficiently probable that $woman(X - p)$ holds (**8**): it will be ignored. Finally, DPH will consider $lives\text{-}in(X - p, Y - l)$. Unlike the previous properties, this has two unbound variables. DPH will thus use (**9**) $cross\_bindings$ to create a set of candidate variable bindings for this property, each of which leaves exactly one variable for which p is responsible unbound. Suppose l knows of locations l_1, l_2, and l_3: $cross\_bindings$ will return $(lives\text{-}in(X - p, Y - l), \{Y \to ls_1\})$, $(lives\text{-}in(X - p, Y - l), \{Y \to ls_2\})$, and $(lives\text{-}in(X - p, Y - l), \{Y \to ls_3\})$, each of which will be added onto P for DPH to consider. (Lines 10- 15).

Suppose it is sufficiently probable (**10**) that $(lives\text{-}in(X - p, l_1))$ applies to p_5 but not to the lone remaining distractor (p_2), allowing p_2 to be ruled out (**11**). $lives\text{-}in(X - p, Y - l)$ will be added (**12**) to d and $\{p_2\}$ will be removed from X. Since X is now empty, the sub-description $p_5 \to \{jim(p_5), lives\text{-}in(p_5, l_1)\}$ will be returned (**13**) to DP (Line 28). Notice that this sub-description refers to an entity (l_1) which itself needs to be described. Accordingly, l_1 will be added to Q (**14**), and because it is the only entity on the queue, immediately popped and sent back to DPH.

As before, DPH begins by asking the consultant responsible for l_1 for a set of distractors X (e.g., $\{p_2, l_3\}$) and a set of properties P to consider (e.g., c_m^Λ = somerville(X-l), cambridge(X-l), massachusetts(X-l), in(X-l,Y-l)), which it considers one at a time. Suppose it is sufficiently probable that $somerville(X - l)$ applies to l_1 (**15**) but not to distractors l_2 or l_3 (**16**): it will be added (**17**) to d, $\{l_2, l_3\}$ will be removed from X, and $l_1 \to \{somerville(l_1)\}$ will be returned (**18**) to DP. Finally, since Q is empty, DP will return $\{p_5 \to \{jim(p_5), lives\text{-}in(p_5, l_1)\}, l_1 \to \{somerville(l_1)\}\}$ (Algorithm 1, Line 15). It will be the responsibility of the next component of the natural language pipeline to translate this into an RE along the lines of "Jim, who lives in Somerville"[2].

---

[2]The integration of *DIST-PIA* with the remaining natural language components of our robot architecture is described in our other recent work (Williams and Scheutz, 2017b).

5 Evaluation

Traditional REG evaluation metrics (e.g., *Dice* (Gatt et al., 2007) and *MASI* (Passonneau, 2006)) compare algorithm- and human-chosen attributes by measuring the distance (e.g., set difference) between machine- and human-generated attribute sets. Recently, however, this methodology has come under criticism, as the semantic similarity of two attribute sets does not imply similarity between the *effectiveness* of those two sets. That is, this methodology does not necessarily assess how well a generated RE actually allows a target to be picked out by a hearer – the presumed purpose of REG algorithms (Van Deemter and Gatt, 2009). Recently, there has been a shift towards *task-based* evaluations (e.g., (Byron et al., 2009; Koller et al., 2010; Viethen and Dale, 2006)), in which algorithms are compared by how well they allow some task to be achieved.

The previously discussed uncertainty-handling REG algorithms have mainly used task-based evaluations in which an image provided to participants is also provided to the algorithm. This necessarily conflates the evaluation of the algorithm with the evaluation of the visual classifiers used to process that image. Furthermore, it prevents direct comparison between the algorithm and both other algorithms (unless they use identical classifiers) and humans. It is thus imperative to develop a *new* evaluation framework that allows an REG algorithm to receive information about attribute uncertainty without visually processing the scene.

We will now present an evaluation framework that achieves this goal through two stages. In Stage One, participants are shown an environment, and are asked to provide (1) an RE referring to an indicated entity, and (2) probability judgments that particular attributes hold for indicated entities. The probability judgments can be used to train REG algorithms to assess whether various attributes hold without committing to particular classifiers. In Stage Two, new participants are shown the same environments, along with either human- or machine-generated REs, and asked to indicate the described entity. This framework thus allows REG algorithms to be compared to both other algorithms and humans under uncertainty.

5.1 Stage One

In the first stage of the evaluation, participants were each shown three randomly-ordered scenes (a kitchen, an office, and a near-featureless room, as seen in Fig. 1)[3], one of which contained a red bounding box around an object. This object was either an object that only appeared in that scene, an object for which an identical object appeared in a different scene, or an object for which one of the same type (but, for example, of a different color) appeared in a different scene, yielding five task-relevant objects in each scene. Each image also contained around five salient irrelevant objects. Finally, because each participant was simultaneously shown three scenes, the rooms themselves also serve as anchors with respect to which referents could be described.

Participants were told to imagine that a future participant would tour the three rooms shown in the pictures in a random order, and in one of the rooms, receive a description of an object. Participants were told to write the description that the future participant should receive. After each participant provided a description, they were asked to evaluate how well the target object matched each of twenty attributes (randomly selected from a total of 52 informally collected attributes such as "is blue", "is a marker", and "is in the kitchen" by re-positioning [0-100] sliders from an initial position of 50.

Participants (56 male, 33 female; mean age 35 (sd=11.65)) were recruited through Amazon Mechanical Turk and paid small cash. Each participant was shown a random target object, providing us with an average of 10 REs per target object and 3.8 probability judgments for each attribute for each object. Gold standard semantic parses (i.e., sets of logical formulae representing properties and relations) were then crafted for each human-generated RE.

Next, two consultants were created which were provided with, respectively, a subset of the objects and locations found in the three scenes. When these consultants are asked for the probability that an entity has a particular attribute, they return the mean probability judgment provided by participants. Finally, each consultant was provided with a preference ordering over properties. While this ordering

---

[3]In future work it would of course be valuable to perform a more comprehensive evaluation with a larger variety of scenes.

Figure 1: Scenes Shown to Participants

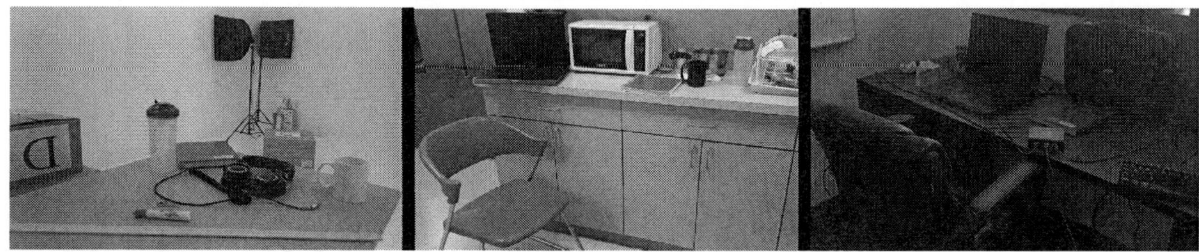

In the scene to the left, the possible target referents in the two evaluation stages were the waterbottle, headphones, and mug; in the middle scene, these were the laptop, chair, and notebook; in the right scene, these were the briefcase, book, and marker.

was hand constructed, we would eventually like to learn similar orderings from data.

DIST-PIA was then used to generate attribute sets for each of the nine target referents, as shown in Tab. 2. We then combined these with the attribute sets derived from human utterances, yielding an average of 9.56 (sd=3.13) unique sets of attributes per target object. For each attribute set, we crafted one RE using a predefined template. This conversion from REs to logical form and back allows us to control for consistent phrasing. Because one RE was produced for each unique property set, an average of 9.56 (sd=3.13) REs were created per target object.

5.2 Stage Two

In the second stage, a new set of participants were shown the same images, but without bounding boxes, shown a randomly selected human- or machine-driven RE for that referent, and asked to click on the described object. After each image, participants were notified as to whether they had clicked on the correct object.

Participants were recruited through Amazon Mechanical Turk (62 male, 46 female; mean age 35.07 (sd=10.14)) and paid small cash. Each of the 85 unique REs was thus shown to an average of 11.44 participants. Recall, however, that these utterances were crafted based on property sets either chosen by *DIST-PIA* or extracted from the utterances collected from participants in Stage One. Because some of these property sets were identical, each of the unique REs in this section really corresponds to a *cluster* of human- or machine-driven property sets. We thus computed how accurately each property set allowed the true target referent to be picked out. Ranking clusters by accuracy, we can then compute an overall

accuracy percentile for *DIST-PIA*, i.e., the percent of RE generators (in this case, humans) compared to which *DIST-PIA* achieved higher accuracy.

5.3 Results and Discussion

Overall, *DIST-PIA* allowed successful identification in 91.4% of cases. On average, the REs crafted using *DIST-PIA*-chosen properties were as or more successful than those crafted using the properties chosen by 45.7% (sd−23.9) of human participants, suggesting that *DIST-PIA* was nearly as effective as humans in choosing properties. *DIST-PIA's* performance would further improve if given more sophisticated consultants. To fairly evaluate *DIST-PIA*, we provided it with consultants that only made judgments based on the attributes used in our pilot study. Even simple knowledge of what relations were *symmetric* would have increased performance.

It is important to note that because *DIST-PIA* is domain independent, it does not *compete* with the classifiers used by previous approaches, which could be integrated into our framework as consultants, allowing for direct comparison of disparate classifiers. And, while our evaluation *presented* all information visually (as we needed participants to be able to unambiguously select referents in an intuitive, static, online environment) it is critical to point out that our evaluation avoided *reliance* on specific visual classifiers: the generality of our consultant framework means that, like the *IA* (but unlike previous REG algorithms which have handled uncertainty), we could easily use consultants that assess non-visual traits (e.g., object costs, utterance sentiments, people professions, room temperatures).

Finally, *DIST-PIA* did not "nicely overspecify" in some conditions where humans did. For example,

Table 2: Properties Chosen by *DIST-PIA*

ID	Properties	Translation	Acc.	Rank
1	notebook(X)	The notebook	80%	11 of 11
2	Dell(X),laptop(X),blue(Y), chair(Y),in-front-of(Y,X)	The Dell laptop that the blue chair is in front of.	85.7%	5* of 10
3	blue(X),chair(X)	The blue chair.	97.8%	2 of 3
4	laptop-bag(X)	The laptop-bag.	100%	1 of 5
5	textbook(X),laptop-bag(Y), behind(Y,X)	The textbook that the laptop-bag is behind.	63.6%	5 of 10
6	red(X),whiteboard-marker(X)	The red whiteboard-marker.	86.7%	6 of 10
7	headphones(X)	The headphones.	100%	1* of 13
8	shaker-bottle(X), headphones(Y),next-to(X,Y)	The shaker-bottle next to the head-phones.	85.7%	3* of 13
9	coffee-mug(X)	The coffee-mug.	100%	1* of 10

"Accuracy" denotes percent of participants who chose the correct object when given the machine-driven RE. "Rank" compares this with human-driven REs. * denotes a tie. For example, when "The notebook" was used, 80% of participants chose the correct object, but all other REs for that object yielded higher accuracy. In contrast, "The textbook that the laptop-bag is behind" had only 63.6% accuracy, but this was a higher than was achieved by all but four of the unique human-driven REs for that object.

DIST-PIA's choice of simply $notebook(X)$ for the first target object achieved 80% success rate, but had the lowest ranking for that object, in part because most humans used descriptions involving $red(X)$ to draw the eye away from distractors like the green book. The traditional *IA* captures this effect by placing colors at a high priority. However, unlike the traditional *IA*, we chose to handle the object's "type" (e.g., "bottle") and variants thereof (e.g., "waterbottle") just like any other properties, so that we would not need to specify an additional mandatory consultant capability (i.e., the ability to provide the "type" of a candidate object). This required us to place these type-like properties at the top of the preference orderings, to make sure that *type* was always used. When presented the trade-off, we chose generality of architectural mechanisms over performance gain.

6 Conclusion

In this paper, we make three main contributions. First, we presented a domain independent algorithm for REG under uncertainty, which separates the problems of referring expression generation and reference resolution from the task of *property assessment*. Second, we presented a novel evaluation framework which allows REG algorithms designed for uncertain contexts to be evaluated without conflating the performance of the *algorithm* with the performance of the *classifiers used by the algorithm*, and which uses human probability judgments to better facilitate comparison to human performance. Using this framework, we showed that *DIST-PIA* exhibited REG capabilities comparable to those of humans. Finally, we have taken the realities of modern integrated agent architectures into account through our *consultant framework*, which allows information to be distributed across multiple heterogeneous KBs (Williams and Scheutz, 2016).

In future work, our thresholds should be learned from data, and Dempster-Shafer Theoretic uncertainty representations should be used to better handle ignorance (Williams et al., 2015). *DIST-PIA* should also be modified to incorporate audience design considerations, similar to Horacek (2005). Finally, *DIST-PIA* should be modified to use use Givenness-Hierarchy Theoretic mechanisms (Williams et al., 2016) in conjunction with a multi-modal reference model to generate deictic and anaphoric REs.

Acknowledgments

This research was in part funded by grant N00014-14-1-0149 from the US Office of Naval Research. We would also like to thank Lars Kunze for constructive conversations which contributed to our evaluation framework.

References

Donna Byron, Alexander Koller, Kristina Striegnitz, Justine Cassell, Robert Dale, Johanna Moore, and Jon Oberlander. 2009. Report on the first NLG challenge on generating instructions in virtual environments (GIVE). In *Proceedings of the 12th European Workshop on Natural Language Generation (ENLG)*, pages 165–173. Association for Computational Linguistics.

Robert Dale and Ehud Reiter. 1995. Computational interpretations of the gricean maxims in the generation of referring expressions. *Cognitive Science*, 19(2):233–263.

Robert Dale. 1989. Cooking up referring expressions. In *Proceedings of the 27th annual meeting on Association for Computational Linguistics (ACL)*, pages 68–75.

Rui Fang, Changsong Liu, Lanbo She, and Joyce Y Chai. 2013. Towards situated dialogue: Revisiting referring expression generation. In *Proceedings of Empirical Methods on Natural Language Processing (EMNLP)*, pages 392–402.

Rui Fang, Malcolm Doering, and Joyce Y Chai. 2015. Embodied Collaborative Referring Expression Generation in Situated Human-Robot Interaction. In *Proceedings of the 10th International Conference on Human-Robot Interaction (HRI)*, pages 271–278.

Albert Gatt, Ielka van der Sluis, and Kees van Deemter. 2007. Evaluating algorithms for the generation of referring expressions using a balanced corpus. In *Proceedings of the Eleventh European Workshop on Natural Language Generation (ENLG)*, pages 49–56, Stroudsburg, PA, USA. Association for Computational Linguistics.

Helmut Horacek. 2005. Generating referential descriptions under conditions of uncertainty. In *Proceedings of the 10th European Workshop on Natural Language Generation (ENLG)*, pages 58–67.

Alexander Koller, Kristina Striegnitz, Andrew Gargett, Donna Byron, Justine Cassell, Robert Dale, Johanna Moore, and Jon Oberlander. 2010. Report on the second NLG challenge on generating instructions in virtual environments (GIVE-2). In *Proceedings of the 6th International Conference on Natural Language Generation (INLG)*, pages 243–250. Association for Computational Linguistics.

Sébastien Konieczny. 2000. On the difference between merging knowledge bases and combining them. In *Proceedings of Knowledge Representation (KR)*, pages 135–144.

Emiel Krahmer and Kees Van Deemter. 2012. Computational generation of referring expressions: A survey. *Computational Linguistics*, 38(1):173–218.

Paolo Liberatore and Marco Schaerf. 1998. Arbitration (or how to merge knowledge bases). *IEEE Transactions on Knowledge and Data Engineering*, 10(1):76–90.

Jinxin Lin. 1996. Integration of weighted knowledge bases. *Artificial Intelligence*, 83(2):363–378.

Timothy Meo, Brian McMahan, and Matthew Stone. 2014. Generating and resolving vague color references. *Proceedings of The 18th Workshop on the Semantics and Pragmatics of Dialogue (SemDial)*, pages 107–115.

Rebecca Passonneau. 2006. Measuring agreement on set-valued items (MASI) for semantic and pragmatic annotation. In *In Proceedings of the International Conference on Language Resources and Evaluation (LREC)*.

Morgan Quigley, Josh Faust, Tully Foote, and Jeremy Leibs. 2009. ROS: an open-source robot operating system. In *ICRA Workshop on Open Source Software*.

Deb K Roy. 2002. Learning visually grounded words and syntax for a scene description task. *Computer Speech & Language*, 16(3):353–385.

Amir Sadovnik, Andrew Gallagher, and Tsuhan Chen. 2013. Not everybody's special: Using neighbors in referring expressions with uncertain attributes. In *Proceedings of the IEEE Conference on Computer Vision and Pattern Recognition Workshops (CVPR)*, pages 269–276.

Matthias Scheutz, Gordon Briggs, Rehj Cantrell, Evan Krause, Tom Williams, and Richard Veale. 2013. Novel mechanisms for natural human-robot interactions in the DIARC architecture. In *Proceedings of the AAAI Workshop on Intelligent Robotic Systems*.

Kees Van Deemter and Albert Gatt. 2009. Beyond DICE: measuring the quality of a referring expression. In *n Proceedings of the Workshop on Production of Referring Expressions: Bridging Computational and Psycholinguistic Approaches (preCogSci-09)*.

Kees Van Deemter. 2016. *Computational Models of Referring: A Study in Cognitive Science*. MIT Press.

Jette Viethen and Robert Dale. 2006. Towards the evaluation of referring expression generation. In *Proceedings of the 4th Australasian Language Technology Workshop*, pages 115–122, Sydney, Australia.

Tom Williams and Matthias Scheutz. 2016. A framework for resolving open-world referential expressions in distributed heterogeneous knowledge bases. In *Proceedings of the 30th AAAI Conference on Artificial Intelligence (AAAI)*, pages 3958–3964.

Tom Williams and Matthias Scheutz. 2017a. Referring expression generation under uncertainty in integrated robot architectures. In *Proceedings of Robotics: Science and Systems Workshop on Human-Centered*

Robotics: Interaction, Physiological Integration and Autonomy.

Tom Williams and Matthias Scheutz. 2017b. Resolution of referential ambiguity in human-robot dialogue using dempster-shafer theoretic pragmatics. In *Proceedings of Robotics: Science and Systems (RSS)*.

Tom Williams, Gordon Briggs, Bradley Oosterveld, and Matthias Scheutz. 2015. Going beyond command-based instructions: Extending robotic natural language interaction capabilities. In *Proceedings of 29th AAAI Conference on Artificial Intelligence*, pages 1387–1393.

Tom Williams, Saurav Acharya, Stephanie Schreitter, and Matthias Scheutz. 2016. Situated open world reference resolution for human-robot dialogue. In *Proceedings of the 11th ACM/IEEE International Conference on Human-Robot Interaction*, pages 311–318.

Sina Zarrieß and David Schlangen. 2016. Towards generating colour terms for referents in photographs: Prefer the expected or the unexpected? In *Proceedings of the 9th International Natural Language Generation conference (INLG)*.

Natural Language Descriptions for Human Activities in Video Streams

Nouf Al Harbi

Department of Computer Science, University of Sheffield, Sheffield, United Kingdom
Department of Computer Science and Engineering, Taibah University, Medina, Saudi Arabia
`nmalharbi1@sheffield.ac.uk`

Yoshihiko Gotoh

Department of Computer Science, University of Sheffield, Sheffield, United Kingdom
`y.gotoh@sheffield.ac.uk`

Abstract

There has been continuous growth in the volume and ubiquity of video material. It has become essential to define video semantics in order to aid the searchability and retrieval of this data. We present a framework that produces textual descriptions of video, based on the visual semantic content. Detected action classes rendered as verbs, participant objects converted to noun phrases, visual properties of detected objects rendered as adjectives and spatial relations between objects rendered as prepositions. Further, in cases of zero-shot action recognition, a language model is used to infer a missing verb, aided by the detection of objects and scene settings. These extracted features are converted into textual descriptions using a template-based approach. The proposed video descriptions framework evaluated on the NLDHA dataset using ROUGE scores and human judgment evaluation.

1 Introduction

The field of computer vision has advanced to detect humans, identify their activities, or to discriminate between a large number of object classes and assign them attributes. The outcome is usually a compact semantic representation that encodes activities associated with object categories. Such representations could be easily processed and interpreted by automatic systems. However, the natural way to convey this kind of information to humans is through natural language. Thus, this paper addresses the issue of producing textual descriptions for human activities in videos. This task has a range of applications, such as human-computer/robot interaction,

video summarising, indexing and retrieval. Furthermore, translation between visual video content and language provides a solid foundation for understanding relations between vision and linguistics, as they are the closest modalities to interact with humans.

Generating textual descriptions of visual content is an intriguing task that requires a combination of two major research aspects: visual recognition approaches and natural language generation (NLG) techniques. To generate descriptions for videos and images, a template-based approach is a powerful tool though one which needs to be manually identified (Kulkarni et al., 2011; Barbu et al., 2012; Gygli et al., 2014a; Khan et al., 2015). An alternative approach is to retrieve descriptive sentences from a training corpus based on visual similarity, or to utilise externally textual-based corpora to help rank the visual detections (Farhadi et al., 2010; Kuznetsova et al., 2012; Mitchell et al., 2012; Hanckmann et al., 2012; Das et al., 2013b).

The most relevant researches to us are the (Khan et al., 2015) and (Barbu et al., 2012). Both of these approaches identify high-level features (HLFs) such as humans, chairs, and so forth, and generate textual descriptions using a template-based approach. (Khan et al., 2015) propose a method that relies on treating a video as a sequence of frames, and performs image detection for each frame independently, to identify HLFs without exploiting the temporal domain. Alternatively, (Barbu et al., 2012) have used a dataset with simple video settings where only one action is performed. Consequently, their natural language descriptions consist of one sentence.

In contrast, this study focuses on generating de-

Proceedings of The 10th International Natural Language Generation conference, pages 85–94,
Santiago de Compostela, Spain, September 4-7 2017. ©2017 Association for Computational Linguistics

scriptions of human activities in videos sequences at a shot-based level, relying mainly on visual detections. Specifically, objects tracks and their visual attributions are extracted from each shot, along with their spatial and temporal relations. In cases of zero-shot action recognition, where no verb (action class) is assigned for a given track, the detected objects classes are used to mine the relative verb from web-scale textual corpora via incorporated text-mined likelihoods. Structuring videos at shot-level enables us to utilise the temporal information associated with video data. Finally, the set of detected HLFs will be used to generate the final description for the video using a template-based approach.

2 Related Work

Video data introduces the additional dimension of time, with an associated set of challenges, such as temporal continuity. The majority of the literature pertaining to video descriptions has centred around two fundamental themes: deriving the description from semantic visual content and/or mining the relevant description from text-based corpora.

(Barbu et al., 2012) demonstrate a method whereby a single sentential description of a short video is generated by visual recognition techniques to render the language entities; specifically an event recognition approach is utilised to identify object tracks, role assignment and body posture variability. Finally, generation is achieved by pre-defined templates for each event class, in the form of subject-action-object. (Khan et al., 2015) and (Hanckmann et al., 2012) introduce a video description framework which starts with the extraction of the set of HLFs by the implementation of conventional image processing techniques. Context-free grammar (CFG) is used next to convert the extracted concepts into natural language descriptions. The drawback of these techniques is that they rely on only a limited set of high-level concepts, without exploiting text mined from text-based corpora. Moreover, videos are manipulated as sequences of images; hence no interaction between objects is considered over the time domain.

(Guadarrama et al., 2013) introduce a new framework that addresses the challenges associated with describing activities 'in-the-wild'. The method encompasses a wide range of verbs, objects and functions in an out-of-domain manner that does not necessitate videos consisting of the precise activity. If it is unable to provide a precise prediction by using the pre-trained model, it will generate a more concise and credible answer. The semantic hierarchies are learned from web-based corpora in order to decide upon the most suitable degree of generalisation. However, this work focuses on short videos clips that depict one activity; hence the resulting descriptions consist of single sentences, without investigation of any temporal associations between objects.

(Gygli et al., 2014b) describe a novel way to carry out video summarisation, the process of which is initiated by segmenting the video via the use of a 'super-frame'. Then, the degree to which the visuals are appealing is approximated for every super-frame with the use of low-, mid- and high-level characteristics. On the basis of this scoring method, an ideal subset of super-frames is chosen to produce an informative summary. However, this approach concentrates mainly on subject, verb, object (SVO) triples, without taking into account the spatial and temporal associations between objects.

(Thomason et al., 2014) integrate the use of linguistics and computer vision techniques in order to enhance the description of objects in real-life videos. They propose a method through which textual descriptions of videos could be generated by combining visual detections with language statistics, via the use of a factor graph model. A conventional visual detection system was used to detect and score objects, activities and scenes involved in the video. Then, the factor graph model combines these detection confidences with probabilistic knowledge mined from text corpora to estimate the most likely subject, verb, object, and place. Again, this study targets videos with single activity without identification of spatial and temporal relations.

In contrast to earlier researches, through which individual presences have been determined through the use of the DPM model (Felzenszwalb et al., 2010) at a frame-based level, our approach is different in several important ways. We consider the video as 3D (x, y, t), and consequently individual detection is achieved by the recent human body segmentation approach introduced in (Al Harbi and Gotoh,

verbs:	clap, wave, jog, run, walk, dive, kick, lift, ride, skate, swing, answer phone, drive, eat, fight, kiss, hug, sit down, sit up, stand up, get out, hand shake, approach, carry, catch, collide, drop, high five, depart and touch
nouns:	man, women, baby, child , person, bird, cat, cow, dog, horse, sheep, aeroplane, bicycle, boat, bus, car, motorbike, train, bottle, chair, dining table, potted plant, sofa, phone, TV/monitor, home, road, bedroom, park, hotel , kitchen, living room , office, restaurant and shop
prepositions:	in, on, next to, to the left, to the right, under, beside, above and inside
conjunctions:	and, after, before, while, later, then, next, finally
adverbs:	away and toward
adjectives:	small, big, young, old, angry, happy, sad, surprised, serious and disgust
pronouns:	he, she, they, him and her
articles:	a, an, the
auxiliary:	is

Table 1: The set of vocabulary used to produce textual descriptions of video.

2015b). This approach is designed for video data, to alleviate the shortcomings of the DPM model, such as partial occlusion, background noise and temporal variation. As a result it provides reliable physical interpretations. Visual attributes for regions of detected salience are extracted, along with their spatial and temporal relations, to avoid generating long, complex and unnatural textual descriptions. The video in this approach is structured as a sequence of shots, to preserve the order of activities, combining the sentence description of each shot to generate a coherent multi-sentence video description at the required level of detail. Additionally, our work utilises a language model trained on text-based corpora only in cases of zero-shot action recognition, where no action class is detected, drawing on detected object tracks and scene setting information.

3 Framework for Generating Textual Video Description

Figure 1 shows the overall approach for the video description task, while Table 1 illustrates the set of vocabulary used to generate textual descriptions of video. The generating of video descriptions task basically includes two main modules: content planning and a surface realizer. In our system, the content planning is mainly accomplished by improved visual recognition techniques, with the exception of the case of zero-shot action recognition, where language statistics are utilised to infer the verb class, given the detected subject and object classes. For the surface realizer stage, the template-based approach is used to generate a single sentence shot-based description. The following describes each of these components in turn.

3.1 Visual recognition of Subjects

As humans are the main participants in the video activities, in this study the role of subject is assigned to human objects if they are present. A recent model that detects and segments human body regions across video frames is utilised (Al Harbi and Gotoh, 2015b), rather than using the human detector of (Felzenszwalb et al., 2010), which is used by all previous works in generating video descriptions. This approach improves visual detection by focusing only on human regions rather than on holistic features (*e.g.*dense trajectories). As a result, a list of human objects tracks is extracted which will be used for further processing to identify their adjective attributes, such as gender (Bekios-Calfa et al., 2011), age (Horng et al., 2001) and emotion (Garg and Choudhary, 2012), using conventional image processing techniques.

3.2 Visual recognition of Objects

We used the discriminatively trained part-based models from (Felzenszwalb et al., 2010) in order to detect the non-human objects present in each video, creating a store of twenty object classes: bird, cat, cow, dog, horse, sheep, aeroplane, bicycle, boat, bus, car, motorbike, train, bottle, chair, dining table, potted plant, sofa, phone and TV/monitor. As these object detectors are mainly designed for images, they are applied to each keyframe, in order to obtain the maximum scores allocated to each objects, and top two objects are chosen per frame to reduce the false positive detections.

3.3 Visual recognition of Verbs

We aim to process and represent complex actions that are difficult to track efficiently using conventional descriptors. To this end a recent model for action representation that relies on extracted human regions is used from (Al Harbi and Gotoh, 2015b). It formulates a descriptor that encompasses the static and dynamic features of detected segments. After several trials the classifier is applied every ten frames, to assign a human objects track with the appropriate action class. In our experiment, 30 different action classes are used to train the model, with an extra negative class that is assign to any action that doesnt appear in the training data.

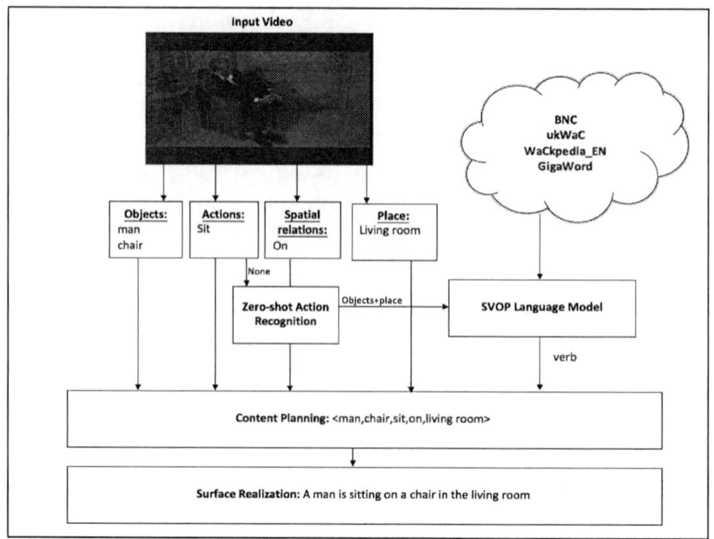

Figure 1: Summary of proposed framework of generation of video description.

3.4 Visual recognition of Prepositions

Generating elaborate textual descriptions demands more than simply applying object detection and event recognition. Producing a sentence with the embedding of spatial relations as a prepositional phrase requires the extraction of spatial relations between the detected interacting objects. To efficiently and accurately represent the relationships between the interacting objects present in a video stream, the AngledCORE-9 is adopted in (Al Harbi and Gotoh, 2015a) is utilised. Firstly, an approximated region of OBB is replaced with a space-time volume for detected objects and for each extracted region a tight OBB is drawn. Finally, the compact CORE-9 representation is used to extract the spatial and temporal aspects for multiple inter-related object bodies by analysing the nine cores and six intervals in each binary relation. Compared to the commonly used representation CORE-9, the object-volume based method has a higher chance of generating reliable results regarding the direction of objects, topologies, size, distances and temporal changes. Symmetric relations are not allowed between any pairs, to eliminate the redundancy. In this study, the following prepositions are identified, including in, on, away from, next to, to the left, to the right, under, toward, beside, above and inside.

3.5 Visual recognition of Scene Settings

In order to accurately identify the scene featured in the corpus for this study, the environment recognition method suggested by (Zhou et al., 2014) was employed. The method was used to identify the scene setting of the first frame in each shot whether it was an indoor or an outdoor scene, with a ranked list of the five most likely place categories. For this experiment, 12 different scenes settings are exist and recognised for both between indoor and outdoor settings, for each of which the associated preposition is assigned manually.

3.6 Zero-shot Language Statistics

Our approach to generating a textual video description relies mainly on visual semantic content. However, there is a case called zero-shot action recognition where is the action recognition system is unable to identify the performed action, as the action has not previously appeared in the training data; in this case a negative class is assigned. Subsequently, language statistics will be used to predict the missing verb (action class), given a detected objects classes and recognised scene settings.

Language statistics are mined from four large text-based English corpora. As in (Thomason et al., 2014) the dependency parser[1] is used to parse

---

[1]The spacy's API: https://spacy.io

text from the following corpora: English Giga-word, British National Corpus (BNC), ukWac and WaCkypedia-EN. The quadruple of SVOP (subject, verb, object, place) are extracted using the dependency parser. The subject-verb relations are extracted on the basis of nsubj dependencies, while the verb-object relations are identified by dobj and prep dependencies (prep dependencies are used in order to account for intransitive verbs that occur with prepositional objects). Object-place relations are extracted by utilising the prep dependencies where the noun affected by the preposition belong to the recognisable places list.

The quadruple frequency of SVOP are maintained and if no object or place is present in the sentence, their values in the quadruple are None. For the best performance, the frequency counts are a python dictionary with verbs as keys, and for each verb we keep the count of each context (subject, object, place) that co-occurs with that verb. To propose the best verb for a given context, the conditional probability $P(V|S, O, P)$ is calculated by maximum likelihood estimate (MLE) as follows:

$$P(V|S, O, P) = \frac{P(V,S,O,P)}{P(S,O,P)} = \frac{Count(V,S,O,P)}{Count(S,O,P)} \tag{1}$$

The verb with high probability given the context of subject, object and place is chosen to generate the sentence.

3.7 Sentence Generation

Finally, the extracted information from previous stages will be used to generate informative descriptions for each shot. For this purpose the template-based approach will be used. The same template will be used to create a description for each human track present in the video shot, if no human track is detected the object is considered as a subject and described in term of it motion. The list of generated sentences will be further processed to generate a coherent description. Like (Thomason et al., 2014), the following template will be used for the generation task:

'Determiner (A, The) - Adjective (optional)- Subject - Verb (Present Continuous) - Preposition (optional) - Determiner (A, The) - Adjective (optional) - Object (optional) - Preposition (optional) - Deter-miner (A,The) - Place (optional)'.

For implementation purposes, the surface realizer simpleNLG is utilised (Gatt and Reiter, 2009). This package also provides some extra processing applied automatically to the generated sentence: (1) the first letter is capitalised for each sentence; (2) -ing is attached to the verb if the progressive tense is chosen; (3) the words are assembled in the correct grammatical order; (4) white spaces are automatically added to separate words; and (5) at the end of each sentence a full stop is inserted.

3.8 Creating Cohesive Descriptions

Our system independently describes each video shot. The generated multi-sentence descriptions for the video as a whole tend to be a 'list of sentences' rather than a coherent 'text'. Generating coherent natural language descriptions requires linking sentences at a surface level without any need for deep understanding of the text produced. Hence, the generated list of sentences for each video is automatically post-processed at two levels shot-level and video-level in order to create more cohesive and informative descriptions. First, each human track in each shot will be described independently in a complete sentence, which results in a list of sentences describing a given shot. The following set of rules is applied in order to generate compact and coherent sentence:

1. When multiple subjects perform the same action at the same time, the subjects of these sentences are combined by 'and'. (*e.g.*If (i) 'A man is eating.' and (ii) 'A woman is eating.' these are combined to become (iii) 'A man and woman are eating.')

2. If multiple subjects perform different action simultaneously, they will be combined using 'while'. (*e.g.*in Figure 2 (a)(b)).

3. In the case where multiple subjects interact to create certain common actions (*e.g.*hug or fight), one is considered as the subject while the other(s) serve as objects in the sentence. (*e.g.*If (i) 'A man is fighting.' and (ii) 'A man is fighting.' these are combined to become (iii) 'A man is fighting another man.')

4. Proper pronouns (co-reference) are added if multiple verbs are allocated to the same subject during the same video shot. In this case, when a subject is mentioned again after its debut, a proper pronoun is used to improve the sentences concision. (*e.g.*in Figure 2 (c)(d)).

Secondly, shot-based descriptions are combined to produce the final video description. For this purpose the following rules are applied:

1. Temporal adverbials (*e.g.*next, then and finally) are incorporated between subsequent sentences as a powerful device for conserving the logical order of events performed over different shots.

2. Scene-setting information is added only to the leading sentence and discarded from subsequent sentences if the event take place in the same setting to eliminate redundancy.

3. The phrase 'In this video,' is added to the leading sentence of each video description.

4 Experiments and results

This section presents the evaluation procedure of our video description framework on the NLDHA dataset introduced in (Al Harbi and Gotoh, 2016). First, a brief overview of the baseline approach used to provide a comparison with our system is presented. Next, the results of quantitative evaluation with the ROUGE Metric, along with qualitative human judgements, are discussed.

4.1 Frame-based Video Description Baseline

To put our performance in perspective, we compare our proposed approach against the baseline video description framework of (Khan et al., 2015). This approach is chosen as the baseline as it augments the sentence components largely on the basis of semantic video content by applying conventional image processing techniques. Additionally, in order to make a fair comparison, the same set of detected objects are used for both systems. However, we advanced the detection to accommodate temporal information from the videos. The baseline approach processes the video as a sequence of frames. For each frame, conventional image processing methods are implemented to extract a set of high-level visual features (*e.g.*humans and their activities). A limited set of spatial relations are calculated between the extracted HLFs geometric features, though no temporal information is considered. These HLFs are translated into sentential descriptions utilising the SimpleNLG, a template-based approach with a context free grammar.

4.2 Evaluation with ROUGE Metric

The complexity of evaluating video textual descriptions comes from the fact that defining the criteria is a challenging task. To evaluate our method, we examine the metrics commonly used for this purpose in machine translation. These metrics include the BLEU (bilingual evaluation understudy) (Papineni et al., 2002) and ROUGE (Recall Oriented Understudy for Gisting Evaluation) (Lin, 2004) metrics, among others. The BLEU score calculates precision on a word basis or n-grams, and for this reason is not suitable for our task of lingual video description, as has already suggest by (Mitchell et al., 2012) and (Das et al., 2013a).

By contrast, ROUGE score is an n-gram recall oriented measure of the information coverage of human annotation references compared to automatic summaries produced by a system. A higher ROUGE score denotes a higher degree of match between them. In general, a score of '1' indicates a perfect match whereas a score close to '0' means the match occurs in only a small portion of the data. Four different ROUGE scores are used in this experiment, ROUGE-1 (unigram) recall is the perfect option to compare descriptions based on predicted keywords only (Das et al., 2013a). ROUGE-2 (bigram) and ROUGE-SU4 (skip-4 bi-gram) scores are best to evaluate lingual video descriptions for coherence and fluency, whereas ROUGE-L scores depend on the longest common subsequence. ROUGE metrics are chosen for this study following (Das et al., 2013a) who used it to evaluate lingual video summarisation.

Table 2 present the average ROUGE scores achieved between the automatic descriptions produced by the baseline and our system, averaged over all twelve different human action categories, with respect to manual annotations. Manual annotations tend to be subjective as they depend on the annota-

Figure 2: Example of applying post-processing rules to the system-generated description of 'actionclipautoautotrain00463' video from the AnswerPhone category, with two shots.

		Baseline	Our approach
ROUGE-1	R	0.2480	**0.3513**
	P	**0.3443**	0.2474
	F	0.2749	**0.2806**
ROUGE-2	R	0.0532	**0.0737**
	P	**0.0801**	0.0500
	F	**0.0592**	0.0577
ROUGE-L	R	0.2353	**0.33365**
	P	**0.3275**	0.2354
	F	0.2609	**0.26689**
ROUGE-SU4	R	0.0939	**0.1526**
	P	**0.1745**	0.0951
	F	0.1064	**0.1098**

Table 2: ROUGE scores calculated for the baseline and our approach, with respect to hand annotations. For each ROUGE metric, the recall (R), precision (P), and F-measure (F) are averaged over all twelve categories from the NLDHA dataset.

	Grammar	Correctness	Relevance
Baseline	3.40	3.40	2.25
Our approach	3.54	3.75	3.74

Table 3: Human evaluation for the baseline and our approach, with respect to three aspects: grammatical correctness, cognitive correctness, and relevance.

it captures similarity at sentence-level between the automatic generated descriptions and hand annotations. There is also an observable improvement for ROUGE-2 and ROUGE-SU4. This is not surprising since attributes (such as adjectives and prepositions) and co-reference enhance the quality of description by generating richer and less verbose descriptions. However, this kind of improvement in quality does not usually contribute considerably to the ROUGE score, which is based on n-gram comparisons.

4.3 Human Evaluation

The ROUGE metrics produce only a rough estimate of the informativeness of an automatically produced summary, as it does not consider other significant aspects, such as readability or overall responsiveness. To evaluate these types of aspects there is an urgent need for manual evaluation. For this task Amazon Mechanical Turk was used to collect human judgements of automatic video descriptions. We follow (Kuznetsova et al., 2012) and asked 10 Turk workers to rate video descriptions generated by the baseline and our description. Each worker watched each video and rated the description on a scale of 1 to 5, where 5 means 'perfect description', and 1 indicates 'bad description'.

The description rating was based on three different criteria: grammar, correctness, and relevance.

tors perception and understanding. Moreover, this subjectivity might be affected by personal education level, interests, background and experiences. As a result, the ROUGE metric inevitably penalises many automatically generated sentences where these do not match the manual annotations, despite being technically correct.

Clearly, the best results were obtained by ROUGE-1, as our method involves an extended language vocabulary compared to the baseline. This richness comes from a varied set of verbs included along with their scene setting, especially when the language model is involved for the case of zero-shot action recognition. (*e.g.*When 'person' and 'TV' are detected in the scene without a connected verb, the language model will infer the verb 'watch' to complete the sentence.) Additionally, ROUGE-L results confirm the efficiency of our approach as

For both the correctness and relevance aspects, the video was displayed with its description. The correctness evaluates to what extent the textual description depicted the video semantic content, while the relevance rates if the sentence captures the most salient actions and objects. For the grammar correctness, only lingual descriptions were presented to the worker, without the video, to evaluate the sentence. Table 3 shows the results of human evaluation of both the baseline and our approach. It can be observed that our system improves on the baseline in all three aspects. However, the relevance score significantly outperforms the baseline with margin of 1.61. This indicates that our approach is able to describe much more semantic video content, especially in terms of activities, attributes and scene setting.

4.4 Discussion

The majority of previous works, including the baseline system, rely on the image-based detector deformable parts model (DPM) (Felzenszwalb et al., 2010) which is applied to each frame to augment a store of detected objects, without preserving any temporal dependency between video frames. As a result, the descriptions generated using this detector suffer from several weaknesses, mainly redundancy and lack of coherence. The redundancy issue basically results from applying the object detector at each frame without maintaining any temporal correlation; hence if the object changes its position gradually between frames it will be considered as a new detection.

Moreover, consistent co-reference of pronouns to visual objects across multiple sentences cannot be reliably identified for image-based detections, as prior information is required from the preceding frames to prove the previous detection. As a result, the generated description will be verbose, unnatural and contain irrelevancies. The Figure 3(c) shows an example of co-reference identification achieved successfully by the proposed system in '*she* is sitting next to *him*', while the baseline was unable to identify such information as its detection based on individual frames rather than tracking the detection over video frames and exploiting the temporal continuity. See Figure 3 for some examples of automatic video descriptions.

Generating elaborate textual descriptions demands more than action recognition and object detection. Identifying spatial and temporal relations between entities allows them to be mapped onto prepositions and adverbs in the output description. Figure 3(b) shows an example of improvement over the baseline as the proposed system was able to identify the scene layout by formalising spatial relations in 'a man is standing *next to* a car; while a woman is standing *to the right of* him'. Additionally, temporal relations are captured by the system in Figure 3(c) 'a woman is walking *toward* a man' and in Figure 3(a) 'a man is walking away from her' as this relation is calculated by comparing the distance between two objects over sequence of frames.

The proposed framework is applicable to any video genre with human actions and even if no human is detected, the video will be described based on detected non-human objects and scene setting. Although this framework produces a syntactically and grammatically correct description, the current immaturity of computer vision techniques can lead to false positive detections or missing information. As a result, the generated description can be inaccurate and mismatch the real action performed in the video sequences. There is a room for improvement, especially in object detections and their associated attributes, such as actions, colour and dress, which can significantly enhance the accuracy and quality of automatically generated description.

5 Conclusion

This paper has introduced a framework that produces textual descriptions of video based on extracted semantic video content. In an extensive experimental evaluation we show the improvements of our framework compared to the recent baseline frame-based video description system. The improvements are consistent among both automatic evaluation with ROUGE metrics and manual human evaluations of correctness and relevance. This improvement offered by the proposed system stems from the fact that the main sentence components are extracted by visually parsing the video content with respect to temporal information.

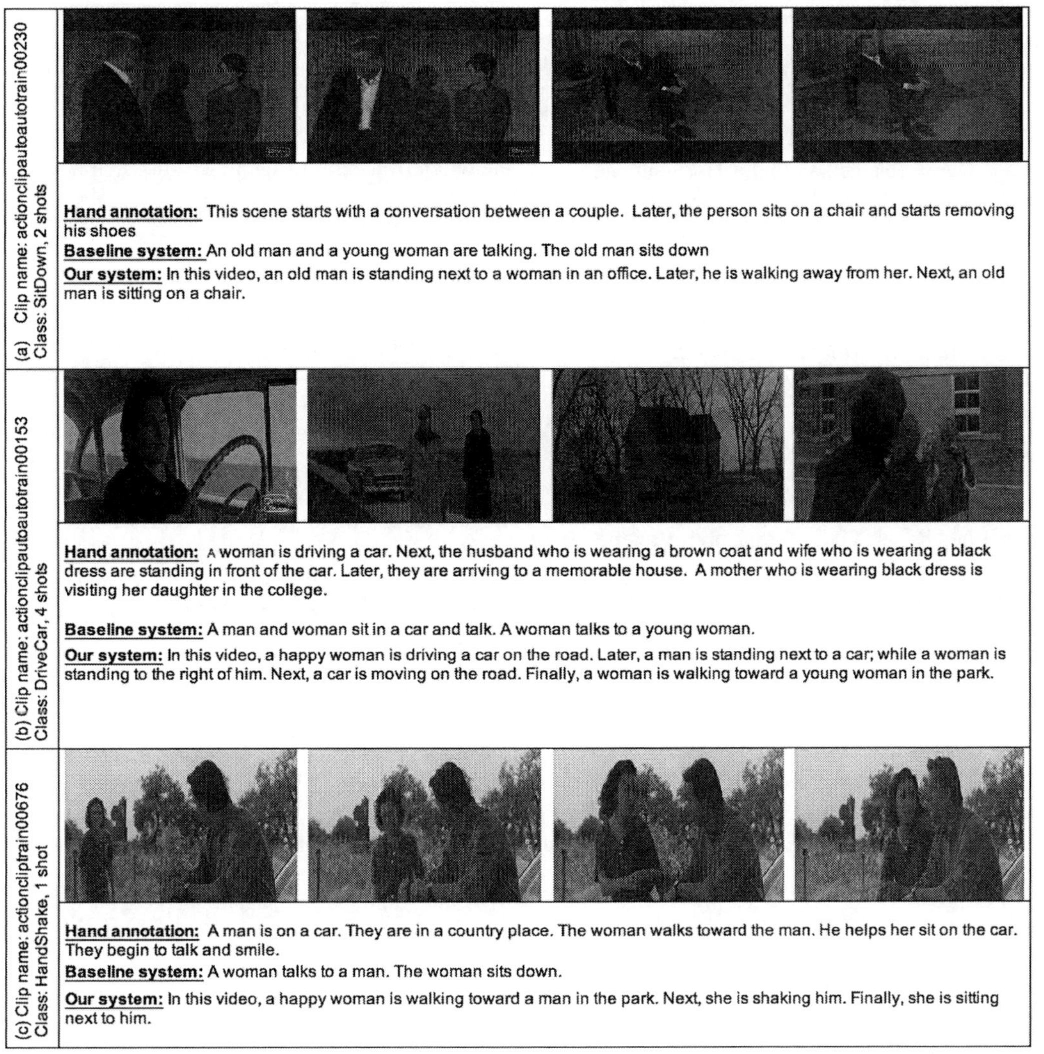

Figure 3: Sample of textual video descriptions along with their video shots from different categories from the NLDHA dataset.

References

Nouf Al Harbi and Yoshihiko Gotoh. 2015a. Describing spatio-temporal relations between object volumes in video streams. In *Workshops at the Twenty-Ninth AAAI Conference on Artificial Intelligence*.

Nouf Al Harbi and Yoshihiko Gotoh. 2015b. A unified spatio-temporal human body region tracking approach to action recognition. *Neurocomputing*, 161:56–64.

Nouf Al Harbi and Yoshihiko Gotoh. 2016. Natural language descriptions of human activities scenes: Corpus generation and analysis. pages 39–47.

Andrei Barbu, Alexander Bridge, Zachary Burchill, Dan Coroian, Sven Dickinson, Sanja Fidler, Aaron Michaux, Sam Mussman, Siddharth Narayanaswamy, Dhaval Salvi, et al. 2012. Video in sentences out. *arXiv preprint arXiv:1204.2742*.

Juan Bekios-Calfa, Jose M Buenaposada, and Luis Baumela. 2011. Revisiting linear discriminant techniques in gender recognition. *IEEE Transactions on Pattern Analysis and Machine Intelligence*, 33(4):858–864.

Pradipto Das, Rohini K Srihari, and Jason J Corso. 2013a. Translating related words to videos and back through latent topics. In *Proceedings of the sixth ACM international conference on Web search and data mining*, pages 485–494. ACM.

Pradipto Das, Chenliang Xu, Richard F Doell, and Jason J Corso. 2013b. A thousand frames in just a few words: Lingual description of videos through latent topics and sparse object stitching. In *Proceedings of the IEEE Conference on Computer Vision and Pattern Recognition*, pages 2634–2641.

Ali Farhadi, Mohsen Hejrati, Mohammad Amin Sadeghi, Peter Young, Cyrus Rashtchian, Julia Hockenmaier, and David Forsyth. 2010. Every picture tells a story: Generating sentences from images. In *European conference on computer vision*, pages 15–29. Springer.

Pedro F Felzenszwalb, Ross B Girshick, David McAllester, and Deva Ramanan. 2010. Object detection with discriminatively trained part-based models. *IEEE transactions on pattern analysis and machine intelligence*, 32(9):1627–1645.

Akshat Garg and Vishakha Choudhary. 2012. Facial expression recognition using principal component analysis. *Int. J. Sci. Eng. Res. Technol.*

Albert Gatt and Ehud Reiter. 2009. Simplenlg: A realisation engine for practical applications. In *Proceedings of the 12th European Workshop on Natural Language Generation*, pages 90–93. Association for Computational Linguistics.

Sergio Guadarrama, Niveda Krishnamoorthy, Girish Malkarnenkar, Subhashini Venugopalan, Raymond Mooney, Trevor Darrell, and Kate Saenko. 2013. Youtube2text: Recognizing and describing arbitrary activities using semantic hierarchies and zero-shot recognition. In *Proceedings of the 14th International Conference on Computer Vision (ICCV-2013)*, pages 2712–2719, Sydney, Australia, December.

Michael Gygli, Helmut Grabner, Hayko Riemenschneider, and Luc Van Gool. 2014a. Creating summaries from user videos. In *European conference on computer vision*, pages 505–520. Springer.

Michael Gygli, Helmut Grabner, Hayko Riemenschneider, and Luc Van Gool. 2014b. Creating Summaries from User Videos. In *ECCV*.

Patrick Hanckmann, Klamer Schutte, and Gertjan J Burghouts. 2012. Automated textual descriptions for a wide range of video events with 48 human actions. In *European Conference on Computer Vision*, pages 372–380. Springer.

Wen-Bing Horng, Cheng-Ping Lee, and Chun-Wen Chen. 2001. Classification of age groups based on facial features. *Tamkang Journal of Science and Engineering*, 4(3):183–192.

Muhammad Usman Ghani Khan, Nouf Al Harbi, and Yoshihiko Gotoh. 2015. A framework for creating natural language descriptions of video streams. *Information Sciences*, 303:61–82.

Girish Kulkarni, Visruth Premraj, Sagnik Dhar, Siming Li, Yejin Choi, Alexander C Berg, and Tamara L Berg. 2011. Baby talk: Understanding and generating image descriptions. In *Proceedings of the 24th CVPR*. Citeseer.

Polina Kuznetsova, Vicente Ordonez, Alexander C Berg, Tamara L Berg, and Yejin Choi. 2012. Collective generation of natural image descriptions. In *Proceedings of the 50th Annual Meeting of the Association for Computational Linguistics: Long Papers-Volume 1*, pages 359–368. Association for Computational Linguistics.

Chin-Yew Lin. 2004. Rouge: A package for automatic evaluation of summaries. In *Text summarization branches out: Proceedings of the ACL-04 workshop*, volume 8. Barcelona, Spain.

Margaret Mitchell, Xufeng Han, Jesse Dodge, Alyssa Mensch, Amit Goyal, Alex Berg, Kota Yamaguchi, Tamara Berg, Karl Stratos, and Hal Daumé III. 2012. Midge: Generating image descriptions from computer vision detections. In *Proceedings of the 13th Conference of the European Chapter of the Association for Computational Linguistics*, pages 747–756. Association for Computational Linguistics.

Kishore Papineni, Salim Roukos, Todd Ward, and Wei-Jing Zhu. 2002. Bleu: a method for automatic evaluation of machine translation. In *Proceedings of the 40th annual meeting on association for computational linguistics*, pages 311–318. Association for Computational Linguistics.

Jesse Thomason, Subhashini Venugopalan, Sergio Guadarrama, Kate Saenko, and Raymond J Mooney. 2014. Integrating language and vision to generate natural language descriptions of videos in the wild. In *Coling*, volume 2, page 9.

Bolei Zhou, Agata Lapedriza, Jianxiong Xiao, Antonio Torralba, and Aude Oliva. 2014. Learning deep features for scene recognition using places database. In *Advances in neural information processing systems*, pages 487–495.

PASS: A Dutch data-to-text system for soccer, targeted towards specific audiences

Chris van der Lee and **Emiel Krahmer** and **Sander Wubben**
Tilburg center for Cognition and Communication (TiCC)
Tilburg University
The Netherlands
`{c.vdrlee, e.j.krahmer, s.wubben}@tilburguniversity.edu`

Abstract

We present PASS, a data-to-text system that generates Dutch soccer reports from match statistics. One of the novel elements of PASS is the fact that the system produces corpus-based texts tailored towards fans of one club or the other, which can most prominently be observed in the tone of voice used in the reports. Furthermore, the system is open source and uses a modular design, which makes it relatively easy for people to add extensions. Human-based evaluation shows that people are generally positive towards PASS in regards to its clarity and fluency, and that the tailoring is accurately recognized in most cases.

1 Introduction

For the past few years, news organizations worldwide have begun to show interest in automating various types of news reports. One of the domains that is especially viable for automation is the domain of sports, since the outcomes of most sports matches can be extracted from the data. Additionally, sports statistics (who played, who scored, etcetera) are stored for many games that are neither visited, nor reported on by sports reporters. Automated text generation systems can generate reports for these games.

However, most of the current text generation systems used for journalistic purposes (e.g. Wordsmith[1], Quill[2]) are closed systems that are inaccessible for the general public and for interested researchers. As a result, it is not fully transparent how

[1] `https://www.automatedinsights.com/`
[2] `https://www.narrativescience.com/`

these systems work. At the same time, early NLG systems on sports-reporting (André et al., 1988; Robin, 1994; Theune et al., 2001, among others) are also inaccessible because the code for these systems has become obsolete or abandoned. The goal of this paper, therefore, is to present a new data-to-text system, which we call Personalized Automated Soccer texts System (hereafter: PASS). PASS is inspired by earlier NLG research and capable of generating soccer reports from data. The system is open-source and freely available, and set-up in modular way, so that interested researchers can use the system as a testbed for their own, possibly specialized NLG algorithms.

As we argue below, this project is inspired by a previous system and fits with the increased emphasis on replication in science, but this project is more than a straightforward reimplementation. In particular, we show and evaluate how the core system can be used to generate tailored reports for specific audiences.

One of the strengths of data-to-text generation is that texts can easily be tailored towards specific audiences (Gatt and Krahmer, 2017). In order to showcase this strength, PASS produces two texts for fans of each of the teams participating in a soccer match. The difference between these two texts is the tone of voice in the reports. One of the goals in the development of PASS was to generate emotional language that would be expected when people report on an event they are emotionally invested in. In the context of soccer, this means that if the club of the targeted audience loses, the tone of a PASS report would be more disappointed or frustrated and if the

95

Proceedings of The 10th International Natural Language Generation conference, pages 95–104,
Santiago de Compostela, Spain, September 4-7 2017. ©2017 Association for Computational Linguistics

club of the targeted audience wins, the tone would be more upbeat. The language of these reports was made to look similar to the reports written by professional journalists by using a corpus-driven approach in the development of the PASS system.

2 Related work

Data-to-text systems, systems that "generate texts from non-linguistic data, such as sensor data and event logs" (Reiter, 2007, p. 97), have been around for a long time and still remain a popular topic for Natural Language Generation. Some of the data-to-text language generation tasks that have been investigated recently include weather forecast generation (Belz and Kow, 2010; Angeli et al., 2010; Gkatzia et al., 2016a, among others), medical reports (Gatt et al., 2009; Gkatzia et al., 2016b; Schneider et al., 2013, among others), and financial reports (Nesterenko, 2016, among others).

The domain of sports is also a domain that is investigated quite frequently. This domain is appealing because the content organization could be (partly) fixed for many sports. At the same time, the sports domain is complex enough that it gives rise to many challenges at almost every stage of the data-to-text pipeline (Barzilay and Lapata, 2005). Data-to-text systems in the sports domain can be roughly divided into two categories. The first category is the **commentary** category. Systems in this category produce texts in a style that is similar to the live commentary that can be heard when watching a live sports event. This means that content selection and organization is relatively simple: most, if not all, observable events are covered and this is done in a chronological order. Examples of data-to-text systems that fall into this category are Tanaka-Ishii et al. (1998), Chen and Mooney (2008), and Konstas and Lapata (2012), which all produce soccer reports.

The second, **summary** category could provide a bigger challenge for content selection and organization. These texts are more similar to texts that can be read in newspapers or websites after the sports event and should provide a report on the most interesting elements of the game. This means that content selection is more important and a chronological order is not necessarily used. Examples of systems in this category are Robin (1994), and McKeown et al. (1995), which produced basketball reports, and Theune et al. (2001), and Barzilay and Lapata (2005), which produced reports on soccer matches.

The current system falls in the latter category. PASS is a data-to-text system that produces Dutch summaries of soccer matches and that uses a template-based approach. Template-based systems can generally be characterized by their slot-filler structure: texts with gaps that can be filled with information. while this approach is sometimes contrasted with "real" NLG, research has shown that template-based approaches generally result in texts of relatively high quality (van Deemter et al., 2005), that are generated relatively quickly (Sanby et al., 2016).

The current project is in line with the ongoing concerns about replication in science in general. However, it is important to stress that PASS is a reimplementation of GoalGetter, not a replication. We aimed to make PASS generate soccer reports somewhat similar to those generated by GoalGetter, but we did not use any of the source code of GoalGetter. Instead, we have built a new system from the ground up, using the description and results of GoalGetter as inspiration, while simultaneously adding new techniques to emphasize the variety of the system's output.

In the last few years, people have become increasingly interested in replicating published research (Ioannidis, 2005; Nosek et al., 2015; Mieskes, 2017, among others). However, in order to replicate previous studies in this field, reimplementation of previous systems is often necessary. Many older systems such as GoalGetter have become abandonware. They are not (any longer) publicly available, their code is obsolete, and sometimes have never been properly evaluated. Reimplementation is required for these older systems before they can be replicated. Therefore, our goal was to develop a system according to modern standards that produces output that is similar to GoalGetter. Furthermore, we have made our implementation publicly available[3], and have performed a human-based evaluation of the system. This makes it possible for others to attempt replication of the current study.

---

[3]`https://github.com/TallChris91/PASS`

Type	Match information
General	League, date, time, stadium, city, referee, attendees, final score, teams, goal scorers
Match events	Assists, regular goals, own goals, penalty goals, penalty misses, yellow cards, red cards (2x yellow), red cards (direct)
Last game	League, date, opponent, final score, played home/away, won/tied/lost, changes in lineup
Players in lineup, substitutes and managers	Name, full name, nickname, birth date, birth place, height, weight, position, kit number, name in *Goal.com*, *Goal.com* player page, youth clubs, senior clubs, national teams represented, current team
Last five games	Opponent, final score, played home/away, won/tied/lost
Relative strength	Wins per team for previous meetings, draws in previous meetings, percentage of people predicting win for the home team/win for the away team/tie, date of previous meetings, which team played home/away in previous meetings, final score previous meetings, most predicted results
Match statistics	Total shots, shots on target, completed passes, passing accuracy, possession, corners, offsides, fouls, total passes, short passes, long passes, forward/left/right/back passes, percentage of forward passes, blocked shots, shots on the left/right/centre of the goal, percentage of shots outside the 18-yard box, total crosses, successful crosses, crosses accuracy, crosses inside/outside 18-yard box, left crosses, right crosses, total attempted take-ons, successful take-ons, successful left/right/centre/total take-ons in the final third of the match, blocks, interceptions, clearances, recoveries, total tackles, successful tackles, tackle accuracy

Table 1: Information stored from *Goal.com*.

3 Data collection

3.1 Gathering the data

GoalGetter scraped data from *Teletext*: a system that broadcasts textual data to television and Internet. While this system still exists, the amount of data available on *Teletext* is limited, is not stored, and many sources nowadays offer more data. Therefore, an application was built to automatically scrape soccer match data from *Goal.com*[4], and store this data in XML-format. Similarly to *Teletext*, *Goal.com* contains information about teams that played, final score, goal scorers, referee, attendees and players that were given a yellow or red card. However, *Goal.com* keeps track of a sizable amount of data in addition to this, such as the players that participated in the game, score predictions, the results of previous match-ups between the teams and a sizable amount of detailed statistical information; cf. Table 1. While most of this *Goal.com*-specific data has not been used in the current version of PASS, the availability of this information makes it relatively easy to use this data in future versions.

3.2 Designing the templates

With PASS, an attempt was made to produce reports where the tone of voice is emotional, while the report still appears to be relatively professional. The language in the templates therefore needed to be close to what could be encountered in human-written soccer reports. To achieve this, the templates were derived from sentences in the MeMo FC corpus (Braun et al., 2016). The MeMo FC corpus contains match reports copied directly from the websites of the soccer clubs that participated in the match. These reports are intended for the supporters of their respective club and often contain an emotional tone. These characteristics made the corpus particularly suitable for PASS.

Three steps were undertaken to convert reports in the MeMo FC corpus to templates. The first step was to manually label a sample of reports in the corpus: for each sentence in the sample, we examined what event it described. This first step was done to cluster sentences that described similar events and to get a general idea which categories could be distinguished. Separate databases were made for reports that described a win, a tie or a loss for the team of the website it originates from. The template categories were the same for all these databases, but the templates were different. After the first step followed a reduction step: for every extracted category and sentence we judged if there was *Goal.com*-data available for the information it conveyed and if the information would have been present in GoalGetter.

Section	Category	Variants
Title		All-purpose, deciding goal, 2+ goal difference, 6+ total goals, no goals, red card targeted team, final goal targeted team, targeted team played away, late equalizer for targeted team, late equalizer other team
Introduction	Won/tied/lost	All-purpose, red card targeted team, red card other team
	Final score	All-purpose, final goal targeted team, late equalizer other team, focus team tie after being 2+ goals down
Game course	Regular goal	All-purpose, goal with assist, deciding goal, deciding goal with assist, 2 goal difference, 2+ goal difference, two successive goals for one team, early goal, goal giving the lead, equalizer, anschlusstreffer, ergebniskosmetik, 2+ goal by a player, final goal, only goal
	Own goal	All-purpose, deciding goal, 2 goal difference, 2+ goal difference, early goal, goal giving the lead, equalizer, final goal, only goal
	Penalty goal	All-purpose, deciding goal, 2 goal difference, 2+ goal difference, goal giving the lead, equalizer, anschlusstreffer, ergebniskosmetik, 2+ goal by a player, final goal
	Penalty miss	All-purpose
Debriefing	Yellow card	Multiple in match, one in match, none in match
	Red card (2x yellow)	Multiple in match, one in match, second yellow for targeted team
	Red card (direct)	All-purpose, early red, red for targeted team

Table 2: Template categories and their variants.

This led to a reduction of roughly half of the categories and sentences; cf. Table 2. This means that a sizable portion of the content found in most human-written reports is not conveyed in the reports generated by PASS. However, the most crucial information about a match was still present after the second step. In the last step, the sentences were converted to templates. This means that the parts in the sentence containing specific information on a match were replaced by empty gaps and information about which type of data should be used to fill in the gap. Sentences were rephrased if this was necessary to make the template applicable to multiple soccer matches. However, these changes were kept to a minimum in order to stay as close to the source material as possible.

The templates used for PASS are somewhat different from the templates used in GoalGetter. Goal-Getter contains less categories and templates, but Theune et al. (2001) ensured variation in the text by using 'syntactic templates'. They made a syntactic structure for each template, so that small changes could automatically be made to the original template if the circumstances required these changes. For instance, the template changed from (1) to (2) if the second goal of a player had to be described.

(1)   *"<goal scorer> scored **a** goal"*

(2)   *"<goal scorer> scored **his second goal**"*

We did not add a syntactic system to the templates, but stored templates such as (1) and (2) as separate categories. PASS, contains a larger amount of categories and templates per category, compared to GoalGetter. This makes PASS produce a similar, if not greater amount of variation in the generated reports.

3.3   Content selection and document structure

We used a sample of articles from the MeMo FC corpus to get a feeling for the document structure used in human-written soccer reports. We found that a roughly similar document structure like the one in GoalGetter reports is often used for human-written soccer reports. This means that, a four-part division of a soccer report can often be found in human-written reports. These four parts are:

Title Usually the result (win/tie/loss) and the final score of the match.

Introduction A match preview and the most important results of the match. For example, information about the opponent, expectations about the match difficulty, previous results and current ranking, did the team win/tie/lose, and the final score.

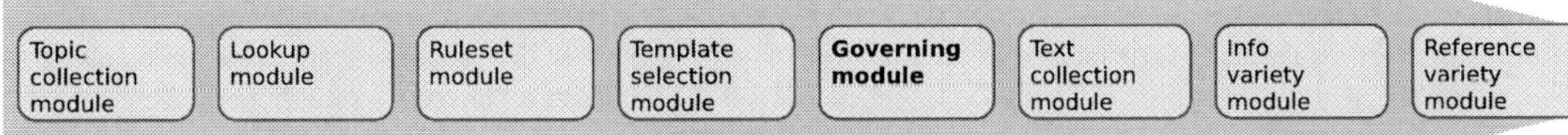

Figure 1: Modules used in PASS.

Game course A chronological report on the most important events of a match, usually linked together with the subjective evaluations of the writer. For example, a report on the goals, biggest scoring chances, most noteworthy fouls, and which team plays better.

Debriefing The consequences of the match and general information about future matches. For example, information on bookings and suspensions, rankings after the match, date of the next match.

Not all commonly found types of information in the MeMo FC corpus were used in PASS reports, since not all information was adequately represented in the *Goal.com*-data and to make the output of PASS more similar to GoalGetter. This means that the introduction-part only expresses win/tie/loss information and the final score. The game course-part focuses on goals and missed penalties, and the debriefing-part merely displays information on bookings. Every part was represented in a separate paragraph.

4   PASS system

In this section, we will describe the process PASS takes to go from data to text. The system uses handwritten rules and templates to achieve this goal and produces short reports on a soccer match personalized for each team that played, like the ones in Table 3.

4.1   Algorithm

While PASS is similar to GoalGetter in terms of output, the method to achieve this output is different (Theune et al., 2001, for a description of GoalGetter's architecture). The biggest difference is that a modular approach was used in the design of PASS.

By using a modular design, it is easy to make adjustments, improvements and extensions. This means that the modules shown in Figure 1 can easily by replaced by other modules.

PASS starts with the module that governs the generation of the title and introduction. The order in which the topics for this part are reported on is fixed for the current version of the system: title, win/tie/loss information and the final score. The **governing module** will walk through every topic in a stepwise order and interact with all the other modules necessary to generate the text for the introduction-part. We will give an overview of these other modules that it uses for each step.

First, when the governing module starts with a new step, a *unused_topic* will become a *current_topic*. Then, the **lookup module** is activated that opens the template database and retrieves all the template categories and corresponding templates that could be used for the *current_topic*. Part of these template categories can only be used if certain conditions are met, while there is also a general-purpose category containing templates that can be used in every situation.

After a collection has been found of all the template categories corresponding to *current_topic*, the **ruleset module** is activated. This module checks for each template category if the conditions to use said category have been matched. If this is the case, the ruleset module will return `True` to the governing module. If not, it will return `False`. If the governing module receives `True` for a template category, it will add the templates from the category to a list of the *possible_templates*.

If every category has been checked by the ruleset module, the **template selection module** will select a template from the *possible_templates* list in a weighted random fashion. We observed in the MeMo FC corpus that if the right conditions are met, human writers tend to prefer language describing

	Report for fans of Achilles '29	Report for fans of Dordrecht
Dutch	**Thoone velt Dordrecht: 2-1** Jop van Steen en Freek Thoone hebben ervoor gezorgd dat de uitploeg zonder punten achterbleef. In Groesbeek werd voor 1022 toeschouwers met 2-1 gewonnen van Dordrecht. De uitploeg kwam na 10 minuten uit het niets op een 0-1 voorsprong door een prachtige treffer van Janga. Jop van Steen schoot in de 48e minuut de dik verdiende gelijkmaker tegen de touwen. Thoone bracht na 88 minuten de winnende treffer op het scorebord: 2-1. Scheidsrechter Van den Kerkhof was genoodzaakt 3 gele kaarten te geven, aan Arnaud De Greef, Boy van de Beek en Josimar Lima.	**Het zit Dordrecht niet mee tegen Achilles '29: 2-1** De uitploeg leed een zure nederlaag uit tegen de ploeg van manager Eric Meijers. Dordrecht verloor na een hoopvol begin met 2-1 van Achilles '29. Aanvaller Janga zette de ploeg van manager Gérard de Nooijer op een 0-1. Achilles '29 kwam door twee gelukkige treffers van Van Steen en Freek Thoone op een 2-1 voorsprong. Er werden 3 gele kaarten uitgedeeld: aan de zijde van Dordrecht voor Arnaud de Greef en Josimar Lima en aan de zijde van de thuisploeg voor Boy van de Beek.
English	**Thoone slays Dordrecht: 2-1** Jop van Steen and Freek Thoone have ensured that the away team did not get any points. In Groesbeek, a 2-1 victory against Dordrecht was achieved before 1022 attendees. Out of nowhere, the away team got a 0-1 lead because Janga made a beautiful goal after 10 minutes. Jop van Steen shot the well deserved equalizer against the ropes in the 48th minute. Thoone put the winning goal on the score board after 88 minutes: 2-1. Referee Van den Kerkhof was forced to give 3 yellow cards, to Arnaud De Greef, Boy van de Beek and Josimar Lima.	**Dordrecht does not have much luck against Achilles '29: 2-1** The away team conceded a sour defeat away against the team of manager Eric Meijers. Dordrecht lost after a promising start with 2-1 against Achilles '29. Attacker Jaga gave the team of manager Gérard de Nooijer the 0-1. Achilles '29 got a 2-1 lead by two lucky goals of Van Steen and Freek Thoone. 3 yellow cards were issued: on the side of Dordrecht to Arnaud de Greef and Josimar Lima and on the side of the home team to Boy van de Beek.

Table 3: Two variants of a match report generated by PASS.

details that apply specifically to the situation, as is shown in (3), rather than language that can be used in every situation, as is shown in (4).

(3)   *"Joachim Andersen made the equalizer directly after the opening goal"*

(4)   *"Joachim Andersen scored the 1-1"*

Therefore, the more conditions were required to be true, the higher the weight we assigned to the template when selecting a template. This increased the chance that a template was selected that was more tailored to the situation at hand, although general-purpose templates still had a decent chance to be selected.

When one template has been selected to convey the *current_topic*, the empty slots in the template need to be filled with the right kind of information. This is done by the **template filler module**.

Every empty slot had been given a tag in the template database (e.g. <stadium>, <referee>, <attendees>). The template filler module uses these tags to find the corresponding piece of information in the match data, then fills the empty slot with this data and returns the filled-in template to the governing module.

The game course and the debriefing were both generated in a largely similar way. With one exception: unlike the introduction, these parts had no fixed order. The topics for the game course and debriefing depended on the match events. For example, a 1-0 result with a missed penalty requires two topics to be reported on in the game course, while a 6-4 result and no missed penalties means ten topics (every goal) in the game course. This meant that an extra module was added, the **topic collection module**. This module extracted the topics from the match data and gave them the right order. After the topics were collected and ordered, the exact same modules were used as for the introduction.

After every governing module has produced text for their respective parts, they activate the **text collection module**. This module simply had the task of taking the text for every part and combine them in the right order.

While the system produced reasonable output with the described modules, three more modules were added to increase the variety within and between reports. The **information variety module** ensured that certain types of information in the report would not be repeated. Before the information variety module, certain constructions such as the following could exist:

(5)　　*"Ajax obtained the victory before the eyes of **16,673 attendees**. **16,673 attendees** saw the match against AZ end with a 0-3 score."*

Reporting on the attendee information a second time would be redundant in this context. The information variety checks the finished report to see if templates are used with redundant information. If this is the case, the module interacts with the template selection and template filler modules to get an alternative template for the template with redundant information. The information variety module keeps going through the finished report until it cannot find any more redundant information.

Like repetition of information, repetition of references can also have a negative impact on the text quality of the report. This can be observed in the following example:

(6)　　*"**Ajax** obtained the victory before the eyes of 16,673 attendees. **Ajax** beat AZ with 0-3."*

The **reference variety module** crawls through the text to spot the same referent in two subsequent sentences. If the module is able to find this, it will use a different form to address the referent in the second sentence (e.g. *Ajax* becomes *the club of manager Peter Bosz*). General-purpose templates have been designed to refer to a person or a soccer team. These templates are picked randomly and the empty slots are then filled in with the template selection and template filler modules, respectively. While this module

works for the current version of PASS, it is possible that the module is too simple for longer, more complicated reports. Therefore, this module will probably be replaced by a probabilistic module as is seen in Ferreira et al. (2016) in future versions of PASS.

Finally, we wanted to demonstrate the variety in outcomes PASS can generate. Therefore, the **between-text variety module** was implemented. This module keeps track of the templates that were used when generating a soccer report. When generating a new report, this module interacts with the template selection module, deleting all templates from the *possible_templates* list if they had been used in the previous soccer report. This ensures that every generated report is completely different from the previous one, thus increasing overall variety.

5　Evaluation

We conducted a human-based evaluation to measure the text quality of PASS. For the purpose of the evaluation, a sample was taken of 10 soccer matches played in the Dutch second league in the 2015/2016 season. This means that a total of 20 reports (2 per soccer match) were evaluated by participants. Each participant got to see all 20 reports.

20 Dutch students (13 male, average age 20.6 years) participated in the evaluation. For every match, these participants were asked to answer five questions. The first question was a multiple choice question and served as a manipulation check: 'For fans of which team was the report written: the intended team/the other team'. This question was asked since one of the main functions of PASS is the generation of reports targeted towards fans of each team. After the manipulation check, participants were asked to rate the clarity and fluency of the reports. Clarity refers to how clear and understandable the report is, and was measured using two seven-point Likert-scale questions ('The message of this text is completely clear to me', 'While reading, I immediately understood the text'). Fluency refers to how fluent and easy to read the report is and was also measured using two seven-point Likert-scale questions ('This text is written in proper Dutch', 'This text is easily readable').

An analysis of the manipulation check results showed that people were able to correctly tell towards fans of which team the text was tailored in 91% of all cases. A chi-square test also showed a significant correlation between the intended and perceived tailoring towards fans of the clubs ($\chi^2(1) = 233.33$, $p < .001$). Furthermore, the results showed that participants were overall positive in regards to the clarity and fluency of the reports. The average scores of clarity ($M = 5.64$, $SD = 0.88$) and fluency ($M = 5.36$, $SD = 0.79$) were well above the neutral score of 4.

6 Discussion

We have presented a data-to-text system, PASS, that converts data of a soccer match to a textual soccer report. This system was a partial reimplementation of GoalGetter (Theune et al., 2001). Like GoalGetter, a template and rule-based approach was used to design PASS, but there were also several differences between GoalGetter and PASS. For instance, the data source was changed from *Teletext* to *Goal.com*, which provided us with more data. The templates were also constructed in a different fashion. Theune et al. (2001) used syntactically enriched templates, which made a template applicable for several conditions so that more variety in the reports was achieved. PASS uses regular templates, but a corpus-driven approach made it possible to produce a sizable amount of templates and categories, which positively impacted the variety of the PASS reports. However, the biggest change was the implementation of text personalization. GoalGetter generated one 'neutral' report, while PASS generated two reports: one for fans of each club that participated in the match. Personalization was achieved through the use of more 'biased' emotional language as was found in the MeMo FC corpus (Braun et al., 2016). Human-based evaluation showed that this manipulation of the bias in the text was successful. In 91% of all cases, people were able to perceive the tailoring in the intended way. Furthermore, the human-based evaluation showed a positive perception of the text quality in regards to clarity, as well as fluency.

6.1 Future work

While GoalGetter was the end result of the research project, the current version of PASS is a first version that will be expanded upon in future research. A simple way of expansion would be to use more template categories and templates and to include more of the available *Goal.com* information in the reports. This is a feasible way to potentially increase the text quality. Additionally, the current version of PASS produces language that could be seen as evaluative (e.g. 'the well deserved equalizer', 'lucky goals'). This evaluative content is currently not backed up by objective data, but can be seen as the subjective view in favor of one side. An interesting future topic would be to explore the usage of these evaluative remarks in connection with statistical data.

Another way of expansion that we are currently investigating is to convert the rule-based content selection and surface realization to a trainable approach. Like most of the template-based data-to-text systems, a sizable amount of manual work was necessary to build PASS. All the templates and rules were written by hand with the specific goal to produce reports for the domain of soccer. This means that the current PASS system cannot easily be adapted to produce reports for other domains. One way of solving this problem would be to build a module that could produce and apply templates with a minimal amount of supervision. Trainable approaches to content selection have been tried previously (Gkatzia, 2016, for an overview). However, most of these approaches only attempt to extract sentences that are aligned with the data. We would also want these sentences to automatically be converted to usable templates, and that these templates could subsequently be applied to produce reports with a minimal amount of rules. To our knowledge, this is a relatively unexplored area of research. The rare study (Kondadadi et al., 2013) that does try to execute all these steps, attempts to produce reports where the topics are always fixed. However, for many domains such as soccer this approach would be problematic, since the topics for these domains could differ greatly as many different events could have taken place. These, and other ideas, are easily explorable with the base that is the current PASS system. The modular design of the system makes all kinds of expansions easily achievable.

References

Elisabeth André, Gerd Herzog, and Thomas Rist. 1988. On the simultaneous interpretation of real world image sequences and their natural language description: the system soccer. In Yves Kodratoff, editor, *Proceedings of the 8th European Conference on Artificial Intelligence*, page 449–454, London, August. Pitman.

Gabor Angeli, Percy Liang, and Dan Klein. 2010. A simple domain-independent probabilistic approach to generation. In *Proceedings of the 2010 Conference on Empirical Methods in Natural Language Processing*, pages 502–512, Stroudsburg, PA, October. Association for Computational Linguistics.

Regina Barzilay and Mirella Lapata. 2005. Collective content selection for concept-to-text generation. In *Proceedings of the Conference on Human Language Technology and Empirical Methods in Natural Language Processing*, pages 331–338, Stroudsburg, PA, October. Association for Computational Linguistics.

Anja Belz and Eric Kow. 2010. Extracting parallel fragments from comparable corpora for data-to-text generation. In John Kelleher, Brian MacNamee, and Ielka van der Sluis, editors, *Proceedings of the 6th International Natural Language Generation Conference*, pages 167–171, Stroudsburg, PA, July. Association for Computational Linguistics.

Nadine Braun, Martijn Goudbeek, and Emiel Krahmer. 2016. The multilingual affective soccer corpus (masc): compiling a biased parallel corpus on soccer reportage in english, german and dutch. In Amy Isard, Verena Rieser, and Dimitra Gkatzia, editors, *Proceedings of the 9th International Natural Language Generation Conference*, pages 74–78, Stroudsburg, PA, September. Association for Computational Linguistics.

David Chen and Raymond Mooney. 2008. Learning to sportscast: a test of grounded language acquisition. In *Proceedings of the 25th International Conference on Machine Learning*, pages 128–135, Cambridge, MA, July. ACM.

Thiago Castro Ferreira, Emiel Krahmer, and Sander Wubben. 2016. Towards more variation in text generation: developing and evaluating variation models for choice of referential form. In *Proceedings of the 54th Annual Meeting of the Association for Computational Linguistics*, pages 568–577, Stroudsburg, PA, August. Association for Computational Linguistics.

Albert Gatt and Emiel Krahmer. 2017. Survey of the state of the art in natural language generation: Core tasks, applications and evaluation. *arXiv preprint arXiv:1703.09902*, pages 1–111.

Albert Gatt, Francois Portet, Ehud Reiter, Jim Hunter, Saad Mahamood, Wendy Moncur, and Somayajulu Sripada. 2009. From data to text in the neonatal intensive care unit: using nlg technology for decision support and information management. *AI Communications*, 22(3):153–186.

Dimitra Gkatzia, Oliver Lemon, and Verena Rieser. 2016a. Natural language generation enhances human decision-making with uncertain information. In *Proceedings of the 54th Annual Meeting of the Association for Computational Linguistics*, pages 264–268, Stroudsburg, PA, August. Association for Computational Linguistics.

Dimitra Gkatzia, Verena Rieser, and Oliver Lemon. 2016b. How to talk to strangers: generating medical reports for first-time users. In *Proceedings of the 2016 IEEE International Conference on Fuzzy Systems*, pages 579–586, Redhook, NY, July. Curran Associates, Inc.

Dimitra Gkatzia. 2016. Content selection in data-to-text systems: A survey. *arXiv preprint arXiv:1610.08375*.

John Ioannidis. 2005. Why most published research findings are false. *PLoS Medicine*, 2(8):696–701.

Ravi Kondadadi, Blake Howald, and Frank Schilder. 2013. A statistical nlg framework for aggregated planning and realization. In *Proceedings of the 51st Annual Meeting of the Association for Computational Linguistics*, pages 1406–1415, Stroudsburg, PA, August. Association for Computational Linguistics.

Ioannis Konstas and Mirella Lapata. 2012. Unsupervised concept-to-text generation with hypergraphs. In *Proceedings of the 2012 Conference of the North American Chapter of the Association for Computational Linguistics: Human Language Technologies*, page 752–761, Stroudsburg, PA, June. Association for Computational Linguistics.

Kathleen McKeown, Jacques Robin, and Karen Kukich. 1995. Generating concise natural language summaries. *Information Processing & Management*, 31(5):703–733.

Margot Mieskes. 2017. A quantitative study of data in the nlp community. In *Proceedings of the First Workshop on Ethics in Natural Language Processing*, pages 1–7, Stroudsburg, PA, April. Association for Computational Linguistics.

Liubov Nesterenko. 2016. Building a system for stock news generation in russian. In Amy Isard, Verena Rieser, and Dimitra Gkatzia, editors, *Proceedings of the 9th International Natural Language Generation Conference*, Stroudsburg, PA, September. Association for Computational Linguistics.

Brian Nosek, Alexander Aarts, Christopher Anderson, Joanna Anderson, and Heather Barry Kappes. 2015. Estimating the reproducibility of psychological science. *Science*, 349(6251).

Ehud Reiter. 2007. An architecture for data-to-text systems. In Stephan Busemann, editor, *Proceedings of the Eleventh European Workshop on Natural Language Generation*, pages 97–104, Stroudsburg, PA, June. Association for Computational Linguistics.

Jacques Robin. 1994. *Revision-based Generation of Natural Language Summaries Providing Historical Background*. Ph.D. thesis, Columbia University.

Lauren Sanby, Ion Todd, and Maria Keet. 2016. Comparing the template-based approach to gf: the case of afrikaans. In Amy Isard, Verena Rieser, and Dimitra Gkatzia, editors, *Proceedings of the 9th International Natural Language Generation Conference*, Stroudsburg, PA, September. Association for Computational Linguistics.

Anne Schneider, Alasdair Mort, Chris Mellish, Ehud Reiter, Phil Wilson, and Pierre-Luc Vaudry. 2013. Mime-nlg in pre-hospital care. In *Proceedings of the 14th European Workshop on Natural Language Generation*, pages 152–156, Stroudsburg, PA, August. Association for Computational Linguistics.

Kumiko Tanaka-Ishii, Kôiti Hasida, and Itsuki Noda. 1998. Reactive content selection in the generation of real-time soccer commentary. In *Proceedings of the 17th International Conference on Computational linguistics*, pages 1282–1288, Stroudsburg, PA, August. Association for Computational Linguistics.

Mariët Theune, Esther Klabbers, Jan-Roelof de Pijper, Emiel Krahmer, and Jan Odijk. 2001. From data to speech: a general approach. *Natural Language Engineering*, 7(1):47–86.

Kees van Deemter, Emiel Krahmer, and Mariët Theune. 2005. Real vs. template-based natural language generation. *Computational Linguistics*, 31(1):15–23.

Evaluation of a Runyankore grammar engine for healthcare messages

Joan Byamugisha and **C. Maria Keet** and **Brian DeRenzi**
Department of Computer Science, University of Cape Town, South Africa,
{jbyamugisha,mkeet,bderenzi}@cs.uct.ac.za

Abstract

Natural Language Generation (NLG) can be used to generate personalized health information, which is especially useful when provided in one's own language. However, the NLG technique widely used in different domains and languages—templates—was shown to be inapplicable to Bantu languages, due to their characteristic agglutinative structure. We present here our use of the grammar engine NLG technique to generate text in Runyankore, a Bantu language indigenous to Uganda. Our grammar engine adds to previous work in this field with new rules for cardinality constraints, prepositions in roles, the passive, and phonological conditioning. We evaluated the generated text with linguists and non-linguists, who regarded most text as grammatically correct and understandable; and over 60% of them regarded all the text generated by our system to have been authored by a human being.

1   Introduction

The vast majority of doctor-patient interactions in a healthcare setting is through verbal communication. The provision of written information to patients, to complement and augment the face-to-face session, increases the amount of information they retain (DiMarco et al., 2005). Additionally, studies in health communication identified that patient information is likely to be more effective if it is personalized for a specific patient (Cawsey et al., 2000) and presented in an understandable form and manner (DiMarco et al., 2009). This however assumes that such information is communicated in one's first language, which,

however, may not be the case in multilingual societies. Language is important here because problems with language exacerbate literacy difficulties, which are further confounded in situations of health (DiMarco et al., 2009).

There are several Natural Language Generation (NLG) systems that generate customized patient information (Cawsey et al., 2000; DiMarco et al., 1995; de Rosis et al., 1999; Hussain et al., 2015; Lindahl, 2005; Mahamood and Reiter, 2011). These systems generate text in English, and one strategy to account for other languages could be to translate the generated English text to the target language. However, this requires correct machine translation for medical information, which does not exist for most languages, including our language of interest, Runyankore. Runyankore is a Bantu language indigenous to the south western part of Uganda (Asiimwe, 2014; Tayebwa, 2014; Turamyomwe, 2011), a country where English is the official language, whereas indigenous languages are still predominantly spoken in rural areas. There is therefore a need to investigate NLG for Runyankore.

We have limited our scope to generating patient summaries, drug prescription explanations, and treatment instructions. The kind of text generated could include: the number of pills to be taken, listing the active ingredient(s), what the medication does not contain, and the general classification of the medication (for example, that hydrocodone is an opiate). These are largely knowledge-to-text cases, for which ontologies, such as the medical terminology SNOMED-CT, can easily be used. There are several NLG systems that take ontologies as input,

105

Proceedings of The 10th International Natural Language Generation conference, pages 105–113,
Santiago de Compostela, Spain, September 4-7 2017. ©2017 Association for Computational Linguistics

mainly for English (Kaljurand and Fuchs, 2007), but also Latvian and Lithuanian (Gruzitis et al., 2010; Gruzitis and Barzdins, 2011), and Greek (Androutsopoulos et al., 2013). These systems apply the template NLG technique. However, as was demonstrated in (Keet and Khumalo, 2017), templates are inapplicable to agglutinating Bantu languages, such as Runyankore.

Runyankore, like other Bantu languages has a complex verbal morphology (14 tenses), noun class system with 20 noun classes, and is highly agglutinative. A noun class (NC) determines the affixes of the nouns belonging to it, and this in turn determines the agreement markers on the associated lexical categories such as adjectives and verbs. To illustrate the agglutinative nature of Runyankore (taken from (Turamyomwe, 2011)):

Verb: *titukakimureeterahoganu*

English: 'We have never ever brought it to him'

Decomposition: *ti-tu-ka-ki-mu-reet-er-a-ho-ga-nu*

Our previous work for Runyankore NLG (Byamugisha et al., 2016a; Byamugisha et al., 2016b) is not adequate, as it neither covers cardinality constraints (e.g., 'take [exactly] 3 pills'); nor the passive (e.g., 'operated by'); and ignore phonological conditioning of vowels in the agglutination process. Additionally, no evaluation on grammatical correctness of the generated text was done. All these aspects are needed for our scope of medical text generation. We undertook to address these shortcomings by: analyzing further details of the language to also process minimum, maximum, and exact cardinality, and devising algorithms for them; adding the phonological conditioning rules required for the scope; and extending the CFG of (Byamugisha et al., 2016b) with the passive. Their algorithms together with these novel ones were implemented and evaluated with 100 Runyankore speakers in rural Uganda and three Runyankore linguists. Most of the evaluated sentences were regarded as grammatically correct and understandable, and all computer-generated text was considered by a majority to have been written by a human being.

The paper is structured as follows: Section 2 introduces the new rules and algorithms required to generate more expressive text. Section 3 presents the experimental evaluation. We discuss in Section 4 and conclude in Section 5.

2 New rules and algorithms

Due to the limitations in our previous work for Runyankore NLG, as well as the structure of information in our domain of interest, healthcare, we developed new rules and algorithms to account for these gaps. These rules are added to those which already take care of the basic constructors in ontology languages, being named class subsumption ('is a' $\sqsubseteq$), conjunction ('and' $\sqcap$), negation ('not' $\neg$), existential quantification ('at least one' $\exists$), and universal quantification ('all/each' $\forall$) (Byamugisha et al., 2016a).

2.1 Cardinality constraints

In terns of the knowledge-to-text input, our previous language coverage was the description logic (DL) language $\mathcal{ALC}$. Adding qualified cardinality constraints brings the language feature coverage to $\mathcal{ALCQ}$, which is an important fragment of OWL 2 DL (Motik et al., 2009). We describe the verbalization patterns for maximum ($\leq$), minimum ($\geq$), and exact cardinality ($=$) in this section.

Maximum cardinality is worded in English typically as 'a maximum of', 'not more than', or 'at most'. We use the Runyankore equivalent of 'not more than', *-tarikurenga*, which is the preferred word use. However, to form the full word for 'not more than', the subject prefix of the concept quantified over is required. We illustrate this in the following example. Consider Axiom 1 below, where 'symptom' has to be pluralized to 'symptoms', which is in noun class (NC) 4. The plural prefix for NC4 is *emi* (making *emicucumo* 'symptoms') that has a subject prefix *gi* that is attached to the *-tarikurenga*, 'not more than'. Compare this with Axiom 2, where 'courses' *amashomo* is in NC 6, and therewith goes with the subject prefix *ga*.

Axiom1: Diabetes $\sqsubseteq$ $\leq$ 3 has.Symptoms

> *Buri ndwara ya shukari eine **emi**cucumo **gi**tarikurenga 3.*
>
> 'Every disease of diabetes has at most 3 symptoms'

Axiom2: Student $\sqsubseteq$ $\leq$ 10 takes.Course

> *Buri mwegi natwaara **ama**shomo **ga**tarikurenga 10.*
>
> 'Every student takes not more than 10 courses'

The algorithm to generate these coordinating elements is included in Algorithm 2.1.

Algorithm 2.1 Verbalization of Maximum Cardinality ($\leq$)

1: A axiom; Variables: a_1, o, n_1, n_p, nc_p, and sp_p; and functions: $getNumber(A)$, $getNext(A)$, $getNoun(o)$, $getPlural(n)$, $getNC(n_p)$, and $getSubjectPrefix(nc_p)$
2: $a_1 \leftarrow getNumber(A)$ {get the number after $\leq$}
3: $o \leftarrow getNext(A)$ {get the role after the number}
4: $n_1 \leftarrow getNoun(o)$ {obtain the noun from the role}
5: **if** $a_1 = 1$ **then**
6:    $nc_1 \leftarrow getNC(n_1)$ {get the noun class of the noun}
7:    $sp_1 \leftarrow getSubjectPrefix(nc_1)$ {use the noun class to obtain the subject prefix}
8:    Result $\leftarrow$ " sp_1tarikurenga a_1"   {verbalize with the appropriate subject prefix}
9: **else**
10:    $n_p \leftarrow getPlural(n_1)$ {pluralize the noun}
11:    $nc_p \leftarrow getNC(n_p)$ {get the plural noun class}
12:    $sp_p \leftarrow getSubjectPrefix(nc_p)$ {get the plural subject prefix}
13:    Result $\leftarrow$ " sp_ptarikurenga a_1"   {verbalize with the plural noun and subject prefix}
14: **end if**
15: **return** Result

Minimum cardinality ($\geq$) is typically rendered in English as 'a minimum of', 'not less than', or 'at least'. We apply 'at least' as the Runyankore verbalization, again because this is a more directly translatable version. Like the verbalization of existential quantification ($\exists$) in (Byamugisha et al., 2016a), it uses *hakiri* for 'at least'. However, unlike $\exists$ where we always have *-mwe* for 'one', $\geq$ has the number instead (unless the number is 1). Thus, a verbalization similar to $\exists$ is used, also using the subject prefix of the concept quantified over. The examples below illustrate this case; e.g., *e* is the subject prefix of NC 9, for *diguri* 'degree':

Axiom1: Panado $\sqsubseteq$ $\geq$ 4 has.ActiveIngredient
    *Buri Panado **hakiri** eine ebirungo by'amaani 4*
    'Every Panado has at least 4 active ingredients'
Axiom2: Student $\sqsubseteq$ $\geq$ 1 has.Degree

*Buri mwegi **hakiri** aine diguri emwe*
'Every student has at least 1 degree'

Similar to the verbalization of $\leq$, there is a need to pluralize the noun whenever the number after $\geq$ is greater than 1 (as is the case in Axiom 1, above). Due to space limitations, we omit the algorithm, as it is similar to Algorithm 2.1.

The English verbalization of exact cardinality ($=$) is 'exactly'. However, Runyankore does not have a direct translation for 'exactly', but uses 'only' instead. The word for 'only', *-onka*, requires the subject prefix to form the full word. In the following examples, **bw** and **ky** are the subject prefixes of NC 14 and 7, respectively, to which the nouns *obujuma* 'pills' and *ekitabo* 'book' belong, respectively:

Axiom1:   Patient $\sqsubseteq$ $=$ 2 takes.Pill
    *Buri murweire natwara obujuma 2 **bw**onka*
    'Every patient takes only 2 pills'
Axiom2:   Child $\sqsubseteq$ $=$ 1 has.Book
    *Buri mwana aine ekitabo 1 **ky**onka*
    'Every child has only 1 book'

As is the case with $\leq$ and $\geq$, the noun is pluralized whenever the number is greater than 1. The algorithm is fairly similar to the others and therefore omitted due to space limitations.

2.2   Processing of Prepositions

The presence of prepositions in roles (relations), such as 'works *for*', and passives, such as 'operated *by*' changes the pattern in which the role is verbalized. While the algorithms cannot yet deal with any arbitrary preposition, we cover those that appeared in our test ontologies. These include: 'with' *na*, 'in' *omu*, 'of' (depends on the NC of the noun), and 'by' *w*. Our implementation of 'of' and 'by' is limited to the situation where the former is present after a noun, and where the verb is in past tense for the latter. Examples of roles containing these prepositions are: works **with** $\rightarrow$ *naakora **na***; offered **in** $\rightarrow$ *neherezibwa **omu***; part **of** $\rightarrow$ *ekicweka **kya***; and driven **by** $\rightarrow$ *naavugwa*. 'With' and 'in' are translated as *na* and *omu* respectively, except when the verb is in the past tense, then the passive is introduced (as is the case with *neeherezibwa*). This case is similar to the verbalization of 'by' (see also Section 2.3). The verbalization of 'of' is different, as the NC of the noun (NC 7 in the example above) is required to obtain the genitive **ekya**, which then drops its initial vowel to form *kya*. Algorithm 2.2 shows the verbalization process of 'of'. The corresponding rules have been added to the ruleset.

Algorithm 2.2 Verbalization of 'of')

1: A axiom; Variables: n_1 g_1, nc_1, and p_1; and functions: $getNoun(A)$, $getNC(n_1)$, $getPreposition(n_1)$, $getGenitive(nc_1)$, and $dropIV(g_1)$
2: $n_1 \leftarrow getNoun(A)$ {obtain the main noun in the axiom}
3: $p_1 \leftarrow getPreposition(n_1)$ {obtain the preposition from the XML file}
4: $nc_1 \leftarrow getNC(n_1)$ {obtain the noun class}
5: $g_1 \leftarrow getGenitive(nc_1)$ {use the NC to obtain the genitive}
6: $g_1' \leftarrow dropIV(g_1)$ {Drop the initial vowel of the genitive}
7: Result $\leftarrow n_1$ g_1' {Verbalize with the noun and the genitive}
8: **return** Result

2.3 The Passive in Context-Free Grammars

In Byamugisha et al., (2016b), we used a CFG for verb conjugation. In order to cater for the passive as explained in Section 2.2, we added a new non-terminal to our original CFG that had 6 non-terminals. The passive is under the 'extensions' grammatical slot (Turamyomwe, 2011), represented here as non-terminal EX, which is placed between the verb stem VS and the final vowel FV. The new CFG is now as follws:

$S \rightarrow IG\ FM\ VS\ EX\ FV$

$IG \rightarrow PN\ IT$

$PN \rightarrow$ ti | ni

$IT \rightarrow$ a | o | n | tu | mu | ba | gu | gi | ri | ga | ki | bi | e | zi | ru | tu | ka | bu | ku | gu | ga

$FM \rightarrow \emptyset$

$VS \rightarrow$ kyendez | gw | vug | gend

$EX \rightarrow$ w | er | erer | ir | zi | is | n | ur | uur | gur | VS | isPN

$FV \rightarrow$ a | e | ire

This extended CFG was also added to our ruleset.

2.4 Phonological Conditioning

Due to the agglutinative nature of Runyankore, the text resulting from our algorithms sometimes con-tains letter combinations that do not exist in Runyankore phonology. When this happens, phonological rules are used to make the required changes that reflect the sound change in language. This is referred to as phonological conditioning, which is considered as a last step of text generation. Table 1 shows a sample of the inputs into this step, under which process it occurs, the output after phonological conditioning, and the reason why this is the case. Note that while some cases that require phonological conditioning appear similar, and would thus be assumed to have the same solution, this is actually not the case. Take the example of *baona* and *baonka*, which could be assumed to both be solved by a double vowel, leading to *boona* and *boonka* respectively. Instead, each case is assessed individually, due to the presence of the nasal compound *nk*, which therefore results in *boona* and *bonka*.

All algorithms and rules have been implemented and first verified with four ontologies: SNOMED-CT, university[1], people[2], and family[3]. We were able to generate text for all axioms which contained our selected constructors.

3 Evaluation of Generated Text

The typical method of evaluating the performance of NLG systems is to ask subjects to read and judge the generated text, as compared to human-authored text (Bouayad-Agha et al., 2012). Another form of evaluating NLG systems is to present people with a text composed of both human-authored and computer generated text, and ask them to identify which is which (de Rosis et al., 1999; Hussain et al., 2015). We used both methods in our evaluation. Similar to Hussain et al., (2015), we both rated the generated text for grammatical correctness and understandability, as well as distinguished between human-authored and computer generated text.

3.1 Materials and Methods

A questionnaire survey was used to evaluate the generated text. The questionnaire had three main sec-

---

[1]http://www.mindswap.org/ontologies/debugging/university.owl
[2]http://owl.man.ac.uk/2005/07/sssw/people
[3]http://www.mindswap.org/ontologies/family.owl

Table 1: Examples of when phonological conditioning is required.

Before	Process	After	Reason
abaegi	Pluralization	*abeegi*	Vowel coalescence
kiona	Agglutination	*kyona*	Whenever *i* is followed by a vowel, it is converted to *y*
baona	Agglutination	*boona*	Vowel coalescence
baonka	Agglutination	*boonka*, then *bonka*	When a double vowel (*oo*) precedes a nasal compound (*-nk-*), vowel elision occurs
niavuga	Conjugation	*navuga*, then *naavuga*	First, vowel elision occurs with *ni*, then the vowel is doubled due to vowel harmony

tions: (1) age, highest level of education, occupation, and first language; (2) 10 generated sentences, which were varied based on the DL constructor being verbalized, as well as the presence of special conditions like prepositions, the passive, and definitions; and (3) 10 sentences, of which 5 human-authored and 5 computer generated. The study was conducted in Mbarara, a district in Uganda, where Runyankore is ethnically and predominantly spoken. We used purposive sampling by only selecting participants who could read, write, and speak Runyankore. We evaluated with both linguists and non-linguists. We obtained 100 non-linguists from a single village, Mirama. In order to inform our target population that we were looking for study participants, an announcement was made at the local catholic church after the Sunday service. This information was related to the headmaster of a nearby school, who agreed to let his students and staff take part in our study. All our study participants were at least 18 years old. We also contacted 3 linguists from the Department of African Languages, College of Humanities and Social Sciences, Makerere University in Uganda.

We used a modified version of the questionnaire for linguists, which had 4 sections. The first 3 were similar to the questionnaire given to non-linguists; but we added a forth section to evaluate the output from the CFG. This section had 99 conjugated verbs, testing both the standard CFG and deviations from the standard CFG, negation, several verb stems from the ontologies, and phonological conditioning.

Grammatical Correctness and/or understandability The 10 sentences were required to be graded each according to four criteria: grammatically correct and understandable, incorrect grammar but understandable, grammatically correct but not understandable, and incorrect grammar and not understandable. Table 2 shows all the sentences in the questionnaire, as well as the DL axioms they verbalize, and the specific constructor whose verbalization we were testing for.

Sentence G originally had 'ProfessorInHCIorAI' and 'AIStudent' as concepts in the axiom. However, 'AI' and 'HCI' were replaced with 'Science' before the evaluation, because they were unfamiliar to the study participants, and this could have negatively affected how the sentence was graded.

Computer Generated versus Human-Authored 10 sentences, with 5 authored by a Runyankore Linguist (H) and 5 computer generated (C), were presented to study participants. They were then required to grade each sentence either as human-authored or computer generated, based on its construction. The sentences used in this part of the questionnaire are presented in Table 3.1, along with the DL axioms verbalized.

All study participants received a questionnaire containing the questions for evaluating grammatical correctness and understandability, and computer generated vs. human-authored.

3.2 Results and Analysis

99% of the 100 study participants were aged between 18 and 30 years of age. 94% were students, 5% were teachers, and 1% were retired nurse. 54% were female, and 94% had high school as their highest level of education. All study participants spoke Runyankore as their first language.

Table 2: Sentences evaluated for grammatical correctness and understandability.

	DL Axiom	Constructor Investigated	Runyankore Sentence
A	Chlordiazepoxide_hydro chloride $\sqsubseteq$ $\exists$ Has_active_ingredient(Chlordiazepoxide)	$\exists$ in medical domain	*Buri mubazi gwa hydrochloride ya Chlordiazepoxide hakiri gwine ekirungo ekyamaani kimwe kiri omubazi gwa Chlordiazepoxide.*
B	Giraffe $\sqsubseteq$ $\forall$ eats.Leaf	$\forall$	*Buri ntwiga nerya amapapa goona.*
C	Leaf $\sqsubseteq$ $\exists$ part_of.Leaf	$\exists$ with preposition	*Buri eipapa hakiri n'ekicweka kya omuti gumwe.*
D	Newspaper $\sqsubseteq$ Publication	$\sqsubseteq$	*Buri rupapura rwamakuru n'ekihandiiko ekishohoziibwe.*
E	Person $\sqsubseteq$ = 2 has.Parent	=	*Buri muntu aine abazaire 2 boonka.*
F	Student $\sqsubseteq$ $\geq$ 1 hasDegree	$\geq$	*Buri mwegi hakiri aine diguri emwe.*
G	ScienceProfessor $\sqsubseteq$ $\forall$ advisorOf.ScienceStudent	$\forall$ with preposition	*Buri purofeesa wa sayansi n'omuhabuzi wa boona abari abeegi ba sayansi.*
H	Man $\sqsubseteq$ $\neg$ Woman	disjointness ($\sqsubseteq \neg$)	*Omukazi ti mushaija.*
I	Old_Lady $\sqsubseteq$ $\exists$ has_pet.Animal $\sqcap$ $\forall$ has_pet.Cat	$\sqcap$	*Buri mukaikuru hakiri aine enyamaishwa erikutungwa abantu kuzaanisa emwe eri enyamishwa, kandi aine enyamaishwa erikutungwa abantu kuzaanisa zoona eziri enjangu.*
J	LecturerTaking4Courses $\sqsubseteq$ = 4 takes.Course	= with noun phrase	*Buri mushomesa orikushomesa amashomo ana natwara amashomo 4 goonka.*

Grammatical Correctness and/or Understandability Our preferred outcome during this evaluation was to have all sentences graded as 'grammatically correct and understandable' by more than 50% of study participants. The results are summarised in Figure 1. Sentences A, D, E, G, and H, which evaluated the verbalization of: medical $\exists$, $\sqsubseteq$, =, $\forall$ with preposition, and $\neg$, were regarded as 'grammatically correct and understandable' by over 50% of the study participants (66%, 80%, 86%, 71%, and 92% respectively), which was a very positive outcome. Sentences B and J received the highest scores of 'grammatically correct and understandable' among its scores (47% and 38% respectively), but this was followed closely by 'incorrect grammar but understandable' (with 41% for B and 35% for J).

Sentences C, F, and I, which evaluated the verbalization of $\exists$-with preposition, $\geq$, and $\sqcap$, were regarded as 'grammatically correct and understandable' by only 8%, 34%, and 26% of the study participants, respectively. They were graded for the worst outcome (incorrect grammar and not understandable) by 18%, 13%, and 35% of study partic-

ipants respectively. The grading of sentences C, F,

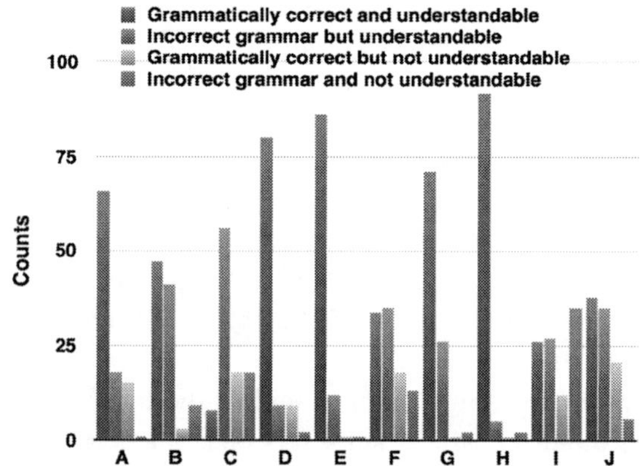

Figure 1: Evaluation results: A, D, E, G, and H performed very well ($>$ 65%); C, F, and I performed poorly ($<$ 35%); B and J performed marginally

and I was due to a lack of vowel assimilation, issues of syntax versus semantics, and wrong pluralization of definitions, respectively. The algorithms were updated to perform vowel assimilation and pluralize definitions accordingly.

Table 3: Sentences evaluated as either computer generated (C) or human-authored (H)

Label	DL Axiom	Runyankore Sentence
C1	Dog ⊑ ∃ eats.Bone	*Buri mbwa hakiri nerya eigufa rimwe.*
C2	Hydrocodone ⊑ Morphine_derivative	*Buri mubazi gwa Hydrocodone n'omubazi gwokukyendeeza obusaasi.*
H1	Lecturer ⊑ ¬ Professor	*Omushomesa wa yunivasite ti purofeesa.*
C3	Sheep ⊑ ∀ eats.Grass	*Buri ntaama nerya ebinyaansi byoona.*
H2	Student ⊑ ≤ 7 studies.Course	*Buri mwegi naashoma amashomo gatarikurenga 7.*
C4	TeachingFaculty ⊑ ≤ 3 takes.Course	*Abashomesa omu kitongore boona nibatwara amashomo gatarikurenga 3.*
H3	Hydrocodone ⊑ Opiate	*Buri mubazi gwa Hydrocodone gurimu ebirungo ebirikukyendeeza obusaasi.*
H4	Parent ⊑ ∃ hasChild	*Buri muzaire nomuntu oine haakiri omwana omwe.*
C5	Cat ⊑ ¬ Dog	*Enjangu ti mbwa.*
H5	Van ⊑ Vehicle	*Buri vaani nemotoka.*

Computer Generated Versus Human-Authored
The desired outcome for this part of the evaluation was to have all computer generated sentences graded as human-authored by at least 66% of study participants. Hussain et al., (2015) evaluated for the same, but with 3 professionals, and their best result was that 64% of the overall text were regarded as human-authored. Our results are summarised in Figure 2. All computer generated sentences (C) except for C4 (with 64%) were above this bar. C1, C2, C3, and C5 were regarded as human-authored by 78%, 71%, 90%, and 97% of study participants respectively.

On the other hand, some human-authored text performed under the desired threshold. H2 just made it with 66%, while H3 and H5 were below with 64% and 56% of study participants respectively, regarding them as human-authored. They actually performed worse than computer generated text.

The implication that most study participants (> 60%) regarded all generated text as having been written by a human being is positive outcome.

Results from Linguist We have so far received feedback from one of the 3 linguists we contacted, and we present that feedback here. From the same sentences in Table 2 (except I) for evaluating grammatical correctness and/or understandability, A, D, E, and G were graded as 'incorrect grammar but understandable', due to: the issue of translating medical terminologies, the nature of the text from the axiom, a lack of proper phonological conditioning,

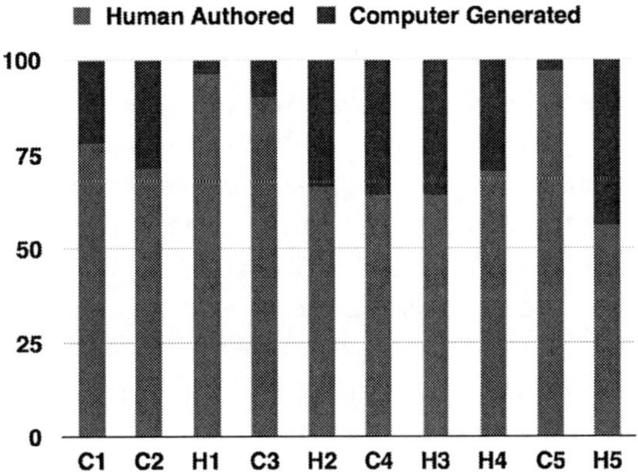

Figure 2: Computer vs Human: C1, C2, C3, C5 considered human authored by more than 66%; H2, H3, H5 performed worse than C

and the incorrect arrangement of the prepositional phrase respectively. C was graded as both incorrect and not understandable because of an error in the algorithm. This led to a modification of the grammar rules and algorithms. After the poor performance of sentence I in the non-linguists' questionnaire, arising from the translation of 'pet', we used a different axiom for the linguists, in order to focus their evaluation on the verbalization of conjunction. We used: Old_Lady ⊑ ∃ reads.Publication ⊓ ∀ reads.Tabloid. This was verbalized as: *Buri mukaikuru hakiri nashoma ekihandiiko ekishohozi-ibwe kimwe, kandi naashoma taburoyidi zoona.* It was regarded as 'grammatically correct but not understandable' because 'tabloid' was naturalized as *taburoyidi*. This is however the conventional way of translating loan words, and its negative effect on the grading of the sentence was unexpected. Sentences B, F, H, and J (except for the issue with the nasal compound) were graded as 'grammatically correct and understandable'. Except for H, the rest differ from the evaluation by non-linguists, where F was regarded as 'incorrect grammar but understandable' by 35%, 1% more than those who regarded it as 'grammatically correct and understandable'. Sentences B and J were only marginally regarded as being grammatically correct and understandable. It will be interesting to see whether all linguists will have a similar evaluation. From the same sentences in Table 3.1, C1, C2, H2, C4, and H3 were graded as human-authored; while H1, C3, H4, C5, and H5 were graded as computer generated. The reasons for differences in assessing this between linguists and non-linguists are unclear, as neither group explained their choice. It is however encouraging that more computer generated text was considered human-authored by a linguist.

When evaluating the performance of the CFG, 11 of the 99 conjugated verbs presented in the questionnaire were considered as incorrect: 1 due to a wrong subject prefix, 2 due to the need for an extra suffix, and 8 because vowel harmony was not implemented. The subject prefix and vowel harmony errors have since been fixed. The need for an extra suffix was only identified for the verb stem for 'eat' (*ry*). We are still investigating this error.

4   Discussion

Our work here adds to the growing efforts to verbalize ontologies in multiple languages. It has also provided a basis to consider that the underlying theories could be generalizable to other Bantu languages. In our previous work (Byamugisha et al., 2016a; Byamugisha et al., 2016c), we showed that the factors affecting verbalization in isiZulu and Runyankore are the same, and both Runyankore and isiZulu had similar exceptions to pluralizing nouns according to the standard NC table. Further, the passive as a grammatical slot is present in the verbal morphologies of both languages.

Perhaps most interestingly for our domain of in-terest, is that the use of a small sample of SNOMED-CT, a very large healthcare ontology, during testing, helped to investigate how to translate medical jargon to Runyankore. In some cases, the term is maintained, which is the case for common terms like 'Panado'; in others, it is given context, e.g., hydrocodone translated as *omubazi gwa hydrocodone* 'medicine of hydrocodone'; or a mixed transslation and context approach, e.g., *endwara ya shukari* 'disease of sugar', where 'sugar' is a common translation for 'diabetes' in a healthcare context; while in extreme cases, the term is defined, e.g., opiate translated as *omubazi ogukusinza ogukwejunisibwa kukyendeza obusaasi* 'medicine which intoxicates as treatment to reduce pain'. There are several terms for anatomy, diseases, and drugs which are not directly translatable to Runyankore, but this offers a starting point to show alternative ways to handle it.

Further, the results from the evaluation of the generated text are very encouraging, both from a linguist and non-linguists. Additionally, important feedback was obtained, which enabled us to make modifications to the initial rules and algorithms.

5   Conclusion

New algorithms for knowledge-to-text verbalisation into Runyankore have been developed. These include: i) rules and algorithms for cardinality constraints (maximum, minimum, and exact), therewith extending the language coverage, ii) handling some prepositions in complex roles; iii) processing the passive with a CFG, and iv) phonological conditioning. We have evaluated the text generated by the algorithms and rules with a group from the general population on grammatical correctness, understandability, and whether they were computer generated and human-authored text. The data demonstrated that most sentences were evaluated as grammatically correct and understandable, and human authored. We are currently investigating the architecture required to implement this as a NLG system.

Acknowledgements   This work is based on the research supported by the Hasso Plattner Institute (HPI) Research School in CS4A at UCT and the National Research Foundation of South Africa (Grant Number 93397).

References

Ion Androutsopoulos, Gerasimos Lampouras, and Dimitrios Galanis. 2013. Generating natural language descriptions from owl ontologies: The naturalowl system. *Journal of Artificial Intelligence Research*, 48:671–715.

Allen Asiimwe. 2014. *Definiteness and Specificity in Runyankore-Rukiga*. Ph.D. thesis, Stallenbosch University, Cape Town, South Africa.

Nadjet Bouayad-Agha, Gerard Casamayor, and Leo Wanner. 2012. Natural language generation in the context of the semantic web. *Semantic Web Journal*.

Joan Byamugisha, C. Maria Keet, and Brian DeRenzi. 2016a. Bootstrapping a runyankore cnl from an isizulu cnl. In *CNL 2016*, Aberdeen, Scotland. Springer LLNCS.

Joan Byamugisha, C. Maria Keet, and Brian DeRenzi. 2016b. Tense and aspect in runyankore using a context-free grammar. In *INLG 2016*, Edinburgh, Scotland.

Joan Byamugisha, C. Maria Keet, and Langa Khumalo. 2016c. Pluralizing nouns in isizulu and related languages. In *CICLing 2016*, Konya, Turkcy.

J. Alison Cawsey, B. Ray Jones, and Janne Pearson. 2000. The evaluation of a personalized health information system for patients with cancer. *User Modeling and User-Adapted Interaction*, 10(1):47–72.

Fiorella de Rosis, Floriana Grasso, and C. Dianne Berry. 1999. Refining instructional text generation after evaluation. *Artificial Intelligence in Medicine*, 17(1):1–36.

Chrysanne DiMarco, Graeme Hirst, Leo Wanner, and John Wilkinson. 1995. Healthdoc: Customizing patient information and health education by medical condition and personal characteristics. In *Workshop on Artificial Intelligence in Patient Education*, Glasgow, Scotland.

Chrysanne DiMarco, Peter Bray, Dominic Covvey, Don Cowan, Vic DiCiccio, Eduard Hovy, Joan Lipa, and Cathy Yang. 2005. Authoring and generation of tailored preoperative patient education materials. In *Workshop on Personalization in e-Health User Modeling, Conference*, Edinburgh, Scotland.

Chrysanne DiMarco, David Wiljer, and Eduard Hovy. 2009. Self-managed access to personalized healthcare through automated generation of tailored health educational materials from electronic health records. In *AAAI Fall Symposium on Virtual Health Interaction*, Washington D. C.

Normunds Gruzitis and Guntis Barzdins. 2011. Towards a more natural multilingual controlled language interface to owl. In *IWCS*, pages 335–339.

Normunds Gruzitis, Gunta Nespore, and Baiba Saulite. 2010. Verbalizing ontologies in controlled baltic languages. In *4th International Conference on Human Language Technologies-The Baltic Perspective*, Riga, Latvia.

Sazzad Mohammed Hussain, A. Rafael Calvo, Louise Ellis, Juchen Li, Laura Ospina-Pinillos, Tracey Davenport, and Ian Hickie. 2015. Nlg-based moderator response generator to support mental health. In *CHI'2015*, Seoul, South Korea. ACM.

Kaarel Kaljurand and E. Norbert Fuchs. 2007. Verbalizing owl in attempto controlled english. In *Third International Workshop on OWL: Experiences and Directions*, Innsbruck, Austria.

C. Maria Keet and Langa Khumalo. 2017. Towards a knowledge-to-text controlled natural language of isizulu. *Language Resources and Evaluation*, 51:131–157.

Fredrik Lindahl. 2005. Practical text generation in clinical medicine. Chalmers Computer Science Department Winter Meeting.

Saad Mahamood and Ehud Reiter. 2011. Generating affective natural language for parents of neonatal infants. In *ENLG 2011*, pages 12–21, Stroudsburg, Pa, USA. ACM.

Boris Motik, Peter F. Patel-Schneider, and Bijan Parsia. 2009. OWL 2 web ontology language structural specification and functional-style syntax. W3c recommendation, W3C, 27 Oct. http://www.w3.org/TR/owl2-syntax/.

Doreen Daphine Tayebwa. 2014. Demonstrative determiners in runyankore-rukiga. Master's thesis, Norwegian University of Science and Technology, Norway.

Justus Turamyomwe. 2011. Tense and aspect in runyankore-rukiga: Linguistic resources and analysis. Master's thesis, Norwegian University of Science and Technology, Norway.

**Invited Speaker

Talking about the world with a distributed model

Gemma Boleda
Universitat Pompeu Fabra

Abstract

We use language to talk about the world, and so reference is a crucial property of language. However, modeling reference is particularly difficult, as it involves both continuous and discrete aspects of language. For instance, referring expressions like "the big mug" or "it" typically contain content words ("big", "mug"), which are notoriously fuzzy or vague in their meaning, and also function words ("the", "it") that largely serve as discrete pointers. Data-driven, distributed models based on distributional semantics or deep learning excel at the former, but struggle with the latter, and the reverse is true for symbolic models. I present ongoing work on modeling reference with a distributed model aimed at capturing both aspects, and learns to refer directly from reference acts.

Proceedings of The 10th International Natural Language Generation conference, page 114,
Santiago de Compostela, Spain, September 4-7 2017. ©2017 Association for Computational Linguistics

The Code2Text Challenge: Text Generation in Source Code Libraries

Kyle Richardson[†], **Sina Zarrieß**[‡] and **Jonas Kuhn**[†]

[†]Institute for Natural Language Processing, University of Stuttgart, Germany
`kyle@ims.uni-stuttgart.de`
[‡]Dialogue Systems Group // CITEC, Bielefeld University, Germany
`sina.zarriess@uni-bielefeld.de`

Abstract

We propose a new shared task for tactical data-to-text generation in the domain of source code libraries. Specifically, we focus on text generation of function descriptions from example software projects. Data is drawn from existing resources used for studying the related problem of semantic parser induction (Richardson and Kuhn, 2017b; Richardson and Kuhn, 2017a), and spans a wide variety of both natural languages and programming languages. In this paper, we describe these existing resources, which will serve as training and development data for the task, and discuss plans for building new independent test sets.


```
                1. Java Documentation

*Returns the greater of two long values
*/ ...
public static long max(long a, long b)
```

```
                2. Python Documentation

# from decimal.Context

max(self, a, b):
    """Compares two values numerically
    and returns the maximum"""
```

```
3. aNALoGuE Challenge (Novikova and Rieser, 2016)

MR input:   name[Bibmbap House] food[French]
priceRange[cheap], area[riverside] near[Clare Hall]
NL output:  Near Clare Hall, in the riverside area,
Bibimbap serves French food in the price range cheap.
```

Figure 1: Example source code documentation, or *docstrings* in 1-2, and an example MR/text pair.

1 Introduction

Source code libraries are collections of computer programs/instructions expressed in a target programming language that aim to solve some set of problems. Within these libraries, the designers of the code often use natural language to describe how various internal components work. For example, Figure 1.1 shows a docstring description (in red) for the `max` function in the Java standard library, which explains what the function does (i.e., *Returns the greater of*), and the types of arguments that the function takes (i.e., *two long values*). Similarly, a related function and its documentation for the Python programming language is shown in Figure 1.2.

Given the tight coupling between such high-level text and lower-level representations, automatically extracting parallel datasets in this domain, consisting of short text descriptions and code templates, is rather straightforward. Such datasets can then be used to study various translation problems, including translating text to code templates (i.e., semantic parsing), or generating representations to text (i.e., data-to-text generation). In previous work (Richardson and Kuhn, 2017b), we looked at using source code libraries to study the first problem, and have collected datasets for 43 software libraries across 7 natural languages. We have also created a tool, called `Function Assistant`, for extracting new datasets from arbitrary software projects (Richardson and Kuhn, 2017a).

In this paper, we propose using these resources for studying the second problem. The task can be described as follows: given a source code library dataset or collection of datasets consisting of text and code template pairs, e.g., the text *Returns the greater of two..* and the function representation `static long max(..)` in Figure 1.1, create a model that generates well-formed natural language descriptions of these formal code inputs. This task involves solving several sub-tasks, chief among them being *lexicalization*, or the problem of how to

115

Proceedings of The 10th International Natural Language Generation conference, pages 115–119,
Santiago de Compostela, Spain, September 4-7 2017. ©2017 Association for Computational Linguistics

verbalize the function name and return value (here using a VP *returns the greater of*), and the function's arguments (expressed here as a plural expression, *two long values*). As shown in Figure 1.3, existing lexicalization tasks tend to involve input representations that have considerable lexical overlap with the verbal output, which is not the case with our datasets and therefore makes our problem more difficult. In addition, there is the problem of *realization*, or here aggregating the description as a sentence with an implied subject containing a transitive verb and a complex object, where the referring expression is attached as a PP.

The available resources make the task highly multilingual, both in terms of the input programming languages and output natural languages. Since programming languages differ in terms of representation conventions, each formal language provides unique challenges related to these differences. For example, statically-typed languages, such as Java in Figure 1.1., contain more information about argument and return values than dynamically-typed languages, such as Python in Figure 1.2.

In what follows, we motivate this task by discussing related work. We also discuss the current datasets and plans to build new independent test sets.

2 Related Work

Data-to-text generation concerns the problem of generating well-formed, natural language descriptions from non-linguistic, formal meaning representations (Gatt and Krahmer, 2017). In our case, the input to a given generation system is a source code representation. In order to learn a natural language generation (NLG) system from data, a parallel corpus containing pairs of inputs and outputs must be constructed. In many studies on data-to-text generation, these parallel resources are relatively small, cf. work on sportscasting (Chen and Mooney, 2008), weather reporting (Belz, 2008; Liang et al., 2009), or biology facts (Banik et al., 2013). We follow similar efforts to build automatic parallel resources (Belz and Kow, 2010) by mining example software libraries for (raw) pairs of short text descriptions and function representations.

A recent trend is the use of crowd-sourcing to obtain parallel NLG data (Wen et al., 2016; Novikova et al., 2016; Gardent et al., 2017). Crowd-workers are presented with some meaning representation (MR, e.g., triples from a knowledge base) and asked to verbalize these representations in natural language. For example, the **MR input** in Figure 1.3 in the restaurant domain is verbalized as the **NL output** text. While this method allows for fast annotation, and thus solves the data scarcity problem, it also raises some new issues. For instance, sentences or utterances are produced by crowd-workers without much context, which puts to question the naturalness of the resulting text. Novikova et al. (2016) compare collecting data from logic-based MRs, of the type shown in Figure 1.3, and pictorial MRs, and find that the former approach leads to less natural and less informative descriptions. This seems to be related to the problem that the natural language sentence is a very close verbalization of the "logic" input, i.e., many terms in the MR can be simply taken up in the sentence.

Our approach relies on naturally occurring verbal descriptions produced by human developers. Our input data (source code representations) seems more abstract than previously used representations e.g. in the restaurant domain where many lexical items in the target utterance already appear in the MR. Thus, our input data is more "naturally occurring" in the sense that it has not been designed specifically for an NLG system (as compared to Wen et al. (2016) who randomly generate input representations) yet it still corresponds to a formal language. We expect that there is relatively little lexical correspondence between source code representations and verbal descriptions and that this is an interesting challenge for data-driven NLG, as simple "alignment" methods might fail to predict lexicalization.

While natural language generation in technical domains has long been of interest to the NLG community (Reiter et al., 1995), there has been renewed interest in this and other closely related topics over the last few years in NLP (Allamanis et al., 2015; Iyer et al., 2016; Yin and Neubig, 2017), making a shared task on the topic rather timely. While preparing the final version of this paper, we learned about the work of (Miceli Barone and Sennrich, 2017), who similarly look at generating text from automatically mined Python projects, using a similar set of tools as ours. This interest seems largely related to the wider availability of new data resources in the technical domain, especially through technical websites such as Github and StackOverflow. Rather than focus on unconstrained source code representations, as done in some of these studies, we believe that limiting the expressivity of the generation input to function representations within *known* software libraries allows for more controlled experimentation.

On the resource side, our datasets are taken from (Richardson and Kuhn, 2017b; Richardson and Kuhn, 2017a). These resources have been used to study the problem of semantic parser induction, which is the inverse of the proposed data-to-text task. Given the close connection between the two tasks, there is often considerable overlap between the techniques used to solve either problem, techniques that are largely drawn from work on statistical machine translation (Wong and Mooney, 2006; Belz and Kow, 2009) and parsing (Zettlemoyer and Collins, 2012; Konstas and Lapata, 2012). While some approaches to generation explicitly use semantic parsing methods (Wong and Mooncy, 2007; Zarrieß and Richardson, 2013), a more systematic investigation into the relation between these two tasks seems missing, which is a topic that we hope to address in this shared task.

3 Task Description

Given a collection of datasets consisting of text x and function representation z pairs, or $D = \{(x, z)_i\}_i^n$, the goal is to create a generation system that can produce well-formed, natural language descriptions from these representations, or $\text{gen} : z \rightarrow x$. As discussed above, such descriptions should not only cover what the associated function does in general, but should also describe the function's various parameters. As a secondary (optional) task, we will allow generation systems that accommodate processing in the other direction to compete on the task of semantic parsing, $\text{sp} : x \rightarrow z$, or generating function representations from text input.

3.1 Main Research Questions

Recent data-driven approaches in NLG have been successful in modeling end-to-end generation from unaligned input-output, cf. (Angeli et al., 2010; Mairesse and Young, 2014; Dušek and Jurcicek,

2015; Wen et al., 2016). However, these system have been mostly tested on datasets (e.g., in the restaurant domain) that require describing very similar entities, entities that are encoded in MRs that have considerable lexical overlap with the target text output. A central research question is whether these end-to-end approaches scale to NLG settings that involve substantially harder lexicalization problems, such as with our datasets where the overlap is considerably less. Similarly, generating source code documentation also involves describing a wide variety of functions from many different libraries, meaning that many more lexical concepts need to be learned.

A more general question is the following: to what extent can one build a function to text generation system by relying only on example input-output pairs? This question is partly about the sufficiency of function representations for natural language generation, namely, are these representations detailed enough to serve as a reasonable knowledge representation for natural language? If not, what is missing? How do hybrid approachcs, pcrhaps approaches that rely on linguistically well-founded translation constraints and information about natural language syntax, fare against purely data-driven systems that rely solely on input-output as evidence?

Finally, the semantic parsing task addresses the following questions: what is the precise relationship between semantic parsing and data-to-text generation? Does an improvement in one task lead to an improvement in the other task? Is data-to-text generation simply an *inverse* semantic parsing task (Gatt and Krahmer, 2017) or are the two tasks fundamentally different?

4 Datasets

4.1 Train and Development Sets

Figure 2 shows information about the two datasets that will be available for model development, which were first introduced in (Richardson and Kuhn, 2017b) and (Richardson and Kuhn, 2017a) respectively[1]. None of these datasets have been previously used for data-to-text generation. The first dataset consists of the standard library documentation for 9 programming languages, including Java, Ruby, PHP,

---

[1]Please see the original papers to get more detailed information about each dataset

Dataset	# Software Projects	# Training Pairs	# Programming Languages	# Natural Languages
Standard Library Docs	16	38,652	9	7
Python 27	27	37,567	1	1

Figure 2: A description of the currently available software datasets for model development.

Python, Elisp, Haskell, Clojure, C, and Scheme. In addition, this resource includes documentation in 7 natural languages, including English, French, Spanish, Russian, Japanese, Turkish, and German. The second resource includes 27 publicly available Python projects, taken from the well-known *awesome Python* list of (Chen, 2017).

Each individual standard library documentation set or Python project consists of short text descriptions with function representations. While each function representation typically has only a *single* text description, background information in the documentation allows one to find related functions, and therefore related descriptions, which can be taken into account for training and evaluation. We note that there is wide variability in the size of each individual dataset, and some datasets are low-resource. One interesting research question is whether it is feasible to build a NLG system in these low-resource scenarios, and whether training on multiple languages can help. In our previous experiments, we built individual models for each parallel dataset, though participants will be free to build models that are trained on multiple projects if desired.

We also note that these datasets are constructed automatically, and our existing extraction tool does not do extensive text preprocessing. The motivation for this is that we can quickly construct new resources for model development and evaluation, though the result is that some of available text descriptions are noisy. We however regard this "noisiness" as an interesting technical challenge, and contrasts with other shared tasks where more carefully curated data is assumed.

4.2 Test Sets

The publicly available test sets will be used for evaluation (see details of the evaluation below). In order to ensure that participants are not fitting their models to these sets, we are proposing to build three additional evaluation sets, each corresponding to a different programming language. These resources will be built using the `Function Assistant`

toolkit (Richardson and Kuhn, 2017a), which already supports building parallel datasets from arbitrary Python source code projects, and will soon have functionality for the Java language.

The first two test sets, or *evaluation tracks*, will be specific to the Python and Java language, and will consist of unseen function representation-text pairs for each language. By having two separate sets according to language, we can see whether generation quality differs between different types of programming languages. Taking an idea from the recent CoNLL 2017 shared task on dependency parsing, the third evaluation track will include examples from a *surprise* programming language that has not been observed during the training phase. The idea is to see how generation systems generalize to unobserved languages where the inputs vary slightly.

5   Evaluation, Baselines and Scheduling

Following other data-to-text shared tasks (Banik et al., 2013; Colin et al., 2016) and previous work on text generating from code (Iyer et al., 2016), we will use automatic evaluation metrics such as BLEU and METEOR to evaluate system output. We will also perform fluency-based human evaluation on a subset of each test set using student volunteers from the Institute for Natural Language Processing (IMS), at the University of Stuttgart, Germany.

To establish baseline results, we have already started a pilot study that uses phrase-based SMT to do generation. Such models have previously been used to establish strong baseline generation results (Belz and Kow, 2009; Wong and Mooney, 2007), and have the advantage of being easy to run using known open-source tools. Since these models only require parallel data, they also show what a purely input-output driven model is capable of achieving on these datasets.

All publicly available datasets are immediately available for system development. The goal is to develop the new test sets before the end of 2017, and for the evaluation to be carried out in summer 2018.

Acknowledgement

This work and the current data collection effort is funded by the German Research Foundation (DFG) via SFB 732, project D2, at the University of Stuttgart. In addition, we acknowledge support by the Cluster of Excellence "Cognitive Interaction Technology" (CITEC; EXC 277) at Bielefeld University, which is also funded by the DFG.

References

Miltos Allamanis, Daniel Tarlow, Andrew Gordon, and Yi Wei. 2015. Bimodal modelling of Source Code and Natural Language. In *Proceedings of ICML*.

Gabor Angeli, Percy Liang, and Dan Klein. 2010. A Simple Domain-Independent Probabilistic Approach to Generation. In *Proceedings of EMNLP*.

Eva Banik, Claire Gardent, and Eric Kow. 2013. The KBGen Challenge. In *Proceedings of ENLG*.

Anja Belz and Eric Kow. 2009. System Building Cost vs. Output Quality in Data-to-Text Generation. In *Proceedings of ENLG*.

Anja Belz and Eric Kow. 2010. Extracting Parallel Fragments from Comparable Corpora for Data-to-Text Generation. In *Proceedings of INGL*.

Anja Belz. 2008. Automatic Generation of Weather Forecast Texts using Comprehensive Probabilistic Generation-space Models. *Natural Language Engineering*, 14(4):431–455.

David L Chen and Raymond J Mooney. 2008. Learning to Sportscast: a Test of Grounded Language Acquisition. In *Proceedings of ICML*.

Vinta Chen. 2017. Awesome Python: A curated list of awesome Python frameworks, libraries, software and resources. `https://github.com/vinta/awesome-python`.

Emilie Colin, Claire Gardent, Yassine Mrabet, Shashi Narayan, and Laura Perez-Beltrachini. 2016. The WebNLG Challenge: Generating Text from DBPedia Data. In *Proceedings of INLG*.

Ondřej Dušek and Filip Jurcicek. 2015. Training a natural language generator from unaligned data. In *Proceedings of the ACL-IJCNLP*.

Claire Gardent, Anastasia Shimorina, Shashi Narayan, and Laura Perez-Beltrachini. 2017. Creating Training Corpora for NLG Micro-Planning. In *Proceedings of ACL*.

Albert Gatt and Emiel Krahmer. 2017. Survey of the State of the Art in Natural Language Generation: Core tasks, applications and evaluation. *arXiv preprint arXiv:1703.09902*.

Srinivasan Iyer, Ioannis Konstas, Alvin Cheung, and Luke Zettlemoyer. 2016. Summarizing Source Code using a Neural Attention Model. In *Proceedings of ACL*.

Ioannis Konstas and Mirella Lapata. 2012. Unsupervised Concept-to-text Generation with Hypergraphs. In *Proceedings of NAACL*.

Percy Liang, Michael I Jordan, and Dan Klein. 2009. Learning Semantic Correspondences with Less Supervision. In *Proceedings of ACL*.

François Mairesse and Steve Young. 2014. Stochastic language generation in dialogue using factored language models. *Computational Linguistics*, 40(4).

Antonio Valerio Miceli Barone and Rico Sennrich. 2017. A parallel corpus of Python functions and documentation strings for automated code documentation and code generation. *arXiv preprint arXiv:1707.02275*.

Jekaterina Novikova and Verena Rieser. 2016. The aNALoGuE Challenge: Non Aligned Language GEneration. In *Proceedings of INLG*.

Jekaterina Novikova, Oliver Lemon, and Verena Rieser. 2016. Crowd-sourcing NLG Data: Pictures Elicit Better Data. In *Proceedings of INLG*.

Ehud Reiter, Chris Mellish, and John Levine. 1995. Automatic Generation of Technical Documentation. *Applied Artificial Intelligence*, 9(3):259–287.

Kyle Richardson and Jonas Kuhn. 2017a. Function Assistant: A Tool for NL Querying of APIs. In *Proceedings of EMNLP*.

Kyle Richardson and Jonas Kuhn. 2017b. Learning Semantic Correspondences in Technical Documentation. In *Proceedings of ACL*.

Tsung-Hsien Wen, Milica Gašic, Nikola Mrkšic, Lina M Rojas-Barahona, Pei-Hao Su, David Vandyke, and Steve Young. 2016. Multi-domain Neural Network Language Generation for Spoken Dialogue Systems. In *Proceedings of NAACL-HLT*.

Yuk Wah Wong and Raymond J Mooney. 2006. Learning for Semantic Parsing with Statistical Machine Translation. In *Proceedings of NACL*.

Yuk Wah Wong and Raymond J Mooney. 2007. Generation by Inverting a Semantic Parser that Uses Statistical Machine Translation. In *Proceedings of HLT-NAACL*.

Pengcheng Yin and Graham Neubig. 2017. A Syntactic Neural Model for General-Purpose Code Generation. In *Proceedings of ACL*.

Sina Zarrieß and Kyle Richardson. 2013. An Automatic Method for Building a Data-to-Text Generator. In *Proceedings of ENLG*.

Luke S Zettlemoyer and Michael Collins. 2012. Learning to Map Sentences to Logical Form: Structured Classification with Probabilistic Categorial Grammars. *arXiv preprint arXiv:1207.1420*.

Shared Task Proposal: Multilingual Surface Realization Using Universal Dependency Trees

Simon Mille
UPF
Barcelona, ES
simon.mille@upf.edu

Bernd Bohnet
Google Research
London, UK
bohnetbd@google.com

Leo Wanner
ICREA and UPF
Barcelona, ES
leo.wanner@upf.edu

Anja Belz
U of Brighton
Brighton, UK
A.S.Belz@brighton.ac.uk

Abstract

We propose a shared task on multilingual Surface Realization, i.e., on mapping unordered and uninflected universal dependency trees to correctly ordered and inflected sentences in a number of languages. A second deeper input will be available in which, in addition, functional words, fine-grained PoS and morphological information will be removed from the input trees. The first shared task on Surface Realization was carried out in 2011 with a similar setup, with a focus on English. We think that it is time for relaunching such a shared task effort in view of the arrival of *Universal Dependencies* annotated treebanks for a large number of languages on the one hand, and the increasing dominance of *Deep Learning*, which proved to be a game changer for NLP, on the other hand.

1 Introduction

In 2017, three shared tasks on Natural Language Generation (NLG) take place: Task 9 of SemEval (May and Priyadarshi, 2017), WebNLG[1] and E2E[2]. The first starts from *Abstract Meaning Representations* (AMRs), the second from *RDF triples*, and the third from dialog act-based *Meaning Representations* (MRs) respectively. With these efforts, the focus is put on "real-life" generation, since the respective inputs come from existing analyzers (for AMRs) or existing databases (for RDF triples and

MRs). This shows that the research on NLG is on the right track and that there is an interest in large scale "deep" NLG. However, both the 2017 and the past shared tasks (including the 2011 Surface Realization Shared Task (Belz and et al., 2011)) focus on English; multilingual generation has been neglected largely so far.

On the other side, the last years saw a push in the annotation of multilingual treebanks with so-called *Universal Dependencies* (UDs), such that nowadays resources for a number of languages are available and can be used for shared tasks.[3] Furthermore, recent years witnessed a shift of the processing paradigm in applications such as parsing and machine translation from traditional supervised machine learning techniques to deep learning.[4] This is also a chance for NLG, which could benefit from deep learning to a greater extent than it currently does.

Our objective is to set up a follow-up of the 2011 Surface Realization Shared Task (SR'11) at Generation Challenges (Belz and et al., 2011); this time with an emphasis of multilingual surface generation from UD treebanks. The success of deep learning techniques in a number of areas of natural language processing furthermore opens the avenue to a broader range of system designs than have been seen before.

As in SR'11, the proposed shared task comprises

---

[1]http://talcl.loria.fr/webnlg/stories/challenge.html

[2]http://www.macs.hw.ac.uk/InteractionLab/E2E/

[3]See the recent parsing shared task based on UDs (Nivre and de Marneffe et al., 2016): http://universaldependencies.org/conll17/.

[4]See for instance the 1st NMT workshop, in which the NLG topic is also addressed: https://sites.google.com/site/acl17nmt/.

Proceedings of The 10th International Natural Language Generation conference, pages 120–123,
Santiago de Compostela, Spain, September 4-7 2017. ©2017 Association for Computational Linguistics

two tracks with different levels of difficulty:[5]

- Shallow Track: This track will start from genuine UD structures from which word order information has been removed and the tokens have been lemmatized, i.e., from unordered dependency trees with lemmatized nodes that hold PoS tags and morphological information as found in the original annotations. It will consist in determining the word order and inflecting words.

- Deep Track: This track will start from UD structures from which functional words (in particular, auxiliaries, functional prepositions and conjunctions) and surface-oriented morphological information have been removed. In addition to what has to be done for the Shallow Track, the Deep Track will thus consist of the introduction of the removed functional words and morphological features.

The participating teams will be expected to produce outputs at least for the Shallow Track.

2 Data

Universal Dependencies[6] (UD) have attracted in recent years interest from many researchers across different fields of NLP. Currently, 70 treebanks covering about 50 languages can be downloaded freely[7].

UD Treebanks facilitate the development of an application that works potentially across all of the UD treebank languages in a uniform fashion, which is a big advantage for system developers. These treebanks are also a good basis for a multilingual shared task: a system that has been built for some of the languages may work for most of the other languages as well.

For the SR'18 Task, we will use a subset of the UD treebanks, selecting about 10 languages with an annotation of high quality, which provides PoS tags and morphological annotation (number, tense, verbal finiteness, etc.). A subset of at least 4 treebanks will be used for the Deep Track. The treebanks will be selected according to (i) the expertise

of the task organizers in the corresponding language, (ii) the availability of native speakers for conversion and evaluation, (iii) the size of the treebank, (iv) the feasibility of the format conversion, (v) the variety of linguistic features captured in the annotation.

For the input to the Shallow Track, the UD structures will be processed as follows:

1. the information on word order will be removed by randomized scrambling;

2. the words will be replaced by their lemmas or stems, depending on the availability of lemmatization and stemming tools, respectively.

For the Deep Track, additionally:

3. functional prepositions and conjunctions that can be inferred from other lexical units or from the syntactic structure will be removed, as e.g., "by" and "of" in Figure 2;

4. determiners and auxiliaries will be replaced (when needed) by attribute/value pairs, as, e.g., "Definiteness" and "Aspect" in Figure 3;

5. edge labels will be generalized into predicate argument labels, following the PropBank/NomBank edge label nomenclature (Meyers and et al., 2004; Palmer et al., 2005), with three main differences: (i) there will be no special label for external arguments (i.e., no "A0"), which means that all first arguments of a predicate will be mapped to A1, and the rest of the arguments will be labeled starting from A2; (ii) all modifier edges "AM-..." will be generalized to "AM"; (iii) there will be a coordinative relation; and (iv) any relation that does not fall into the first three cases will be assigned an underspecified edge label.

6. morphological information coming from the syntactic structure or from agreements will be removed; in other words, only "semantic" information such as nominal number and verbal tense will be maintained in the Deep input, as opposed to verbal finiteness (which comes from the structure) or verbal number (which comes from agreement with the subject);

---

[5]In what follows, we refer to the proposed task as 'SR'18'.
[6]http://universaldependencies.org/#en
[7]https://lindat.mff.cuni.cz/repository/xmlui/handle/11234/1-1983

7. fine-grained PoS labels found in some tree-banks (as, e.g., column 5 in Figure 2) will be removed, and only coarse-grained ones will be maintained (column 4 in Figures 2 and 3).

The idea beyond the Deep Track is to make the input closer to a real-life input to NLG systems, in which no syntactic or language-specific information is available (see, e.g., the inputs in the SemEval, WebNLG, E2E shared tasks), while keeping it relatively simple. The main differences between the proposed Deep input and AMRs are the following: (i) no linking with NE databases; (ii) no abstraction of nominal VS verbal events; (iii) no OntoNotes labeling; (iv) no shared arguments; (v) no typed circumstancials.

The inputs to the Shallow and Deep Tracks will be distributed in the CoNLL-U format[8], and in the Human-Friendly Graph (HFG) format, as in SR'11 (Belz and et al., 2011). Figures 1, 2 and 3 show a sample original UD annotation for English, a sample input for the Shallow Track, and a sample input for the Deep Track respectively, in the 10-column CoNLL-U format.

3 Evaluation

We will perform both automatic and manual evaluations of the outputs of the systems.

For the automatic evaluation, we will compute scores with the following metrics:

1. BLEU as geometric mean of 1 to 4-grams with smoothing to compute sentence level scores,

2. NIST n-gram similarity weight,

3. METEOR lexical similarity based on stem, synonym and paraphrase matches.

We will apply text normalization before scoring. For n-best ranked system outputs, we will compute a single score for all outputs by computing the weighted sum of their individual scores, with a weight assigned to an output in inverse proportion to its rank. For a subset of the test data we may obtain additional alternative realizations via Mechanical Turk for use in the automatic evaluations.

For the human-assessed evaluation, we are planning to use a type of evaluation that is based on preference judgements (Kow and Belz, 2012, p.4035), using the existing evaluation interface described in Kow and Belz's paper. As in SR'11, we plan to use students in the third year of an undergraduate degree, from Cambridge, Oxford and Edinburgh. Two candidate outputs[9] will be presented to the evaluators, who will assess them for Clarity, Fluency and Meaning Similarity. For each criterion, they will be asked not only to state which system output they prefer, but also how strong is their preference.

We plan to organize a workshop collocated with ACL '18, COLING '18, or EMNLP '18 at which the results of the SR'18 will be presented. To ensure a smooth setup of the Shared Task and a swift evaluation of the system outputs, the organizers will contribute with their research funds. Furthermore, Google sponsorship will be solicited.

4 Conclusion

With this shared task, we aim to continue a very successful first shared task on surface realization. We think it is a good moment to take this topic up again due to emerging new techniques and system designs, new available data sets that can be used as basis for data-preparation, and a broad interest in deep generation techniques that emerges from new applications such as chat bots and personal assistants. We hope to attract a number of submissions within these application contexts (not only from the generation, but also, for instance, from the parsing community) and deepen the interest in text generation.

Beyond the possible impact of the tools developed in the context of this shared task due to the standard input sets and thus their easier reuse, we also see the shared task as an interesting experiment on the usability of UDs in the context of NLG. Our secondary objective is to assess how feasible it is to connect UD representations to predicate argument structures commonly used in deep NLG systems.

A valuable by-product of the shared task will be a set of input structures derived from UD data on a shallow and deep levels, which will be useful for further system development, application and research.

---

[8]http://universaldependencies.org/format.html

[9]Candidate outputs can also include a gold sentence, in addition to the system output.

```
1    The        the         DET     DT    Definite=Def|PronType=Art                       2     det         _     _
2    third      third       ADJ     JJ    Degree=Pos|NumType=Ord     5      nsubj_pass       _     _
3    was        be          AUX     VBD   Mood=Ind|Number=Sing|Person=3|Tense=Past|VerbForm=Fin   5   aux     _     _
4    being      be          AUX     VBG   VerbForm=Ger     5      aux_pass        _     _
5    run        run         VERB    VBN   Tense=Past|VerbForm=Part|Voice=Pass     0      root     _     _
6    by         by          ADP     IN    _       8      case      _     _
7    the        the         DET     DT    Definite=Def|PronType=Art      8      det       _     _
8    head       head        NOUN    NN    Number=Sing     5      obl       _     _
9    of         of          ADP     IN    _       12     case      _     _
10   an         a           DET     DT    Definite=Ind|PronType=Art      12     det       _     _
11   investment investment  NOUN    NN    Number=Sing    12      compound          _     _
12   firm       firm        NOUN    NN    Number=Sing     8      nmod      _     SpaceAfter=No
13   .          .           PUNCT   .     _       5      punct     _     _
```

Figure 1: A sample UD structure in English

```
1    the        _    DET     DT    Definite=Def|PronType=Art             _     2     det         _     _
2    third      _    ADJ     JJ    Degree=Pos       _      3      nsubj_pass       _     _
3    run        _    VERB    VBN   Tense=Past|VerbForm=Part       _      0      ROOT      _     _
4    be         _    AUX     VBD   Tense=Past|Mood=Ind|VerbForm=Fin|Person=3       _     3     aux     _     _
5    be         _    AUX     VBG   VerbForm=Ger     _      3      aux_pass        _     _
6    head       _    NOUN    NN    Number=Sing      _      3      obl       _     _
7    .          _    PUNCT   .     _       _      3      punct     _     _
8    by         _    ADP     IN    _       _      6      case      _     _
9    the        _    DET     DT    Definite=Def|PronType=Art      _      6      det       _     _
10   firm       _    NOUN    NN    Number=Sing      _      6      nmod      _     _
11   a          _    DET     DT    Definite=Ind|PronType=Art      _      10     det       _     _
12   investment _    NOUN    NN    Number=Sing      _      10     compound          _     _
13   of         _    ADP     IN    _       _      10     case      _     _
```

Figure 2: A sample Shallow input

```
1    third       _    ADJ     _    Degree=Pos       _      2      A2        _     _
2    run         _    VERB    _    Tense=Past|Aspect=Progr     _      0      ROOT      _     _
3    head        _    NOUN    _    Number=Sing|Definiteness=Def     _      2      A1        _     _
4    firm        _    NOUN    _    Number=Sing|Definiteness=Indef     _      3      A2        _     _
5    investment  _    NOUN    _    Number=Sing      _      4      AM        _     _
```

Figure 3: A sample Deep input

5 Proposed Timeline

Assuming that the presentation of the results will not take place before mid-July 2018, the proposed timeline for the shared task would be the following:

- **Oct 1, 2017**: Completion of the consultation process regarding SR'18 input specifications and concerned languages.
- **Oct 1–Dec 8, 2017**: Implementation of conversion scripts and production of new inputs.
- **Oct 6, 2017**: Announcement of SR'18 and website.
- **Nov 13, 2017**: Call for interest in participation in SR'18.
- **Nov 13, 2017**: SR'18 Trial datasets and documentation.
- **Dec 11, 2017**: Registration for the task.
- **Dec 11, 2017**: SR'18 training and development sets.
- **April 2, 2018**: Evaluation scripts available.
- **May 14, 2018**: SR'18 test sets available.
- **May 18, 2018**: SR'18 system outputs collected.
- **May 21–June 30, 2018**: Evaluation period.

References

Anja Belz and Mike White et al. 2011. The first Surface Realisation Shared Task: Overview and evaluation results. In *Proceedings of ENLG*, pages 217–226, Nancy, France.

Eric Kow and Anja Belz. 2012. Lg-eval: A toolkit for creating online language evaluation experiments. In *Proceedings of LREC*, pages 4033–4037, Istambul, Turkey.

Jonathan May and Jay Priyadarshi. 2017. Semeval-2017 task 9: Abstract meaning representation parsing and generation. In *Proceedings of SemEval*, pages 534–543, Vancouver, Canada, August. Association for Computational Linguistics.

Adam Meyers and Ruth Reeves et al., 2004. *The Nom-Bank project: An interim report*, pages 24–31.

Joakim Nivre and Marie-Catherine de Marneffe et al. 2016. Universal dependencies v1: A multilingual treebank collection. In *Proceedings of LREC*, Portorož, Slovenia.

Martha Palmer, Daniel Gildea, and Paul Kingsbury. 2005. The proposition bank: An annotated corpus of semantic roles. *Computational Linguistics*, 31(1):71–105.

The WebNLG Challenge: Generating Text from RDF Data

Claire Gardent   Anastasia Shimorina
CNRS, LORIA, UMR 7503
Vandoeuvre-lès-Nancy, F-54500, France
claire.gardent@loria.fr
anastasia.shimorina@loria.fr

Shashi Narayan   Laura Perez-Beltrachini
School of Informatics, University of Edinburgh
10 Crichton Street, Edinburgh, EH8 9AB, UK
shashi.narayan@ed.ac.uk
lperez@ed.ac.uk

Abstract

The WebNLG challenge consists in mapping sets of RDF triples to text. It provides a common benchmark on which to train, evaluate and compare "microplanners", i.e. generation systems that verbalise a given content by making a range of complex interacting choices including referring expression generation, aggregation, lexicalisation, surface realisation and sentence segmentation. In this paper, we introduce the microplanning task, describe data preparation, introduce our evaluation methodology, analyse participant results and provide a brief description of the participating systems.

1 Introduction

Previous Natural Language Generation (NLG) challenges have focused on surface realisation (Banik et al., 2013; Belz et al., 2011), referring expression generation (Belz and Gatt, 2007; Gatt et al., 2008; Gatt et al., 2009; Belz et al., 2008; Belz et al., 2009; Belz et al., 2010) and content selection (Bouayad-Agha et al., 2013).

In contrast, the WebNLG challenge focuses on microplanning, that subtask of NLG which consists in mapping a given content to a text verbalising this content. Microplanning is a complex choice problem involving several subtasks referred to in the literature as referring expression generation, aggregation, lexicalisation, surface realisation and sentence segmentation. For instance, given the WebNLG data unit shown in (1a), generating the text in (1b) involves choosing to lexicalise the JOHN_E_BLAHA

entity only once (*referring expression generation*), lexicalising the OCCUPATION property as the phrase *worked as* (*lexicalisation*), using PP coordination to avoid repeating the word born (*aggregation*) and verbalising the three triples by a single complex sentence including an apposition, a PP coordination and a transitive verb construction (*sentence segmentation* and *surface realisation*).

(1) a. Data: (JOHN_E_BLAHA BIRTHDATE 1942_08_26)
(JOHN_E_BLAHA BIRTHPLACE SAN_ANTONIO)
(JOHN_E_BLAHA OCCUPATION FIGHTER_PILOT)

    b. Text: *John E Blaha, born in San Antonio on 1942-08-26, worked as a fighter pilot*

2 Data

As illustrated by the above example, the WebNLG dataset was designed to exercise the ability of NLG systems to handle the whole range of microplanning operations and their interactions. It was created using a content selection procedure specifically designed to enhance data and text variety (Perez-Beltrachini et al., 2016). In (Gardent et al., 2017), we compared a dataset created using the WebNLG process with existing benchmarks in particular, (Wen et al., 2016)'s dataset (RNNLG) which was produced using a similar process. In what follows, we give various statistics about the WebNLG dataset using the RNNLG dataset as a reference point.

Size. The WebNLG dataset consists of 25,298 (data,text) pairs and 9,674 distinct data units. The data units are sets of RDF triples extracted from DB-Pedia and the texts are sequences of one or more sentences verbalising these data units.

Proceedings of The 10th International Natural Language Generation conference, pages 124–133,
Santiago de Compostela, Spain, September 4-7 2017. ©2017 Association for Computational Linguistics

Lexicalisation. As illustrated by the examples in (2), different properties can induce different lexical forms (a property might be lexicalised as a verb, a relational noun, a preposition or an adjective). Therefore, the larger the number of properties, the more likely the data is to allow for a wider range of lexicalisation patterns.

(2) X TITLE Y ⇒ *X served as Y*   Verb
    X NATIONALITY Y ⇒ *X's nationality is Y*
                                        Relational noun
    X COUNTRY Y ⇒ *X is in Y*   Preposition
    X NATIONALITY USA ⇒ *X is American*   Adjective

To promote diverse lexicalisation patterns, we extracted data from 15 DBPedia categories (Astronaut, University, Monument, Building, ComicsCharacter, Food, Airport, SportsTeam, WrittenWork, Athlete, Artist, City, MeanOfTransportation, CelestialBody, Politician) resulting in a set of 373 distinct RDF properties (more than three times the number of properties contained in the RNNLG dataset). The corrected type token ratio (CTTR[1]) and the number of word types is roughly twice as large in theWebNLG dataset than in RNNLG.

Surface Realisation. To increase *syntactic variety*, we use a content selection procedure which extracts data units of various shapes. The intuition is that different input shapes may induce distinct linguistic constructions. This is illustrated in Figure 2. Typically, while triples sharing a subject (SIBLING configuration) are likely to induce a VP or a sentence coordination, a CHAIN configuration (where the object of one triple is the subject of the other) will more naturally give rise to object relative clauses or participials.

Another factor impacting syntactic variation is the set of properties (input patterns) cooccuring in a given input. This is illustrated by the examples in (3) where two inputs of the same length (3 triples hence 3 properties) result in text with different syntax. That is, a larger number of input patterns is more likely to induce texts with greater syntactic variety. By extracting data units from a large number of distinct domains (DBPedia categories), we seeked to produce a large number of distinct input patterns.

---

[1]Following (Perez-Beltrachini and Gardent, 2017), we use (Lu, 2008)'s system to compute the CTTR (Carroll, 1964).

CHAIN 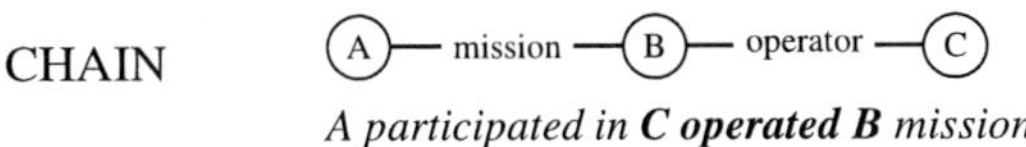

*A participated in **C** operated **B** mission*

SIBLING 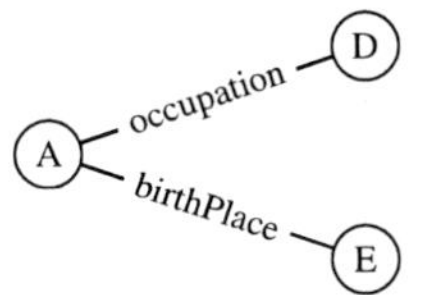

*A was born in E. **She** worked as a D.*
*A was born in E **and** worked as a D.*

(3) a. LOCATION-COUNTRY-STARTDATE
      ⇒ Passive-Apposition-Active
      108 St. Georges Terrace is located in Perth, Australia. Its construction began in 1981.

    b. BIRTHPLACE-ALMAMATER-SELECTION
      ⇒ Passive-VP coordination
      William Anders was born in British Hong Kong, graduated from AFIT in 1962, and joined NASA in 1963.

As shown in Table 3, the WebNLG dataset contains twice as many distinct input patterns and ten times more input shapes than the RNNLG dataset. It is also less redundant with a ratio between number of inputs and number of input patterns of 2.34 against 10.31 for RNNLG.

Aggregation, Sentence Segmentation and Referring Expression Generation. Finally, the need for aggregation, sentence segmentation and referring expression generation mainly arise when texts contains more than one sentence. As Table 3 shows, although data units are overall smaller in the WebNLG dataset than in RNNLG, the WebNLG dataset has a higher number of texts containing more than one sentence and contains texts of longer length.

3 Participating Systems

The WebNLG challenge received eight submissions from six participating teams: the ADAPT Centre, Ireland (ADAPTCENTRE), the University of Melbourne, Australia (UMELBOURNE), Peking University, China (PKUWRITER), Tilburg University, The Netherlands (UTILBURG), University of Information Technology, VNU-HCM, Vietnam (UIT-VNU-

	WebNLG	RNNLG
Size		
# data-text pairs	25,298	30,842
# distinct inputs	9,674	22,225
Lexicalisation		
# properties	373	108
# domains	15	4
# CTTR	6.51	3.42
# Words (Type)	6,547	3,524
Syntactic Variety		
# input patterns	4,129	2,155
# input / # input patterns	2.34	10.31
# input shapes	62	6
Aggregation, GRE, Segmentation		
# input with 1 or 2 triples	11,111	4,087
# input with 3 or 4 triples	8,172	6,690
# input with 5 to 7 triples	6,015	20,065
# text with 1 sentence	16,740	24,234
# text with 2 sentences	6,798	5,729
# text with $\geq$ 3 sentences	1,760	879
# words/text (avg/min/max)	22.69/4/80	18.37/1/76

Table 1: Some Statistics about the WebNLG Dataset

HCM) and Universitat Pompeu Fabra, Barcelona, Spain (UPF-FORGE). Each team submitted outputs from a single system except UTILBURG who submitted outputs from three different systems. As a result, there were nine systems in total: eight participating systems and our baseline (BASELINE) system. These can be grouped into three categories: pipeline systems, statistical machine translation (SMT) and neural machine translation (NMT) systems. Table 3 shows the system categorisations.

Pipeline Systems. Three submissions used a template or grammar-based pipeline framework with some NLG module: UTILBURG-PIPELINE, UIT-VNU-HCM and UPF-FORGE.

The first two systems, UTILBURG-PIPELINE and UIT-VNU-HCM, extracted rules or templates from the training data for surface realisation, whereas the third system, UPF-FORGE, used the FORGe grammar (Mille et al., 2017).

UTILBURG-PIPELINE extracted rules mapping a triple (or a triple set) to a text observed in the training data; both the triple and the associated text were delexicalised. Given a RDF triple set to generate

System ID	Institution
PIPELINE Systems	
UTILBURG-SMT	Tilburg University
UIT-VNU-HCM	University of Information Technology
UPF-FORGE	Universitat Pompeu Fabra
SMT Systems	
UTILBURG-SMT	Tilburg University
NMT Systems	
ADAPTCENTRE	ADAPT Centre, Ireland
UMELBOURNE	University of Melbourne
UTILBURG-NMT	Tilburg University
PKUWRITER	Peking University
BASELINE	

Table 2: Categorisation of participating systems.

from, UTILBURG-PIPELINE first ordered triples to maintain discourse order. Extracted rules were then applied to generate a delexicalised text. Missing entities were added using a referring expression generation module (Castro Ferreira et al., 2016). Finally, a 6-gram language model trained on the Gigaword corpus was used to rank the system output.

UIT-VNU-HCM did not resort to delexicalisation in their rules. Instead of using the text to extract templates, it used the typed-dependency structure of the text to facilitate rule extraction from the training data. In addition, at run time, WordNet was used to estimate similarity between predicates in the test and train sets.

UPF-FORGe mostly focused on sentence planning with predicate-argument (PredArg) templates. For each of the DBPedia properties found in the training and evaluation data, they manually defined PredArg templates encoding various DBPedia-specific and linguistic features. Given a RDF triple set to generate from, PredArg templates were used to convert these triples to PredArg structures and to further aggregate them to form a PredArg graph structure. The FORGe generator took this linguistic PredArg structure as input and generated a text.

SMT Systems. UTILBURG-SMT was the only system which used the statistical machine translation framework. It was trained on the WebNLG dataset using the Moses toolkit (Koehn et al., 2007). The dataset was pre-processed whereby each entity in the input and each corresponding referring expression in the output were delexicalised and annotated with the entity Wikipedia ID. The alignments from the training set were obtained using MGIZA and model weights were tuned using 60-batch MIRA with BLEU as the evaluation metric. Similar to UTILBURG-PIPELINE, the system used a 6-gram language model trained on the Gigaword corpus using KenLM.

NMT Systems. Four systems (ADAPTCENTRE, UMELBOURNE, UTILBURG-NMT and PKUWRITER) build upon the attention-based encoder-decoder architecture proposed in (Bahdanau et al., 2014). Most of them make use of existing NMT frameworks. There are however important differences among systems with respect to both the concrete architecture and the sequence representations they use.

ADAPTCENTRE makes use of the Nematus (Sennrich et al., 2017) system. They opt for sub-word representations rather than delexicalisation to deal with rare words and sparsity. They linearise the input sequence and insert tuple separation special tokens.

UMELBOURNE does a combined delexicalisation procedure and enrichment of the input sequence. Entities are delexicalised using an entity identifier (ENTITY-ID). When available, the DBPedia type of the entity is appended. An n-gram search is used to assure the most accurate target sequence delexicalisation. They use a standard encoder-decoder with attention model.

UTILBURG-NMT is based on the Edinburgh Neural Machine Translation submission for the 2016 machine translation shared task (WMT 2016). The target sequences are the delexicalised texts (cf. UTILBURG-PIPELINE) and the input sequences are the linearisation of the delexicalised input set of triples. The REG module from their pipeline system is used to post-process the decoder outputs.

The PKUWRITER system relies upon two extra mechanisms, namely a ranking module and an extra Reinforcement Learning (RL) training objective. It uses an ensemble of attention-based encoder-decoder models based on the TensorFlow seq2seq API in addition to the baseline (7 models in total). They propose an output ranking module to choose the best verbalisation among those output by the generation models. The ranker is trained on supervised data generated automatically. Input triple sets are paired with verbalisations produced by each of the generation models. Then, each pair is associated with a quality score, i.e. the BLEU score of the verbalisation and the reference. Word and sentence level features are extracted to train the ranker. The generation models and ranker are trained on different data partitions. The RL objective encourages the generation of output texts which include subjects occurring in the input RDF triples. In addition, PKUWRITER uses a set of hand-crafted rules to handle input cases where the model fails.

4 Evaluation Methodology

The WebNLG challenge includes both an automatic and a human-based evaluation. Due to time constraints, only the results of the automatic evaluation are presented in this paper. The results of the human-based evaluation will be provided on the WebNLG website[2] in October 2017.

---

[2] http://talc1.loria.fr/webnlg/stories/
challenge.html

4.1 Automatic Evaluation

Three automatic metrics were used to evaluate the participating systems:

- BLEU-4[3] (Papineni et al., 2002). BLEU scores were computed using up to three references.

- METEOR (v1.5)[4] (Denkowski and Lavie, 2014);

- TER[5] (Snover et al., 2006).

For statistical significance testing, we followed the bootstrapping algorithm described in (Koehn and Monz, 2006).

To assess the ability of the participating systems to generalise to out of domain data, the test dataset consists of two sets of roughly equal size: a test set containing inputs created for entities belonging to DBpedia categories that were seen in the training data (Astronaut, University, Monument, Building, ComicsCharacter, Food, Airport, SportsTeam, City, and WrittenWork), and a test set containing inputs extracted for entities belonging to 5 unseen categories (Athlete, Artist, MeanOfTransportation, CelestialBody, Politician). We call the first type of data *seen categories*, the second, *unseen categories*. Correspondingly, we report results for 3 datasets: the seen category dataset, the unseen category dataset and the total test set made of both the seen and the unseen category datasets.

Table 3 gives more detailed statistics about the number of properties, objects and subject entities occurring in each test set.

- $|Test|$ is the number of distinct properties, subjects and objects in the test set;

- $|Test \cap TnDv|$ is the number of distinct properties, subjects and objects which are in the test set and were seen in the training or the development set;

- $|Test \setminus TnDv|$ is the number of distinct properties, subjects and objects which occur in the

---

test set, but not in the training and development set.

		Seen	Unseen	All
Prop.	$|Test|$	188	159	300
	$|Test \cap TnDv|$	188	51	192
	$|Test \setminus TnDv|$	0	108	108
Obj.	$|Test|$	1033	898	1888
	$|Test \cap TnDv|$	1011	57	1025
	$|Test \setminus TnDv|$	22	841	863
Subj.	$|Test|$	343	238	575
	$|Test \cap TnDv|$	342	6	342
	$|Test \setminus TnDv|$	1	232	233

Table 3: Test data statistics on properties, objects and subjects for seen, unseen and all datasets.

While in the seen test data (first column) almost all triple elements are present in the training and development sets, in the unseen test data (second column) the vast majority of subjects, objects, and, more importantly, properties (which need to be lexicalised) has not been seen in the training and development data.

Participants were requested to submit tokenised and lowercased texts. To ensure consistency between submissions, we pre-processed the submitted results one more time to double-check that those requirements were fullfilled. As teams used different strategies of tokenisation, we had to modify submissions using our own scripts. In particular, all punctuation signs were separated from alphanumeric sequences (e.g. a two-token group *65.6 feet* was modified to a four-token *65 . 6 feet*). Moreover, we converted both references and submission outputs to the ASCII character set.

4.2 Baseline System

We developed a baseline system using neural networks and delexicalisation. Before training, we preprocess the data by linearising triples, performing tokenisation and delexicalisation using exact matching.

While delexicalising, we make the following replacements:

- given a triple of the form *(s p o)* where s is of the category C for which the triple set has been produced (e.g., *Alan_Bean* for the category Astronaut), we replace s by C.

---

[3]https://github.com/moses-smt/
mosesdecoder/blob/master/scripts/generic/
multi-bleu.perl
[4]http://www.cs.cmu.edu/~alavie/METEOR/
[5]http://www.cs.umd.edu/~snover/tercom/

- given a triple of the form *s p o*, we replace *o* by *p*. E.g., *(s country Indonesia)* becomes *(s country COUNTRY)*. The replacements were made using the exact match and as a result not all the entities were replaced.

Examples 4 and 5 show a (data,text) pair before and after delexicalisation. Note that *noodles* was not substituted by the corresponding entity category in the target text (because there is no exact match with the NOODLE object in the input). Table 4 shows the number of distinct tokens occurring in the original and delexicalised data.

(4) a. Set of triples: (INDONESIA LEADERNAME JUSUF_KALLA) (BAKSO INGREDIENT NOODLE) (BAKSO COUNTRY INDONESIA)

b. Text: *Bakso is a food containing noodles; it is found in Indonesia where Jusuf Kalla is the leader.*

(5) a. Source: (COUNTRY LEADERNAME LEADERNAME) (FOOD INGREDIENT INGREDIENT) (FOOD COUNTRY COUNTRY)

b. Target: *FOOD is a food containing noodles ; it is found in COUNTRY where LEADERNAME is the leader .*

On this delexicalised data-to-text corpus, we trained a vanilla sequence-to-sequence model with attention mechanism using the OpenNMT toolkit (Klein et al., 2017) with default parameters for training and decoding. The network consists of a two-layered bidirectional encoder-decoder model with LSTM units. We use a batch size of 64 and a starting learning rate of 1.0. The size of the hidden layers is 500. The network was trained for 13 epochs with a stochastic gradient descent optimisation method and a dropout probability of 0.3. We used the entire vocabulary for the baseline due to its rather small size.

	Original	Delexicalised
Source	2703	1300
Target	5374	5013
Total	8077	6313

Table 4: Vocabulary size in tokens.

After training we relexicalised sentences with corresponding entities if of course their counterparts are present in generated output. The performance of the baseline is shown in Tables 5, 6, 7 along with other teams' results.

5 Results

We briefly discuss the automatic scores distinguishing between results on the whole dataset, on data extracted from previously unseen categories and on data extracted from seen categories.

Global Scores. Table 5 shows the global results that is, results on the whole test set. Horizontal lines group together systems for which the difference in scores is not statistically significant. The names of the teams are coloured according to system type: neural-based systems are in red, pipeline systems in blue, and SMT systems in light grey.

Most systems (6 out of 8) outperform the baseline, four of them obtaining scores well above it. In terms of BLEU and TER scores, the first four systems include systems of each type (neural, SMT-based and pipelines).

While BLEU and METEOR yield almost identical rankings, METEOR does not, suggesting that the systems handle synonyms and morphological variation differently. In particular, the fact that UPF-FORGE ranks first under the METEOR score suggests that it often generates text that differs from the references because of synonymic or morphological variation.

Scores on Seen Categories. For data extracted from DBPedia categories that were seen in the training data, machine learning based systems (neural and SMT) mostly outperform rule-based systems. In particular, in terms of BLEU and TER scores, the three pipeline systems are at the low end of the ranking. Again though, the METEOR scores show a much higher ranking (3rd rather than 6th) for the UPF-FORGE systems.

Scores on Unseen Categories. On unseen categories, the UPF-FORGE systems ranks first as the system could quickly be adapted to handle properties that had not been seen in the training data. The ranking of the other systems is more or less unchanged with the exception of the ADAPTCENTRE system. This neural system does not use delexicalisation and the subword approach that was adopted

BLEU			TER			METEOR		
1	MELBOURNE	45.13	1	MELBOURNE	0.47	1	UPF-FORGE	0.39
2	TILB-SMT	44.28	2	TILB-SMT	0.53	2	TILB-SMT	0.38
3–4	PKUWRITER	39.88	3–4	PKUWRITER	0.55	3	MELBOURNE	0.37
3–4	UPF-FORGE	38.65	3–5	UPF-FORGE	0.55	4	TILB-NMT	0.34
5–6	TILB-PIPELINE	35.29	4–5	TILB-PIPELINE	0.56	5–6	ADAPT	0.31
5–6	TILB-NMT	34.60	6–7	TILB-NMT	0.60	5–7	PKUWRITER	0.31
7	BASELINE	33.24	6–7	BASELINE	0.61	6–7	TILB-PIPELINE	0.30
8	ADAPT	31.06	8–9	UIT-VNU	0.82	8	BASELINE	0.23
9	UIT-VNU	7.07	8–9	ADAPT	0.84	9	UIT-VNU	0.09

Table 5: Results for all categories. Lines between systems indicate a difference in scores which is statistically significant ($p <$ 0.05). A colour for a team name indicates a type of the system used (NMT, SMT, Pipeline).

BLEU			TER			METEOR		
1	ADAPT	60.59	1	ADAPT	0.37	1	ADAPT	0.44
2–3	MELBOURNE	54.52	2	MELBOURNE	0.40	2	TILB-SMT	0.42
2–4	TILB-SMT	54.29	3–4	BASELINE	0.44	3–4	MELBOURNE	0.41
3–4	BASELINE	52.39	3–4	PKUWRITER	0.45	3–4	UPF-FORGE	0.40
5	PKUWRITER	51.23	5	TILB-SMT	0.47	5–6	TILB-NMT	0.38
6	TILB-PIPELINE	44.34	6	TILB-PIPELINE	0.48	5–8	TILB-PIPELINE	0.38
7	TILB-NMT	43.28	7	TILB-NMT	0.51	6–8	PKUWRITER	0.37
8	UPF-FORGE	40.88	8	UPF-FORGE	0.55	6–8	BASELINE	0.37
9	UIT-VNU	19.87	9	UIT-VNU	0.78	9	UIT-VNU	0.15

Table 6: Results for seen categories.

BLEU			TER			METEOR		
1	UPF-FORGE	35.70	1	UPF-FORGE	0.55	1	UPF-FORGE	0.37
2	MELBOURNE	33.27	2	MELBOURNE	0.55	2	TILB-SMT	0.33
3	TILB-SMT	29.88	3	TILB-SMT	0.61	3	MELBOURNE	0.33
4–5	PKUWRITER	25.36	4–5	TILB-PIPELINE	0.65	4	TILB-NMT	0.31
4–5	TILB-NMT	25.12	4–5	PKUWRITER	0.67	5	PKUWRITER	0.24
6	TILB-PIPELINE	20.65	6	TILB-NMT	0.72	6	TILB-PIPELINE	0.21
7	ADAPT	10.53	7	BASELINE	0.80	7	ADAPT	0.19
8	BASELINE	06.13	8	UIT-VNU	0.87	8	BASELINE	0.07
9	UIT-VNU	0.11	9	ADAPT	1.4	9	UIT-VNU	0.03

Table 7: Results for unseen categories.

S   John Clancy is a labour politican who leads Birmingham, where architect John Madin, who designed 103 Colmore Row, was born.

$\mathbf{M}_S$ { BIRMINGHAM|LEADERNAME|JOHN_CLANCY_(LABOUR_POLITICIAN),
JOHN_MADIN|BIRTHPLACE|BIRMINGHAM,
103_COLMORE_ROW|ARCHITECT|JOHN_MADIN}

$\mathbf{T}_1$ Labour politician, John Clancy is the leader of Birmingham.

$\mathbf{M}_{T_1}$ { BIRMINGHAM|LEADERNAME|JOHN_CLANCY_(LABOUR_POLITICIAN)}

$\mathbf{T}_2$ John Madin was born in Birmingham.

$\mathbf{M}_{T_2}$ { JOHN_MADIN|BIRTHPLACE|BIRMINGHAM }

$\mathbf{T}_3$ He was the architect of 103 Colmore Row.

$\mathbf{M}_{T_3}$ { 103_COLMORE_ROW|ARCHITECT|JOHN_MADIN}

Figure 1: An example pair out of the Split-and-Rephrase Dataset. **S** is a single complex sentence with meaning $\mathbf{M}_S$. $\mathbf{T}_1$, $\mathbf{T}_1$, $\mathbf{T}_1$ form a text of three simple sentences whose joint meaning $\mathbf{M}_{T_1} \cup \mathbf{M}_{T_2} \cup \mathbf{M}_{T_3}$ is the same as the meaning $\mathbf{M}_S$ of the corresponding single complex sentence **S**.

to handle unseen data does not seem to work well.

6   Conclusion

The WebNLG challenge was novel in that it was the first challenge to provide a benchmark on which to evaluate and compare microplanners. Despite a tight schedule (we released the training data in April for a submission in August), it generated a high level of interest among the NLG community: 62 groups from 18 countries[6] downloaded the data, 6 groups submitted 8 systems and 3 groups developped a system but did not submit.

The training data for the WebNLG 2017 challenge is available on the WebNLG website[7] and evaluation on the test data can be run by the organisers on demand. A larger dataset consisting of 40,049 (data, text) pairs, 15,095 distinct data input and 15 DBpedia categories is also available. Both datasets are under the creative common licence "CC Attribution-Noncommercial-Share Alike 4.0 International license". We hope that these resources will enable a long and fruitful strand of research on microplanning.

The usefulness of the WebNLG dataset reaches far beyond the WebNLG challenge. It can be used for instance to train a semantic parser which would convert a sentence into a set of RDF triples. It can also be used to derive new datasets for related tasks. Thus in (Narayan et al., 2017), we show how to derive from the WebNLG dataset, a dataset for sentence simplification which we call the Split-and-Rephrase dataset. In this dataset, each pair consists of (i) a single, complex sentence with its meaning representation in terms of RDF triples and (ii) a sequence of at least two sentences and their corresponding sets of RDF triples whereby these sets form a partition on the set of RDF triples associated with the input complex sentence. In other words, the Split-and-Rephrase dataset associates a complex sentence with a sequence of at least two sentences whose meaning is the same as that of the complex sentence. As explained in (Narayan et al., 2017), this dataset was created using the meaning represen-

tations (sets of RDF triples) as pivot. The Split-and-Rephrase dataset consists of 1,100,166 pairs of the form $\langle (M_C, T_C), \{(M_1, T_1) \ldots (M_n, T_n)\}\rangle$ where T_C is a complex sentence and $T_1 \ldots T_n$ is a sequence of texts with semantics $M_1, \ldots M_n$ expressing the same content M_C as T_C. Figure 1 shows an example pair. It was used to train four neural systems and the associated meaning representations were shown to improve performance.

In the future, we are planning to build a multilingual resource in which the English text present in the WebNLG dataset will be translated into French, Russian and Maltese. In this way, morphological variation can be explored which is an interesting avenue of research in particular for neural systems which have a limited ability to handle unseen input: how well will these systems be able to handle the generation of morphologically rich languages ?

The analysis of the participants results presented in this paper will be complemented in an arxiv report by the results of a human-based evaluation. Using human judgcmcnts obtaincd through crowdsourcing, this human evaluation will assess the system results on three criteria, namely fluency, grammaticality and appropriateness (does the text correctly verbalise the input data?). We will also provide a more in depth analysis of the participant results on data extracted from different categories and data of various length.

Acknowledgments

The research presented in this paper has been supported by the following grants and projects: "WebNLG", Project ANR-14-CE24-0033 of the French National Research Agency and "SUMMA", H2020 project No. 688139.

References

Dzmitry Bahdanau, Kyunghyun Cho, and Yoshua Bengio. 2014. Neural machine translation by jointly learning to align and translate. In *Proceedings of ICLR-2015 (abs/1409.0473)*.

Eva Banik, Claire Gardent, and Eric Kow. 2013. The kbgen challenge. In *the 14th European Workshop on Natural Language Generation (ENLG)*, pages 94–97.

Anja Belz and Albert Gatt. 2007. The attribute selection for gre challenge: Overview and evaluation results.

---

[6]Australia, Canada, China, Croatie, France, Germany, India, Iran, Ireland, Italy, Netherlands, Norway, Poland, Spain, Tunisia, UK, USA, Vietnam

[7]`http://talc1.loria.fr/webnlg/stories/challenge.html`

Proceedings of UCNLG+ MT: Language Generation and Machine Translation, pages 75–83.

Anja Belz, Eric Kow, Jette Viethen, and Albert Gatt. 2008. The grec challenge: Overview and evaluation results.

Anja Belz, Eric Kow, and Jette Viethen. 2009. The grec named entity generation challenge 2009: overview and evaluation results. In *Proceedings of the 2009 Workshop on Language Generation and Summarisation*, pages 88–98. Association for Computational Linguistics.

Anja Belz, Eric Kow, Jette Viethen, and Albert Gatt. 2010. Generating referring expressions in context: The grec task evaluation challenges. In *Empirical methods in natural language generation*, pages 294–327. Springer.

Anja Belz, Michael White, Dominic Espinosa, Eric Kow, Deirdre Hogan, and Amanda Stent. 2011. The first surface realisation shared task: Overview and evaluation results. In *Proceedings of the 13th European Workshop on Natural Language Generation*, ENLG '11, pages 217–226, Stroudsburg, PA, USA. Association for Computational Linguistics.

Nadjet Bouayad-Agha, Gerard Casamayor, Leo Wanner, and Chris Mellish. 2013. Overview of the first content selection challenge from open semantic web data. In *ENLG*, pages 98–102.

J. B. Carroll. 1964. *Language and thought*. NJ: Prentice-Hall. Englewood Cliffs.

Thiago Castro Ferreira, Emiel Krahmer, and Sander Wubben. 2016. Towards more variation in text generation: Developing and evaluating variation models for choice of referential form. In *Proceedings of the 54th Annual Meeting of the Association for Computational Linguistics (Volume 1: Long Papers)*, pages 568–577.

Michael Denkowski and Alon Lavie. 2014. Meteor universal: Language specific translation evaluation for any target language. In *Proceedings of the EACL 2014 Workshop on Statistical Machine Translation*.

Claire Gardent, Anastasia Shimorina, Shashi Narayan, and Laura Perez-Beltrachini. 2017. Creating training corpora for nlg micro-planners. In *Proceedings of the 55th Annual Meeting of the Association for Computational Linguistics (Volume 1: Long Papers)*, volume 1, pages 179–188.

Albert Gatt, Anja Belz, and Eric Kow. 2008. The tuna challenge 2008: Overview and evaluation results. In *Proceedings of the Fifth International Natural Language Generation Conference*, pages 198–206. Association for Computational Linguistics.

Albert Gatt, Anja Belz, and Eric Kow. 2009. The tuna-reg challenge 2009: Overview and evaluation results. In *Proceedings of the 12th European Workshop on Natural Language Generation*, pages 174–182. Association for Computational Linguistics.

G. Klein, Y. Kim, Y. Deng, J. Senellart, and A. M. Rush. 2017. OpenNMT: Open-Source Toolkit for Neural Machine Translation. *ArXiv e-prints*.

Philipp Koehn and Christof Monz. 2006. Manual and automatic evaluation of machine translation between european languages. In *Proceedings of the Workshop on Statistical Machine Translation*, StatMT '06, pages 102–121.

Philipp Koehn, Hieu Hoang, Alexandra Birch, Chris Callison-Burch, Marcello Federico, Nicola Bertoldi, Brooke Cowan, Wade Shen, Christine Moran, Richard Zens, Chris Dyer, Ondřej Bojar, Alexandra Constantin, and Evan Herbst. 2007. Moses: Open source toolkit for statistical machine translation. In *Proceedings of the 45th Annual Meeting of the ACL on Interactive Poster and Demonstration Sessions*, pages 177–180.

Xiaofei Lu. 2008. Automatic measurement of syntactic complexity using the revised developmental level scale. In *FLAIRS Conference*, pages 153–158.

Simon Mille, Roberto Carlini, Alicia Burga, and Leo Wanner. 2017. FORGe at SemEval-2017 task 9: Deep sentence generation based on a sequence of graph transducers. In *Proceedings of SemEval-2017*, pages 917–920.

Shashi Narayan, Claire Gardent, Shay B. Cohen, and Anastasia Shimorina. 2017. Split and rephrase. In *Proceedings of EMNLP*.

Kishore Papineni, Salim Roukos, Todd Ward, and Wei-Jing Zhu. 2002. Bleu: a method for automatic evaluation of machine translation. In *Proceedings of the 40th annual meeting on association for computational linguistics*, pages 311–318. Association for Computational Linguistics.

Laura Perez-Beltrachini and Claire Gardent. 2017. Analysing data-to-text generation benchmarks. In *Proceedings of the tenth International Natural Language Generation Conference*, INLG.

Laura Perez-Beltrachini, Rania Sayed, and Claire Gardent. 2016. Building rdf content for data-to-text generation. In *COLING*, pages 1493–1502.

Rico Sennrich, Orhan Firat, Kyunghyun Cho, Alexandra Birch-Mayne, Barry Haddow, Julian Hitschler, Marcin Junczys-Dowmunt, Samuel Laubli, Antonio Miceli Barone, Jozef Mokry, and Maria Nadejde. 2017. Nematus: A toolkit for neural machine translation. In *Proceedings of the EACL 2017 Software Demonstrations*, pages 65–68, 4.

Matthew Snover, Bonnie Dorr, Richard Schwartz, Linnea Micciulla, and John Makhoul. 2006. A study of translation edit rate with targeted human annotation.

In *Proceedings of association for machine translation in the Americas*, volume 200.

Tsung-Hsien Wen, Milica Gašić, Nikola Mrkšić, Lina M. Rojas-Barahona, Pei-Hao Su, David Vandyke, and Steve Young. 2016. Multi-domain neural network language generation for spoken dialogue systems. In *Proceedings of NAACL-HLT*.

A Commercial Perspective on Reference

Ehud Reiter
Arria NLG PLC
ehud.reiter@arria.com

Abstract

I briefly describe some of the commercial work which Arria NLG is doing in referring expression algorithms, and highlight differences between what is commercially important (at least to Arria) and the NLG research literature. Arria's focus is on high-quality algorithms for types of reference which are important in its systems. These algorithms need to be parametrisable for different genres and domains, usable in hybrid systems which include some canned text, and support variation.

1   Introduction

There is an extensive academic literature in NLG on generating referring expressions. In this paper I partially describe the types of reference which are important to Arria NLG, a company which builds commercial NLG systems (I cannot fully describe what Arria does because of commercial confidentiality).

In general terms, the high-level concepts behind Arria's work are similar to the high-level concepts behind academic NLG work. However there is a difference in emphasis, and hence in the specifics of algorithms. In particular, Arria has focused less on the task of identifying salient visual or physical entities, and more on specialized reference tasks such as referring to a specific component in a complex machine, and referring to a company in a contextually appropriate way. Arria also wants its reference algorithms (and indeed all of its NLG algorithms) to support a number of practical criteria:

- *Configuration*: Easily configurable and parametrisable for different genres and domains.

- *Hybrid NLG/template systems*: Usable in systems which produce documents which include canned text as well as NLG text.

- *Variation*: Allow random or systematic variation (when desirable), so users who regularly read generated texts don't see the same referring expression used again and again.

In this paper I will give some examples of the reference algorithms Arria has developed, and explain how they meet the above criteria.

2   Background: Reference

Referring expression generation has been a focus of NLG research since the 1990s (van Deemter 2016a); a good recent survey is Krahmer and van Deemter (2012). Much of this research has been on choosing definite NPs (such as "the dog" or "the big black dog") to refer to physical objects which are already salient to the hearer. As described by Krahmer and van Deemter, many algorithms have been developed for this task, and there also has been work on data sets and evaluation criteria, and a shared task (e.g., Gatt and Belz 2008). A substantial amount of work has also been done on using pronouns, and on generating references to sets. Less research has been done on reference to non-physical entities such as dates or companies. In terms of the above criteria:

Proceedings of The 10th International Natural Language Generation conference, pages 134–138,
Santiago de Compostela, Spain, September 4-7 2017. ©2017 Association for Computational Linguistics

- *Configurability*: Some algorithms are parametrisable, for example the incremental algorithm (Dale and Reiter 1995) allows a genre/domain specific preference order to be specified between features. But this has not been a focus of research.

- *Hybrid systems*: Similarly some work has been done on reference in systems which include canned text (e.g., van Deemter et al 2005, Belz and Kow 2010), but this has not been a research focus.

- *Variation*: This has been addressed indirectly via research (motivated by cognitive modelling) on probabilistic reference algorithms (e.g., Gatt et al 2013, Mitchell et al 2013).

In short, while the criteria of interest to Arria have been addressed in academic research, they have been peripheral and not the main focus of this work.

3 Background: Arria

Arria NLG is a company which specializes in selling NLG solutions and technology, especially data-to-text systems. As described on Arria's webpage[1], Arria uses a fairly standard data-to-text NLG pipeline (Reiter 2007). This pipeline is incorporated into Articulator Pro (A-Pro), which is Arria's NLG software development kit (SDK). One of Arria's systems was described (including evaluation) in an earlier INLG paper (Sripada et al, 2014).

Most of Arria's systems generate texts which are intended to support professionals such as engineers, doctors, and financial analysts. Thus, Arria focuses on language used in professional contexts, not everyday language.

4 Reference at Arria

A-Pro has a generic API for reference modules. This means that different reference modules can be plugged into a system, depending on what is being referred to (e.g., person, place, time, company, machine, etc.), and the genre. Reference modules can access a domain model (which describes reference targets) and a discourse model (which records linguistic context). Below I briefly describe some of the specific reference modules which Arria has developed for A-Pro.

It is of course essential that Arria's reference algorithms be fast computationally, robustly implemented and tested, well documented, and interface easily to external data sources and domain models. I will not further discuss such software engineering issues in this paper, but they are very important.

4.1 Component Reference

Arria has developed and indeed obtained a patent on a reference algorithm for components in complex machinery (Reiter, 2016). This algorithm arose out of work that Arria did in the oil industry, where it was necessary to refer to specific components in a complex machine in a narrative text which described the status of the machine. The specific context is confidential and also quite complex, but a related problem is referring to body parts (Fig 1). For example, suppose a mother is talking to her three children, Ann, Bob, and Charlotte, and wishes to refer to the index finger of Ann's left hand. Depending on the discourse context and previous utterances, the mother could say

1. The index finger of Ann's left hand
2. The left hand index finger
3. The index finger
4. It

For instance, reference (1) would be appropriate in a null context, or if the previous utterance had been about Bob. Reference (2) might be appropriate if the previous utterance had been about Ann's face. Reference (3) would make sense if the previous utterance had been about Ann's left hand, and reference (4) could be used if the previous utterance had been about the Ann's left-hand index finger.

Arria's algorithm assumes there is domain model which specifies a part-of hierarchy of the machine (or body) in question, and a discourse model which keeps track of previous references to entities in the domain model. When a new reference is needed, the algorithm essentially looks for the lowest common parent of the most recent previous referent and the new reference target, and constructs a referring expression by traversing the part-of hierarchy from the common parent to the reference target.

---

[1] www.arria.com

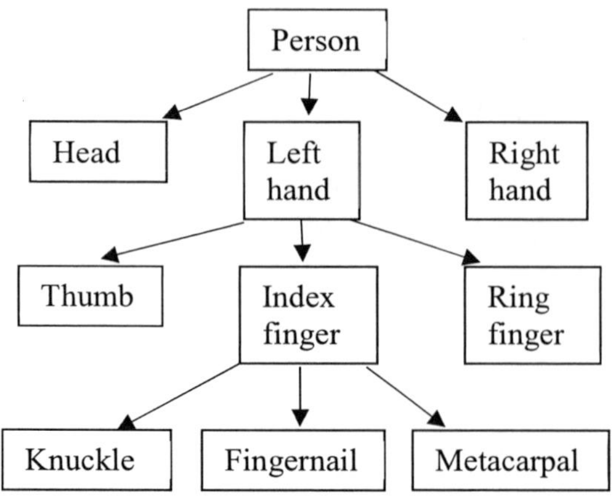

Fig 1: part-of hierarchy for body (extract)

For example, if the previous reference was (1) below, then the algorithm might produce (2)

(1) Ann's left thumb is scratched.

(2) The index finger is bleeding.

In this case

PreviousRef: thumb of left hand of Ann

TargetRef: index finger of left hand of Ann

Lowest common parent: left hand of Ann

PartofHiererachy from parent to referent: index finger

Referring expression: index finger

In terms of the criteria mentioned above

- *Configurability*: At the semantic/content level, the algorithm allows levels in the part-of hierarchy to be skipped, and special names to be used. For example, we can configure the algorithm so that the thumb of the left hand is referred to as the "left thumb", not the "thumb of the left hand". Realisation of referring expressions (e.g., the maximum number of noun-noun modifiers) can also be configured.

- *Hybrid systems*: Excluding pronouns, the algorithm works as long as all component references are generated via the algorithm; everything else can be canned text. In other words, the algorithm can be used with structures such as "I am worried about [X]",

where X is a component reference and everything else is canned text.

- *Variation*: This is supported by allowing algorithm to occasionally start from a higher node than the lowest-common parent (e.g., produce "left-hand index finger" instead of "index finger", even if the latter is sufficient in the context), and to vary realization (e.g., "the index finger of the left hand").

4.2 Named Entity Reference

Arria has also developed an algorithm for referring to named entities such as companies. This is very important in financial services, which is one of the sectors which Arria is targeting.

For example, suppose that a financial report wished to refer to Arria as a company. Should it say

1. Arria NLG
2. Arria
3. It

Reference (1) would be appropriate when the company was first mentioned in a text, or when the full name was contextually required. Reference (2) would be appropriate when the company had already been introduced in the text, and a short name was unambiguous. References (3) would be appropriate when the discourse context made it clear what the pronoun referred to. Note that the algorithm needs access to an external data source of name variants, otherwise it would not know, for example, that International Business Machines and IBM referred to the same entity.

The algorithm basically looks for the shortest referring expression which works in the current discourse context. Crucially, it is customizable for different genres and clients. For example, some genres require a full legal name (e.g., Arria NLG PLC), and in other genres a stock name (e.g. GOOGL) should be used to refer to a company.

Appropriate use of pronouns also depends on genre and client. In particular, some clients are relatively "relaxed" about pronoun usage, because they think semantic context will disambiguate pronoun references; however for other clients pronouns should only be used if there is no possibility of confusion. For example, consider "Yahoo had a poor year. It may need a new CEO". Using "It" to refer to Yahoo is acceptable under a relaxed strategy which assumes that semantic context will rule out "a poor year" as a potential reference target. However under a strict reference policy "it" could not be used here, since (at least from a purely syntactic perspective) it could refer to the year.

From the perspective of the above criteria

- *Configurability*: supporting configurability (including pronoun strategies) is the most complex aspect of the algorithm.

- *Hybrid systems*: Similar to the previous algorithm, template structures such as "I recommend buying [X]" can be used provided that all company name references are generated via the algorithm.

- *Variation*: The algorithm can be configured so that a specific form cannot be repeated more than N times in a row.

4.3 Time and date reference

Arria also has an algorithm for time and date reference; date reference in particular is very important in financial reporting. This algorithm allows timestamps to be referred to at different levels of granularity (e.g., minute, day, year), using discourse-appropriate references. For example, if granularity is day, then the timestamp 00:00:00 28 April 2017 could be referred to as

1. 28 April 2017
2. 28 April
3. the next day

Formatting can be configured, for example we can get April 28, 2017 in USA. In any case, reference (1) could be used in a null context, reference (2) in a context where the previous date reference was to another day in 2017, and reference (3) when the previous date mentioned in the text was 27 April 2017.

From the perspective of the above criteria

- *Configurability*: Developers can control which forms are allowed in the text (which depends on genre), as well as formatting.

- *Hybrid systems*: Similar to the previous algorithms, templates such as "I went to New York on [X]" can be used provided that all time/date references are generated via the algorithm.

- *Variation*: The algorithm can be configured to vary the forms used in a specific context.

5 Discussion

High-quality referring expressions are important to Arria, in part because they distinguish Arria's systems from text-generation systems built with non-NLG technology. However from Arria's perspective, academic research on generating referring expressions has been less useful than originally anticipated. What would be ideal from Arria's perspective is research on specific types of reference which are common in the domains Arria works in, focusing on algorithms which are sensitive to linguistic and discourse context, configurable, usable in hybrid systems which include some canned text, and which support variation.

There are definitely encouraging signs, for example the recent resurgence of interest in contextually appropriate named entity reference (e.g., Belz and Kow 2010, van Deemter 2016b), although this has mostly focused on people rather than companies. It is also encouraging to see recent work on variation (e.g., Baltaretu and Ferreira 2016) and on configuring reference for different genres and domains (e.g. Koolen et al, 2012).

Of course NLG researchers do not need to focus on Arria's needs. But there are many interesting research issues in specific types of reference, variation, etc. Also human speakers arguably use different reference strategies for different types of entities, vary reference strategies depending on domain and genre, insert referring expressions into fixed (formulaic) language, and vary reference in order to keep text interesting. Investigating these issues could lead to important insights about language and reference.

Acknowledgements

Many thanks to the many people on the Arria team (too many to list here) who have worked on developing, testing, and documenting the above-mentioned algorithms. My thanks also to Kees van Deemter and other members of the Aberdeen University CLAN research group for their very valuable advice and suggestions; and to the anonymous reviewers for their comments and suggestions.

References

A Baltaretu and T Ferreira (2016). Task demands and individual variation in referring expressions. In *Proceedings of INLG-2016*.

A Belz and E Kow (2010). The GREC Challenges 2010: Overview and Evaluation Result. In *Proceedings of INLG-2010*.

R Dale and E Reiter (1995). Computational Interpretations of the Gricean Maxims in the Generation of Referring Expressions. *Cognitive Science* 19:233-263

K van Deemter, E Krahmer, M Theune (2005). Real vs. template-based natural language generation: a false opposition? *Computational Linguistics* **31**:15-24.

K van Deemter (2016a). *Computational Models of Referring*. MIT Press.

K van Deemter (2016b). Designing Algorithms for Referring with Proper Names. In *Proceedings of INLG-2016*.

A Gatt and A Belz (2008). Attribute Selection for Referring Expression Generation: New Algorithms and Evaluation Methods. *Proceedings of INLG-2008*.

A Gatt, R van Gompel, K van Deemter, E Kramer (2013). Are we Bayesian referring expression generators. *Proceedings of CogSci 2013*.

E Krahmer and K van Deemter. 2012 Computational Generation of Referring Expressions: A Survey. *Computational Linguistics* **38**:173-218

R Koolen, E Krahmer, M Theune (2012). Learning Preferences for Referring Expression Generation: Effects of Domain, Language and Algorithm. *Proceedings of INLG-2012*.

M Mitchell, K van Deemter, E Reiter (2013). Generating Expressions that Refer to Visible Objects. *Proceedings of NAACL-2013*, pages 1174-1184.

R de Oliveira, S Sripada, E Reiter (2015). Designing an Algorithm for Generating Named Spatial References. *Proceedings of ENLG-2015*, pages 127-135

E Reiter (2007). An Architecture for Data-to-Text Systems. *Proceedings of ENLG-2007*, pages 97-104.

E Reiter (2016). Method and apparatus for referring expression generation. US Patent 9355093.

S Sripada, N Burnett, R Turner, J Mastin, D Evans (2014). A Case Study: NLG meeting Weather Industry. *Proceedings of INLG 2014*.

R Turner, S Sripada, and E Reiter (2010) Generating Approximate Geographic Descriptions. In E Krahmer and M Theune (eds). *Empirical Methods in Natural Language Generation*, pages 121-140. Springer.

Integrated sentence generation with charts

Alexander Koller and **Nikos Engonopoulos**
Saarland University, Saarbrücken, Germany
`{koller|nikos}@coli.uni-saarland.de`

Abstract

Integrating surface realization and the generation of referring expressions (REs) into a single algorithm can improve the quality of the generated sentences. Existing algorithms for doing this, such as SPUD and CRISP, are search-based and can be slow or incomplete. We offer a chart-based algorithm for integrated sentence generation which supports efficient search through chart pruning.

1 Introduction

It has long been argued (Stone et al., 2003) that the strict distinction between surface realization and sentence planning in the classical NLG pipeline (Reiter and Dale, 2000) can cause difficulties for an NLG system. Generation decisions that look good to the sentence planner may be hard or impossible for the realizer to express in natural language. Furthermore, a standalone sentence planner must compute each RE separately, thus missing out on opportunities for succinct REs that are ambiguous in isolation but correct in context (Stone and Webber, 1998).

Algorithms such as SPUD (Stone et al., 2003) and CRISP (Koller and Stone, 2007) perform surface realization and parts of sentence planning, including RE generation, in an integrated fashion. Such integrated algorithms for sentence generation can balance the needs of the realizer and the sentence planner and take advantage of opportunities for succinct realizations. However, integrated sentence planning multiplies the complexities of two hard combinatorial problems, and thus existing, search-based algorithms can be inefficient or fail to find a good solu-

tion; SPUD's greedy search strategy may even find no solution at all, even when one exists.

By contrast, chart-based algorithms have been shown in parsing to remain efficient and accurate even for large inputs because they support structure sharing and very effective pruning techniques. Chart algorithms have been successfully applied to surface realization (White, 2004; Gardent and Kow, 2005; Carroll and Oepen, 2005; Schwenger et al., 2016), but in RE generation, most algorithms are not chart-based, see e.g. (Dale and Reiter, 1995; Krahmer et al., 2003). One exception is the chart-based RE generation of Engonopoulos and Koller (2014).

In this paper, we present a chart-based algorithm for integrated surface realization and RE generation. This makes it possible – to our knowledge, for the first time – to apply chart-based pruning techniques to integrated sentence generation. Our algorithm extends the chart-based RE generation algorithm of Engonopoulos and Koller (2014) by keeping track of the semantic content that has been expressed by each chart item. Because it is modular on the string side, the same algorithm can be used to generate with context-free grammars or TAGs, with or without feature structures, at no expense in runtime efficiency. An open-source implementation of our algorithm, based on the Alto system (Gontrum et al., 2017), can be found at `bitbucket.org/tclup/alto`.

2 Chart-based integrated generation

We first describe the grammar formalism we use. Then we explain the sentence generation algorithm and discuss its runtime performance.

139

Proceedings of The 10th International Natural Language Generation conference, pages 139–143,
Santiago de Compostela, Spain, September 4-7 2017. ©2017 Association for Computational Linguistics

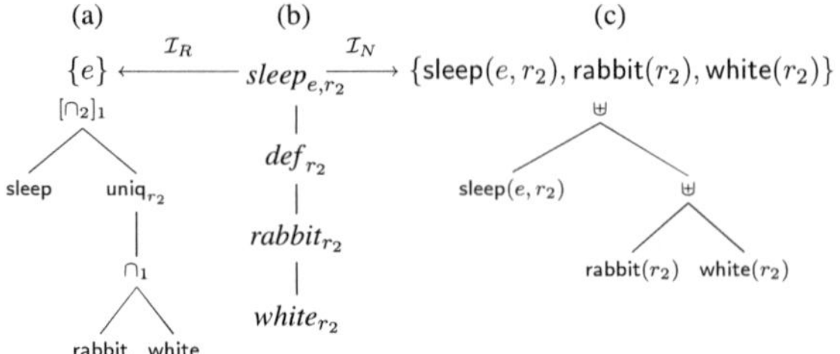

(d) $\mathcal{I}_S : \bullet(\bullet(\text{the}, \bullet(\text{white}, \text{rabbit})), \text{sleeps}) = $ "the white rabbit sleeps"

Figure 1: A derivation tree (b) with its interpretations (a, c, d).

2.1 Semantically interpreted grammars

We describe the integrated sentence generation problem in terms of *semantically interpreted grammars (SIGs)* (Engonopoulos and Koller, 2014), a special case of Interpreted Regular Tree Grammars (Koller and Kuhlmann, 2011). We introduce SIGs by example, and refer to Engonopoulos and Koller (2014) for detailed definitions.

An example SIG grammar is shown in Fig. 2. At the core of each grammar rule is a rule of the form $A_a \rightarrow f(B_b, \ldots, Z_z)$. The symbols $A, \ldots, Z$ are nonterminals such as S, NP, VP, and $a, \ldots, z$ are semantic indices, i.e. constants for individuals indicating to which object in the model a natural-language expression is intended to refer. These core rules allow us to recursively derive a *derivation tree*, such as the one shown in Fig. 1b, representing the abstract syntactic structure of a natural-language expression.

Each derivation tree t is mapped to a string through a function $\mathcal{I}_S$. This function is defined recursively for each rule of the grammar. In the example grammar of Fig. 2, we have $\mathcal{I}_S(white_{r_2}) = $ white, i.e. the word "white". Given a string w_1, we have $\mathcal{I}_S(rabbit_{r_2})(w_1) = w_1 \bullet \text{rabbit}$, where "$\bullet$" is string concatenation. This means that given a subtree t' which evaluates to the string w_1, a string for the tree $rabbit_{r_2}(t')$ is constructed by appending the word "rabbit" after w_1. For the complete derivation tree t in Fig. 1, we obtain $\mathcal{I}_S(t) = $ "the white rabbit sleeps".

At the same time and in the same way, the derivation tree is also evaluated to a set of referents through a function $\mathcal{I}_R$. Constants, such as rabbit and sleep, are interpreted as subsets of and relations between the individuals in a given model. For instance, in the model of Fig. 3, rabbit denotes the set $\{r_1, r_2\}$, whereas in denotes the relation $\{(r_1, h_1), (f_1, h_2)\}$.

for all $e, a \in$ sleep:
$S_e \rightarrow sleep_{e,a}(\text{NP}_a)$
$\mathcal{I}_S(sleep_{e,a})(w_1) = w_1 \bullet \text{sleeps}$
$\mathcal{I}_R(sleep_{e,a})(R_1) = [\text{sleep} \cap_1 \text{uniq}_a(R_1)]_1$
$\mathcal{I}_N(sleep_{e,a})(N_1) = \{\text{sleep}(e,a)\} \uplus N_1$

for all $a \in$ rabbit:
$N_a \rightarrow rabbit_a(\text{Adj}_a)$
$\mathcal{I}_S(rabbit_a)(w_1) = w_1 \bullet \text{rabbit}$
$\mathcal{I}_R(rabbit_a)(R_1) = \text{rabbit} \cap_1 R_1$
$\mathcal{I}_N(rabbit_a)(N_1) = \{\text{rabbit}(a)\} \uplus N_1$

for all $a \in U$:
$\text{NP}_a \rightarrow def_a(\text{N}_a)$
$\mathcal{I}_S(def_a)(w_1) = \text{the} \bullet w_1$
$\mathcal{I}_R(def_a)(R_1) = R_1$
$\mathcal{I}_N(def_a)(N_1) = N_1$

for all $a \in U$:
$\text{N}_a \rightarrow thing_a(\text{Adj}_a)$
$\mathcal{I}_S(thing_a)(w_1) = w_1 \bullet \text{thing}$
$\mathcal{I}_R(thing_a)(R_1) = R_1$
$\mathcal{I}_N(thing_a)(N_1) = N_1$

for all $a \in$ white:
$\text{Adj}_a \rightarrow white_a$
$\mathcal{I}_S(white_a) = \text{white}$
$\mathcal{I}_R(white_a) = \text{white}$
$\mathcal{I}_N(white_a) = \{\text{white}(a)\}$

for all $a \in U$:
$\text{Adj}_a \rightarrow nop_a$
$\mathcal{I}_S(nop_a) = \epsilon$
$\mathcal{I}_R(nop_a) = U$
$\mathcal{I}_N(nop_a) = \emptyset$

for all $e, a, b \in$ takefrom(e, a, b):
$S_e \rightarrow takefrom_{e,a,b}(\text{NP}_a, \text{NP}_b)$
$\mathcal{I}_S(takefrom_{e,a,b})(w_1, w_2) = \text{take} \bullet w_1 \bullet \text{from} \bullet w_2$
$\mathcal{I}_R(takefrom_{e,a,b})(R_1, R_2) = [[\text{takefrom} \cap_2 \text{uniq}_a(R_1 \cap_1 [\text{in} \cap_2 R_2])_1]) \cap_3 \text{uniq}_b(R_2 \cap_1 [\text{in} \cap_1 R_1]_2)]_1$
$\mathcal{I}_N(takefrom_{e,a,b})(N_1, N_2) = \{\text{takefrom}(e,a,b)\} \uplus N_1 \uplus N_2$

Figure 2: An example grammar.

Figure 3: An example model.

These relations are then combined using intersection $R_1 \cap_i R_2$ (yielding the subset of elements of R_1 whose i-th component is an element of the set R_2), projection $[R]_i$ (yielding the set of i-th components of the tuples in R), and the uniqueness checker $\text{uniq}_a(R)$ (yielding R if $R = \{a\}$ and $\emptyset$ otherwise). Under this interpretation, the derivation tree in Fig. 1 maps to the set $\{e\}$, given the model in Fig. 3.

Observe, finally, that each rule is annotated with a "for all" clause, which creates instances of the rule for each tuple of individuals that satisfies the condition. We also mention that although we only use unary attributes such as "rabbit" and "white" in this example grammar, SIGs deal easily with relational attributes such as "in" or "next to"; see Engonopoulos and Koller (2014).

2.2 Integrated sentence generation with SIGs

Engonopoulos and Koller (2014) describe an algorithm which, given a SIG grammar G and a set R

$$\frac{[B_1, R_1, N_1] \quad \ldots \quad [B_k, R_k, N_k] \qquad A \to r(B_1, \ldots, B_k) \text{ in } G}{[A, \mathcal{I}_R(r)(R_1, \ldots, R_k), \mathcal{I}_N(r)(N_1, \ldots, N_k)]}$$

Figure 4: The chart computation algorithm.

of target referents, will compute a chart describing all derivations t of G with $\mathcal{I}_R(t) = R$ – that is, all semantically valid REs for R.

Here we extend both SIGs and this algorithm to include surface realization. We assume that the generation algorithm is given a set N of *semantic atoms* in addition to the grammar G and referent set R, and should return only derivations that refer to R while expressing at least all the atoms in N. We achieve this by adding an interpretation $\mathcal{I}_N$ to SIGs, such that $\mathcal{I}_N(t)$ will return a set of semantic atoms expressed by the derivation tree t. We have added such $\mathcal{I}_N$ clauses to the grammar in Fig. 2. For example, the rule for $white_{r_2}$ expresses the set $\{\text{white}(r_2)\}$ of semantic atoms. The rule for $rabbit_{r_2}$ evaluates to the disjoint union of $\{\text{rabbit}(r_2)\}$ with whatever its "Adj" subtree expressed. Thus, the $\mathcal{I}_N$ interpretation keeps track of the semantic atoms expressed by each subtree of a derivation tree; in the example of Fig. 1, we see that the derivation tree as a whole expresses the semantic atoms $\{\text{sleep}(e, r_2), \text{rabbit}(r_2), \text{white}(r_2)\}$.

Given a grammar G, target referent set R, and target semantic content N, we can now compute a chart that describes all derivation trees t of G such that $\mathcal{I}_R(t) = R$ and $\mathcal{I}_N(t) \supseteq N$; thus this algorithm performs surface realization and RE generation at the same time. The algorithm, shown in Fig. 4 in the form of a parsing schema (Shieber et al., 1995), computes *chart items* $[A, R, N]$ in a bottom-up fashion. Such an item states that there is a tree t such that t can be derived from A, and we have $\mathcal{I}_R(t) = R$ and $\mathcal{I}_N(t) = N$. Given k items for subtrees derived from the nonterminals $B_1, \ldots, B_k$ as premises and a rule r that can combine these into a nonterminal A, the algorithm creates a new item for A in which the $\mathcal{I}_R$ and $\mathcal{I}_N$ functions for that rule were applied to the referent sets and semantic contents of the subtrees. Given the inputs R and N, we define a *goal item* to be an item $[S, R, N']$ where S is the start symbol of the grammar and $N' \supseteq N$. Each goal item the algorithm discovers thus represents a sentence that achieves the given communicative goals.

An example run of the algorithm, for the inputs

1	$[\text{Adj}_{r_2}, \{r_2\}, \{white_{r_2}\}]$	$(white_{r_2})$
2	$[\text{Adj}_{r_2}, U, \emptyset]$	(nop_{r_2})
3	$[\text{N}_{r_2}, \{r_2\}, \{white_{r_2}, rabbit_{r_2}\}]$	$(rabbit_{r_2}, 1)$
4	$[\text{N}_{r_2}, \{r_2\}, \{white_{r_2}\}]$	$(thing_{r_2}, 1)$
5	$[\text{N}_{r_2}, \{r_1, r_2\}, \{rabbit_{r_2}\}]$	$(rabbit_{r_2}, 2)$
6	$[\text{NP}_{r_2}, \{r_2\}, \{white_{r_2}, rabbit_{r_2}\}]$	$(the_{r_2}, 3)$
7	$[\text{NP}_{r_2}, \{r_2\}, \{white_{r_2}\}]$	$(the_{r_2}, 4)$
8	$[\text{NP}_{r_2}, \{r_1, r_2\}, \{rabbit_{r_2}\}]$	$(the_{r_2}, 5)$
9	$[\text{S}_e, \{e\}, \{white_{r_2}, rabbit_{r_2}, sleep_{e, r_2}\}]$	$(sleep_e, 6)$
10	$[\text{S}_e, \{e\}, \{white_{r_2}, sleep_{e, r_2}\}]$	$(sleep_e, 7)$
11	$[\text{S}_e, \emptyset, \{rabbit_{r_2}, sleep_{e, r_2}\}]$	$(sleep_e, 8)$

Figure 5: Excerpt from the chart for "The white rabbit sleeps."

$R = \{e\}$ and $N = \{\text{rabbit}(r_2)\}$, is shown in Fig. 5. Each row in the chart corresponds to one application of the rule in Fig. 4. The grammar rule that was used, along with any premises, is given in brackets to the right. Observe that the only goal item, (9), corresponds to the derivation in Fig. 1, and hence the output string "the white rabbit sleeps"; the derivation can be reconstructed by following the backpointers to the premise items recursively. Observe also that (10) – for "the white thing sleeps" – is not a goal item because its semantic content is not a superset of N. The item (11) – for "the rabbit sleeps" – is not a goal item either: Its referent set is empty because (8) is not a unique RE for r_2, and thus the term $\text{uniq}_{r_2}(R_1)$ in the "sleep" rule evaluates to the empty set. Thus, the algorithm performs both surface realization and RE generation.

2.3 Generating succinct REs in context

One advantage of integrating surface realization with RE generation is that REs can be more succinct in the context of a larger grammatical construction than in isolation. The shortest standalone RE for r_1 in Fig. 3 is "the brown rabbit", but it is perfectly felicitous to say "take *the rabbit* from the hat". Stone and Webber (1998) explain this in terms of the presuppositions of the verb "take X from Y", which say that X must be in Y, and thus the REs X and Y can mutually constrain each other. They also show how the SPUD algorithm can generate such succinct REs in the context of the verb, by global reasoning over the referent sets of all REs in the sentence.

Our algorithm can generate such REs as well, and can do it in an efficient, chart-based way. Assume $R = \{e_2\}$ and $N = \{\text{takefrom}(e_2, r_1, h_1)\}$ and the grammar in Fig. 2. The chart algorithm will construct items for the sub-derivation-trees $t_1 = def_{r_1}(rabbit_{r_1}(nop_{r_1}))$ ("the rabbit") and $t_2 = def_{h_1}(hat_{h_1}(nop_{h_1}))$ ("the hat"), with $R_1 = \mathcal{I}_R(t_1) = \{r_1, r_2\}$ and $R_2 = \mathcal{I}_R(t_2) = \{h_1, h_2\}$; thus, these REs are not by themselves unique. These trees are then combined with the rule $takefrom_{e_2,r_1,h_1}$. This rule intersects R_1 with the set of things that are "in" an element of R_2, encoding the presupposition of "take X from Y". Thus $R_1 \cap_1 [\text{in} \cap_2 R_2]_1$ evaluates to $\{r_1\}$, satisfying the uniqueness condition. Thus, the algorithm returns $t = takefrom_{e_2,r_1,h_1}(t_1, t_2)$ as a valid realization.

Note that we achieved the ability to let REs mutually constrain each other by moving the requirement for semantic uniqueness to the verb that subcategorizes for the RE. This is in contrast to the standard assumption that it is the definite article that requires uniqueness, but permits us a purely grammar-based treatment of mutually constraining REs which requires no further reasoning capabilities.

2.4 Chart generation with heuristics

Our algorithm can enumerate all subsets N of the true semantic atoms in the model, and thus has worst-case exponential runtime. This is probably unavoidable, given that surface realization and the generation of shortest REs are both NP-complete (Koller and Striegnitz, 2002; Dale and Reiter, 1995).

However, because it is a chart-based algorithm, we can use heuristics to avoid computing the whole chart, and thus speed up the search for the best solution. To get an impression of this, assume that we are looking for a *short* sentence; other optimization criteria are also possible. We first compute the full chart $C_{\mathcal{R}}$ for the $\mathcal{I}_R$ part of the input alone, using essentially the same algorithm as Engonopoulos and Koller (2014). From $C_{\mathcal{R}}$ we compute the *distance* of each chart item to a goal item, i.e. the minimal number of rules that must be applied to the item to produce a goal item. We then refine the items of $C_{\mathcal{R}}$ by adding the $\mathcal{I}_N$ parts to each chart item. Unprocessed chart items $[A, R, N]$ are organized on an agenda which is ordered lexicographically by the number of atoms in the target semantic content that are not yet realized in N and then the distance of $[A, R]$ to a goal item in $C_{\mathcal{R}}$. We stop the chart computation once the first goal item has been found.

Using this pruning strategy, we measured runtimes with problems from the GIVE Challenge (Koller et al., 2010) on an 2.9 GHz Intel Core i5 CPU.[1] We compared the performance of our system against CRISP, which uses the FF planner (Hoffmann and Nebel, 2001) to perform the search. For CRISP, we only measured the time spent in running the planner. On the most complex scene from GIVE that we tried, our system took 13 ms to generate the sentence "Push the button to the left of the flower", outperforming CRISP which generated the same sentence in 50 ms. Note that it is possible to construct (not entirely realistic) inputs for the generator on which FF's much more sophisticated search strategy outperforms the heuristic described above. By incorporating such a heuristic into chart generation, e.g. as in Schwenger et al. (2016), our system could be accelerated further.

3 Conclusion

We have presented a chart-based algorithm for integrated surface realization and RE generation. Compared to earlier approaches to integrated sentence generation, our algorithm can exploit the capabilities of charts for structure-sharing and pruning to achieve higher runtime performance in practice. We have only presented a simple pruning strategy here, but it would be astraightforward extension to incorporate pruning strategies from surface realization (White, 2004; Schwenger et al., 2016).

One advantage of our algorithm is that it is agnostic of the grammar formalism that is used on the string side. We have used context-free rules for reading off string representations from the generated derivation trees, but because SIGs are special case of IRTGs, we could instead use a tree-adjoining grammar to construct strings instead (Koller and Kuhlmann, 2012). In fact, the runtime experiments in Section 2.4 were based on a TAG grammar to allow direct comparison with CRISP.

With the algorithm presented here, it may become feasible for the first time to perform integrated sentence generation in the context of practical applications. So far, grammars that support this lag far behind grammars for surface realization in size and complexity. It would thus be interesting to either convert existing surface realization grammars to SIGs, or to learn such grammars from data.

---

[1] We let the Java VM warm up before measuring runtimes.

References

John Carroll and Stephan Oepen. 2005. High efficiency realization for a wide-coverage unification grammar. In *Proceedings of the 2nd IJCNLP*.

Robert Dale and Ehud Reiter. 1995. Computational interpretations of the Gricean Maxims in the generation of referring expressions. *Cognitive Science*, 19(2):233–263.

Nikos Engonopoulos and Alexander Koller. 2014. Generating effective referring expressions using charts. In *Proceedings of the 8th International Conference on Natural Language Generation (INLG)*, Philadelphia.

Claire Gardent and Eric Kow. 2005. Generating and selecting grammatical paraphrases. In *Proceedings of ENLG*.

Johannes Gontrum, Jonas Groschwitz, Alexander Koller, and Christoph Teichmann. 2017. Alto: Rapid prototyping for parsing and translation. In *Proceedings of the EACL Demo Session*.

Jörg Hoffmann and Bernhard Nebel. 2001. The FF planning system: Fast plan generation through heuristic search. *Journal of Artificial Intelligence Research*, 14:253–302.

Alexander Koller and Marco Kuhlmann. 2011. A generalized view on parsing and translation. In *Proceedings of the 12th International Conference on Parsing Technologies (IWPT)*.

Alexander Koller and Marco Kuhlmann. 2012. Decomposing TAG algorithms using simple algebraizations. In *Proceedings of the 11th TAG+ Workshop*.

Alexander Koller and Matthew Stone. 2007. Sentence generation as a planning problem. In *Proceedings of the 45th ACL*.

Alexander Koller and Kristina Striegnitz. 2002. Generation as dependency parsing. In *Proceedings of the 40th Annual Meeting of the Association for Computational Linguistics*, pages 17–24, Philadelphia, PA, USA.

Alexander Koller, Kristina Striegnitz, Donna Byron, Justine Cassell, Robert Dale, Johanna Moore, and Jon Oberlander. 2010. The First Challenge on Generating Instructions in Virtual Environments. In E. Krahmer and M. Theune, editors, *Empirical Methods in Natural Language Generation*, number 5790 in LNCS, pages 337–361. Springer.

Emiel Krahmer, Sebastiaan van Erk, and André Verleg. 2003. Graph-based generation of referring expressions. *Computational Linguistics*, 29(1):53–72.

Ehud Reiter and Robert Dale. 2000. *Building Natural Language Generation Systems*. Cambridge University Press, Cambridge, England.

Maximilian Schwenger, Álvaro Torralba, Jörg Hoffmann, David M. Howcroft, and Vera Demberg. 2016. From OpenCCG to AI planning: Detecting infeasible edges in sentence generation. In *Proceedings of the 26th International Conference on Computational Linguistics (COLING)*.

Stuart Shieber, Yves Schabes, and Fernando Pereira. 1995. Principles and implementation of deductive parsing. *Journal of Logic Programming*, 24(1–2):3–36.

Matthew Stone and Bonnie Webber. 1998. Textual economy through close coupling of syntax and semantics. In *Proceedings of the 9th INLG*.

Matthew Stone, Christine Doran, Bonnie Webber, Tonia Bleam, and Martha Palmer. 2003. Microplanning with communicative intentions: The SPUD system. *Computational Intelligence*, 19(4):311–381.

Michael White. 2004. Reining in CCG chart realization. In Anja Belz, Roger Evans, and Paul Piwek, editors, *Proceedings of the Third International Conference on Natural Language Generation (INLG04)*.

Adapting SimpleNLG to Spanish

Alejandro Ramos-Soto and **Julio Janeiro-Gallardo** and **Alberto Bugarín**
Centro Singular de Investigación en Tecnoloxías da Información (CiTIUS)
University of Santiago de Compostela, Spain
`{alejandro.ramos,julio.janeiro,alberto.bugarin.diz}@usc.es`

Abstract

We describe SimpleNLG-ES, an adaptation of the SimpleNLG realization library for the Spanish language. Our implementation is based on the bilingual English-French SimpleNLG-EnFr adaptation. The library has been tested using a battery of examples that ensure that the most common syntax, morphology and orthography rules for Spanish are met. The library is currently being used in three different projects for the development of data-to-text systems in the meteorological, statistical data information, and business intelligence application domains.

1 Introduction

In recent times, natural language generation (NLG) is receiving increased attention beyond its research community. Commercial success is nowadays a fact for several NLG companies and this trend is likely to expand in coming years, as many opportunities will arise for the development of NLG systems that provide useful interpretable information and address different needs within organizations.

In this context, software for NLG purposes which is freely available is an exception rather than a norm. In fact, according to Reiter (Reiter, 2017), this problem is worsened by a lack of visibility of available software. In other words, there is not much software for NLG and most of it is unknown to the wide public. However, among the different tasks that can be identified within an NLG system according to (Reiter and Dale, 2000), software for the realization task (the actual text generation process from the inter-

mediate representation of the information to be conveyed) is actually plentiful when compared to other tasks like referring expression generation.

In this paper we focus on a specific realizer for the English language, namely SimpleNLG, which was originally presented in (Gatt and Reiter, 2009), but has been improved over the years and has become a popular and active project. As a Java library, SimpleNLG honours its name by providing an intuitive object-oriented API for generating text from a lexical-syntactic specification.

Moreover, different adaptations of SimpleNLG have been made to support other languages. Among them, the bilingual English-French version developed by Vaudry (Vaudry and Lapalme, 2013), provided an abstraction of the common linguistic features shared by both languages. Subsequent adaptations include German (Bollmann, 2011), Brazilian Portuguese (de Oliveira and Sripada, 2014) and Italian (Mazzei et al., 2016), based on different versions of the original and the bilingual versions of the library. SimpleNLG has also served as inspiration for a realizer for the Indian Telugu language (Dokkara et al., 2015).

2 Adapting SimpleNLG-EnFr to Spanish

Given that Spanish is one of the most spoken languages in the world in terms of native speakers, there are many potential benefits about providing a realizer that supports this language. To our knowledge, there has been a previous attempt at developing a Spanish version of SimpleNLG, as in (Trzpis, 2015). However, this project was not made publicly available and, according to its description, several fea-

Proceedings of The 10th International Natural Language Generation conference, pages 144–148,
Santiago de Compostela, Spain, September 4-7 2017. ©2017 Association for Computational Linguistics

tures were missing or incomplete, such as interrogative questions, gerund and participle verb forms or an extensive lexicon.

In order to address this, we provide an adaptation of the bilingual English-French version of SimpleNLG for the Spanish language. Specifically, we have opted for the creation of a bilingual English-Spanish version that follows the original class structure of SimpleNLG-EnFr, instead of adding a third language to the existing implementation of SimpleNLG-EnFr. While we believe that creating a more general framework based on SimpleNLG with multilingual support is a necessary task that should be undertaken in the future, our main interest is to provide an useful NLG tool which is not currently available for NLG developers that may need use the Spanish language.

Thus, as in SimpleNLG-EnFr, most of the basic framework is shared between both languages, such as document elements and some grammar rules which are common for both English and Spanish. Based on the abstract classes, we have subclassed several functionalities regarding syntax, morphology, and orthography and adapted an already existing lexicon which provides a very extensive collection of Spanish words and inflections. The Spanish grammar used as reference is the *"Nueva gramática de la lengua española"* (RAE, 2011).

2.1 Lexicon

Instead of building our own lexicon, we opted for reusing already well-known and reputed existing resources in the literature. In particular, we have used the Spanish dictionary provided by the FreeLing project (Padró and Stanilovsky, 2012) to develop and test SimpleNLG-ES. This dictionary provides 555,000 forms corresponding to more than 76.000 lemma-PoS (Part of Speech) combinations. Since the dictionary cannot be used directly with SimpleNLG, we converted the original file format into an XML file format which is compatible with the realizer.

3 Features of the Spanish language

We describe here some of the most interesting features of the Spanish language which have been incorporated into SimpleNLG-ES. These involve syntax, orthography, morphology and morphophonology elements.

3.1 Syntax

Some of the most relevant features in terms of syntax include the adjective positioning, the use of reflexive pronouns for passive clauses, relatively simple interrogative clauses, and the subjunctive conversion of imperative statements that are used as relative clauses.

Verb phrase: Verb phrases are in structure similar to English verb phrases. Among the most interesting verb phrase features of the Spanish language for which we have added support, the construction of verb clauses without subject using the verb *"haber"*, is expressed as *"hay"* (which actually means *"there is/are"*). Likewise, passive clauses, which are less common in Spanish, can be constructed by adding the reflexive pronoun *"se"*. For instance, *"se crearon tres prototipos"* means *"three prototypes were created"*.

Noun phrase: Noun phrases follow a similar pattern to their English counterpart, with a determiner, a noun, and one or more adjectives. The main difference is that adjectives are usually positioned after the noun, although they can also be positioned before the noun for emphatic purposes or slight differences in meaning. For instance, *"that **good man**"* can be expressed as *"ese hombre **bueno**"* or *"ese **buen** hombre"*.

A specific feature involving noun phrases when used as indirect objects is that a preposition *'a'* has to be attached before the noun phrase. For instance, *"I gave **the kids** a toy"* would be expressed as *"Le di un juguete **a los niños**"*. This actually coincides with the less used English alternative, *"I gave a toy **to the kids**"*.

Interrogative clause: Interrogative clauses are formed in many cases by simply adding the proper punctuation signs at the beginning and end of a sentence. For instance, a simple statement converted into a yes/no question like *"you want to eat"* → *"do you want to eat?"* would be expressed as *"quieres comer"* → *"¿quieres comer?"*.

In the case of a 'who' question, where this particle plays the role of an indirect object, the beginning of the question incorporates a preposition 'a', just like in the indirect object case described above for the noun phrase. For instance, *"**Who** do you prefer?"* would be expressed as *"¿A **quién** prefieres?"*.

Relative clause: In the case of relative clauses, subordinate imperative sentences are transformed into subjunctive. For instance, *"Throw away the stones." → "I want you to throw away the stones."*, would be expressed as *"Tira las piedras." → "Quiero que **tires** las piedras."* (*"I want that you throw away the stones"*, literally translated).

3.2 Orthography

Most general orthography rules that are used in English also apply to Spanish, such as beginning sentences with capital letters or punctuation using commas and dots. Thus, in SimpleNLG-ES most orthography code is shared for both languages.

In Spanish there exist orthographic rules that determine whether specific letters within words must include a tilde, a diacritical mark that helps determine the word pronunciation. For example, in 'pretérito' the tilde over the 'e' letter implies a stress in the pronunciation for that syllable. In our case, the Freeling lexicon already provides the correct forms of the words, including tildes. This allowed us to avoid including the related orthography rules for determining tildes, which involve identifying syllables and ending letters for words.

In fact, the only Spanish orthographic rule we had to add is the inclusion of the interrogative particle '¿' that marks the beginning of an interrogative sentence.

3.3 Morphology

Gender and number: Determiners, adjectives and some nouns must be inflected in gender and number. In our case the lexicon supports all inflections for base words, but we have also included several rules for inflection of plurals for regular nouns.

Verb tenses: As in other languages, in Spanish there exist regular and irregular verbs. We have included in SimpleNLG-ES the standard rules for inflecting regular verbs, while irregular verbal forms are provided by the lexicon. Moreover, verbs in Spanish can be inflected for several modalities (indicative, subjunctive, imperative) and many different tenses. Tenses involve simple and compound forms using the auxiliar verb *"haber"* (to have). All of them are correctly supported by SimpleNLG-ES.

In order to illustrate the complexity of the verbal system in Spanish, which is supported by SimpleNLG-ES, consider the English sentence *"I had eaten"*. In Spanish, depending on the context, this could correspond to the indicative compound tense named *pretérito pluscuamperfecto "yo había comido"* or to the *preterito perfecto compuesto "yo hube comido"*. At the same time, *"if I had eaten"* would correspond to the subjunctive *pretérito pluscuamperfecto "si yo hubiera comido"* or *"si yo hubiese comido"* (this tense admits two different forms). Thus, depending on the context of the sentence, *"I had eaten"* could correspond in Spanish to three different tenses, four different realizations, and two different modalities.

3.4 Morphophonology

The Spanish language is not as rich as other close languages in terms of morphophonology rules. However, there exist two main contractions between the prepositions *'a'* and *'de'*, and the masculine singular determinant *'el'* that are always used:

- *"a el"* → *'al'* (to the)

- *"de el"* → *'del'* (of the)

Other contractions are used in a more colloquial spoken context, such as *"para atrás"* → *"patrás"* (backwards) and *"para adelante"* → *"palante"* (forwards), but these are not officially recognized by the Real Academia Española (the official organism that regulates the Spanish language). Thus, SimpleNLG-ES includes only support for *'al'* and *'del'*.

4 Test and use

We have tested our adaptation of SimpleNLG for Spanish in different ways. Firstly, we adapted the existing tests for the English language version, as many of the features tested also apply to Spanish. These tests, built using a unit testing framework, check the functioning of the library at different levels, by comparing if the text strings generated by the library match the correct expected results. SimpleNLG-ES passed all these tests successfully.

Secondly, we tested SimpleNLG-ES in the real data-to-text service GALiWeather (Ramos-Soto et al., 2015), which is a template-based NLG system that was deployed in May 2015 as a public service for the Official Meteorology Agency (MeteoGalicia, 2000) of Galicia (NW Spain). GALiWeather produces automatically daily operational weather forecasts for each of the 314 municipalities in Galicia.

Specifically, we refactorized and adapted GALiWeather, to perform realization using SimpleNLG for Spanish. Tests consisted of 76 different real weather forecasts produced since November 2016, which were generated for the same input data. The corresponding forecast texts were generated using both approaches (GALiWeather's original template-based and SimpleNLG-ES realizations) and their strings were matched using unit testing assertion methods.

Only in 7 out of the 76 testing examples (9%), the same non-relevant difference was found between pairs of texts generated for the same input data. This corresponded to the case where the Spanish reflex ive pronoun *'se'* appeared. In Spanish, this pronoun can be placed separately or attached to a verb with no changes in meaning, as in *"se podrán encontrar"* or *"podrán encontrarse"*. The templates use the latter case, while our adaptation of SimpleNLG applies the former rule:

- Expected (template-based GALiWeather): *"Se espera que los cielos alternen periodos muy nubosos con otros parcialmente nubosos, aunque ocasionalmente **podrán encontrarse** poco nubosos o despejados."*

- Actual (SimpleNLG-ES): *"Se espera que los cielos alternen periodos muy nubosos con otros parcialmente nubosos, aunque ocasionalmente **se podrán encontrar** poco nubosos o despejados."*

In order to further test and refine the library, we are also currently using SimpleNLG-ES in three different projects for the development of data-to-text systems in new domains, with satisfactory results. The first project is in the environmental information domain, also in cooperation with the Galician Meteorology Agency, for automatically generating textual meteorological warnings following the guidelines of the European Meteoalarm service (EUMET-Net, 2007). The second project focuses on providing textual descriptions and explanations in natural language about a number of official statistical data and indicators. Finally, the third project is in the business intelligence information realm.

5 Documentation and release

SimpleNLG-ES has been thoroughly documented. Specifically, the source code maintains the original documentation style of SimpleNLG in English. We have also adapted and translated the original documentation and tutorial into Spanish.

The source code of SimpleNLG-ES and its associated documentation are available on GitHub (Alejandro Ramos-Soto, 2017).

6 Conclusions

We have described in this paper the most relevant features of our adaptation SimpleNLG-ES of the realizer SimpleNLG for the Spanish language. This version provides an extensive support for the most common usage of Spanish, using a comprehensive lexicon that covers most of the common Spanish vocabulary and all its inflections.

SimpleNLG-ES has been tested through various means. Moreover, the library is currently being used in three different projects for the development of real D2T systems in the meteorological, statistical data information, and business intelligence application domains. As current and near future work, we will extend the library to also support the Galician language.

Acknowledgments

This work has been funded by TIN2014-56633-C3-1-R and TIN2014-56633-C3-3-R projects from the Spanish "Ministerio de Economía y Competitividad" and by the "Consellería de Cultura, Educación e Ordenación Universitaria" (accreditation 2016-2019, ED431G/08) and the European Regional Development Fund (ERDF). A. Ramos-Soto is funded by the "Consellería de Cultura, Educación e Ordenación Universitaria" (under the Postdoctoral Fellowship accreditation ED481B 2017/030).

References

Alberto Bugarín Alejandro Ramos-Soto, Julio Janeiro-Gallardo. 2017. SimpleNLG-ES on GitHub. `https://github.com/citiususc/simplenlg-es`. Accessed: 2017-10-03.

Marcel Bollmann, 2011. *Proceedings of the 13th European Workshop on Natural Language Generation*, chapter Adapting SimpleNLG to German, pages 133–138. Association for Computational Linguistics.

Rodrigo de Oliveira and Somayajulu Sripada, 2014. *Proceedings of the 8th International Natural Language Generation Conference (INLG)*, chapter Adapting SimpleNLG for Brazilian Portuguese realisation, pages 93–94. Association for Computational Linguistics.

Sekhar Sasi Raja Dokkara, Verma Suresh Penumathsa, and Gowri Somayajulu Sripada, 2015. *Proceedings of the 15th European Workshop on Natural Language Generation (ENLG)*, chapter A Simple Surface Realization Engine for Telugu, pages 1–8. Association for Computational Linguistics.

EUMETNet. 2007. Meteoalarm website. www.meteoalarm.eu. `http://www.meteoalarm.eu`. Accessed: 2017-05-12.

Albert Gatt and Ehud Reiter, 2009. *Proceedings of the 12th European Workshop on Natural Language Generation (ENLG 2009)*, chapter SimpleNLG: A Realisation Engine for Practical Applications, pages 90–93. Association for Computational Linguistics.

Alessandro Mazzei, Cristina Battaglino, and Cristina Bosco, 2016. *Proceedings of the 9th International Natural Language Generation conference*, chapter SimpleNLG-IT: adapting SimpleNLG to Italian, pages 184–192. Association for Computational Linguistics.

MeteoGalicia. 2000. Meteogalicia operational forecasting website for municipalities. www.meteogalicia.gal. `http://www.meteogalicia.gal/web/predicion/localidades/localidadesIndex.action?idZona=15078`. Accessed: 2017-05-12.

Lluís Padró and Evgeny Stanilovsky. 2012. Freeling 3.0: Towards wider multilinguality. In *Proceedings of the Language Resources and Evaluation Conference (LREC 2012)*, Istanbul, Turkey, May. ELRA.

RAE. 2011. Nueva gramática de la lengua española. `http://www.rae.es/recursos/gramatica/nueva-gramatica`. Accessed: 2017-05-10.

A. Ramos-Soto, A. Bugarín, S. Barro, and J. Taboada. 2015. Linguistic descriptions for automatic generation of textual short-term weather forecasts on real prediction data. *IEEE Transactions on Fuzzy Systems*, 23(1):44 – 57.

Ehud Reiter and Robert Dale. 2000. *Building Natural Language Generation Systems*. Cambridge University Press.

Ehud Reiter. 2017. Why isnt there more open-source NLG software? `https://ehudreiter.com/2017/03/17/open-source-nlg-software/`. Accessed: 2017-05-10.

Damian Jozef Trzpis. 2015. Adaptación de una herramienta de generación de lenguaje natural al idioma español. Master Thesis.

Pierre-Luc Vaudry and Guy Lapalme, 2013. *Proceedings of the 14th European Workshop on Natural Language Generation*, chapter Adapting SimpleNLG for Bilingual English-French Realisation, pages 183–187. Association for Computational Linguistics.

G-TUNA: a corpus of referring expressions in German, including duration information

David M. Howcroft and **Jorrig Vogels** and **Vera Demberg**
Department of Language Science and Technology
Saarland Informatics Campus, Saarland University
66123 Saarbrücken, Germany
{howcroft, jorrig, vera}@coli.uni-saarland.de

Abstract

Corpora of referring expressions elicited from human participants in a controlled environment are an important resource for research on automatic referring expression generation. We here present G-TUNA, a new corpus of referring expressions for German. Using images of furniture as stimuli similarly to the TUNA and D-TUNA corpora, our corpus extends on these corpora by providing data collected in a simulated driving dual-task setting, and additionally provides exact duration annotations for the spoken referring expressions. This corpus will hence allow researchers to analyze the interaction between referring expression length and speech rate, under conditions where the listener is under high vs. low cognitive load.

1 Introduction

Referring expression generation (REG) is an important problem in natural language generation (Dale, 1989; Dale and Reiter, 1995; van Deemter, 2002; Krahmer et al., 2003). The challenge of generating referring expressions (REs) that can pick out a specific object among a set of similar objects represents a prominent subtask in REG. One important goal for REG is to produce human-like referring expressions which are not only logically correct but also sound natural to native speakers of the target language.

Corpora that include referring expressions and contain transparent semantic annotation are an important resource for being able to evaluate the naturalness of an REG algorithm. Because naturally occurring corpora vary wildly with respect to domain and genre, van Deemter et al. (2006) pro-

posed the systematic construction of the TUNA corpus of REs by eliciting them from human subjects in a controlled setting. In their experiment, participants wrote descriptions of target objects in a scene of similar distractor objects and were told that they were interacting with a computer. While this provided the first systematic collection of REs written by humans that could be used to evaluate REG algorithms, Koolen & Krahmer (2010) argued that the written modality was not natural enough to be representative of typical language use. Indeed, most language use is spoken and involves an interlocutor, so when they collected the D-TUNA corpus of REs in Dutch, Koolen & Krahmer included two spoken-language conditions: one where the interlocutor was visible to the speaker and one where they were not.

Including a human addressee was a marked improvement over the text-only modality of the TUNA corpus, and showed that REs were longer on average and more overspecified (although the latter not significantly) in the spoken modality. However, the addressee was a confederate of the experimenters and explicitly instructed to give no feedback to the speaker. This is problematic as speakers usually expect a reaction from their listeners, and so a neutral interlocutor is unrealistic. It is also difficult to emulate the reactions of a naive subject throughout many experimental sessions. In addition, the D-TUNA corpus does not include any acoustic information about the recorded speech, such as RE duration, which is important to be able to assess reduction processes in human language production, and identify possible trade-offs between referring expression length and speaking rate.

Proceedings of The 10th International Natural Language Generation conference, pages 149–153,
Santiago de Compostela, Spain, September 4-7 2017. ©2017 Association for Computational Linguistics

2 Corpus Collection

We built a corpus of spoken referring expressions, aimed at investigating how speakers accommodate listeners who are under cognitive load. We created a more natural speech environment by having pairs of naive participants describe objects to each other in a simulated driving context, while retaining the same collection of furniture images used in both previous TUNA corpora. We did not use the people domain (Gatt et al., 2007; Koolen and Krahmer, 2010), because previous analyses on the TUNA corpora made clear that this domain results in a large amount of linguistic variation that is hard to capture by a semantic annotation. In addition, the detail in the images did not show up well in the driving simulator.

Furthermore, the fact that this corpus was collected in German means that it provides a third language for cross-linguistic comparison. There are two other corpora associated with the analysis of REs in German, namely the GIVE-2 corpus (Gargett et al., 2010) and the PENTOREF corpus (Zarrieß et al., 2016). However, the virtual environment in which the data for the GIVE-2 corpus were collected, coupled with the freedom subjects had to move around the environment, makes the corpus poorly suited to the sort of systematic evaluation of REs that is enabled by the TUNA, D-TUNA, and now the G-TUNA corpora. While the PENTOREF corpus provides data for both English and German accompanied by utterance-level timing information, the task-oriented dialogue with feedback from 'Instruction Followers' and the different target objects make comparisons to the TUNA corpora more challenging. Our corpus thus provides a testing ground for evaluating referring expression generation algorithms for German in a similarly controlled context to the TUNA and D-TUNA corpora in a more natural spoken language context without introducing the further confounds of collaborative dialogue.

2.1 Participants

Twenty pairs of Saarland University students participated in our experiment, with mean age 23.0 (*SD*=4.1). Twenty-one participants were women and the rest were men. We paid the students 10 euros each for their participation.

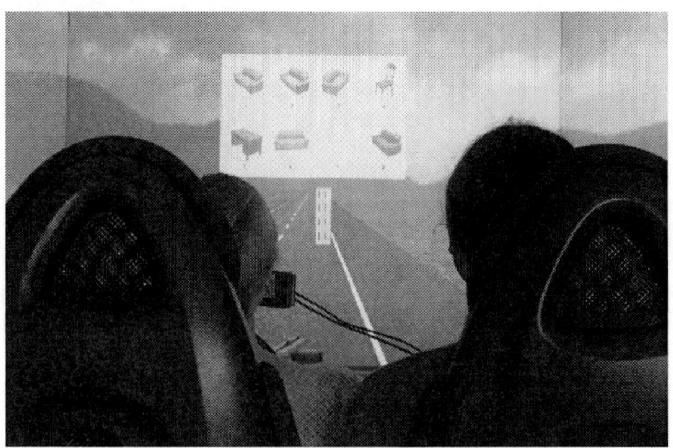

Figure 1: Driving simulator with 2 subjetcs and a stimulus. From left-to-right, top-to-bottom, the stimulus depicts a green sofa, a grey sofa, a green sofa, a green chair, a green desk, a green sofa, a blank space, and a red sofa. #1 was the target.

2.2 Materials

The stimuli were based on those used for the TUNA and D-TUNA corpora. They consist of scenes containing 7 images in a 2×4 grid, where each grid position is numbered 1-8.[1] The target image was identified for the speaker by a number appearing on a separate display not visible to the driver.

The images in a scene are furniture, taken from the Object Databank[2]. The image set in this domain is highly systematic, consisting of four different object types (chair, sofa, desk, fan) in four different colors (blue, red, green, grey), three different orientations (front-, left-, right-facing)[3], and two different sizes (large, small).

The scenes were constructed so that different numbers of modifiers are necessary for the listener to pick out the correct referent with a minimal description (MD). We systematically varied the length of the minimal description for each target, so that objects could be uniquely identified by mentioning 0 (i.e. mentioning only the object type), 1, 2, or 3 attributes. For example, in Figure 1, image #1 is identifiable by the attributes 'orientation=left' and 'color=green', allowing for descriptions like "Das

---

[1] We used a different grid size than in the previous TUNA experiments, which used a 3×5 grid, in order to accommodate the presentation of the images in the driving simulator.

[2] Available from: `http://wiki.cnbc.cmu.edu/Objects`

[3] We removed the backward-facing objects from the original image set as it was difficult to distinguish them from the forward-facing objects in the driving simulator.

grüne Sofa, das nach links zeigt"[4]. Each image appeared at most once as the target referent.

We created two lists of 60 items, each comprising two blocks of 30 items, such that each participant in a pair would describe different items in their role as speaker. Most items on a list required either one (18 trials) or two (26 trials) attributes to be mentioned. Each block began with 4 practice trials, one for each length of minimal description.

2.3 Procedure

Pairs of participants performed a referential communication task in a driving simulator A coin toss determined which participant in each pair was assigned to the role of speaker first. Speakers were instructed to describe the target referents in such a way that the listener-driver could identify the correct object from an array displayed on the driving simulator screen. They had 15 seconds to provide their description and were told that they were not allowed to use the image's location as a cue. All speech was recorded. To keep speakers aware of the listener's cognitive state, they were prompted to assess the driver's degree of cognitive load after every 10 trials.

The listener-drivers were instructed to verbally respond with the number of the object that they believed was described. They were allowed to ask for clarification if the description was not clear. During the identification task, drivers were either holding the steering wheel stationary (EASY driving condition) or steering to follow a moving object on the road (HARD driving condition). We refrained from the use of a confederate for the listener role, because experience with the dual task may decrease cognitive load, and visibly performing the role of a driver under increased cognitive load was expected to be too difficult for reliable results. Since both participants played both roles, an additional factor was whether the subject played the role of the driver first or the speaker first. A complete experimental session took about 1.5 hours.

3 Corpus Format and Statistics

3.1 Format

The corpus uses the same XML format as the earlier TUNA corpora to facilitate comparisons (Gatt et al., 2008). This annotation scheme includes information about the target image and distractors along with the transcribed referring expression and a flat semantic representation of the mentioned attributes.

We supplement the annotation scheme with duration information for each trial to facilitate more detailed analyses. So far results are mixed as to whether speakers vary word durations based on communicative setting (Bard et al., 2000; Galati and Brennan, 2010), so it is important to provide this information for studies on accommodation, in addition to variation in the number of words used and the degree of over- or under-specification.

3.2 Statistics and Comparison to other Corpora

The current version of the G-TUNA corpus contains data from 40 native speakers of German, each of which completed 60 trials as a driver and 60 trials as a speaker. This resulted in 2331 descriptions after removing problematic items[5], which is comparable to the other two corpora. Table 1 compares the three TUNA corpora on their main properties.

Out of all referring expressions, 45.5% were over-specified, 51.4% were minimally specified, 1.9% were underspecified, and 1.2% were wrongly specified (e.g. mentioning color and orientation where color and size were required). These figures are similar to those found for the TUNA and D-TUNA corpora (Koolen and Krahmer, 2010; Koolen et al., 2011), confirming that referential overspecification is ubiquitous for these items in German as well as in English and Dutch. The rate of overspecification was very similar between the EASY (M=0.53; SD=0.70) and HARD (M=0.56; SD=0.72) driving conditions, which is also in line with the findings for D-TUNA that the communicative situation does not affect the degree of overspecification.

An important addition in G-TUNA is the duration annotation for the descriptions. Both the average duration of referring expressions and the number of words showed an influence of the task manipulation. Referring expressions were significantly shorter on

---

[4]English: The green sofa facing left

[5]We removed items where subjects described the wrong item, identified the target by number, took too long to respond, or made reference to earlier trials as well as items which involved experimental errors, interruptions, etc. Any additions triggered by listener feedback were also removed.

	TUNA	D-TUNA	G-TUNA
# subjects	45	60	40
language	English	Dutch	German
# trials	20	40	60
grid size	3×5	3×5	2×4
# targets/grid	1–2	1–2	1
# distractors/grid	6	6	6
communicative situation	human-computer	no v. invisible v. visible addressee	driver & passenger in driving simulation
modality	written	written + spoken	spoken
domains	furniture, people	furniture, people	furniture
# comparable REs / total	420 / 2280	400 / 2400	2331 / 2331

Table 1: Comparison table for the three versions of TUNA released so far. The 'comparable' RE counts are based on domain & cardinality matches. The TUNA corpus' REs are all in the textual modality, while the 400 D-TUNA REs listed here are in the spoken modality as in our experiments. There are an additional 200 textual furniture REs in the D-TUNA corpus as well.

average in the HARD condition than in the EASY condition, but only for those speakers that had already experienced the driving task themselves (5.9 words / 2464 ms vs. 6.3 words / 2687 ms). This suggests that speakers do adapt some aspects of their descriptions to the communicative situation.

As shown in Figure 2, our corpus provides a balanced middle ground between the TUNA and D-TUNA corpora with respect to description length. Here we observe that the D-TUNA descriptions are often longer, involving longer full sentences, where the time pressure of our experimental setting encouraged subjects to use shorter utterances on average. At the same time, our utterances are longer than the TUNA expressions on average, perhaps due to the difference in modalities as well as the difference in language. That differences between the corpora are already visible with such a coarse analysis suggests that there are many more interesting nuances available to study while accounting for differences in modality and presentation as appropriate.

4   Conclusion

We presented a German corpus of referring expressions, designed to examine listener accommodation in an image identification task where listeners are under cognitive load. The stimuli and design were crafted to make the corpus comparable to the existing TUNA and D-TUNA corpora of referring expressions in English and Dutch. Moreover, we extended our annotations to include word durations, enabling us to evaluate more nuances of speaker adaptation, and to investigate the relationship between referring expression length and speech rate.

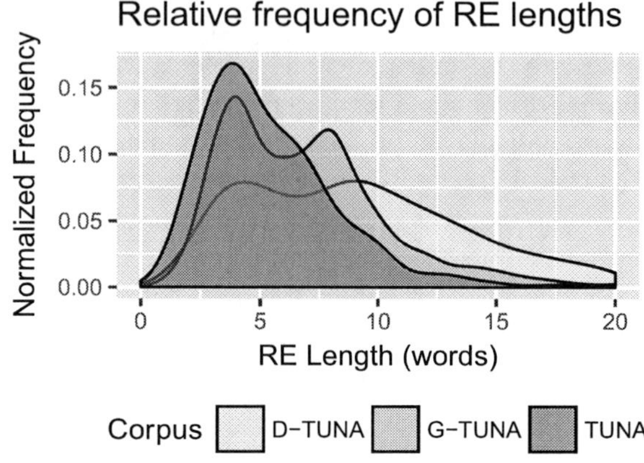

Figure 2: Density plot of RE lengths in the 3 TUNA corpora for comparable REs. The density plot is used so the distribution over different lengths is more easily compared across corpora despite the different numbers of REs in each corpus.

In addition to enabling cross-linguistic comparison and the evaluation of algorithms for referring expression generation in German, this corpus will provide insight into human behavior when describing objects for identification by listeners with varying levels of linguistic attention.

Acknowledgments

Thank you to student research assistants Fabio Lu & Matthias Lindemann. Thanks to Dietrich Klakow for feedback on drafts and Marc Schulder, Elisabeth Rabs, & Sebastien Le Maguer for photography. This work was supported by the DFG through SFB 1102 'Information Density and Linguistic Encoding'.

References

Ellen Gurman Bard, Anne H Anderson, Catherine Sotillo, Matthew Aylett, Gwyneth Doherty-sneddon, and Alison Newlands. 2000. Controlling the Intelligibility of Referring Expressions in Dialogue. *Journal of Memory and Language*, 42(1):1–22, jan.

Robert Dale and Ehud Reiter. 1995. Computational interpretations of the Gricean maxims in the generation of referring expressions. *Cognitive science*, 19(2):233–263.

Robert Dale. 1989. Cooking up referring expressions. In *Proceedings of the 27th Annual Meeting on Association for Computational Linguistics*, pages 68–75. Association for Computational Linguistics.

Alexia Galati and Susan E. Brennan. 2010. Attenuating information in spoken communication: For the speaker, or for the addressee? *Journal of Memory and Language*, 62(1):35–51.

Andrew Gargett, Konstantina Garoufi, Alexander Koller, and Kristina Striegnitz. 2010. The GIVE-2 Corpus of Giving Instructions in Virtual Environments. In *LREC*.

Albert Gatt, Ielka van der Sluis, and Kees van Deemter. 2007. Evaluating algorithms for the Generation of Referring Expressions using a balanced corpus. In *Proceedings of the Eleventh European Workshop on Natural Language Generation (ENLG)*, pages 49–56, Schloss Dagstuhl, Germany. Association for Computational Linguistics.

Albert Gatt, Ielka van der Sluis, and Kees van Deemter. 2008. XML format guidelines for the TUNA corpus. Technical report, Technical report, Computing Science, Univ. of Aberdeen, http://www. csd. abdn. ac. uk/ agatt/home/pubs/tunaFormat. pdf.

Ruud Koolen and Emiel Krahmer. 2010. The D-TUNA Corpus: A Dutch Dataset for the Evaluation of Referring Expression Generation Algorithms. In *LREC*.

Ruud Koolen, Albert Gatt, Martijn Goudbeek, and Emiel Krahmer. 2011. Factors causing overspecification in definite descriptions. *Journal of Pragmatics*, 43(13):3231–3250.

Emiel Krahmer, Sebastiaan Van Erk, and André Verleg. 2003. Graph-based generation of referring expressions. *Computational Linguistics*, 29(1):53–72.

Kees van Deemter, Ielka van der Sluis, and Albert Gatt. 2006. Building a semantically transparent corpus for the generation of referring expressions. In *Proceedings of the Fourth International Natural Language Generation Conference*, pages 130–132. Association for Computational Linguistics.

Kees van Deemter. 2002. Generating Referring Expressions: Boolean Extensions of the Incremental Algorithm. *Computational Linguistics*.

Sina Zarrieß, Julian Hough, Casey Kennington, Ramesh Manuvinakurike, David DeVault, Raquel Fernndez, and David Schlangen. 2016. Pentoref: A corpus of spoken references in task-oriented dialogues. In *Proc. of the Language Resources and Evaluation Conference (LREC)*.

Toward an NLG System for Bantu languages: first steps with Runyankore (demo)

Joan Byamugisha and **C. Maria Keet** and **Brian DeRenzi**
Department of Computer Science, University of Cape Town, South Africa,
{jbyamugisha,mkeet,bderenzi}@cs.uct.ac.za

Abstract

There are many domain-specific and language-specific NLG systems, which are possibly adaptable across related domains and languages. The languages in the Bantu language family have their own set of features distinct from other major groups, which therefore severely limits the options to bootstrap an NLG system from existing ones. We present here our first proof-of-concept application for knowledge-to-text NLG as a plugin to the Protégé 5.x ontology development system, tailored to Runyankore, a Bantu language indigenous to Uganda. It comprises a basic annotation model for linguistic information such as noun class, an implementation of existing verbalisation rules and a CFG for verbs, and a basic interface for data entry.

1 Introduction

Natural Language Generation systems require content planning and format for the selected subject domain as input and specifics about the natural language in order to generate text (Staykova, 2014), of which the latter tend to be bootstrappable for related languages (de Oliveira and Sripada, 2014). Our NLG system uses ontologies to represent domain knowledge. As for language, we are interested in Runyankore, a Bantu language indigenous to south western Uganda. The highly agglutinative structure and complex verbal morphology of Runyankore make existing NLG systems based on templates inapplicable (Keet and Khumalo, 2017). There have been efforts undertaken to apply the grammar engine

technique instead (Byamugisha et al., 2016a; Byamugisha et al., 2016b; Byamugisha et al., 2016c), which resulted in theoretical advances in verbalization rules for ontologies, pluralization of nouns, and verb conjugation that address the text generation needs for Runyankore. We present our implementation of these algorithms and required linguistic annotations as a Protégé 5.x plugin.

2 Linguistic Annotations for NLG

Most NLG systems for ontology verbalization require some annotations to the ontology's vocabulary so as to make the generated sentence sound more natural language-like. For instance, the *lemon* model for ontologies (McCrae and others, 2012). However, it has been shown to be insufficient for covering grammar constructs for Bantu languages, most notably due to the noun class system and complex morphological rules (Chavula and Keet, 2014). Other systems use tailor-made annotation schemata, e.g. (Androutsopoulos et al., 2013; Keet and Chirema, 2016). While they differ in number of linguistic annotation properties, what they share in common is the separation of annotation from ontology, as proposed in (Buitelaar et al., 2009), and storing that annotation in a separate XML file for further processing. We thus also annotated using an XML-based model, but limited our structure to our information of interest: NC, part-of-speech, and translation. The annotation functionality was implemented as a view tab in the Protégé 5.x plugin, so that it can be used during either multi-lingual or mono-lingual ontology development, or validation of the represented knowledge in an easily accessible way. The interface

Proceedings of The 10th International Natural Language Generation conference, pages 154–155,
Santiago de Compostela, Spain, September 4-7 2017. ©2017 Association for Computational Linguistics

also ensures no typographical errors are made in the XML file. These annotation fields are mandatory, and we allowed for the use of 0 as the NC for the POS which is not a noun. These restrictions to input were achieved using document filters. The XML file is queried during the verbalization process so as to obtain the required annotations that are needed for the algorithms.

3 Implementation of the Grammar Engine

We implemented the algorithms for verbalization and pluralization presented in (Byamugisha et al., 2016a; Byamugisha et al., 2016c) as a Java application. The CFG specified in (Byamugisha et al., 2016b) was implemented using the CFG Java tool (Xu et al., 2011). We used this tool for three main reasons: our grammar engine implementation was done in Java, so we wanted a Java tool as well; we wanted a small CFG implementation for reasonable performance; and their tool extended Purdom's algorithm to fulfill Context-Dependent Rule Coverage (CDRC), which generates more and simpler sentences. A sample of the generated text is presented below:

- **Buri** rupapura rwamakuru **n'**ekihandiiko ekishohoziibwe, (generated from: Newspaper ⊑ Publication)
- **Buri** ntaama nerya ebinyaansi byo*ona*, (generated from: Sheep ⊑ ∀ eats.Grass)

The generated text is saved in a text file, which ensures that the text can be linked to other application scenarios. We are working on a better design to present the sentences within the tool, for interaction during multi-modal ontology development. The grammar engine can be launched through the 'Runyankore>Verbalize' submenu under the 'Tools' menu in Protégé 5.x. The jar file is available from `https://github.com/runyankorenlg/RunyankoreNLGSystem`.

4 Conclusion

We briefly presented the core components of the Runyankore grammar engine Protégé 5.x plugin. It implements algorithms for verbalization patterns, noun pluralization, and verb conjugation. To make this work, the grammar engine requires linguistic information about each noun and verb (OWL class and object property) in the ontology in order to generate text. This linguistic information is stored in as separate XML file. The demo will show the working system and further details of the architecture.

Acknowledgements This work is based on the research supported by the Hasso Plattner Institute (HPI) Research School in CS4A at UCT and the National Research Foundation of South Africa (Grant Number 93397).

References

I. Androutsopoulos, G. Lampouras, and D. Galanis. 2013. Generating natural language descriptions from OWL ontologies: The NaturalOWL system. *JAIR*, 48:671–715.

P. Buitelaar, P. Cimiano, P. Haase, and M. Sintek. 2009. Towards linguistically grounded ontologies. In *ESWC'09, LNCS 5554*, pages 111–125.

J. Byamugisha, C. M. Keet, and B. DeRenzi. 2016a. Bootstrapping a Runyankore CNL from an isiZulu CNL. In *CNL 2016*, Aberdeen, Scotland. Springer LL-NCS.

J. Byamugisha, C. M. Keet, and B. DeRenzi. 2016b. Tense and aspect in Runyankore using a context-free grammar. In *INLG 2016*, Edinburgh, Scotland.

J. Byamugisha, C. M. Keet, and L. Khumalo. 2016c. Pluralizing nouns in isiZulu and related languages. In *CICLing 2016*, Konya, Turkey.

C. Chavula and C. M. Keet. 2014. Is lemon sufficient for building multilingual ontologies for bantu languages? In *OWLED'14*, volume 1265, pages 61–72, Riva del Garda, Italy.

R. de Oliveira and S. Sripada. 2014. Adapting simplenlg for brazilian portuguese realisation. In *Proc of INLG'14*, pages 93–94. ACL.

C. M. Keet and T. Chirema. 2016. A model for verbalizing relations with roles in multiple languages. In *Poc. of EKAW'16*, volume 10024 of *LNAI*, pages 384–399, Bologna, Italy. Springer.

C. M. Keet and L. Khumalo. 2017. Towards a knowledge-to-text controlled natural language of isizulu. *LRE*, 51:131–157.

John McCrae et al. 2012. Interchanging lexical resources on the semantic web. *LRE*, 46(4):701–719.

K. Staykova. 2014. Natural language generation and semantic technologies. *Cybern. and Info. Tech.*, 14.

Z. Xu, L. Zheng, and H. Zhen. 2011. A toolkit for generating sentences from context-free grammars. *Int. J. of Software and Informatics*, 5:659–676.

A working, non-trivial, topically indifferent NLG System for 17 languages

Robert Weißgraeber and **Andreas Madsack**
AX Semantics
`[robert.weissgraeber|andreas.madsack]@ax-semantics.com`

Abstract

We present a fully fledged practical working application for a rule-based NLG system that is able to create non-trivial, human sounding narrative from structured data, in any language (e.g., English, German, Arabic and Finnish) and for any topic.

1   Introduction

Use cases for Natural Language Generation are abundant and vary widely from theoretically interesting to practically relevant. Topically limited systems are already being used in different areas like weather reports (Ramos-Soto et al., 2013) or financial analysis (Nesterenko, 2016). Our topically unlimited software has an abstraction layer for text planning, structure, semantics, and content that can be fitted to any kind of subject. In addition, this abstraction layer includes a cross-language abstraction as well, making it feasible to write texts in multiple languages at the same time, independent from data source language or grammatical differences in the output. This demonstrates a feature complete NLG system (Reiter et al., 2000) with a rule-based non-template approach (Van Deemter et al., 2005). Most important, this is available as a web-based tool for everyone including eLearning elements. A free sandbox license for playing around is available, as well as free licenses for educational use – `https://cockpit.ax-semantics.com/signup`.

2   Topicality Free NLG abstraction

The basic level of the realisation is based in a container, which implements the basic NLG notation for a phrase. The notation is written in Automated Text Markup Language (ATML3) syntax, which is an open specification.

Example:
```
Máte [property1,adj=yes,case=acc,
cardinal=property2].
```

This ATML3 expression will generate in *Czech:* *Máte jednu novou zprávu* (You have one new message) or *Máte sedm nových zpráv* (You have seven new messages) from the noun *zpráva*, the adjective *nový* and a numerical value coming from the data. Noun and adjective are provided by *property1* and the numerical value is taken from *property2* which abstracts the data itself. Both properties are supplied by the planner component.

Containers are used inside statements, which implement the content determination, together with story types and statement groups which are responsible for the document structuring. Lexical choices can be defined by the configuration in the property output, and are related to the data they are interpreting, removing the limitations of topicality inside of the NLG core. Data intake and interpretation is done in so-called properties, which relate the data to extractable meaning, and are then referenced inside the linguistics configuration. Together, these configurations build the text and logic ruleset as a training for a certain topic and text output. If cross-language output is desired, word-level and phrase-level lookups can be used to identify uninflected word pairs across languages, which will automatically be inflected correctly during realization of the phrases.

Proceedings of The 10th International Natural Language Generation conference, pages 156–157,
Santiago de Compostela, Spain, September 4-7 2017. ©2017 Association for Computational Linguistics

3 Components and Compilation workflow

The data intake for a text is one data document, which is combined with the ruleset to form the basis for the text production. The NLG core then interprets the data and ruleset together, and combines this with grammatical information about the selected output language and a lexicon for word-based grammar information.

4 NLG Core Capabilities

The core grammar module allows for all possible language features. Each distinct used language has a unique configuration that combines those features according to the required phenomena. This allows for adding "new" languages within a few days.

5 User Access

ATML3 is designed as a markup language that, in contrast to programming approaches, allows everyone to create the required configuration. No developer skills are required, making the system suitable to be used by any kind of user. A GUI is available as well. To decrease manual effort, the software combines NLP and data analysis features: (1) properties are automatically generated from the training data; (2) part-of-speech tagging is used to transform a manual written sample text to an ATML3 ruleset automatically.

6 Examples

The sentence "A camera, Wi-Fi and bluetooth are just a few of its features." in ATML3 will render the pluralization and the verb based on the number of features in the dataset (`DATA_Features`), handling conjunction, capitalization and articles as well:

```
[DATA_Features.all(),conj=and,
det=indef,id=subject] [G:verb=be,
grammar-from=subject] just [Text:a few;
On,true=LOGIC_more_than_one_features;
Alt:one] of its features.
```

will return in English:

"A camera, Wi-Fi and bluetooth are just a few of its features." OR "Bluetooth is just one of its features."

The same containers are used in Spanish:

```
[Text:Algunas;
On,true=LOGIC_more_than_one_features]
```

```
de sus características
[G:verb=ser,grammar-from=subject;Alt:Una]
[DATA_Features.all(),conj=y,id=subject]
```

"Algunas de sus características son cámara, WiFi y Bluetooth." OR "Algunas de sus características es Bluetooth."

7 Overcoming Limitations

As of now, no limitations exist as intrinsic or conceptual barriers, proven by (1) in use large scale text production in milliseconds, (2) the current 17 languages, and a wide range of topics from personalized communication, live dialogue systems or static text outputs. Practical limits relate to two categories: one being the feasibility in reference to effort by implementing a set of rules by the user to define inference and text output, the second one being the predictability of possible input data errors (Graefe, 2016).

These Limitations are already being solved by integrating the progress from other related fields from the language analysis side and machine translation improvements: An implementation for integrating NLP-based tools like POS-tagging allow for suggesting possible ATML3 rules, reducing the effort and error rate of human rule creation; and machine learning based toolchains for data analysis can be used to predict inference-oriented rules.

References

Andreas Graefe. 2016. Guide to automated journalism.

Liubov Nesterenko. 2016. Building a system for stock news generation in russian. In *Proceedings of the 2nd International Workshop on Natural Language Generation and the Semantic Web (WebNLG 2016)*.

A. Ramos-Soto, A. Bugarin, S. Barro, and J. Taboada. 2013. Linguistic descriptions for automatic generation of textual short-term weather forecasts on real prediction data. In *International Conference on Flexible Query Answering Systems*.

Ehud Reiter, Robert Dale, and Zhiwei Feng. 2000. *Building natural language generation systems*, volume 33. MIT Press.

Kees Van Deemter, Emiel Krahmer, and Mariët Theune. 2005. Real versus template-based natural language generation: A false opposition? *Comput. Linguist.*, 31(1):15–24, March

Generating titles for millions of browse pages on an e-Commerce site

Prashant Mathur, Nicola Ueffing and Gregor Leusch
Machine Translation Science Lab,
eBay Inc.
Kasernenstrasse 25
Aachen, Germany

Abstract

We present three approaches to generate titles for browse pages in five different languages, namely English, German, French, Italian and Spanish. These browse pages are structured search pages in an e-commerce domain. We first present a rule-based approach to generate these browse page titles. In addition, we also present a hybrid approach which uses a phrase-based statistical machine translation engine on top of the rule-based system to assemble the best title. For the two languages English and German, we have access to a large amount of rule-based generated and human-curated titles. For these languages, we present an automatic post-editing approach which learns how to post-edit the rule-based titles into curated titles.

1 Introduction

Natural language generation has a broad range of applications, from question answering systems to story generation, summarization etc. In this paper, we target a particular use case common to many e-Commerce websites. In e-Commerce sites, multiple items can be grouped on a common page called *browse page*. Each browse page contains an overview of various items which share some characteristics. However, the items do not necessarily share all characteristics. The characteristics can be expressed as slot/value pairs. For example, we can have a browse page for all items which share the characteristics (*Watch Type: wrist watch*) and (*Band: stainless steel*). These watches can have additional characteristics such as (*Feature: day clock*)

Figure 1: Example of a browse page

or (*Feature: date indicator*) or (*Feature: chronograph*), which can differ between all items grouped on one browse page. Different combinations of characteristics bijectively correspond to different browse pages, and consequently to different browse page titles. To show customers which items are grouped on a browse page, we need a human-readable description of the content of that particular page. A lack of such description negatively impacts the user experience.

Figure 1 shows an example of a browse page with a title, with navigation elements leading to related browse pages as well as the individual items listed in this page. The corresponding meta-data for the browse page is shown in Table 1. Note that in our problem definition slot names are already given; the task is to generate a title for a set of slots. Moreover, we do not perform any selection on the slots, all the slots needs to be realized in order to have a unique browse page title.

Proceedings of The 10th International Natural Language Generation conference, pages 158–167,
Santiago de Compostela, Spain, September 4-7 2017. ©2017 Association for Computational Linguistics

Slot Name	Value
Category	*Cell Phones & Smart Phones*
Brand	*ACME*
Color	*white*
Storage Capacity	*32GB*

Table 1: The underlying meta-data for Figure 1

We have access to a few thousand human-created titles (curated titles) for English and German. To generate these titles, humans annotators were given a set of slot name-value pairs and were asked to generate a title for that within a set of guidelines, the important one being that all slots need to be realized in the title.

Large e-Commerce sites can easily have tens of millions of such browse pages in many different languages. The problem gets more complex as each browse page can have one to six slots to be realized. On top of that, the number of unique slot-value pairs are in the order of hundreds of thousand. All these factors render the task of human creation of all the browse page titles infeasible. In this paper, we propose several strategies to generate these human-readable titles automatically for any possible browse page, aiming for a high average title quality.

These different strategies address the existence (or non-existence) of human-curated titles across the different languages we are dealing with. In section 3, we present a rule-based system which can be used if there are no human-curated titles at all. We show that title quality can be improved by combining this rule-based system with a machine translation system, exploring monolingual data, as described in section 4. If there are human-curated titles available, we can use automatic post-editing on top of the rule-based system, as described in section 5, to achieve even higher quality titles.

2 Previous works

Generating titles for pages containing structured data, for example in e-Commerce, is a frequent problem. Dale et al. (1998) describe the problem of generating natural language titles and short descriptions of structured nodes which consist of slot/value pairs. There are many publications which deal with learning a generation model from parallel data. These parallel data consist of the structured data and

natural-language text, so that the model can learn to transform the structured data into text. Konstas and Lapata (2012) compare 1-*best* vs k-*best* approaches in the verbalization of database records; the k-*best* is implemented as hypergraph decoding under a trigram language model. Duma and Klein (2013) generate short natural-language descriptions, taking structured DBPedia data as input. Their approach learns text templates which are filled with the information from the structured data. Mei et. al. (2015) use recurrent LSTM models to generate text from facts given in a knowledge base.

Several recent papers tackle the problem of generating a one-sentence introduction for a biography given structured biographical slot/value pairs. Lebret et al (2016) introduced a neural model for this concept-to-text generation and evaluated on a large dataset of biographies from Wikipedia. Chisholm et. al. (2017) solve the same problem by applying a machine translation system to a linearized version of the pairs. All of these approaches require a large set of parallel training data to learn from.

In the work presented here, however, we need to generate titles also in languages for which we do not have parallel (slot/value pairs to natural language) training data. For the romance languages (French, Italian and Spanish), no curated titles are available for training. For these languages, we resort to rule-based language generation. These systems are time-consuming and require significant human effort, but a lot of research work has been done in this area such as the FoG system (Goldberg et al., 1994), the Sum-Time system (Reiter et al., 2005) and the PLAN-DOC system (McKeown et al., 1994).

For the languages English and German, we have parallel data available, so we can directly learn with a machine translation (MT) approach to "translate" from rule-based generated titles to curated titles. Note that, both source and target language are identical in our case. This problem is widely studied in the MT community under the umbrella of Automatic Post-Editing (APE) (Simard et al., 2007). APE systems are mostly used to correct the output of a traditional MT system (with different source and target language), thereby producing higher quality translations. To the best of our knowledge, there is no work in the prior art that leverages an APE system to improve the quality of a rule-based generation system.

Another difference between our work and some of the papers described above, (Konstas and Lapata, 2012), (Mei et al., 2015) and (Chisholm et al., 2017), is that they perform selective generation, i.e. they run a selection step that determines the slot/value pairs which will be included in the verbalization. For our e-Commerce browse pages, all slot/value pairs are relevant and need to be verbalized.

The work of (Zajic and Dorr, 2002) is related in that they add morphological variation of verbs into a HMM approach for headline generation. In our hybrid approach described in section 4, we also incorporate many alternative lexicalizations and let the decoding process find the optimal sequence. However, our work is different in that we generate titles from slot/value pairs instead of news stories, and we allow for much more variation than those used in (Zajic and Dorr, 2002).

3 Rule-based approach

The first title generation system described in this paper is a strictly rule-based approach with a manually created grammar. These approaches are especially useful when the amount of human-curated training data is limited. Since on an e-Commerce site, different categories will have different possible slots and slot-value pairs, the total number of potential slots can be huge. In this case, creating individual rules for each slot is not feasible. But we can heuristically classify slot/value pairs into a small set of slot types. With Table 1 as an example, we classify

- All slot/value pairs with an adjective value as *Adjective slots*, e.g. *Color: white*

- All slots mentioning a brand, model, series, maker as *Brand slots*, e.g. *Brand: ACME*

- All slots with a numerical value as *Numerical slots*, e.g. *Storage Capacity: 32GB*

- All slots with a Boolean (Yes/No) value as *Boolean slots*, etc.

Furthermore, in the slot classification phase, we can use a language model trained on related-domain texts (product titles and description, search queries, . . .) to identify whether certain nominal aspect values typically go with specific prepositions, e.g. *"in*

English" for (*Language: English*) slots, *"for* children" for (*Age group: Children*) slots.

Each of these slot types then gets a hand-written language-dependent rule for lexicalization[1], using parts of the slot value as well as the slot name, if required: For example, adjective slot values are inflected to match the category head noun inflection[2] and realized by themselves (*Category: Schuhe*) + (*Farbe: Grün*) → "grüne (Schuhe)"[3]. Numeric aspects are realized as combination of an optional preposition, the slot name including units, and the numeric value (*Diamètre (cm): 20*) → "diamètre 20 cm"[4]). Certain slots can also replace parts of the category name; e.g. (*Category: RC Boats & Watercrafts*) + (*Type: Submarine'*) is combined into "RC Submarines".

We then create a language-dependent grammar which combines all these realizations by slot type in a defined order, e.g. for English, BRAND | NUMERIC | ADJECTIVES | NOMINAL | CATEGORY+TYPE | FROM | WITH | FOR | LANGUAGE | BOOLEAN.

4 Hybrid approach

4.1 Motivation

This section describes the hybrid generation approach which combines the rule-based language generation approach (Section 3) and statistical machine translation for situations in which monolingual data for the language is available, but human-curated titles are not.

The approach described in Section 3 requires creating and maintaining individual rules for all potential slots in all categories for all languages, which is next to impossible on a large e-Commerce site. The structure of categories and slots is dynamic and typically evolves over time. Furthermore, there are many combinations of slots that lead to redundancies and non-fluent generations, which are hard to cover with individual rules. For example, if we have a "Room" slot, any mentions of "interior-" in a title become redundant. We therefore developed a model

---

[1]Lexicalization is the same as verbalization or realization in this context.

[2]We use a shallow tagger for that

[3]"green shoes"

[4]"diameter 20cm"

which is able to learn and generalize the realizations from data.

4.2 Statistical machine translation

The process of generating a title from category information and slot/value pairs can be modeled by leveraging phrase-based statistical machine translation (PBSMT). Translation from source into target language using PBSMT works as follows:

1. the source sentence is split into all possible sequence of words called *phrases*[5],

2. each of these source phrases is looked up in a phrase translation table (learned from the training data) and translated into a target phrase,

3. these target phrases are then combined to form a translation candidate,

4. a language model scores the translation candidates, and

5. the system outputs the best scoring translation.

We use the open-source Moses translation system (Koehn et al., 2007) for our hybrid system. In order to combine the rule-based generation approach with machine translation decoding, we leverage the so-called cache-based translation model (Bertoldi et al., 2014). This model uses an additional dynamic phrase table providing one score per phrase pair, originally implemented for dynamic adaptation. CBTM has been integrated into Moses, and we extended the available implementation to match our use case of title generation:

- CBTM is intended to work at the document level, while we are working on the title level. We extended this so that each title has a separate cache model which is not accessible to any other thread but the thread assigned to that sentence, thus also making the model thread-safe;

- The original CBTM score decays over time, i.e. the recent phrase pairs are scored higher than the old phrase pairs, where recency refers to document history. We modified this so that

Slot/*Value*	Lexicalizations
Category/*Cell Phones & Smart Phones*	"Cell Phones & Smart Phones"
Brand/*ACME*	"ACME"
Color/*white*	"white", "in white"
Storage Capacity/*32GB*	"32GB", "with 32GB", "with storage capacity 32GB", ", 32GB", …

Table 2: Alternative lexicalizations for the slot/value pairs for the browse page in Figure 1

the cache entries do not decay over time. Instead, the cache entries are deleted once the sentence is processed;

- CBTM generates only one score based on recency of the phrase pair. We extended this multiple static scores for each cache entry, similar to a standard phrase-table.

4.3 Combining rule-based and PBSMT

The rule-based generation approach generates exactly one lexicalization for each slot/value pair. In the hybrid approach, we extend this and generate many different alternative lexicalizations[6] for a slot/value pair.

For the example browse page from Table 1, alternative lexicalizations for the slot/value pairs are shown in Table 2. Note that we also add the category as a slot and the category name as its lexicalization. This is done in order to generate distinct title for products that have same slot/value pairs across categories.

We use the cache-based translation model described in section 4.2 to represent these alternative realizations. The slot/value pairs are represented as the source phrases, and their alternative lexicalizations are represented as different target phrases, i.e. different possible "translations" of this source phrase. For each browse page, we dynamically create a specific phrase table containing source representations and their possible target phrases.

These target phrases are then combined and scored by a language model, and the system returns the best scoring title. This language model

---

[5]These are sequences of contiguous words and not necessarily linguistically well-defined phrases.

[6]We use a shallow tagger to lexicalize the slot names and values.

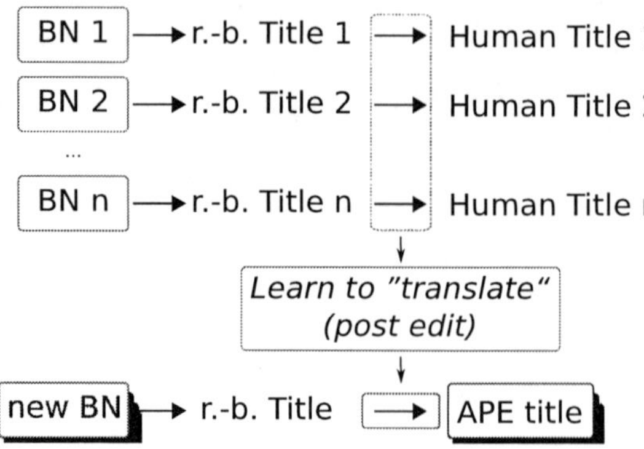

Figure 2: Principle of Automatic Post Editing. "r.-b. Title" denotes an auto-generated (rule-based) title as described in Section 3.

is trained on a large corpus of monolingual out-of-domain data. As mentioned in the introduction, we have set up the hybrid system for languages where no curated browse page titles are available. However, we do have access to monolingual data which can be used to build a language model.

5 Automatic Post-Editing approach

Rule-based title generation causes some errors in the output which are recurrent and consistent. For English and German, we have access to a reasonably large amount of already available curated titles (refer Table 3). By generating titles using the rule–based system for the same browse pages, we can create parallel data, where the source side is the – sometimes erroneous – automatically created title, and the target is the – desired human–curated title. Note that in this case, both source and target text are in the same language.

These parallel data can be used to train an automatic post-editing (APE) system (Simard et al., 2007) which will then learn how to correct the errors made by the rule-based system. In this work, we are learning to automatically correct the titles generated by the rule-based system. As proposed in APE, we train a phrase-based statistical MT system on the "parallel" data where the source corpus is the rule-based generated data and the target corpus is the human curated title data. The principle behind this approach is sketched in Figure 2. We use the Moses toolkit (Koehn et al., 2007) for training and decoding.

The APE approach has several advantages: it is straightforward to implement, automatic post-editing is a well-studied topic, and we can apply all features and models used within the current state-of-the-art MT systems.

We leverage the following MT models:

1. Phrase translation model, including a simple string-matching penalty that is used to control for higher faithfulness with regard to the raw machine translation output (Junczys-Dowmunt et al., 2016). This penalty is added as phrase score in the phrase translation model.

2. Operation Sequence Model (OSM): This models the translation process as a Markov chain of sequence of operations. OSM basically clubs the benefits of both translation and language model into one model (Durrani et al., 2011).

3. Language Model (LM): The 5-gram LM was trained only on the target side of our "parallel" data, i.e. the human-curated titles, because this is clean in-domain data.

At the same time, there are some disadvantages of using an APE system:

- Only errors seen in training can be corrected by APE;

- When the data is noisy, APE learns to generate artifacts from the data.

- Data that is lost in the rule-based generation cannot be reconstructed.

6 Experiments

6.1 Data

We evaluated our rule-based, HybridMT and APE approach for the generation of browse page titles in English (En), German (De), French, Italian and Spanish (FrItEs). The rule-based system does not require any training data. The HybridMT system requires a language model (LM) which we trained on large monolingual data extracted from descriptions of items in the e-Commerce inventory. For FrItEs, we do not have access to many human-curated titles (we have access to small development and evaluation sets), but we do have these item description data available. We heuristically filter the description data by making sure that each sentence has at least one preposition and the number of tokens are greater than 3. Parallel data is used to train, tune and evaluate the APE system.

For development and testing purposes, we use a manually-generated set of 500 browse page titles per language. Statistics on the amount of parallel and monolingual data for the languages are given in Table 3. "AlgoTok" represents the number of tokens in browse page titles which were generated using the rule-based system, while "CuratedTok" represents those in human curated titles.

	Curated		Monolingual
Language	#SrcTok	#TrgTok	#TrgTok
English	5.21M	4.97M	4.97M
German	3.68M	3.76M	3.76M
French	-	-	47.3M
Italian	-	-	39.8M
Spanish	-	-	56.7M

	Dev		Test	
Language	#Src	#Trg	#Src	#Trg
English	7.5K	6.7K	6.7K	6.6K
German	8.5K	8.8K	8.6K	8.8K
French	-	3.2K	-	3.8K
Italian	-	10K	-	3.7K
Spanish	-	6.7K	-	3.6K

Table 3: Statistics of training (Curated, Monolingual), development (Dev) and evaluation (Test) datasets. For French, Italian, Spanish there is no parallel training data. M, K stands for million and thousand respectively.

6.2 Systems

This section describes the various language generation systems we have applied. All the language models are 5-grams with modified Kneser-Ney smoothing trained with KenLM (Heafield, 2011). We use the modified cache-based translation model (cf. Section 4) for the HybridMT systems. For the APE system, we train the translation and operation sequence model with scripts provided under Moses (Koehn et al., 2007). For tuning the weights we use the k-best batch MIRA implementation (Cherry and Foster, 2012) provided in the Moses toolkit. A combination of BLEU (Papineni et al., 2002) and word error rate (WER) (Nießen et al., 2000) is used for tuning the system, because tuning on BLEU only resulted

in overly long translations. Performance of all systems are reported in terms of BLEU, character F1-score CHRF1 (Popović, 2016) and WER. Statistical significance tests were conducted using approximate randomization tests (Clark et al., 2011).

7 Results

This section collects the results from the three different generation systems, namely the rule-based system (RBNLG), the Hybrid Machine Translation system (HybridMT) and the automatic post-editing system (APE), for 5 different languages. We group the results based on the amount of curated titles available per language. For English and German, we have curated titles and can thus train an APE system. For FrItEs, we do not have such data, so we compare the RBNLG system with the HybridMT approach. In addition, we also run a contrastive experiment on English with the HybridMT system, comparing the quality for all three systems on this language.

7.1 English and German

Table 4 collects results for English and German. In general, the results obtained by the APE systems are significantly better than the rule-based system. For English, the APE system shows an absolute improvement of almost 10 BLEU points over the rule-based system. The effect of in-domain data can be clearly seen in this experiment.

Our rule-based approach for German in comparison with English does not fare well. German is a morphologically rich language and to manually cover all the grammar rules in German requires a lot of effort. This is one of the reasons why the metric scores on German are far lower than on English. These errors by the rule-based system, such as re-ordering errors, usage of prepositions etc., are however systematic and consistent across titles. These consistent errors are captured well by the APE system which results in a very impressive improvement: the APE system outperforms the rule-based approach by almost 30 BLEU points and reduces WER by 29% absolute.

The HybridMT system on English is also better than the RBNLG system by almost 3 BLEU points. In this particular case, HybridMT benefits from the large monolingual in-domain language model trained on the curated titles. The tuned weight of the in-domain LM is 0.41 in comparison to the out-of-domain LM with a weight of 0.13.

Language	System	BLEU	CHRF1	WER
English	RBNLG	69.96	87.30	25.82
English	HybridMT	72.71	88.44	22.25
English	APE	80.29	91.71	15.89
German	RBNLG	41.68	76.68	56.00
German	APE	65.10	89.6	29.51

Table 4: Cased BLEU, Character F-score and WER on the human post-edited data for English and German.

7.2 FRITES

Table 5 collects results for French, Italian and Spanish. We see a similar trend for these three languages as we saw for English and German. In all cases, the HybridMT system is significantly better than the RBNLG system. The largest gains are observed in French and Italian (7–10 BLEU points) and relatively moderate improvements in Spanish (∼4.5 BLEU points).

Language	System	BLEU	CHRF1	WER
French	RBNLG	66.47	86.79	27.20
French	HybridMT	73.32	89.42	22.87
Italian	RBNLG	49.92	79.08	38.28
Italian	HybridMT	60.63	83.67	30.98
Spanish	RBNLG	65.33	85.83	26.57
Spanish	HybridMT	69.92	87.40	23.14

Table 5: Cased BLEU, Character F-score and WER on the human post-edited data for French, Italian and Spanish.

7.3 Analysis of HybridMT

We have seen that HybridMT takes advantage of the alternative phrase pairs generated in the output of the rule-based system and then leverages the LM to score the title. With this system, we can also generate an n-best list of titles for a particular browse page. The HybridMT system picks the best title as scored by the decoder. This one title might indeed be the best title the system can generate. However, there might be even better alternatives which the system can generate, but which receive a worse score from the decoder models.

To find this out, we did several experiments with the HybridMT system for the FrItEs languages. We looked for the best possible title in the n-best list by comparing sentence-level BLEU scores of the candidates in the n-best against the curated title. This gives us the upper bound of the quality of translation that can be achieved. With the increasing size of the n-best list we found out that we can find better generated titles. Figure 3 plots the BLEU scores against the increasing size of n-best list respectively. As we can observe in these figures, BLEU score continuously increases with the increasing size of n-best and plateaus after a while.

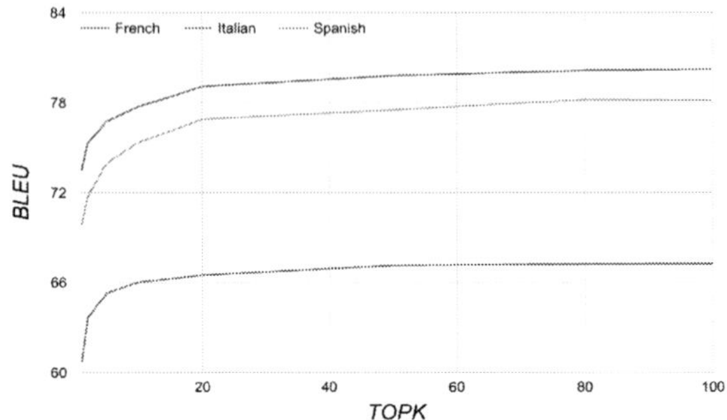

Figure 3: Learning curve of HybridMT system with increasing size of n-best list against BLEU score.

This experiment basically shows that there is a large scope of improvement in the quality of titles if we have access to a large amount of in-domain data or curated titles in these languages.

7.4 Qualitative Evaluation

In Table 6 we show examples from the evaluation set where our HybridMT and APE systems solved the problems occurring in the rule-based RBNLG system.

One of the most common issues we encountered in the RBNLG system is redundancy. In this rule-based system, all slot/value pairs are realized independently of each other in the title. This realization approach can cause redundancy in the title if there is overlap between two slot/value pairs. For example, consider the browse page with slot/value pairs (*Category: Lamps, Type: Side lamps, Color: Blue, Style: Decorative*). The RBNLG system will generate the title "Decorative blue lamps side lamps", whereas the reference title is "Decorative blue side lamps". This happens because RBNLG system does not know that side lamps are also lamps.

164

Language	System	Title
English	RBNLG	Album Suite Classical SACD Music CDs
	HybridMT	SACD Album Suite Classical Music CDs
	APE	Album Suite Classical Music SACDs
	Ref	Album Suite Classical Music SACDs
German	RBNLG	Ab 12 LEGO Baukästen & Sets mit Weltraum
	APE	LEGO Weltraum-Baukästen & - Sets ab 12 Jahren
	Ref	LEGO Weltraum-Baukästen & - Sets ab 12 Jahren
French	RBNLG	Réflecteurs pour automobiles Marque du véhicule BMW
	HybridMT	Réflecteurs pour automobiles BMW
	Ref	Réflecteurs pour automobiles BMW

Table 6: Examples of English, German and French titles generated by rule-based, HybridMT and APE systems.

A similar problem occurs in the first English example in Table 6: RBNLG realizes all slot/value pairs independently, and ends up generating both "SACD" (Super Audio CD) and "CDs" in the title. The same happens in the HybridMT system, which generates a title containing both "SACD" and "Music CDs". The automatic post-editing system, on the other hand, learns to fix this redundancy in the title and drops "CDs" and at the same time inflects "SACD" to its plural form.

While realizing the slot/value pairs, the rule-based system has an option to either verbalize the "slot" or drop it and just output the "value". This is done in order to not generate any redundant information in the title. In the German example[7] in Table 6, we see that the RBNLG system incorrectly dropped the slot and did not verbalize it. For the slot/value pair (*Jahre: Ab 12*), RBNLG generates the incomplete verbalization "Ab 12" and puts it in the wrong position within the title. APE learns to correct these kind of errors from the parallel data, and fixes both the ordering and the missing word.

The French titles[8] generated by RBNLG and HybridMT in Table 6 are another example of the same issue. In this case, the slot/value (*Marque du véhicule: BMW*) is realized as "Marque du véhicule BMW" by the RBNLG system, i.e. both slot and value are output. This is not needed since "pour automobiles" already contains the information about the "véhicule". In HybridMT, the cache-based translation model has the option of realizing the slot/value pair as "Marque du véhicule BMW" or "BMW", and in this case the language model chooses the latter option, thereby improving over the rule-based system.

8 Conclusion

We have described three different approaches for automatic generation of browse page titles. The rule-based approach can be applied on languages for which we do not have in-domain data at all. The hybrid machine translation approach extends this approach and uses monolingual in-domain data, yielding substantial gains over the rule-based system. For settings where we have large amounts of human-curated browse page titles already, we developed an automatic post-editing system which can be applied on top of a rule-based system and leads to very impressive improvements.

In future work we are planning to extend the hybrid approach to German by adding the generation of realization alternatives, and compare this with the APE approach. We will also investigate on combining learned and rule-generated realizations, and on using different Machine Translation approaches for APE and the Hybrid model. We will also work on generating the browse page titles directly from the realized form of meta-data (i.e. concatenation of all slots and slot-values pairs) using a sequence to sequence model with attention mechanism as described in Bahdanau et. al. (Bahdanau et al., 2014).

Acknowledgments

We would like to thank our colleagues Alex Zhicharevich and Daniel Hurwitz for developing the initial rule-based approach for English and German that was the foundation of this work.

---

[7] Translation: LEGO Space kits & sets from 12 years

[8] Translation: Reflectors for BMW cars

References

Dzmitry Bahdanau, Kyunghyun Cho, and Yoshua Bengio. 2014. Neural machine translation by jointly learning to align and translate. *CoRR*, abs/1409.0473.

Nicola Bertoldi, Patrick Simianer, Mauro Cettolo, Katharina Wäschle, Marcello Federico, and Stefan Riezler. 2014. Online adaptation to post-edits for phrase-based statistical machine translation. *Machine Translation*, 28:309–339.

Colin Cherry and George Foster. 2012. Batch tuning strategies for statistical machine translation. In *Proceedings of the 2012 Conference of the North American Chapter of the Association for Computational Linguistics: Human Language Technologies*, pages 427–436, Montréal, Canada, June. Association for Computational Linguistics.

Andrew Chisholm, Will Radford, and Ben Hachey. 2017. Learning to generate one-sentence biographies from Wikidata. In *Proceedings of the 15th Conference of the European Chapter of the Association for Computational Linguistics: Volume 1, Long Papers*, pages 633–642. Association for Computational Linguistics.

Jonathan H Clark, Chris Dyer, Alon Lavie, and Noah A Smith. 2011. Better hypothesis testing for statistical machine translation: Controlling for optimizer instability. In *Proceedings of the 49th Annual Meeting of the Association for Computational Linguistics: Human Language Technologies: short papers-Volume 2*, pages 176–181. Association for Computational Linguistics.

Robert Dale, Stephen J Green, Maria Milosavljevic, Cécile Paris, Cornelia Verspoor, and Sandra Williams. 1998. The realities of generating natural language from databases. In *Proceedings of the 11th Australian Joint Conference on Artificial Intelligence*, pages 13–17.

Daniel Duma and Ewan Klein. 2013. Generating natural language from linked data: Unsupervised template extraction. In *Proceedings of the 10th International Conference on Computational Semantics (IWCS 2013) – Long Papers*, pages 83–94. Association for Computational Linguistics.

Nadir Durrani, Helmut Schmid, and Alexander M. Fraser. 2011. A joint sequence translation model with integrated reordering. In *Proceedings of the 49th Annual Meeting of the Association for Computational Linguistics*, pages 1045–1054, June.

Eli Goldberg, Norbert Driedger, and Richard I. Kittredge. 1994. Using natural-language processing to produce weather forecasts. *IEEE Expert: Intelligent Systems and Their Applications*, 9(2):45–53, April.

Kenneth Heafield. 2011. Kenlm: Faster and smaller language model queries. In *Proceedings of the Sixth Workshop on Statistical Machine Translation*, pages 187–197. Association for Computational Linguistics.

Marcin Junczys-Dowmunt, Tomasz Dwojak, and Rico Sennrich. 2016. The AMU-UEDIN submission to the WMT16 news translation task: Attention-based NMT models as feature functions in phrase-based SMT. In *Proceedings of the First Conference on Machine Translation*, pages 319–325, Berlin, Germany, August. Association for Computational Linguistics.

Philipp Koehn, Hieu Hoang, Alexandra Birch, Chris Callison-Burch, Marcello Federico, Nicola Bertoldi, Brooke Cowan, Wade Shen, Christine Moran, Richard Zens, Chris Dyer, Ondrej Bojar, Alexandra Constantin, and Evan Herbst. 2007. Moses: Open Source Toolkit for Statistical Machine Translation. In *Proceedings of the 45th Annual Meeting of the Association for Computational Linguistics Companion Volume Proceedings of the Demo and Poster Sessions*, pages 177–180, Prague, Czech Republic.

Ioannis Konstas and Mirella Lapata. 2012. Concept-to-text generation via discriminative reranking. In *Proceedings of the 50th Annual Meeting of the Association for Computational Linguistics: Long Papers-Volume 1*, pages 369–378. Association for Computational Linguistics.

Rémi Lebret, David Grangier, and Michael Auli. 2016. Generating text from structured data with application to the biography domain. *Computing Research Repository (CoRR)*, abs/1603.07771.

Kathleen McKeown, Karen Kukich, and James Shaw. 1994. Practical issues in automatic documentation generation. In *Proceedings of the Fourth Conference on Applied Natural Language Processing*, ANLC '94, pages 7–14, Stroudsburg, PA, USA. Association for Computational Linguistics.

Hongyuan Mei, Mohit Bansal, and Matthew R. Walter. 2015. What to talk about and how? Selective generation using LSTMs with coarse-to-fine alignment. *Computing Research Repository (CoRR)*, abs/1509.00838.

Sonja Nießen, Franz Josef Och, Gregor Leusch, and Hermann Ney. 2000. An evaluation tool for machine translation: Fast evaluation for MT research. In *Language Resources and Evaluation (LREC)*, pages 39–45, Athens, Greece, May.

Kishore Papineni, Salim Roukos, Todd Ward, and Wei-Jing Zhu. 2002. BLEU: a method for automatic evaluation of machine translation. In *Proceedings of the 40th annual meeting on association for computational linguistics*, pages 311–318. Association for Computational Linguistics.

Maja Popović. 2016. chrF deconstructed: beta parameters and n-gram weights. In *Proceedings of the First Conference on Machine Translation*, pages 499–504,

Berlin, Germany, August. Association for Computational Linguistics.

Ehud Reiter, Somayajulu Sripada, Jim Hunter, and Ian Davy. 2005. Choosing words in computer-generated weather forecasts. *Artificial Intelligence*, 167:137–169.

Michel Simard, Cyril Goutte, and Pierre Isabelle. 2007. Statistical phrase-based post-editing. In *Proceedings of the Human Language Technology Conference of the North American Chapter of the Association of Computational Linguistics, NAACL*. The Association for Computational Linguistics, April.

David Zajic and Bonnie Dorr. 2002. Automatic headline generation for newspaper stories. In *Proceedings of the DUC 2002 workshop on text summarization*, July.

Towards Automatic Generation of Product Reviews from Aspect-Sentiment Scores

Hongyu Zang and **Xiaojun Wan**

Institute of Computer Science and Technology, Peking University

The MOE Key Laboratory of Computational Linguistics, Peking University

{zanghy, wanxiaojun}@pku.edu.cn

Abstract

Data-to-text generation is very essential and important in machine writing applications. The recent deep learning models, like Recurrent Neural Networks (RNNs), have shown a bright future for relevant text generation tasks. However, rare work has been done for automatic generation of long reviews from user opinions. In this paper, we introduce a deep neural network model to generate long Chinese reviews from aspect-sentiment scores representing users' opinions. We conduct our study within the framework of encoder-decoder networks, and we propose a hierarchical structure with aligned attention in the Long-Short Term Memory (LSTM) decoder. Experiments show that our model outperforms retrieval based baseline methods, and also beats the sequential generation models in qualitative evaluations.

1 Introduction

Text generation is a central task in the NLP field. The progress achieved in text generation will help a lot in building strong artificial intelligence (AI) that can comprehend and compose human languages.

Review generation is an interesting subtask of data-to-text generation. With more and more online trades, it usually happens that customers are lazy to do brainstorming to write reviews, and sellers want to benefit from good reviews. As we can see, review generation can be really useful and worthy of study. But recent researches on text generation mainly focus on generation of weather reports, financial news, sports news (Konstas, 2014; Kim et al., 2016; Zhang et al., 2016), and so on. The task of review generation still needs to be further explored.

Think about how we generate review texts: we usually have the sentiment polarities with respect to product aspects before we speak or write. Inspired by this, we focus on study of review generation from structured data, which consist of aspect-sentiment scores.

Traditional generation models are mainly based on rules. It is time consuming to handcraft rules. Thanks to the quick development of neural networks and deep learning, text generation has achieved a breakthrough in recent years in many domains, e.g., image-to-text (Karpathy and Fei-Fei, 2015; Xu et al., 2015), video-to-text (Yu et al., 2016), and text-to-text (Sutskever et al., 2014; Li et al., 2015), etc. More and more works show that generation models with neural networks can generate meaningful and grammatical texts (Bahdanau et al., 2015; Sutskever et al., 2011). However, recent studies of text generation mainly focus on generating short texts of sentence level. There are still challenges for modern sequential generation models to handle long texts. And yet there is very few work having been done in generating long reviews.

In this paper, we aim to address the challenging task of long review generation within the encoder-decoder neural network framework. Based on the encoder-decoder framework, we investigate different models to generate review texts. Among these models, the encoders are typically Multi-Layer Perceptron (MLP) to embed the input aspect-sentiment scores. The decoders are RNNs with LSTM units, but differ in architectures. We proposed a hierarchi-

Proceedings of The 10th International Natural Language Generation conference, pages 168–177,
Santiago de Compostela, Spain, September 4-7 2017. ©2017 Association for Computational Linguistics

cal generation model with a new attention mechanism, which shows better results compared to other models in both automatic and manual evaluations based on a real Chinese review dataset.

To the best of our knowledge, our work is the first attempt to generate long review texts from aspect-sentiment scores with neural network models. Experiments proved that it is feasible to general long product reviews with our model.

2 Problem Definition and Corpus

To have a better understanding of the task investigated in this study, we'd like to introduce the corpus first.

Without loss of generality, we use Chinese car reviews in this study and reviews in other domains can be processed and generated in the same way. The Chinese car reviews are crawled from the website AutoHome[1]. Each review text contains eight sentences describing eight aspects[2], respectively: 空间/*Space*, 动力/*Power*, 控制/*Control*, 油耗/*Fuel Consumption*, 舒适度/*Comfort*, 外观/*Appearance*, 内饰/*Interior*, and 性价比/*Price*. Each review text corresponds to these eight aspects and the corresponding sentiment ratings, and the review sentences are aligned with the aspects and ratings. So we may split the whole review into eight sentences when we need. Note that the sentences in each review are correlated with each other, so if we regard them as independent sentences with respect to individual aspect-sentiment scores, they probably seem pretty mendacious when put altogether. We should keep each review text as a whole and generate the long and complete review at one time, rather than generating each review sentence independently. Specifically, we define our task as generating long Chinese car reviews from eight aspect-sentiment scores.

The raw data are badly formatted. In order to clean the data, we keep the reviews whose sentences corresponding to all the eight aspects. And we skip the reviews whose sentences are too long or too short. We accept length of 10 to 40 words per sentence. We use Jieba[3] for Chinese word segmentation. Note that each review text contains eight sentences, where each sentence has 24 Chinese characters on average. The review texts in our corpus are actually very long, about 195 Chinese characters per review.

The rating score for each aspect is in a range of [1, 5], and we regard rating 3 as neutral, and normalize ratings into [-1.0, 1.0] by Equation (1)[4], and the sign of a normalized rating means the sentiment polarity. For instance, if the original ratings for all eight aspects are [1,2,3,4,5,4,3,2], we will normalize it into[-1.0,-0.5,0.0,0.5,1.0,0.5, 0.0,-0.5] and use the normalized vector as the input for review generation.

$$x' = \frac{x - \frac{Max+Min}{2}}{\frac{Max-Min}{2}} \tag{1}$$

And finally, we get 43060 pairs of aspect-sentiment vectors and the corresponding review texts, in which there are 8340 different inputs[5]. Then we split the data randomly into training set and test set. The training set contains 32195 pairs (about 75%) and 6290 different inputs, while the test set contains the rest 10865 pairs with 2050 different inputs. The test set does not overlap with the train set with respect to the input aspect-sentiment vector.

Furthermore, we transform the input vector into aspect-oriented vectors as input for our models. For each aspect, we use an additional one-hot vector to represent the aspect, and then append the one-hot vector to the input vector. For example, if we are dealing with a specific aspect *Power* corresponding to a one-hot vector [0,1,0,0,0,0,0,0] for the above review with input vector [-1.0,-0.5,0.0,0.5,1.0,0.5,0.0,-0.5], the new input vector with respect to this aspect is actually [-1.0,-0.5,0.0,0.5,1.0,0.5,0.0,-0.5,0,1,0,0,0,0,0,0]. Each new input vector is aligned with a review sentence. Similarly, we can get eight new vectors with respect to the eight aspects as input for our models.

---

[1]www.autohome.com.cn

[2]In fact, there may be multiple grammatical sentences describing one single aspect. But for simplification, we define the sequence of characters describing the same aspects as a sequence.

[3]github.com/fxsjy/jieba

[4]We set the origin rating as x, and the normalized rating as x'. Max and Min is the maximum and minimum value out of all the original ratings in the dataset, or rather, 5 and 1.

[5]We allow multiple gold-standard answers to one input.

3 Preliminaries

In this section, we will give a brief introduction to LSTM Network (Hochreiter and Schmidhuber, 1997).

3.1 RNN

RNN has been widely used for sequence generation tasks (Graves, 2012a; Schuster and Paliwal, 1997). RNN accepts sequence of inputs $X = \{x_1, x_2, x_3, ..., x_{|X|}\}$, and gets h_t at time t according to Equation (2).

$$h_t = W_H \times \begin{bmatrix} h_{t-1} \\ x_t \end{bmatrix} \quad (2)$$

3.2 LSTM Network

An LSTM network contains LSTM units in RNN and an LSTM unit is a recurrent network unit that excels at remembering values for either long or short durations of time(Graves, 2012b; Sundermeyer et al., 2012). It contains an input gate, a forget gate, an output gate and a memory cell. Respectively, at time t, we set the above parts as i_t, f_t, o_t, c_t. In an LSTM network, we propagate as Equation (3)(4)(5).

$$\begin{bmatrix} i_t \\ f_t \\ o_t \end{bmatrix} = sigmoid\left(\begin{bmatrix} W_I \\ W_F \\ W_O \end{bmatrix} \times \begin{bmatrix} h_{t-1} \\ x_t \end{bmatrix} \right) \quad (3)$$

$$c_t = i_t \times tanh\left(W_C \times \begin{bmatrix} h_{t-1} \\ x_t \end{bmatrix} \right) + f_t \times c_{t-1} \quad (4)$$

$$h_t = c_t \times o_t \quad (5)$$

In the past few years, many generation models based on LSTM networks have given promising results in different domains (Xu et al., 2015; Shang et al., 2015; Wu et al., 2016). Compared to other network units of RNN, like GRU (Chung et al., 2014), LSTM is considered the best one in most cases.

4 Review Generation Models

4.1 Notations

We define our task as receiving a vector of aspect-sentiment scores V_s to generate review texts, which is a long sequence of words $Y\{y_1, y_2, \ldots, y_{|Y|-1}, \langle EOS \rangle\}$ ($\langle EOS \rangle$ is the special word representing the end of a sequence). As mentioned in section 2, we also transform an input vector V_s into a series of new input vectors $\{V_1, V_2, \ldots, V_8\}$ with respect to eight aspects for our models. More specifically, in order to obtain each V_i, we append a one-hot vector representing a specific aspect to V_s. That is, $V_i = [V_s, O]$, where O is a one-hot vector with the size of eight, and only the ith element of O is 1.

We have three different kinds of embeddings: E^W stands for word embedding, E^V stands for embedding of the input vector by a MLP encoder, and E^C stands for embedding of context sentences. There will be subscripts specifying the word, the vector, and the context.

And in LSTM, h is a hidden vector, x is an input vector, P is the possibility distribution, y' is the predicted word, and t is the time step.

4.2 Sequential Review Generation Models (SRGMs)

SRGMs are similar to the popular Seq2Seq models (Chung et al., 2014; Sutskever et al., 2011), except that it receives inputs of structured data (like aspect-sentiment scores) and encodes them with an MLP.

The encoder's output E_s^V is treated as the initial hidden state h_0 of the decoder. And the initial input vector is set as the word embedding of $\langle BOS \rangle$ ($\langle BOS \rangle$ is the special word representing the begin of a sequence). Then the decoder proceeds as a standard LSTM network.

At time $t(t \geq 1)$, the hidden state of the decoder h_t is used to predict the distribution of words by a softmax layer. We will choose the word with max possibility as the word predicted at time t, and the word will be used as the input of the decoder at time $t + 1$.

This procedure can be formulated as follows:

$$h_0 = E_s^V = MLP(V_s) \quad (6)$$

$$x_1 = E^W_{\langle BOS \rangle} \quad (7)$$

$$h_t = LSTM(h_{t-1}, x_t) \quad (8)$$

$$P_t = softmax(h_t) \quad (9)$$

$$y'_t = argmax_w(P_{t,w}) \quad (10)$$

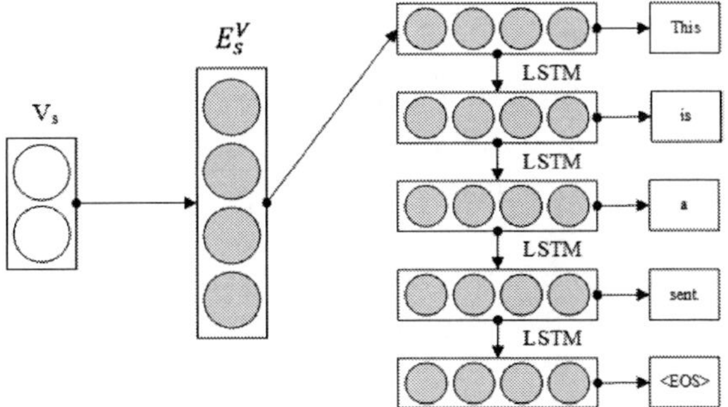

Figure 1: The architecture of SRGM-w.

$$x_{t+1} = E_{y'_t}^W \tag{11}$$

In each training step, we adopt the negative likelihood loss function.

$$Loss = -\frac{1}{|Y|}\sum_t logP_{t,y_t} \tag{12}$$

However, Sutskever et al. (2014) and Pouget-Abadie et al. (2014) have shown that standard LSTM decoder does not perform well in generating long sequences. Therefore, besides treating the review as a whole sequence, we also tried splitting the reviews into sentences, generating the sentences separately, and then concatenating the generated sentences altogether. Respectively, we name the sequential model generating the whole review as SRGM-w, and the one generating separate sentences as SRGM-s.

4.3 Hierarchical Review Generation Models (HRGMs)

Inspired by Li et al. (2015), we build a hierarchical LSTM decoder based on the SRGMs. Note that we have two different LSTM units in hierarchical models, in which the superscript S denotes the sentence−level LSTM, and the superscript P denotes the paragraph−level one. And t is the time step notation in the sentence decoder, while T is the time step notation in the paragraph decoder. Both the time step symbols are put in the position of subscripts.

There is a one-hidden-layer-MLP to encode the input vector into E_s^V. $LSTM^P$ receives E_s^V as the initial hidden state, and the initial input x_1^P is a zero vector. At time $T(T \geq 1)$, the output of $LSTM^P$ is used as the initial hidden state of $LSTM^S$. And then $LSTM^S$ works just like the LSTM decoder in

SRGMs. The final output of $LSTM^S$ is treated as the embedding of the context sentences E_T^C, which is also the input of $LSTM^P$ at time $T + 1$. We call this hierarchical model HRGM-o.

$$h_0^P = E_s^V = MLP(V_s) \tag{13}$$

$$x_1^P = \mathbf{0} \tag{14}$$

$$h_T^P = LSTM^P(h_{T-1}^P, x_T^P) \tag{15}$$

$$h_{T,0}^S = h_T^P \tag{16}$$

$$h_{T,t}^S = LSTM^S(h_{T,t-1}^S, x_{T,t}^S) \tag{17}$$

$$P_{T,t} = softmax(h_{T,t}^S) \tag{18}$$

$$y'_{T,t} = argmax_w(P_{T,t,w}) \tag{19}$$

$$x_{T,t+1}^S = E_{y'_{T,t}}^W \tag{20}$$

$$x_{T+1}^P = E_T^C = h_{T,|Y_T|}^S \tag{21}$$

In the experiment results of HRGM-o, we find that the model has its drawback. In some test cases, the output texts miss some important parts of the input aspects.

As many previous studies have shown that the attention mechanism promises a better result by considering the context (Bahdanau et al., 2015; Fang et al., 2016; Li et al., 2015). We adopt attention to the generation of each sentence, which is aligned to the sentence's main aspect.

Different from the attention mechanism mentioned in previous studies, in our situation, we have the alignment relationships between aspect-sentiment ratings and sentences, which are natural attentions to be used in the generation process. By applying additional input vector V_T at each time step T, we obtain the initial hidden state of $LSTM^S$ from two source vectors E_T^V and h_T^P. Therefore, we simply train a gate vector g to control the two parts of information. The encoding of V_T is similar to Equation (13), but with different parameters. In brief, we change Equation (16) to Equation (22)(23).

$$E_T^V = MLP'(V_T) \tag{22}$$

$$h_{T,0}^S = \begin{bmatrix} h_T^P \\ E_T^V \end{bmatrix} \times [g, \mathbf{1} - g] \tag{23}$$

Based on all of these, we propose a hierarchical model with a special aligned attention mechanism as shown in Figure 2. We call the model HRGM-a.

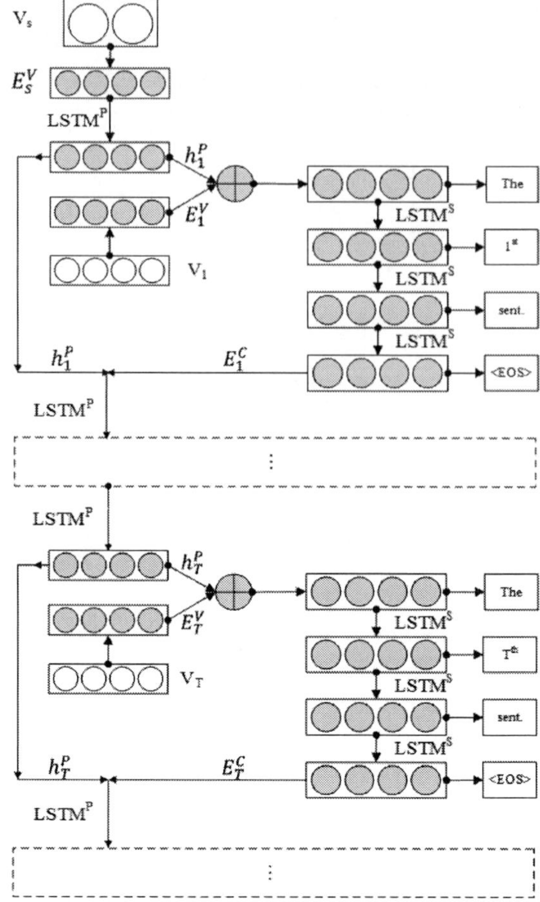

Figure 2: The architecture of HRGM-a.

5 Experiments

5.1 Training Detail

We implemented our models with TensorFlow 1.10[6], and trained them on an NVIDIA TITANX GPU (12G).

Because the limitation of our hardware, we only do experiments with one layer of encoder and one layer of LSTM network. The batch size is 4 in HRGMs, and 32 in SRGMs. The initial learning rate is set to 0.5, and we dynamically adjust the learning rate according to the loss value. As experiments show that the size of hidden layer does not affect the results regularly, we set all of them to 500.

All the rest parameters in our model can be learned during training.

---

[6]github.com/tensorflow/tensorflow/tree/r0.10

5.2 Baselines

Apart from SRGM-w and SRGM-s, we also developed several baselines for comparison.

- **Rand-w**: It randomly chooses a whole review from the training set.

- **Rand-s**: It randomly choose a sentence for each aspect from the training set and concatenates the sentences to form a review.

- **Cos**: It finds a sentiment vector from the training set which has the the largest cosine similarity value with the input vector, and then returns the corresponding review text.

- **Match**: It finds a sentiment vector from the training set which has the maximum number of rating scores matching exactly with that in the input vector, and then returns the corresponding review text.

- **Pick**: It finds one sentence for each aspect respectively in the training set by matching the same sentiment rating, and then concatenates them to form a review.

Generally speaking, models in this paper are divided into four classes. The first class is lower bound methods (Rand-w, Rand-s), where we choose something from the training set randomly. The second one is based on retrieval (Cos, Match, Pick), and we use similarity to decide which to choose. The third one is sequential generation models based on RNNs (SRGM-w, SRGM-s). And the last one is hierarchical RNN models to handle the whole review generation (HRGM-o, HRGM-a).

5.3 Automatic Evaluation

We used the popular BLEU (Papineni et al., 2002) scores as evaluation metrics and BLEU has shown good consistent with human evaluation in many machine translation and text generation tasks. High BLEU score means many n-grams in the hypothesis texts meets the gold-standard references. Here, we report BLEU-2 to BLEU-4 scores, and the evaluation is conducted after Chinese word segmentation.

The only parameters in BLEU is the weights W for n-gram precisions. In this study, we set W as average weights ($W_i = \frac{1}{n}$ for BLEU-n evaluation). As for multiple answers to the same input, we put all of them into the reference set of the input.

The results are shown in Table 1. Retrieval based

	BLEU-2	BLEU-3	BLEU-4
Rand-w	0.1307	0.0378	0.0117
Rand-s	0.1406	0.0412	0.0124
Cos	0.1342	0.0403	0.0129
Match	0.1358	0.0423	0.0136
Pick	0.1427	0.0434	0.0133
SRGM-w	0.1554	0.0713	0.0307
SRGM-s	0.1709	0.0829	0.0369
HRGM-o	0.1850	0.0854	0.0334
HRGM-a	**0.1985**	**0.0942**	**0.0412**

Table 1: The results of BLEU evaluations.

baselines get low BLEU scores in BLEU-2, BLEU-3 and BLEU-4. Among these models, Cos and Match even get lower BLEU scores than the lower bound methods in some BLEU evaluations, which may be attributed to the sparsity of the data in the training set. Pick is better than lower bound methods in all of the BLEU evaluations. Compared to the retrieval based baselines, SRGMs get higher scores in BLEU-2, BLEU-3, and BLEU-4. It is very promising that HRGMs get the highest BLEU scores in all evaluations, which demonstrates the effectiveness of the hierarchical structures. Moreover, HRGM-a achieves better scores than HRGM-o, which verifies the helpfulness of our proposed new attention mechanism.

In all, the retrieval models and sequential generation models can not handle long sequences well, but hierarchical models can handle long sequences. The reviews generated by our models are of better quality according to BLEU evaluations.

5.4 Human Evaluation

We also perform human evaluation to further compare these models. Human evaluation requires human judges to read all the results and give judgments with respect to different aspects of quality.

We randomly choose 50 different inputs in the test set. For each input, we compare the best models in each class, specifically, Rand-s, Pick, SRGM-s, HRGM-a, and the Gold (gold-standard) answer. We employ three subjects (excluding the authors of this paper) who have good knowledge in the domain of car reviews to evaluate the outputs of the models. The outputs are shuffled before shown to subjects. Without any idea which output belongs to

which model, the subjects are required to rate on a 5-pt Likert scale[7] about readability, accuracy, and usefulness. In our 5-pt Likert scale, 5-point means "very satisfying", while 1-point means "very terrible". The ratings with respect to each aspect of quality are then averaged across the three subjects and the 50 inputs.

To be more specific, we define readability, accuracy, and usefulness as follows. Readability is the metric concerned with the fluency and coherence of the texts. Accuracy indicates how well the review text matches the given aspects and sentiment ratings. Usefulness is more subjective, and subjects need to decide whether to accept it or not when the text is shown to them. The readability, accuracy, even the length of the review text will have an effect on the usefulness metric.

	Readability	Accuracy	Usefulness
Gold	4.61	4.41	4.39
Rand-s	4.44	3.21	3.52
Pick	**4.55**	4.15	4.20
SRGM-s	4.51	4.21	4.21
HRGM-a	4.52	**4.33**	**4.26**

Table 2: Human evaluation results of typical models. We set the best result of each metric in bold except for Gold-Standard.

The results are shown in Table 2. We can see that in human evaluations, all the models get high scores in readability. The readability score of our model HRGM-a is very close to the highest readability score achieved by Pick. Rand-s gets the worst scores for accuracy and usefulness, while the rest models perform much better in these metrics. Compared to the strong baselines Pick and SRGM-s, although our model is not the best in readability, it performs better in accuracy and usefulness. The results also demonstrate the efficacy of our proposed models.

5.5 Samples

To get a clearer view of what we have done and have an intuitive judgment of the generated texts, we present some samples in Table 3.

In Table 3, the first three samples are output texts of Gold-Standard, Pick, and our model HRGM-a for the same input. And in the last sample, we

[7]en.wikipedia.org/wiki/Likert_scale

Inputs	Outputs
Gold-Standard Space: 3 Power: 4 Control: 5 Fuel: 3 Comfort: 3 Appearance: 5 Interior: 4 Price: 4	后备箱的空间还是蛮大的，就是后排的空间比较小，座椅也不平整。动力还行吧，只要舍得给油，还说的过去。方向盘精准度高，路况反应清晰。可能是因为轮胎薄的原因吧，自动档的油耗有点高，市区油耗在10个左右，高速最多7个油。座椅还是蛮舒适的，就是行车中噪音比较大，建议做个全车隔音比较好。小⟨UNK⟩的颜值在同级别里算高的了，这点比较不错，特别是那个战斧轮毂。用料还行，偶尔会有点小异响，这个价位的车差不多⟨UNK⟩这样。不错，对得起这个价了，毕竟价钱摆在那里。 Translation: Trunk space is quite large, but the rear space is relatively small, and the seat is not smooth. Power is also okay, as long as willing to give oil. Steering wheel has high precision. Probably because of the reasons for thin tires, fuel consumption of automatic transmission is a bit high, urban fuel consumption in 10 or so, while on high way up to 7 oil. The seat is still quite comfortable, but there is large noise when driving. I propose the car to have a better sound insulation. Little ⟨UNK⟩'s appearance is better than others in the same class, and this is quite good. I especially like the Tomahawk wheels. Materials are okay, there is occasionally a little abnormal sound. The price of the car is acceptable. Yeah, worthy of the price ⟨UNK⟩. After all, the price is not that high.
Pick Space: 3 Power: 4 Control: 5 Fuel: 3 Comfort: 3 Appearance: 5 Interior: 4 Price: 4	略显狭小，如果坐4个人就很拥挤了。1.4T双增压带来的直观动力表现是不错的，不输给家里的锐志，毕竟1.4的车。新款也把双增压换成单增压，感觉有点不厚道。指哪打哪，宝马的公路操控，应该是比较不错了，很精准，无虚伪，路感强，现在400公里纯市内全程空调12个多，没平均速度可看，2.5的排量这个油耗能够接受。由于空间较大，所以随之舒适性也加了不少分。这个不多说OK！！！满意！！！一般吧，希望有些小细节要改进一下，多听听大家的意见。优惠完之后，觉得性价比还好，要是优惠⟨UNK⟩就不考虑宝来了 Translation: The space is slightly narrow, not enough for four people. The intuitional performance given by 1.4T double booster is good, better the Reiz of mine. After all, 1.4T. The new dual-pressure supercharger is replaced by a single one, where I feel a little unkind. The car goes anywhere I want. BMW's road control should be relatively good. Very accurate, no hypocrisy, strong sense of the road. I have driven the car 400 km along with air condition, the fuel consumption is about 12. I didn't pay attention to the average speed, but I think a displacement of 2.5 is acceptable to have such fuel consumption. Because of the large space, it's very comfortable in the car. I'm very satisfactory with the appearance! About interior, I think there are some small details to improve. The price is good with discount, if not for the discount ⟨UNK⟩, I won't consider Bora.
HRGM-a Space: 3 Power: 4 Control: 5 Fuel: 3 **Comfort: 3** Appearance: 5 Interior: 4 Price: 4	空间一般，后排空间有点小。动力方面，提速很快。超车很轻松。操控很好，指向精准，方向盘很轻，高速容易上手。油耗在市区内比较高，高速在7个左右，市区的话油耗在10个左右。**舒适性一般，毕竟是运动型的车**。外观很满意，我喜欢。内饰做工还可以，就是中控的塑料感太强了。性价比很高，这个价位的车，这个配置的值价位，这个价格。性价比配置，这个价位。值！ Translation: The space is just so so, as the rear space is a little small. As for power, it can speed up very quickly, which makes it pretty easy to overtake. The control is good. It's very precise. And the steering wheel is very light, easy to use on highway. Fuel consumption in the urban area is relatively high, about 7 on highway, about 10 in urban roads. **It's not comfortable enough in the car. After all, it is a sports car.** The appearance is very satisfactory. I like it very much. Interiors are ok. But there is too much plastic in center control area. The price/performance ratio is very high. A car at this price, with these configurations, worths buying.
HRGM-a Space: 3 Power: 4 Control: 5 Fuel: 3 **Comfort: 5** Appearance: 5 Interior: 4 Price: 4	空间一般，后排空间有点小，后备箱空间也不错，就是后排座椅不能放倒。动力还不错，提速很快。操控很好，指向精准。油耗还可以，毕竟是2.0的排量，油耗也不高，毕竟是2.0的排量，也不可能我个人开车的原因。**舒适性很好，座椅的包裹性很好，坐着很舒服**。外观很满意，就是喜欢。很有个性。内饰做工一般，但是用料还是很好的，不过这个价位的车也就这样了！性价比不错，值得购买。 Translation: The space is just so so, as the rear space is a little small. The trunk space is also good, but the rear seat cannot be tipped. Power is also OK. The car can speed up very quickly. Control is very good. It goes wherever you want. Fuel consumption is acceptable. After all, with a 2.0 displacement, fuel consumption is not that high. But it can't be my problem. **It's comfortable in the car. The seats are well wrapped, which makes them really comfortable.** The appearance is very satisfactory. I just like the cool features. Interiors are ok. The materials are ok. After all, you can't want more from cars at this price. It's worth buying the car, and I can say that the price/performance ratio is pretty good.

Table 3: Sample reviews. Given the same input, our model can generate long reviews that matches the input aspects and sentiments better than the baseline methods. When we change the input rating for *Comfortable* from middle (3) to high (5), our model can also detect the difference and change the outputs accordingly.

change one rating in the input to show how our model changes the output according to the slight difference in the input.

As we can see, Pick is a little better than our model HRGM-a in text length and content abundance. But the output of Pick has a few problems. For example, there is a serious logic problem in the reviews of *Space* and *Comfort*. It says the car is narrow in *Space*, but the car has a large space in *Comfort*, which violates the context consistency.

What's more, it gives improper review to *Comfort*. Although *Comfort* gets 3-point, the review sentence is kind of positive. And that can be considered as a mismatch with the input. On the contrary, our model produces review texts as a whole and the texts are aligned with the input aspect-sentiment scores more appropriately. All 3-point aspects get neutral or slightly negative reviews, while all 5-point aspects get definitely positive comments. And 4-point aspects also get reviews biased towards being positive.

As for the last example after changing the rating of *Comfort* from 3-point to 5-point, we can see that except for the review sentence for *Comfort*, other sentences do not change apparently. But the review sentence of *Comfort* changes significantly from neutral to positive, which shows the power of our model.

6 Related Work

Several previous studies have attempted for review generation (Tang et al., 2016; Lipton et al., 2015; Dong et al., 2017) . They generate personalized reviews according to an overall rating. But they do not consider the product aspects and whether each generated sentence is produced as the user requires. The models they proposed are very similar to SRGMs. And the length of reviews texts are not as long as ours. Therefore, our work can be regarded as a significant improvement of their researches.

Many researches of text generation are also closely related to our work. Traditional way for text generation (Genest and Lapalme, 2012; Yan et al., 2011) mainly focus on grammars, templates, and so on. But it is usually complicated to make every part of the system work and cooperate perfectly following the traditional techniques, while end-to-end generation systems nowadays, like the ones within encoder-decoder framework (Cho et al., 2014; Sordoni et al., 2015), have distinct architectures and achieve promising performances.

Moreover, the recent researches on hierarchical structure help a lot with the improvement of the generation systems. Li et al. (2015) experimented on LSTM autoencoders to show the power of the hierarchical structured LSTM networks to encode and decode long texts. And recent studies have succefully generated Chinese peotries(Yi et al., 2016) and Song iambics(Wang et al., 2016) with hierarchical RNNs.

The attention mechanism originated from the area of image (Mnih et al., 2014), but is widely used in all kinds of generation models in NLP (Bahdanau et al., 2015; Fang et al., 2016). Besides, attention today is not totally the same with the original ones. It's more a thinking than an algorithm. Various changes can be made to construct a better model.

7 Conclusion and Future Work

In this paper, we design end-to-end models to challenge the automatic review generation task. Retrieval based methods have problems generating texts consistent with input aspect-sentiment scores, while RNNs cannot deal well with long texts. To overcome these obstacles, we proposed models and find that our model with hierarchical structure and aligned attention can produce long reviews with high quality, which outperforms the baseline methods.

However, we can notice that there are still some problems in the texts generated by our models. In some generated texts, the contents are not rich enough compared to human-written reviews, which may be improved by applying diversity decoding methods (Vijayakumar et al., 2016; Li et al., 2016). And there are a few logical problems in some generated texts, which may be improved by generative adversarial nets (Goodfellow et al., 2014) or reinforcement learning (Sutton and Barto, 1998).

In future work, we will apply our proposed models to text generation in other domains. As mentioned earlier, our models can be easily adapted for other data-to-text generation tasks, if the alignment between structured data and texts can be provided. We hope our work will not only be an exploration of review generation, but also make contributions to general data-to-text generation.

Acknowledgments

This work was supported by 863 Program of China (2015AA015403), NSFC (61331011), and Key Laboratory of Science, Technology and Standard in Press Industry (Key Laboratory of Intelligent Press Media Technology). We thank the anonymous reviewers for helpful comments. Xiaojun Wan is the corresponding author.

References

Dzmitry Bahdanau, Kyunghyun Cho, and Yoshua Bengio. 2015. Neural machine translation by jointly learning to align and translate. *ICLR*.

Kyunghyun Cho, Bart Van Merriënboer, Caglar Gulcehre, Dzmitry Bahdanau, Fethi Bougares, Holger Schwenk, and Yoshua Bengio. 2014. Learning phrase representations using rnn encoder-decoder for statistical machine translation. *EMNLP*.

Junyoung Chung, Caglar Gulcehre, KyungHyun Cho, and Yoshua Bengio. 2014. Empirical evaluation of gated recurrent neural networks on sequence modeling. *NIPS, Deep Learning and Representation Learning Workshop*.

Li Dong, Shaohan Huang, Furu Wei, Mirella Lapata, Ming Zhou, and Ke Xu. 2017. Learning to generate product reviews from attributes. In *Proceedings of the 15th Conference of the European Chapter of the Association for Computational Linguistics: Volume 1, Long Papers*, pages 623–632, Valencia, Spain, April. Association for Computational Linguistics.

Wei Fang, Juei-Yang Hsu, Hung-yi Lee, and Lin-Shan Lee. 2016. Hierarchical attention model for improved machine comprehension of spoken content. *IEEE Workshop on Spoken Language Technology (SLT)*.

Pierre-Etienne Genest and Guy Lapalme. 2012. Fully abstractive approach to guided summarization. In *Proceedings of the 50th Annual Meeting of the Association for Computational Linguistics: Short Papers-Volume 2*, pages 354–358. Association for Computational Linguistics.

Ian Goodfellow, Jean Pouget-Abadie, Mehdi Mirza, Bing Xu, David Warde-Farley, Sherjil Ozair, Aaron Courville, and Yoshua Bengio. 2014. Generative adversarial nets. In *Advances in neural information processing systems*, pages 2672–2680.

Alex Graves. 2012a. Sequence transduction with recurrent neural networks. *International Conference of Machine Learning (ICML) Workshop on Representation Learning*.

Alex Graves. 2012b. Supervised sequence labelling. In *Supervised Sequence Labelling with Recurrent Neural Networks*, pages 5–13. Springer.

Sepp Hochreiter and Jürgen Schmidhuber. 1997. Long short-term memory. *Neural computation*, 9(8):1735–1780.

Andrej Karpathy and Li Fei-Fei. 2015. Deep visual-semantic alignments for generating image descriptions. In *Proceedings of the IEEE Conference on Computer Vision and Pattern Recognition*, pages 3128–3137.

Soomin Kim, JongHwan Oh, and Joonhwan Lee. 2016. Automated news generation for tv program ratings. In *Proceedings of the ACM International Conference on Interactive Experiences for TV and Online Video*, pages 141–145. ACM.

Ioannis Konstas. 2014. Joint models for concept-to-text generation.

Jiwei Li, Minh-thang Luong, and Dan Jurafsky. 2015. A hierarchical neural autoencoder for paragraphs and documents. In *Proceedings of ACL*. Citeseer.

Jiwei Li, Michel Galley, Chris Brockett, Jianfeng Gao, and Bill Dolan. 2016. A diversity-promoting objective function for neural conversation models. In *Proceedings of NAACL-HLT*, pages 110–119.

Zachary C Lipton, Sharad Vikram, and Julian McAuley. 2015. Generative concatenative nets jointly learn to write and classify reviews. *arXiv preprint arXiv:1511.03683*.

Volodymyr Mnih, Nicolas Heess, Alex Graves, et al. 2014. Recurrent models of visual attention. In *Advances in neural information processing systems*, pages 2204–2212.

Kishore Papineni, Salim Roukos, Todd Ward, and Wei-Jing Zhu. 2002. Bleu: a method for automatic evaluation of machine translation. In *Proceedings of the 40th annual meeting on association for computational linguistics*, pages 311–318. Association for Computational Linguistics.

Jean Pouget-Abadie, Dzmitry Bahdanau, Bart van Merriënboer, Kyunghyun Cho, and Yoshua Bengio. 2014. Overcoming the curse of sentence length for neural machine translation using automatic segmentation. *Syntax, Semantics and Structure in Statistical Translation*, page 78.

Mike Schuster and Kuldip K Paliwal. 1997. Bidirectional recurrent neural networks. *IEEE Transactions on Signal Processing*, 45(11):2673–2681.

Lifeng Shang, Zhengdong Lu, and Hang Li. 2015. Neural responding machine for short-text conversation. *ACL*.

Alessandro Sordoni, Yoshua Bengio, Hossein Vahabi, Christina Lioma, Jakob Grue Simonsen, and Jian-Yun Nie. 2015. A hierarchical recurrent encoder-decoder for generative context-aware query suggestion. In *Proceedings of the 24th ACM International on Conference on Information and Knowledge Management*, pages 553–562. ACM.

Martin Sundermeyer, Ralf Schlüter, and Hermann Ney. 2012. Lstm neural networks for language modeling. In *Interspeech*, pages 194–197.

Ilya Sutskever, James Martens, and Geoffrey E Hinton. 2011. Generating text with recurrent neural networks. In *Proceedings of the 28th International Conference on Machine Learning (ICML-11)*, pages 1017–1024.

Ilya Sutskever, Oriol Vinyals, and Quoc V Le. 2014. Sequence to sequence learning with neural networks. In *Advances in neural information processing systems*, pages 3104–3112.

Richard S Sutton and Andrew G Barto. 1998. *Reinforcement learning: An introduction*, volume 1. MIT press Cambridge.

Jian Tang, Yifan Yang, Sam Carton, Ming Zhang, and Qiaozhu Mei. 2016. Context-aware natural language generation with recurrent neural networks. *arXiv preprint arXiv:1611.09900*.

Ashwin K Vijayakumar, Michael Cogswell, Ramprasath R Selvaraju, Qing Sun, Stefan Lee, David Crandall, and Dhruv Batra. 2016. Diverse beam search: Decoding diverse solutions from neural sequence models. *arXiv preprint arXiv:1610.02424*.

Qixin Wang, Tianyi Luo, Dong Wang, and Chao Xing. 2016. Chinese song iambics generation with neural attention-based model. *arXiv preprint arXiv:1604.06274*.

Yonghui Wu, Mike Schuster, Zhifeng Chen, Quoc V Le, Mohammad Norouzi, Wolfgang Macherey, Maxim Krikun, Yuan Cao, Qin Gao, Klaus Macherey, et al. 2016. Google's neural machine translation system: Bridging the gap between human and machine translation. *arXiv preprint arXiv:1609.08144*.

Kelvin Xu, Jimmy Ba, Ryan Kiros, Kyunghyun Cho, Aaron C Courville, Ruslan Salakhutdinov, Richard S Zemel, and Yoshua Bengio. 2015. Show, attend and tell: Neural image caption generation with visual attention. In *ICML*, volume 14, pages 77–81.

Rui Yan, Liang Kong, Congrui Huang, Xiaojun Wan, Xiaoming Li, and Yan Zhang. 2011. Timeline generation through evolutionary trans-temporal summarization. In *Proceedings of the Conference on Empirical Methods in Natural Language Processing*, pages 433–443. Association for Computational Linguistics.

Xiaoyuan Yi, Ruoyu Li, and Maosong Sun. 2016. Generating chinese classical poems with rnn encoder-decoder. *arXiv preprint arXiv:1604.01537*.

Haonan Yu, Jiang Wang, Zhiheng Huang, Yi Yang, and Wei Xu. 2016. Video paragraph captioning using hierarchical recurrent neural networks. In *Proceedings of the IEEE Conference on Computer Vision and Pattern Recognition*, pages 4584–4593.

Jianmin Zhang, Jin-ge Yao, and Xiaojun Wan. 2016. Toward constructing sports news from live text commentary. In *Proceedings of ACL*.

A model of suspense
for narrative generation

Richard Doust
Open University, UK
richard.doust@gmail.com

Paul Piwek
Open University, UK
paul.piwek@open.ac.uk

Abstract

Most work on automatic generation of narratives, and more specifically suspenseful narrative, has focused on detailed domain-specific modelling of character psychology and plot structure. Recent work on the automatic learning of narrative schemas suggests an alternative approach that exploits such schemas for modelling and measuring suspense. We propose a domain-independent model for tracking suspense in a story which can be used to predict the audience's suspense response on a sentence-by-sentence basis at the content determination stage of narrative generation. The model lends itself as the theoretical foundation for a suspense module that is compatible with alternative narrative generation theories. The proposal is evaluated by human judges' normalised average scores correlate strongly with predicted values.

1 Introduction

Research on computational models of narrative has a long tradition, with important contributions from researchers in natural language generation, such as the AUTHOR system (Callaway and Lester, 2002), which provides the blueprint for a prose generation architecture including a narrative planner and organiser with traditional NLG pipeline components (sentence planner, realiser) and a revisor.

Two features are found in much of such research. Firstly, work on content determination and organisation has often centred on use of detailed representations for character goals and plans – see for example Cavazza et al. (2002) and Cavazza and Charles (2005). According to such approaches, a good and, more specifically, a suspenseful story should arise out of the complex interaction of the system components. It is often hard to separate the different contributions of the system choices from the quality of the underlying domain-specific plans and story templates (Concepción et al., 2016).

Secondly, existing approaches to suspense often interlock with the concept of a story protagonist under some kind of threat. For example, the suspense modelling in the SUSPENSER system Cheong and Young (2015) - which aims to enable choices that can maximise suspense in narrative generation - is entirely based on Gerrig and Bernardo (1994)'s definition, according which suspense varies inversely with the number of potential actions of the central protagonist which could allow him or her to escape a threat. Similarly, Zillman's definition (Zillmann, 1996) links suspense to the reader's fearful apprehension of a story event that threatens a liked protagonist. Delatorre et al. (2016) proposed a computational model based on Zillman's definition from which they derived the use of emotional valence, empathy and arousal as the key components of suspense. Interestingly, their experimental results led the authors to question the usefulness of empathy for measuring suspense.

In this paper, we approach the problem of suspenseful story generation from a different angle. Our main contribution is a domain-independent model of suspense together with a method for measuring the suspensefulness of simple chronological narratives. Thus we identify a separately testable measure of story suspensefulness. By separating out emotional salience and character empathy considerations from informational and attentional processes at the heart of the suspense reaction, we construct a modular definition of suspense that could in theory encompass the definitions cited above. The method builds on the psychological model of narrative proposed by Brewer

Proceedings of The 10th International Natural Language Generation conference, pages 178–187,
Santiago de Compostela, Spain, September 4-7 2017. ©2017 Association for Computational Linguistics

and Lichtenstein (1982), and was first developed in Doust (2015).

Inspired by Brewer and Lichtenstein's informal model, we build a formal model in which the concept of a *narrative thread* plays a pivotal role. Narrative threads model the reader's expectations about what might happen next in a given story. As a story is told, narrative threads are activated and de-activated. Different threads may point to conflicting events that are situated in the future. As more of the story is revealed, the moment of resolution of the conflict may appear more or less proximal in time. We capture this by formally defining the concept of *Imminence*. Imminence is based on the potential for upcoming storyworld events to conflict with one another and on the narrative proximity with these conflicts. It is the key factor in what we call *conflict-based suspense*. Additionally, as the story is told, conflicting *interpretations* about certain events in the story may prevail. This leads us to define a distinct second type of suspense which we call *revelatory suspense*.

Our approach has a number of advantages. Firstly, by disentangling suspense from story protagonist-based modelling, our approach can deal with scenes that have no discernable human-like protagonist. An example could be an ice floe slowly splitting up or a ball slowly rolling towards the edge of a table[1]. Thus the empirical coverage of the theory is extended.

Secondly, the model lends itself as the theoretical foundation for a suspense module that is compatible with alternative narrative generation theories. Such a module could be used to evaluate story variants being considered in the search space of a narrative generation program. This is possible because the model operates at a level of abstraction where character motivations are subsumed by higher level properties of an unfolding story, such as imminence.

Thirdly, the underlying world knowledge that our model relies on, makes use of a format, narrative threads, which meshes with recent work in computational linguistics on the automatic learning of narrative schemas as proposed in Chambers and Jurafsky (2009) and Chambers and Jurafsky (2010).

The remainder of this paper is organised as follows. In Section 2 we discuss previous primarily compu-

tational work on suspense. The section concludes with a description of Brewer and Lichtenstein's psychological theory of suspense, which forms the basis for our model. Section 3.1 introduces our formal model. Section 3.2 presents our model of the reader's response to a suspenseful narrative and the algorithm for calculating suspense. Section 3.3 presents an overview of *revelatory suspense*. Section 4 reports on the evaluation of the model by human judges. Finally, in Section 5 we present our conclusions and avenues for further research.

2 Related work on computational models of narrative and suspense

In computational models of narrative, a common approach is to determine some basic element, which, when manipulated in certain ways, will produce a skeletal story-line or plot. For example, TALE-SPIN (Meehan, 1977) uses the characters' *goals*, whereas MINSTREL (Turner, 1992) uses *both* authorial and character goals. MEXICA (Pérez y Pérez and Sharples, 2001) uses a *tension curve* to represent *love*, *emotion* and *danger* in order to drive the generation process. Riedl and Young (2010) and later the GLAIVE narrative planner (Ware and Young, 2014) introduce a novel refinement search planning algorithm that combines intentional and causal links and can reason about character intentionality.

The focus in the aforementioned work is on the *global* story-modelling task and the automatic generation of new narratives. Suspense is seen as one of a set of by-products of story generation. There is no re-usable model of what makes a suspenseful story.

Other approaches have been more specifically aimed at generating *suspenseful* stories. Cheong and Young (2015)'s SUSPENSER and O'Neill and Riedl (2014)'s DRAMATIS propose cognitively motivated heuristics for suspense using the planning paradigm. Characters have goals and corresponding plans, and suspense levels are calculated as a function of these. The measurement of suspense in these algorithms was evaluated using alternate versions of a story. In particular, O'Neill and Riedl (2014) asked human judges to make a decision about which story was more suspenseful and then compared these results to the story their system identified as most suspenseful.

Several psychological theories of narrative under-

---

[1] One could postulate the existence of imaginary protagonists for such scenarios, but this seems unnecessarily complex.

standing have attempted to approach suspense modelling. For example, Kintsch (1980) considers the schemata and frames that readers call upon to actually learn from the text they are reading. They examine the additional focus generated by expectation violations, i.e., surprise rather than suspense.

Our suspense measurement method is grounded in Brewer and Lichtenstein (1982)'s psychological theory of narrative understanding. They suggest that three major discourse structures account for the 'enjoyment' of a large number of stories: surprise, curiosity and suspense. This approach is based on the existence of Initiating Events (*IE*) and Outcome Events (*OE*) in a given narrative.

For suspense, an *IE* is presented which triggers the prediction of an *OE* which corresponds to a significant change in the state of the storyworld. The reader feels concern about this outcome event, and if this state is maintained over time, the feeling of suspense will arise. Such a change in the state of the storyworld can have a positive or negative valence for the reader, and may often be significant because it concerns the fate of a central character in the story. However, this link to a character's fate is not a requirement of our model.

Also, as Brewer & Lichtenstein say: 'often additional discourse material is placed between the initiating event and the outcome event, to encourage the build up of suspense' (Brewer and Lichtenstein, 1982, p. 17). Thus, to produce suspense, the *IE* and *OE* are ordered chronologically and other events are placed between them.

We propose a computational extension of this model based on what we call *narrative threads*, a concept grounded in psychological research such as Zwaan et al. (1995), the constructionist and prediction-sustantiation models of narrative comprehension (Graesser et al., 1994) and scripts (Lebowitz, 1985; Schank and Abelson, 1977). Our narrative threads include both causal and intentional links as do for example Ware and Young (2014) and also include the concept of *recency* (see for example Jones et al. (2006)).

The research reported in this paper differs in two key respects from the computational approaches described above.

Firstly, it eschews a planning approach to story generation that makes use of detailed modelling of character intentions and goals. In our view, suspense is *not dependent* on the existence of characters' goals: we can experience suspense about a piece of string breaking under the strain of a weight. Nor does our approach require the existence of a central protagonist and his or her predicament.

Secondly, our model tracks suspense throughout the telling of a story. Unlike much previous work, rather than evaluate only the predicted *overall* suspense level of a story, in our evaluation we compare predicted suspense levels with human judgements at *multiple steps* throughout the telling of the story. This provides us with a much more fine-grained evaluation of our suspense measurement method than has hitherto been used.

Brewer and Lichtenstein's work has been the basis of further work such as Hoeken and van Vliet (2000) and Albuquerque et al. (2011). The former found that 'suspense is evoked even when the reader knows how the story will end' whereas the latter explored story-line variation to evoke suspense, surprise and curiosity. However, neither presents a model of how suspense fluctuates during the telling of a story nor any empirical evaluation of such a model.

In the following section, we present our computational model of suspense that extends that of Brewer and Lichtenstein (1982).

3 Formalism and Algorithm for Suspense Generation

3.1 Formalism

A *story* can be considered the work of a hypothetical author, who first chooses some events from a *storyworld* and orders them into a *fabula* (this includes all relevant events from the storyworld, not just those that get told). The author then chooses events and orderings of events from this fabula to create a story designed to trigger specific reactions from its readers.

3.1.1 A storyworld

A storyworld $\mathbb{W} = (\mathbb{E}, \mathbb{N}, \mathbb{D})$ is made up of the following elements:

- $\mathbb{E}$, the set of possible events,

- $\mathbb{N}$, the set of narrative threads. Each narrative thread $Z \in \mathbb{N}$ consists of a fixed sequence of distinct events chosen from the set $\mathbb{E}$ and an *Importance* value, $\text{Value}(Z)$,

- $\mathbb{D}$, the set of ordered pairs (a, b) of disallowing events where $a, b \in \mathbb{E}$ and a disallows b.

We will be dealing in this research only with *chronological stories*. For a given set of narrative threads, a story will satisfy the chronological constraint if and only if:

> For all pairs of events a and b where a precedes b in the story, if there *are* any narrative threads in which both a and b occur, then in at least *one* of these threads a precedes b.

Using the chronological qualities of narrative threads, we can now define a *fabula* as a chronologically ordered list of n events chosen from $\mathbb{E}$, the set of possible events in the storyworld $\mathbb{W}$. We define a *story* as an ordered list of events chosen from a given *fabula*. In the general case, a story for a fabula can reorder, repeat or skip any of the fabula's events. Because we are only dealing with chronological stories, in our current model, the only allowable difference between a fabula and a story is that some elements of the fabula can be skipped.

We now give two constraints on fabulas for a given storyworld $\mathbb{W} = (\mathbb{E}, \mathbb{N}, \mathbb{D})$. An (optional) completeness relation between the set of events, $\mathbb{E}$, and the set of narrative threads, $\mathbb{N}$, is a useful constraint to include in most storyworlds. It excludes the possibility that an event in a fabula has no narrative thread which contains it, thus avoiding the situation where an event is 'uninterpretable' in storyworld terms.

Concerning $\mathbb{D}$, the set of disallowing event-pairs, $(a, b) \in \mathbb{D}$ means that if a is told, then b is predicted *not* to occur in storyworld $\mathbb{W}$, or we can also say, b *should not* be one of the subsequent events to be told. We will therefore require that no event that is a member of a fabula disallows any other[2].

3.1.2 Telling the story

Telling a story is equivalent to going through an ordered list of events one by one. To 'tell an event in the story', we take the next event from a list of *Untold* events and add it to the tail of a list of *Told* events. Each new told event may have an effect on one or more narrative threads.

Each narrative thread also has a *Conveyed* and *Unconveyed* event list. Events in a thread become *conveyed* in two cases: when they are *told* in a story, or when they are *presumed* to have occurred in the storyworld because in some thread they *precede* an event which has been told (see also 3.1.3).

If the new story event matches a member of the *Unconveyed* list of any narrative thread, then we move it (and all the events before it) into the thread's *Conveyed* list. Additionally, the thread also becomes active (if previously, it was not).

Finally, certain threads may be deactivated by the new story event. Any active narrative thread with an event α in its Unconveyed list will be deactivated if an event γ is told in the story and $(\gamma, \alpha) \in \mathbb{D}$.

For each thread Z, we designate $\text{state}(Z)$ which indicates both whether Z is *active* or *inactive*, which events in Z have been conveyed, and which are as yet unconveyed. Before the story starts to be told, all narrative threads are *inactive* and all their events are in their respective *Unconveyed* lists. *Inactive* threads always have this form and have no effect on suspense calculations. When the last event in a narrative thread Z gets conveyed in the story, we can say: 'Z succeeds'.

3.1.3 Implicated events

An *implicated prior event* is any event in the Conveyed list of some active narrative thread that has *not* been told in the story, but is 'presumed to have occurred'. If α and γ are implicated prior events (in different active threads), and $(\gamma, \alpha) \in \mathbb{D}$, then α is a *conflicted* implicated prior event. In a similar way to implicated *upcoming* events, implicated prior events in different threads may remain in conflict with each other over several story steps. A *conflicted thread* is a thread whose Conveyed list contains at least one conflicted implicated prior event.

An *implicated upcoming event* is just any member of the *Unconveyed* list of an active thread. Such an event is predicted to be told in the current story with a confidence level that depends on the confidence we have in the narrative thread of which it is a member. It is conflicts between implicated upcoming events that create suspense.

---

[2]This is in fact a transposition of the constraints used in the GLAIVE narrative planner (Ware and Young, 2014).

3.1.4 Confirmed and unconfirmed threads

Active threads may be confirmed or unconfirmed. An active *confirmed* thread is any thread whose *Conveyed* list contains at least one told event. Active *unconfirmed* threads with *no told events* are important in our system because they allow for a degree of flexibility in the linking together of different narrative threads. Thus, an inactive thread which shares at least one event with some other active thread can become *active* but *unconfirmed* for the purposes of suspense calculation. For example, a set of threads which detail the different things that someone might do when they get home can under this rule be activated before the story narrates the moment when they open their front door. We can formalise this in the following way:

> An inactive thread Z can become an *active unconfirmed thread* if any of its (unconveyed) events appears in the Unconveyed list of some other *active* confirmed thread (and as long as it has no event that is disallowed by some told event).

Thus, in such a case, an inactive (and thus unconfirmed) thread Z becomes active even though none of its events have yet been told in the story. We can say that 'the confirmation of thread Z is predicted'.

3.2 Modelling the reader's predicted reactions: the suspense algorithm

For each narrative thread, we first determine the following intermediate values: *Imminence, Importance, Foregroundedness*, and *Confidence*. We then combine these values to calculate the suspense contribution from each *individual* narrative thread. Finally we propose a heuristic to combine all these individual narrative thread suspense values and produce the *global* suspense level for each moment in the story.

3.2.1 Imminence

Each active narrative thread Z generates two values for Imminence. Completion Imminence is related to the number of events in Z still to be conveyed for it to be completed or to 'succeed'. Figure 1 shows a thread with a Completion Imminence number of 4.

Interruption Imminence is related to the smallest number of events still to be conveyed in some other thread Y before an event is told which can interrupt Z

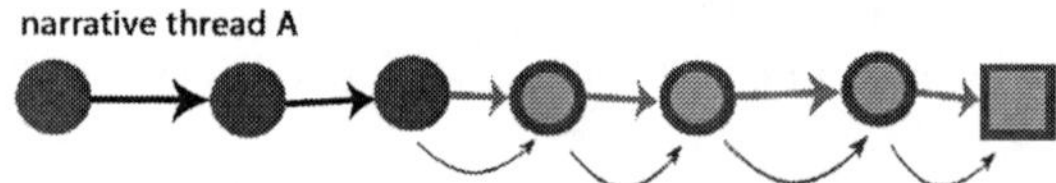

Figure 1: Completion Imminence
Conveyed events are black, *unconveyed* grey.

by disallowing one of its events. In the case where no thread can interrupt Z, the Interruption Imminence of Z is zero. In Figure 2, thread A has an Interruption Imminence number of 3 due to thread B.

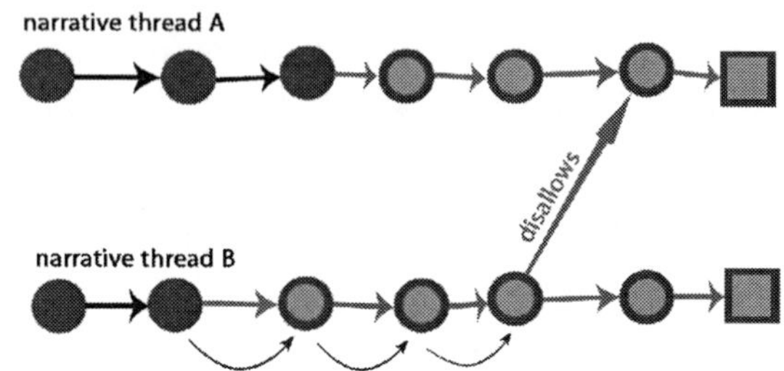

Figure 2: Interruption Imminence

If a *large* number of events must be told for a thread to be completed, the Imminence is *low*, and vice versa. To model this behaviour, we adopted the ratio $1/x$. Also, to enable exploration of the relative effects of Completion and Interruption Imminence on this measure, we used a factor ρ to vary the relative weighting of these two effects.

We can now give a first definition of the Total Imminence$_n(Z)$ of a narrative thread Z after the nth event in the story.

$$\text{Total Imminence } = \rho\frac{1}{H} + (1 - \rho)\frac{1}{R} \quad (1)$$

where H is the number of events to the completion of Z and R is the minimum number of events before an event in some other narrative thread could be told which would disallow some unconveyed event in Z.

Experimentation with the implementation of our model led us to choose $\rho = 0.7$, in effect boosting the relative effect of *Completion imminence*.

3.2.2 Foregroundedness

We use a parameter called *Foregroundedness* to represent how present a given narrative thread is in the reader's mind. This is similar to the concept of *recency* in the psychological literature[3]. The Foregroundedness of each narrative thread changes with each new event in the story and varies between 0 and 1. Threads which *contain* the current story event are considered to be very present and get ascribed the maximum level of Foregroundedness, that is 1.

In our current model, the Foregroundedness of all *other* narrative threads is simply set to decrease at each story step due to the following decay function:

$$\text{decayFunction}(x) = \beta x, \text{where } 0 < \beta < 1 \quad (2)$$

Experimentation led us to use $\beta = 0.88$.

3.2.3 Confidence

Depending on the number of its conflicted prior events, a thread will have varying degrees of *Confidence* as the story progresses. In Figure 3, we show narrative threads *A* and *B* that share an event, the event which has just been told in the story.

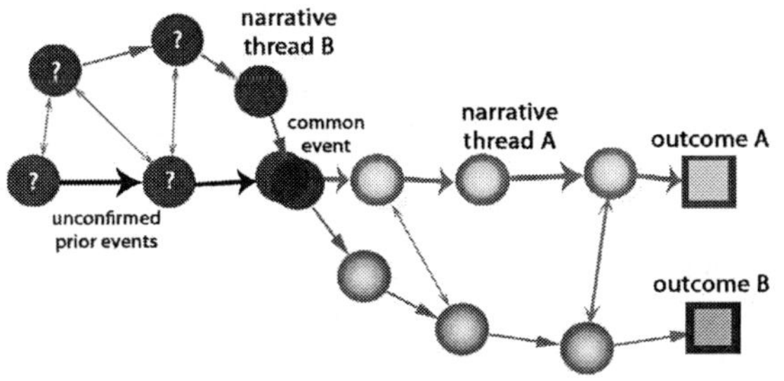

Figure 3: Threads with a shared event. *Implicated prior events* have a question mark. Bidirectional arrows show *mutual disallowing* relations.

We see that two implicated prior events in *A* are in conflict with implicated prior events in *B*. Overall then, thread *A* has *two* conflicted prior events and *one* confirmed event. Narrative threads with many *conflicted* prior events will have a low Confidence level, reducing their potential effect on suspense. We define the $\text{Confidence}_n(Z)$ of a narrative thread Z after the nth event in the story as follows:

$$\text{Confidence} = \frac{1}{\left(1 + \frac{\phi Q}{P}\right)} \text{where } \phi = 1.5 \quad (3)$$

where P is the (non-zero) number of *told events* and Q the number of *conflicted implicated prior events* in Z and $0 \leq \text{Confidence} \leq 1$. Note that

---

[3]See for example, Jones et al. (2006).

if the threads containing events conflicting with Z get deactivated, then Z may come to no longer have *any* conflicted prior events. In such a case, as long as Z has at least *one* confirmed event, its confidence level would reach the maximum value of 1. In other words, if $P > 0, Q = 0$, then Confidence = 1. Empirical work on our implementation led us to use a 'conflicted-to-told ratio' of $\phi = 1.5$.

3.2.4 Importance

We next define $\text{Value}(Z)$ as the measure of the *Importance* of a narrative thread Z.

> $\text{Value}(Z) =$ the predicted degree of positive or negative appraisal of the storyworld situation that the reader would have, were Z to succeed.

In our model, we use the range $(-10, +10)$ for this value, where -10 and $+10$ correspond to events about which the reader is very negative (sad, dissatisfied) and very positive (happy, satisfied) respectively.

3.2.5 Our suspense algorithm

After the telling of the nth story event, we calculate the $\text{Imminence}_n(Z)$, $\text{Foregroundedness}_n(Z)$, $\text{Confidence}_n(Z)$ and $\text{Importance}_n(Z)$ for each active narrative thread Z. For the general case, we assumed that all four variables were independent and chose *multiplication* to combine them and create a measure of the suspense contribution of each narrative thread after story event n:

$$
\begin{aligned}
\text{Suspense}_n(Z) = \quad & \text{Imminence}_n(Z) \\
& \times \text{Importance}_n(Z) \\
& \times \text{Foregroundedness}_n(Z) \\
& \times \text{Confidence}_n(Z)
\end{aligned}
\quad (4)
$$

Once we have the suspense level of each active thread, we assume that the thread with the *highest suspense value* is the one that will be responsible for the story's evoked suspense at that point. We therefore define this thread's suspense value as equivalent to the suspense level of the narrative as a whole at that point in the story.

3.3 Revelatory suspense

As well as the general case of conflict-based suspense described above, our thread-based model allows us to deal with a type of suspense we call *revelatory suspense*, or *curiosity-based* suspense. This kind of suspense is linked to the potential disambiguation of a story event that belongs to several narrative threads. There is suspense about which thread will provide the 'correct' interpretation of the event.

To understand this, we can imagine that in a given storyworld, event δ is present in several different threads. When δ is told in the story, *several* threads become activated as candidates to uniquely 'explain' it. Subsequent story events may disallow some candidate threads. Exactly which thread turns out to be the correct 'explanation' of δ in the storyworld will be determined by the rest of the story. In Figure 3 already mentioned, there is therefore revelatory suspense about which of threads A and B will remain active to explain the shared event. Revelatory suspense is potentially present as soon as the storyworld has threads with shared events.

We can contrast this disambiguation process with Cheong and Young (2015)'s SUSPENSER system, where suspense varies inversely with the number of possible actions of a central protagonist. Similarly, because the decrease in conflicted events boosts the thread's Confidence level, in our model, the suspenseful effect of a thread will go up as ambiguity is reduced. However, in the SUSPENSER system, the suspense depends on the *protagonist's* options, whereas in our model, it depends on the reduced number of options for the *reader*.

4   Evaluation

We implemented our formal model and suspense metric computationally. To test our implementation, we designed and wrote a short suspenseful story, the *Mafia story*, where an important judge drives towards his home with a bomb ticking in his car. The story was inspired by the story used in Brewer and Lichtenstein (1982)'s experiment.[4]

4.1   Original story and storyworld calibration

First we used Zwaan's protocol (Zwaan et al., 1995) to split the story into separate events each time there was a significant change in either time, space, interaction, subject, cause or goal.

The next step was to create the storyworld information. Our model is designed to rely on information in a form which could be generated automatically from real-world data or corpora. The actual generation of this information lay however outside the scope of this research. We therefore created the events, $\mathbb{E}$, the narrative threads $\mathbb{N}$, their importance values $\mathrm{Value}(Z)$ and the set of disallowing events $\mathbb{D}$ by hand, partly modelling our work on the event chains described in Chambers and Jurafsky (2009).

We then conducted an experiment to calibrate the importance values and check the validity of the events in our hand-made narrative threads. The online interface created for the experiment presented a warm-up story and then the *Mafia story* to the participants (N=40 for 33 story steps, 1320 individual judgements), recording step-by-step self-reported suspense ratings using magnitude estimation (see for example Bard et al. (1996)). The raw suspense ratings were converted to normalised z-scores.

Next, we used our suspense algorithm to produce suspense level predictions for all the steps in the Mafia story. Once we had obtained both predicted and experimental values for suspense levels in the Mafia story, we examined their degree of match and mismatch for different sections of the story. We then adjusted some importance values and made minor modifications to some narrative threads.

4.2   Variant of the original story

Next, we created the *Mafia-late* story variant, which differed only from the original (henceforth) *Mafia-early* story in that the vital information suggesting the presence of a bomb in the judge's car is revealed at a later point in the story. Apart from this change in the event order, we strove to create as realistic a story as possible that used exactly the same events.

With the calibrated importance values from the first study, we then used our implementation to create new predictions for this story variant. For comparison, we show these together with the original *Mafia-early* predictions in Figure 4[5].

We then collected human suspense level judgements (N=46 for 31 steps, 1426 individual judge-

---

[4]Both the PROLOG implementation and story variants are available at https://doi.org/10.6084/m9.figshare.5208862.

[5]The *Mafia-late* story has two events fewer than the *Mafia-early* story. To facilitate comparison, we have aligned the *Mafia-late* and *Mafia-early* results so that as far as possible the same events occur at the same point on the x-axis.

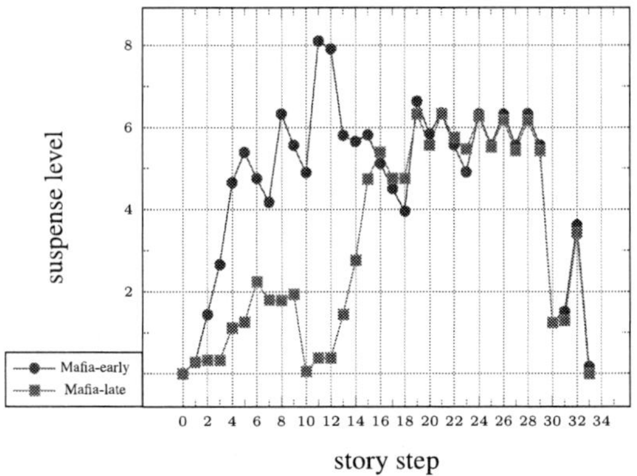

Figure 4: Predicted suspense for the story variants. The Mafia-early and Mafia-late stories mention the bomb at steps 4 and 15 respectively.

ments) for the *Mafia-late* story. We predicted that the suspense levels calculated by our calibrated model for the *Mafia-late* story variant would agree with the step-by-step averaged z-scores of ratings for this story given by a new set of participants.

4.3 Results and Statistical Analysis

The magnitude estimation ratings obtained for each participant were first converted to z-scores. For each story step, we then calculated the mean and standard deviation of the z-scores for all participants which, for comparison, we present together with the predicted values in Figure 5.

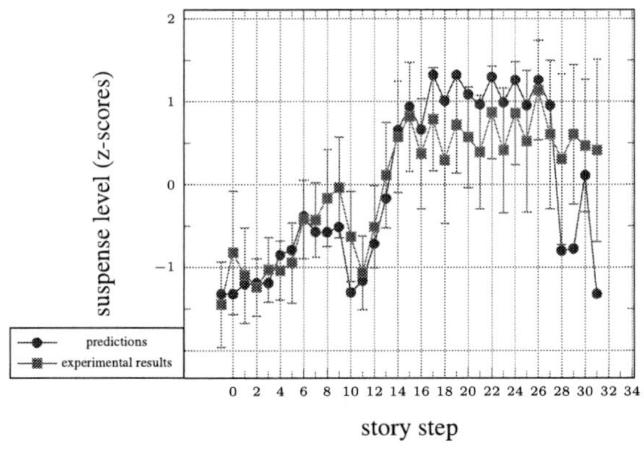

Figure 5: Experimental and predicted suspense for the Mafia-late story

For these two curves, the *Pearson Correlation Coefficient* is 0.8234 and the *Spearman's Rho Coefficient* is 0.794, both values indicating a strong positive correlation. However, the vertical standard deviation values for the z-scores are large, suggesting large variations between participants' responses. To check inter-coder reliability, we performed Fleiss' Kappa test and achieved a value of 0.485. Landis and Koch (1977) interprets this value as signifying *moderate* inter-coder agreement. Levels of agreement as measured by Fisher's test between predicted and experimental suspense levels for our story-variant show *highly significant* success in prediction (P=0.002).

5 Conclusions and further work

We believe that narrative and more specifically suspense is an important topic of study. As discussed in Delatorre et al. (2016), suspense is a pervasive narrative phenomenon that is associated with greater enjoyment and emotional engagement.

In this paper, we describe a formal model of suspense based on four variables: Imminence, Importance, Foregroundedness and Confidence together with a method for measuring suspense as a story unfolds. The model enabled us to predict step-by-step fluctuations in suspensefulness for a short story which correlate well with average self-reported human suspense judgements.

Our method for obtaining suspense judgements was intrusive and may have created some interference with the reading process. Ideally, future research should explore less intrusive methods that use direct physiological measurements of the participants. So far, the search for measurement methods that correspond with perceived suspense has been unsuccessful (Cheong and Young, 2015).

A key difference with previous work is that our model predicts and evaluates suspense at multiple stages *within* the same story. This is why we focussed on variations in one storyworld instead of a large corpora of stories. Indeed, our goal is to create the first model of the suspense evoked as a narrative is being received, and not just a single overall suspense rating. Also, instead of starting from character goals and plans, our basic construct is the narrative thread which is akin to narrative schemas that can be harvested automatically (Chambers and Jurafsky, 2009). In future work, we aim to apply our method to such automatically harvested schemas and extend our model to different storyworlds and story variants.

References

Alexandre C Albuquerque, Cesar Tadeu Pozzer, and Angelo EM Ciarlini. 2011. The usage of the structural-affect theory of stories for narrative generation. In *Games and Digital Entertainment (SBGAMES), 2011 Brazilian Symposium on Games and Digital Entertainment*, pages 250–259. IEEE.

Ellen Gurman Bard, Dan Robertson, and Antonella Sorace. 1996. Magnitude estimation of linguistic acceptability. *Language*, 72(1):32–68.

W.F. Brewer and E.H. Lichtenstein. 1982. Stories are to entertain: A structural-affect theory of stories. *Journal of Pragmatics*, 6(5-6):473–486.

Charles B Callaway and James C Lester. 2002. Narrative prose generation. *Artificial Intelligence*, 139(2):213–252.

Marc Cavazza and Fred Charles. 2005. Dialogue Generation in Character-based Interactive Storytelling. *AAAI, AIIDE2005,*, pages 21–26.

Marc Cavazza, Fred Charles, and Steven J Mead. 2002. Character-Based Interactive Storytelling. *IEEE Intelligent Systems,*, 17(4):17–24.

Nathanael Chambers and Dan Jurafsky. 2009. Unsupervised learning of narrative schemas and their participants. In *Proceedings of the Joint Conference of the 47th Annual Meeting of the ACL and the 4th International Joint Conference on Natural Language Processing of the AFNLP*, volume 2, pages 602–610. Association for Computational Linguistics.

Nathanael Chambers and Daniel Jurafsky. 2010. A database of narrative schemas. In *Proceedings of the 7th International Conference on Language Resources and Evaluation (LREC'10), Valletta, Malta. European Language Resources Association (ELRA)*.

Yun-Gyung Cheong and R Michael Young. 2015. Suspenser: A story generation system for suspense. *IEEE Transactions on Computational Intelligence and AI in Games*, 7(1):39–52.

Eugenio Concepción, Gonzalo Méndez, Pablo Gervás, and Carlos León. 2016. A Challenge Proposal for Narrative Generation Using CNLs. In *9th International Natural Language Generation Conference, INLG*, pages 171–173, Edinburgh, Scotland, UK.

Pablo Delatorre, Barbara Arfe, Pablo Gervás, and Manuel Palomo-Duarte. 2016. A component-based architecture for suspense modelling. *Proceedings of AISB, 3rd International on Computational Creativity (CC2016)*, pages 32–39.

Richard Doust. 2015. *A domain-independent model of suspense in narrative*. Ph.D. thesis, The Open University.

R.J. Gerrig and A.B.I. Bernardo. 1994. Readers as problem-solvers in the experience of suspense. *Poetics*, 22(6):459–472.

Arthur C Graesser, Murray Singer, and Tom Trabasso. 1994. Constructing inferences during narrative text comprehension. *Psychological review*, 101(3):371.

H. Hoeken and M. van Vliet. 2000. Suspense, curiosity, and surprise: How discourse structure influences the affective and cognitive processing of a story. *Poetics*, 27(4):277–286.

Matt Jones, Bradley C Love, and W Todd Maddox. 2006. Recency effects as a window to generalization: separating decisional and perceptual sequential effects in category learning. *Journal of Experimental Psychology: Learning, Memory, and Cognition*, 32(2):316–332.

Walter Kintsch. 1980. Learning from text, levels of comprehension, or: Why anyone would read a story anyway. *Poetics*, 9(1):87–98.

J Richard Landis and Gary G Koch. 1977. The measurement of observer agreement for categorical data. *Biometrics*, 33(1):159–174.

Michael Lebowitz. 1985. Story-telling as planning and learning. *Poetics*, 14(6):483–502.

J.R. Meehan. 1977. Tale-spin, an interactive program that writes stories. In *Proceedings of the Fifth International Joint Conference on Artificial Intelligence (IJCAI), Cambridge, MA, USA*, volume 1, pages 91–98.

Brian O'Neill and Mark Riedl. 2014. Dramatis: A computational model of suspense. In *Proceedings of the 28th AAAI Conference on Artificial Intelligence, Québec City, Québec, Canada*, pages 944–950.

Rafael Pérez y Pérez and Mike Sharples. 2001. Mexica: A computer model of a cognitive account of creative writing. *Journal of Experimental and Theoretical Artificial Intelligence*, 13(2):119–139.

Mark O Riedl and Robert Michael Young. 2010. Narrative planning: balancing plot and character. *Journal of Artificial Intelligence Research*, 39(1):217–268.

Roger C Schank and Robert P Abelson. 1977. *Scripts, plans, goals and understanding: an inquiry into human knowledge structures*. Lawrence Erlbaum Associates Publishers, Hillsdale, NJ.

S.R. Turner. 1992. *MINSTREL: a computer model of creativity and storytelling*. University of California at Los Angeles, CA, USA.

Stephen G Ware and R Michael Young. 2014. Glaive: A state-space narrative planner supporting intentionality and conflict. In *Proceedings of the 10th International Conference on Artificial Intelligence and Interactive Digital Entertainment, AIIDE2014*, pages 80–86, North Carolina State University, Raleigh, NC USA.

Dolf Zillmann, 1996. *The psychology of suspense in dramatic exposition*, pages 199–231. Vorderer, P, Wulff, HJ and Friedrichsen, M.

Rolf A Zwaan, Mark C Langston, and Arthur C Graesser. 1995. The construction of situation models in narrative comprehension: An event-indexing model. *Psychological Science*, 6(5):292–297.

Data-Driven News Generation for Automated Journalism

Leo Leppänen and **Myriam Munezero** and **Mark Granroth-Wilding** and **Hannu Toivonen**
Department of Computer Science
University of Helsinki
Helsinki, Finland

Abstract

Despite increasing amounts of data and ever improving natural language generation techniques, work on automated journalism is still relatively scarce. In this paper, we explore the field and challenges associated with building a journalistic natural language generation system. We present a set of requirements that should guide system design, including transparency, accuracy, modifiability and transferability. Guided by the requirements, we present a data-driven architecture for automated journalism that is largely domain and language independent. We illustrate its practical application in the production of news articles upon a user request about the 2017 Finnish municipal elections in three languages, demonstrating the successfulness of the data-driven, modular approach of the design. We then draw some lessons for future automated journalism.

1 Introduction

Traditional media companies around the world are confronted by many challenges stemming from the radical digital transformation of the publishing industry. This includes the increase in availability of and access to data, on a scale that prohibits journalists from handling it and using it for news reporting. An essential development in this area is the automation of editorial processes, with capabilities to work with scalable, data-driven content (Linden, 2017). Noticeably, while natural language generation (NLG) as a field has made huge strides in recent years, few NLG systems have been developed to meet the journalistic automation needs of newsrooms (Linden, 2017).

In this paper, we investigate the design and development of NLG systems for generating news. Specifically, we aim to address the question: *How should an NLG system be designed to meet journalistic requirements?*

Based on a review of literature on automation of journalistic processes, we identify a set of six requirements (e.g., transparency, accuracy, modifiability) that should be considered when developing NLG systems for the newsroom. We then describe a data-driven architecture that is modular and to a large extent domain and language independent. We demonstrate the applicability of the design by implementing a real-world automatic news generation system[1] that was capable of producing hundreds of thousands of news articles about the Finnish municipal elections that took place in April 2017, in three languages. Responding to user requests, the system was able to generate hyper-localized news, e.g. on how one candidate fared at a single polling station.

2 Related work

Carlson (2015) defines automated journalism as programs or algorithms capable of converting structured data into publishable news stories without human intervention. A recent review (Linden, 2017) of the state of automated journalism found that, while NLG as a field has taken huge strides, these changes have not so far manifested themselves in newsrooms. While many media companies, such as the Associated Press, Forbes, and the New Yorker, have

---

[1] https://www.vaalibotti.fi

Proceedings of The 10th International Natural Language Generation conference, pages 188–197,
Santiago de Compostela, Spain, September 4-7 2017. ©2017 Association for Computational Linguistics

started to automate production of news content due to the demands and pressures of reduced resources in newsrooms, the majority of news generation efforts have been in domains where structured data is abundant and the domains are well understood, such as weather forecasting (Sripada et al., 2003; Goldberg et al., 1994), weather news summaries (Chen and Huang, 2014), finance (Nesterenko, 2016; Mendez-Nunez and Trivino, 2010; Andersen et al., 1992) and sports (Bouayad-Agha et al., 2012; Theune et al., 2001; United Robots, 2017).

As most systems used in newsrooms are built by private companies, details of their architectures and operation are scarce. From what information is available, the majority appear to be heavily rule- and template-based. For instance, the widely used Wordsmith (Automated Insights, nd) enables journalists to easily build templates for whole stories. Homicide Report (Los Angeles Times, 2007) and Quakebot (Los Angeles Times, 2014) by the Los Angeles Times, use templates with simple, hand-written rules (Young and Hermida, 2015). In contrast, Quill (Narrative Science, nd) uses a data ontology, together with user input, to generate text, relying less on application-specific templates. A development manager from a Nordic news company points out: "It is difficult to create generic solutions, [newsrooms] have to start from scratch for each new case, and relatively little is reusable" (Linden, 2017). Newsrooms use primarily whole-story templates and custom software that is not easy to port across domains and produces news in one language.

NLG systems generally range from the classical type of multi-staged architecture described by Reiter and Dale (2000) to end-to-end architectures, such as recurrent neural networks. For reasons discussed below, we here focus on the pipeline architecture common in earlier NLG work (Reiter, 2007; Mahapatra et al., 2016), consisting of document planning, micro planning, and surface realization stages.

3 Requirements for Journalistic Natural Language Generation

An NLG system for news production must try to meet some if not all requirements that are placed on journalists. From literature on journalism, we iden-

tify a set of six requirements that are important in journalism in general and should adequately be reflected in journalistic NLG. These stem from three primary motivations: the journalistic process (requirements for transparency and accuracy), the system itself (modifiability and transferability, fluency) and the application of the system (data availability and topicality).

Transparency While trust in the underlying data is not strictly an NLG problem, trust in the system that transforms the data into an article is a concern. This is related to journalistic transparency and accountability. Transparency has been defined by Deuze (2005) as the "ways in which people both inside and external to journalism are given a chance to monitor, check, criticize and even intervene in the journalistic process." In the case of automated journalism, transparency might include making public the steps taken to process the data, the analysis code, the model or inferences made with it, software used, or data sources (Diakopoulos and Koliska, 2016). This transparency in turn reinforces the goal of media accountability (McBride and Rosenstiel, 2013; Stark and Diakopoulos, 2016). This requirement, however, may be in opposition to the possible business benefits of keeping the algorithmic processes hidden (Diakopoulos, 2015).

For end-to-end (e.g. neural network-based) NLG systems, transparency can become an issue, since their 'black box' design prohibits inspection of the generation process, which makes tracing the decisions of the system often impossible. Traditional pipeline systems are better suited to providing transparency, as they allow the processing to be logged and observed to a high degree and individual decisions to be traced to specific components.

Accuracy Like journalists, a journalistic NLG system must meet basic standards of journalistic accuracy. The produced text must be supported by factual data and should not provide any misleading statements (Wright, 2015; Smiley et al., 2017). It may be appropriate to add a disclaimer on the accuracy or correctness of data (Smiley et al., 2017).

Modifiability and transferability of the system Software modifiability is a desirable characteristic of NLG systems, as well as other software systems

(Oskarsson, 1982). In particular, for journalistic NLG systems, easy modifiability of system components in order to incorporate new knowledge will allow for transferability to other domains. This is especially important for newsrooms that have a declining budget and resources, where it would be desirable for one NLG system to produce news over several domains.

Fluency of output Just as humans, NLG systems are expected to output natural sounding texts that are coherent and fluent (Gatt and Krahmer, 2017). Fluency helps make NLG systems more usable (Oberlander and Brew, 2000), which would help maintain or increase newsrooms' customers' satisfaction.

Data availability Although availability of (structured) data is a requirement for all NLG systems, for newsrooms it affects or dictates a number of areas. For instance, it affects the domains and topicality of generated news and the speed of content production (Dörr, 2016). In addition, the data must be newsworthy and available in good quality for accurate reporting. Frequency of availability further affects how regularly an NLG system can produce news. Thus newsrooms first have to be aware of available data sources before investing in NLG systems.

Topicality of news To ensure user interest, the produced news should be topical, discussing recent events that are relevant to the reader (Dörr, 2016). One way to increase topicality is to focus on locality, covering stories for small, local audiences which currently go unreported (Van Dalen, 2012). This might take the form of tailoring the content, style or even the language of the article (Dörr, 2016; Linden, 2017). Highly localized news needs to be targeted to readers, either by automated means or by allowing the user to interact with the service (Dörr, 2016).

4   A Data-Driven NLG Architecture

We present an architecture for a journalistic NLG system, addressing the above process- and system-oriented requirements. An overview of the design is given in Figure 1. It aims to be modular with respect to application domain, language, and representation of individual facts. We next describe how the design supports these goals, and in the following section describe an instantiation of this architecture.

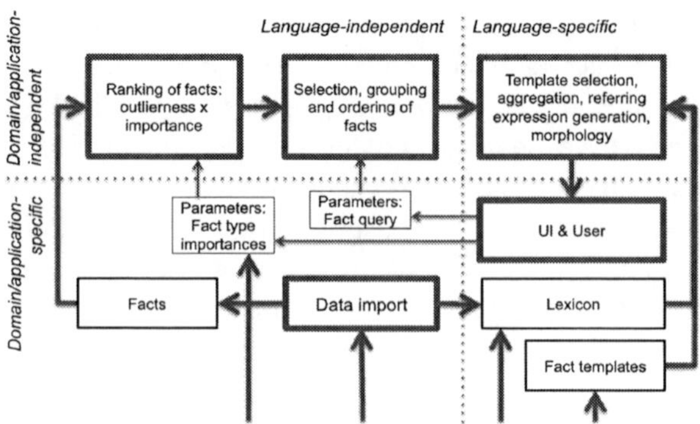

Figure 1: Overview of the architecture. Thick boxes represent software components and thin boxes data structures.

Generic representation of facts Aiming for wide applicability and domain independence, all facts are represented using identical data structures. Inspired by the informal need for news stories to communicate *what* took place, *where* and *who* was involved, we represent a fact as a triplet of *(entity, location, value)*. This minimal set of information could be extended as necessary to cover aspects such as *when*.

To allow explicit handling of different types of entities, locations, and values, each field will in practice need to specify a category or type. For example, the system may distinguish 'person' and 'party' entity types. The triplets thus become sextuplets *(entity_type, entity, location_type, location, value_type, value)*. The domains of types and values are open; the core components are made application independent by allowing such meta-information to be specified later for a particular domain.

Use of Flat Sets of Facts The sets of facts obtained as input data are assumed to have no structure beyond their sextuplet forms. All facts are initially considered equal such that stories could, in principle, express each fact and in any order.

The design uses templates for short natural language expressions. The templates are typically specified at the fact level, which gives the system the possibility to order and aggregate them to create richer sentences or paragraphs.

These assumptions together allow for application independence in core components: there is no need for application-specific data structures or story structures. It is easy to make incremental changes or additions to the possible fact types, adding templates as necessary without changes to the existing ones.

Data-Driven, Application-Independent Fact Ranking Method   A measure of *newsworthiness* is computed for facts as the product of two factors.

Outlierness: evaluates how exceptional a given value is when compared to other values of the same *value_type* within the same location. It is completely data driven and calculated with respect to the interquartile range of the distribution of the values.

Importance: depends on the application and the user. In the design, we parameterize its computation, so that parameters can be expressed for a specific application in a modular fashion and changes to importance can be made at run-time according to the user's interests. The parameters specify weights for different *entity_types*, *location_types* and *value_types*; the overall interestingness is their product.

This parameterization makes it easy to generate highly tailored and localized news, by adjusting parameters in response to, e.g., user profile data or user interaction.

Data-Driven, Application-Independent Selection, Grouping and Ordering of Facts   A document plan is created with application-independent methods using the newsworthiness-ranked list of facts, potentially constrained to a particular location or entity by the user. Since no fixed story structures are assumed, the most newsworthy fact is chosen as the *nucleus* – the most important part (Forsbom, 2005) – of the first paragraph, to which other supporting facts, or *satellites*, are added.

Isolation of Language-Specific Aspects   Language-specific aspects are isolated in a modular fashion. First, each new language requires fact templates and a lexicon, providing language-specific expressions for entities in the input data, for use in referring expression generation (REG). Second, aggregation, REG, and morphology components must be modified for the language; existing tools and methods can often be used. The templates, realization component, and user interface are the only language-dependent parts of the architecture.

Application-Independent Microplanning Based on Fact Templates   The final story is constructed from small templates, typically each representing one fact. The templates are the only application-dependent input to the process aside from the data itself; the proposed design allows microplanning (template selection, aggregation, and REG) and surface realization (morphology) to be performed in an application-independent manner.

5   A Data-Driven Election News System

5.1   Finnish Municipal Elections

The architecture presented above was implemented and applied to the Finnish municipal elections of 2017. These occur every four years and are a large political event in Finland, comparable to presidential and parliamentary elections in voter turnout.

The election results, as released immediately after the first count by the Finnish Ministry of Justice (MoJ), offer ample opportunities for automated news production. The data is made available in a machine-readable format. The files include the results for each party on the level of the whole country, each of the 13 electoral districts, 311 municipalities, and 2,012 polling stations. For each of the 33,316 candidates, the data includes details of their success in their own municipality (each candidate is only votable in a single municipality) and all of the municipality's polling stations.

In total, 727,404 valid combinations of locations and entities (party, candidate, or none) are possible. Each of these combinations corresponds to a distinct topic for a news story, satisfying the goal of producing news at varying levels of locality.

The Finnish context further calls for multilinguality. Finland is bilingual, with both Finnish and Swedish being official languages. This situation, not uncommon in other countries with several official languages or minority languages, exemplifies the modifiability and transferability requirements discussed in Section 3. With international audiences in mind, it was also desirable to produce articles in English.

5.2   Implementation

The design of the election news system follows Figure 1. Software components corresponding to the top part of the figure are generic, and any information about the election domain is provided to them as parameters or data at run-time. The bottom part of the figure is domain and application specific.

Fact Types Components in the lower part of the figure work with specific fact types, while the upper part treats them as abstract symbols. In the election system, fact types consist of three components: the types of the entity, the location and the value concerned. Entity has two types: party and candidate. Location has four types: the whole country, electoral district, municipality, and polling station.

Value types are more varied. They capture numerical information such as the absolute number of votes received by an entity in a location, the percentage of votes received, and the number of seats obtained (distinction A in computing importance, below). For each of these types of information, we also have the corresponding numbers from the previous municipal elections, and thus also the change in each of them (B). In addition, for each of these nine numbers, we can compute ranks, e.g., who received most votes, or who won most new seats (C). We can also compute reverse ranks, which are interesting especially for changes: who lost most votes or most seats. With the addition of some facts providing background information about candidates and the removal of some redundant types, we have a total of 14 value types per candidate and 21 per party, for each applicable location.

Data Import Data is imported from the MoJ online system with custom-built software. Facts are extracted and derived according to the sextuplet schema *(entity_type, entity, location_type, location, value_type, value)*. Slightly over 10 million facts were obtained.

Lexicon Finnish and Swedish lexicons are automatically extracted from the MoJ dataset at data import, providing natural language expressions for entities and locations. In the English lexicon we use the Finnish names. For this application, we had no use for lexical entries of values, which are largely numeric or boolean.

Some additional entries were specified for each language: alternative short names for parties, as well as pronouns and other generic referring expressions used for entities and locations, such as "the party" and "it" for parties.

Templates We use a simple templating language. A template expression consists of (1) a sentence expressed in natural language with slots that can be filled with information from facts, such as "`{entity} won {value} new seats in {location}`", and (2) conditions on what facts the template can be used for, such as "`value_type = nr_of_seats, value > 0`". Slots are optionally associated with cases to instruct the morphological component.

Multi-linguality is supported by allowing expressions in different languages to be specified within the same template. This allows different languages to share the conditions and logic of templates. One template can also have multiple expressions for the same language.

We supplied the system with 100 templates for Finnish, averaging 5.7 tokens; 102 for English, averaging 9.4 tokens; and 70 for Swedish, averaging 8.3 tokens. A separate, smaller set of templates was used for generating headlines. Templates were written by journalists who are native speakers of the respective languages.

Fact Type Importance Value types have a compositional structure, corresponding to distinctions A, B and C in Fact Types above: they talk about the absolute or relative number of votes or of seats (A), of the current or previous election results or the change (B), and possibly about the ranking or reverse ranking of the values (C).

From a news reporting perspective, some of these value types are more important than others. For instance, the number of seats is important because it directly reflects the power of a party, and changes are usually interesting to readers; on the other hand, the absolute numbers of votes are mostly minutiae.

The importance of any given value type is defined as the product of factors reflecting distinctions A, B, and C. This allows developers to tune their view of fact importance in a modular way. In future, the same tuning could also be performed, either directly or implicitly, by the user at generation time.

In the same way, factors are specified for different entity types and location types and included in the importance of a fact. The overall newsworthiness of a fact is the product of the fact type importance and of the outlierness of the value (cf. Section 4).

Fact Selection, Grouping and Ordering To support locality and selectivity of news, the system allows users to make queries based on an entity and a location. The system then extracts only those facts that have the specified location and entity, letting the user specify what is relevant for them.

Among the extracted facts, the system picks the most newsworthy as a nucleus. Satellite facts that share the nucleus' location and entity are then selected, ordered by their newsworthiness. Satellites are added until the paragraph is considered full (in our case, consisting of five facts) or the newsworthiness drops below 20% of the most newsworthy fact in the story.

Nuclei for subsequent paragraphs are selected in order of newsworthiness, but giving preference to facts with a different location or entity to the previous nucleus. Paragraphs are added in this way until either a maximum number (five) is reached or there are no newsworthy candidate nuclei remaining.

Additionally, the system handles context changes. If a fact talks about a new location, this change in context will need to be expressed in the resulting text. If no suitable template that expresses the location exists, the fact is disallowed at that point in the document plan.

Template Selection Realization of facts in a given language is performed by instantiating matching templates to obtain initial sentences. Each fact in the document plan is associated with a template. If there are several choices meeting all requirements, one is picked at random.

Aggregation The aggregation component simply checks whether two subsequent templates contain a common prefix of one or more tokens. If they do, and the first sentence is not already a product of aggregation, the two sentences are joined together by a conjunction (e.g., "and"), with the common prefix removed from the second sentence.

Referring Expression Generator The REG consults the lexicon for names of entities. When an entity is first encountered in the document plan, the full name (e.g. "Kansallinen Kokoomus") is always used. On subsequent encounters, the short name (e.g. "Kokoomus") or the pronoun form is used depending on whether the previously men-

tioned named entity is a different entity or not. Instead of the pronoun form, an equivalent general expression (e.g. "the party") can be also used.

Morphology To produce morphologically correct forms of filled slots, a few simple rules suffice for Swedish and English. Finnish morphology is significantly more complex, with 15 cases. We use Omorfi (Pirinen, 2015) to perform inflection, with some additional rules for uncommon names.

User Interface The system is accessed via a web interface. The user can specify a query via an entity or a location, or both, or neither, and the system produces the corresponding story. After the generated story, headlines linking to random recently read articles are displayed.

5.3 Deployment

The web application was launched at the night of Finnish municipal elections in April 2017 on a website not associated with any news organization or university, at `https://www.vaalibotti.fi`.

During its first day of operation, it saw 398 unique visitors accessing 573 unique news stories. Out of these, 343 (60%) stories were viewed only by one user each. This indicates a need for a high degree of tailoring of news stories in this application.

The system and the reports it generates were made freely available for reuse. At least one Finnish newspaper published stories generated by the system on their website, as-is without any editing.

An example of the system's English language output is presented in Figure 2. A formal quantitative evaluation of the output is outside the scope of this article: we concentrate here on how the constraints set by the journalistic domain influence system design. However, we make some brief, subjective and informal remarks of the produced reports.

Overall, the generated news is expressed in clear language. The few linguistic errors are mostly due to the complexity of Finnish morphology. The texts are fluent, but not always as fluent as human-written texts. There seem to be two main reasons for this: fact ordering sometimes is suboptimal (e.g., the second-last sentence in Figure 2), and the simple aggregation method sometimes combines sentences in unnatural or misleading ways (e.g., the last sentence in Figure 2; "17.5%" refers to current elections, not

Perussuomalaiset drop most seats across Finland

Perussuomalaiset dropped the most council seats throughout Finland and got 3.5 percentage points fewer votes than in the last municipal election. Perussuomalaiset decreased their voter support by the greatest margin and has 769 seats in the new council. The party secured 4th most council seats.

Throughout Finland, Vihreä Liitto secured the largest gain in council seats. The party increased their voter support by the greatest margin and got 3.9 percentage points more votes than in the last municipal election. 12.4% of the vote went to the party. The party got 319440 votes.

Suomen Keskusta lost 254 seats and the second most council seats. The party has 2823 seats in the new council and won the most council seats nationwide in the previous election. The party secured 17.5% of the vote and had 3077 seats in the previous council.

Figure 2: Excerpt of the system's output. The user has requested an overview article on country-wide results without any specific candidate or party as focus.

the previous ones). These results are unsurprising given the simplicity of the corresponding components in our implemented system.

Fact ranking, selection and grouping work well. Stories generated for different queries exhibit a wide range of different story structures and contents, reflecting the corresponding election results in a natural way. The balance of story diversity and quality is in our view striking, given that stories are composed of sentence-long components.

6 Discussion

Reflecting on the requirements for journalistic NLG systems described in Section 3, in this section we discuss, based on our experiences, how the presented data-driven NLG design manages to satisfy them.

Transparency A journalistic NLG system should be transparent at least to the editorial staff of the newsroom, to give it accountability and ensure trust. The simple and modular architecture we described is easier to understand than a large and complex system, not to mention black-box architectures. It allows journalists to observe the generation processes in detail via fine-grained logging, and any decisions made by the system can be explained if needed. For instance, the reason for including any specific fact in the story can be traced back to nucleus-satellite rela-

tions in the story structure and to the weights of fact types given as parameters.

The implemented election system is, however, not as transparent as systems built around a story template with explicit, human-written rules of how to apply the templates. There seems to be a trade-off here between general-purpose architectures and custom-built ones. However, in the long run, it may be easier for journalists to understand the principles of one generic system rather than many manually built ones.

Accuracy The accuracy of a news story is paramount and it is critical that any journalistic NLG system truthfully describes the underlying facts. In the proposed design, it is clear that facts are not modified or faked. Two questions remain: are the "right" facts selected, and are they shown in a manner that accurately conveys their meanings.

Fact selection is based on parameters that adjust fact type importances as well as the data point outlierness. It is possible – or even likely – that the result does not correspond exactly to what a journalist would report, but we can expect disagreement among journalists too on this. The benefit of transparency, and here especially of the explicit fact type importance parameters, is that they can be discussed and modified in the light of a system's behaviour.

Fact templates need to be carefully written to not misrepresent any situation. For example, the template "{party} got the most votes in {location}" can be technically true even when two distinct parties were tied for the most votes received, but the reader would be misled to think that there was one winner.

Aggregation of templates by the simple, surface-level technique our system uses, can also produce misleading sentences. For example, aggregating "X got most votes", and "X got 5 seats in the previous elections" into "X got most votes and 5 seats in the previous elections" changes the meaning of the first text snippet. Avoiding this sort of error requires a more sophisticated aggregation component with, at least, an awareness of syntactic structure – a well-studied task in NLG (Dalianis, 1999).

Modifiability and transferability of system Our case study shows that it is possible to design an NLG system so that the domain-specific, language-specific, and general subsystems are separated. Transferring a system to a new language or a new domain then entails only localized changes in the respective components. In the multilingual election application we added English last, and the additional effort required was minimal, consisting mostly of translating template sentences to English.

The design and its successful implementation in the election system also demonstrate that language- and domain-independent software components can have a central role in content determination and document planning, and any information that is dependent on either the language or the domain is provided as parameters or small extensions.

Modularity also opens up interesting avenues for automation of parts of the architecture that were built by hand in our election system. Modularity with respect to fact types, for instance, allows for the possibility of automated acquisition of templates.

Fluency of output The requirement for the fluency of a journalistic NLG system is dependent on the intended audience and use of the system. If the intention is to produce stories to subscribers (rather than drafts to journalists, or short fragments of text), the system must produce near-flawless text. In a data-driven architecture like ours, it is safer to use simpler sentence structures than more complex, aggregated structures, for reasons discussed above.

Based on our experience, a large balancing act exists between transferability of the system and the fluency of the produced text. Long and complex templates are less transferable to different domains or languages, while general rules end up not producing the kind of idiomatic language one would expect from a human journalist.

Data availability and topicality of news These requirements have more to do with the application domain than the system or processes. Since the focus of this paper is on the latter, we only make some general remarks.

The data source used in this case study was an example of a rarely published but large data set. Other domains might have data sources that produce smaller amounts of data near-constantly. Evaluating whether the amount and frequency of published data is enough in any particular scenario to make automa-

tion worthwhile is an important step when considering potential applications (Reiter and Dale, 2000).

7 Conclusions

Automated journalism is an interesting and under-studied application area for NLG. We examined the needs of journalistic systems and extracted six key requirements. We proposed a data-driven, modular architecture to address the requirements and described its instantiation in news generation for municipal elections.

The architecture allows for the implementation of an NLG pipeline using application- and language-independent software components, parameterized with application-specific information about fact types. The design as well as the election system successfully demonstrate that the data-driven, modular approach is able to select and structure content in an accurate and transparent manner and output fluent text. The high modularity further made it straightforward to produce text in three languages as well as tailor the text based on user request.

In future work, we will conduct a more formal evaluation of the texts output by the election system. Whilst the support for multiple languages validates some of our design decisions, it is also crucial to test the proposed design principles by transferring the system to new domains. Potential improvements during this process include more versatile fact types (e.g., adding a time element to facts) and identifying generic alternatives for the flat fact structure (e.g., stories that have a causal structure), possibly using existing, general formalisms, such as Abstract Meaning Representations. Finally, we aim to apply machine learning to specific components within the architecture, such as automatic acquisition of templates.

Acknowledgements

This work is part of the "Immersive Automation" research project which has received funding from Tekes, the Finnish Funding Agency for Innovation, and from companies.

References

Peggy M Andersen, Philip J Hayes, Alison K Huettner, Linda M Schmandt, Irene B Nirenburg, and Steven P

Weinstein. 1992. Automatic extraction of facts from press releases to generate news stories. In *Proceedings of the third conference on Applied natural language processing*, pages 170–177. Association for Computational Linguistics.

Automated Insights. n.d. Wordsmith. `https://automatedinsights.com/wordsmith`. Accessed: 2017-04-07.

Nadjet Bouayad-Agha, Gerard Casamayor, Simon Mille, and Leo Wanner. 2012. Perspective-oriented generation of football match summaries: Old tasks, new challenges. *ACM Trans. Speech Lang. Process.*, 9(2):1–31.

Matt Carlson. 2015. The robotic reporter: Automated journalism and the redefinition of labor, compositional forms, and journalistic authority. *Digital Journalism*, 3(3):416–431.

Shyi-Ming Chen and Ming-Hung Huang. 2014. Automatically generating the weather news summary based on fuzzy reasoning and ontology techniques. *Information Sciences*, 279:746–763.

Hercules Dalianis. 1999. Aggregation in natural language generation. *Computational Intelligence*, 15(4):384–414.

Mark Deuze. 2005. What is journalism? professional identity and ideology of journalists reconsidered. *Journalism*, 6(4):442–464.

Nicholas Diakopoulos and Michael Koliska. 2016. Algorithmic transparency in the news media. *Digital Journalism*, pages 1–20.

Nicholas Diakopoulos. 2015. Algorithmic accountability: Journalistic investigation of computational power structures. *Digital Journalism*, 3(3):398–415.

Konstantin Nicholas Dörr. 2016. Mapping the field of algorithmic journalism. *Digital Journalism*, 4(6):700–722.

Eva Forsbom. 2005. Rhetorical structure theory in natural language generation. *Téléchargé le*, 10(08):2008.

Albert Gatt and Emiel Krahmer. 2017. Survey of the state of the art in natural language generation: Core tasks, applications and evaluation. *arXiv preprint arXiv:1703.09902*.

Eli Goldberg, Norbert Driedger, and Richard I Kittredge. 1994. Using natural-language processing to produce weather forecasts. *IEEE Expert*, 9(2):45–53.

Carl-Gustav Linden. 2017. Decades of automation in the newsroom: Why are there still so many jobs in journalism? *Digital Journalism*, 5(2):123–140.

Los Angeles Times. 2007. Homicide report. `http://homicide.latimes.com/`. Accessed: 2017-04-07.

Los Angeles Times. 2014. Quakebot. `http://www.latimes.com/local/lanow/earthquake-27-quake-strikes-near-westwood-california-rdivor-story.html`. Accessed: 2017-04-07.

Joy Mahapatra, Sudip Kumar Naskar, and Sivaji Bandyopadhyay. 2016. Statistical natural language generation from tabular non-textual data. In *INLG*, pages 143–152.

Kelly McBride and Tom Rosenstiel. 2013. *The new ethics of journalism: Principles for the 21st century.* CQ Press.

Sheila Mendez-Nunez and Gracian Trivino. 2010. Combining semantic web technologies and computational theory of perceptions for text generation in financial analysis. In *Fuzzy systems (fuzz), 2010 IEEE international conference on*, pages 1–8. IEEE.

Narrative Science. n.d. Quill. `http://www.quillcontent.com/`. Accessed: 2017-04-07.

Liubov Nesterenko. 2016. Building a system for stock news generation in Russian. In C Gardent and A Gangemi, editors, *Proc. of the 2nd International Workshop on Natural Language Generation and the Semantic Web (WebNLG 2016)*, pages 37–40, Stroudsburg, PA. ACL.

Jon Oberlander and Chris Brew. 2000. Stochastic text generation. *Philosophical Transactions of the Royal Society of London A: Mathematical, Physical and Engineering Sciences*, 358(1769):1373–1387.

Östen Oskarsson. 1982. *Mechanisms of modifiability in large software systems.* Linkping Studies in Science and Technology. Dissertations,0345-7524; 77.

Tommi A Pirinen. 2015. Omorfi free and open source morphological lexical database for Finnish. In *Proceedings of the 20th Nordic Conference of Computational Linguistics, NODALIDA 2015, May 11-13, 2015, Vilnius, Lithuania*, number 109, pages 313–315. Linköping University Electronic Press.

Ehud Reiter and Robert Dale. 2000. *Building natural language generation systems.* Studies in Natural Language Processing. Cambridge University Press.

Ehud Reiter. 2007. An architecture for data-to-text systems. In *Proceedings of the Eleventh European Workshop on Natural Language Generation*, pages 97–104. Association for Computational Linguistics.

Charese Smiley, Frank Schilder, Vassilis Plachouras, and Jochen L Leidner. 2017. Say the right thing right: Ethics issues in natural language generation systems. *EACL 2017*, page 103.

Somayajulu Sripada, Ehud Reiter, and Ian Davy. 2003. SumTime-Mousam: Configurable marine weather forecast generator. *Expert Update*, 6(3):4–10.

Jennifer A Stark and Nicholas Diakopoulos. 2016. Towards editorial transparency in computational journalism. *Computation + Journalism Symposium*.

Mariët Theune, Esther Klabbers, Jan-Roelof de Pijper, Emiel Krahmer, and Jan Odijk. 2001. From data to speech: a general approach. *Natural Language Engineering*, 7(01):47–86.

United Robots. 2017. Rosalinda for sports. retrieved on 24th April 2017, `http://www.unitedrobots.se/produkter-1/`.

Arjen Van Dalen. 2012. The algorithms behind the headlines: How machine-written news redefines the core skills of human journalists. *Journalism Practice*, 6(5-6):648–658.

Alex Wright. 2015. Algorithmic authors. *Communications of the ACM*, 58(11):12–14.

Mary Lynn Young and Alfred Hermida. 2015. From Mr. and Mrs. outlier to central tendencies: Computational journalism and crime reporting at the Los Angeles Times. *Digital Journalism*, 3(3):381–397.

Data Augmentation for Visual Question Answering

Kushal Kafle, Mohammed Yousefhussien, and **Christopher Kanan**[*]
Rochester Institute of Technology
{kk6055, mxy7332, kanan}@rit.edu

Abstract

Data augmentation is widely used to train deep neural networks for image classification tasks. Simply flipping images can help learning by increasing the number of training images by a factor of two. However, data augmentation in natural language processing is much less studied. Here, we describe two methods for data augmentation for Visual Question Answering (VQA). The first uses existing semantic annotations to generate new questions. The second method is a generative approach using recurrent neural networks. Experiments show the proposed schemes improve performance of baseline and state-of-the-art VQA algorithms.

1 Introduction

In recent years, both computer vision and natural language processing (NLP) have made enormous progress on many problems using deep learning. Visual question answering (VQA) is a problem that fuses computer vision and NLP to build upon these successes. In VQA, an algorithm is given an image and a question about the image, and it predicts the answer to the question (Malinowski and Fritz, 2014; Antol et al., 2015). Although progress has been rapid, there is still a significant gap between the performance of the best VQA systems and humans. For example, on the open-ended 'The VQA Dataset' that uses real images, the best systems in 2016 are at around 65% accuracy (e.g., Fukui et al. (2016)) compared to 83% for humans (Antol et al., 2015). Analysis of VQA algorithm performance as a function of the amount of training data show that existing algorithms would benefit greatly from more training data (Kafle and

Figure 1: We explore two methods for data augmentation for VQA. The Template method uses semantic image annotations. The LSTM method is a generative approach. For this image, the original questions are: 1) 'Where are the people sitting at?' 2) 'How many orange cups are there?' and 3) 'What is the coffee table made of?' The Template augmentation method generates the questions (4 of 13 total): 1) 'Is there a person in the picture?' 2) 'Is there a couch?' 3) 'How many people are there?' and 4) 'What room is this?' The LSTM method generates the questions: 1) 'How many people are there?' 2) 'How many people are in the picture?' and 3) 'Are they playing a video game?'

Kanan, 2017). One way to address this would be to annotate additional questions about images, but this is time-consuming and expensive. Data augmentation is a much cheaper alternative.

Data augmentation is generating new training data from existing examples. In this paper, we explore two data augmentation methods for generating new question-answer (QA) pairs for images. The first method uses existing semantic annotations and templates to generate QA pairs, similar to the method in Kafle and Kanan (2017). The second method is a generative approach using a recurrent neural network (RNN). Fig. 1 shows an example image from 'The VQA Dataset' along with the original questions and the questions generated using our methods. Our methods improve the variety and the number of questions for the image. We evaluate how well each augmentation method performs on two VQA datasets. Our results show that augmentation increases performance for both datasets.

---

[*]Corresponding author.

198

Proceedings of The 10th International Natural Language Generation conference, pages 198–202,
Santiago de Compostela, Spain, September 4-7 2017. ©2017 Association for Computational Linguistics

1.1 Related Work

For supervised computer vision problems, e.g., image recognition, labels are scarcer than images. This is especially a problem with deep convolutional neural networks (CNNs) that have millions of parameters. Although more human labeled data would be ideal, it is easier to exploit the training dataset to generate new examples. For image classification, common ways to exploit training images to create more labeled examples include mirror reflection, random crops etc. Many of these methods were used in training the seminal AlexNet (Krizhevsky et al., 2012), which increased the training data by more than ten folds and produced relative improvement of over 4% for image classification.

Compared to vision, where augmentation is common, little work has been done on augmenting text for classification problems. A notable exception is Zhang et al. (2015), where a thesaurus was used to replace synonymous words to create more training data for text classification. However, this augmentation produced little improvement and sometimes even hurt performance. The authors' argued that because large quantities of real data are available, models generalize properly without augmentation. Although *training* using augmented text data is rare, generating new questions about images has been studied. The COCO-QA dataset (Ren et al., 2015) for VQA was created by parsing COCO captions with a syntactic parser, and then used this to create QA pairs for four kinds of questions using hand-crafted rules. However, due to inability of the algorithm to cope with complex sentence structures, a significant portion of COCO-QA questions have grammatical errors or are oddly phrased. Visual question generation was also studied in (Mostafazadeh et al., 2016), with an emphasis on generating questions about images that are beyond the literal visual content of the image. They endeavored to avoid simple questions such as counting and color, which were emphasized in COCO-QA. Unlike our work, their objective was not data augmentation and they did not try to answer the generated questions.

1.2 Datasets and Algorithms for VQA

We conduct experiments on two of the most popular VQA datasets: 'The VQA Dataset' (Antol et al., 2015) and COCO-QA (Ren et al., 2015). 'The VQA Dataset' is currently the most popular VQA dataset and it contains both synthetic and real-world images. The real-world images are from the COCO dataset (Lin et al., 2014). All questions were generated by human annotators. We refer to this portion as COCO-VQA, and use it for our experiments. COCO-QA (Ren et al., 2015) also uses images from COCO, with the questions generated by an NLP algorithm that uses COCO's captions. All questions belong to four categories: object, number, color, and location.

Many algorithms have been proposed for VQA. Some notable formulations include attention based methods (Yang et al., 2016; Xiong et al., 2016; Lu et al., 2016; Fukui et al., 2016), Bayesian frameworks (Kafle and Kanan, 2016; Malinowski and Fritz, 2014), and compositional approaches (Andreas et al., 2016a,b). Detailed reviews of existing methods can be found in Kafle and Kanan (2017) and Wu et al. (2016). However, simpler models such as linear classifiers and multilayer perceptrons (MLPs) perform only slightly worse on many VQA datasets. These baseline methods predict the answer using a vector of image features concatenated to a vector of question features (Ren et al., 2015; Zhou et al., 2015; Kafle and Kanan, 2016). We use the MLP model to conduct the bulk of the experiments, but we show that the proposed method is also effective on more sophisticated VQA systems like multimodal compact bilinear pooling (MCB) (Fukui et al., 2016).

2 Methods for Data Augmentation

The impact of using data augmentation to improve VQA has not been studied. We propose two methods for generating QA pairs about images: 1) a template based generation method that uses image annotations and 2) a long short term memory (LSTM) based language model. The number of questions generated using both methods are shown in Table 1.

2.1 Template Augmentation Method

The template data augmentation method uses the semantic segmentation annotations in COCO to generate new QA pairs. COCO contains detailed segmentation annotations with labels for 80 objects typically found in the images. We synthesize four kinds of questions from the COCO annotations: yes/no, counting, object recognition, scene, activity and sport recognition.

Yes/No Questions: First, we make a list of the

Table 1: Number of questions in COCO-VQA compared to the number generated using the LSTM and template methods.

Type	COCO-VQA(Antol et al., 2015)	LSTM	Template	Total Augmentation
Yes/No	140,780 (38.0%)	31,595 (29.2%)	1,023,594 (86.2%)	1,055,189 (81.5%)
Number	45,813 (12.4%)	2,727 (2.52%)	60,547 (5.1%)	63,274 (4.8%)
Other	183,286 (49.6%)	73,617 (68.2%)	102,617 (8.6%)	176,234 (13.6%)
Total	369,879	107,939	1,186,758	**1,294,697**

COCO objects present in an image. If the object has an area greater than 2000 pixels, we can generate an object presence question, e.g., 'Is there a OBJECT in the picture?' with 'yes' as the answer. We use 10 templates to allow some variation in phrasing. For example, 'Is there a person in the image?' and 'Are there any people in the photo?' are variations of the same question. To avoid question imbalance, we ask equal number of 'no' questions about the objects that are absent from the image.

Counting Questions: To make counting questions, we count the number of separate annotations of all the objects of a particular category that have an area greater than 2000 pixels, and ask 12 variations of a counting question template.

Object Recognition Questions: Object recognition questions such as 'What is in the picture?' can be ambiguous because multiple objects may be present. So, we ask questions about COCO 'super-categories' (e.g., 'food,' 'furniture,' 'vehicle,' etc.) to specify the type of object in the question. However, ambiguity may persist if there are multiple objects belonging to same supercategory. For example, 'What vehicles are shown in the photo?' becomes ambiguous if both 'cars' and 'trucks' are present. So, we ensure only a single object of a supercategory is present before asking a recognition question. We use 12 variations of 'What SUPERCATEGORY is in the image?'

Scene and Activity Questions: If a object in an image belongs to the COCO supercategory *indoor* or *outdoor*, we generate questions such as 'Is this indoor or outdoors?' Similarly, we ask about different rooms in the house by identifying the common objects in the room. For example, if there are least two common kitchen appliances in the picture(e.g., toaster, microwave, etc.), then we infer the room is a kitchen and ask 'What room is this?' with 'kitchen' as the answer. We employ similar strategies for 'living room' and 'bathroom.' We used six variations for 'indoor/outdoor' questions and four variations for room classification questions. For sports, we check if any sports equipment is present in the image and generate a question about the type of sport being depicted in the image. We use four variations of questions to ask about each of the six common sports activities.

2.2 LSTM Augmentation Method

One major issues with our template-based augmentation method is that the questions are rigid and may not closely resemble the way questions are typically posed in the VQA dataset. To address this, we train a stacked LSTM that generates questions about images. The network consists of two LSTM layers each with 1000 hidden units followed by two fully connected layers, with 7000 units each, which is the size of our vocabulary constructed by tokening training questions into individual words. The first fully connected layer has a ReLU activation function, while the second layer has the 7000-way softmax. The output question is produced one word at a time until the ¡end-of-question¿ token. The network is trained using the COCO-VQA training data. During the generation process, we start by passing the ¡start-question¿ token concatenated with the image features. To predict the next word, we sample from a multinomial distribution characterized by the prediction probabilities. Sometimes such sampling generates questions unrelated to image content. To compensate for this, we repeat the sampling for every word multiple times and pick the word occurring most frequently. We then generate 30 initial questions per image, and only retain the 3 most frequent questions. Any generated question that already exists in the original dataset is removed.

We use the MLP VQA method described in Sec. 3 to create answers for the generated questions, but it is trained without augmented data. Used alone, this can produce many incorrect answers. To mitigate this problem, we tried to identify the kinds of questions the MLP VQA algo-

COCO-VQA: What instrument does the person who lives here play? **A:** Guitar

COCO-QA: What is in front of a computer looking at the screen as if browsing? **A:** Cat

Figure 2: Examples of questions and predicted answers from COCO-VQA and COCO-QA datasets. The results are from model trained jointly on original and temple based QA pairs.

rithm tends to get correct. To do this, we use k-means to cluster the training question features concatenated to a one-hot vector with the answer for each question type ($k = 25$). We assign each validation QA pair to one of these clusters and compute each cluster's accuracy. QA pairs assigned to clusters that have a validation accuracy of less than 70% are removed from the dataset.

3 Experiments And Results

First, we use the simple MLP baseline model used in Kafle and Kanan (2016) to assess the two data augmentation methods. Kafle and Kanan (2016) showed that MLP worked well across multiple datasets despite its simplicity. The MLP model treats VQA as a classification problem with concatenated image and question features given to the model as features and answers as categories. CNN features from ResNet-152 (He et al., 2016) and the skip-thought vectors (Kiros et al., 2015) are used as image and question features respectively. We evaluate the MLP model on COCO-VQA and COCO-QA datasets. For COCO-QA, we excluded all the augmented QA pairs derived from COCO's validation images during training, as the test portion of COCO-QA contains questions for these images. Table 2 shows the results for the MLP model when trained with and without augmentation. Some examples for the model trained with augmentation are are shown in Fig. 2.

Next, to demonstrate that the data augmentation scheme also helps improve more complex models, we train the state-of-the-art MCB model with attention (MCB+Att.+GloVe) (Fukui et al., 2016) with the template augmentation and compare the accuracy when the same model trained only on the COCO-VQA dataset (Table 3).

Table 2: Results on COCO-VQA (test-dev) and COCO-QA datasets for the MLP model trained with and without augmentation.

Method	COCO-QA	COCO-VQA
MLP (Our Baseline)	60.80	58.65
MLP (LSTM Augmentation)	61.31	58.11
MLP (Template Augmentation)	62.21	**59.61**
MLP (Joint Augmentation)	**62.28**	58.45

Table 3: Results on COCO-VQA (test-dev) for the MCB+Att.+GloVe model trained with and without template augmentation.

Method	COCO-VQA
MCB+Att.+GloVe	64.7
MCB+Att.+GloVe (Template Aug.)	**65.28**

4 Discussion and Conclusion

Referring to Table 2, we can see that both forms of augmentation improved accuracy on COCO-QA compared to the baseline, and the template-based approach worked better than LSTM. For COCO-VQA, the template-based augmentation helped considerably, producing a relative increase of 1.6% compared to when it was not used. We did not observe an improvement from using the LSTM method, perhaps due to label noise. While we tried to mitigate label noise by rejecting QA pairs that were likely to be wrong, this was not sufficient. We are exploring alternative training methods that are robust to label noise (e.g., Reed et al. (2014)) to help improve results using LSTM.

Additionally, we also evaluated which types of questions benefit the most from data augmentation. For the MLP model trained on COCO-VQA with the template augmentation, counting category answer is improved the most (1.74%), followed by others (1.01%), and yes/no (0.7%).

The results are promising and demonstrate that VQA algorithms can benefit from data augmentation, even for hard question types like counting. Furthermore, there is a lot of room for expansion in both the LSTM and the template based methods to produce a larger number and variety of questions. Template augmentation worked best in our experiments, but if we can control for label noise, the LSTM method can be more flexible than the template method, and could be used to generate virtually unlimited amount of training data using images from the Internet.

References

Jacob Andreas, Marcus Rohrbach, Trevor Darrell, and Dan Klein. 2016a. Deep compositional question answering with neural module networks. In *The IEEE Conference on Computer Vision and Pattern Recognition (CVPR)*.

Jacob Andreas, Marcus Rohrbach, Trevor Darrell, and Dan Klein. 2016b. Learning to compose neural networks for question answering. In *Annual Meeting of the North American Chapter of the Association for Computational Linguistics (NAACL)*.

Stanislaw Antol, Aishwarya Agrawal, Jiasen Lu, Margaret Mitchell, Dhruv Batra, C. Lawrence Zitnick, and Devi Parikh. 2015. VQA: Visual question answering. In *The IEEE International Conference on Computer Vision (ICCV)*.

Akira Fukui, Dong Huk Park, Daylen Yang, Anna Rohrbach, Trevor Darrell, and Marcus Rohrbach. 2016. Multimodal compact bilinear pooling for visual question answering and visual grounding. In *Conference on Empirical Methods on Natural Language Processing (EMNLP)*.

Kaiming He, Xiangyu Zhang, Shaoqing Ren, and Jian Sun. 2016. Deep residual learning for image recognition. In *The IEEE Conference on Computer Vision and Pattern Recognition (CVPR)*.

Kushal Kafle and Christopher Kanan. 2016. Answer-type prediction for visual question answering. In *The IEEE Conference on Computer Vision and Pattern Recognition (CVPR)*.

Kushal Kafle and Christopher Kanan. 2017. Visual question answering: Datasets, algorithms, and future challenges. *Computer Vision and Image Understanding* .

Ryan Kiros, Yukun Zhu, Ruslan Salakhutdinov, Richard S Zemel, Antonio Torralba, Raquel Urtasun, and Sanja Fidler. 2015. Skip-thought vectors. In *Advances in Neural Information Processing Systems (NIPS)*.

Alex Krizhevsky, Ilya Sutskever, and Geoffrey E Hinton. 2012. Imagenet classification with deep convolutional neural networks. In *Advances in Neural Information Processing Systems (NIPS)*.

Tsung-Yi Lin, Michael Maire, Serge Belongie, James Hays, Pietro Perona, Deva Ramanan, Piotr Dollár, and C Lawrence Zitnick. 2014. Microsoft coco: Common objects in context. In *European Conference on Computer Vision (ECCV)*.

Jiasen Lu, Jianwei Yang, Dhruv Batra, and Devi Parikh. 2016. Hierarchical question-image co-attention for visual question answering. In *Advances in Neural Information Processing Systems (NIPS)*.

Mateusz Malinowski and Mario Fritz. 2014. A multi-world approach to question answering about real-world scenes based on uncertain input. In *Advances in Neural Information Processing Systems (NIPS)*.

Nasrin Mostafazadeh, Ishan Misra, Jacob Devlin, Larry Zitnick, Margaret Mitchell, Xiaodong He, and Lucy Vanderwende. 2016. Generating natural questions about an image. *CoRR* abs/1603.06059.

Scott E. Reed, Honglak Lee, Dragomir Anguelov, Christian Szegedy, Dumitru Erhan, and Andrew Rabinovich. 2014. Training deep neural networks on noisy labels with bootstrapping. *CoRR* abs/1412.6596.

Mengye Ren, Ryan Kiros, and Richard Zemel. 2015. Exploring models and data for image question answering. In *Advances in Neural Information Processing Systems (NIPS)*.

Qi Wu, Damien Teney, Peng Wang, Chunhua Shen, Anthony Dick, and Anton van den Hengel. 2016. Visual question answering: A survey of methods and datasets. *arXiv preprint arXiv:1607.05910* .

Caiming Xiong, Stephen Merity, and Richard Socher. 2016. Dynamic memory networks for visual and textual question answering. In *International Conference on Machine Learning (ICML)*.

Zichao Yang, Xiaodong He, Jianfeng Gao, Li Deng, and Alexander J. Smola. 2016. Stacked attention networks for image question answering. In *The IEEE Conference on Computer Vision and Pattern Recognition (CVPR)*.

Xiang Zhang, Junbo Zhao, and Yann LeCun. 2015. Character-level convolutional networks for text classification. In *Advances in Neural Information Processing Systems (NIPS)*.

Bolei Zhou, Yuandong Tian, Sainbayar Sukhbaatar, Arthur Szlam, and Rob Fergus. 2015. Simple baseline for visual question answering. *arXiv preprint arXiv:1512.02167* .

Personalized Questions, Answers and Grammars: Aiding the Search for Relevant Web Information

Marta Gatius
Computer Science Department, Technical University of Catalonia,
Jordi Girona Salgado, 1-3, 08034 Barcelona, Spain
gatius@cs.upc.edu

Abstract

This work is about guiding the user web search by generating most relevant questions, answers and grammars from web documents. The proposed approach is based on the representation of the main domain concepts as a set of attributes and relating these attributes to the user models and to a syntactico-semantic taxonomy, that describes the general relationships between conceptual and linguistic knowledge. This taxonomy is used for both generating questions and answers and also for extracting data from the web. The data extracted from the web documents is represented as instances of the domain concepts. Questions, answers and grammars are generated from these instances.

1 Introduction

The large amount of data and services available on the web has increased the need of tools that may assist the different types of users when looking for information. The approach described in this paper to guide the user search consists of providing the most relevant data in a particular domain as a set of questions and their corresponding answers.

Presenting the main questions (and their answers) could be valuable in different types of scenarios, especially when the information to search is voluminous and/or when the user is looking for relevant data that has to be understood perfectly. For example, including most relevant questions and answers in the web description of academic courses could result useful for students, as described in the next sections.

The generation of personalized questions for a specific domain involves reasoning skills as well

as domain and linguistic knowledge. To reduce the human effort needed in this process, this work proposes a general organization of the conceptual and linguistic knowledge involved, thus limiting the specific data that has to be incorporated for a new domain. In this proposal, the main domain concepts are described by a set of attributes and those attributes are related to user models and to a syntactico-semantic taxonomy, which represents the general relationships between conceptual and linguistic knowledge. This taxonomy, described in a previous work (Gatius, 2013), was defined following (Bateman et al, 1994). It is used for generating questions, answers and grammar and also for extracting data from the web.

This work is focused on the generation of questions and answers from (semi)structured web documents describing particular cases of general concepts (i.e., university courses and types of foods). Information from these documents can be automatically extracted and represented as instances of the general concepts, previously described by the expert. Questions, answers and grammars can be automatically generated from the resulting instances.

The next section gives an overview of the approach proposed together with its adaptation in several languages (English, Catalan and Spanish) for two different domains: university courses and cultural events. The Section 3 describes the implementation and evaluation done. Finally, related work and discussion is given in the last section

2 Approach Overview

The approach proposed to generate personalized questions, answers and grammars from web documents in a particular domain is based in a separated representation of the different types of

Proceedings of The 10th International Natural Language Generation conference, pages 203–207,
Santiago de Compostela, Spain, September 4-7 2017. ©2017 Association for Computational Linguistics

knowledge involved. This approach consists of the following five steps:

1. Representing the most relevant domain concepts as a set of attributes.
2. Relating the attributes to the taxonomy.
3. Relating the attributes to the users groups.
4. Extracting the web data.
5. Generating the personalized questions and answers (or grammars).

The first three steps, studied in a previous work (Gatius, 2015), have to be done by a human expert. First, the main concepts have to be defined by a set of attributes and these attributes by *facets*, which describe details such as the cardinality.

In a second step, the conceptual attributes have to be associated with the classes in the syntactico-semantic taxonomy, defined in previous work. These classes are associated with the linguistic structures involved in the questions and answers about the conceptual attributes. They can be easily adapted to new languages.

Figure 1 shows a partial description of the concepts involved in this scenario: **Course** and **Exam**. The course description is represented by a set of attributes. Each of the course exam is represented by an attribute, which value is an instance of the concept **Exam**. As can be seen in the Figure, the conceptual attributes have been associated with the corresponding syntactico-semantic classes. For example, the attributes **code** and **content** are related to the class **of**, corresponding to general descriptions and there are others attributes related to its subclasses, describing more precise information: **of_quantity** (i.e., the **credits**, **assessment** and **weight**), **of_time**, **of_date** and **of_place**.

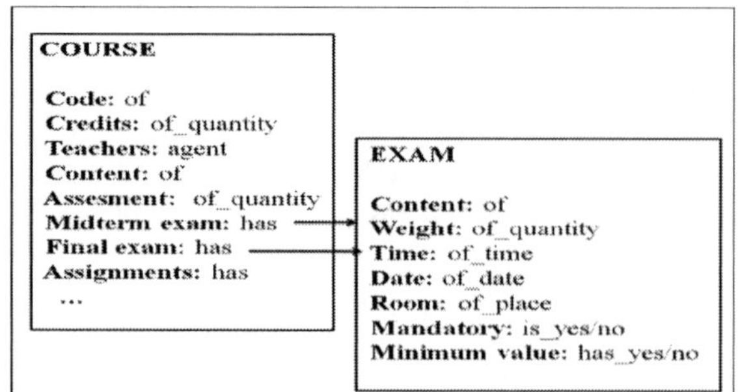

Figure 1: The main concepts describing a course

User models can also be incorporated by classifying users in groups and associating each conceptual attribute with the group interested on it. In several scenarios, stereotypes could also be related to different values of the attribute. For example, in the nutrition domain, the values of the attributes describing the number of calories and physical activity needed daily are different for each group (women, men and children).

In the academic scenario two user groups can be distinguished: students and teachers. The attributes describing the course are considered relevant for the two groups, except for the attribute **Code**, only interesting for teachers.

The two last steps proposed can be done automatically, although human supervision of the data obtained is needed. First, from the web documents selected, the appropriate data is extracted and represented as instances of the domain concepts. The values of the conceptual attributes are obtained using general rules defined for that purpose. Finally, the questions and answers (or grammars) are generated from the conceptual instances.

2.1 Personalized Questions and Answers

Most university web sites include clear and detailed descriptions about their courses. However, frequently, students ask teachers about this information, especially that related to the exams. For this reason, including relevant questions and their answers in the course description could help.

The extraction of the data in this domain requires a limited human effort, because the descriptions of university courses usually include similar content and are presented in a (semi)structured form. Several web documents from different faculties in the same university have been analyzed.

The web description of the courses analyzed, is placed in separated documents, with different formats: The particular data related to the exams (date, time and room) is presented by tables while more general information is in textual form.

The data related to a particular course is extracted from the web documents and represented as instances of the concepts **Course** and **Exam**. For this purpose, domain independent rules that use the facets describing the attributes (type, related terms and cardinality) are used. The data extracted is represented as the values of the instance attributes.

The general rule for obtaining the value of an attribute from a textual document is: *"If the attribute related terms (or synonyms) are found, then extract the **context** words that correspond to the type of the attribute"*.

In this rule, **context** is a variable that indicates the maximum number of words before or after the attribute terms that have to be considered. Its value is obtained by analyzing the domain documents.

A condition to this general rule has been added to extract all possible values of the attributes, considering its cardinality.

Using this rule, the data describing the final exam of a particular course is obtained from the document giving general data and represented as the instance shown in Figure 2 (which belongs to concept **Exam** in Figure 1).

FINAL EXAM
Content: all units
Weight : 40%
Date: June
Mandatory: Yes
Minimun value: No

Figure 2: Representation of data extracted as an instance

> 1. **Which is the content of the final exam?**
>   **The content of the final exam is all units.**
> 2. **How much is the final exam worth?**
>   **The final exam is worth 40% (of the final mark).**
> 3. **When is the final exam?**
>   **The final exam is on June.**
> 4. **At what time is the final exam?**
>   **The place will be detailed in the web course.**
> 5. **Where is the final exam?**
>   **The place will be detailed in the web course.**
> 6. **Is the final exam compulsory?**
>   **Yes, it is.**
> 7. **Is there a minimum grade of the final exam?**
>   **No, there is not.**

Figure 3: Generated questions and answers about the exam

More specific details about the exam have to be obtained from a separated document, where the date, time and room for the exams of several courses in the faculty are presented in a table. For this type of document a new rule is used:

If one of the course identifiers is found in a row then extract the next words in the row that correspond to the type of the attribute.

Figure 3 shows examples of the generated questions and answers obtained from the instance **Final Exam** in Figure 2.

2.2 Generating Personalized Grammars

Language interfaces have also been used to assist the user when accessing the web. They can incorporate domain-restricted grammars to help the user about the contents and the terms to be used to build the query, as can be seen in Figure 4. Those semantic grammars can also be generated following the approach proposed. The processing of the resulting query is simple, because the language to be considered is limited, i.e., the user will describe time by selecting one of the forms in the screen.

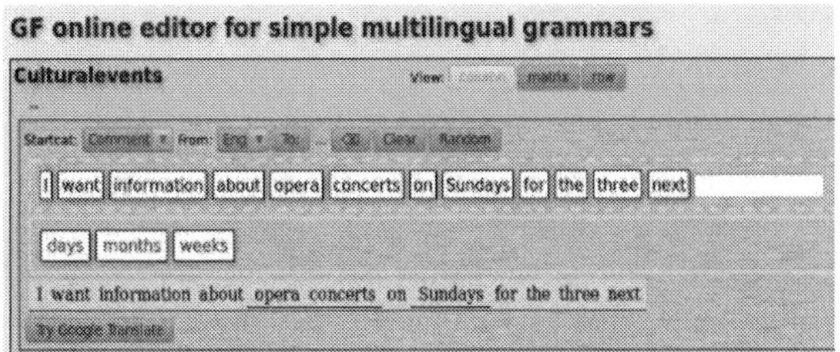

Figure 4: Guiding the user to build the query to the service

Figure 4 shows an example of how the user is guided to build a query to a web service giving information about the cultural events in a particular city. In this scenario, the grammar used has been generated from the concept **Event**, described by a set of attributes that correspond to the parameters of the service: **title**, **type**, **place**, **time** and **audience**. The same concept could be adapted for many of the web services about cultural activities. Two different user groups are distinguished, considering the value of the attribute **audience**, if they are interested on activities for adults or for children.

The interface shown in Figure 4 has been generated by the Grammatical Framework (GF, www.gramaticalframework.org), from the grammar written in the GF formalism, although other formalisms and environments could also be used.

3 Implementation and Evaluation

The web documents are first analyzed and classified in two groups considering their structure. Domain and language independent rules to extract the relevant data from these two types of documents have been defined and implemented in *C* language.

To automatically generate the personalized linguistic resources from the domain concepts, a *Prolog* program has also been developed. *Prolog* is an appropriate language because its unification mechanism facilitates the association of general conceptual categories with features indicating additional information: stereotype, language and syntactic details (such as gender, number and tense).

Average punctuation for the 3 questions	Group 1 (0..10)	Group 2 (0..10)
1. Do you think the questions and answers about the course assessment have helped you to solve doubts?	8.10	8.43
2. Do you think is useful to incorporate questions and answers about the course assessment in the course web page?	9.14	8.78
3. Do you think you are going to consult again those questions?	7.8	7.74

Table 1: Results of the questionnaire

The questions and answers related to the exams of a particular course on introduction to programming were generated in three languages (English, Catalan and Spanish) and included in the course web page. In order to evaluate their usability, the students of two different degrees were asked to complete, anonymously, an online questionnaire, included in the same web page. There were 26 students in the Group 1, enrolled in the Bachelor's Degree of *Aerospace Vehicle Engineering* and 27 in Group 2, in the Bachelor's Degree of *Industrial Technology Engineering*. Table 1 shows the questions and their results, rating scales are from 0 to 10, 0 strongly disagree, 10 strongly agree. This result indicates that students think the generated questions and answers are useful: 8.4 over 10 in Group 1 and 8.12 in Group 2. Similar results were obtained from students in the same degrees, in an informal evaluation, done the previous semester.

4   Related Work and Discussion

The generation of questions and answers has focused many research works in different areas, such as educational (Wyse and Piwek, 2009) and conversational systems (Varges et al., 2006), (Okoye et al., 2011).

There are different techniques that can be used for generation, based on rules (Mazidi and Tarau, 2009) and/or statistical methods (Jin and Le, 2016). Those techniques can be adapted to textual documents and/or to structured data (Duma and Klein, 2013). In the first case, the generation process is usually done by applying rules to the trees obtained from the syntactic analysis (Nouri et al., 2011), although there are also works that use the resulting semantic structure (Kuyten et al., 2012) and other use both (Heilman, 2011).

Generation from structured data has been studied for years in language interfaces, which usually obtain the system inquiries and responses from application specifications and domain-restricted bases. Domain knowledge representation has been incorporated into a considerable number of relevant dialogue systems (Guzzoni et al., 2006; Sonntag et al., 2007), because they facilitate the adaptation of knowledge to different domains, languages, user types and modes of communication. Additionally, they provide synonyms, hyponyms and hyperonyms terms to improve the query.

There is an increasing interest in the combination of language and user model techniques to obtain personalized linguistic resources (Brusilovsky and Millán, 2007; Milosavljevic and Oberlander, 1998; Stock et al., 2007; Han et al., 2014).

This article describes an approach to guide the user about the web contents based on the generation of personalized questions, answers and grammars from web documents, because they could result useful in different scenarios, as the students opinion on the questions generated about course exams (shown in Table 1) indicates.

This work proposes an organization of the different type of knowledge involved (conceptual, linguistic and about the user) that minimizes the human effort needed for a new domain and/or a new language, by separating the general facts that can be reused across domains from those more specific. The representation is based on relating the set of attributes describing main domain concepts to the user models and to a taxonomy representing general relationships between conceptual and linguistic knowledge. The linguistic information associated with the taxonomy classes is used for both generating questions and answers and grammars and also for extracting data from the web.

Future work could include the study of the adaptation of the set of rules developed to extract the data from the web documents to new domains.

Acknowledgments

This work has been partially supported by the FreeLing project http://nlp.cs.upc.edu/freeling.

References

John Bateman and Bernardo Magnini and Fabio Rinaldi. The generalized *{Italian, German, English}* upper model, In Proceedings of the ECAI94 Workshop: Comparison of Implemented Ontologies, Amsterdam, 1994.

Peter Brusilovsky and Eva Millan. 2007. User models for adaptive hypermedia and adaptive educational systems. The Adaptive Web, 4321:3–53.

Daniel Duma and Ewan Klein. Generating natural language from linked data: Unsupervised template extraction. In the proceedings of the 10th International Conference on Computational Semantics, pages 83–94, Potsdam, Germany, 2013.

Marta Gatius. Adaptive Generation of Multilingual Questions and Answers from Web Content. In: 26th International Workshop on Database and Expert Systems Applications, Valencia 2015.

Marta Gatius. Improving Knowledge Representation to Speed up the Generation of Grammars for a Multilingual Web Assitant. In Fernandez Raquel AND Isard Amy (ed.). Proceedings of the 17th Workshop on the Semantics and Pragmatics of Dialogue semdial, December, 2013.

Didier Guzzoni, Charles Baur and Adam Cheyer. Active : A unified platform for building intelligent web interaction assistants. In: IEEE/WIC/ACM International Conference on Web Intelligence and Intelligent Agent Technology (WI-IAT 2006 Workshops), pp. 417-420.

Xiwu Han, Somayajulu Sripada, Kit Macleod and Antonio Ioris. Latent User Models for Online River Information Tailoring. In the proceedings of the 7th International Natural Language Generation conference, 2014.

Michael Heilman. 2011. Automatic Factual Question Generation from Text. Ph.D. thesis, Carnegie Mellon University.

Yiping Jin and Phu Le. Selecting Domain-Specific Concepts for Question Generation with Lightly-Supervised Method. In the proceedings of the 9th International Natural Language Generation conference, pages 133–142, Edinburgh, UK, September 5-8 2016.

Pascal Kuyten, Timothy Bickmore, Svetlana Stoyanchev, Paul Piwek, Helmut Prendinger, and Mitsuru Ishizuka. 2012. Fully Automated Generation of Question-Answer Pairs for Scripted Virtual Instruction, volume 7502 of LNAI. Springer-Verlag.

Karen Mazidi and Paul Tarau. Infusing NLU into Automatic Question Generation . In the proceedings of the 9th International Natural Language Generation conference, 2016.

Maria Milosavljevic and Jon Oberlander. Dynamic hypertext catalogues: helping users to help themselves. In: HYPERTEXT, ACM, 1998.

Elnaz Nouri, Ron Artstein, Anton Leuski, and David Traum. 2011. Augmenting conversational characters with generated question-answer pairs. In the proceedings of the AAAI Fall Symposium.

Ifeyinwa Okoye, Jalal Mahmud, Tessa Lau, and Julian Cerruti. 2011. Find this for me: mobile information retrieval on the open web. In Proceedings of the 16th international conference on Intelligent user interfaces (IUI '11). ACM, New York, NY, USA, 3-12. DOI: https://doi.org/10.1145/1943403.1943407.

Daniel Sonntag, Ralf Engel, Gerd Herzog, Alexander Pfalzgraf, Norbert Pfleger, Massimo Romanelli, Norbert Reithinger, (2007), "SmartWeb Handheld — Multimodal Interaction with Ontological Knowledge Bases and semantic web services", Proceedings of the ICMI 2006 and IJCAI 2007 international conference on Artificial intelligence for human computing Pages 272-295.

Oliviero Stock, Massimo Zancanaro, Paolo Busetta, Charles Callaway, Antonio Krüger, Michael Kruppa, Tsvi Kuflik, Elena Not, and Cesare Rocchi. 2007. Adaptive, intelligent presentation of information for the museum visitor in PEACH. User Modeling and User-Adapted Interaction 17, 3 (July 2007), 257-304.

Sebastian Varges, Fuliang Weng, and Heather Pon-Barry. 2009. Interactive question answering and constraint relaxation in spoken dialogue systems. Natural Language Engineering.

Wyse, Brendan and Piwek, Paul (2009). Generating questions from OpenLearn study units. In AIED 2009 Workshop Proceedings Volume 1. The 2nd Workshop on Question Generation, 6-9 July 2009, Birghton, UK.

A Comparison of Neural Models for Word Ordering

Eva Hasler[1,2], Felix Stahlberg[1], Marcus Tomalin[1], Adrià de Gispert[1,2], Bill Byrne[1,2]

[1]Department of Engineering, University of Cambridge, UK
[2]SDL Research, Cambridge, UK
`{ech57,fs439,mt126,ad465,wjb31}@cam.ac.uk`
`{ehasler,agispert,bbyrne}@sdl.com`

Abstract

We compare several language models for the word-ordering task and propose a new *bag-to-sequence* neural model based on attention-based *sequence-to-sequence* models. We evaluate the model on a large German WMT data set where it significantly outperforms existing models. We also describe a novel search strategy for LM-based word ordering and report results on the English Penn Treebank. Our best model setup outperforms prior work both in terms of speed and quality.

1 Introduction

Finding the best permutation of a multi-set of words is a non-trivial task due to linguistic aspects such as "syntactic structure, selective restrictions, subcategorization, and discourse considerations" (Elman, 1990). This makes the word-ordering task useful for studying and comparing different kinds of models that produce text in tasks such as general natural language generation (Reiter and Dale, 1997), image caption generation (Xu et al., 2015), or machine translation (Bahdanau et al., 2015). Since plausible word order is an essential criterion of output fluency for all of these tasks, progress on the word-ordering problem is likely to have a positive impact on these tasks as well. Word ordering has often been addressed as *syntactic linearization* which is a strategy that involves using syntactic structures or part-of-speech and dependency labels (Zhang and Clark, 2011; Zhang et al., 2012; Zhang and Clark, 2015; Liu et al., 2015; Puduppully et al., 2016). It has also been addressed as *LM-based linearization* which relies solely on language models and obtains better

scores (de Gispert et al., 2014; Schmaltz et al., 2016). Recently, Schmaltz et al. (2016) showed that recurrent neural network language models (Mikolov et al., 2010, RNNLMs) with long short-term memory (Hochreiter and Schmidhuber, 1997, LSTM) cells are very effective for word ordering even without any explicit syntactic information.

We continue this line of work and make the following contributions. We compare several language models on the word-ordering task and propose a *bag-to-sequence* neural architecture that equips an LSTM decoder with explicit context of the bag-of-words (BOW) to be ordered. This model performs particularly strongly on WMT data and is complementary to an RNNLM: combining both yields large BLEU gains even for small beam sizes. We also propose a novel search strategy which outperforms a previous heuristic. Both techniques together surpass prior work on the Penn Treebank at ∼4x the speed.

2 Bag-to-Sequence Modeling with Attentional Neural Networks

Given the BOW {*at, bottom, heap, now, of, the, the, we, 're, .*}, a word-ordering model may generate an output string **w** = "*now we 're at the bottom of the heap .*". We can use an RNNLM (Mikolov et al., 2010) to assign it a probability $P(\mathbf{w})$ by decomposing into conditionals:

$$P(w_1^T) = \prod_{t=1}^{T} P(w_t | w_1^{t-1}) \qquad (1)$$

Since we have access to the input BOWs, we extend the model representation by providing the network additionally with the BOW to be ordered, thereby allowing it to focus explicitly on all tokens it generates

Work partially supported by U.K. EPSRC grant EP/L027623/1.

208

Proceedings of The 10th International Natural Language Generation conference, pages 208–212,
Santiago de Compostela, Spain, September 4-7 2017. ©2017 Association for Computational Linguistics

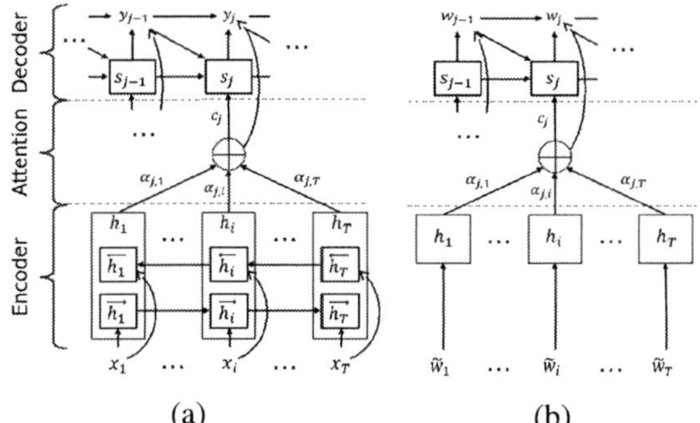

Figure 1: (a) Attention-based *seq2seq* model and (b) *bag2seq* model used in this work.

in the output during decoding. Thus, instead of modeling the *a priori* distribution of sentences $P(\mathbf{w})$ as in Eq. 1, we condition the distribution on $\textsc{Bow}(\mathbf{w})$:

$$P(w_1^T|\textsc{Bow}(\mathbf{w})) = \prod_{t=1}^{T} P(w_t|w_1^{t-1}, \textsc{Bow}(\mathbf{w}))$$

(2)

This dependency is realized by the neural attention mechanism recently proposed by Bahdanau et al. (2015). The resulting bag-to-sequence model (*bag2seq*) is inspired by the attentional sequence-to-sequence model RNNSEARCH (*seq2seq*) proposed by Bahdanau et al. (2015) for neural machine translation between a source sentence $\mathbf{x} = x_1^I$ and a target sentence $\mathbf{y} = y_1^J$. Fig. 1a illustrates how *seq2seq* generates the j-th target token y_j using the decoder state s_j and the context vector c_j. The context vector is the weighted sum of source side *annotations* h_i which encode sequence information.

To modify *seq2seq* for problems with unordered input, we make the encoder architecture order-invariant by replacing the recurrent layer with non-recurrent transformations of the word embeddings, as indicated by the missing arrows between source positions in Fig. 1b. For convenience, we formalize $\textsc{Bow}(\mathbf{w})$ as sequence $\langle \tilde{w}_1, \ldots, \tilde{w}_T \rangle$ in which words are sorted, e.g. alphabetically, so that we can refer to the t-th word in the $\textsc{Bow}$. The model can be trained to recover word order in a sentence by using $\textsc{Bow}(\mathbf{w}) = \langle \tilde{w}_1, \ldots, \tilde{w}_T \rangle$ as input and the original sequence $\langle w_1, \ldots, w_T \rangle$ as target. This network architecture does not prevent words outside the $\textsc{Bow}$ to appear in the output. Therefore, we explicitly *constrain* our beam decoder by limiting its available output vocabulary to the remaining tokens in the input bag at each time step, thereby ensuring that all model outputs are *valid permutations* of the input.

3 Search

Beam search is a popular decoding algorithm for neural sequence models (Sutskever et al., 2014; Bahdanau et al., 2015). However, standard beam search suffers from search errors when applied to word ordering and Schmaltz et al. (2016) reported that gains often do not saturate even with a large beam of 512. They suggested adding external unigram probabilities of the remaining words in the $\textsc{Bow}$ as future cost estimates to the beam-search scoring function and reported large gains for an n-gram LM and RNNLM. We re-implement this future cost heuristic, $f(\cdot)$, and further propose a new search heuristic, $g(\cdot)$, which collects internal unigram statistics during decoding. We keep hypotheses in the beam if their score is close to a theoretical upper bound, the product of the best word probabilities given any history within the explored search space. For each word $\tilde{w} \in \textsc{Bow}(\mathbf{w})$ we maintain a heuristic score estimate $\hat{P}(\tilde{w})$ which we initialize to 0. Each time the search algorithm visits a new context, we update the estimates such that $\hat{P}(\tilde{w})$ is the current best score for $\tilde{w}$:

$$\hat{P}(\tilde{w}) = \max_{c \in \mathcal{C}_t} P(\tilde{w}|c, \textsc{Bow}(\mathbf{w}))$$

(3)

where $\mathcal{C}_t$ is the set of contexts (i.e. ordered prefixes in the form of w_1^t) explored by beam search so far. Thus, instead of computing a future cost, we compare the actual score of a partial hypothesis with the product of heuristic estimates of its words. This is especially useful for model combinations since all models are taken into account. We also implement hypothesis recombination to further reduce the number of search errors. More formally, at each time step t our beam search keeps the n best hypotheses according to scoring function $S(\cdot)$ using partial model score $s(\cdot)$ and estimates $g(\cdot)$:

$$
\begin{aligned}
S(w_1^t) &= s(w_1^t) - g(w_1^t) \\
s(w_1^t) &= \log P(w_1^t|\textsc{Bow}(\mathbf{w})) \\
g(w_1^t) &= \sum_{w' \in w_1^t} \log \hat{P}(w')
\end{aligned}
$$

(4)

4 Experimental Setup

We evaluate using data from the English-German news translation task (Bojar et al., 2015, WMT) and using the English Penn Treebank data (Marcus et al., 1993, PTB). Since additional knowledge sources are often available in practice, such as access to the source sentence in a translation scenario, we also report on bilingual experiments for the WMT task.

4.1 Data and evaluation

The WMT parallel training data includes *Europarl v7*, *Common Crawl*, and *News Commentary v10*. We use *news-test2013* for tuning model combinations and *news-test2015* for testing. All monolingual models for the WMT task were trained on the German *news2015* corpus ($\sim$51.3M sentences). For PTB, we use preprocessed data by Schmaltz et al. (2016) for a fair comparison ($\sim$40k sentences for training).[1] We evaluate using the multi-bleu.perl script for WMT and mteval-v13.pl for PTB.

4.2 Model settings

For WMT, the *bag2seq* parameter settings follow the recent NMT systems trained on WMT data. We use a 50k vocabulary, 620 dimensional word embeddings and 1000 hidden units in the decoder LSTM cells. On the encoder side, the input tokens are embedded to form annotations of the same size as the hidden units in the decoder. The RNNLM is based on the "large" setup of Zaremba et al. (2014) which uses an LSTM. NPLM, a 5-gram neural feedforward language model, was trained for 10 epochs with a vocabulary size of 100k, 150 input and output units, 750 hidden units and 100 noise samples (Vaswani et al., 2013). The n-gram language model is a 5-gram model estimated with SRILM (Kneser and Ney, 1995). For the bilingual setting, we implemented a *seq2seq* NMT system following Bahdanau et al. (2015) using a beam size of 12 in line with recent NMT systems for WMT (Sennrich et al., 2016). RNNLM, *bag2seq* and *seq2seq* were implemented using TensorFlow (Abadi et al., 2015)[2] and we used *sgnmt* for beam decoding[3].

Following Schmaltz et al. (2016), our neural models for PTB have a vocabulary of 16,161 incl. two different *unk* tokens and the RNNLM is based on the "medium" setup of Zaremba et al. (2014). *bag2seq* uses 300 dimensional word embeddings and 500 hidden units in the decoder LSTM. We also compare to GYRO (de Gispert et al., 2014) which explicitly targets the word-ordering problem. We extracted 1-gram to 5-gram phrase rules from the PTB train-

---

[1]We thank the authors for help to reproduce their results.
[2]https://github.com/ehasler/tensorflow
[3]https://github.com/ucam-smt/sgnmt

RNNLM	NPLM	n-gram	bag2seq	seq2seq	BLEU
✓					29.4
	✓				30.3
		✓			32.5
			✓		**33.6**
✓	✓	✓			34.9
✓	✓	✓	✓		**39.4**
				✓	49.7
			✓	✓	**52.6**
✓	✓	✓		✓	51.3
✓	✓	✓	✓	✓	**53.1**

Table 1: German word ordering on *news-test2015* with *beam=12*, single models/combinations. Monolingual models use heuristic $f(\cdot)$, *bag2seq* as a single model and bilingual models use no heuristic.

ing data and used an n-gram LM for decoding. For model combinations, we combine the predictive distributions in a log-linear model and tune the weights by optimizing BLEU on the validation set with the BOBYQA algorithm (Powell, 2009).

5 Results

5.1 Word Ordering on WMT data

The top of Tab. 1 shows that *bag2seq* outperforms all other language models by up to 4.2 BLEU on ordering German (bold numbers highlight its improvements). This suggests that explicitly presenting all available tokens to the decoder during search enables it to make better word order choices. A combination of RNNLM, NPLM and n-gram LM yields a higher score than the individual models, but further adding *bag2seq* yields a large gain of 4.5 BLEU confirming its suitability for the word-ordering task.

In the bilingual setting in the bottom of Tab. 1, the *seq2seq* model is given English input text and the beam decoder is constrained to generate permutations of German BOWs. This is effectively a translation task with knowledge of the target BOWs and *seq2seq* provides a strong baseline since it uses source sequence information. Still, adding *bag2seq* yields a 2.9 BLEU gain and adding it to the combination of all other models still improves by 1.8 BLEU. This suggests that it could also help for machine translation rescoring by selecting hypotheses that constitute good word orderings.

5.2 Word Ordering on the Penn Treebank

Tab. 2 shows the performance of different models and search heuristics on the Penn Treebank: using

Model	none	$f(\cdot)$	$g(\cdot)$
Previous work		*beam=512*	
GYRO[5]	42.2	–	–
NGRAM-512	–	38.6	–
LSTM-512	–	42.7	–
This work		*beam=512*	
n-gram	35.7	38.6	**38.9**
RNNLM	38.6	43.2	**44.2**
bag2seq	**37.1**	33.6	**37.1**

Table 2: BLEU scores for PTB word-ordering task (test). NGRAM-512 and LSTM-512 are quoted from Schmaltz et al. (2016).

no heuristic (*none*) vs. $f(\cdot)$ and $g(\cdot)$ described in Section 3. Numbers in bold mark the best result for a given model. We compare against the LM-based method of de Gispert et al. (2014) and the n-gram and RNNLM (LSTM) models of Schmaltz et al. (2016), of which the latter achieves the best BLEU score of 42.7. We can reproduce or surpass prior work for n-gram and RNNLM and show that $g(\cdot)$ outperforms $f(\cdot)$ for these models. This also holds when adding a 900k sample from the English Gigaword corpus as proposed by Schmaltz et al. (2016).[4] However, *bag2seq* underperforms RNNLM at this large beam size.

Since decoding is slow for large beam sizes, we compare *bag2seq* to the n-gram and RNNLM using a small beam of size 5 in Tab. 3. The first three rows show that decoding without heuristics is much easier with *bag2seq* and outperforms n-gram and RNNLM by a large margin with 33.4 BLEU. The RNNLM needs heuristic $f(\cdot)$ to match this performance. For *bag2seq*, using heuristic estimates is worse than just using its partial scores for search. We suspect that its partial model scores are obfuscated by the heuristic estimates and the amount of their contribution should probably be tuned on a heldout set. Using the same beam size, ensembles yield better results but the best results are achieved by combining RNNLM and *bag2seq* (37.9 BLEU). This confirms our findings on WMT data that these models are highly complementary for word ordering. The results for beam=64 follow this pattern and identify an interaction between heuristics and beam size. While we get the best results for beam=5 using $f(\cdot)$, heuristic $g(\cdot)$ seems to perform better for larger beams,

---

⁴Results omitted from Tab. 2 to save space.
⁵Note that this model has an advantage because longer sentences are processed in chunks of maximum length 20.

Model	none	$f(\cdot)$	$g(\cdot)$
	beam=5		
n-gram	23.3	**30.1**	26.5
RNNLM	24.5	**33.6**	29.7
bag2seq	**33.4**	27.0	31.7
RNNLM-ensemble	25.5	**34.2**	30.6
bag2seq-ensemble	34.8	**35.1**	32.8
RNNLM+*bag2seq*	35.7	**37.9**	34.4
	beam=64		
RNNLM	34.6	40.9	**42.5**
bag2seq	36.2	31.4	**36.5**
RNNLM-ensemble	35.4	42.4	**43.2**
RNNLM+*bag2seq*	40.5	43.1	**43.5**

Table 3: BLEU scores for PTB word-ordering task for different search heuristics and beam sizes (test).

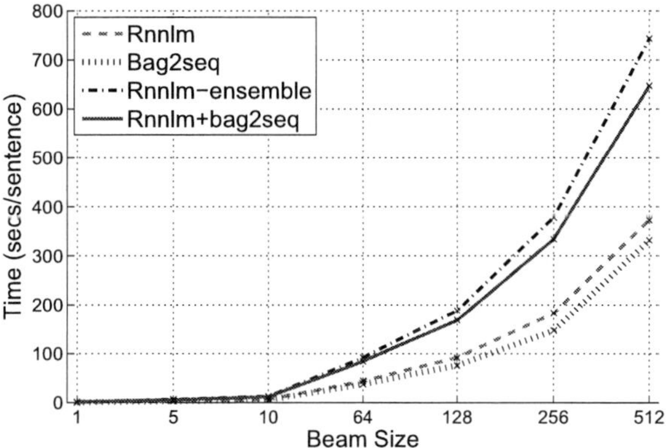

Figure 2: Decoding time in relation to beam size for PTB word ordering task (test).

perhaps because the internal unigram statistics become more reliable. Finally, RNNLM+*bag2seq* with $g(\cdot)$ and beam=64 outperforms LSTM-512 by 0.8 BLEU. This is significant because decoding in this configuration is also ∼4x faster than decoding with a single RNNLM and beam=512 as shown in Fig. 2.

6 Conclusion

We have compared various models for the word-ordering task and proposed a new model architecture inspired by attention-based sequence-to-sequence models that helps performance for both German and English tasks. We have also proposed a novel search heuristic and found that using a model combination together with this heuristic and a modest beam size provides a good trade-off between speed and quality and outperforms prior work on the PTB task.

References

Martın Abadi, Ashish Agarwal, Paul Barham, Eugene Brevdo, Zhifeng Chen, Craig Citro, Greg S Corrado, Andy Davis, Jeffrey Dean, Matthieu Devin, et al. 2015. TensorFlow: Large-scale machine learning on heterogeneous systems, 2015. 1. Software available from http://www.tensorflow.org/.

Dzmitry Bahdanau, Kyunghyun Cho, and Yoshua Bengio. 2015. Neural machine translation by jointly learning to align and translate. In *ICLR*.

Ondřej Bojar, Rajen Chatterjee, Christian Federmann, Barry Haddow, Matthias Huck, Chris Hokamp, Philipp Koehn, Varvara Logacheva, Christof Monz, Matteo Negri, Matt Post, Carolina Scarton, Lucia Specia, and Marco Turchi. 2015. Findings of the 2015 workshop on statistical machine translation. In *Proceedings of the Tenth Workshop on Statistical Machine Translation*, pages 1–46. Association for Computational Linguistics.

Adrià de Gispert, Marcus Tomalin, and W Byrne. 2014. Word ordering with phrase-based grammars. In *EACL*, pages 259–268.

Jeffrey L Elman. 1990. Finding structure in time. *Cognitive science*, 14(2):179–211.

Sepp Hochreiter and Jürgen Schmidhuber. 1997. Long short-term memory. *Neural computation*, 9(8):1735–1780.

Reinhard Kneser and Hermann Ney. 1995. Improved backing-off for m-gram language modeling. In *ICASSP*, volume 1, pages 181–184.

Yijia Liu, Yue Zhang, Wanxiang Che, and Bing Qin. 2015. Transition-based syntactic linearization. In *NAACL*.

Mitchell P Marcus, Mary Ann Marcinkiewicz, and Beatrice Santorini. 1993. Building a large annotated corpus of English: The Penn Treebank. *Computational linguistics*, 19(2):313–330.

Tomas Mikolov, Martin Karafiát, Lukas Burget, Jan Cernockỳ, and Sanjeev Khudanpur. 2010. Recurrent neural network based language model. In *Interspeech*, volume 2, page 3.

Michael JD Powell. 2009. The BOBYQA algorithm for bound constrained optimization without derivatives. *Cambridge NA Report NA2009/06, University of Cambridge, Cambridge*.

Ratish Puduppully, Yue Zhang, and Manish Shrivastava. 2016. Transition-based syntactic linearization with lookahead features. In *Proceedings of NAACL-HLT*, pages 488–493.

Ehud Reiter and Robert Dale. 1997. Building applied natural language generation systems. *Natural Language Engineering*, 3(01):57–87.

Allen Schmaltz, Alexander M Rush, and Stuart M Shieber. 2016. Word ordering without syntax. In *EMNLP*.

Rico Sennrich, Barry Haddow, and Alexandra Birch. 2016. Edinburgh neural machine translation systems for wmt 16. In *Proceedings of the First Conference on Machine Translation*, pages 371–376.

Ilya Sutskever, Oriol Vinyals, and Quoc V. Le. 2014. Sequence to sequence learning with neural networks. In *Proceedings of NIPS*.

Ashish Vaswani, Yinggong Zhao, Victoria Fossum, and David Chiang. 2013. Decoding with large-scale neural language models improves translation. In *EMNLP*.

Kelvin Xu, Jimmy Lei Ba, Ryan Kiros, Kyunghyun Cho, Aaron Courville, Ruslan Salakhutdinov, Richard S. Zemel, and Yoshua Bengio. 2015. Show, attend and tell: Neural image caption generation with visual attention. *arXiv preprint arXiv:1502.03044*.

Wojciech Zaremba, Ilya Sutskever, and Oriol Vinyals. 2014. Recurrent neural network regularization. *arXiv preprint arXiv:1409.2329*.

Yue Zhang and Stephen Clark. 2011. Syntax-based grammaticality improvement using CCG and guided search. In *EMNLP*, pages 1147–1157.

Yue Zhang and Stephen Clark. 2015. Discriminative syntax-based word ordering for text generation. *Computational Linguistics*, 41(3):503–538.

Yue Zhang, Graeme Blackwood, and Stephen Clark. 2012. Syntax-based word ordering incorporating a large-scale language model. In *EACL*, pages 736–746.

Investigating the Content and Form of Referring Expressions in Mandarin: Introducing the Mtuna Corpus

Kees van Deemter
University of Aberdeen

Le Sun
Institute of Software
Chinese Academy of Sciences

Rint Sybesma
Leiden University

Xiao Li
University of Aberdeen

Bo Chen
Institute of Software
Chinese Academy of Sciences

Muyun Yang
Harbin Institute of Technology

Abstract

East Asian languages are thought to handle reference differently from English, particularly in terms of the marking of definiteness and number. We present the first Data-Text corpus for Referring Expressions in Mandarin, and we use this corpus to test some initial hypotheses inspired by the theoretical linguistics literature. Our findings suggest that function words deserve more attention in Referring Expression Generation than they have so far received, and they have a bearing on the debate about whether different languages make different trade-offs between clarity and brevity.

1   Introduction

East Asian languages can differ considerably from the languages of Western Europe, which have often dominated formal and computational studies of language. One phenomenon where these differences are obvious is Referring Expressions (REs), where languages such as Mandarin differ markedly from, for example, English, in terms of their expression of *number* (e.g., Am I referring to 1 thing or more?), *maximality* (Am I talking about all the things that have a certain combination of properties, or only some of them?), and *givenness* status (Am I talking about something that the hearer is familiar with?).

To gain an insight in these matters, and to assist future research, we have embarked on a data gathering enterprise focussing on East Asian languages, starting with a language elicitation experiment in which speakers of Mandarin were asked to produce one-shot REs in a carefully balanced range of situations. The present paper introduces the corpus and offers an initial assessment of some of our research questions. The Mtuna data-text corpus is freely available from `homepages.abdn.ac.uk/k.vdeemter-/pages/mtuna-webpage/`, containing the original Chinese characters, their transcription into (phonetic) pinyin notation, and an informal English gloss. Each RE is coupled with a pictorial scene that shows the referent and its distractors in the same way as participants in the experiment saw it.

2   Initial Research Questions

According to the linguistics literature, REs without a numeral can take three different shapes, namely (1) Demonstrative + Classifier + Noun Group (e.g., *Na ge laoren*, "That (person) old person"), (2) Demonstrative + Noun Group (*Na laoren*, "That old person") , and (3) (bare) Noun Group *Laoren*, "Old person") (Cheng and Sybesma 1999, 2015).[1] We call these the DCN pattern, the DN pattern, and the N pattern respectively. Together we call them the *Canonical* Patterns of reference in Mandarin.

Noun Groups (the third pattern) can be strikingly open to interpretation: they can be understood as indefinite, generic, or definite; moreover, they are not marked for number. Thus, a bare Noun Group like *lüse de yizi* (lit: *green colour chair*) can mean *the green chair*, but equally, *the green chairs*, *green chairs* (in general), and *a green chair*. We are in-

---

[1]Classifiers are words that attribute entities to ontological classes; in certain contexts classifiers are obligatory. Noun Groups are combinations of Nouns and their modifiers (e.g., adjectives).

Proceedings of The 10th International Natural Language Generation conference, pages 213–217,
Santiago de Compostela, Spain, September 4-7 2017. ©2017 Association for Computational Linguistics

terested how frequently each of these NPs occur because it will give us a first insight into the role of underspecification in Mandarin. Following a small pilot experiment with 10 speakers, we set out to address the following questions:

Research Questions: *Are the three Canonical patterns the ones that are used predominantly when people refer? Is this only true for sentence positions where definiteness is the norm (in Mandarin this is the pre-verbal position), or is it equally true for other positions? How frequently are REs underspecified for number, maximality,[2] and givenness?*

The original English TUNA corpora were collected in 2006 and used for multiple shared tasks (Gatt and Belz 2010) on Referring Expression Generation (REG) and other work in this area (van Deemter et al. 2012). Each corpus consists of REs produced by humans presented with a target item (1 or 2 pieces of furniture, or 1 or 2 people's faces) and a set of distractors (other pieces of furniture or faces), in a web-based elicitation paradigm. A Dutch TUNA was conducted in 2011 (DTuna, Koolen et al. 2011) and an Arabic one in 2015 (Khan 2015).

Though a number of other REG data gathering exercises have followed (see e.g., van Deemter 2016), the TUNA setup suits our research questions well. However, the analysis of the corpus is very different this time. For whereas earlier TUNAs focussed on the properties expressed by a given RE (chair, green, etc.), our research questions mean that function words (English: *the, a, one, two, this, those, both*) are key. Although these are sometimes considered to be part of Linguistic Realisation, they are not just "syntactic sugar", since they contribute much to the information conveyed by these REs (e.g., Kamp and Reyle 1993, and many other treatments of the semantics and pragmatics of English).

3 The Mtuna Experiment and Corpus

The 44 stimuli of our experiment (40 + 4 items originally used for training only) resemble closely those of earlier TUNAs; like these, they were semantically balanced (e.g. the number of cases when the target could be identified by means of colour was identical to the number of cases when the target could

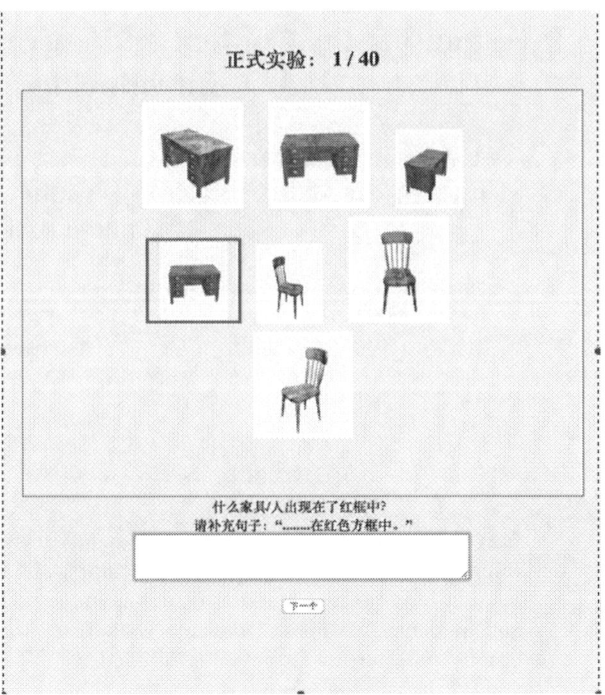

Figure 1: *A furniture trial, with the RE in pre-verbal position.*

be identified by means of size). They include references to sets as well as individual items. Instructions to participants were translated from Dtuna, except that the new instructions did not include examples of actual REs in the target language (i.e., Mandarin), since these could have biased participants towards particular syntactic patterns. Also, where earlier TUNAs had always asked subjects essentially the same question, namely "Which object/objects appears/appear in a red window?", the new experiment distinguished between REs in pre-verbal and post-verbal position.

Participants were recruited from the Chinese Academy of Sciences (Institute of Software) and the Harbin Institute of Technology. Data from 37 participants have been obtained. 35/37 were self-assessed native speakers of Mandarin, 2/37 were merely fluent. 29/37 were from the North of China and 8/37 from the South. Subjects were discouraged from using location in their REs, being told that the recipient might view the scenes on a page that uses a different layout. Items were presented in random order and with random layout where all entities were allotted to cells in a 3-by-5 grid invisible to participants.

Sentence position was varied in a between-

---

[2]An occurrence of the above-mentioned NP *lüse de yizi* would be *maximal* if it denoted *all* the green chairs in the scene.

Figure 2: *A people trial with RE in post-verbal position.*

subjects design: Participants who were asked to produce REs in pre-verbal position were asked this trigger question: *Shenme jiaju/ren chuxian zai le hongkuang zhong?* (What furniture / person occur(s) in red frame(s)?) Immediately below this question, the page continues: *Qing buchong juzi: .... zai hongse fangkuang zhong* (Please complete the sentence: "......is in the red frame(s)".) Participants who were asked to produce REs in post-verbal position were asked: *Nin xiwang shoushizhe xuanze shenme jiaju/ren?* (What furniture / person do you want the participants to choose?) The page continues: *Qing buchong juzi: Hongse fangkuang zhong de shi........* (Please complete the sentence: "What's in the red frame is ....."

4 Initial Analysis of the Mtuna corpus

The corpus was subjected to an initial analysis of all descriptions elicited. Our conclusions need to be handled with care, because further analysis is needed and the narrowness of our participant base (recruited from two Language Technology groups) may have biassed our results.

1. Are the three Canonical Patterns the ones that are actually used? Table 2 shows the numbers for

Pattern	Pre-verbal	Post-verbal
N	315	326
DN	0	0
DCN	0	0
Other D	5	4
Indefinite	98	54
Ordinal	4	0

Table 2: Raw frequencies of referential patterns for singular (i.e., non-set) references. *Other D* are structures such as *Lan yizi, zui da de nage* ("The blue chair, that largest one"), where the Demonstrative takes a different position than in DN and DCN. Indefinites tended to be of the form *"Yi ..."* ("One ...") Ordinals were expressions such as ("First from the left""). Not all participants answered all the questions, with different numbers of entries for Pre-verbal and Post-verbal.

references to singular referents only. The N Pattern dominated, whereas no DN or DCN Patterns were found. We did found a small number of Ordinal Patterns, all of which came from a small number of subjects who had ignored the instruction to avoid mentioning the location of the referent (saying things like "the first ... from the left"). Indefinite NPs occurred quite often, even in pre-verbal position, where we had expected not to see them (though the bulk of these REs were produced by just 3 participants). These results appear to be at odds with linguists' views about the dominant patterns; one possible explanation is that Demonstratives are restricted to situations in which the antecedent is either pointed at or mentioned in earlier text (Jenks 2015).

2. Was the choice of RE pattern influenced by sentence position? A Chi-Square calculation on the figures of Table 2 suggests a cautiously affirmative answer ($p < .05$), caused by the larger number of indefinites in pre-verbal position. We had expected to see fewer N Patterns in post- than in pre-verbal position, but this expectation was not borne out.

3. How often were REs non-specific as to number, maximality, and givenness? Mandarin's explicit markers for *maximality* were used very rarely (14 occurrences of *dou* ("all")). No explicit markers for *givenness* were found. In both cases, we may have missed out on less obvious markers (e.g., syntactic position may play a role), therefore we plan a new experiment that will investigate readers' or listeners' interpretation of the REs produced in the corpus.

Mandarin (transcribed into pinyin)	Approximate English Gloss
Furniture	
Xiaode lüsede xiangqian de zhuozi	Small green [sub] forward table
Yizhang lüse de shuzhuo	One[cla] green [sub] desk
Zhengmian chao qian de xiezitai, chicun jiaoxiaode nage	Front facing [sub] writing desk, the smaller size [sub] of those
Yige chouti chaowai de lüse xiao shuzhuo	One[cla] small desk with a drawer facing out [sub]
Lüse zhuozi	Green table
Yige zhengmian chaoxiang guancezhe de xiangdui xiao de zhuozi	A[cla] relatively small table facing observer [sub]
People	
Dai yanjing hei toufa de liang ge ren	Wear glasses black hair [sub] two [cla] people
Liang ge dai yanjing de nianqing nanxing	Two [cla] wear glasses [sub] young men
Hei toufa liang ge ren	Black hair two [cla] people
Liang ge dai yanjing chuan heise xifu de heise toufa de nanren zai hongse fangkuang zhong	Two [cla] wear glasses wear black clothes [sub] black hair man in red box
Dai yanjing hei toufa de liangwei kexuejia	Wear glasses black hair [sub] two[cla] scientists
Yige zhengmian de chaowai de dai yanjing, chuan xizhuang da lingdai hei toufa de nanren	One[cla] face outward [sub] wear glasses, wear suit and tie black-haired man

Table 1: Some REs as found in the corpus referring to the target referents in Figures 1 and 2. [cla] denotes a classifier, [sub] denotes a subordinating *de*. The modelling of classifier and subordinator use is a topic to which we will turn in later research.

	Number was marked	Number was not marked
singular post-verbal	59	325
singular pre-verbal	106	312
plural post-verbal	231	157
plural pre-verbal	297	121

Table 3: A singular RE was counted as marked for number if it was of the form *Yi* ... ("One ..."). A plural RE was marked for number if it contained the numeral *liang* ("two") or an ordinal or if it used a conjunction.

Number can be marked by numerals, by ordinals or by the use of logical conjunction (e.g., *he* ("and"), as in *hongse yizi he lüse dianfengshan* ("red chair AND green fan")). Table 3 suggests that number tended to be marked when the referent was plural but not when it was singular; number was marked more often in pre-verbal than in post-verbal position.

5 Discussion

It has often been suggested that East Asian languages handle the trade-off between brevity and clarity differently to those of Western Europe, with the former (as typical instances of languages that are "cool" rather than "hot") allegedly leaning more towards brevity, and relying more on communicative context for disambiguation (Newnham 1971, Huang 1984). If this was true, one would expect that Mandarin REs use less over-specification (i.e., REs from which one or more properties can be removed without causing referential confusion) and more under-specification than in English and Dutch; equally, one might expect that Mandarin REs are less fully specified in terms of number, maximality, and givenness. In future, we want to investigate these hypotheses and their implications for REG more thoroughly.

Based on a first look at our data, a nuanced picture is emerging, where defaults are likely to play a role. Based on the literature (e.g., Chao 1968), Mandarin NPs in pre-verbal position may be interpreted as definite unless there is information to the contrary; based on our data, it may be that a Mandarin NP denotes a singular entity by default, and that plural interpretations only arise when the context enforces this (e.g., by means of a numeral). These issues need to be investigated further.

Some aspects of the unexpected distribution of patterns in Mandarin reported in section 4 may have been caused by ususual features of the communicative situation in which we placed our participants, for instance because only written input was available to them. If this was true, then this would also cast doubt on earlier results that were obtained with the same, TUNA-style, data gathering method.

Acknowledgments

This work is partly supported by the National Natural Science Foundation of China, Grant no. 61433015. We thank Stephen Matthews, University of Hong Kong, for comments, and Albert Gatt, University of Malta, for access to Dutch TUNA.

6 References

Chao 1968. Y. R. Chao. *A Grammar of Spoken Chinese.* University of California Press.

Cheng and Sybesma, 1999. L. Cheng and R. Sybesma. Bare and Not-So-Bare Nouns and the Structure of NP. *Linguistic Inquiry* **30** (4).

Cheng and Sybesma, 2015. L. Cheng and R. Sybesma. [Syntactic sketch of] Mandarin, Syntax Theory and Analysis. An International Handbook. Handbooks of Linguistics and Communication Science, ed. Tibor Kiss and Artemis Alexiadou, 42.1-3, Berlin: Mouton de Gruyter.

Gatt and Belz, 2010. A. Gatt and A. Belz. Introducing shared task evaluation to NLG: The TUNA shared task evaluation challenges. In Krahmer, E. and Theune, M., editors, Empirical Methods in Natural Language Generation, p. 264 - 293. Springer Verlag, Berlin.

Huang 1984. C. -T. J. Huang. On the distribution and reference of empty pronouns. *Linguistic Inquiry* **15** (4), p.531 − 574.

Jenks, 2015. P. Jenks. Two kinds of definites in numeral classifier languages. In Proceedings of Semantics and Linguistic Theory (SALT) 25.

Kamp and Reyle, 1993. H. Kamp and U. Reyle. *From Discourse to Logic.* Kluwer, Dordrecht.

Khan, 2015. I.H. Khan. Do Speakers Produce Different Referring Expressions in Their Native Language Than A Non-native Language? *International Journal of Computational Linguistics Research* **6** (2), p. 41 - 47.

Koolen et al. 2011. R. Koolen, A.Gatt, M. Goudbeek, E. Krahmer. Factors causing overspecification in definite descriptions. *Journal of Pragmatics* **43**, p. 3231 - 3250.

Newnham, 1971. R. Newnham. About Chinese. Harmondsworth, Middlesex: Penguin Books.

van Deemter et al., 2012. K. van Deemter, A. Gatt, I. van der Sluis, and R. Power. Generation of Referring Expressions: Assessing the Incremental Algorithm. Cognitive Science, **36** (5): p. 799 - 836.

van Deemter, 2016. K. van Deemter. Computational Models of Referring: a Study in Cognitive Science. MIT Press, Cambridge Mass.

Westerbeek et al. 2015. H. Westerbeek, R. Koolen, and A. Maes. Stored object knowledge and the production of referring expressions: The case of color typicality. *Frontiers in Psychology* **6**.

Realization of long sentences using chunking

Ewa Muszyńska
Computer Laboratory
University of Cambridge
emm68@cam.ac.uk

Ann Copestake
Computer Laboratory
University of Cambridge
aac10@cam.ac.uk

Abstract

We propose sentence chunking as a way to reduce the time and memory costs of realization of long sentences. During chunking we divide the semantic representation of a sentence into smaller components which can be processed and recombined without loss of information. Our meaning representation of choice is Dependency Minimal Recursion Semantics (DMRS). We show that realizing chunks of a sentence and combining the results of such realizations increases the coverage for long sentences, significantly reduces the resources required and does not affect the quality of the realization.

1 Introduction

Surface realization, or generation, is a task of producing sentences from a representation. Realization can be thought of as the inverse of parsing and constraint-based approaches, implemented, for instance, using chart algorithms, make it possible to use the same reversible grammar for both parsing and realization.

Large semantic representations present a challenge to generators. In the worst-case scenario chart generation has exponential complexity with respect to the size of the representation, although the algorithm can be modified to improve the performance (Carroll et al., 1999; White, 2004).

In this paper we propose chunking (Muszyńska, 2016) as a way to reduce memory and time cost of realization. The general idea of chunking is that strings and semantic representations can be divided

into smaller parts which can be processed independently and then recombined without a loss of information. For realization we chunk input semantic representations. There may be multiple chunking points in one sentence. Here we show that the efficient realization of a full sentence is possible through a principled composition of realizations of the chunks.

We show that the technique noticeably reduces the cost of realization and in some cases it allows for realization where no result was found using the standard approach. This effect is achieved without significantly degrading realization quality.

2 DELPH-IN framework

The semantic representation we use in our experiments is Dependency Minimal Recursion Semantics (DMRS) (Copestake, 2009), developed as part of the DELPH-IN initiative[1], together with several wide-coverage HPSG-based grammars, notably the English Resource Grammar (ERG) (Flickinger, 2000; Flickinger et al., 2014). The ERG is a broad-coverage, symbolic, bidirectional grammar of English. The DELPH-IN realization systems have been used successfully in a number of applications, such as question generation (Yao et al., 2012), paraphrasing logic forms for teaching purposes (Flickinger, 2016) and abstractive summarisation (Fang et al., 2016).

An example of a DMRS graph is shown in Fig. 1. Nodes correspond to predicates, edges (links) represent relations between them. It is inter-convertible

---

[1]Deep Linguistic Processing with HPSG, www.delph-in.net

Proceedings of The 10th International Natural Language Generation conference, pages 218–222,
Santiago de Compostela, Spain, September 4-7 2017. ©2017 Association for Computational Linguistics

with Minimal Recursion Semantics (MRS) format (Copestake et al., 2005).

DMRS graphs can be manipulated using two existing Python libraries. The `pyDelphin` library[2] is a more general MRS-dedicated library which we use for conversions between MRS and DMRS. The `pydmrs` library[3] (Copestake et al., 2016) is dedicated solely to DMRS.

In these experiments, we work with DMRS graphs which are the output of parsing with the 1214 version of the ERG. The realizer we use, ACE[4], is one of the processors designed to work with DELPH-IN grammars. It is a more efficient re-implementation of the chart parser and generator of the LKB (Carroll et al., 1999; Copestake, 2002; Flickinger, 2016). Parsing and realization results are ranked by a maximum entropy language model (Velldal, 2008).

In this paper we refer to the realization using default ACE settings as the standard realization. We introduce two adjustments to this set-up: a fixed time-out of 30s after which a realization attempt is abandoned even if it did not produce a result, and a mechanism to deal with unknown words. The time-out chosen is quite high and does not affect most realizations.

The ACE generator does not currently have a mechanism to cope with unknown predicates, i.e. predicates which do not appear in the grammar's lexicon. They can be parsed, however, and assigned a part-of-speech tag. Based on this information, we substitute each unknown predicate with a known predicate with the same part-of-speech tag before the semantic representation is input to the generator. Afterwards, the known surface form of the substitute predicate is replaced in the realization string with the surface form of the original unknown predicate (Horvat, 2017).

We retrieve all possible realizations for the given semantic representation together with their ranking scores. We also note the amount of memory and time needed for the realization, and the number of edges produced in the chart generation process.

We do not expect full realization coverage, even though the generator uses the same grammar as the parser which produced the representations. Some lexical items, such as infinitival *to*, are semantically empty according to the ERG analysis, i.e. they are not assigned their own predicates (Carroll et al., 1999). During realization with ERG/ACE, hand-written rukes are used to signal that particular semantically empty lexical items may be required. Missing rules sometimes cause realization failure.

3 Realization with chunking

Realization from chunks consists of four phases. After chunking a sentence (§ 3.1), we convert each chunk into a well-formed DMRS, introducing small place-holder graphs where necessary (§ 3.2). During the realization phase we generate from each of the chunk DMRSs separately. Finally, we use the information about how chunks are related to combine the chunk realizations into a full sentence realization (§ 3.4).

3.1 Chunking

Here we use an approach to chunking based on DMRS graphs. We chunk a semantic representation by dividing it into subgraphs, without access to any information about the surface form of the represented sentence. The link structure of the DMRS graph reveals appropriate chunk boundaries. Currently chunking is based on three grammatical constructions: clausal coordination, subordinating conjunctions and clausal complements.

For each chunking decision, we identify a functional chunk which plays the role of a trigger for chunking, i.e. its presence indicates the chunking possibility. For example, if a semantic representation contains a subordinating conjunction, it can be chunked as shown in Fig. 1. A functional chunk in this case consists of a single node with `_since_x_subord` predicate representing the subordinating lexeme. Each chunking decision also identifies two clauses. In Fig. 1 they are simple main and subordinate clauses, but in more complicated sentences these clauses could contain further chunking triggers, forming a tree-like hierarchy of chunks.

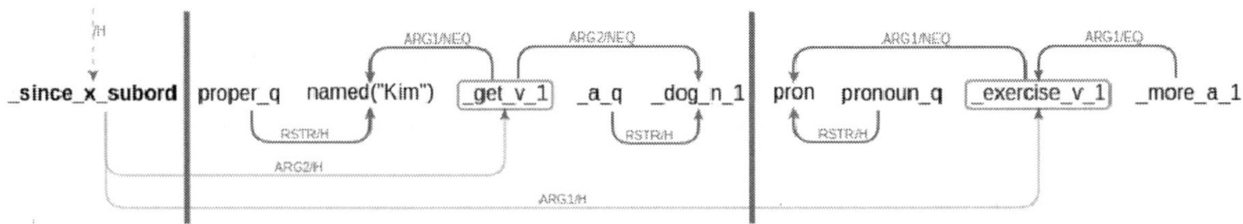

Figure 1: A DMRS graph for the sentence *Since Kim got a dog, she exercises more.* Chunk boundaries are marked in red.

3.2 Substitution

Functional chunks are not well-formed DMRSs – they typically consist of a single node. During chunking we preserve information about severed links between the chunks (trigger links, highlighted in Fig. 1) and in the substitution phase we introduce small pre-defined DMRSs at the end of the trigger links, where we would originally find other chunks. This ensures the well-formedness of the functional chunk.

In the experiment we use two minimalistic substitution DMRSs corresponding to clauses *It was snowing* and *it was raining*. Their DMRS graphs consist of single nodes and have one possible realization, which is important for the assembly phase. For coordination and subordinating conjunction we substitute both clauses and for clausal complements we substitute the complement. The resulting DMRS for the functional chunk of the example in Fig. 1 would consist of three nodes: `_since_x_subord`, `_snow_v_1` at the end of the highlighted ARG1 link and `_rain_v_1` at the end of the ARG2 link.

3.3 Realization

In this phase we simply feed chunk DMRSs into the ACE generator. In the case of functional chunks these are the DMRSs obtained through substitution. Collected data and realization settings are the same as for the standard realization.

3.4 Surface assembly

After all possible realizations are collected for all chunks, we replace realizations of the substitute DMRSs with realizations of appropriate chunks. Based on the chunk hierarchy preserved during chunking, we know which chunk was originally at the end of each trigger link and following this information we can assemble the full sentence recursively.

	Percentage	Count
Both	40.6	128
Only chunking	17.5	55
Only full	8.9	28
Neither	33.0	104

Table 1: The percentage and absolute counts of examples for which the standard realization and/or realization with chunking were successful or not.

4 Dataset

We use the 1214 release of WeScience (Ytrestøl et al., 2009), a fragment of a 2008 Wikipedia snapshot. It is a part of the Redwoods treebank (Oepen et al., 2004), so the analyses it contains are verified by humans as optimal for the original sentence.

Out of the entire dataset, we took 315 sentences which have DMRSs with more than 40 nodes and which can be chunked. There are on average 3.6 chunks per sentence (st. dev. 1.3, max. 12). We do not have space to illustrate the sentences here, but see `tinyurl.com/y9ghd35x`.

5 Coverage and performance

In the experiment we compare the results of the standard realization from a full sentence and realization from a chunked sentence (Table 1).

Realization with chunking allowed realization from some semantic graphs which do not produce a sentence using the standard ACE set-up. The coverage is about 9% higher overall. Some sentences cannot be realized with the new method even though the standard system works. This is because of the presence of grammatical structures not covered by the chunking algorithm, which lead to incorrect subgraphs. Limitations of the chunking algorithm are discussed in detail elsewhere (Muszyńska, 2016).

We investigated the performance of the two approaches in terms of time and memory usage. Fig. 2

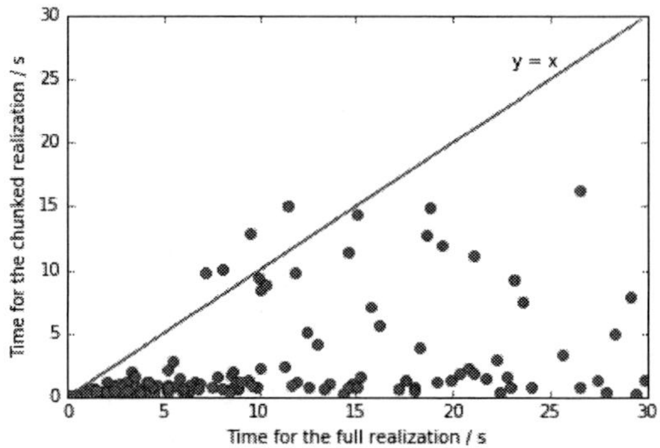

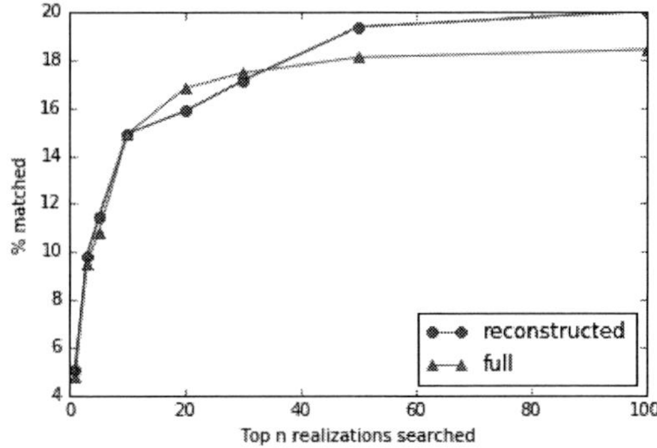

Figure 2: The time needed for realization with chunking against the time taken by the standard realization.

Figure 3: Percentage of exact matches in top n realizations.

shows CPU time for all examples where sentences were successfully realized with both methods or where the standard realization failed without a time-out. The time measured for realization with chunking was the sum across all chunks. The maximum time needed for realization with chunking was 16s. The outliers in the upper half of the graph correspond to sentences where the standard realization failed or chunking was incorrect.

We also recorded the maximum memory used. For space reasons, we do not show the graph but its shape matches that for time, including the outliers. The maximum number of passive edges produced in chart generation also follows a similar pattern and is consistently smaller for chunking than for the standard realization.

The ACE generator ranks its results with a maximum entropy language model and assigns a score to each result. We assign a score to a result of realization with chunking by adding logarithms of scores of the constituent chunk realizations.

Following the original work on the ERG generator by Velldal (2008), we evaluate the ranking quality by comparing the top-ranked realization result with the original sentence on which the semantic representation was based. We use two metrics: the exact match percentage and the BLEU score.

We report an exact match in top n realizations if the original and realized surface strings are identical after removing capitalization and punctuation. Realization with chunking yields comparable results for all n for the examples where both methods produced results (Fig 3). In fact, it slightly overtakes the stan-

dard approach for $n \approx 40$ as some lower ranked realizations are produced only with chunking.

The BLEU score is evaluated only for the top ranked realizations, again after removing punctuation and capitalization. The average score for the standard realization is 0.79 ± 0.14 (st. dev.), and 0.77 ± 0.15 (st. dev.) for realization with chunking. The standard approach achieved a higher score for 17.1% examples, while realization with chunking scored higher for 12.4%. However, there is no statistically significant difference between the two approaches.

6 Conclusions

Chunking noticeably reduces the realization cost for long sentences without affecting the quality of results. In fact, some sentences can be realized only after applying chunking (given time-out). We expect that refinements in chunking will further improve the realization coverage. In future we will also investigate whether the chunking information can be used to improve realization ranking.

Acknowledgements

The authors would like to thank Dan Flickinger for helpful discussions and Matic Horvat for assistance with resolving unknown words. The research is funded by EPSRC Doctoral Research Studentship (EP/M508007/1).

References

John Carroll, Ann Copestake, Dan Flickinger, and Victor Poznanski. 1999. An efficient chart generator for (semi-)lexicalist grammars. In *Proceedings of the 7th European Workshop in Natural Language Generation (ENLG)*, pages 86–95.

Ann Copestake, Dan Flickinger, Carl Pollard, and Ivan A. Sag. 2005. Minimal Recursion Semantics: An introduction. *Research on Language and Computation*, 3(2):281–332.

Ann Copestake, Guy Emerson, Michael Wayne Goodman, Matic Horvat, Alexander Kuhnle, and Ewa Muszyńska. 2016. Resources for building applications with Dependency Minimal Recursion Semantics. In *Proceedings of the Tenth Language Resources and Evaluation Conference (LREC '16)*.

Ann Copestake. 2002. *Implementing typed feature structure grammars*, volume 110 of *CSLI Lecture Notes*. Center for the Study of Language and Information, Stanford, CA.

Ann Copestake. 2009. Slacker semantics: Why superficiality, dependency and avoidance of commitment can be the right way to go. In *Proceedings of the 12th Conference of the European Chapter of the ACL (EACL 2009)*, pages 1–9, Athens, Greece.

Yimai Fang, Haoyue Zhu, Ewa Muszyńska, Alexander Kuhnle, and Simone Teufel. 2016. A proposition-based abstractive summariser. In *Proceedings of COLING 2016, the 26th International Conference on Computational Linguistics*, pages 567–578, Osaka, Japan.

Dan Flickinger, Emily M. Bender, and Stephan Oepen. 2014. Towards an encyclopedia of compositional semantics. Documenting the interface of the English Resource Grammar. In *Proceedings of the Ninth Language Resources and Evaluation Conference (LREC '14)*, pages 875–881, Reykjavik, Iceland.

Dan Flickinger. 2000. On building a more efficient grammar by exploiting types. *Natural Language Engineering*, 6(1):15–28.

Dan Flickinger. 2016. Generating English paraphrases from logic. In Martijn Wieling, Martin Kroon, Gertjan Van Noord, and Gosse Bouma, editors, *From Semantics to Dialectometry*, chapter 11. College Publications.

Matic Horvat. 2017. *Hierarchical statistical semantic translation and realization*. Ph.D. thesis, University of Cambridge, Computer Laboratory.

Ewa Muszyńska. 2016. Graph- and surface-level sentence chunking. In *Proceedings of the ACL 2016 Student Research Workshop*, pages 93–99, Berlin, Germany.

Stephan Oepen, Dan Flickinger, Kristina Toutanova, and Christopher D. Manning. 2004. LinGO Redwoods. *Research on Language and Computation*, 2(4):575–596.

Erik Velldal. 2008. *Empirical Realization Ranking*. Ph.D. thesis, University of Oslo, Department of Informatics.

Michael White. 2004. Reining in CCG chart realization. In Anja Belz, Roger Evans, and Paul Piwek, editors, *Natural Language Generation. Lecture Notes in Computer Science*, volume 3123. Springer, Berlin, Heidelberg.

Xuchen Yao, Gosse Bouma, Yi Zhang, Paul Piwek, and Kristy Elizabeth Boyer. 2012. Semantics-based question generation and implementation. *Dialogue and Discourse*, 3(2):11–42.

Gisle Ytrestøl, Dan Flickinger, and Stephan Oepen. 2009. Extracting and annotating Wikipedia subdomains - towards a new eScience community resource. In *Proceedings of the Seventh International Workshop on Treebanks and Linguistic Theories (TLT 7)*, pages 185–197, Groningen, The Netherlands.

SaToS: Assessing and Summarising Terms of Services from German Webshops

Daniel Braun and **Elena Scepankova** and **Patrick Holl** and **Florian Matthes**
Technical University of Munich
Department of Informatics
{daniel.braun,elena.scepankova,patrick.holl,matthes}@tum.de

Abstract

Every time we buy something online, we are confronted with Terms of Services. However, only a few people actually read these terms, before accepting them, often to their disadvantage. In this paper, we present the SaToS browser plugin which summarises and simplifies Terms of Services from German webshops.

1 Introduction

The phrase "I have read and understood the terms of service" is often referred to as "the biggest lie on the internet" (Pridmore and Overocker, 2014; Binns and Matthews, 2014). In a study conducted by Obar and Oeldorf-Hirsch (2016), participants were asked to register for a made-up social network. 74% of the participants did not read the Terms of Service (ToS) at all and those who did read it spent on average 13.6 seconds on it, hardly enough to read let alone understand a juridical text with more than 4,300 words. Nevertheless, all participants agreed to the ToS.

General terms and conditions (German: *Allgemeine Geschäftsbedingungen - AGB*; in the following: ToS) included in standard form contracts are of significant economic value, as most companies use these terms when entering into contractual relationships with their customers. Historically, ToS trace back to the age of industrialisation in the 19th century. In the course of mass production, entering into contracts has been accompanied by the unilateral use of these terms and conditions as a set of pre-formulated rules - tailored to one party's own purposes and thus resulting in an imbalance of powers between the contracting parties. (Zerres, 2014)

In this paper, we present the ongoing interdisciplinary computer and legal science research project SaToS (Software aided analysis of ToS) and a prototype which automatically identifies ToS on German webshops and summarises them with regard to their lawfulness and customer friendliness, in a simplified language. These summarisations are presented through an adblocker-like browser plugin. In this way, SaToS aims to empower customers to make educated decisions about where to buy or not within seconds, directly addressing the imbalance of powers and fostering the constitutional principle of Legal Clarity[1].

2 Related Work

Generally speaking, automatically generated summarisations can be divided into extractive and abstractive (cf. e.g. Das and Martins (2007)). As mentioned before, many people do not read ToS at all and even if they do, these texts are often difficult to understand. Therefore, in order to make ToS understandable for customers, it is necessary to create abstractive, simplified summaries, rather than extractive ones. Currently, there are mainly two projects trying to create automatic summarisations of legal texts: the SUM project from Grover et al. (2003) and the LetSum project from Farzindar and Lapalme (2004). However, both systems create extractive summaries for English texts, while we aim to create abstractive summaries for German texts. In order to create abstractive summaries, a system first

---

[1] Art. 20 Abs. 3 GG (Grundgesetz - German Constitution)

223

Proceedings of The 10th International Natural Language Generation conference, pages 223–227,
Santiago de Compostela, Spain, September 4-7 2017. ©2017 Association for Computational Linguistics

has to obtain the relevant information from the text. Information Retrieval (IR) for legal texts has gained a lot of attraction in recent years. Examples are Mc-Callum (2005), Grabmair et al. (2015), Francesconi et al. (2010), and Shulayeva et al. (2017), or, for German texts, Walter and Pinkal (2006), and Waltl et al. (2017). The issue of simplifying legal texts was e.g. addressed by Bhatia (1983) and Collantes et al. (2015). A general architecture for simplifying texts was presented by Siddharthan (2002). From a legal perspective, ToS;DR (Binns and Matthews, 2014) and janolaw[2] pursue a similar aim by evaluating ToS. Whereas we use a natural language processing and artificial intelligence in order to assess and evaluate ToS, they are crowed-sourced, which affects their scalability and topicality.

3 Legal Assessment

The assessment of ToS is of enormous value. Firstly, they affect many important issues of contractual relationships - details of performance and payment, liability, revocation rights, the place of jurisdiction - and thus have a significant impact on the customer. Being drafted unilaterally by one party, they bear risks like limiting liability or revocation rights, granting permission to increase prices or imposing penalties in case of delay etc.

Secondly, legal language is written in a way that is often difficult to understand. The reason is that law by itself has to be written with a certain degree of abstractness, in order to fulfil its function of regulating our social behaviour. This abstractness, however, leads to a low level of comprehensibility. Although law has to satisfy both principles - abstractness and comprehensibility -, it implicitly favours the former at costs of the latter. Against the background of this, it is not surprising that people avoid reading general terms and conditions at all.

Finally, the imbalance of powers resulting from the fact, that ToS are imposed unilaterally by one party, is mirrored by the number of laws[3] and courts decisions[4] assessing the lawfulness of those clauses.

---

[2]https://www.janolaw.de/

[3]Relevant laws concerning general terms and conditions are in §§305 -310 BGB (Bürgerliches Gesetzbuch - German Civil Code).

[4]According to the data base *Juris*, there are currently about 27,600 judgments addressing the lawfulness of ToS.

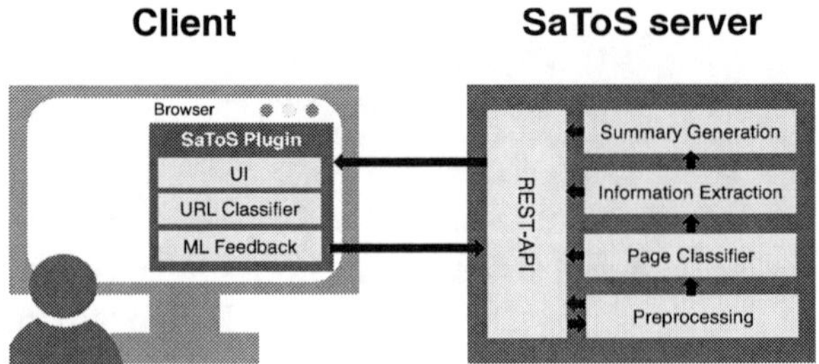

Figure 1: Architecture of the SaToS prototype

We try to adjust this imbalance of powers by identifying unlawful clauses and indicating differences between them so that customers will finally know their rights, without any previously required legal knowledge.

4 Prototype Architecture

The client-server architecture of the SaToS prototype is shown in Figure 1. While most of the natural language processing and generation is done on the server, the client handles the output and collects feedback from the user. A REST-API is used for the communication between client and server. The server itself is a Node.js application and internally based on a pipes and filters architecture (Meunier, 1995).

4.1 SaToS server

In this section, we will describe the components of the SaToS server. The REST-API consists of routes for every of these components. While it is possible to exit the pipeline after every module, it can only be entered through the first module. All routes take a URL as input.

4.1.1 Preprocessing

In the first module, the content of the webpage is retrieved and pre-processed. First, the main content is extracted and elements like navigation and header, are removed. Afterwards, all HTML tags are removed. Depending on further analysis that will be conducted, additional pre-processing is conducted, like tokenization, stemming, and POS tagging.

4.1.2 Page Classifier

The Page Classifier is a binary classifier that labels each page either "ToS" or "Other". In our current prototype, we use a naive Bayes classifier. Our aim is to incrementally improve its quality based on user feedback (cf. Section 4.2.1). In Section 5, we present an evaluation of the classifier.

4.1.3 Information Extraction

The Information Extraction (IE) module contains the domain knowledge, which is necessary to extract the information and identify unlawful clauses by examining the used legal language formulations, in accordance with the rules used by German courts. An excerpt of these rules is shown in Table 1.

There is not a single module for IE, but one for every aspect. Currently, our prototype has two of these modules, one for the right of withdrawal and one for the right of warranty. We decided to start with these, because they are very valuable for potential customers, included in most ToS, and relatively similar because they both essentially describe a timespan. Therefore, in order to extract this information, we first look for sentences which describe a timespan, i.e. a number or numeral word followed by a "unit" like day, month, or year. Afterwards, we identify the topic of the sentence. Thanks to the legal nature of the texts, there is a relatively small variety of permissible formulations to describe the right of withdrawal (*"Widerrufsrecht"*) and the warranty period (*"Gewährleistungsfrist"*). Once the information is extracted, it is returned in JSON-format. The sentence *"Der Kunde kann von uns erhaltene Ware ohne Angabe von Gründen innerhalb von 30 Tagen durch Rücksendung der Ware zurückgeben."*[5] would, for example, generate the output shown in Listing 1.

```
1  {
2      "topic": "Widerrufsrecht",
3      "dataType": "Timespan",
4      "value": 30,
5      "unit": "Tag"
6  }
```

Listing 1: Format of extracted Information

4.1.4 Summary Generation

The summary generator gets an array of extracted information in the above-described format as input and is leant on the architecture described by Reiter (2007). Since we do not have purely numerical data

---

[5]https://www.thomann.de/de/compinfo_terms.html; last accessed 12 May 2017

input, we do not have a *Signal Analysis* stage, however, the above-described information extraction fulfils a similar goal. The next stage is *Data Interpretation*. In this stage, we interpret the extracted information mainly regarding their legality. In this way, we distinguish between unlawful, lawful, and customer friendly regulations. Under German law, for example, customers always have to have at least 14 days of time to withdraw their order. Hence, a shorter timespan would be unlawful, a timespan of 14 days would be lawful, and anything beyond would be classified as customer friendly.

During *Document Planning*, so far, only the order of the messages is determined, starting with unlawful messages, followed by customer friendly messages, followed by lawful messages.

Finally, during *Realisation*, the actual summaries are created based on templates that have been written by a jurist. These templates are designed to be easily understandable while still containing all the necessary information and have to be created for each individual information extraction module.

4.2 Browser Plugin

The SaToS browser plugin works passively and does usually not require any user input.

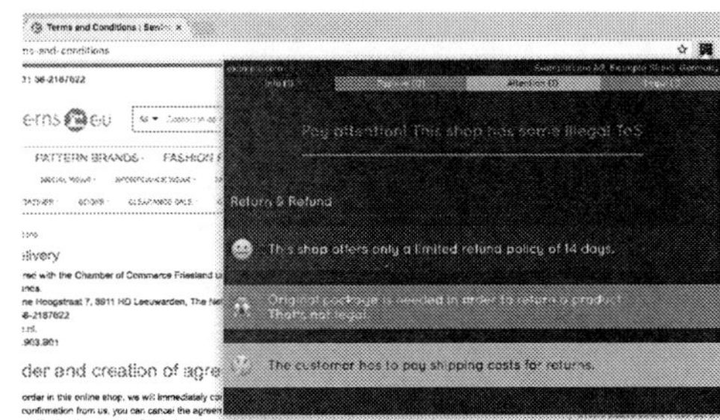

Figure 2: SaToS Browser Plugin

4.2.1 User Interface

Figure 2 shows the UI of the Plugin, including an overall recommendation for the shop and three categorised summary excerpts. The summary excerpts are split into the four categories: *Info* (neutral information for the user, grey), *Positive* (anything that improves customer friendliness and which goes beyond the legal requirements, green), *Attention* (warns the user if the ToS contains clauses which are legal but unusual, orange), and *Illegal* (any invalid or illegal

	unlawfull	rules (translated from German)
Right of warranty	New goods: less than 2 years; used goods: less than 1 year	-warranty ... ([0-9]* I [one I two I ...]) [day(s) I month(s) I year(s)] AND used OR NOT used (goods I products) -warranty ... used (goods I products) ... excluded
Right of withdrawal	Products have to be send back using the original packaging	-product ... original (packaging I packed I ...) ... (return I send back) -original (packaging I packed I ...) ... (return I send back)
Period for withdrawal	Period of less than 14 days for shops trading in the EU	-withdraw ... ([0-9]* I [one I two I ...]) [day(s) I month(s) I year(s)]
Obligation to inspect product	Warranty rights only if customer inspects and/or reports any product defects	-warranty ... [inspect I report] AND NOT merchant
Risk of loss	In case of shipped sales the customer bears the risk of loss	[risk of loss I bearing the risk] ... [shipped I carriage of goods] ... consumer

Table 1: Extraction rules for ToS (excerpt)

statement, red). The summaries are assigned to a certain category and highlighted accordingly. Furthermore, based on the categorizations, we generate a recommendation for the shop as a whole. Users can also give feedback whether the ToS were classified correctly. We use this feedback to realise an online learning approach for our ML algorithms.

4.2.2 URL Classifier

Usually, when a user visits a webshop, he enters it via a specific landing or product page. However, for the summarisation, we have to process the content of the shops' ToS page. The goal of the URL classifier is to pre-select links that potentially lead to the ToS page and hence restrict the set of pages that have to be classified by the server. The classification is done by using a rule-based approach that matches common patterns for ToS links. One common pattern we identified is that the URL often contains *"AGB"*. The classifier separates URL strings into the following components: scheme specifier, network location part, path, query parameters. The path and query parameters are matched against a set of pre-defined, weighted rules. If the matches reach a certain threshold, we consider that a given URL points to a potential ToS page.

5 Evaluation ToS Classification

As mentioned before, we use a hybrid approach of client-based rules and server-based ML. Since all further analyses are based on the correct classification of ToS pages, we conducted an evaluation of both components. We collected a dataset of 3424 URLs. 2592 from ToS pages, manually labelled by a price comparison website, and 832 from other web-

shop pages. We split the dataset into training (200 ToS and 200 Other) and test (2392 ToS and 632 Other). The results of the evaluation are shown in Table 2. It is obvious, that the ML approach performed significantly better, with regard to precision, recall, and F-score. Given the fact, that the ML classifier was trained with a relatively small, non-optimized, dataset, the results are promising, keeping in mind that we use an online learning approach and expect the system to improve over time. One might wonder, why one should use a hybrid approach, although ML performs better in every category. The fifth column in Table 2 shows the average time in seconds, that was needed to classify a URL. If successful, the rule-based approach is not only faster, but its calculation is also "free" for SaToS, since it happens on the client.

approach	precision	recall	F-score	$\emptyset t$ in s
ML	0.9115	0.8219	0.8644	1.435
rule-based	0.7953	0.5393	0.6428	0.001

Table 2: Evaluation ToS Classification

6 Conclusion

By combining legal expertise with state-of-the-art technology, we want to empower customers to understand ToS and exercise their rights towards companies. In this paper, we presented a first research prototype, called SaToS, which automatically detects, summarises, and analyses ToS from German webshops regarding their lawfulness and customer-friendliness. We have evaluated the ToS Classifier and argued for a hybrid solution, combining rule-based approaches and ML. In the future, we want to expand the prototype for other ToS clauses.

References

Vijay K Bhatia. 1983. Simplification v. easification-the case of legal texts. *Applied linguistics*, 4:42.

Reuben Binns and David Matthews. 2014. Community structure for efficient information flow in'tos; dr', a social machine for parsing legalese. In *Proceedings of the 23rd International Conference on World Wide Web*, pages 881–884. ACM.

Miguel Collantes, Maureen Hipe, Juan Lorenzo Sorilla, Laurenz Tolentino, and Briane Samson. 2015. Simpatico: A text simplification system for senate and house bills. In *Proceedings of the 11th National Natural Language Processing Research Symposium*, pages 26–32.

Dipanjan Das and André FT Martins. 2007. A survey on automatic text summarization. *Literature Survey for the Language and Statistics II course at CMU*, 4:192–195.

Atefeh Farzindar and Guy Lapalme. 2004. Letsum, an automatic legal text summarizing system. *Legal knowledge and information systems, JURIX*, pages 11–18.

Enrico Francesconi, Simonetta Montemagni, Wim Peters, and Daniela Tiscornia. 2010. *Semantic processing of legal texts: Where the language of law meets the law of language*, volume 6036. Springer.

Matthias Grabmair, Kevin D Ashley, Ran Chen, Preethi Sureshkumar, Chen Wang, Eric Nyberg, and Vern R Walker. 2015. Introducing luima: an experiment in legal conceptual retrieval of vaccine injury decisions using a uima type system and tools. In *Proceedings of the 15th International Conference on Artificial Intelligence and Law*, pages 69–78. ACM.

Claire Grover, Ben Hachey, Ian Hughson, and Chris Korycinski. 2003. Automatic summarisation of legal documents. In *Proceedings of the 9th international conference on Artificial intelligence and law*, pages 243–251. ACM.

Andrew McCallum. 2005. Information extraction: Distilling structured data from unstructured text. *Queue*, 3(9):48–57.

Regine Meunier. 1995. The pipes and filters architecture. In *Pattern languages of program design*, pages 427–440. ACM Press/Addison-Wesley Publishing Co.

Jonathan A Obar and Anne Oeldorf-Hirsch. 2016. The biggest lie on the internet: Ignoring the privacy policies and terms of service policies of social networking services.

Jeannie Pridmore and John Overocker. 2014. Privacy in virtual worlds: a us perspective. *Journal For Virtual Worlds Research*, 7(1).

Ehud Reiter. 2007. An architecture for data-to-text systems. In *Proceedings of the Eleventh European Workshop on Natural Language Generation*, pages 97–104. Association for Computational Linguistics.

Olga Shulayeva, Advaith Siddharthan, and Adam Wyner. 2017. Recognizing cited facts and principles in legal judgements. *Artificial Intelligence and Law*, 25(1):107–126.

Advaith Siddharthan. 2002. An architecture for a text simplification system. In *Language Engineering Conference*, page 64. IEEE Computer Society.

Stephan Walter and Manfred Pinkal. 2006. Automatic extraction of definitions from german court decisions. In *Proceedings of the workshop on information extraction beyond the document*, pages 20–28. Association for Computational Linguistics.

B. Waltl, J. Landthaler, E. Scepankova, F. Matthes, T. Geiger, C. Stocker, and C. Schneider. 2017. Automated extraction of semantic information from german legal documents. In *IRIS: Internationales Rechtsinformatik Symposium*. Association for Computational Linguistics.

Thomas Zerres. 2014. Principles of the german law on standard terms of contract. *Jurawelt*.

Textually Summarising Incomplete Data

Stephanie Inglis, Ehud Reiter and Somayajulu Sripada
Department of Computing Science, University of Aberdeen
Aberdeen, UK, AB24 3UE
r01si14@abdn.ac.uk, e.reiter@abdn.ac.uk, yaji.sripada@abdn.ac.uk

Abstract

Many data-to-text NLG systems work with data sets which are incomplete, ie some of the data is missing. We have worked with data journalists to understand how they describe incomplete data, and are building NLG algorithms based on these insights. A pilot evaluation showed mixed results, and highlighted several areas where we need to improve our system.

1 Introduction

Natural language generation systems which produce texts based on incomplete data can produce low quality or inaccurate reports (Reiter & Dale. 2000). Improving the quality of these reports means more accurate information can be concluded from datasets, which increases the impact of data being collected. All tasks described in this paper use the Em-Dat database (Guha-Sapir, Below, and Hoyois).

2 Related Work

Daniel et al. (2008) identified three major data quality issues which occur in a large number of datasets – incompleteness, inconsistency and incorrectness. The paper describes scenarios where data quality has a profound knock on effect, such as when ordering incorrect quantities of medical supplies. Based on findings from preliminary experiments involving non-experts, missing data was the most important of these issues. Therefore, missing data is the quality focus of this paper.

With automated journalism being used to report news in an unbiased fashion, care needs to be taken to improve generated texts. One way this has been done is through research on human written news (Van der Kaa & Krahmer, 2014).

3 Experts

3.1 Expert Identification

To design a system which models human behavior accurately, knowledge was elicited from experts – people who use datasets to create texts for humans. One such domain is journalism. The Guardian newspaper has a section dedicated specifically for this type of journalism called Datablog[1]. They use datasets to produce texts allowing non-experts to access the stories being told by the data. Some journalists from Datablog agreed to take part in a protocol analysis, which encourages the participant to speak aloud as they complete a task (Ericsson, 2006). This allows insight into how a data journalist produces text from a dataset, which can later be used to create an algorithm.

3.2 Normal Process

We first asked the journalists to describe in general terms how they would write an article based on incomplete data. Both journalists agreed that they

---

[1] https://www.theguardian.com/data

Proceedings of The 10th International Natural Language Generation conference, pages 228–232,
Santiago de Compostela, Spain, September 4-7 2017. ©2017 Association for Computational Linguistics

would not extrapolate gaps in the data and would only report the raw data to ensure accurate reports. Instead, they would contact the source of the data and enquire about the reasoning behind the gaps. If gaps could be remedied by contacting experts in the dataset's domain, this avenue would be explored. Otherwise, academic papers on the dataset would be consulted to see if another solution had been identified. If not, an attempt to locate an alternative dataset would be made. Both journalists also agreed they would not use a dataset if more than half the data was missing.

If no other datasets exist, they would question whether this story is appropriate. In one instance, journalists wanted to write a story about the number of sexual assaults on university campuses, and found that this data was not recorded. The story became that universities were not accurately recording sexual assaults on campuses (McVeigh, 2015).

If an incomplete dataset was used for a story, gaps would be communicated to the reader, for example by giving this information as footnotes.

3.3   Knowledge Elicitation

We asked journalists to participate in a formal knowledge elicitation task. They were asked to write texts to summarise data from the EM-Dat database.

The first dataset had no missing data. While unrealistic, this acted as a baseline to observe their methodology when missing data was not an issue. The second dataset had some data missing, but with enough data present to allow a report to be created. The final dataset had a large amount of missing data, which would likely be unsuitable for an article.

The journalists were asked to imagine they had to write an article using these datasets. For each dataset, they had to describe their steps to produce an article. They had access to the data in a spreadsheet on a laptop to allow them to manipulate data as they would normally to simulate normal working conditions as closely as possible.

> "I wouldn't say well the average looks to be between these periods this so therefore let's just extrapolate. I would not do that at all."

Figure 1 - Quote from transcript of Journalist 1, Dataset 3

A dictaphone recorded the journalists throughout.

3.4   Outcome Methodology

Both journalists followed similar methodologies. The journalists wanted to investigate the metadata first, such as the validity of the dataset itself, any bias that may be present from the database creator, and column headers definitions. They both also disregarded the current year as this was deemed incomplete since the year itself is currently incomplete.

Next, columns with no missing data were identified. The maximum value and minimum values of these columns were noted along with which years the maximum and minimum occurred. This was compared with the years of the maximum and minimum of other columns.

If no columns were complete, a threshold of present data would be decided, and applied consistently across all columns in the dataset. If data is missing, the phrase "of the data reported" was added.

Next the journalists looked at the rows for complete time periods, such as decades, otherwise for time periods with years divisible by 5. This was not always possible as events did not happen every year. However, just because a year is not present in the dataset does not mean an event did not occur; the entry may be missing from the database.

One journalist said they would not report an average figure as it did not make sense in this context. Events occur at different magnitudes and it would be highly inaccurate to assume all variables are evenly distributed across all events.

4   Algorithm

The algorithm that mimics the journalist methodology first computes the best block data and generates text to describe it as described below.

4.1   Preprocessing

A CSV file with the dataset is read, and columns with meaningful information are identified. Columns with redundant information were removed. These are columns acting as metadata which never have empty cells – such as year and occurrences, and columns that are the sum of other columns, which can later be calculated if required later.

If the current year has an entry, this is put to one side. The remaining data can now be used to search for the "best" block of data to talk about. A block is defined as a subset of the dataset of any size, where data is either missing, or present. Rows within a block must remain contiguous, however all possible sets of columns, regardless of whether the columns in the set are next to each other are considered. Any gaps in the data are replaced with -1, to indicate that this cell has no data. Using 0 may be ambiguous as this is a legitimate number that could be reported.

4.2 Best Blocks

Instead of using the entire dataset with large areas of missing data to produce texts, blocks with more present data than missing data were identified.

We select the block with the highest score using the scoring function below:

$$Score(block) = \#DataElements(block) - \#MissingData(block)$$

If the total score is a negative number, more than 50% of the data is missing, and the block should be rejected for being too sparse.

If more than one block has the highest score, the block with the smallest percentage of missing data is chosen as the single "optimal" block.

4.3 Algorithm Functions

Once the optimal block has been selected, the algorithm looks for interesting elements to talk about.

If the block does not cover all rows of the dataset, text is added to give the time period discussed, in the form "Between *firstYear* and *lastYear*", with firstYear being the year of the first event, and lastYear being the year of the final event.

As each text output gives text for each column, one column was selected as the focus for the text. Both years and occurrences were ruled out as possible foci since they were not "meaningful" variables. For each column in the optimal block, the maximum values are reported in the form "the worst year for *column* as a result of *disaster* in *country* was *year* when there was *value*". This was the first thing both journalists considered with regards to the data itself:

"Let's just sort it to start with because usually in headlines we think of like what was the worst year." – Journalist 1

"When I look at the data I look at the year, the time series for the total deaths and the biggest number" – Journalist 2

This is supported by research that people are more interested in negative headlines than positive headlines (Trussler & Soroka, 2014). Therefore, only the worst years are reported.

Next, the years in which there is a recorded event are investigated in descending order. The algorithm detects the number of consecutive years. This number is rounded down to the nearest multiple of 5. If this number is a multiple of 10, a sentence can report information about "the last x decades". Alternatively, if it is a multiple of 5 but not a multiple of 10, a sentence can report information about "the last x years". The rationale behind this is demonstrated from an excerpt from the transcript of participant 1 for dataset 2:

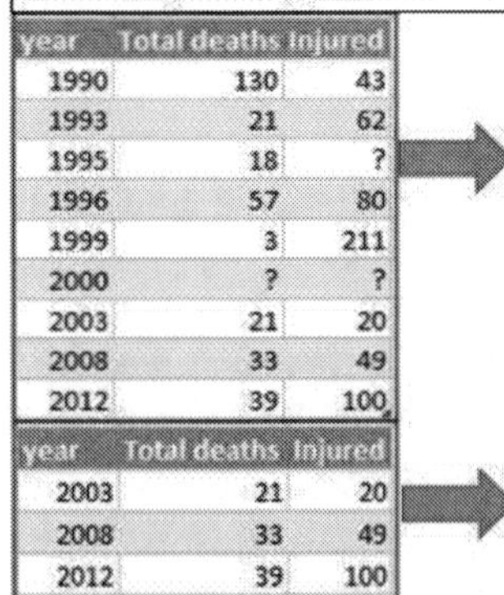

Hong Kong Technological

year	Total deaths	Injured	Affected	Homeless	Total damage
1948	135	?	?	?	?
1983	?	?	?	9000	?
1984	?	?	?	4650	?
1990	130	43	?	?	?
1993	21	62	?	?	?
1995	18	?	?	?	?
1996	57	80	?	?	?
1999	3	211	?	?	?
2000	?	?	?	300	?
2003	21	20	?	?	?
2008	33	49	7	?	?
2012	39	100	?	?	?
2014	12	?	?	?	?
2015	?	100	?	?	?

"The worst year for injured as a result of technological disasters in Hong Kong was 1999 when there were 211 injuries. However, there were 9000 people made homeless and 7 people affected by technological disasters in Hong Kong in 1983 and 2008 respectively."

year	Total deaths	Injured
1990	130	43
1993	21	62
1995	18	?
1996	57	80
1999	3	211
2000	?	?
2003	21	20
2008	33	49
2012	39	100

"Between 1990 and 2012, the worst year for injured as a result of technological disasters in Hong Kong was 1999 when there were 211 injuries."

year	Total deaths	Injured
2003	21	20
2008	33	49
2012	39	100

"Between 2003 and 2012, the worst year for injured as a result of technological disasters in Hong Kong was 2012 when there were 100 injuries. In the same year, there were 39 total deaths."

Figure 2 – The full dataset for technological events in Hong Kong, the "optimal" block with missing data, and the "optimal" block without missing data (selected by the algorithm). This figure also shows the corresponding generated texts (also produced by the algorithm) for each data block.

"There are years missing in the sequence...we don't have any period that would give us something to talk about a decade, and definitely not the most recent."

These sentences are produced in the same way the sentences about columns are produced – giving the time period, and the maximum values for each column. Like the definition of the current year, the current decade is also classed as being incomplete, and should not be used. A separate sentence is added to report the current year so far.

5 Pilot Evaluation

An experiment was designed to judge the output texts generated by the algorithm using SimpleNLG (Gatt & Reiter, 2009). Six datasets with varying degrees of missing data were chosen, and three texts were generated for each dataset. One text was generated using the entire dataset, another with the "optimal" block, and the third with the largest block containing no missing data.

The text structure was kept the same for all outputs to minimise any unwanted bias in the writing style. All texts report only the worst figures.

The datasets were ordered alphabetically, and the order in which the texts were shown were randomly generated by numbering them (1 for full dataset text, 2 for no missing data block text, and 3 for the "optimal" algorithm output), and a random sequence generator to create the order.

Participants were asked to choose which of the three texts they thought was the most appropriate in describing the dataset. 20 participants were recruited using social media. A space was also left for participants to leave comments.

We hypothesised that the text produced by our algorithm would be preferred over the control texts. Although not statistically significant, we found participants preferred texts generated by the full dataset (40.8% against 32.5% (optimal) and 26.7% (full)). Comments left by participants (detailed in section 6) allow improvements to be made.

6 Future Work

6.1 Missing Data

Text with missing data should be highlighted as having missing data by adding phrases such as "of the data recorded" or "of the data available". This ensures the reader of the text is aware that not all data was available when generating this text. One participant did not think this was clear and remarked *"for me, appropriate [text] would be 'the worst year recorded'"*.

Secondly, business rules can be added to improve plausibility and confidence. If there are a large number of deaths but no one injured or affected, the number of deaths may be too high, or there may be data missing from the other columns. This was considered by one participant who commented that it was *"easy to find the outliers"* and that *"simply stating the biggest number could lead to false information"*.

Additionally, a weighting factor will be added to the scoring function to model the importance of missing data. For instance:

$$Score(block) = \#DataElements(block) - Weight * \#MissingData(block)$$

6.2 Text

Multiple participants commented on the language used, particularly conjunctives. One participant said *"there are some texts where the connective 'however' does not seem to fit well"*, while another pointed out *"'however' shouldn't be used as it refers to the same year thus making this statement confusing"*. Care will be taken to resolve this. Also, reporting *"large figures as $158230000 in so many digits"* was confusing for participants, so presentation of such values will be made more appropriate.

Participants felt the time period should also be made explicit for the full dataset as one participant noted: *"I would never find 'the worst year ever' without a date range to be appropriate"*. Therefore, the date range will be added for all texts.

The content of the text could be ordered by importance. Importance could be measured by how important the information is e.g. if a death toll is particularly large. The importance could be investigated by revisiting the interview with the journalists from the experiment, or run a corpus analysis and look at the frequency of words in the text.

7 Conclusion

Knowledge has been gathered from domain experts and used to design and create an algorithm. While the pilot evaluation had mixed results, the feedback is crucial in taking steps to improve the algorithm.

References

Daniel, F., Casati, F., Palpanas, T., Chayka, O. and Cappiello, C. (2008*). Enabling Better Decisions Through Quality-Aware Reports In Business Intelligence Applications.*

Ericsson, K. A. (2006). Protocol Analysis and Expert Thought: Concurrent Verbalizations of Thinking during Experts' Performance on Representative Tasks. In: *The Cambridge Handbook of Expertise and Expert Performance*. Cambridge: Cambridge University Press. p223-242.

Gatt, A and Reiter, E (2009). *SimpleNLG: A realisation engine for practical applications*. Proceedings of ENLG-2009

Guha-Sapir, D., Below, R., and Hoyois, Ph. *EM-DAT: International Disaster Database*. Available: www.emdat.be. Last accessed 10th May 2017.

McVeigh, K. (2015). *Top universities fail to record sexual violence against students, The Guardian,* 24th May. Available: https://www.theguardian.com/education/2015/may/24/top-universities-fail-record-sexual-violence-against-students-russell-group. Last accessed 10th May 2017.

Reiter, E. and Dale, R. (2000). *Building Natural Language Generation Systems*. Cambridge University Press.

Trussler, M and Soroka, S. (2014). Consumer Demand for Cynical and Negative News Frames. *The International Journal of Press/Politics*. 19 (3), p360-379.

Van der Kaa, H. & Krahmer, E. (2014). Journalist versus news consumer: The perceived credibility of machine written news. *Proceedings of the Computation + Journalism conference.*

Improving the generation of personalised descriptions

Thiago Castro Ferreira
Tilburg center for Cognition and Communication (TiCC)
Tilburg University, The Netherlands
tcastrof@tilburguniversity.edu

Ivandré Paraboni
School of Arts, Sciences and Humanities
University of São Paulo, Brazil
ivandre@usp.br

Abstract

Referring expression generation (REG) models that use speaker-dependent information require a considerable amount of training data produced by every individual speaker, or may otherwise perform poorly. In this work we propose a simple personalised method for this task, in which speakers are grouped into profiles according to their referential behaviour. Intrinsic evaluation shows that the use of speaker's profiles generally outperforms the personalised method found in previous work.

1 Introduction

In natural language generation systems, referring expression generation (REG) is the microplanning task responsible for generating references of discourse entities (Krahmer and van Deemter, 2012). Choice of referential form (Ferreira et al., 2016), i.e., deciding whether a reference should be a proper name ('Ayrton Senna'), a pronoun ('He') or a description ('The racing driver'), is the first decision to be made in this task.

Albeit notable studies on pronominalisation (Callaway and Lester, 2002) and proper name generation (Ferreira et al., 2017), research on REG has largely focused on the generation of descriptions or, more specifically, on content selection. For instance, in the previous example, Ayrton Senna's *occupation* is the content selected to describe him. This work focuses on this kind of content selection task, hereby called REG for brevity.

Existing work in computational REG and related fields have identified a wide range of factors that may drive content selection. To a considerable extent, however, content selection is known to be influenced by human variation (Viethen and Dale, 2010). In other words, under identical circumstances (i.e., in the same referential context), different speakers will often produce different descriptions, and a single entity may be described by different speakers as 'the racing driver', 'the McLaren pilot', etc.

Existing REG algorithms as in Bohnet (2008) and Ferreira and Paraboni (2014) usually pay regard to human variation by computing personalised features from a training set of descriptions produced by each speaker. This highly personalised training method may of course be considered an ideal account of human variation but, in practice, will only be effective if every speaker in the domain is represented by a sufficiently large number of training instances.

As means to improve REG results when the amount of training data is limited, in this work we propose a simple training method for speaker-dependent REG in which training referring expressions are grouped into profiles according to the speaker's referential behaviour. The method relies on the observation that speakers tend to be consistent in their choices of referential overspecification, and it is shown to outperform the use of personalised information.

2 Related Work

Existing methods for speaker-dependent REG generally consist of computing the relevant features for each speaker. In what follows we summarise a number of studies that follow this method. In Bohnet (2008), the Incremental algorithm (Dale and Reiter,

Proceedings of The 10th International Natural Language Generation conference, pages 233–237,
Santiago de Compostela, Spain, September 4-7 2017. ©2017 Association for Computational Linguistics

1995) and a number of extensions of the Full Brevity algorithm (Dale, 1989) are evaluated on a corpus of furniture items and famous mathematicians (TUNA) (Gatt et al., 2007). In the case of the Incremental algorithm, human variation is accounted for by computing individual preference lists based on the attribute frequency of each speaker as observed in the training data. In the case of Full Brevity, all possible descriptions for a given referent are computed, and the description that most closely resembles those produced by the speaker is selected using a nearest neighbour approach.

The work in Viethen and Dale (2010) makes use of decision-tree induction to predict content patterns (i.e., full attribute sets representing actual referring expressions) to describe geometric objects on Google SketchUp scenes (GRE3D3/7 corpus) (Dale and Viethen, 2009; Viethen and Dale, 2011). Human variation is accounted for by modelling speaker identifiers as machine learning features.

Finally, the work in Ferreira and Paraboni (2014) presents a SVM-based approach to speaker-dependent REG tested also on the description of geometric objects (GRE3D3/7 and Stars/Stars2 (Teixeira et al., 2014; Paraboni et al., 2016) corpora). Once again, human variation is accounted for by computing individual preference lists from the subset of descriptions produced by each speaker.

3   Current work

In all the studies discussed in the previous section, personalised REG outperforms standard algorithms on domains in which a sufficient large number of training instances (i.e., referring expressions) is available for every speaker under consideration. However, the number of available instances per speaker tends to be small even in purpose-built REG corpora. For instance, there are only about 7 descriptions per speaker in the TUNA (singular) domain (Gatt et al., 2007), and 10-16 descriptions per speaker in GRE3D3/7 (Dale and Viethen, 2009; Viethen and Dale, 2011) and Stars/Stars2 (Teixeira et al., 2014; Paraboni et al., 2016).

To improve REG results in these situations, in what follows we consider a grouping personalised method that relies on psycholinguistic studies on referential overspecification (Koolen et al., 2011).

3.1   Basic REG model

We designed a REG experiment that makes use of a speaker-dependent REG model adapted from Ferreira and Paraboni (2014) as follows. Given a set D of domain objects, a set A of referential attributes, a set R of spatial relations between object pairs, and a target object $t \in D$ to be identified, content selection is implemented with the aid of a set of classifiers $C_{atom} = \{c^{(1)}, c^{(2)}, ..., c^{(|A|)}\}$, in which $c^{(i)} \in C_{atom}$ predicts whether $a^{(i)} \in A$ should be selected or not, and a multi-class classifier C_{rel} predicts the kind of relation ($r \in R$) that may hold between the target t and the nearest landmark lm. R includes the special *no-relation* property to denote situations in which no relation between a certain object pair is predicted. When a relation to a landmark object lm exists, we also consider a set of classifiers $C_{atom}^{lm} = \{c^{(1)}, c^{(2)}, ..., c^{(|A|)}\}$ to describe lm.

Part of the input to the classifiers consists of feature vectors extracted from the referential context. These features - hereby called context features - are based on the ones proposed in Viethen and Dale (2010), and are intended to model target and landmark properties (if any), and similarities between objects. More specifically, context features represent the size of the target and its nearest landmark, the relation (horizontal or vertical) between the two objects, and the number of distractors that share a certain property (e.g., *type*, *colour* etc.)

In order to model human variation, we also consider two kinds of speaker-dependent feature: those that model personal information about the speakers, and those that model their content selection preferences. Speaker's personal features consist of a unique speaker identifier as in Viethen and Dale (2010), gender and age bracket. Speaker's preferences consist of lists of preferred attributes for reference to target and landmark objects sorted by frequency. Attributes and relations of the main target t and nearby landmark lm are combined to form a description L according to Algorithm 1.

The input to the algorithm is a target t and a domain D. The algorithm also makes use of a history list H to prevent self-reference (e.g., 'the ball next to a box that is next to a ball that...') and the initially empty list L representing the output description (to be built recursively).

Method	TUNA-f		TUNA-p		GRE3D3		GRE3D7		Stars		Stars2		Overall	
	Dice	Acc.	Dice	Acc.	Dice	Acc.	Dice	Acc.	Dice	Acc.	Dice	Acc.	Dice	Acc.
Speaker	0.85	0.41	0.71	0.24	0.88	0.61	0.92	0.72	0.75	**0.39**	0.70	0.31	0.87	0.60
Profile	0.85	0.43	**0.78**	**0.35**	**0.93**	**0.74**	**0.94**	**0.77**	0.73	0.32	**0.78**	**0.40**	**0.90**	**0.66**

Table 1: Content selection results

Algorithm 1: Classification-based REG

```
 1  Algorithm getDescription(t, L, D, H)
 2      L[t] ← {}
 3      H ← H ∪ t
 4      level ← |H|
 5      Pr_atom ← getPredictions(level)
 6      Pr_rel ← getRelationPrediction(level)
 7      for A_i ∈ Pr_atom do
 8          if Pr_atom[A_i] == 1 then
 9              L[t] ← L[t] ∪ ⟨A_i, value(t, A_i)⟩
10      if Pr_rel ≠ no-relation then
11          lm ← value(t, Pr_rel)
12          if lm ≠ null and lm ∉ H then
13              L[t] ← L[t] ∪ ⟨rel, lm⟩
14              L ← getDescription(lm, L, D, H)
15      return L
```

An auxiliary function $level$ is assumed to return 1 when t corresponds to the main target, 2 when t corresponds to the first landmark object, and so on. This information is taken into account to invoke the appropriate set of classifiers, which are implemented by the auxiliary functions $getPredictions$ and $getRelationPrediction$. The former is assumed to invoke the set of binary classifiers for every attribute of t, and the latter invokes the multivalue prediction for the $relation$ class.

Content selection is performed by selecting all atomic attributes of the target t that were predicted by the corresponding binary classifiers. When a relation between t and its nearest distractor lm is predicted, the relation is included in L and the algorithm is called recursively to describe lm as well.

3.2 Personalised method

As an alternative to standard speaker-dependent REG (which relies on a set of descriptions produced by each speaker as in, e.g., Bohnet (2008)), we propose a personalised method based on the simple observation - made by Viethen and Dale (2010) and others - that some speakers follow a consistent pattern in reference production, whereas others do not.

In the present method - hereby called *Profile* - speakers are divided into three simple categories: those that always produced overspecified descriptions, those that always produced minimally distinguishing descriptions, and those that do not follow a consistent pattern. Knowing in advance the category of a particular speaker, the REG model will be trained on the descriptions produced by that category only. This will effectively allow us to use more training data than in standard personalised methods.

4 Evaluation

Data Six REG datasets: TUNA-Furniture and TUNA-People (Gatt et al., 2007) (in both cases, only descriptions to single objects were considered), GRE3D3 (Dale and Viethen, 2009), GRE3D7 (Viethen and Dale, 2011), Stars (Teixeira et al., 2014) and Stars2 (Paraboni et al., 2016).

Models As in Ferreira and Paraboni (2014), all classifiers were built using Support Vector Machines (SVMs) with a Gaussian Kernel. For the relation prediction, we use an "one-against-one" multi-class method. All models were evaluated using cross-validation with a balanced number of referring expressions per participant within each fold. For TUNA and Stars, descriptions were divided into six folds each. For GRE3D3/7 and Stars2, descriptions were divided into ten folds each. Grid-search was used to obtain an optimal model setting by testing values for the SVM C parameter (1, 10, 100 and 1000) and the Gaussian kernel γ (1, 0.1, 0.01, and 0.001) in a validation set before the test step.

Baseline We make use of a baseline method called *Speaker*. In this method, classifiers are trained on the set of referring expressions produced by each individual speaker.

Metrics We measured Dice coefficients (Dice, 1945) to assess the similarity between each description generated by the model and the corpus description. We also computed the overall REG Accuracy

Method	TUNA-f	TUNA-p	GRE3D3	GRE3D7	Stars	Stars2	Overall
Speaker	0.75	0.70	0.54	0.80	0.70	0.65	0.75
Profile	0.78	0.78	0.61	0.82	0.68	0.78	0.79

Table 2: Reference type classification for each corpus

by counting the number of exact matches between each description pair.

5   Results

Table 1 presents the results of the REG model using the *Speaker* and *Profile* personalised methods on each of the test domains. Overall results suggest that *Profile* outperforms *Speaker* both in terms of Dice (Wilcoxon W=3188296.5, p<0.01) and Accuracy (Chi-Square χ^2 =104.28, p<0.01) scores.

Regarding the results in individual domains, we notice that *Profile* outperforms *Speaker* in terms of Dice scores in the case of TUNA-People, GRE3D3, GRE3D7 and Stars2. A pairwise comparison shows that these differences are significant at p<.01. In the case of TUNA-Furniture and Stars the difference was not significant. *Profile* also outperforms *Speaker* in terms of Accuracy in TUNA-People, GRE3D3, GRE3D7 and Stars2, with pairwise comparisons significant at p<0.01. In the case of TUNA-Furniture, the difference was not significant, and in the case of Stars a significant effect in the opposite direction was observed (χ^2 =9.38, p<0.01).

Finally, Table 2 shows how often the *Speaker* and *Profile* methods were able to reproduce the level of referential specification found in the corpus, that is, how often each method correctly produced underspecified, overspecified and minimally distinguishing descriptions. Results show that predictions made by the *Profile* method generally outperform those made by the *Speaker* method, the exception being the case of the Stars corpus.

6   Discussion

This paper presented a machine-learning approach to REG that takes speaker-dependent information into account by making use of a personalised method to circumnavigates the issue of data sparsity. By grouping speakers according to a simple model of referential overspecification, we were arguably able to sketch a more general approach to speaker-dependent REG that was shown to outperform the standard use of individual speaker's information proposed in previous work.

Since using more training data - as we did by considering groups of similar speakers - improved results, we may of course argue that by simply training our REG models on the data provided by *all* speakers may improve results even further. Although we presently do not seek to validate this claim, there is plenty of evidence to suggest that this would not be the case. Studies such as in Bohnet (2008) have consistently shown that using individual training datasets for each speaker outperforms speaker-independent REG and, in particular, the work in Ferreira and Paraboni (2014) has shown that the current SVM model produces best results when trained on personalised datasets.

7   Future Work

The low availability of training data is not the only challenge to be dealt with in speaker-dependent REG. We notice that there is also the related issue of domain complexity. Existing REG models usually assume the existence of a pre-defined knowledge base of entities and their properties (Dale and Haddock, 1991; Dale and Reiter, 1995) or, as in the present case, take into account an overly simplified domain that restricts content selection. As a result, the variation in the output descriptions is limited by the knowledge base.

In future, the issue may be addressed by using the *semantic web* as the input to the REG model. This strategy, which has been shown succeed in the generation of proper names (Ferreira et al., 2017), may provide more information about the entities and their relations, and allow the generation of descriptions with greater variation (and possibly closer to the descriptions produced by any particular individual).

Acknowledgements

This work has been supported by the National Council of Scientific and Technological Development from Brazil (CNPq) and FAPESP 2016/14223-0.

References

B. Bohnet. 2008. The fingerprint of human referring expressions and their surface realization with graph transducers. In *Fifth International Natural Language Generation Conference*, pages 207–210, Stroudsburg, PA, USA.

C. B. Callaway and J. L. Lester. 2002. Pronominalization in generated discourse and dialogue. In *Proceedings of 40th Annual Meeting of the Association for Computational Linguistics*, pages 88–95, Philadelphia, Pennsylvania, USA, July. Association for Computational Linguistics.

R. Dale and N. J. Haddock. 1991. Content determination in the generation of referring expressions. *Computational Intelligence*, 7(4):252–265.

R. Dale and E. Reiter. 1995. Computational interpretations of the Gricean maxims in the generation of referring expressions. *Cognitive Science*, 19(2):233–263.

R. Dale and J. Viethen. 2009. Referring expression generation through attribute-based heuristics. In *Proceedings of ENLG-2009*, pages 58–65.

R. Dale. 1989. Cooking up referring expressions. In *Proc. ACL-1989*, pages 68–75, Stroudsburg, USA.

L. R. Dice. 1945. Measures of the amount of ecologic association between species. *Ecology*, 26(3):297–302.

T. C. Ferreira and I. Paraboni. 2014. Referring expression generation: taking speakers' preferences into account. *Lecture Notes in Artificial Intelligence*, 8655:539–546.

T. C. Ferreira, E. Krahmer, and S. Wubben. 2016. Towards more variation in text generation: Developing and evaluating variation models for choice of referential form. In *Proceedings of the 54th Annual Meeting of the Association for Computational Linguistics (Volume 1: Long Papers)*, pages 568–577, Berlin, Germany, August. Association for Computational Linguistics.

T. C. Ferreira, E. Krahmer, and S. Wubben. 2017. Generating flexible proper name references in text: Data, models and evaluation. In *Proceedings of the 15th Conference of the European Chapter of the Association for Computational Linguistics: Volume 1, Long Papers*, pages 655–664, Valencia, Spain, April. Association for Computational Linguistics.

A. Gatt, I. van der Sluis, and K. van Deemter. 2007. Evaluating algorithms for the generation of referring expressions using a balanced corpus. In *Proceedings of ENLG-07*.

R. Koolen, A. Gatt, M. Goudbeek, and E. Krahmer. 2011. Factors causing overspecification in definite descriptions. *Journal of Pragmatics*, 43(13):3231–3250.

E. Krahmer and K. van Deemter. 2012. Computational generation of referring expressions: A survey. *Computational Linguistics*, 38(1):173–218.

I. Paraboni, M. Galindo, and D. Iacovelli. 2016. Stars2: a corpus of object descriptions in a visual domain. *Language Resources and Evaluation*.

C. V. M. Teixeira, I. Paraboni, A. S. R. da Silva, and A. K. Yamasaki. 2014. Generating relational descriptions involving mutual disambiguation. *LNCS*, 8403:492–502.

J. Viethen and R. Dale. 2010. Speaker-dependent variation in content selection for referring expression generation. In *Australasian Language Technology Association Workshop 2010*, pages 81–89, Melbourne, Australia.

J. Viethen and R. Dale. 2011. GRE3D7: A corpus of distinguishing descriptions for objects in visual scenes. In *Proceedings of UCNLG+Eval-2011*, pages 12–22.

Analysing Data-To-Text Generation Benchmarks

Laura Perez-Beltrachini
School of Informatics, University of Edinburgh
10 Crichton Street, Edinburgh EH8 9AB
Scotland

Claire Gardent
CNRS, LORIA, UMR 7503
Vanoeuvre-lès-Nancy, F-54506
France

Abstract

A generation system can only be as good as the data it is trained on. In this short paper, we propose a methodology for analysing data-to-text corpora used for training microplanner i.e., systems which given some input must produce a text verbalising exactly this input. We apply this methodology to three existing benchmarks and we elicite a set of criteria for the creation of a data-to-text benchmark which could help better support the development, evaluation and comparison of linguistically sophisticated data-to-text generators.

1 Introduction

In some scenarios, generation datasets provide linguistic descriptions of a specific domain and application (e.g. (Reiter et al., 2005)). However, in other scenarios generation datasets aim at broader syntactic (e.g. the surface realisation shared-task (Belz et al., 2011)) or domain (Wen et al., 2015a) coverage. Recently, several datasets have been created to train data-to-text generators (Wen et al., 2015a; Liang et al., 2009; Lebret et al., 2016; Novikova et al., 2016; Chen and Mooney, 2008). It is unclear however to what extent the generation task exercised by these datasets is linguistically challenging. Do these datasets provide enough variety to support the development of high-quality data-to-text generators ? In this paper, we propose a methodology for characterising the variety and complexity of these datasets. We exemplify its use by applying it to three existing training corpora for NLG and we conclude by eliciting a set of criteria for the creation of data-to-text

benchmarks which could better support the development, evaluation and comparison of linguistically sophisticated data-to-text generators.

2 Approach

Our classification aims to assess to what extent a data-to-text corpus will allow for the learning of a linguistically sophisticated microplanner i.e., a microplanner which can handle a wide range of linguistic constructions and their interaction. We focus on the following four criteria: *linguistic and computational diversity* (How complex or varied are the data and the texts?), *lexical richness* (Is the dataset lexically varied ?), *syntactic variety* (Is the dataset syntactically varied and in particular, does it include text of varied syntactic *complexity* ?) and *informational adequacy* (Does the text match the information contained in the data ?).

Linguistic and Computational Diversity. Linguistic and computational diversity can be assessed using the following metrics[1]:

Size: the number of training instances in the dataset
Nb. of Rel: the number of distinct relations
Sub.Ent: the number of distinct subject entities
Rel.Obj.Ent: the number of relation-object pairs
Da Len: the average length of the input data computed as the number of subject-relation-object triples
Da Ptns: the number of distinct relation combinations
Da Inst: the number of distinct data inputs

---

[1] We assume that a data-to-text corpus for NLG includes entities, concepts and binary relations. Following RDF terminology, we refer to the first argument of a binary relation as a subject entity and to the second as an object entity.

Proceedings of The 10th International Natural Language Generation conference, pages 238–242,
Santiago de Compostela, Spain, September 4-7 2017. ©2017 Association for Computational Linguistics

PPxDa Inst: the average (min/max) number of paraphrases per data input.

Lexical Richness. (Lu, 2012)'s system automatically measure various dimensions of lexical richness. Two measures are particularly relevant here.

Type-token ratio (TTR) is a measure of diversity defined as the ratio of the number of word types to the number of words in a text. To address the fact that this ratio tends to decrease with the size of the corpus, Mean segmental TTR (MSTTR) is computed by dividing the corpus into successive segments of a given length and then calculating the average TTR of all segments.

Lexical sophistication (LS) measures the proportion of relatively unusual or advanced word types in the text. In practice, LS is the proportion of lexical word types which are not in the list of 2,000 most frequent words from the British National Corpus.

Syntactic Variation To support the training of generators with wide syntactic coverage, a benchmark needs to show a balanced distribution of the various syntactic phenomena present in the target language. To characterise the syntactic coverage of a dataset, we use a complexity classification proposed in the domain of language learning development assessment which consists of eight levels: (0) simple sentences, including questions (1) infinitive or -ing complement with subject control; (2) conjoined noun phrases in subject position; conjunctions of sentences, of verbal, adjectival, or adverbial construction; (3) relative or appositional clause modifying the object of the main verb; nominalization in object position; finite clause as object of main verb; subject extraposition; (4) subordinate clauses; comparatives; (5) nonfinite clauses in adjunct positions; (6) relative or appositional clause modifying subject of main verb; embedded clause serving as subject of main verb; nominalization serving as subject of main verb; (7) more than one level of embedding in a single sentence.

We use (Lu, 2010)'s system for the automatic measurement of syntactic variability. Briefly, this system decomposes parse trees[2] into component sub-trees and scores each of these sub-trees based

---

[2]Parses are obtained using Collins' constituent parser (Collins, 1999).

	M	A	MA	E
RNNLG$_{Laptop}$	16%	2%	0	82%
RNNLG$_{TV}$	12%	4%	0	84%
RNNLG$_{Hotel}$	0	6%	0	94%
RNNLG$_{Restaurant}$	0	6%	0	94%
IMAGEDESC	50%	6%	0	44%
WIKIBIOASTRO	30%	0	70%	0

Table 1: Match between Text and Data. M: Missing content in the text, A: Additional content in the text, MA: both additional and missing, E:Exact.

on the type of the syntactic constructions detected in it using a set of heuristics. Sentences are then assigned to a syntactic level based on the scores assigned to the sub-trees it contains as follows. If all sub-trees found in that sentence are assigned to level zero, the sentence is assigned to level 0; if one and only one non-zero level is assigned to one or more sub-trees, the sentence is assigned to that non-zero level; if two or more different non-zero scores are assigned to two or more of the sub-trees, the sentence is assigned to level 7. When evaluated against a gold standard of 500 sentences independently rated by two annotators with a very high inter-annotator agreement (kappa = 0.91), the system achieves an F-Score of 93.2% (Lu, 2010).

Informational Adequacy A microplanner should express all or part of the content expressed in the input data. It is therefore important to verify that this is the case through manual examination of a random subset of the dataset. A data/text pair will be considered an "Exact" match if all data is verbalised by the text. It will be labelled as "Missing" if part of the data is not present in the text (content selection) and as "Additional" if the text contains information not present in the input data.

3 Case Study

To illustrate the usage of the evaluation grid proposed in the preceding section, we apply it to three datasets recently proposed for data-to-text generation by (Lebret et al., 2016), (Wen et al., 2015b; Wen et al., 2016) and (Novikova and Rieser, 2016).

(Lebret et al., 2016)'s dataset (WIKIBIO) focuses on biographies and associates Wikipedia infoboxes with the first sentence of the corresponding article in Wikipedia. As the dataset is much larger than the other datasets and is not domain specific, we extract two subsets of it for better comparison: one whose size is similar to the other datasets (WIKIBIO$_{16317}$) and one which is domain specific in that all biographies are about astronauts (WIKIBIOASTRO).

The other two datasets were created manually with humans providing text for dialogue acts in the case of (Wen et al., 2015b; Wen et al., 2016)'s RNNLG datasets (laptop, TV, hotel, restaurant) and image descriptions in the case of (Novikova and Rieser, 2016)'s dataset (IMAGEDESC).

We also include a text-only corpus for comparison with the texts contained in our three datasets. This corpus (GMB) consists of the texts from the Groningen Meaning Bank (Version 1.0.0, (Basile et al., 2012)) and covers different genres (e.g., news, jokes, fables).

Linguistic and Computational Diversity. Table 2 gives the descriptive statistics for each of these three datasets. It shows marked differences in terms of size (WIKIBIO$_{16317}$ being the largest and IMAGEDESC the smallest), number of distinct relations (from 16 for IMAGEDESC to 2367 for WIKIBIO$_{16317}$) and average number of paraphrases (15.11 for IMAGEDESC against 1 to 3.72 for the other two datasets). The number of distinct data inputs (semantic variability) also varies widely (from 77 distinct data inputs for the IMAGEDESC corpus to 12527 for RNNLG$_{Laptop}$). Overall the number of distinct relations is relatively small.

Lexical Richness. The WIKIBIO dataset, even when restricted to a single type of entity (namely, astronauts) has a higher MSTTR. This higher lexical variation is probably due to the fact that this dataset also has the highest number of relations (cf. Table 2): more relations brings more diversity and thus better lexical range. Indeed, there is a positive correlation between the number of relations in the dataset and MSTTR (Spearman's rho +0.385).

Again the WIKIBIO dataset has a markedly higher level of lexical sophistication than the other datasets. The higher LS might be because the WIKIBIO text are edited independently of input data thereby leaving more freedom to the authors to include additional information. It may also result from the fact that the WIKIBIO dataset, even though it is restricted to biographies, covers a much more varied set of domains than the other datasets as people's lives may be very diverse and consequently, a more varied range of topics may be mentioned than in a domain restricted dataset.

Syntactic variation. Figure 1 summarises the results for the various datasets. A first observation is that the proportion of simple texts (Level 0) is very high across the board (42% to 68%). In fact, in all data sets but two, *more than half of the sentences are of level 0 (simple sentences)*. In comparison, only 35% of the GMB corpus sentences are of level 0.

Second, levels 1, 4 and to a lesser extent level 3, are absent or almost absent from the data sets. We conjecture that this is due to the shape and type of the input data. Infinitival clauses with subject control (level 1) and comparatives (level 4) involve coreferential links and relations between entities which are absent from the simple binary relations comprising the input data. Similarly, non finite complements with their own subject (e.g., *"John saw Mary leaving the room"*, Level 3) and relative clauses modifying the object of the main verb (e.g., *"The man scolded the boy who stole the bicycle"*, Level 3) require data where the object of a literal is the subject of some other literal. In most cases however, the input data consists of sets of literals predicating facts about a single entity.

Third, datasets may be more or less varied in terms of syntactic complexity. It is in particular noticeable that, for the WIKIBIO dataset, three levels (1, 3 and 7) covers 84% of the cases. This restricted variety points to stereotyped text with repetitive syntactic structure. Indeed, in WIKIBIO, the texts consist of the first sentence of biographic Wikipedia articles which typically are of the form *"W (date of birth - date of death) was P"*. where P usually is an arbitrarily complex predicate potentially involving relative clauses modifying the object of main verb (Level 3) and coordination (Level 7).

Informational Adequacy. Each data-text pair was independently rated by two annotators resulting in a kappa score ranging between 0.566 and 0.691 depending on the dataset. The results shown in Table 1 highlight some important differences. While the RNNLG datasets have a high percentage of exact entries (82% to 94%), the IMAGEDESC dataset is less precise (44% of exact matches). The WIKIBIO datasets does not contain a single example where data and text coincide. These differences can be

Dataset	Size	Nb. of Rel	Sub.Ent[‡]	Rel.Obj.Ent	Da Len.	Da Ptns	Da Inst	PPxDa Inst.
WIKIBIO$_{16317}$	16317	2367	16317	149484	19.65	9990	16317	1
WIKIBIOASTRO	615	68	615	5290	15.46	293	615	1
RNNLG$_{Laptop}$	13242	34	123	451	5.86	2068	12527	1.03(1/3)
RNNLG$_{TV}$	7035	30	92	300	5.79	1024	6808	1.01(1/6)
RNNLG$_{Hotel}$	5373	22	138	535	2.66	112	940	3.72(1/149)
RNNLG$_{Restaurant}$	5192	22	223	869	2.86	182	1950	1.82(1/101)
IMAGEDESC	1242	16	33	117	5.33	21	77	15.11(8/22)

Table 2: Datasets descriptive statistics. [‡]Note that we consider as distinct entities those given by the *name* relations and that in the RNNLG datasets not all dialogue acts describe entities (e.g. inform_count or ?select).

Dataset	Tokens	Types	LS	MSTTR
WIKIBIO$_{16317}$	377048	36712	**0.92**	**0.82**
WIKIBIOASTRO	14720	2335	0.81	0.8
RNNLG$_{Laptop}$	295492	1757	0.46	0.74
RNNLG$_{TV}$	141606	1171	0.48	0.71
RNNLG$_{Hotel}$	48982	967	0.43	0.59
RNNLG$_{Restaurant}$	45791	1187	0.43	0.62
IMAGEDESC	20924	598	0.47	0.56
GMB	75927	7791	0.75	0.81

Table 3: Lexical Sophistication (LS) and Mean Segmental Type-Token Ratio (MSTTR).

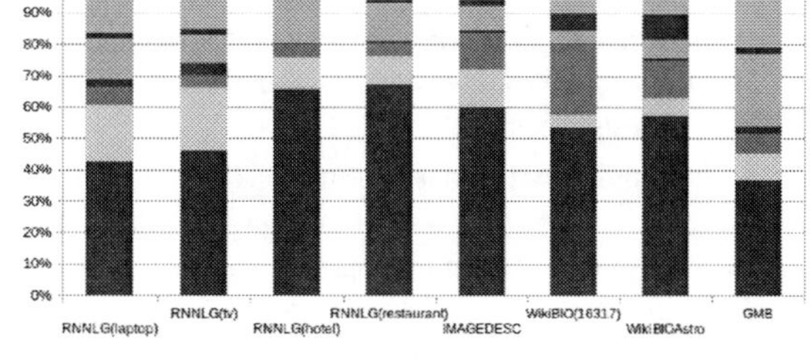

Figure 1: Syntactic complexity. D-Level sentence distribution.

traced back to the way in which each resource was created. The WIKIBIO dataset is created automatically from Wikipedia infoboxes and articles while information adequacy is not checked for. In the IMAGEDESC dataset, the texts are created from images using crowdsourcing. It seems that this method, while enhancing variety, makes it easier for the crowdworkers to omit some information.

4 Conclusion

The proposed measures suggest several key aspects to take into account when constructing a data-to-text dataset for the development and evaluation of NLG systems. Lexical richness can be enhanced by including data from different domains, using a large number of distinct relations and ensuring that the total number of distinct inputs is high. Wide and balanced syntactic coverage is difficult to ensure and probably requires input data of various size and shape, stemming from different domains. Informational adequacy is easiest to achieve using crowdsourcing which also facilitates the inclusion of paraphrases. In future work, it would be interesting to further exploit such analyses of data-to-text corpora (i) to better characterise the generators that can be learnt from a given corpus, (ii) to perform a graded analysis of generation systems on data of various syntactic complexity or (iii) to support error mining (which type of data is most often associated with generation failure ?).

More specifically, our classification could be useful to identify sources of under-performance and thus directions for improvements. For instance, BLEU results reported by (Wen et al., 2015a) on three different datasets indicate that the same systems are facing different difficulties on each of these. Indeed, lexical richness is higher (Table 3) for the RNNLG$_{Laptop}$ dataset for which (Wen et al., 2015a) reports the lowest BLEU score. But also the proportion of simple sentences is lower (Figure 1) in this dataset. A focused evaluation could report on BLEU scores aggregated on the syntactic classification of sentences into levels.

Acknowledgments

This research was partially supported by the French National Research Agency within the framework of the WebNLG Project (ANR-14-CE24-0033).

References

Valerio Basile, Johan Bos, Kilian Evang, and Noortje Venhuizen. 2012. Developing a large semantically annotated corpus. In *LREC*, volume 12, pages 3196–3200.

Anja Belz, Mike White, Dominic Espinosa, Eric Kow, Deirdre Hogan, and Amanda Stent. 2011. The first surface realisation shared task: Overview and evaluation results. In *Proceedings of the Generation Challenges Session at the 13th European Workshop on Natural Language Generation*, pages 217–226, Nancy, France, September. Association for Computational Linguistics.

David L Chen and Raymond J Mooney. 2008. Learning to sportscast: a test of grounded language acquisition. In *Proceedings of the 25th international conference on Machine learning*, pages 128–135. ACM.

M. Collins. 1999. *Head-Driven Statistical Models for Natural Language Parsing*. Ph.D. thesis, University of Pennsylvania, Philadelphia, PA.

Rémi Lebret, David Grangier, and Michael Auli. 2016. Neural text generation from structured data with application to the biography domain. In *Proceedings of the 2016 Conference on Empirical Methods in Natural Language Processing*, pages 1203–1213, Austin, Texas, November. Association for Computational Linguistics.

P. Liang, M. I. Jordan, and D. Klein. 2009. Learning semantic correspondences with less supervision. In *Association for Computational Linguistics and International Joint Conference on Natural Language Processing (ACL-IJCNLP)*, pages 91–99.

Xiaofei Lu. 2010. Automatic analysis of syntactic complexity in second language writing. *International Journal of Corpus Linguistics*, 15(4):474–496.

Xiaofei Lu. 2012. The relationship of lexical richness to the quality of esl learners oral narratives. *The Modern Language Journal*, 96(2):190–208.

Jekaterina Novikova and Verena Rieser. 2016. The analogue challenge: Non aligned language generation. In *The 9th International Natural Language Generation conference*, page 168.

Jekaterina Novikova, Oliver Lemon, and Verena Rieser. 2016. Crowd-sourcing nlg data: Pictures elicit better data. In *Proceedings of the 9th International Natural Language Generation conference*, pages 265–273, Edinburgh, UK, September 5-8. Association for Computational Linguistics.

Ehud Reiter, Somayajulu Sripada, Jim Hunter, Jin Yu, and Ian Davy. 2005. Choosing words in computer-generated weather forecasts. *Artificial Intelligence*, 167(1-2):137–169.

Tsung-Hsien Wen, Milica Gašic, Nikola Mrkšic, Lina M Rojas-Barahona, Pei-Hao Su, David Vandyke, and Steve Young. 2015a. Toward multi-domain language generation using recurrent neural networks. In *The Proceedings of the 29th Annual Conference on Neural Information Processing Systems (NIPS), Workshop on Machine Learning for Spoken Language Understanding and Interaction*.

Tsung-Hsien Wen, Milica Gasic, Nikola Mrksic, Pei-Hao Su, David Vandyke, and Steve Young. 2015b. Semantically conditioned lstm-based natural language generation for spoken dialogue systems. *arXiv preprint arXiv:1508.01745*.

Tsung-Hsien Wen, Milica Gasic, Nikola Mrksic, Lina M Rojas-Barahona, Pei-Hao Su, David Vandyke, and Steve Young. 2016. Multi-domain neural network language generation for spoken dialogue systems. *arXiv preprint arXiv:1603.01232*.

Linguistic Description of Complex Phenomena with the rLDCP R Package

Jose M. Alonso
Centro de Investigación en
Tecnoloxías da Información (CiTIUS)
University of Santiago de Compostela,
Santiago de Compostela, Spain
`josemaria.alonso.moral@usc.es`

Patricia Conde-Clemente
Universidad de Oviedo,
Asturias, Spain

Gracian Trivino
Phedes Lab,
Asturias, Spain

Abstract

Monitoring and analysis of complex phenomena attract the attention of both academy and industry. Dealing with data produced by complex phenomena requires the use of advance computational intelligence techniques. Namely, linguistic description of complex phenomena constitutes a mature research line. It is supported by the Computational Theory of Perceptions grounded on the Fuzzy Sets Theory. Its aim is the development of computational systems with the ability to generate vague descriptions of the world in a similar way how humans do. This is a human-centric and multi-disciplinary research work. Moreover, its success is a matter of careful design; thus, developers play a key role. The rLDCP R package was designed to facilitate the development of new applications. This demo introduces the use of rLDCP, for both beginners and advance developers, in practical use cases.

1 Introduction

Trivino and Sugeno (2013) defined a framework for Linguistic Description of Complex Phenomena (LDCP). It is based on the Computational Theory of Perceptions (CTP) introduced by Zadeh (2001) as a new tool for paving the way from computing with numbers to computing with words (Zadeh, 1999). CTP is rooted in the computational intelligence technique best suited to deal with approximate reasoning and vague concepts, i.e., the Fuzzy Sets Theory (Zadeh, 1965; Trillas and Eciolaza, 2015).

LDCP has already been successfully applied in several multi-disciplinary projects. For example:

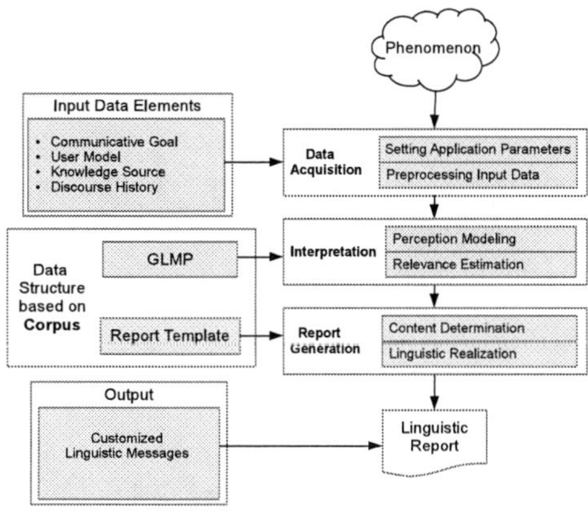

Figure 1: The LDCP Architecture for NLG/D2T.

describing big data (Conde-Clemente et al., 2017b); advising how to save energy at home (Conde-Clemente et al., 2016); describing physical activity (Sanchez-Valdes et al., 2016); describing drivers' behavior in driving simulations (Eciolaza et al., 2013); or describing double stars in astronomy (Arguelles and Trivino, 2013).

Figure 1 depicts the LDCP architecture for Natural Language Generation in Data-to-text applications (NLG/D2T). It is inspired on the well-known NLG pipeline proposed by Reiter and Dale (2000). The development of new applications with LDCP comprises the following steps:

- Careful analysis of the phenomenon under consideration, regarding: communicative goal, audience background, and the set of natural language expressions (corpus) most commonly used in the context of the application domain.

243

- Design of a computational structure (the so-called Granular Linguistic Model of the Phenomenon, GLMP) which organizes all related perceptions in a similar way how humans usually organize their experience by means of natural language.

- Design of a Report Template easy to customize in accordance with the audience requirements.

- Implementation of a computational system able to collect and process raw data, interpret them according to the previously defined GLMP, and producing the Report with the most relevant information to convey to end-users.

Conde-Clemente et al. (2017a) have developed an R package called rLDCP[1] which constitutes a first implementation in R of the steps enumerated above. Thus, it facilitates the use of the LDCP architecture in new applications.

2 Structure of the Demo

This demo describes how to use rLDCP from scratch. Firstly, we explain how to download and install rLDCP. Secondly, we detail how to run step by step the toy example *ComfortableRoom* from the point of view of beginners and advance developers. The goal is describing the comfort in a room with respect to temperature and light intensity data values previously stored in a ".csv" file.

Then, we show how to use rLDCP for building a real application: The *inProfilePhoto* mobile app. We implement with rLDCP the application described in (Conde-Clemente et al., 2013) where an NLG system guided a person with visual disabilities to take his/her own profile photos.

Acknowledgments

This work is supported by the Spanish Ministry of Economy and Competitiveness [grant numbers TIN2014-56633-C3-3-R, TIN2014-56633-C3-1-R]; the "Consellería de Cultura, Educación e Ordenación Universitaria" (accreditation 2016-2019, ED431G/08) and the European Regional Development Fund (ERDF); and the Spanish Ministry of Science and Innovation [grant number FPI-MICINN BES-2012-057427].

References

Luis Arguelles and Gracian Trivino. 2013. I-struve: Automatic linguistic descriptions of visual double stars. *Engineering Applications of Artificial Intelligence*, 26(9):2083–2092.

Patricia Conde-Clemente, Jose M. Alonso, and Gracian Trivino. 2013. Interpretable fuzzy system allowing to be framed in a profile photo through linguistic expressions. In *Proceedings of 8th Conference of the European Society for Fuzzy Logic and Technology (EUSFLAT)*, pages 463–468, Milano, Italy.

Patricia Conde-Clemente, Jose M. Alonso, and Gracian Trivino. 2016. Towards automatic generation of linguistic advice for saving energy at home. *Soft Computing*, pages 1–15.

Patricia Conde-Clemente, Jose M. Alonso, and Gracian Trivino. 2017a. rldcp: R package for text generation from data. In *IEEE International Conference on Fuzzy Systems (FUZZ-IEEE)*, pages 1–6, Naples, Italy.

Patricia Conde-Clemente, Gracian Trivino, and Jose M. Alonso. 2017b. Generating automatic linguistic descriptions with big data. *Information Sciences*, 380:12–30.

Luka Eciolaza, Martin Pereira-Fariña, and Gracian Trivino. 2013. Automatic linguistic reporting in driving simulation environments. *Applied Soft Computing*, 13(9):3956–3967.

Ehud Reiter and Robert Dale. 2000. *Building natural language generation systems*, volume 33. MIT Press.

Daniel Sanchez-Valdes, Alberto Alvarez-Alvarez, and Gracian Trivino. 2016. Dynamic linguistic descriptions of time series applied to self-track the physical activity. *Fuzzy Sets and Systems*, 285:162–181.

Enric Trillas and Luka Eciolaza. 2015. *Fuzzy Logic: An Introductory Course for Engineering Students*. Springer.

Gracian Trivino and Michio Sugeno. 2013. Towards linguistic descriptions of phenomena. *International Journal of Approximate Reasoning*, 54(1):22–34.

Lotfi A. Zadeh. 1965. Fuzzy sets. *Information and Control*, 8(3):338–353.

Lotfi A. Zadeh. 1999. From computing with numbers to computing with words. from manipulation of measurements to manipulation of perceptions. *IEEE Transactions on Circuits and Systems*, 46(1):105–119.

Lotfi A. Zadeh. 2001. A new direction in AI: Toward a computational theory of perceptions. *Artificial Intelligent Magazine*, 22(1):73–84.

---

[1]rLDCP is an R package for text generation from data. It is freely available at [http://www.phedes.com/rLDCP]

A demo of FORGe: the Pompeu Fabra Open Rule-based Generator

Simon Mille [1], **Leo Wanner** [1,2]

[1] Universitat Pompeu Fabra, Roc Boronat 138, 08018 Barcelona, Spain
[2]Institució Catalana de Recerca i Estudis Avançats (ICREA),
Lluis Companys 23, 08010 Barcelona, Spain
`firstname.lastname@upf.edu`

Abstract

This demo paper presents the multilingual deep sentence generator developed by the TALN group at Universitat Pompeu Fabra, implemented as a series of rule-based graph-transducers.

1 Introduction

FORGe (Mille et al., 2017)[1] is a pipeline of graph transducers which, coupled with lexical resources, allows for generating texts, starting from a variety of abstract input structures. The current generator has been mainly developed for English on the dependency Penn Treebank (Johansson and Nugues, 2007) automatically converted to predicate-argument structures, and on Abstract Meaning Representations, using the SemEval'17 data (May and Priyadarshi, 2017). It is currently being adapted to languages such as Spanish, German French, and Polish, in the context of ontology-to-text generation as part of a dialogue system. Our generator follows the theoretical model of the Meaning-Text Theory (Mel'čuk, 1988), and performs the following actions: (i) syntacticization of predicate-argument graphs; (ii) introduction of function words; (iii) linearization and retrieval of surface forms.

2 Overview of the system

In this section, we briefly describe the input to the system and the successive transductions .

---

[1]See this paper for an evaluation of the system in the context of the SemEval AMR-to-text generation challenge.

2.1 Inputs

The input structures can be trees or acyclic graphs that contain linguistic information only, which includes meaning bearing units and predicate-argument relations such as *ARG0* (if licensing external arguments, as in PropBank (Kingsbury and Palmer, 2002)), *ARG1*, *ARG2*, ..., *ARGn*). In order to allow for more compact representations, the generator can also handle "non-core" predicates as edges, be it with a generic label *nonCore*, or with a typed label such as *purpose*; see, for example two alternative representations of a *purpose* meaning between two nodes N_1 and N_2:

$$N_1 \; N_{purpose} \; N_2 \qquad N_1 \; N_2$$

2.2 Generation of the deep syntactic structure

First of all, parts of speech are assigned to each node of the structure. Then, during this transduction, a top-down recursive syntacticization of the semantic graph is performed. It looks for the syntactic root of the sentence, and from there for its syntactic dependent(s), for the dependent(s) of the dependent(s), and so on. We first identify the root of a syntactic tree in case the original input structure does not contain one, and then, produce a well-formed tree that covers as much of the input graph as possible, while avoiding the possible dependency conflicts. In the following example, "peek" is chosen as the root (Left: predicate-argument; Right: Deep-Syntax):

he peek dog black bark   *he peek dog black bark dog*

Proceedings of The 10th International Natural Language Generation conference, pages 245–246,
Santiago de Compostela, Spain, September 4-7 2017. ©2017 Association for Computational Linguistics

2.3 Introduction of function words

The next step towards the realization of the sentence is the introduction of all idiosyncratic words (prepositions, auxiliaries, determiners, etc.) and of a fine-grained (surface-)syntactic structure that gives enough information for linearizing and resolving agreements between the different words. For this task, we use a valency (subcategorization) lexicon built automatically from PropBank and Nom-Bank (Meyers et al., 2004). During this transduction, anaphora are resolved, and personal pronouns are introduced in the tree (this includes possessive, relative and personal pronouns). See, e.g., how the preposition "at" is introduced in the following surface-syntactic structure:

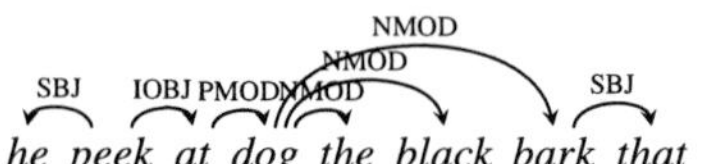

2.4 Resolution of morpho-syntactic agreements, linearization, and retrieval of surface forms

In order to resolve agreements, the rules for this transduction check the governor/dependent pairs, together with the syntactic relation that links them together. Some other rules order governor-dependent pairs and siblings with one another. We then match the triple <lemma><POS><morpho-syntactic features> with an entry of a morphological dictionary and simply replace the triple by the surface form. The final sentence corresponding to the running example would be *He peeks at the black dog that barks*.

3 A flexible multilingual generation pipeline

The presented pipeline is flexible from several perspectives. First, it is quite easily adaptable to different types of inputs; for instance, it took only one week to adapt it to the AMRs of SemEval'17. Second, many rules are language-independent, and others can be easily adapted to other languages, which means that, with good quality lexical resources, the effort for building a generator in a new language is minimal. Finally it is possible to substitute some parts of the pipeline with statistical modules, as, e.g., the transition between deep-and surface-syntax

(Ballesteros et al., 2015) or the linearization step (Bohnet et al., 2011), in order to overcome a possible lack of coverage of the rules.

During the demo session, participants will be encouraged to play with the generator through a graphical interface, in order to see all the details of a generation process (in English, with some examples in German and Polish).

Acknowledgments

The work described in this paper has been partially funded by the European Commission under the contract numbers FP7-ICT-610411, H2020-645012-RIA, H2020-700024-RIA, and H2020-700475-RIA.

References

Miguel Ballesteros, Bernd Bohnet, Simon Mille, and Leo Wanner. 2015. Data-driven sentence generation with non-isomorphic trees. In *Proceedings of NAACL:HLT*, pages 387–397, Denver, CO, May–June. ACL.

Bernd Bohnet, Simon Mille, Benoît Favre, and Leo Wanner. 2011. StuMaBa: From deep representation to surface. In *Proceedings of ENLG*, pages 232–235, Nancy, France.

Richard Johansson and Pierre Nugues. 2007. Extended constituent-to-dependency conversion for English. In *Poceedings of NODALIDA*, pages 105–112, Tartu, Estonia.

Paul Kingsbury and Martha Palmer. 2002. From Tree-Bank to PropBank. In *Proceedings of LREC*, pages 1989–1993, Las Palmas, Canary Islands, Spain.

Jonathan May and Jay Priyadarshi. 2017. Semeval-2017 task 9: Abstract meaning representation parsing and generation. In *Proceedings of SemEval-2017*, pages 534–543, Vancouver, Canada, August. Association for Computational Linguistics.

Igor Mel'čuk. 1988. *Dependency Syntax: Theory and Practice*. SUNY Press, Albany.

Adam Meyers, Ruth Reeves, Catherine Macleod, Rachel Szekely, Veronika Zielinska, Brian Young, and Ralph Grishman. 2004. The NomBank Project: An interim report. In *Proceedings of the Workshop on Frontiers in Corpus Annotation, (HLT/NAACL)*, pages 24–31, Boston, MA, USA.

Simon Mille, Roberto Carlini, Alicia Burga, and Leo Wanner. 2017. Forge at semeval-2017 task 9: Deep sentence generation based on a sequence of graph transducers. In *Proceedings of SemEval-2017*, pages 917–920, Vancouver, Canada, August. Association for Computational Linguistics.

Referential Success of Set Referring Expressions with Fuzzy Properties

Nicolás Marín, Gustavo Rivas-Gervilla, and **Daniel Sánchez**
Dept. Computer Science and A.I., University of Granada, Spain
`nicm@decsai.ugr.es`

Abstract

We introduce the properties to be satisfied by measures of referential success of set referring expressions with fuzzy properties. We define families of measures on the basis of k-specificity measures and we illustrate some of them with a toy example.

1 Introduction

The classical referring expression generation (REG) problem intends to determine a noun phrase which univocally identify an object in a collection. From a knowledge representation perspective, the problem is to determine (if possible) a collection of object properties that can be employed in the noun phrase for the abovementioned purpose (van Deemter, 2016).

The most usual version of the REG problem can be formalized as follows: given a context formed by a collection of objects O and a set of properties P of objects in O, determine a subset $re \subseteq P$ such that

$$\bigcap_{p_i \in re} [\![p_i]\!] = \{o\} \tag{1}$$

where $[\![p_i]\!]$ is the set of objects that satisfy p_i. This formalization assumes that properties in re are combined conjunctively; other logical combinations are possible (van Deemter, 2016).

There are many different extensions of the classical REG problem. One such extension is that of referring to sets (Krahmer and van Deemter, 2012; van Deemter, 2016), where the objective is to generate a referring expression able to identify an distinguish

a subset of objects $O^i \subset O$, that is, to determine a subset $re \subseteq P$ such that

$$\bigcap_{p_i \in re} [\![p_i]\!] = O^i \tag{2}$$

Note that the classical problem is a particular case of set referring where O^i is a singleton.

Another extension considers that properties in P may be vague or uncertain in several respects (van Deemter, 2012). When the fulfilment of properties in P is *gradual* in nature, they may be modelled by means of fuzzy sets (Gatt et al., 2016). Fuzzy properties are modelled by means of fuzzy sets, corresponding to membership functions of the form $p_i : O \rightarrow [0,1]\ \forall p_i \in P$, where 0 means "no fulfilment" and 1 means "total fulfilment", allowing intermediate degrees. Note that classical crisp properties are particular cases of fuzzy ones in which no intermediate degrees are allowed, and hence the classical REG problem is again a particular case of the REG problem with fuzzy properties.

In the aforementioned crisp versions of the problem, when Eq. (1) (resp. Eq. (2)) holds, it is said that re has *referential success* for o (resp. O^i). One problem that arises in REG with fuzzy properties is that, as the fulfilment of properties by objects is a matter of degree, so it is the referential success. Several proposals for determining the degree of referential success have been provided in the literature (Gatt et al., 2016; Marín et al., 2016; Marín et al., 2017c), some of them based on the notion of specificity introduced by R. Yager (Yager, 1982; Yager, 1990; Yager, 1992; Garmendia et al., 2003; Garmendia et al., 2006).

247

Proceedings of The 10th International Natural Language Generation conference, pages 247–251,
Santiago de Compostela, Spain, September 4-7 2017. ©2017 Association for Computational Linguistics

In this paper we show a preliminary proposal for extending referential success measures to the case of set referring expressions with fuzzy properties.

2 Referential Success for Individual Objects with Fuzzy Properties

Let us assume that properties in P are fuzzy and let $p_i(o)$ be the accomplishment degree of property p_i for object o. The accuracy of the referring expression is then calculated as (Gatt et al., 2016):

$$O_{re}(o) = \bigotimes_{i=1}^{n} p_i(o) \qquad (3)$$

where $\otimes$ is a t-norm. Unless otherwise stated, we shall employ the minimum, that is, $O_{re}(o) = \min\{p_i(o)\}$. O_{re} can be seen as the fuzzy set induced by re on O.

In (Marín et al., 2016), a minimal set of properties that a referential success measure $rs(re, o)$ must fulfill in relation to the induced O_{re} is presented:

Property 2.1 $rs(re, o_i) = 1$ iff $O_{re} = \{o_i\}$.

Property 2.2 If $O_{re}(o_i) = 0$ then $rs(re, o_i) = 0$.

Property 2.3 If $O_{re}(o) \leq O_{re'}(o)$ $\forall o \in O \backslash \{o_i\}$ and $O_{re}(o_i) \geq O_{re'}(o_i)$ then $rs(re, o_i) \geq rs(re', o_i)$.

Additionally, a general family of measures is provided in (Marín et al., 2016) on the basis of Yager's specificity measures, as follows:

Definition 2.1 *(Marín et al., 2016) Let t be a t-norm and Sp be a specificity measure. The referential success measure associated to Sp and t is defined as follows:*

$$\overrightarrow{RS}_t(Sp)(re, o_i) = \begin{cases} t(O_{re}(o_i), Sp(O_{re}^*)) & condmax \\ 0 & otherwise \end{cases} \qquad (4)$$

where

$$O_{re}^*(o_j) = \frac{O_{re}(o_j)}{\max\limits_{o \in O} O_{re}(o)} \qquad (5)$$

and condmax *stands for the following condition:*

$$\max\limits_{o \in O} O_{re}(o) = O_{re}(o_i) > 0.$$

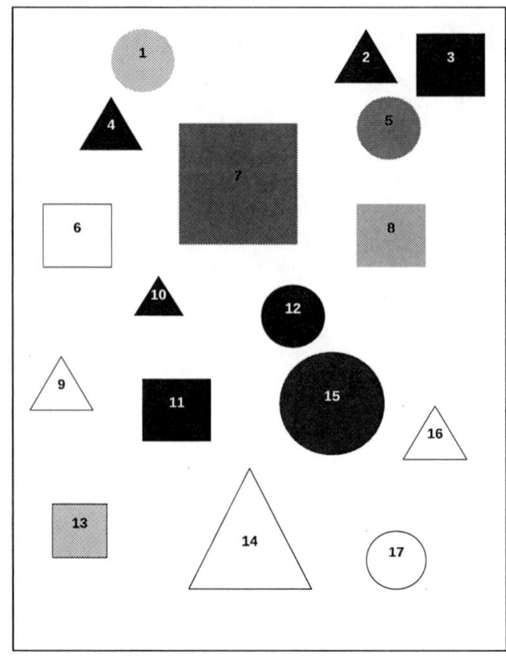

Figure 1: Example scene

3 Referential success of Set Referring Expressions

We propose the following minimal set of properties to be fulfilled by a referential success measure rs of set referring expressions:

Property 3.1 $rs(re, O^i) = 1$ iff $O_{re} = O^i$.

Property 3.2 If $\exists o \in O^i$ such that $O_{re}(o) = 0$ then $rs(re, O^i) = 0$.

Property 3.3 If $O_{re}(o) \leq O_{re'}(o)$ $\forall o \in O \backslash O^i$ and $O_{re}(o) \geq O_{re'}(o)$ $\forall o \in O^i$ then $rs(re, O^i) \geq rs(re', O^i)$.

Our proposal of measures in this paper is based on the measures of k-specificity introduced in (Sánchez et al., 2016) and related to cardinality in (Marín et al., 2017a). The measure Sp_k indicates to which degree the cardinality of a fuzzy set is exactly k. Eqs. (6) to (8) show three such measures:

$$Sp_k^f(A) = \begin{cases} \dfrac{\prod\limits_{i=0}^{k} a_i^2}{\prod\limits_{i=0}^{k} a_i + \sum\limits_{i=k+1}^{m} a_i} & a_k > 0 \\ 0 & otherwise \end{cases} \qquad (6)$$

	1	2	3	4	5	6	7	8	9	10	11	12	13	14	15	16	17
top-right	0	1	1	0	1	0	0.1	0.3	0	0	0	0	0	0	0	0	0
dark	0.3	1	1	1	0.6	0	0.7	0.4	0	1	1	1	0.3	0	0.9	0	0
square	0	0	1	0	0	1	1	1	0	0	1	0	1	0	0	0	0
triangle	0	1	0	1	0	0	0	0	1	1	0	0	0	1	0	1	0
circle	1	0	0	0	1	0	0	0	0	0	0	1	0	0	1	0	1

Table 1: Membership degrees of properties by objects in Fig. 1.

	Sp_3^f		$Sp_{\Lambda,3}$		$Sp_{L,3}$	
	$t = min$	$t = prod$	$t = min$	$t = prod$	$t = min$	$t = prod$
Fig. 2(a)	1	1	1	1	1	1
Fig. 2(b)	1/3	1/3	0	0	0	0
Fig. 2(c)	5/7	5/7	0.7	0.7	0.7	0.7
Fig. 2(d)	0.35	0.245	0.21	0.147	0.3	0.21

Table 2: Different referential success measures applied to scenes in Fig. 2.

$$Sp_{\Lambda,k}(A) = a_k(a_k - a_{k+1}) \qquad (7)$$

$$Sp_{L,k}(A) = a_k - a_{k+1} \qquad (8)$$

We define the following family of measures of referential success:

Definition 3.1 *Let t be a t-norm, let $|O^i| = n > 0$ and Sp_k be a measure of k-specificity. The referential success measure associated to Sp_k and t is defined as follows:*

$$\overrightarrow{RS}_t(Sp_k)(re, O^i) = \begin{cases} t(O^i_{re}, Sp_k(O^*_{re})) & condmax \\ 0 & otherwise \end{cases} \qquad (9)$$

where O^i_{re} is the conjunction via t of the memberships of all the objects in O^i. Also

$$O^*_{re}(o_j) = \frac{O_{re}(o_j)}{\max\limits_{o \in O} O_{re}(o)} \qquad (10)$$

and condmax *holds iff $\forall o \in O \backslash O^i, o' \in O^i$ it is $O_{re}(o) \leq O_{re}(o')$.*

4 Examples

Fig. 1 shows an scene containing several objects, that have been numbered for easier identification. Table 1 shows several fuzzy properties for objects in the scene, and the corresponding fulfilment degrees.

Fig. 2 shows four sets of three objects O^i, marked with an "x" in each case, intended to be referred to by referring expressions "The dark triangles" (Fig. 2(a)), "The circles" (Fig. 2(b)), "The objects at the top-right" (Fig. 2(c)), and "The dark squares" (Fig. 2(d)). Table 2 shows the referential success obtained using Def. 3.1 with the three k-specificity measures of Eqs. (6) to (8) and minimum and product as t-norms. The best behaviour is that of measures $C_{\Lambda,3}$ and $C_{L,3}$, since they yield the expected values 1 and 0 for the first two cases, and reasonable intermediate values in the other two cases. Measure C_3^f, as discussed in (Marín et al., 2017b) for its corresponding specificity measure, is more suitable for ranking intermediate results when generating the referring expression by means of Greedy approaches.

5 Conclusions

The measures proposed are to be employed in REG algorithms for set referring expressions with fuzzy properties. We are about to begin testing which measures are more suitable for providing good results in such setting, in order to validate the proposal.

Acknowledgments

This work has been partially supported by the Spanish Ministry of Economy and Competitiveness and the European Regional Development Fund - ERDF (Fondo Europeo de Desarrollo Regional - FEDER) under project TIN2014-58227-P *Descripción lingüística de información visual mediante técnicas de minería de datos y computación flexible.*

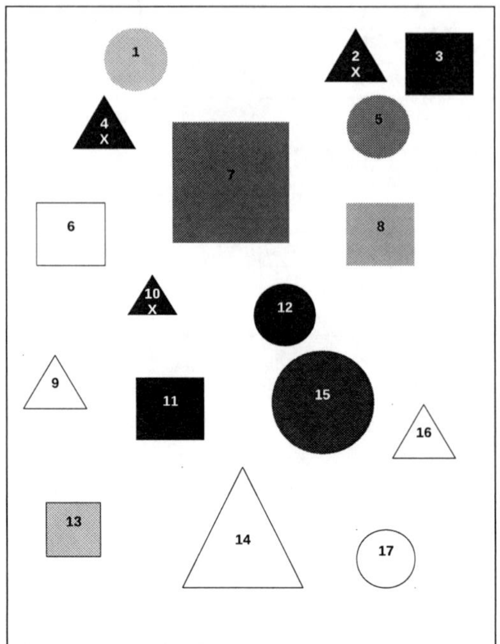

(a) "The dark triangles" matches the marked objects.

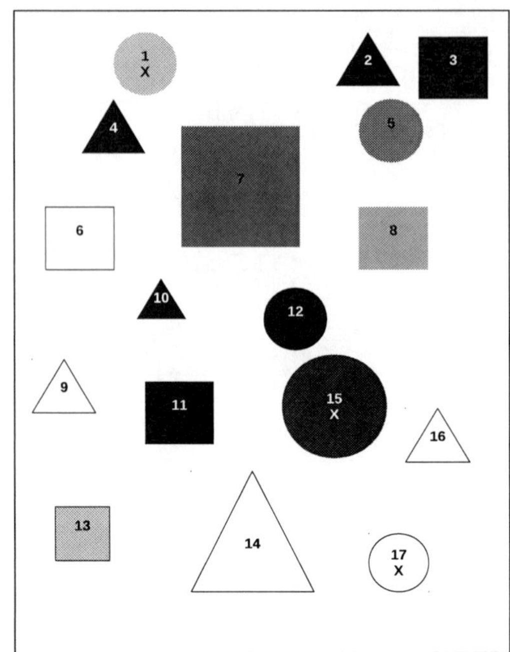

(b) "The circles" does not match the marked objects (also refers to objects 5 and 12).

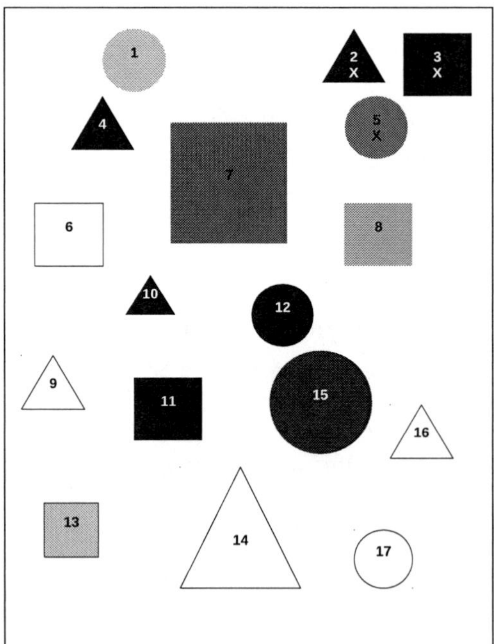

(c) "The objects at the top right" matches the marked objects to a certain degree because of object 8.

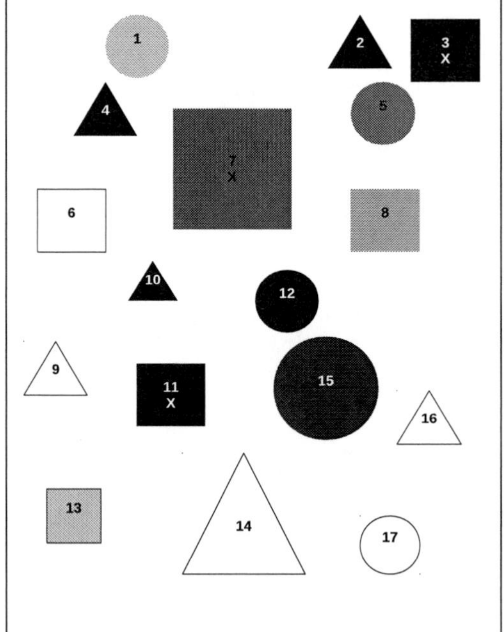

(d) "The dark squares" matches the marked objects to a certain degree because of objects 8 and 13.

Figure 2: Example scenes and (some valid, some not) expressions.

References

L. Garmendia, R. R. Yager, E. Trillas, and A. Salvador. 2003. On t-norms based specificity measures. *Fuzzy Sets and Systems*, 133(2):237–248.

L. Garmendia, R. R. Yager, E. Trillas, and A. Salvador. 2006. Measures of specificity of fuzzy sets under t-indistinguishabilities. *IEEE Transactions on Fuzzy Systems*, 14(4):568–572.

A. Gatt, N. Marín, F. Portet, and D. Sánchez. 2016. The role of graduality for referring expression generation in visual scenes. In *Proceedings IPMU 2016, Part I, CCIS 610*, pages 191–203.

E. Krahmer and K. van Deemter. 2012. Computational generation of referring expressions: A survey. *Computational Linguistics*, 38(1):173–218.

N. Marín, G. Rivas-Gervilla, and D. Sánchez. 2016. Using specificity to measure referential success in referring expressions with fuzzy properties. In *Proceedings FUZZ-IEEE 2016*, pages 563–570.

N. Marín, G. Rivas-Gervilla, and D. Sánchez. 2017a. Using measures of k-specificity for the management of count restrictions in flexible querying. In *Proceedings SUM 2017*.

N. Marín, G. Rivas-Gervilla, D. Sánchez, and R. R. Yager. 2017b. On families of bounded specificity measures. In *IEEE International Conference on Fuzzy Systems, FUZZ-IEEE Naples, Italy*.

N. Marín, G. Rivas-Gervilla, D. Sánchez, and R. R. Yager. 2017c. Specificity measures and referential success. *IEEE Transactions on Fuzzy Systems*, In press. DOI: 10.1109/TFUZZ.2017.2694803.

J. Luis González Sánchez, R. González del Campo, and L. Garmendia. 2016. Some new measures of k-specificity. In *Advances in Artificial Intelligence - 17th Conference of the Spanish Association for Artificial Intelligence, CAEPIA 2016, Salamanca, Spain, September 14-16, 2016. Proceedings*, pages 489–497.

K. van Deemter. 2012. *Not Exactly: In Praise of Vagueness*. Oxford University Press, Inc., New York, NY, USA.

K. van Deemter. 2016. *Computational Models of Referring: A Study in Cognitive Science*. MIT Press.

R. R. Yager. 1982. Measuring tranquility and anxiety in decision-making: An application of fuzzy sets. *Internat. J. Gen. Systems*, 8:139–146.

R. R. Yager. 1990. Ordinal measures of specificity. *Internat. J. Gen. Systems*, 17:57–72.

R. R. Yager. 1992. On the specificity of a possibility distribution. *Fuzzy Sets and Systems*, 50:279–292.

Neural Response Generation for Customer Service
based on Personality Traits

Jonathan Herzig, **Michal Shmueli-Scheuer**, **Tommy Sandbank** and **David Konopnicki**

IBM Research - Haifa
Haifa 31905, Israel
`{hjon,shmueli,tommy,davidko}@il.ibm.com`

Abstract

We present a neural response generation model that generates responses conditioned on a target personality. The model learns high level features based on the target personality, and uses them to update its hidden state. Our model achieves performance improvements in both perplexity and BLEU scores over a baseline sequence-to-sequence model, and is validated by human judges.

1 Introduction

Automated conversational agents are becoming popular for various tasks, such as personal assistants, shopping assistants, or as customer service agents. Automated agents benefit from adapting their personality according to the task at hand (Reeves and Nass, 1996; Tapus and Mataric, 2008) or to the customer (Herzig et al., 2016). Thus, it is desirable for automated agents to be capable of generating responses that express a target personality.

Personality is defined as a set of traits which represent durable characteristics of a person. Many models of personality exist while the most common one is the *Big Five* model (Digman, 1990) , including: *Openness, Conscientiousness, Extraversion, Agreeableness,* and *Neuroticism.* These traits were correlated with linguistic choices including lexicon and syntax (Mairesse and Walker, 2007).

In this paper we study how to encode personality traits as part of neural response generation for conversational agents. Our approach builds upon a sequence-to-sequence (SEQ2SEQ) architecture (Sutskever et al., 2014) by adding an additional

> **Example 1**
> Customer: *Why isn't your service working???*
> Consensus-agent: *We are aware of the issue and are working to fix it.*
> Agreeableness-agent: *We're here to help! Are you getting any error messages or codes?*
>
> **Example 2**
> Customer: *You guys messed up my delivery today.*
> Consensus-agent: *Please contact us if you don't get it by the end of the week.*
> Conscientiousness-agent: *Please email us with your tracking #, details and contact #. We'll check on it.*

Figure 1: Examples of a customer utterance followed by a consensus agent response and a high agreeableness or high conscientiousness response.

layer that represents the target set of personality traits, and a hidden layer that learns high-level personality based features. The response is then generated conditioned on these features.

Specifically, we focus on conversational agents for customer service; in this context, many studies examined the effect of specific personality traits of human agents on service performance. Results indicate that **conscientiousness** (a person's tendency to act in an organized or thoughtful way) and **agreeableness** (a person's tendency to be compassionate and cooperative toward others) correlate with service quality (Blignaut et al., 2014; Sackett, 2014).

Figure 1 shows examples of customer utterances, followed by two automatically generated responses. The first response (in each example), is generated by a standard SEQ2SEQ response generation system that ignores personality modeling and in effect generates the consensus response of the humans represented in the training data. The second response is generated by our system, and is aimed to generate

Proceedings of The 10th International Natural Language Generation conference, pages 252–256,
Santiago de Compostela, Spain, September 4-7 2017. ©2017 Association for Computational Linguistics

data for an agent that expresses a high level of a specific trait. In example 1, the agreeableness-agent is more compassionate (expresses empathy) and is more cooperative (asks questions). In example 2, the conscientiousness-agent is more thoughtful (will "check the issue").

We experimented with a dataset of 87.5K real customer-agent utterance pairs from social media. We find that leveraging personality encoding improves relative performance up to 46% in BLEU score, compared to a baseline SEQ2SEQ model. To our knowledge, this work is the first to train a neural response generation model that encodes target personality traits.

2   Related Work

Generating responses that express a target personality was previously discussed in different settings. Early work on the PERSONAGE system (Mairesse and Walker, 2007; Mairesse and Walker, 2008; Mairesse and Walker, 2010; Mairesse and Walker, 2011) presented a framework projecting different traits throughout the different modules of an NLG system. The authors explicitly defined 40 linguistic features as generation parameters, and then learned how to weigh them to generate a desired set of traits. While we aim at the same objective, our methodology is different and does not require feature engineering. Our approach utilizes a neural network that automatically learns to represent high level personality based features.

Neural response generation models (Vinyals and Le, 2015; Shang et al., 2015) are based on a SEQ2SEQ architecture (Sutskever et al., 2014) and employ an encoder to represent the user utterance and an attention-based decoder that generates the agent response one token at a time. Models that aim to generate a coherent persona also exist. Li et al. (2016) modified a SEQ2SEQ model to encode a persona (the character of an artificial agent). The main difference with our work is that we focus on modeling the expression of specific personality traits and not an abstract character. Moreover, their persona-based model can only generate responses for the agents that appear in the training data, while our model has no such restriction. Finally, Xu et al. (2017) generated responses for customer service requests on social media using standard SEQ2SEQ, while we modify it to generate a target personality.

3   Sequence-to-Sequence Setup

We review the SEQ2SEQ attention based model on which our model is based.

Neural response generation can be viewed as a sequence-to-sequence problem (Sutskever et al., 2014), where a sequence of input language tokens $x = x_1, \ldots, x_m$, describing the user utterance, is mapped to a sequence of output language tokens $y_1, \ldots, y_n$, describing the agent response.

The **encoder** is an LSTM (Hochreiter and Schmidhuber, 1997) unit that converts $x_1, \ldots, x_m$ into a sequence of context sensitive embeddings $b_1, \ldots, b_m$. An attention-based **decoder** (Bahdanau et al., 2015; Luong et al., 2015) generates output tokens one at a time. At each time step j, it generates y_j based on the current hidden state s_j, then updates the hidden state s_{j+1} based on s_j and y_j. Formally, the decoder is defined by the following equations:

$$s_1 = \tanh(W^{(s)} b_m), \qquad (1)$$

$$p(y_j = w \mid x, y_{1:j-1}) \propto \exp(U[s_j, c_j]), \qquad (2)$$

$$s_{j+1} = LSTM([\phi^{(out)}(y_j), c_j], s_j), \qquad (3)$$

where $i \in \{1, \ldots, m\}$, $j \in \{1, \ldots, n\}$ and the context vector, c_j, is the result of global attention (see (Luong et al., 2015)). The matrices $W^{(s)}$, $W^{(a)}$, U, and the embedding function $\phi^{(out)}$ are decoder parameters. The entire model is trained end-to-end by maximizing $p(y \mid x) = \prod_{j=1}^{n} p(y_j \mid x, y_{1:j-1})$.

4   Personality Generation Model

The model described in section 3 generates responses with maximum likelihood which reflect the consensus of the agents that appear in the training data. This kind of response does not characterize a specific personality and thus can result in inconsistent or unwanted personality cues. In this section we present our PERSONALITY-BASED model (Figure 2) which generates responses conditioned on a target set of personality traits values which the responses should express. The target set of personality traits is represented as a vector p, where p_i represents the desired value for the ith trait. This value encodes

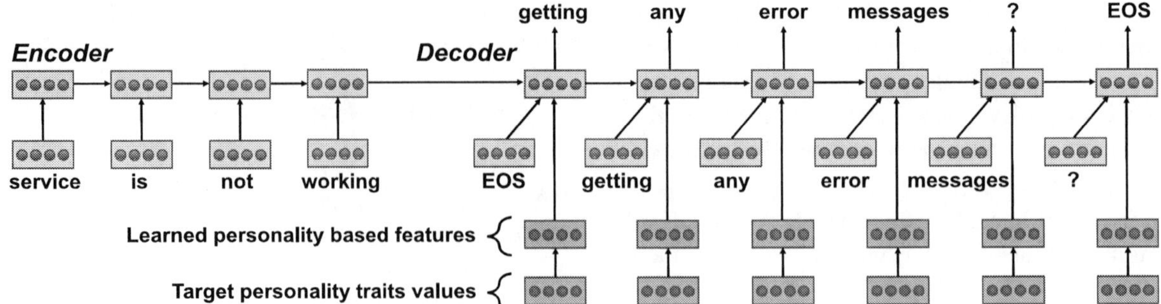

Figure 2: Architecture for the personality based generation model.

how strongly should this trait be expressed in the response. Consequently, the size of p depends on the selected personality model (e.g., five traits for the Big Five model).

As in (Mairesse and Walker, 2011), we argue that personality traits are exhibited as different types of stylistic linguistic variation. Thus, our model's response is conditioned on generation parameters which are based on personality traits. In comparison to (Mairesse and Walker, 2011) where generation parameters were defined manually, we learn these high-level features automatically during training. We introduce a personality based features hidden layer $h_p = \sigma(W^{(p)}p + b)$, where $W^{(p)}$ and b are parameters learned by the model during training. Each personality feature h_i is a weighted sum of the targeted traits values (following a sigmoid activation). Now, at each token generation, the decoder updates the hidden state conditioned on the personality traits features h_p, as well as on the previous hidden state, the output token and the context. Formally, Equation 3 is changed to:

$$s_{j+1} = LSTM([\phi^{(out)}(y_j), c_j, h_p], s_j), \quad (4)$$

Conditioning on h_p captures the relation of text generation to the underlining personality traits.

5 Experiments

Data. Our model is designed to generate text conditioned on a target set of personality traits. Specifically, we verified its performance in a scenario of customer service. For our experiments we utilized the dataset presented in (Xu et al., 2017), which exhibits a large variety of customer service properties. This dataset is a collection of $1M$ conversations over customer service Twitter channels of 62 different

brands which cover a large variety of product categories. Several preprocessing steps were performed for our purposes:

We first split the data to pairs consisting of a single customer utterance and its corresponding agent response. We removed pairs containing non-English sentences. We further removed pairs for agents that participated in less than 30 conversation pairs, so we would have sufficient data for each agent to extract their personality traits (see below). This resulted in $87.5K$ conversation pairs in total including 633 different agents (138 ± 160 pairs per agent on average).

Following (Sordoni et al., 2015; Li et al., 2016) we used BLEU (Papineni et al., 2002) for evaluation. Besides BLEU scores, we also report perplexity as an indicator of model capability. For implementation details, refer to Appendix A.

Results. We experimented with two different settings to measure our model's performance.

Warm Start: In the first experiment, data for each agent in the dataset was split between training, validation and test data sets with a fraction of 80%/10%/10%, respectively. We then extracted the agents' personality traits using an external service (described in Appendix B), from the training data for each agent. These personality traits values are then used during the model training as the values for the personality vector p. In this setting, since all the agents that appear in the test data appear also in the training data, we can also test the performance of (Li et al., 2016), which learns a persona vector for each agent in the training data.

The results in table 1 show that the standard SEQ2SEQ model achieved the lowest performance in terms of both perplexity and BLEU score while the competing models which learn a representation

254

Model	Perplexity	BLEU
SEQ2SEQ	11.49	6.3%
PERSONA-BASED (Li et al., 2016)	9.25	15.55%
PERSONALITY-BASED	9.62	12.46%

Table 1: Warm start performance.

Model	Perplexity	BLEU
SEQ2SEQ	21.04	3.19%
PERSONALITY-BASED	19.64	4.67%

Table 2: Cold start performance (agents in the test data do not appear in the training data).

for the agents achieved higher performance. The PERSONA-BASED model achieved similar perplexity but higher BLEU score than our model. This is reasonable since PERSONA-BASED is not restricted to personality based features. However, this model can not generate content for agents which do not appear in the training data, and thus, it is limited.

Cold Start: In our second experiment, we split the dataset such that 10% of the agents only formed the validation and test sets (half of each agent's examples for each set). Data for the other 90% of the agents formed the training set.

In this setting, data for agents in the test set does not appear in the training set. These agents represent new personality distributions we would like to generate responses for. Note that, we extracted target personality traits for agents in the training set using their training data, or, for agents in the test set, using validation data. In this setting, it is not possible to test the PERSONA-BASED model since no representation is learned during training for agents in the test set. Thus, we only compare our model to the baseline SEQ2SEQ model. Table 2 shows that, in this setting, we get better performance by utilizing personality based representation: our model achieves a relative 6.7% decrease in perplexity, and a 46% relative improvement in BLEU score. Results from both experiments demonstrate that we can better model the linguistic variation in agent responses by conditioning on target personality traits.

Human Evaluation. We conducted a human evaluation of our PERSONALITY-BASED model using a crowd-sourcing service. This evaluation measures whether the responses generated by our model are correlated with the target personality traits. We focused on two personality traits from the *Big Five* model that are important to customer service: *agreeableness* and *conscientiousness* (Blignaut et al., 2014; Sackett, 2014). We extracted 60 customer utterances from the validation set of the **cold start** setting described above. We selected customer utterances that convey a negative sentiment, since re-

sponses to this kind of utterances vary much. After sentences were selected, we generated corresponding agent responses in the following way. We generated a high-*trait* target personality distribution (*trait* was either *agreeableness* or *conscientiousness*), where *trait* was set to a value of 0.9, and all other traits to 0.5. Similarly, we created a low-*trait* version where *trait* was set to 0.1. For each trait and customer utterance we generated a response for the high-*trait* and low-*trait* versions.

Each triplet (a customer utterance followed by high-*trait* and low-*trait* generated responses) was evaluated by five master level judges. To get the judges familiar with personality traits, we first presented clear definitions of the two traits, followed by several examples (from the task's domain), and explanation. Following Li et al. (2016) methodology, the two responses were presented in a random order, and judged on a 5-point zero-sum scale. A score of 2 (-2) was assigned if one response was judged to express the trait more (less) than the other response, and 1 (-1) if one response expressed the trait "somewhat" more (less) than the other. Ties were assigned a score of zero.

The judges rated each pair, and their scores were averaged and mapped into 5 equal-width bins. After discarding ties, we found that the high-*trait* responses generated by our PERSONALITY-BASED model were judged either more expressive or somewhat more expressive than the low-*trait* corresponding responses in 61% of cases. If we ignore the somewhat more expressive judgments, the high-*trait* responses win in 17% of cases.

6   Conclusions and Future Work

We have presented a personality-based response generation model and tested it in customer care tasks, outperforming baseline SEQ2SEQ model. In future work, we would like to generate responses adapted to the personality traits of the customer as well, and to apply our model to other tasks such as education systems.

References

D. Bahdanau, K. Cho, and Y. Bengio. 2015. Neural machine translation by jointly learning to align and translate. In *International Conference on Learning Representations (ICLR)*.

Linda Blignaut, Leona Ungerer, and Helene Muller. 2014. Personality as predictor of customer service centre agent performance in the banking industry: An exploratory study. *SA Journal of Human Resource Management*, 12(1).

John M Digman. 1990. Personality structure: Emergence of the five-factor model. *Annual review of psychology*, 41(1):417–440.

Jonathan Herzig, Guy Feigenblat, Michal Shmueli-Scheuer, David Konopnicki, and Anat Rafaeli. 2016. Predicting customer satisfaction in customer support conversations in social media using affective features. In *UMAP 2016, Halifax, NS, Canada, July 13 - 17, 2016*, pages 115–119.

S. Hochreiter and J. Schmidhuber. 1997. Long short-term memory. *Neural Computation*, 9(8):1735–1780.

Jiwei Li, Michel Galley, Chris Brockett, Georgios P. Spithourakis, Jianfeng Gao, and William B. Dolan. 2016. A persona-based neural conversation model. In *ACL*.

M. Luong, H. Pham, and C. D. Manning. 2015. Effective approaches to attention-based neural machine translation. In *EMNLP*, pages 1412–1421.

Franois Mairesse and Marilyn Walker. 2007. Personage: Personality generation for dialogue. In *ACL*, pages 496–503.

François Mairesse and Marilyn A Walker. 2008. Trainable generation of big-five personality styles through data-driven parameter estimation. In *ACL*, pages 165–173.

François Mairesse and Marilyn A. Walker. 2010. Towards personality-based user adaptation: psychologically informed stylistic language generation. *User Model. User-Adapt. Interact.*, 20(3):227–278.

François Mairesse and Marilyn A. Walker. 2011. Controlling user perceptions of linguistic style: Trainable generation of personality traits. *Computational Linguistics*, 37(3):455–488.

Kishore Papineni, Salim Roukos, Todd Ward, and Wei-Jing Zhu. 2002. Bleu: a method for automatic evaluation of machine translation. In *ACL*, pages 311–318.

Byron Reeves and Clifford Nass. 1996. How people treat computers, television, and new media like real people and places. *CSLI Publications and Cambridge*.

Walmsley P. T. Sackett, P. R. 2014. Which personality attributes are most important in the workplace? *Perspectives on Psychological Science*, 9(5):538–551.

Lifeng Shang, Zhengdong Lu, and Hang Li. 2015. Neural responding machine for short-text conversation. *arXiv preprint arXiv:1503.02364*.

Alessandro Sordoni, Michel Galley, Michael Auli, Chris Brockett, Yangfeng Ji, Margaret Mitchell, Jian-Yun Nie, Jianfeng Gao, and Bill Dolan. 2015. A neural network approach to context-sensitive generation of conversational responses. *CoRR*, abs/1506.06714.

I. Sutskever, O. Vinyals, and Q. V. Le. 2014. Sequence to sequence learning with neural networks. In *NIPS*, pages 3104–3112.

Adriana Tapus and Maja J Mataric. 2008. Socially assistive robots: The link between personality, empathy, physiological signals, and task performance. In *AAAI Spring Symposium: Emotion, Personality, and Social Behavior*, pages 133–140.

Oriol Vinyals and Quoc Le. 2015. A neural conversational model. *arXiv preprint arXiv:1506.05869*.

Anbang Xu, Zhe Liu, Yufan Guo, Vibha Sinha, and Rama Akkiraju. 2017. A new chatbot for customer service on social media.

A Implementation Details

We tuned hyper-parameters based on validation set perplexity for both the baseline SEQ2SEQ and our PERSONALITY-BASED models. We used an LSTM with 800 hidden cells, and a personality based layer with 40 hidden cells. We trained the model for 15 epochs with an initial learning rate of 0.1, and halved the learning rate every epoch, starting from epoch 7. After training was finished we picked the best model according to validation set perplexity. We initialized parameters by sampling from the uniform distribution $[-0.1, 0.1]$. The log likelihood of the correct response was maximized using stochastic gradient descent with a batch size set to 64, and gradients were clipped with a threshold of 5. Vocabulary size is limited to 50,000. Dropout rate is set to 0.2. At test time, we used beam search with beam size 5. All models were implemented in Torch.

B Personality Traits Detection

To extract personality traits for agents in our experiments we utilized the IBM Personality Insights service, which is publicly available. This service infers three models of personality traits, namely, *Big Five*, *Needs* and *Values* from social media text. It extracts percentile scores for 52 traits[1].

---

[1]www.ibm.com/watson/developercloud/doc/
personality-insights/models.html

Neural Paraphrase Generation using Transfer Learning

Florin Brad
Bitdefender, Romania
fbrad@bitdefender.com

Traian Rebedea
University Politehnica of Bucharest
traian.rebedea@cs.pub.ro

Abstract

Progress in statistical paraphrase generation has been hindered for a long time by the lack of large monolingual parallel corpora. In this paper, we adapt the neural machine translation approach to paraphrase generation and perform transfer learning from the closely related task of entailment generation. We evaluate the model on the Microsoft Research Paraphrase (MSRP) corpus and show that the model is able to generate sentences that capture part of the original meaning, but fails to pick up on important words or to show large lexical variation.

1 Introduction

Paraphrase generation is the problem of restating a given sentence such that its overall meaning is preserved. This can be seen as a task useful in and of itself or it can serve in proxy applications such as sentence summarization, sentence simplification, question expansion in question answering or rephrasing utterances generated by a conversational agent.

Paraphrase generation has been previously treated as a monolingual machine translation (MT) problem (Quirk et al., 2004; Finch et al., 2004). Lately, Neural Machine Translation (NMT) has revived interest in statistical machine translation through the use of sequence-to-sequence (SEQ2SEQ) models that learn to maximize the probability of a sentence in a target language, given a sentence in a source language (Cho et al., 2014; Sutskever et al., 2014). The SEQ2SEQ model is composed of an encoder that recurrently consumes the words in the source sentence and a decoder that sequentially predicts words

in the target sentence, conditioned on the encoder's last hidden state and the previously translated words. This model was later improved by using an attention mechanism (Bahdanau et al., 2014) that allowed the decoder to focus on the relevant words from the source sentence.

NMT can then be used for paraphrase generation by maximizing the probability $P(Y|Y')$, where (Y, Y') is a pair of paraphrases. While parallel corpora are abundantly available for machine translation, paraphrase corpora featuring pairs of complex sentences are prohibitively small for training large models. We propose to overcome this aspect by performing transfer learning from a similar task - entailment generation, which is facilitated by the large number of entailment pairs featured in the Stanford Natural Language Inference (Bowman et al., 2015, SNLI) corpus.

2 Related Work

Paraphrase generation has been recently explored as a statistical machine translation problem in a neural setting. Prakash et al. (2016) used a stacked-LSTM (Long Short-Term Memory) SEQ2SEQ network with residual connections and demonstrated strong performance over the simple and attention-enhanced SEQ2SEQ models. They report superior scores on several datasets: the Paraphrase Database corpus (Ganitkevitch et al., 2013, PPDB), captions from Common Objects in Context (Lin et al., 2014, MSCOCO), and question pairs from WikiAnswers (Fader et al., 2013). Mallinson et al. (2017) adapt the NMT architecture to incorporate bilingual pivoting and report improvements over the baseline in simi-

257

Proceedings of The 10th International Natural Language Generation conference, pages 257–261,
Santiago de Compostela, Spain, September 4-7 2017. ©2017 Association for Computational Linguistics

larity prediction, paraphrase identification as well as paraphrase generation.

Our work is different in that we focus on transfer learning to improve performance, using state of the art neural models employed mainly for machine translation.

Transfer learning has been recently investigated by Mou et al. (2016), who distinguish two settings: semantically equivalent transfer (where both source and target tasks are natural language inference) and semantically different transfer (where the source task is natural language inference and the target task is paraphrase detection). They report increased performance only in the former setting. Zoph et al. (2016) train a parent model on a high-resource language pair (such as English-French) in order to improve low-resource language pairs. They manage to improve the baseline with an average 5.6 BLEU points.

3   Experiments

Paraphrases can be seen as mostly bidirectional textual entailments (Androutsopoulos and Malakasiotis, 2010). Sentential paraphrase corpora are prohibitively small for training large neural networks, but textual entailment corpora are quite large thanks to the SNLI dataset. Our aim is to exploit this situation by performing transfer learning from the entailment generation (EG) task (given sentence S, generate sentence T that can be inferred from S) to the paraphrase generation (PG) task. We also fine-tune the weights on the larger PPDB corpus before transferring to the Microsoft Research Paraphrase Corpus (Dolan and Brockett, 2005, MSRP), used for the paraphrase detection task. In addition, we also test the multiple transfer in reverse order.

3.1   Model

We use the state of the art SEQ2SEQ models with attention[1], described in Luong et al. (2015). We train a 2-layer LSTM with 2000 hidden units and word embeddings of size 1000.

3.2   Datasets

We use the MSRP and PPDB datasets featuring paraphrase pairs and the SNLI dataset featuring tex-

---

[1] https://github.com/harvardnlp/seq2seq-attn

Dataset	Train	Validation	Test
MSRP	3,854	1,652	2,294
PPDB(XS)	457,000	114,888	-
SNLI	183,416	3,329	3,368

Table 1: Datasets statistics (number of pairs)

tual entailments. We discard the negative examples from the MSRP dataset. We discard the neutral and contradiction examples and only keep entailment pairs from the SNLI corpus. We also use the small (XS) phrasal subset of the PPDB dataset, due to its higher-scoring pairs as compared to the other variants of PPDB. We also augmented all datasets with the inverse pair (Y, X) for each pair of sentences (X, Y) - this approach is completely justified for paraphrases, but it also makes sense for SNLI if we treat an entailment pair just as a paraphrase pair.

The MSRP dataset is small, but it features long sentences with lots of numbers and proper nouns, which is rather problematic when predicting words from fixed-size vocabularies. The PPDB dataset contains a large number of short, but high-quality paraphrase pairs. We hypothesize that the SNLI entailments could prove useful in paraphrase generation, due to the large lexical overlap between the premise and the hypothesis.

An overview of the datasets and their train/validation/test sizes is shown in Table 1.

3.3   Transfer learning

In order to perform transfer learning in scenarios of type $X \longrightarrow Y$, where X and Y are two datasets for the same or different tasks, we follow the next steps. We train the SEQ2SEQ models on dataset X, keeping the configuration with the lowest perplexity on the validation set of X. We then transfer the parameters to a new model that are retrained on dataset Y.

Transfer learning in scenarios of type $X \longrightarrow Y \longrightarrow Z$ is similar to the process described above, but with the additional transfer from task/dataset Y to task/dataset Z.

All models are compared with the MSRP baseline, where a SEQ2SEQ model is trained on the MSRP training set alone.

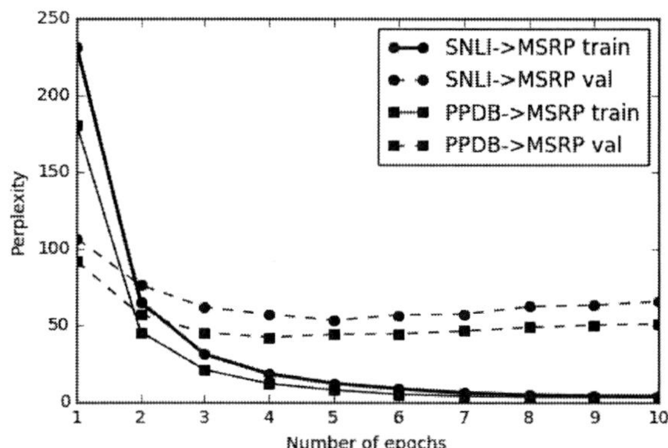

Figure 1: Perplexities with direct transfer

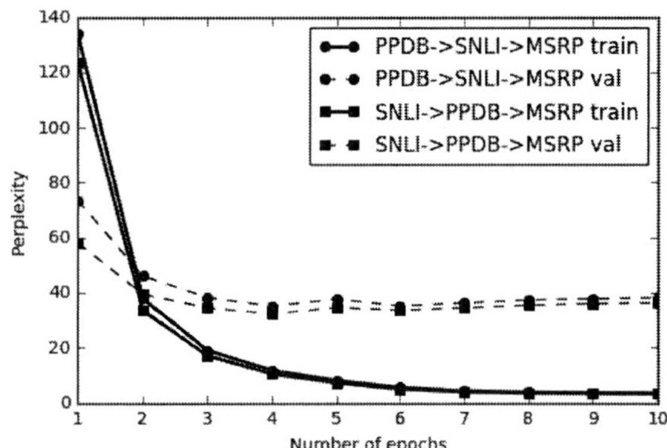

Figure 2: Perplexities with one-hop transfer

Experiment name	test perplexity per word	BLEU score
MSRP	14.37	0.09
SNLI $\longrightarrow$ MSRP	3.97	7.17
PPDB $\longrightarrow$ MSRP	3.73	10.29
SNLI $\longrightarrow$ PPDB $\longrightarrow$ MSRP	3.08	15.76
PPDB $\longrightarrow$ SNLI $\longrightarrow$ MSRP	3.78	12.91

Table 2: BLEU score and perplexity on the MSRP test set over different transfer scenarios

3.4 Training

All models are trained using stochastic gradient descent (SGD), with a learning rate decay of 0.5 if the validation perplexity does not decrease on consecutive epochs. The models are trained for 20 epochs each. We perform early stopping by keeping the configurations with the lowest perplexity on the validation set.

3.5 Evaluation

To generate paraphrases, we use beam-search with a beam size of 5. We report the BLEU score (Papineni et al., 2002) and the perplexity of the reconstructed sentences for the MSRP test corpus. Although no standard metric has proved conclusive for evaluating paraphrase generation, BLEU score has been shown to correlate fairly well with human judgements (Chen and Dolan, 2011), especially when more references are being used. We also plot the perplexity on the training and validations sets of different transfer scenarios.

4 Results

4.1 Quantitative results

Transfer learning improves perplexity and BLEU score

In Figure 1 we notice that transferring from the PPDB paraphrases yields lower perplexities than from the SNLI entailments. Not surprisingly, the additional transfer further lowers perplexity. However, Figure 2 shows that perplexity is slightly lower when transferring from entailments through additional paraphrases than the other way around.

The higher BLEU scores in Table 2 also seem to correlate well with the lower validation perplexities, with SNLI $\longrightarrow$ PPDB $\longrightarrow$ MSRP proving to be the best transfer setting. One possible explanation is that entailment pairs have a stronger lexical, but a weaker semantic overlap. Then phrasal (multi-word) paraphrases from PPDB are used to improve the semantic equivalence needed for paraphrasing. We turn to qualitative analysis, where we generate sentences using the SNLI $\longrightarrow$ PPDB $\longrightarrow$ MSRP model.

4.2 Qualitative results

Results in Table 3 show that the model is able to restate parts of the input sentences, but fails to retain the whole meaning.

In the first two examples, the models drops the proper names and the description following the dialogue. The second example shows little variation in the input sentence. The third example reflects a more diverse vocabulary, but again suffers from dropping parts of the input. The fourth example re-

259

Source sentence	Decoded sentence	Target sentence
current chief operating officer mike butcher and group chief financial officer alex arena will report to so	the chief executive officer and chief financial officer to report to so .	pccw ' s chief operating officer , mike butcher , and alex arena , the chief financial officer , will report directly to mr so .
" there ' s no reason for you to keep your skills up , " the judge told the convicted crack cocaine kingpin .	" there is no reason for you to keep your skills up . "	" there ' s no reason for you to keep your skills up , " u . s . district judge j . frederick motz told mcgriff after he was sentenced .
those reports were denied by the interior minister , prince nayef .	such reports were refused by internal affairs .	however , the saudi interior minister , prince nayef , denied the reports .
the letter bomb sent to prodi exploded in his hands but he was unhurt .	the letter was sent to prodi in his hand but he was surrounded .	it exploded in his hands , but the former italian prime minister was unhurt .

Table 3: Four examples of source sentences from the MSRP test set, along with the decoded and the target sentences

tains part of the original meaning, but doesn't contain important words such as 'bomb' and 'exploded'.

The truncation effect may be due to training on the entailment pairs, because most of the hypotheses featured in the SNLI dataset are shorter than the premises.

Also, without a copying mechanism, it is challenging for SEQ2SEQ models to predict proper names, especially if they are rare or out of training vocabulary.

5   Conclusions and future work

In this paper, we investigated the use of SEQ2SEQ neural models for paraphrase generation. The major limitation in training such models is the shortage of corpora with (complex) sentential paraphrases, which we overcame by performing transfer learning, first using textual entailment and then phrasal paraphrase pairs.

We showed that transfer learning improves the BLEU score of the generated paraphrases in all transfer settings and that transfer works best when transferring entailments to short paraphrases and then to the longer paraphrases from the MSRP corpus.

Qualitative results showed promising results, with the model being able to restate parts of the input sentence fairly well. Further areas of research should address the lexical variety and should look into incorporating copying mechanism into the network so that rare or unknown words are picked up during paraphrasing.

References

Ion Androutsopoulos and Prodromos Malakasiotis. 2010. A survey of paraphrasing and textual entailment methods. *Journal of Artificial Intelligence Research*, 38:135–187.

Dzmitry Bahdanau, Kyunghyun Cho, and Yoshua Bengio. 2014. Neural machine translation by jointly learning to align and translate. *CoRR*, abs/1409.0473.

Samuel R. Bowman, Gabor Angeli, Christopher Potts, and Christopher D. Manning. 2015. A large annotated corpus for learning natural language inference. *CoRR*, abs/1508.05326.

D L Chen and W B Dolan. 2011. Collecting Highly Parallel Data for Paraphrase Evaluation. *Proceedings of the 49th Annual Meeting of the Association for Computational Linguistics*, pages 190–200.

Kyunghyun Cho, Bart van Merrienboer, Caglar Gulcehre, Dzmitry Bahdanau, Fethi Bougares, Holger Schwenk, and Yoshua Bengio. 2014. Learning Phrase Representations using RNN Encoder-Decoder for Statistical Machine Translation. *Proceedings of the 2014 Conference on Empirical Methods in Natural Language Processing (EMNLP)*, pages 1724–1734.

William B. Dolan and Chris Brockett. 2005. Automatically Constructing a Corpus of Sentential Paraphrases. *Proceedings of the Third International Workshop on Paraphrasing (IWP2005)*, pages 9–16.

Anthony Fader, Luke Zettlemoyer, and Oren Etzioni. 2013. Paraphrase-Driven Learning for Open Question Answering. *Acl*, pages 1608–1618.

Andrew Finch, Taro Watanabe, Yasuhiro Akiba, and Eiichiro Sumita. 2004. Paraphrasing as machine translation. *Journal of Natural Language Processing*, 11(5):87–111.

Juri Ganitkevitch, Benjamin Van Durme, and Chris Callison-Burch. 2013. PPDB: the paraphrase database. pages 758–764.

Tsung-Yi Lin, Michael Maire, Serge Belongie, Lubomir D Bourdev, Ross B Girshick, James Hays, Pietro Perona, Deva Ramanan, Piotr Dollár, and C Lawrence Zitnick. 2014. Microsoft {COCO:} Common Objects in Context. *{arXiv}:1405.0312*, pages 740–755.

Minh-Thang Luong, Hieu Pham, and Christopher D. Manning. 2015. Effective approaches to attention-based neural machine translation. *CoRR*, abs/1508.04025.

Jonathan Mallinson, Rico Sennrich, and Mirella Lapata. 2017. Paraphrasing revisited with neural machine translation. In *Proceedings of the 15th Conference of the European Chapter of the Association for Computational Linguistics: Volume 1, Long Papers*, pages 881–893, Valencia, Spain, April. Association for Computational Linguistics.

Lili Mou, Zhao Meng, Rui Yan, Ge Li, Yan Xu, Lu Zhang, and Zhi Jin. 2016. How transferable are neural networks in NLP applications? pages 479–489.

Kishore Papineni, Salim Roukos, Todd Ward, and Wei-Jing Zhu. 2002. Bleu: A method for automatic evaluation of machine translation. In *Proceedings of the 40th Annual Meeting on Association for Computational Linguistics*, ACL '02, pages 311–318, Stroudsburg, PA, USA. Association for Computational Linguistics.

Aaditya Prakash, Sadid A. Hasan, Kathy Lee, Vivek Datla, Ashequl Qadir, Joey Liu, and Oladimeji Farri. 2016. Neural Paraphrase Generation with Stacked Residual LSTM Networks. *Coling*.

Chris Quirk, Chris Brockett, and William B. Dolan. 2004. Monolingual machine translation for paraphrase generation. pages 142–149.

Ilya Sutskever, Oriol Vinyals, and Quoc V Le. 2014. Sequence to sequence learning with neural networks. *Advances in Neural Information Processing Systems (NIPS)*, pages 3104–3112.

Barret Zoph, Deniz Yuret, Jonathan May, and Kevin Knight. 2016. Transfer Learning for Low-Resource Neural Machine Translation. *Emnlp*, page 8.

Author Index